W9-BLV-598

PLAY INDEX

1998-2002

PLAY INDEX

VOLUMES IN PRINT

PLAY INDEX

1998-2002

AN INDEX TO 4,114 PLAYS

Edited by

John Greenfieldt

NEW YORK   DUBLIN

THE H. W. WILSON COMPANY

2003

ISSN 0554-3037

Library of Congress Control Number 64-1054

Printed in the United States of America

CONTENTS

PREFACE

This volume of *Play Index* indexes 4,114 plays that were published during the five-year period 1998-2002. Some plays published before 1998 but omitted from the previous volume of *Play Index* are also included. Like its nine predecessors, the present volume is an index to plays written in English or translated into English, published either separately or in collections.

The policies of the preceding volumes prevail. The symbol *c* indicates a play for children, through grade 6. The symbol *y* indicates a play for young people, grades 7 through 12 inclusive.

Its broad scope—from puppet plays to classical drama—and detailed cast analysis make *Play Index* suitable to a variety of uses. These can be most fully realized by a reading of the Directions for Use.

The indexing staff for this volume includes Stewart Both, Norris Smith, Jennifer Peloso, and Trina King. The production staff is Barbara Delegal, Sandra Watson, and Richard Stein.

The H. W. Wilson Company is grateful to those publishers who provided copies of their books for indexing.

DIRECTIONS FOR USE

Part I. Author, Title, and Subject Index

This section provides detailed information about individual plays. Entries are arranged under author, title, and subject in a single alphabet. The author entry for a play is the most inclusive and contains the following information: name of the author, title of the play, a brief descriptive note, the number of acts and scenes, the size and composition of the cast, and the number of sets required. Where there is no indication of acts or scenes, none is given. For radio and television plays the size of the cast is given but not the number of scenes or settings. For puppet plays the cast is given only as a number of characters.

In the case of separately published plays the author entry includes the publisher, date of publication, pagination, ISBN designation, and Library of Congress control number when available. If the play is contained in a collection, the name of the collection is given. Further information about the collection may be found in Part III of this volume.

Sample author entry:

> **Cleage, Pearl**
> Blues for an Alabama sky. Dramatists
> 1999 81p
> ISBN 0-822-1634-5   LC 99-215184
> Drama about friends living in 1930 Harlem, New York, during the Harlem Renaissance. 2 acts 10 scenes
> 3m 2w Unit set
> —Same
> *In* Cleage, P. Flyin' west and other plays

The entry shows that a play by Pearl Cleage entitled *Blues for an Alabama sky* was published by Dramatists in 1999 and contains eighty-one pages. The play has two acts and ten scenes, and requires a cast of three men and two women plus a unit set for production. This play also appears in the collection *Flyin' west and other plays*. For full information about the collection see Part III, List of Collections Indexed.

All plays are also listed under their titles followed by the name of the author. Fuller information about the play is obtained by consulting the author entry.

Sample title entry:

> **Claudia** meets Fulano Colorado. Farias, J.

Plays dealing in whole or in part with a particular subject are listed under that subject. Plays in a distinctive form, such as masques, mysteries and miracle plays, one-act plays, pageants, pantomimes, puppet plays, plays in verse, radio plays, television plays, etc., are entered under the appropriate form heading as well as under specific subjects. Full information about the play will be found by consulting the author entry.

Sample subject entry:

Museums
    y Francoeur, B. Oh, horrors! It's murder!
       Gilroy, F. D. Contact with the enemy
       Hunt, L. A night under canvas
       Lipkin, D. Pithecus
       Long, Q. The Sixth Floor museum

The symbol *c* preceding an entry indicates that the play is intended for children at elementary school level, through grade six. The symbol *y* identifies material for young adults, in grades seven through twelve approximately.

Part II. Cast Analysis

This section is designed to help the user locate plays by type of cast and number of players or readers. It is divided into six sections by type of cast: (1) all female cast, (2) all male cast, (3) mixed cast, (4) puppet plays, (5) unidentified cast, and (6) variable cast. Unidentified cast is used for non-human characters. Variable cast is used when roles can be acted by either male or female actors, or when an actor can take several parts, so that the exact number of the cast is not easily ascertainable.

Under each type of cast the arrangement is by total number of characters in ascending order. A mixed cast of over thirty-six characters is designated as Large. The word "Extra" or "Extras" indicates that the play requires one or more extra players for non-speaking parts or chorus.

Under each total number of characters the arrangement is then, within the parentheses, by type of character in ascending numbers in this order: boys, girls, men, women, extras. For example, a four-character play for two boys and two girls (2b 2g) would precede one for two boys and two men (2b 2m). Then would follow one for two men and two women (2m 2w) and then one for three men and one woman (3m 1w).

MIXED CAST
5 characters (2m 3w)
Busch, C. The tale of the allergist's wife

The sample entry above indicates that Charles Busch's *The tale of the allergist's wife* has a mixed cast of five characters, two men and three women. Consult the author entry in Part I for the annotation and information about the source of the play.

Translations of Greek and Latin plays are not given cast analysis.

Part III. List of Collections Indexed

This section provides information about the collections indexed, including publisher, date, pagination, ISBN designation, and Library of Congress control number when available.

PLAY INDEX

Play Index, 1998 - 2002

Part 1

Author, Title, and Subject Index

2 1/2 Jews. Brandt, A.
2.5 minute ride. Kron, L.
4.48 psychosis. Kane, S.
4 AM (open all night). Krakower, B.
The **7** stages of grieving. Enoch, W., and Mailman, D.
27 wagons full of cotton. Williams, T.
48 shades of brown. Dean, P.
101 humiliating stories. Kron, L.
140. Norman, M.
187. Rivera, J.
610 Bedford Drive. Ronzoni, M.
1003; or, Don Giovanni's back in town. Hochwälder, F.
16670 (Maximilian Mary Kolbe). Ehn, E.

A

a.m. Sunday. Hairston, J.
Aaron Kelly is dead! McBride-Smith, B.
Abandon all hope. Silverstein, S.

Abbott, Gary W.
y The scarlet letter. Pioneer Drama Service 2001 48p

Dramatization of Hawthorne's novel about adultery and social ostracism in colonial Massachusetts. 5 acts 13m 8w extras 1 interior 3 exteriors
The **abdication.** Wolff, R.
The **abduction.** St. John, B.

Abela, Donna
c Circus caravan.

Teenager joins circus. 1m 2w 1 setting
In International plays for young people
Abenaki Indians

Bruchac, J. Gluskabe and Old Man Winter

Abolitionists

Aiken, G. L. Uncle Tom's cabin
Swayze, J. C. Ossawattomie Brown
Abortion

Macklin, P. Someplace warm
MacLeod, W. The water children
Parks, S.-L. Fucking A
Parnell, P. The cider house rules: part 1
Parnell, P. The cider house rules: part 2
Plata, M. C. Justice for whom?
Price, M. S. That midnight rodeo
Wilson, L. Sympathetic magic
Wimberly, B. Saint Lucy's eyes
About Alice. Laurence, C.
About face. Fo, D.

Abraham (Biblical figure)
c Vogel, L. The patriarchs

Abse, Dannie

The eccentric.

Comedy about a nonconforming businessman. 1 act 1g 4m extras
In Act one Wales; ed. by P. Clark
Abstract expression. Rebeck, T.
Abundance. Henley, B.

Abusive behavior

Baker, E. A. The seventeenth of June
Baker, E. A. Up, down, strange, charmed, beauty, and truth
Mattern, J. Scrapple
Mtshali, T. S. Weemen
Acapulco. Reingold, J.
Accelerando. Loomer, L.
Accents in Alsace: a reasonable tragedy. Stein, G.
Accident. Maloney, P.

Accidents

Bouchard, M. M. Down Dangerous Passes Road

Wilder, T. The message and Jehanne

According to Coyote. Kauffman, J.

Acharnians. Aristophanes

Ackerman, Peter

Things you shouldn't say past midnight. Broadway Play Pub. 2000 85p

ISBN 0-88145-168-1

Sexual comedy about three different couples in bed at three a.m. in the morning. 3 scenes 4m 2w 1 setting

Ackerman, Rob

Tabletop. Dramatists 2001 85p

ISBN 0-8222-1797-X   LC 2002-278647

Comedy about production crew filming commercial. Tempers and egos soon clash, and crew members fight for their jobs. 5m 1w 1 setting

Ackermann, Joan

The batting cage. Dramatists 1999 47p

ISBN 0-8222-1654-X   LC 00-502583

Drama set in St. Augustine, Florida motel room. Two estranged sisters mourn passing of beloved third sister. 2 acts 12 scenes 1m 3w 1 interior

Marcus is walking. Dramatists 1999 53p

ISBN 0-8222-1655-8   LC 00-503493

Comedy about Americans and their cars. 2 acts 11 scenes 3m 3w 1 setting

Off the map. Dramatists 1999 51p

ISBN 0-8222-1591-8   LC 99-222949

Coming-of-age tale. Woman recalls summer she was eleven and living with parents in Nevada desert. 2 acts 25 scenes 1g 3m 2w 1 setting

Acorn. Graziano, D.

The **acorn** planter. London, J.

Across from the garden of Allah. Wood, C.

Across the new frontier. Fredericks, A. D.

Acting

Calarco, J. Shakespeare's R & J

Stroppel, F. Actor!

Activism

Bhagat, D. Routes and escape routes

The **actor**. Foote, H.

Actor!. Stroppel, F.

Actors

Atkins, G. Rep

Chekhov, A. P. Swan song

Cohen, D. J. No way to treat a lady

Foote, H. The actor

Gilroy, F. D. Real to reel

Gotanda, P. K. Yankee dawg you die

Guare, J. New York actor

Healey, M. The drawer boy

Henley, B. Revelers

Howe, T. Rembrandt's gift

Joselovitz, E. Vilna's got a golem

Kaufman, G. S. The royal family

Keyes, S. Moonlight cocktail

Lawler, R. The Piccadilly bushman

Lloyd, M. Dead certain

Ludlam, C. Stage blood

Manzi, W. The audition

Manzi, W. The award

Manzi, W. One for the money

Margulies, D. L.A.

Marowitz, C. Stage fright

c Mason, T. Kidnapped in London

Milligan, J. Any friend of Percy D'Angelino is a friend of mine

Mode, B. Fully committed

Nigro, D. Laestrygonians

Perez, F. Estorias del barrio: special people of international character

Raznovich, D. Inner gardens (Jardín de otoño)

Rebeck, T. The contract

Rushforth, T. The Kerry dance

Sharland, E. Love from Shakespeare to Coward

Sirera, R. The audition

Smith, S. Background artiste

Stroppel, F. Actor!

Van Itallie, J.-C. War

Vreeke, J. The Canterville ghost

Williams, S. Laying the ghost

Williams, T. Out cry

Wood, C. Veterans; or, Hairs in the gates of Hellespont

Yew, C. Red

Actresses

Chekhov, A. P. The sea gull

Chekhov, A. P. The seagull

De Angelis, A. Playhouse creatures

Gould, H. M. Diva

Hare, D. Amy's view

y Kelly, T. Sundown Alley

Actresses—*Continued*

Lynch, J. Take two

MacLeod, J. The hope slide

MacLeod, W. The water children

Manzi, W. The queen of the parting shot

Margulies, D. Pitching to the star

Martin, J. Anton in show business

McConnell, J. Theatrical digs

McPherson, E. Divine Stella Devine

Mérimée, P. The gilded coach (Le carrosse du Saint-Sacrement)

Muschell, D. Amelia, once more

Nigro, D. Beast with two backs

Nigro, D. Laestrygonians

Pedrero, P. A night divided

Pollock, S. Moving pictures

Sandler, S. The burial society

Sondheim, S. A little night music

Stoppard, T. The real thing

Suvorin, A. S. Tatyana Repina

Van Zandt, B. Confessions of a dirty blonde

Wilder, T. Fanny Otcott

Williams, T. Out cry

Williams, T. Sweet bird of youth

Adam (Biblical figure)

Birney, D. The diaries of Adam & Eve

c Vogel, L. The fall into sin

Adamov, Arthur

The invasion; tr. by Robert J. Doan.

Absurdist drama about hopeless search for meaning. Man attempts to decipher illegible manuscript. 4 acts 3m 3w extra 1 setting

In Theater of the avant-garde, 1890-1950; ed. by B. Cardullo and R. Knopf

Adams, Gill

Something blue. Weinberger, J. 2002 65p
ISBN 0-85676-261-X

Drama set September 6, 1997, day of Princess Diana's funeral, in northern English market town. On her wedding day bride-to-be waits for groom to admit he is homosexual. 2 acts 6 scenes 1m 4w extras 2 interiors 1 exterior

Adams, Liz Duffy

Greeks and centaurs.

Woman fantasizes about sex with centaur at British Museum. 2m 1w 1 interior

In Women's project & productions; ed. by J. Miles

Poodle with guitar and dark glasses.

Comedy. Romance novelist, painter, activist, teacher and photographer struggle to find order in chaos of their lives. 4 acts 2m 3w 1 setting

In The Best American short plays, 2000-2001

Adams, Philip

Free's point.

Final violence-filled days in life of Michael Oros, who tried to live alone in remote bush near British Columbia/Yukon border. 3 scenes 2m 1 setting

In Staging the North; ed. by S. Grace, E. D'Aeth and L. Chalykoff

Adamson-Klein, Tessa

c The frog in all of us.

Fairy tale about princess who is obsessed with marrying a frog. 4m 1w 1 setting

In Blast from the future; ed. by D. Yeaton

Adaptive ruse. Beber, N.

Adelchi: a tragedy. Manzoni, A.

The **admissions** officers. Andrews, T.

Adolescence

y Alvarez, L. Analiese

Bradbeer, S. Full bloom

Busch, C. Psycho beach party

Carpenter, B. Fall

Foote, H. Laura Dennis

y Godber, J. Happy families

Gray, S. The late middle classes

y Harden, V. Jessica and Jolene

y Harden, V. Nobody heard mercy

y Hollingsworth, M. B. Johnny Brooke

y Lazarus, J. Secrets

Mérimée, P. The opportunity (L'Occasion)

Nelson, R. Madame Melville

y Newsome, M. The perfect night

Palmieri, M. Prologue

y Rabin, A. The man-child

y Rye, M. S. Turning points

Silberman, B. Walkin' backward

Adolescence—*Continued*

Wallace, N. The trestle at Pope Lick Creek

Wedekind, F. Spring's awakening

Williams, T. This property is condemned

Adoption

Netto, L. Maria

Oates, J. C. The adoption

O'Malley, G. Concertina's rainbow

Taylor, D. H. Only drunks and children tell the truth

The **adoption**. Oates, J. C.

Adult child/dead child. Dowie, C.

Adult entertainment. Walker, G. F.

Adult fiction. Mori, B.

Adultery

y Abbott, G. W. The scarlet letter

Arden of Faversham. Arden of Faversham

Benfield, D. Two and two together

Bobrick, S. Remember me?

Bovell, A. Speaking in tongues

Cabal, F. Passage

Carr, M. Portia Coughlan

Chapman, J. Business affairs

Chappell, E. Haywire

Chappell, E. Something's burning

Chiarelli, L. The mask and the face

Clarvoe, A. Walking on the roof

Coward, N. After the ball

Crommelynck, F. The magnanimous cuckold

Crommelynck, F. The merchant of regrets

Daniels, J. Boom town

Dietz, S. Private eyes

Elwell, J. S. Evening education

Farquhar, S. I do solemnly declare

Farrell, C. The once attractive woman

Feydeau, G. Winner takes all

Filippo, E. de. Those damned ghosts

Foote, H. A coffin in Egypt

Frisby, T. Funny about love

Gilbert, S. The emotionalists

Gilroy, F. D. Match point

Goold, R. The end of the affair

Hare, D. My zinc bed

Herne, J. A. Margaret Fleming

Horovitz, I. Alfred the Great

Janes, H. The perfect murder

Kane, A. Marriage can be hazardous to your health

Kokoschka, O. Sphinx and strawman

Kuruvilla, S. Snapshot: night out

Lipner, N. Pearls

May, E. In and out of the light

McConnell, J. Last post

Menander. Desperately seeking justice

Middleton, T. The changeling

Miller, A. Elegy for a lady

Murray, T. C. Autumn fire

Ogilvy, I. A slight hangover

Orloff, R. August afternoon

Parker, M. The sensuous senator

Pintauro, J. Two eclairs

Plowman, G. There's none so blind

Roth, A. Prelude to a crisis

Smith, C. Four-play

Sondheim, S. A little night music

Stoppard, T. The real thing

Taylor, R. Love poem #98

Weller, M. Mistresses

Whelan, P. The herbal bed

Wilson, L. Book of days

Wiltse, D. To wit and to whom

Adventure and adventurers

Ardito, C. Stoney Bowes

Francis, M. The adventures of Huckleberry Finn

c Grauer, R. Mark Twain's Huckleberry Finn

c Mason, T. The adventures of Huckleberry Finn

c Mason, T. The adventures of Tom Sawyer

Willmott, Phil. Around the world in eighty days

York, Y. Mask of the unicorn warrior

The **adventures** of a black girl in search of God. Sears, D.

The **adventures** of Huckleberry Finn. Francis, M.

The **adventures** of Huckleberry Finn. Mason, T.

The **adventures** of Tom Sawyer. Mason, T.

Advertising

Ackerman, R. Tabletop

Allen, G. Subliminable

Lucie, D. Fashion

Advertising—*Continued*
Powell, D. Big night
Aeolus and the winds. Barchers, S. I.

Aerenson, Benjie
Lighting up the two-year-old. Dramatists
1999 49p il
ISBN 0-8222-1648-5   LC 99-215186
Personal conflicts and shady dealings in horse
racing circles. 2 acts 3 scenes 3m 1 setting

Paradise Island. French 2002 48p
ISBN 0-573-62788-6
Drama about mother and daughter exchanging
verbal blows while on vacation in the Bahamas. 8
scenes 2w

The possum play. French 1998 96p
ISBN 0-573-62436-4   LC 98-213913
Son sabotages mother's efforts to improve lives
of residents of suburban Miami, Florida. 2 acts 28
scenes 7m 3w

Aeschylus
Agamemnon; tr. by Carl R. Mueller.
First play in Oresteia trilogy. Greek classical
drama in verse. Based on legend of murder of Ag-
amemnon by his wife and her lover after the Tro-
jan War. Speaking chorus.
In Aeschylus. Aeschylus: the complete
plays v1
—Same; tr. by David R. Slavitt
In Aeschylus. Aeschylus, 1
—Same; translated by Ted Hughes
In Aeschylus. The Oresteia

Choephori; translated by Ted Hughes.
Variant title: Libation bearers. Orestes and Electra, son and daughter of Agamemnon, meet at their
father's grave and avenge his death by killing their
mother. Orestes then sees the terrible Furies who
pursue matricides.
In Aeschylus. The Oresteia

Eumenides; tr. by Carl R. Mueller.
Variant title: The Furies. Classical tragedy in
verse. Oresteia part III. Based on legend of Orestes and the Furies (Eumenides), the goddesses of
retribution, who refused to absolve him of murder
of his mother.
In Aeschylus. Aeschylus: the complete
plays v1

—Same; tr. by David R. Slavitt
In Aeschylus. Aeschylus, 1
—Same; translated by Ted Hughes
In Aeschylus. The Oresteia
Libation bearers; tr. by Carl R. Mueller.
Variant title: Choephoroe. Greek classical trage-
dy in verse. Oresteia, part II. Based on Greek leg-
end of Orestes and Electra, son and daughter of
Agamemnon, telling how they avenged their fa-
ther's murder. Speaking chorus.
In Aeschylus. Aeschylus: the complete
plays v1
—Same; tr. by David R. Slavitt
In Aeschylus. Aeschylus, 1

Persians; tr. by Carl R. Mueller.
Greek tragedy in verse. Defeat of Xerxes and
Persians by Greeks at Salamis, 480 B.C. Speaking
chorus.
In Aeschylus. Aeschylus: the complete
plays v2
—Same; tr. by David R. Slavitt
In Aeschylus. Aeschylus, 2

Prometheus bound; tr. by Carl R.
Mueller.
Greek tragedy based on legend. Demi-god Pro-
metheus is punished for stealing fire from heaven.
Verse play.
In Aeschylus. Aeschylus: the complete
plays v2
—Same; tr. by William Matthews
In Aeschylus. Aeschylus, 2

Seven against Thebes; tr. by Carl R.
Mueller.
Greek tragedy in verse. Battle between sons of
Oedipus for sovereignty of Thebes. Speaking cho-
rus.
In Aeschylus. Aeschylus: the complete
plays v2
—Same; tr. by Stephen Sandy
In Aeschylus. Aeschylus, 2

Suppliants; tr. by Carl R. Mueller.
Greek legend of the Danaides. 50 daughters of
Danaus who fled from Egypt to escape forced
marriage. Verse play.
In Aeschylus. Aeschylus: the complete
plays v2
—Same; tr. by Gail Holst-Warhaft
In Aeschylus. Aeschylus, 2
about
Aristophanes. Frogs

Aesop

The lion and the mouse (dramatization) See McCullough, L. E. Squeak and maiow!

about

c Lehan, R. Three fables

The **affected** damsels. Molière

Africa

Carter, L. Gulliver redux

African Americans

Aiken, G. L. Uncle Tom's cabin

Alexander, R. The last orbit of Billy Mars

Baraka, A. Dutchman

Baraka, A. The election machine warehouse

Barfield, T. Without skin or breathlessness

Boyd, G. E. Consecrated ground

Brown, W. Life during wartime

Brown, W. W. The escape

Carter, L. Gulliver

Carter, L. Lemuel

Césaire, A. A tempest

Childress, A. Wedding band: a love/hate story in black and white

Cleage, P. Blues for an Alabama sky

Cleage, P. Bourbon at the border

Cleage, P. Chain

Cleage, P. Flyin' west

Cleage, P. Late bus to Mecca

Conquest, N. For they shall see God

Corthron, K. Force continuum

Corthron, K. Splash hatch on the E going down

Dunbar, P. L. Jes lak white fo'ks

Dunbar-Nelson, A. Mine eyes have seen

c Fredericks, A. D. December 1, 1955: Montgomery, Alabama

Gage, C. Harriet Tubman visits a therapist

Gardner, H. I'm not Rappaport

Green, P. Hymn to the rising sun: a drama of man's waste

Green, P. In Abraham's bosom: the tragedy of a southern Negro

c Hines, K. Home on the mornin' train

Hughes, L. Mulatto: a tragedy of the Deep South

Hughes, L. De organizer

Jennings, C. S. Classyass

Kennedy, A. An evening with dead Essex

Kennedy, A. Funnyhouse of a Negro

Kennedy, A. June and Jean in concert (the concert of their lives)

Kennedy, A. Motherhood 2000

Kennedy, A. A movie star has to star in black and white

Kennedy, A. Ohio State murders

Kennedy, A. The owl answers

Kennedy, A. Sun

Lauro, S. Open admissions

Linney, R. A lesson before dying

Long, Q. Snapshot: scene at Mount Rushmore

Martin, J. Shasta Rue

McClelland, C. E. Certain arrangements

McIntyre, D. Split second: a play in two acts

Medley, C. Dearborn Heights

Medley, C. Maiden Lane

Nottage, L. Mud, river, stone

O'Hara, R. Insurrection

Orlandersmith, D. Beauty's daughter

Orlandersmith, D. The gimmick

Orlandersmith, D. Monster

Rahman, A. The Mojo and the Sayso

Rahman, A. Only in America

Redwood, J. H. The old settler

Reed, I. Hubba city

Shephard-Massat, S. M. Waiting to be invited

Smith, C. Knock me a kiss

Smith, C. The Sutherland

y Sundstrom, B. The hundred penny box

y Surface, M. H. Broken rainbows

Taylor, R. It ain't nothin' but the blues

Thompson-Scretching, A. L. You shouldn't have told

Walcott, D. Walker

Wimberly, B. Saint Lucy's eyes

York, Y. The snowflake avalanche

African tales: Kalulu and his monkey farm and Rumpelstiltskin. Mason, T.

Africans

Bandele, 'Biyi. Aphra Behn's Oroonoko

England

Eagleton, T. Disappearances

Africans—*Continued*

United States

Magona, S. House-hunting unlike Soweto

After. Mack, C. K.

After Darwin. Wertenbaker, T.

After Easter. Devlin, A.

After January. Dean, P.

After the ball. Coward, N.

After the rain. Bowen, J.

After you. Dietz, S.

Afterthought. Beber, N.

Agamemnon (Greek mythology)

Aeschylus. Agamemnon

Euripides. Iphigenia at Aulis

Green, G. M. Goodbye, Iphigenia

Teevan, C. Iph. . .

Agamemnon. Aeschylus

The **age** of pie. Hedges, P.

Aging

Maloney, P. Accident

Williams, T. The milk train doesn't stop here anymore

Yew, C. Snapshot: here and now

The **agreement.** Neipris, J.

Agricultural laborers

Gonzalez, S. S. The migrant farmworker's son

Wesker, A. Roots

The **agronomist** (El extensionista). Santander, F.

Ahab (Biblical figure)

c Vogel, L. An Ahab headache and a Jezebelly ache

An **Ahab** headache and a Jezebelly ache. Vogel, L.

Ahlin, Lee

c Cinderella: the true story; book by Henry Fonte & Victoria Holloway; music and lyrics by Lee Ahlin. French 2000 56p

ISBN 0-573-62645-6

Musical based on Charles Perrault's Cinderella, set in New Orleans during Civil War. 2 acts 8 scenes 7m 6w extras 1 setting

Aias. Sophocles

Aidoo, Ama Ata

Anowa.

Set in Ghana in 1870s, explores capitalist and colonial exploitation, as well as patriarchal dominance and gender oppression. Prologue 3 parts 3b 1g 5m 4w extras

In Postcolonial plays; ed. by H. Gilbert

The dilemma of a ghost.

Ghanian student returns to his family with an African American bride. Prologue 5 acts 1b 1g 3m 7w 1 setting

In Modern African drama; ed. by B. Jeyifo

AIDS (Disease)

Alfaro, L. Straight as a line

Bishop, C. A friend from high school

Donaghy, T. The dadshuttle

Gilbert, S. The birth of Casper G. Schmidt

y Harden, V. HIV positive

Harvey, J. Hushabye Mountain

Houston, S. Message sent

Kramer, L. The destiny of me

Kramer, L. The normal heart

Lucas, C. Bad dream

MacLennan, M. L. Beat the sunset

MacLeod, J. The hope slide

Miller, T. Naked breath

Miller, T. Stretch marks

O'Donnell, S. Because I want to say

Osment, P. The undertaking

Rabe, D. A question of mercy

c Saar, D. The yellow boat

Schalchlin, S. The last session

Sheppard, J. Whatever

Sher, E. Denial is a river

Smith, O. Giant steps

Wilson, L. Your everyday ghost story

Aiken, George L.

Uncle Tom's cabin.

Based on Harriet Beecher Stowe's novel about slavery and freedom. 6 acts 30 scenes 1b 20m 7w 8 interiors 8 exteriors

In Fateful lightning; ed. by W. J. Meserve and M. A. Meserve

Air pilots

Aspengren, K. Flyer

Giron, A. Flight

MacLeod, W. Sin

Air to breathe, water to drink. Fredericks, A. D.

Airplanes

Giron, A. Flight

Pritchard, E. Chicken wings

The **airport** play. Gersten-Vassilaros, A.

Airports

Felder, L. Flight of fancy

Filloux, C. Storks

Gersten-Vassilaros, A. The airport play

Lipkin, D. I am Laika

Long, Q. The flight of the last Calhoon

Reitz, D. Where I come from

Roth, A. Terminal connection

Sagal, P. Happenstance

Tarses, J. Cecilia

Yourgrau, T. Peanuts

Ajax. Sophocles

Akalaitis, JoAnne

Ti Jean blues.

Performance piece adapted from the writings of Jack Kerouac, and loosely following the trajectory of his life. 3m 2w 1 setting

In Humana Festival '98

Akhmatova, Anna Adreevna

about

De Groen, A. The woman in the window

Akiba ben Joseph, ca. 50-ca. 132

about

Kushner, T. Notes on Akiba

Al-Hakim, Tawfik

Fate of a cockroach.

Satirical comedy. The do-nothing King of the Cockroaches, whose realm is anatomized, falls into the bathtub of human couple, setting off a marital crisis. 2 acts 7m 3w 2 interiors

In Modern African drama; ed. by B. Jeyifo

Al takes a bride. Sunshine, G.

Aladdin and the magic lamp. Miller, K. S.

Aladdin and the wonderful lamp. Mason, T.

Alarms & excursions. Frayn, M.

Alaska

Brevoort, D. B. Into the fire

Albanian softshoe. Wellman, M.

Albee, Edward

The American dream.

Absurdist satire on the American family. 1 act 2m 3w 1 interior

In Plays of provocation; ed. by F. P. Richmond

The play about the baby. Dramatists 2002

ISBN 0-8222-1814-3

Black comedy about a young couple who have just had a baby, and the strange events that transpire when they are visited by an older man and woman. 2m 2w 1 interior settings

The **Alcestiad.** Wilder, T.

Alcestis. Euripides

The **Alcestis** of Euripides. Euripides

The **alchemist.** Jonson, B.

Alchemy

Jonson, B. The alchemist

Alchemy of desire/dead-man's blues. Svich, C.

Alcoholics Anonymous

Shem, S. Bill W. and Dr. Bob

Alcoholism

Bishop, C. Get happy

Brecht, B. Baal

Farquhar, R. Dust to dust

Foley, D. Sad hotel

Geiogamah, H. Body Indian

Glass, J. M. Play memory

Hughes, D. Digging for fire

McPherson, C. Rum and vodka

Mtshali, T. S. Weemen

Mullins, B. Click

Rintoul, H. Brave hearts

Roth, A. Jeffrey Slugworth: ex-embalmer

y Rye, M. S. Turning points

Shem, S. Bill W. and Dr. Bob

y Surface, M. H. Dancing solo

Alcott, Louisa May, 1832-1888

Little women (dramatization) See Barchers, S. I., and Kroll, J. L. Little women

Aldridge, Ron

You're only young twice. Weinberger, J. 2001 99p

ISBN 0-85676-259-8

Comedy. Widower determined to recapture his youth moves in with his daughter. Music, dancing. 2 acts 3 scenes 3m 4w 1 interior

Alexander, Bill. See Whelan, P. jt. auth.

Alexander, Robert

The last orbit of Billy Mars.

Drama set in lower middle-class African American neighborhood in St. Louis. Musician pursues bisexual woman. 2 acts 3 scenes 2m 2w 1 interior

In Plays from Woolly Mammoth; ed. by R. Alexander and M. Kyrioglou

A preface to the alien garden. Broadway Play Pub. 2001 86p

ISBN 0-88145-191-6

Hip-hop gansta' play set in urban wasteland. Members of a violent crack-dealing gang begin to kill each other. Singing. Prologue 2 acts 11 scenes 5m 3w 1 interior 1 exterior

Alexander, Robert and others

Heaven and hell (on earth): a divine comedy.

Comic anthology of sketches and monologues by 17 playwrights all dealing with issues of good and evil. Variable cast settings

In Humana Festival 2001

Alexander the great

about

Cibber, C. The rival queans

Alexandrine War, 48-47 B.C.

Shaw, B. Caesar and Cleopatra

Alfaro, Luis

Bitter homes and gardens.

Black comedy about dysfunctional family. Social satire about quest of Latina mother and daughter to locate American Dream in suburban Los Angeles. 18 scenes 2m 2w 1 interior

In Latino plays from South Coast Repertory

Downtown.

Monologue about racism, alcoholism, sexual and political diversity, and AIDS awareness. 1m

In O Solo homo; ed. by H. Hughes and D. Román

Straight as a line.

Comical British expat moves her gay son to Las Vegas and tries to mother him as he dies of AIDS. 1 act 13 scenes 1m 1w 1 setting

In Out of the fringe; ed. by C. Svich and M. T. Marrero

Alfred dies. Horovitz, I.

Alfred the Great. Horovitz, I.

Alien boy. Scheffer, W.

Alien creature. Griffiths, L.

Alien teacher. Fredericks, A. D.

Alienor. Chiasson, H.

Alkestis. Euripides

Alki. Overmyer, E.

All about Al. Vogelstein, C.

All cotton. Silverstein, S.

All my sons. Miller, A.

All powers necessary and convenient. Jenkins, M. F.

All the king's horses. Fuson, D.

All the king's men. Warren, R. P.

All the knowledge in the universe. Fredericks, A. D.

All the Verdis of Venice. Chaurette, N.

All things are bright and beautiful. Zapel, A. L.

Allegories

Constable, J. The Southwark Mysteries

Darke, N. The body

Fugard, A. Sorrows and rejoicings

y Hippolyte, K. The song of one; or, The journey of Ti Marie

Jonson, B. Pleasure reconciled to Virtue

Juana Inés de la Cruz. The divine Narcissus (El divino Narciso)

Lavery, B. Origin of the species

c McCullough, L. E. Noah's ark: falsehood and wickedness hitch a ride

Panikkar, K. N. Aramba Chekkan

Pomerance, B. Hands of light

Wertenbaker, T. The Ash Girl

Williams, T. Camino Real

Allegory of whiteness. Wellman, M.

Allen, Greg

Subliminable.

An advertisement for short play entitled Subliminable. Variable cast 1 character

In Humana Festival 2001

Allen, Woody

The floating light bulb. French 2000 80p

ISBN 0-573-62739-8

Comedy about a struggling couple and their stuttering son living in Carnarsie, Brooklyn, New York in 1945. 2 acts 8 scenes 4m 2w 1 interior

Allison, Brian

Titus at the gates of Syon. Minerva Press
   1999 97p
   ISBN 0-75410-572-5

Historical drama about the ancient Jewish historian Josephus, the fall of ancient Jerusalem, and
the mass suicide of the defenders of Masada. 5
acts 16 scenes 16m 1w settings

Almost in Vegas. Neipris, J.

Alonso de Santos, Jose Luis

Hostages in the barrio; tr. by Phyllis
   Zatlin. Estreno 1997 44p
   ISBN 1-888463-02-3

Two unemployed laborers attempt to rob elderly
owner of tobacco shop and her granddaughter,
only to have tables turned and find themselves
trapped by police. 4 scenes 3m 2w extras 1 setting

Alphabet

c McCullough, L. E. The alphabet

The **alphabet**. McCullough, L. E.

alterNatives. Taylor, D. H.

The **altruists**. Silver, N.

Alvarez, Lynne

y Analiese.

Teenage couple find love, lose love, and seek
their own future against backdrop of contrasting
social and physical environments. 12 scenes Variable cast

   In New Plays from A.C.T.'s young
      conservatory v3

—Same

   In Women playwrights: the best plays
      of 1997

Deux marriages: Romola and Nijinsky.

Drama about Nijinsky's marriage to Romola de
Pulsky explores issues of sexuality, love, art and
insanity. 3 acts 16 scenes 5m 6w

   In Women playwrights: the best plays
      of 2001

Don Juan of Seville.

Adaptation of play by Tirso de Molina. Dark humor. Don Juan portrayed as callow "brat-pack"
youth. 3 acts Large mixed cast 2 interiors

   In Alvarez, L. Collected plays: v1

Eddie Mundo Edmundo.

Following mother's death Mexican American
travels to Mexico to explore his heritage. Singing,
dancing. 2 acts 25 scenes 1b 3m 3w 1 setting

   In Alvarez, L. Collected plays: v1

The guitarrón.

Mexican seaside setting for drama about fatal
encounter between noted cellist, two fishermen,
master boatwright and two young lovers. 2 acts 16
scenes 6m 1w 1 setting

   In Alvarez, L. Collected plays: v1

Hidden parts.

Midwest farm family haunted by dark secret. 2
acts 9 scenes 2m 2w 1 setting

   In Alvarez, L. Collected plays: v1

On Sundays.

Symbolic drama about passion, aging and memory. 1 act 6 scenes 1m 1w 1 setting

   In Alvarez, L. Collected plays: v1

The reincarnation of Jaime Brown.

Black comedy about sex, suicide, hair loss and
reincarnation. 2 acts 5m 3w settings

   In Alvarez, L. Collected plays: v1

Thin air: tales from a revolution.

Set in South America. Dream and reality blur in
depiction of revolution and people who disappear
into it. 3 acts 1g 7m 4w extras 2 interiors

   In Alvarez, L. Collected plays: v1

The wonderful tower of Humbert
   Lavoignet.

Comedy drama about faith and sacrifice. Man
believes he has been ordered by God to erect tower of junk. 11 scenes 4m 1w 1 setting

   In Alvarez, L. Collected plays: v1

Alzheimer's disease

Churchill, C. Blue kettle

Kramer, S. World without memory

Vradenburg, T. The apple doesn't fall
   . . .

Am I blue. Henley, B.

Amahl and the night visitors. Menotti,
   G.-C.

Amazing grace. Cristofer, M.

Ambition

Finlayson, A. Winding the ball

Ibsen, H. John Gabriel Borkman

Morgan, E. Christopher Marlowe's Doctor Faustus

Nigro, D. Broadway macabre

Amelia, once more. Muschell, D.

America hurrah (interview, TV, motel).
   Van Itallie, J.-C.

An **American** chronicle. Metcalf, P.

An **American** comedy. Nelson, R.

An **American** daughter. Wasserstein, W.

American drama
19th century
Aiken, G. L. Uncle Tom's cabin
Barras, C. M. The black crook
Belasco, D. The heart of Maryland
Boker, G. H. Francesca da Rimini
Boucicault, D. The octoroon; or, Life in Louisiana
Gillette, W. Secret service
Harrigan, E. The blue and the grey
Herne, J. A. Margaret Fleming
Howard, B. Shenandoah
Jefferson, J. Rip Van Winkle
McCabe, J. D. J. The guerrillas
Mowatt, A. C. Fashion; or, Life in New York
Swayze, J. C. Ossawattomie Brown
Trowbridge, J. T. Neighbor Jackwood
Woolf, B. E. Off to the war

The **American** dream. Albee, E.

American gypsy. Glancy, D.

The **American** plan. Greenberg, R.

Americans
Africa
Nottage, L. Mud, river, stone
Australia
Kim, S. Dreamtime for Alice
China
Neipris, J. A small delegation
England
Vreeke, J. The Canterville ghost
France
Tait, L. The swimming pools of Paris
Ghana
Aidoo, A. A. The dilemma of a ghost
Greece
Sherman, M. A madhouse in Goa
Iceland
Ardal, M. Midnight sun
Italy
Rusconi, P. These two couples went to Italy
Williams, T. The milk train doesn't stop here anymore
Mexico
Shepard, S. Eyes for Consuela
Russia
Congdon, C. Under Lubianka Square

Serbia
Stanley, J. Tesla's letters

Aminta. Tasso, T.

Among friends. Thatcher, K.

Amor de mis amores. Gasteazoro, E.

Amphitryon. Kleist, H. von

Amsterdam (Netherlands)
Robinson, P. Red hot in Amsterdam

Amusement parks
Quilter, P. Respecting your piers

Amy Crockett: M.V.P. Cohen, F.

Amy's view. Hare, D.

An' push da wind down. Harper, L.

Analiese. Alvarez, L.

Anarchists and anarchism
Stoppard, T. Voyage

Anasazi Indians
c Fredericks, A. D. A day in Mesa Verde

Anatol. Schnitzler, A.

Anatomy lesson. Tremblay, L.

Ancestral voices: a family story. Gurney, A. R.

And send forth a raven. Toddie, J. L.

And tell sad stories of the death of queens. Williams, T.

And that's how people burn to death in motel rooms. Reitz, D.

And the girls in their Sunday dresses. Mda, Z.

And the sea shall give up its dead. Wilder, T.

And where was Pancho Villa when you really needed him? Wood, S.

Andeganora. Esson, L.

Andersen, D. R.
Everywhere.

Grungy rock-star patient persuades psychiatrist that a 50-minute nap is the best medicine. Singing. 1 act 1 scene 2m 1 interior

In Andersen, D. R. Crazy and a half

I'll take Manhattan.

Two patients must improvise when their psychiatrist is rushed to the hospital. Fortunately, both patients are themselves psychiatrists. 1 act 1m 1w 1 interior

In Andersen, D. R. Crazy and a half

Andersen, D. R.—*Continued*
In other words.
Psychiatrist treating a Mafia wife achieves a comic breakthrough at gunpoint, possibly resolving some of his own marital problems as well. 1 act 2m 1w 1 interior
In Andersen, D. R. Crazy and a half

They can't take that away from me.
A pair of psychiatrists, on the verge of divorce, schedule a therapy weekend with a couple whose problems involve extraterrestrials. Music. 1 act 1 scene 2m 2w 1 exterior
In Andersen, D. R. Crazy and a half

Yes, sir, that's my baby.
Child psychiatrist brings professional skills to bear on tricky custody battle with her ex-husband. 1 act 1m 1w 1 interior
In Andersen, D. R. Crazy and a half

You oughta be in pictures.
Encouraged by a self-help maven in a bunny suit, a California psychiatrist decides to use video to reach out to her straying lesbian lover. 1 act 1 scene 2w 1 interior
In Andersen, D. R. Crazy and a half

Andersen, Hans Christian

The little match girl (dramatization) See Gollobin, L. B. The match girl's gift: A Christmas story

The nightingale (dramatization) See Mason, T. The nightingale

Thumbelina (dramatization) See Francoeur, B. Tiny Thumbelina

about
c Averill, R. Pixies, kings, and magical things

Parodies, imitations, etc.
c Miller, K. S. The emperor's new clothes

Anderson, Jane

Defying gravity. French 1998 60p
　　ISBN 0-573-60133-X　　　LC 99-199269
Drama revolving around the 1986 Challenger disaster, focusing on the teacher who died along with six other astronauts. Interweaves lives of participants, bystanders, and the painter Claude Monet. 24 scenes 3m 4w
—Same
　In Women playwrights: the best plays of 1997

Looking for normal. Dramatists 2002
　　ISBN 0-8222-1857-7

After twenty-five years of marriage and two children, husband seeks sex change operation. 5m 4w 1 setting

Lynette has beautiful skin.
Young couple and their friend hang out at pizza parlor. 2m 1w 1 interior
　In 30 ten-minute plays for 3 actors from Actors Theatre of Louisville's National Ten-minute Play Contest

Anderson, Sheryl J.

The big one.
Worship program. Coach sends Angel Gabriel to tell Mary of coming of Jesus. 3m 1 interior
　In Anderson, S. J. The twelve plays of Christmas

Echoes of Christmas.
Worship program. Three choral readings from Bible about birth of Christ. Variable cast 4 characters 1 setting
　In Anderson, S. J. The twelve plays of Christmas

Epiphany mosaic.
Worship program. Choir learns meaning of Epiphany. Singing Variable cast 12 characters 1 setting
　In Anderson, S. J. The twelve plays of Christmas

Hanging on the tree.
Worship program. Man explains why he decorates Christmas tree with peculiar ornaments. 2m 1 interior
　In Anderson, S. J. The twelve plays of Christmas

c "Jingle bells" revisited.
Worship program. Children learn new lyrics for seasonal tune. Singing. Variable cast 1 setting
　In Anderson, S. J. The twelve plays of Christmas

Live from Bethlehem.
Worship program. Television news reports on birth of Jesus. 1m 1w 1 setting
　In Anderson, S. J. The twelve plays of Christmas

The night before pageant.
Worship program in verse. Church leaders worry over preparation for Christmas pageant. Unidentified cast 4 characters 1 setting
　In Anderson, S. J. The twelve plays of Christmas

Anderson, Sheryl J.—*Continued*
Now a shepherd, no longer a sheep.

Worship program. Young man is nervous about part in Christmas pageant. 2m 2w 1 interior
> *In* Anderson, S. J. The twelve plays of Christmas

Oh, come on, Emmanuel.

Worship program. Woman explains that true meaning of Christmas stays with you always. 1m 3w extras 1 setting
> *In* Anderson, S. J. The twelve plays of Christmas

Tidings of comfort and joy.

Worship program. Christmas caroller also sings of Easter. Singing. 1m 2w extras 1 setting
> *In* Anderson, S. J. The twelve plays of Christmas

A traditional pageant.

Worship program based on Bible story of birth of Jesus. 10m 2w extras 1 setting
> *In* Anderson, S. J. The twelve plays of Christmas

Traveling with reservations.

Worship program. Traveler and pregnant wife arrive at hotel which has no rooms available. 2m 1 interior
> *In* Anderson, S. J. The twelve plays of Christmas

While you were out.

Worship program. Angel Gabriel reminds family of true meaning of Christmas. 1b 1g 1m 1w 1 setting
> *In* Anderson, S. J. The twelve plays of Christmas

Anderson, Roger
Shine!: the Horatio Alger musical; book by Richard Seff; lyrics by Lee Goldsmith; music by Roger Anderson. French 2002 106p
ISBN 0-573-62928-5

Musical set in summer of 1876 in New York. Adventures of Ragged Dick, who rises from poverty to success on Wall Street. 2 acts 22 scenes 13m 6w settings

Andrews, Tim
The admissions officers.

God and the Devil meet in a diner and discuss humanity. 1m 1w 1 setting
> *In* Blast from the future; ed. by D. Yeaton

Andromache. Euripides
Andy and Claire. Hedges, P.
The **angel** on the ship. Wilder, T.
The **angel** that troubled the waters. Wilder, T.

Angeles, Tony
Tightwad.

Mini-musical about reviving dead guy for money. Music, singing. 3m 4w 1 interior
> *In* HB Playwrights short play festival 2000

Angelica! . . . and the monstrous monster of the deep. Roberts, B.
The **Angelina** project. Canino, F.
Angélique. Gale, L.
Angelo Herndon Jones. Hughes, L.

Angels
> Anderson, S. J. The big one
> Anderson, S. J. While you were out
> Hall, L. I love you, Jimmy Spud
> *y* Jackson, R. E. Touched by an angle
> *c* McCullough, L. E. Tales of angels
> Vogel, L. The angels' locker room: A Christmas play

Angels and saints. Townsend, J.
Angels fall. Wilson, L.
The **angels'** locker room: A Christmas play. Vogel, L.
Angels of war. Box, M.
Angel's trumpet. Pollock, S.

Anglo-Indians
> Khan-Din, A. Last dance at dum dum

Angus, Eric, and Shostak, Cathy
The demon headmaster; book by Paul James; lyrics by Iain Halstead and Paul James; music by Eric Angus and Cathy Shostak. French (London) 2001 102p
ISBN 0-573-08116-6

Based on the novel the Demon Headmaster by Gillian Cross. Students at ultra-disciplined school are out to expose the demon headmaster. Music. singing. 2 acts 6b 6g 5m 3w extras setting

Ania and Esther. Mann, K.

Animal welfare
> *c* McCullough, L. E. Monster in the basement (animal rescue agent)

Animals

c Barchers, S. I. The farmer and the animals

c Bennett, A. Kenneth Grahame's The wind in the willows

Bruchac, J. Possum's tail

c Espinosa, R. The farmer finds his true friends (El granjero descubre a sus verdaderos amigos)

c Jensen, L. Coming around

c Mast, E. Jungalbook

y Mast, E. Wolf child

c McNeff, S. Tom Kitten and his friends

c Smith, J. G. What the animals made known

Anna Christie. O'Neill, E.

Anna Weiss. Cullen, M.

Anne. Ledoux, P.

Anne Boleyn, Queen, consort of Henry VIII, King of England, 1507-1536

about

Luckham, C. The seduction of Anne Boleyn

Annette and Annette. Bogdan, K.

Annie Mae's movement. Nolan, Y.

Annie Wobbler. Wesker, A.

Anniversary. Shields, C., and Williamson, D.

Annunciation, The

Ehn, E. Tree of hope, keep firm (Mary, the Annunciation)

Another American: asking and telling. Wolf, M.

Another Antigone. Gurney, A. R.

Anouilh, Jean, 1910-1987

To Fool the Eye (adaptation) See Hatcher, J. To fool the eye

Antigone; tr. by Jeremy Sams. French 2002 48p

ISBN 0-573-62819-X

This version of Sophocles' tragedy was composed in Vichy, France, in 1942 and is in part a political allegory, pitting plausible arguments for collaboration against the imperatives of justice and personal integrity. 1 act 7m 3w extra 1 setting

Anowa. Aidoo, A. A.

Anthems. Culture Clash (Group)

Anthony, Trey

'Da kink in my hair.

Comic drama using hair as metaphor to explore lives of seven Canadian black women of Caribbean descent. 1 act 9w 1 interior

In Testifyin' v2; ed. by D. Sears

Anthony. Margulies, D.

Anthropology

c McCullough, L. E. Anthropology, the science of us

Anthropology, the science of us. McCullough, L. E.

Anti-Semitism

Horovitz, I. A Rosen by any other name

Rivera, J. The crooked cross

Antichrist

Wilson, S. The glad hand

Antigone (Greek mythology)

y Reader, C. The Oedipus plays

Antigone. Anouilh, J.

Antigone. Sophocles

Anton in show business. Martin, J.

Antonelli, Luigi

A man confronts himself; tr. by Michael Vena.

Older man, allowed to relive his youth, discovers that age does not prevent errors. 3 acts 4m 3w extras 3 exteriors

In Italian grotesque theater

Any friend of Percy D'Angelino is a friend of mine. Milligan, J.

Any given day. Gilroy, F. D.

Anything for you. Celesia, C.

Anything to declare? Hennequin, M., and Veber, P.

Apartment 3A. Daniels, J.

Apartment houses

Ayckbourn, A. Things we do for love

Sherman, J. Romance in D

Aphra Behn's Oroonoko. Bandele, 'Biyi

Apollo (Greek mythology)

Aeschylus. The Eumenides

Euripides. Ion

Kennedy, A. Orestes (Euripides)

Appalachia

c Art, S. S. The Hatfields and the McCoys

Linney, R. Gint

Appalachia—*Continued*
Linney, R. True crimes
c McBride-Smith, B. Cat-skins
Schenkar, J. Cabin fever
y Urquhart, J. Liza and the riddling cave
Appendix two: illumination. Murray, T. C.
Apple. Thiessen, V.
The **apple** doesn't fall . . . Vradenburg, T.
Appleseed, Johnny, 1774-1845

about

c Snyder, G. A. Johnny Appleseed
Approaching Simone. Terry, M.
April in Paris. Godber, J.

Apstein, Theodore
The likeness.

Drama set in 17th century Amsterdam. Jewish man is used to represent face of Jesus in Rembrandt's Christ at Emmaus. 1 act 2m 1w 1 interior

In The Best American short plays 1998-1999

The **Aquarians**. Kleberg, L.
Arabian knights—The panto! Lloyd, R.

Arabian nights

Parodies, imitations, etc.

c Hamlett, C. The prince's dilemma
Arabian nights. Ives, D.

Arabs
Hare, D. Via Dolorosa
Arachne and Athena. McBride-Smith, B.
Aramba Chekkan. Panikkar, K. N.

Araújo, Luis
Vanzetti; tr. by Mary-Alice Lessing. Estreno 1999 36p (Contemporary Spanish Plays, 16)
ISBN 1-888463-08-2

Theater piece about Bartolomeo Vanzetti, an immigrant anarchist tried for murder in Massachusetts in 1921. His actual words alternate with the imagined reactions of his family back in Italy and of the hanging judge at his trial. 1 act 2m 1w 1 setting

Arcadia. Stoppard, T.

Archaeology
Selig, P. Slide show
Wilson, L. The mound builders
Archangels don't play pinball. Fo, D.

Archer, Jeffrey, 1940-
The perfect murder (dramatization) See Janes, H. The perfect murder
Archie of the Amazon. Moriarty, J.
The **architect**. Greig, D.

Architects
Safdie, O. Private jokes, public places
The **archives** at Kanonicza 5. Kraszewski, C. S.

Arctic regions
Kavanagh, G. Ditch
MacEwen, G. Terror and Erebus

Ardal, Maja
Midnight sun. Playwrights Canada 2001 98p
ISBN 0-88754-603-X

Drama set in small northern community during American occupation of Iceland in 1942. Young Icelanders surrender themselves to American popular culture. Music, singing. 2 acts 3m 3w 1 setting

Arden, John
Serjeant Musgrave's dance.

Satire set in Northern England mining town in 1880s. Pacifist sergeant, ostensibly on recruiting mission, intends to teach townspeople horrors of war and colonialism. Music, singing. 3 acts 8 scenes 11m 2w extras 3 interiors 4 exteriors

In The Methuen book of sixties drama

Arden of Faversham
Arden of Faversham.

Also known as The lamentable and true tragedy of Master Arden of Faversham. Domestic tragedy ascribed to Thomas Kyd. Based on case history of murder of a husband by his wife and her lover, 1551, in which miscreants are brought to justice. 18 scenes epilogue 15m 2w extras

In Renaissance drama; ed. by A. F. Kinney

Ardito, Carlo
A bed for the knight.

Through an innocent misunderstanding, a businessman wakes up in the bed of the Home Secretary's wife, setting off farcical complications as characters try to fan or extinguish the potential scandal. 2 acts 8m 5w 1 interior

In Ardito, C. Three plays

Ardito, Carlo—*Continued*
Brief candle.

Drama based on life of painter and diarist Marie Bashkirtseff. Set between 1873 and 1874 in Nice, Paris, Rome, Naples, St. Petersburg, and Moscow. 19 scenes 2m 4w 1 setting

   In Ardito, C. Brief candle; Stoney Bowes; Confessions of Zeno; Da Ponte's last stand

Confessions of Zeno.

Dramatization of novel by Italo Svevo. Comic anti-hero struggles to escape attention of Freudian analyst. 17 scenes 7m 6w 9 interiors 2 exteriors

   In Ardito, C. Brief candle; Stoney Bowes; Confessions of Zeno; Da Ponte's last stand

Da Ponte's last stand.

Drama based on autobiographical recollections of Mozart's librettist Lorenzo Da Ponte. Music. 17 scenes 9m 2w 9 interiors 2 exteriors

   In Ardito, C. Brief candle; Stoney Bowes; Confessions of Zeno; Da Ponte's last stand

St. James's blues.

A traditional London club will have to accept women members to stay afloat. 1 act 14 scenes 6m 2w 1 interior

   In Ardito, C. Three plays

Stoney Bowes.

Drama set in England in late 18th and early 19th century. Unsavory adventures of Stoney Bowes, model for Thackeray's Barry Lyndon. 20 scenes 5m 2w

   In Ardito, C. Brief candle; Stoney Bowes; Confessions of Zeno; Da Ponte

Waiting for the barbarians.

A group of Romans ready themselves for a barbarian invasion but are stuck with the status quo when the enemy fails to appear. Inspired by the Cavafy poem. 2 parts 5m 2w 1 exterior

   In Ardito, C. Three plays

Ardov, Victor

The case of the entry room.

Russian agitational drama featuring monomaniacal characters, transparent scams and absurdist aesthetics. Dispute over use of entry hall goes to trial. 7m 4w extras 1 interior

   In Eight twentieth-century Russian plays; ed. by T. Langen and J. Weir

Are you being served? Lloyd, J., and Croft, D.

Are you ready? Auburn, D.

Argall, T. Gregory

A year in the death of Eddie Jester. French (London) 2003 62p
  ISBN 0-573-62973-0

Stand-up comic is beaten into a coma and goes through much self discovery. 2 acts 7 scenes 3m 2w

Argentina

Mueller, L. The mothers
Raznovich, D. Disconcerted (El disconcierto)

Ariadne (Greek mythology)

c Barchers, S. I. Ariadne
Ariadne. Barchers, S. I.
Arion and his harp. Barchers, S. I.

Aristophanes

The Acharnians; tr. by Jack Flavin.

Greek classical comedy satirizing economic and social effects of militarism. Athenian farmer makes private peace treaty with Sparta. Verse play. Speaking chorus.

   In Aristophanes. Aristophanes, 1

—Same; translated by S. Douglas Olson

   In Greek and Roman Comedy; ed. by S. O'Bryhim

Birds; tr. by Paul Muldoon.

Greek classical comedy. Utopian fantasy. Two Athenians persuade birds to build city in the air called Cloud Cuckooland to cut off gods from men and replace them as ruling powers. Verse play. Speaking chorus.

   In Aristophanes. Aristophanes, 3

—Same; trans. by Kenneth McLeish

   In Six Greek comedies

Celebrating ladies; tr. by David R. Slavitt.

Variant titles: Festival time; Thesmophoriazousai. Greek classical comedy. Farce which burlesques Euripides and eternal battle of the sexes. Verse play. Speaking chorus

   In Aristophanes. Aristophanes, 1

Clouds; tr. by Carol Poster.

Greek classical satire on sophistical system of Socrates' educational methods. Verse play. Speaking chorus.

   In Aristophanes. Aristophanes, 3

Aristophanes—*Continued*

Frogs; tr. by Alfred Corn.

Greek satirical comedy. Dionysus, patron of theater, touring underworld in search of great poet, must choose between Aeschylus and Euripides. Speaking chorus.

In Aristophanes. Aristophanes, 2

—Same; trans. by Kenneth McLeish

In Six Greek comedies

Lysistrata; tr. by X. J. Kennedy.

Greek classical farce. To end war Athenian women organize sex strike. Speaking chorus.

In Aristophanes. Aristophanes, 2

Peace; tr. by Fred Beake.

Greek Classical comedy. Trygiaos enlists aid of other Athenian farmers to rescue goddess Peace after learning gods have left War in control of heaven to punish Greek cities for their squabbling. Verse play. Speaking chorus.

In Aristophanes. Aristophanes, 1

The sexual congress; tr. by R. H. W. Dillard.

Variant titles: Ecclesiazusai; Women in power. Greek classical satire in verse. Athenian women take over government and transform Athens into new society of communal property, food, and sex. Speaking chorus.

In Aristophanes. Aristophanes, 2

The suits; tr. by Greg Delanty.

Greek classical comedy in verse. Satirical attack on Athenian political demagoguery.

In Aristophanes. Aristophanes, 3

Wasps; tr. by Campbell McGrath.

Greek classical satire on demagogues. Philodeon's passion for lawsuits is checked when his son turns their house into a law court. Verse play. Speaking chorus.

In Aristophanes. Aristophanes, 2

Wealth; tr. by Palmer Bovie.

Variant title: Ploutos. Greek classical comedy in verse. God of wealth is cured of blindness and Poverty is defeated. Speaking chorus.

In Aristophanes. Aristophanes, 1

Women in power; tr. by Kenneth Mc-Leish.

Variant titles: Ecclesiazusai; The sexual congress. Greek classical satire. Athenian women take over government and transform Athens into new society of communal property, food, and sex. Speaking chorus

In Six Greek comedies

Arizmendi, Yareli

Nostalgia maldita: 1-900-MEXICO, a Stairmaster piece.

Performance piece for one actress, a recorded voice, and a Stairmaster. Reflections on immigrant experience. Music, singing. 1 scene 1w 1 setting

In Puro teatro; ed. by A. Sandoval-Sánchez and N. S. Sternbach

Arizona

Coen, L. Epic proportions

The **ark**. Griffin, H.

The **Arkansaw** bear. Harris, A.

Arkin, Alan

Virtual reality.

Pair of covert operatives waiting for supplies and instructions start to imagine what the mission will entail, and succumb to their increasingly vivid fantasies. 1 act 2m 1 interior

In May, E. & Arkin, A. Power plays

Armagideon. Dempsey, S.

Armenians

United States

Ayvazian, L. Nine Armenians

Armitage. Nigro, D.

Armory

The gentleman of the chrysanthemums.

Comedy of manners set in 1908 Paris about the homosexual as celebrity. 3 acts 34 scenes variable cast 1 interior

In Lovesick; ed. by L. Senelick

Armstrong, Doug, and others

A Christmas Twist; by Doug Armstrong, Keith Cooper, Maureen Morley. Broadway Play Pub. 2000 69p
ISBN 0-88145-176-2

Parody of Dickens's Christmas carol. Satire on excesses of Christmas sentimentality. Prologue 2 acts 12 scenes Variable cast 17 characters

Of grapes and nuts. Broadway Play Pub. 2000 64p
ISBN 0-88145-174-6

Comedy satire of John Steinbeck's novels The grapes of wrath and Of mice and men. 2 acts 3 scenes 9m 4w

Arnault, Andrew. See Arnault, M. jt. auth.

Arnault, Mary, and Arnault, Andrew

The legend of Sleepy Hollow; comedy with music by Mary and Andrew Arnault. Dramatic Publishing 2003 73p

Comedy with music. Dramatization of Irving's tale of superstitious schoolmaster's encounter with headless horseman. 9m 7w 1 setting

Arnold, Benedict, 1741-1801

about

Nelson, R. The general from America

Aron, Geraldine

My brilliant divorce. French (London) 2003 56p

ISBN 0-573-03021-9

Woman attempts to find a new life after divorcing husband. 1w

Aronson, Billy

The art room.

Twisted love triangle set in mental ward. 2 acts 3 scenes 3m 3w 2 interiors

In Plays from Woolly Mammoth; ed. by R. Alexander and M. Kyrioglou

Dream.

Just before the alarm goes off, a woman's mind is full of the complicated agenda for her day and old memories, in a surrealistic fugue. 1 act 1m 1w 1 setting

In EST marathon '98: the one-act plays; ed. by M. Smith

Light years.

First day of college. 1 act 2m 2w 1 interior

In The Best American short plays 1999-2000

—Same

In Ensemble Studio Theatre marathon 2000: the one-act plays

Around the world in eighty days. Willmott, Phil

Around the world with Nellie Bly. McCullough, L. E.

Arrabal, Fernando

The body-builder's book of love; tr. by Lorenzo Mans. Estreno 1999 43p (Contemporary Spanish plays, 15)

ISBN 1-888463-05-8

A weightlifting contest involving love (platonic and otherwise), menace, mystery, and religious imagery. 1 act 2m 1 setting

Arson

Williams, T. 27 wagons full of cotton

Art, Suzanne Strauss

c Beulah and the feast.

Spoof of Beauty and the beast set in medieval France. 8 scenes variable cast 13 characters settings

In Art, S. S. Quintet

c Cindie Ellis.

Updated version of Cinderella tale. 5 scenes Variable cast 12 characters extras settings

In Art, S. S. Quintet

c The cotton blend horse.

Spoof on Greek legend of the Trojan horse. 5 scenes 8m 7w extras settings

In Art, S. S. Quintet

c The Hatfields and the McCoys.

Spoof on famous Hatfield/McCoy feud set in hills of West Virginia. 6 scenes Variable cast 15 characters 1 setting

In Art, S. S. Quintet

c Joe Knight and the seven serfs.

Combines elements of medieval history with popular fairy tale. 9 scenes Variable cast 18 characters settings

In Art, S. S. Quintet

Art

Buero-Vallejo, A. The sleep of reason

Neilson, A. The censor

Reza, Y. Art

Spencer, S. The Rothko room

Yoon, J. The Yoko Ono project

Yourgrau, T. TH FT

Art. Reza, Y.

Art (condensation). Reza, Y.

Art for art's sake. Sutton, J.

Art galleries and museums

Lonergan, K. The Waverly Gallery

The **art** of remembering. Ruskin, A. L.

The **art** of war. Walker, G. F.

The **art** room. Aronson, B.

Artaud, Antonin

The spurt of blood; tr. by Ruby Cohn.

Experimental theater piece employing surrealist imagery. 7m 3w extra

In Theater of the avant-garde, 1890-1950; ed. by B. Cardullo and R. Knopf

Artemis and Niobe. Barchers, S. I.

Arthur, King

about

c Miller, K. S. The sword in the stone

Artifact. Fredericks, A. D.

Artists

Cruz, M. Frida: the story of Frida Kahlo

Finn, W. Painting you

Howe, T. Rembrandt's gift

Jordan, J. Tatjana in color

Medley, C. Maiden Lane

Murray, T. C. The pipe in the fields

Nigro, D. Beast with two backs

Pedrero, P. The color of August

Rebeck, T. Abstract expression

Shearer, J. Georgia

Spencer, S. In the western garden

Van Itallie, J.-C. The traveler

Witkiewicz, S. I. The cuttlefish; or, The Hyrcanian worldview

Aruman, hero of Java. McCullough, L. E.

Arzner, Dorothy, 1897-1979

about

Vaughan, R. M. Camera, woman

As a man thinks. Thomas, A.

As bees in honey drown. Beane, D. C.

As five years pass. García Lorca, F.

Asch, Sholem, 1880-1957

God of vengeance (adaptation) See Margulies, D. God of vengeance

The **Ash** Girl. Wertenbaker, T.

Ash Wednesday. Kleberg, L.

Asher, Sandra Fenichel

c The wise men of Chelm.

Based on Jewish folklore about town of fools. Background music. 1 act 4m 2w 1 setting

In Theatre for young audiences; ed. by C. A. Jennings

The wolf and its shadows. Anchorage Press 2000 35p

ISBN 0-87602-365-0

Wolf and dog encounter stories about wolf images from around the world. Puppets. 1 act 2m 1w 1 setting

Ashes and sand. Upton, J.

Asian Americans

Gomolvilas, P. Donut holes in orbit

Gomolvilas, P. The theory of everything

Gotanda, P. K. Yankee dawg you die

Lee, C. Carry the tiger to the mountain

Rodgers, R. Flower drum song

Son, D. R. A. W. ('cause I'm a woman)

Yew, C. A beautiful country

Asians

Canada

Yoon, J. The Yoko Ono project

Aspects of Oscar. Day, B.

Aspengren, Kate

Flyer. French 2001 79p

A 1960s female pilot aspiring to become an astronaut, dreams about 1920s black barnstormer, Bessie Coleman, who becomes her role model and mentor. 2 acts 23 scenes Variable cast 21 characters Unit set

The **aspidistra** code. O'Rowe, M.

Astor del Valle, Janis

Transplantations: straight and other jackets para mi.

Monologue by Puerto Rican lesbian. 1 act 13 scenes 1w

In Action; ed. by M. Algarin and L. Griffith

Astronauts

Anderson, J. Defying gravity

Aspengren, K. Flyer

Baron, J. Hershey: a space odyssey

Greig, D. The cosmonaut's last message to the woman he once loved in the former Soviet Union

Astronomy

Hunter, M. Transit of Venus

c McCullough, L. E. "Constellations then arise": astronomy in the age of Copernicus

Astrophysicists

Wilson, L. Sympathetic magic

At Saint Judas's. Fuller, H. B.

At sea. Simon, M.

Atalanta. Barchers, S. I.

Atalanta. McBride-Smith, B.

Athena. Barchers, S. I.

Athens (Greece)

Aeschylus. The Eumenides

c McBride-Smith, B. The contest for Athens

Athletes

Palmieri, M. Rocks

Atkins, Greg

Rep. French 1999 94p

ISBN 0-573-62643-X

Comedy that covers ten years in the lives of actors in a regional repertory theater. 2 acts 8 scenes 4m 2w 1 interior

Atlantis. Hunter, M.

Atomic bomb

Grimsley, J. Math and aftermath

Mueller, L. The confession of many strangers

Attachments. Kearns, M.

Aubrey, John, 1626-1697

Brief lives (dramatization) See Garland, P. Brief lives

Auburn, David

Are you ready?

The fates of three people drawn to the same restaurant are altered in an instant. 2m 1w 1 setting

In Auburn, D. The fifth planet and other plays

Damage control.

Examines a politician and his aide in a moment of crisis. 1m 1w 1 setting

In Auburn, D. The fifth planet and other plays

The fifth planet.

Charts the friendship between two observatory workers as it waxes and wanes over the course of a year. 1m 1w 1 setting

In Auburn, D. The fifth planet and other plays

Miss you.

Two couples rearrange their affairs via callwaiting. 1m 1w 1 setting

In Auburn, D. The fifth planet and other plays

Proof. Faber & Faber 2001 83p

ISBN 0-571-19997-6

Drama set in Chicago about genius and mental stability. Following in his footsteps, daughter of mathematician must cope with attentions of late father's pupil, sister's unsolicited plans for her future, and possibly groundbreaking proof. 2 acts 9 scenes 2m 2w 1 setting

Skyscraper. Dramatists 1998 56p

ISBN 0-8222-1652-3

Dark comedy about six strangers who collide on the rooftop of a historic building targeted for demolition in Chicago. Prologue 2 acts 4 scenes 3m 3w

Three monologues.

Depicts a young woman's solitude. 1w 1 setting

In Auburn, D. The fifth planet and other plays

We had a very good time.

Follows a married couple on a journey to a menacing foreign country. 1m 1w 1 setting

In Auburn, D. The fifth planet and other plays

What do you believe about the future?

Ten people answer the title question. Variable cast 10 characters 1 setting

In Auburn, D. The fifth planet and other plays

The **audition**. Manzi, W.

The **audition**. Sirera, R.

August afternoon. Orloff, R.

Augustine, John

Siobhan.

Monologue. Woman sitting in automat reflects on life. 1w 1 setting

In take ten; ed. by E. Lane and N. Shengold

Aunts

Nigro, D. November

Auschwitz (Concentration camp)

Ehn, E. 16670 (Maximilian Mary Kolbe)

Nelson, T. B. The grey zone

Austen, Jane, 1775-1817

Sense and sensibility (dramatization) See Parsley, R., and Graham, A. Sense and sensibility

Australia

Bower, H. Natural life

Enright, N. Cloudstreet

Esson, L. Australia felix

Esson, L. Mates

Esson, L. Mother and son

Esson, L. Shipwreck

Esson, L. Terra Australis

c Fry, G. Lockie Leonard, scumbuster

Hall, R. A return to the brink

Kim, S. Dreamtime for Alice

Lawler, R. The Piccadilly bushman

Nowra, L. Inside the island

Avarice—*Continued*
Pomerance, B. Hands of light
Ravenhill, M. Shopping and fucking
Aven'u boys. Pugliese, F.

Averill, Ric

c Pixies, kings, and magical things.
Dramatic Publishing 2003 56p

Hans Christian Andersen himself frames four
classic tales, The ugly duckling (with songs), The
swineherd, The pixie and the grocer, and The emperor's new clothes, with the fabulous story of his
own life. Variable cast 1 setting
Avow. Davis, B. C.
The **award**. Manzi, W.
Ax of murder. Cook, P.
Ay, Carmelo! (Ay, Carmelo!). Espinosa, R.

Ayckbourn, Alan

Body language. French (London) 2001
90p
ISBN 0-573-01957-6

Farce set in rural English clinic where wealthy
patients improve looks with plastic surgery. Top
fashion model and radio reporter are decapitated in
freak accident and have their heads reattached, but
on the wrong bodies. 2 acts 6 scenes

c The champion of Paribanou. French
(London) 1998 90p
ISBN 0-573-05123-2

Story about a Sultan who decides to marry one
of his three sons to a princess in a neighboring
kingdom, but the sons and the princess have other
plans. 2 acts 25 scenes Variable cast 14 characters

Comic potential. Faber & Faber 1999
119p
ISBN 0-571-19787-6   LC 99-490746

Satirical love story set in TV studio in near future when programs are performed by androids.
Music. 2 acts 13 scenes Variable cast 22 characters 5 interiors

—Same. French 2002 101p
ISBN 0-573-62797-5

Communicating doors. Faber & Faber
1995 125p
ISBN 0-571-17682-8   LC 96-141022

Time-traveling comedy thriller about three wom-
en trying to undo wrongs and alter their destinies.
3 acts 3m 3w 3 interiors

Garden.

To be staged simultaneously with the same cast
as House. Preparations for a garden fête become
quite chaotic. 2 acts 4 scenes 6m 8w extras settings
In Ayckbourn, A. House & Garden

Gizmo. French (London) 2000 48p
ISBN 0-573-15206-3

Drama about a hospitalized man suffering from
post-traumatic paralysis, who needs a device called
Gizmo in order to walk. When this device falls
into the hands of some violent and dangerous people, complications begin. 6 scenes variable cast 11
characters extras

House.

To be staged simultaneously with the same cast
as Garden. Man who wants to be an MP must
clean up his private life before considering politics. 2 acts 4 scenes 6m 8w extras settings
In Ayckbourn, A. House & Garden

It could be any one of us. French
(London) 1998 89p
ISBN 0-573-01797-2

Murder mystery set in a country house with unusual characters and suspects. 2 acts 4 scenes 1g
3m 2w 1 setting

Things we do for love. French (London)
1998 84p
ISBN 0-573-01914-2

Comedy about the occupants of three apartments
in London. Music, singing. 2 acts 8 scenes 2m 3w
settings

Ayvazian, Leslie

Deaf day.

Speaking and signing, a mother tries to teach her
deaf boy how to deal with hearing people, especially the other children in the playground. Sign
language. 1 act 1 scene 1w extra 1 setting
In Ensemble Studio Theatre marathon
'99: the one-act plays

—Same
In Four from E. S. T. marathon '99

High dive. Dramatists 2002
ISBN 0-8222-1831-3

An American woman, about to turn fifty, is
standing on the high dive at a pool in a hotel in
Greece. She is afraid of heights. She thinks back
on other experiences in her past. Audience participation. 1w 1 exterior settings

Nine Armenians. Dramatists 1998 84p
ISBN 0-8222-1602-7

Ayvazian, Leslie—*Continued*

Young Armenian-American woman travels to Armenia and then returns to the United States with a better understanding of her background. 16 scenes 1b 1g 4m 4w 1 setting

Plan day.

Series of monologues covering mother's relationship with son from her 30s to 70s. 4 scenes 1w 1 interior

In 3 more by E.S.T. '98

Twenty-four years.

He is recovering from knee surgery and she is very tired of playing nurse; nevertheless, it's their wedding anniversary. 1 act 1m 1w 1 interior

In Ensemble Studio Theatre marathon 2000: the one-act plays

Aztecs

Juana Inés de la Cruz. The divine Narcissus (El divino Narciso)

c McCullough, L. E. How Quentzalcoatl found the sun

B

The **B** file. Levy, D.

The **B-I-B-L-E** is L-O-S-T. Vogel, L.

Baal. Brecht, B.

Ba'al Shem Ṭov, ca. 1700-1760

about

c McCullough, L. E. Tale of the Baal Shem Tov

Baba Yaga. Barchers, S. I.

Baba Yaga and the black sunflower. Korty, C.

Babe, Thomas

Great day in the morning. Broadway Play Pub. 1998 88p

ISBN 0-88145-144-4

Drama set in the late 1800s. Wealthy, recently widowed young woman moves from Philadelphia to New York, where she marries decadent society swell. 2 acts 18 scenes 4m 4w

Singleton, the medal winner.

Drama set in 1863 during the Civil War. Wounded soldier dies before receiving medal. 3 scenes 3m

In 30 ten-minute plays for 3 actors from Actors Theatre of Louisville's National Ten-minute Play Contest

—Same

In Actors Theatre of Louisville. Ten-minute plays: v5

The **Babel** of circular labyrinths. Nigro, D.

Babel's in arms. Ives, D.

Babes in the bighouse. Terry, M.

Babes in Toyland. Francoeur, B.

Baby anger. Hedges, P.

The **baby** blues. Taylor, D. H.

Baby doll. Bailey, L.

Baby talk. Wright, D.

Baby with the bathwater. Durang, C.

The **babysitter**. Tait, L.

Babysitting Calvin. Newmeir, J. H.

Bacchae. Euripides

The **bachelor's** daughter. Molloy, M. J.

Bachmann, Ingeborg

The cicadas; translated by Lilian Friedberg.

Radio play about isolation of island life. 9m 2w extras

In Bachmann, I. Three radio plays

A deal in dreams; translated by Lilian Friedberg.

Radio play. Dreams are for sale but the price is high. 3m 1w extras

In Bachmann, I. Three radio plays

The good god of Manhattan.

Experimental radio play about volatility of love. 29 scenes variable cast 17 characters

In Bachmann, I. and Wolf, C. Selected prose and drama

—Same; translated by Lilian Friedberg

In Bachmann, I. Three radio plays

Background artiste. Smith, S.

A **backward** glance. McGee, J.

Bad dream. Lucas, C.

Bad girls. Oates, J. C.

Bad hair day. Jackson, R. E.

Bad penny. Wellman, M.

Bad weather. Holman, R.

Badlam, Robb

Guys.

Two men argue about how to approach a woman. 2m 1 interior

In 30 ten-minute plays for 2 actors from Actors Theatre of Louisville's National Ten-minute Play Contest

Badlam, Robb—*Continued*

Slop-culture.

Comedy. Young woman asks friends for advice on an essay she must submit for job opening. 2m 2w 1 interior

> *In* 30 ten-minute plays for 4, 5 & 6 actors from Actors Theatre of Louisville's National Ten-minute Play Contest

—Same

> *In* Actors Theatre of Louisville. Ten-minute plays; v5

BAFO (Best And Final Offer). Strelich, T.
Bag lady. Van Itallie, J.-C.
Bah, humbug! Francoeur, B.

Bailey, Brett

Ipi zombi?

Drama set in South Africa's Eastern Cape. Tragic deaths divide community along religious lines and spark charges of witchcraft. Music. 1 act Variable cast 15 characters extras 1 setting

> *In* Drama for a new South Africa; ed. by D. Graver

Bailey, Frederick

Keeper.

Woman witnesses act of revenge in Los Angeles theater. 2m 1w 1 interior

> *In* 30 ten-minute plays for 3 actors from Actors Theatre of Louisville's National Ten-minute Play Contest

—Same

> *In* Actors Theatre of Louisville. Ten-minute plays: v4

Bailey, Lucy

Baby doll. French (London) 2003 71p
> ISBN 0-573-01970-3

New stage version based on Tennessee William's Baby Doll. Drama about failed cotton gin owner's sexual frustrations and hatred for rival businessman. 2 acts 1b 14m 2w extras

Bailey, Maxine, and Lewis, Sharon M.

Sistahs. Playwrights Canada 1998 61p
> ISBN 0-88754-553-X

Woman dying of cancer assembles four women she loves most to participate in command preparation of meal. Prologue 18 scenes 5w 1 interior

—Same

> *In* Testifyin' v1; ed. by D. Sears

The **bait** (1953). Merrill, J.
The **bait** (1988). Merrill, J.

Baitz, Jon Robin

Film society.

Dramatic comedy set in South Africa. Tensions in provincial private school reflect those of society at large. 2 acts 15 scenes 4m 2w 1 setting

> *In* Political stages; ed. by E. Mann and D. Roessel

Hedda Gabler. Dramatists 2002
> ISBN 0-8222-1861-5

Ibsen's antiheroine is given a new twist in this adaptation. 3m 4w 1 interior setting

—Same. Grove Press 2000 105p
> ISBN 0-8021-3806-3

Mizlansky/Zilinsky. Dramatists 1999 70p
> ISBN 0-8222-1680-9

Comedy about movie producer who avoids IRS by scheming with partner to produce substandard Bible stories for children.: 2 acts 7 scenes 7m 1w 1 setting

Mizlansky/Zilinsky; or, Schmucks. Theatre Communications Group 1998 82p
> ISBN 1-55936-160-3

Comedy about movie producer who avoids IRS by scheming with partner to produce substandard Bible stories for children. 2 acts 7 scenes 7m 1w 1 setting

Bake off. Wilner, S.

Baker, Edward Allan

Mafia on Prozac.

A Mafia rubout morphs into a free-floating bull session. 1 act 3m 1 exterior

> *In* EST marathon '97: the one-act plays; ed. by M. Smith

The seventeenth of June.

After her husband's death, a battered wife learns how kind he was to her sisters. 1 act 1m 3w 1 interior

> *In* Ensemble Studio Theatre marathon 2000: the one-act plays

Baker, Edward Allan—*Continued*

Up, down, strange, charmed, beauty, and truth.

Two sisters who have always protected each other from their druggie mother make plans to escape. 1 act 1m 2w 1 interior

In Ensemble Studio Theatre marathon '99: the one-act plays

Baker, Jedediah

Male bondage.

Man who wants a friend ties up another man in order to bond with him. 3m 1 setting

In Blast from the future; ed. by D. Yeaton

Bakers

c McCullough, L. E. Roll 'em up, roll 'em up! (pastry chef)

Bakhtin, M. M. (Mikhail Mikhaïlovich), 1895-1975

about

Kleberg, L. Ash Wednesday

Baking competitions

Curran, C. Cake-walk

Bakunin, Mikhail Aleksandrovich, 1814-1876

about

Stoppard, T. Shipwreck

Stoppard, T. Voyage

Bal. Nelson, R.

Balcony. Shafaat, S.

Ballerinas. Nigro, D.

Balls (Parties)

Gilroy, F. D. Dreams of glory

Gurney, A. R. The snow ball

Henley, B. The debutante ball

Wilner, S. Labor Day

Bandele, 'Biyi

Aphra Behn's Oroonoko. Amber Lane Press 1999 105p

ISBN 1-872868-25-8

An African prince is betrayed to slavers and transported to the plantations of Surinam, where he reencounters his wife and dies leading a slave mutiny. Adapted from Aphra Behn's 1688 novel. Music, singing, dancing. 2 parts 6 acts 28 scenes 13m 3w extras 5 interiors 7 exteriors

Two horsemen.

Two philosophical street sweepers trade stories of life, sex and God. 2 acts 2m 1 interior

In Best of the Fest; ed. by Phil Setren

Banks, Julia

c Hercules—The panto!!; a pantomime. French (London) 1999 72p

ISBN 0-573-16440-1

Pantomime with music. Hercules is assigned thirteenth labor by Venus; he must win hand of princess. Music, singing. 2 acts 16 scenes 5m 7w 1 setting

Banks and banking

Chekhov, A. P. The festivities

Chepiga, M. J. Getting and spending

Ibsen, H. John Gabriel Borkman

Banville, John

God's gift; a version of Amphitryon by Heinrich von Kleist; John Banville. Gallery Press 2000 72p

ISBN 1-85235-281-7; 1-85235-280-9 (pa)

LC 00-456925

Adaptation of Heinrich von Kleist's Amphitryon set in County Wexford in 1798. In aftermath of Battle of Vinegar Hill, General Ashburningham, returning home in triumph, experiences night that plays tricks on him, his wife, and sundry characters. 2 acts 12 scenes 4m 2w 2 exteriors

The **bar** plays. Rebeck, T.

Baraka, Amiri

Dutchman.

Subway dialogue between white woman and black man ends in murder. 2 scenes 3m 1w extras 1 interior

In Political stages; ed. by E. Mann and D. Roessel

The election machine warehouse.

Satire. African American family life juxtaposed with history of black culture via radio. Music. 8 scenes variable cast 2 interiors 1 exterior

In Action; ed. by M. Algarin and L. Griffith

Primitive world: an anti-nuclear jazz musical.

Jazz musical set in post-apocalyptic world. Variable cast

In Action; ed. by M. Algarin and L. Griffith

Barbara, Saint

about

Ehn, E. Radio elephant (Barbara)
Barbarians: abide with me. Keeffe, B.
Barbarians: in the city. Keeffe, B.
Barbarians: killing time. Keeffe, B.
The **barber** of Seville. Beaumarchais, P. A. D.

Barbers

Sondheim, S. Sweeney Todd

Barcelona (Spain)

Brossa, J. The quarrelsome party.
Mendez Rodriguez, J. M. Autumn flower

Barchers, Suzanne I.

c Aeolus and the winds.

Each of the winds in Greek mythology describes its history. Variable cast 6 characters
> *In* Barchers, S. I. From Atalanta to Zeus

c Ariadne.

Depicts great resourcefulness and courage of mythical figure of Ariadne. Variable cast 8 characters
> *In* Barchers, S. I. From Atalanta to Zeus

c Arion and his harp.

Greek singer saved from drowning by dolphins enchanted by beauty of his song. Variable cast 5 characters
> *In* Barchers, S. I. Multicultural folktales

c Artemis and Niobe.

Greek myth. Artemis and Apollo slay children of Niobe in fierce defense of their mother Leto. Variable cast 8 characters
> *In* Barchers, S. I. From Atalanta to Zeus

c Atalanta.

Greek myth of Atalanta who was raised by bears, married Melanion and turned into lion by Aphrodite. Variable cast 7 characters
> *In* Barchers, S. I. From Atalanta to Zeus

c Athena.

Athena springs to life fully grown from Zeus's head and becomes a just, stern ruler. Variable cast 8 characters
> *In* Barchers, S. I. From Atalanta to Zeus

c Baba Yaga.

Russian folktale. Brave lad tricks Baba Yaga and her three daughters. Variable cast 7 characters
> *In* Barchers, S. I. Multicultural folktales

c The bee, the harp, the mouse, and the bum-clock.

Irish folk tale variant of Jack and the beanstalk. Jack trades three cows for some entertaining creatures. Variable cast 7 characters
> *In* Barchers, S. I. Multicultural folktales

c Catherine and her destiny.

Italian folk tale. Woman must choose between happiness in youth or in old age. Variable cast 9 characters
> *In* Barchers, S. I. Multicultural folktales

c The clever daughter.

Italian folk tale. King challenges peasant's daughter to solve riddle, offering hand in marriage if she succeeds. Variable cast 6 characters
> *In* Barchers, S. I. Multicultural folktales

c Daedalus and Icarus.

Greek myth about how, ignoring his father's warning, Icarus flew too close to the sun. Variable cast 7 characters
> *In* Barchers, S. I. From Atalanta to Zeus

c Demeter and Persephone.

Greek myth about origins of Winter. Demeter searches world for her daughter Persephone, who was abducted by Hades to the Underworld. Variable cast 9 characters
> *In* Barchers, S. I. From Atalanta to Zeus

c Deucalion and Pyrrha.

Greek myth about how Deucalion and Pyrrha built ark to survive flood and repopulate earth. Variable cast 6 characters
> *In* Barchers, S. I. From Atalanta to Zeus

c Dick Whittington and his cat.

English folk tale. Young orphan gains wealth with help of rat-catching cat. Variable cast 10 characters
> *In* Barchers, S. I. Multicultural folktales

Barchers, Suzanne I.—*Continued*

c Dionysus.

Story of Dionysus, son of Zeus and god of wine. Variable cast 12 characters

In Barchers, S. I. From Atalanta to Zeus

c The doomed prince.

Egyptian folk tale. Young prince is doomed from birth to die from crocodile, serpent, or dog. Variable cast 8 characters

In Barchers, S. I. Multicultural folktales

c Eos, Selene, and Helios.

The dawn, moon, and sun in Greek mythology. Variable cast 7 characters

In Barchers, S. I. From Atalanta to Zeus

c Eros and Psyche.

Greek myth about Psyche, a legendary beauty, and jealous goddess Aphrodite. Variable cast 9 characters

In Barchers, S. I. From Atalanta to Zeus

c The farmer and the animals.

Finnish folk tale. After dispatching farmer, animals turn on each other until fox and wolf make them agree to be friends. Unidentified cast 7 characters

In Barchers, S. I. Multicultural folktales

c Finding the foolish.

Scottish folk tale. Audience participation. Contest to determine most foolish husband. Variable cast 11 characters

In Barchers, S. I. Multicultural folktales

c Fortunée.

French folk tale. Orphaned girl breaks her enchantment and marries prince. Unidentified cast 7 characters

In Barchers, S. I. Multicultural folktales

c Gawain and the Green Knight.

Gawain proves his bravery by keeping his word. 6m

In Barchers, S. I. Multicultural folktales

c The giant in the garden.

Scottish folk tale. Young child tricks giant into returning children to their mother. Variable cast 7 characters

In Barchers, S. I. Multicultural folktales

c Gifts of love.

Korean folk tale. Poor woman restores life to prince. They marry and inherit the throne. Variable cast 8 characters

In Barchers, S. I. Multicultural folktales

c Helen.

Helen's marriage to Menelaus, her elopement with Paris, and the war that followed. Variable cast 11 characters

In Barchers, S. I. From Atalanta to Zeus

c Heracles.

Heracles describes his twelve labors. 3 acts Variable cast 12 characters

In Barchers, S. I. From Atalanta to Zeus

c Hermes.

Explores many roles Hermes plays in Greek myth. Variable cast 7 characters

In Barchers, S. I. From Atalanta to Zeus

c How Fisher went to the skyland.

Anishinabe legend. Explains why half the year remains cold and half warm. Variable cast 10 characters

In Barchers, S. I. Multicultural folktales

c It could always be worse.

Yiddish folk tale. Rabbi teaches poor man how to deal with noisy crowded household. Variable cast 6 characters

In Barchers, S. I. Multicultural folktales

c Jason and the golden fleece.

Story of Jason's legendary quest to find and retrieve golden fleece. Variable cast 13 characters

In Barchers, S. I. From Atalanta to Zeus

c King Midas.

Greek myth of ruler who turned everything he touched into gold. Variable cast 9 characters

In Barchers, S. I. From Atalanta to Zeus

Barchers, Suzanne I.—*Continued*

c Leto.

Hera, always jealous of Zeus's other wives, decreed that Leto could not give birth on any of the lands on Earth. Variable cast 8 characters

In Barchers, S. I. From Atalanta to Zeus

c The magic table.

Adaptation of Grimm tale. Magic table ensures lifetime of feasts and Thanksgiving. Variable cast 8 characters

In Barchers, S. I. Multicultural folktales

c The master-maid.

Norwegian folk tale. Maid helps prince escape from evil giant. They fall in love. Variable cast 9 characters

In Barchers, S. I. Multicultural folktales

c Melampus.

In Greek mythology Melampus learned how to understand the language of animals after showing kindness to some motherless snakes. Variable cast 10 characters

In Barchers, S. I. From Atalanta to Zeus

c Molly Whuppie.

Scottish folktale about girl who outwits giant. Variable cast 9 characters

In Barchers, S. I. Multicultural folktales

c Oedipus.

Greek myth describes tragic tale of man determined to escape his fate. Variable cast 14 characters

In Barchers, S. I. From Atalanta to Zeus

c Orpheus and Eurydice.

Love of Orpheus for Eurydice conquers death. Variable cast 9 characters

In Barchers, S. I. From Atalanta to Zeus

c Pan.

Pan, protector of flocks and agriculture, seeks love with Pitys, Echo, and Syrinx, failing with all three. Variable cast 9 characters

In Barchers, S. I. From Atalanta to Zeus

c The peach boy.

Japanese folk tale. Old man and woman raise boy they find inside peach. Variable cast 8 characters

In Barchers, S. I. Multicultural folktales

c Perseus.

Various gods help Perseus use magic and trickery to defeat terrible gorgon Medusa. Variable cast 14 characters

In Barchers, S. I. From Atalanta to Zeus

c Polly Ann and John Henry.

Railroad steel-driver enters contest to prove that man is more powerful than a machine. Variable cast 7 characters and extras

In Barchers, S. I. Multicultural folktales

c Princess Sivatra.

Folk tale from India. Princess's love saves husband from death and restores his father to throne. Variable cast 6 characters

In Barchers, S. I. Multicultural folktales

c Prometheus and Pandora.

Greek myths about the origin of fire and the moment mortals learned of all the world's ills. Variable cast 8 characters

In Barchers, S. I. From Atalanta to Zeus

c Sally Ann Thunder and Davey Crockett.

Sally Ann Thunder saves Davey Crockett from bear. Variable cast 6 characters

In Barchers, S. I. Multicultural folktales

c The shepherd and the troll.

Icelandic folk tale. Boy outsmarts troll and becomes his friend. Variable cast 7 characters

In Barchers, S. I. Multicultural folktales

c Sisyphus.

Myth about man made to repeatedly push rock up steep hill for eternity. Variable cast 7 characters

In Barchers, S. I. From Atalanta to Zeus

c Spider flies to the feast.

Liberian folk tale. Trickster spider nearly meets tragic end. Unidentified cast 7 characters

In Barchers, S. I. Multicultural folktales

Barchers, Suzanne I.—*Continued*

c The three wishes.

Hungarian folk tale. Poor husband and wife squander three wishes. Variable cast 4 characters
In Barchers, S. I. Multicultural folktales

c To the sun, moon, and wind.

Spanish folktale. Disobedient wife uses her wit and perseverance to rescue husband. Variable cast 8 characters
In Barchers, S. I. Multicultural folktales

c The tree that bled fish.

Micronesian folk tale about tree that provides special nourishment for villagers. Variable cast 8 characters
In Barchers, S. I. Multicultural folktales

c Los tres ratoncitos: a chiste.

Folk tale from Southwestern United States about importance of second language. Unidentified cast 7 characters
In Barchers, S. I. Multicultural folktales

c Water, water will be mine.

Kenyan folk tale. When water dries up, all the animals, except the rabbit, work together to dig new hole. Unidentified cast 13 characters
In Barchers, S. I. Multicultural folktales

c The white-haired old woman.

Native American folk tale. Before she dies old Indian woman plants maize grain so her adopted tribe will never go hungry. Variable cast 4 characters
In Barchers, S. I. Multicultural folktales

c Why ants carry burdens.

Hausa folk tale. Explains how ants were tricked into carrying heavy burdens. Variable cast 6 characters
In Barchers, S. I. Multicultural folktales

c The young chief who played the flute.

Maori folk tale. Young woman risks life to be with young chief who plays beautiful music. Variable cast 6 characters
In Barchers, S. I. Multicultural folktales

c Zeus and Hera.

Zeus cajoles Hera into marrying him even though she knows he cannot remain true to one wife. Variable cast 6 characters
In Barchers, S. I. From Atalanta to Zeus

Barchers, Suzanne I., and Kroll, Jennifer L.

y Captains courageous; adapted by Suzanne I. Barchers.

Dramatization of Kipling's tale. Arrogant, rich young man falls overboard during Atlantic crossing and is rescued by Captain who teaches him about life. 11 scenes Variable cast 15 characters
In Barchers, S. I. and Kroll, J. L. Classic Readers Theatre for Young Adults

y A Christmas carol; adapted by Jennifer L. Kroll.

Dramatization of Dickens's classic holiday ghost story. 5 scenes epilogue Variable cast
In Barchers, S. I. and Kroll, J. L. Classic Readers Theatre for Young Adults

y Dr. Jekyll and Mr. Hyde; adapted by Jennifer L. Kroll.

Dramatization of Stevenson's horror story about scientist and dual nature of man. 10 scenes Variable cast 12 characters
In Barchers, S. I. and Kroll, J. L. Classic Readers Theatre for Young Adults

y Episodes from Don Quixote; adapted by Jennifer L. Kroll.

Dramatization of episodes from novel by Miguel de Cervantes. Several adventures of the eccentric Spanish gentleman. 8 scenes Variable cast
In Barchers, S. I. and Kroll, J. L. Classic Readers Theatre for Young Adults

y Frankenstein; adapted by Jennifer L. Kroll.

Dramatization of Mary Shelley's horror classic. 2 parts 12 scenes Variable cast 13 characters
In Barchers, S. I. and Kroll, J. L. Classic Readers Theatre for Young Adults

y Hard times; adapted by Jennifer L. Kroll.

Dramatization of Dickens's novel set in 19th-century industrial city in northern England about troubled children overseen by stern school superin-

Barchers, Suzanne I., and Kroll, Jennifer L.—*Continued*

tendent. 2 parts 19 scenes epilogue Variable cast 20 characters

In Barchers, S. I. and Kroll, J. L. Classic Readers Theatre for Young Adults

y The lady, or the tiger?; adapted by Suzanne I. Barchers.

Dramatization of Stockton's classic short story. Young man's fate rests upon his choice of doors. Behind one is an alluring young woman, behind the other a ferocious tiger. 4 scenes Variable cast 9 characters

In Barchers, S. I. and Kroll, J. L. Classic Readers Theatre for Young Adults

y The legend of Sleepy Hollow; adapted by Jennifer L. Kroll.

Dramatization of Washington Irving's tale of haunted schoolmaster. 5 scenes Variable cast 17 characters

In Barchers, S. I. and Kroll, J. L. Classic Readers Theatre for Young Adults

y Little women; adapted by Suzanne I. Barchers.

Dramatization of Alcott's novel. A year in the life of the March family. 2 parts 9 scenes 4m 7w extras

In Barchers, S. I. and Kroll, J. L. Classic Readers Theatre for Young Adults

y The luck of Roaring Camp; adapted by Suzanne I. Barchers.

Dramatization of Bret Harte's short story about group of rough frontiersmen who decide to raise orphaned baby. 3 scenes Variable cast 8 characters

In Barchers, S. I. and Kroll, J. L. Classic Readers Theatre for Young Adults

y The necklace; adapted by Suzanne I. Barchers.

Dramatization of Guy de Maupassant short story. Young woman yearning for wealth borrows diamond necklace and loses it. 3 scenes Variable cast 5 characters

In Barchers, S. I. and Kroll, J. L. Classic Readers Theatre for Young Adults

y The oblong box; adapted by Suzanne I. Barchers.

Dramatization of Poe's tale. During storm at sea man dies trying to save contents of mysterious oblong box. 4 scenes Variable cast 10 characters

In Barchers, S. I. and Kroll, J. L. Classic Readers Theatre for Young Adults

y The prince and the pauper; adapted by Suzanne I. Barchers.

Dramatization of Twain's tale of mistaken identity set in 16th century England. 10 scenes Variable cast 21 characters

In Barchers, S. I. and Kroll, J. L. Classic Readers Theatre for Young Adults

y Rappaccini's daughter; adapted by Jennifer L. Kroll.

Dramatization of Hawthorne's story about beautiful young girl who is victim of experiment by her famous medical researcher father. 7 scenes Variable cast 8 characters

In Barchers, S. I. and Kroll, J. L. Classic Readers Theatre for Young Adults.

y A retrieved reformation; adapted by Suzanne I. Barchers.

Dramatization of O. Henry's short story about reformed safe-cracker facing rough decision. Variable cast 12 characters

In Barchers, S. I. and Kroll, J. L. Classic Readers Theatre for Young Adults

y Zorro!; or, The curse of Capistrano; adapted by Jennifer L. Kroll.

Adventures of mysterious outlaw in colonial California. 10 scenes Variable cast 19 characters

In Barchers, S. I. and Kroll, J. L. Classic Readers Theatre for Young Adults

Barefoot boy with shoes on. Sánchez, E.

Barfield, Tanya

Snapshot: defacing patriotic property.

Monologue. Inspired by Mount Rushmore, man seeks plastic surgery. 1 act 1m 1 setting

In Humana Festival 2002

Without skin or breathlessness.

Monologue exploring psyche and persona of beautiful young black lesbian. 1w

In O Solo homo; ed. by H. Hughes and D. Román

Barillet, Pierre
The incomparable LouLou (adaptation) See Clark, R. The incomparable LouLou
Barking sharks. Horovitz, I.

Barlow, Patrick
Love upon the throne. Hern Bks. 1998 64p
ISBN 1-85459-421-4
Comedy based upon the royal marriage of Charles and Diana portrayed by two male actors. 2m 1 interior

Barnes, Peter
The ruling class.
Satire. Aristocratic clan in present-day England is headed by cruel young eccentric who is first convinced that he is God and later Jack the Ripper. Prologue 2 acts 27 scenes epilogue 17m 5w 5 interiors 1 exterior
In The Methuen book of sixties drama

Barnett, Gina
T for 2.
Science fiction set in near-future repressive society. Four lone survivors cobble together underground family. 2 acts 8 scenes 2m 2w 3 interiors
In Women playwrights: the best plays of 2001

Baron, Courtney
The blue room.
Young sailor reminisces about his wedding night. 1m 1w settings
In 30 ten-minute plays for 2 actors from Actors Theatre of Louisville's National Ten-minute Play Contest
—Same
In Actors Theatre of Louisville: Ten-minute plays; v5

Baron, Jeff
Visiting Mr. Green. Dramatists 1999 55p
ISBN 0-8222-1681-7
Comic drama set in New York. Chronicles relationship between 86-year-old Jewish widower and 25-year-old gay corporate executive. 2 acts 9 scenes 2m 1 interior

Baron, Joanne
Hershey: a space odyssey.
Dark comedy about astronauts on the moon arguing over a Hershey bar. 4m 1 setting
In Blast from the future; ed. by D. Yeaton

Barras, Charles M.
The black crook.
Farrago with spectacular effects as airy sprites and water creatures battle a demonic sorcerer for the soul of a young man cheated of his bride. Music, singing, and dancing. Puppets. 4 acts 18 scenes 10m 5w extras settings
In Nineteenth century American plays; ed. by M. Matlaw

Barry, P. J.
Jump the train at Riverpoint. French (London) 1998 135p music, plans
ISBN 0-573-66041-7   LC 99-200351
In a small Rhode Island town in 1911, a group of friends and lovers experience love, betrayal and vengeance. 2 acts 25 scenes 4m 4w

Barry, Sebastian
Our lady of Sligo. Dramatists 1999 62p
ISBN 0-8222-1690-6
Woman stricken with liver cancer reflects upon her life and family from her hospital bed in 1950s Dublin, Ireland. 2 acts 2m 5w
The steward of Christendom. Dramatists 1998 57p
ISBN 0-8222-1609-4
Drama set in 1932 County Wicklow old age home. Ex-superintendent of Dublin police tries to break free of history. 2 acts 3m 2w 1 interior

Barrymore, John, 1882-1942
about
Luce, W. Barrymore
Barrymore. Luce, W.
Bartholomew Fair. Jonson, B.

Basch, Peter
English (it's where the words are).
Spoof of earnest kitchen sink dramas about inarticulate people. 1 act 1m 1w 1 interior
In EST marathon '96: the one-act plays; ed. by M. Smith
Baseball
Greenberg, R. Take me out

Baseball—*Continued*

Palmieri, M. Rocks

Stroppel, F. Judgment call

y Surface, M. H. Most valuable player

The **basement** at the bottom at the end of the world. Graham, N.

Basham, Rebecca

Lot's daughters. French 2001 88p

ISBN 0-573-62751-7   LC 2001-270867

Metaphorical play using the Biblical story of Lot to tell the story of two women who fall in love in eastern Kentucky during summer of 1944. 3 acts 14 scenes 4m 4w 1 setting

Bashkirtseff, Marie, 1860-1884

about

Ardito, C. Brief candle

Bashville in love. Valenti, M.

Basketball

Medoff, M. H. Crunch time

Bass, Alice

The redeemer of minutes.

Easter worship program on theme of perfection 1w 1 interior

In Jubilation: dramas for Easter

Shattering word.

Easter worship program about the word of God. 1m 1 interior

In Jubilation: dramas for Easter

Bass, Tim

Inventory.

Easter worship program about aspects of followers' relationship with Savior. Variable cast 5 characters 1 setting

In Jubilation: dramas for Easter

Letting Mikey go.

Easter worship program about spreading word of risen Christ. 1m 1 interior

In Jubilation: dramas for Easter

Báthory, Erzsébet, 1560-1614

about

King, M. Bathory

Bathory. King, M.

The **batting** cage. Ackermann, J.

Battle of angels. Williams, T.

The **battle** of Bull Run always makes me cry. Real, C.

The **battles** of Coxinga. Chikamatsu, M.

Battlo, Jean

The little theater's production of Hamlet. French 1999 65p

ISBN 0-573-62662-6

Comedy about a New York director who attempts to stage Hamlet in West Virginia with a cast of two hairdressers, a bank executive, and an eager young Ophelia. 2 acts 17 scenes 2m 6w 1 interior

The **bay** at Nice. Hare, D.

Bayiates, Andy

Hype-r-connectivity.

Circular telephone-answering menu prevents calls from going through. Variable cast 1 character

In Humana Festival 2001

Be aggressive. Weisman, A.

Be my guest. Vogel, L.

Bean, Richard

Toast. Oberon Bks. 1999 103p

ISBN 1-84002-104-7

Comedy about seven men working the midnight shift in a bread factory in Hull, England. 2 scenes 7m 1 interior

Bean, Rupert

Pride at Southanger Park.

Amateur cast struggles through a pretentious BBC-type production. 1 act 2 scenes 4m 5w extra 1 interior

In Coarse acting strikes back; ed. by M. Green

Beane, Douglas Carter

As bees in honey drown. Dramatists 1998 75p

ISBN 0-8222-1651-5

Satirical comedy set in Manhattan. Self-invented socialite takes young gay novelist under her wing. 2 acts 17 scenes 3m 3w 1 setting

The country club. Dramatists 2000 63p

ISBN 0-8222-1742-2

Comedy set in small Pennsylvania town. Depicts group of thirty-something WASP members of country club. 2 acts 11 scenes 3m 4w 1 interior

Music from a sparkling planet. Dramatists 2002

ISBN 0-8222-1859-3

Three fans of television personality, Tamara Tomorrow, search to find why she suddenly disappeared from the public eye in the seventies. 4m 1w 1 setting

The **bear**. Bernard, L.

The **bear**. Chekhov, A. P.

Beard, Jocelyn

The Ornamental hermit.

Drama about slavery set in 1854 South Carolina. Mysterious hermit comes to live on plantation and serves as catalyst for the community. 2 acts 4m 4w 1 exterior

In Women playwrights: the best plays of 1998

Bears

c McCullough, L. E. Why bears no longer talk

Bea's niece. Gow, D.

Beast with two backs. Nigro, D.

Beat the sunset. MacLennan, M. L.

Beating heart cadaver. Murphy, C.

Beatrice Chancy. Clarke, G. E.

Beattie, Andrew

c The looking-glass alchemist. Minerva Press 1997 83p

ISBN 1-86106-754-2

Aged schoolmaster, contemplating retirement, decides to tell his class a story instead of reviewing the usual Latin exercises. 2 acts 1b 11m extras

The story of Peter Grimes. Playwrights Canada 1998 42p

ISBN 1-873130-15-5

Mystery inspired by the poem The borough by George Crabbe. Fisherman suspected of killing two apprentice boys in small East Anglian community in early 1800s. 6 scenes 1b 8m 2w extras 1 setting

Beaumarchais, Pierre Augustin De

The barber of Seville; translation and adaptation by Bernard Sahlins. Dee, I. R. 1998 81p

ISBN 1-56663-202-1; 1-56663-203-X (pa)

LC 99-30443

Romantic comedy set in Spain. Heroine evades advances of amorous guardian with aid of barber Figaro and young count she loves. Singing. 4 acts 6m 1w extras 2 interiors 1 exterior

Beaumont, Francis

The knight of the burning pestle.

Jacobean satire on plays, players and 17th century London citizenry. Sometimes attributed to Beaumont and John Fletcher. Background music,

singing, dancing. Prologue 5 acts 25 scenes epilogue 3b 14m 5w

In Renaissance drama; ed. by A. F. Kinney

Beautiful city. Walker, G. F.

A **beautiful** country. Yew, C.

A **beautiful** life. Futcher, M., and Howard, H.

Beauty. Martin, J.

Beauty and the beast. Congdon, C.

Beauty and the beast. Mason, T.

Beauty and the beast. Miller, K. S.

The **beauty** queen of Leenane. McDonagh, M.

The **beauty** queen of Leenane (condensation). McDonagh, M.

Beauty's daughter. Orlandersmith, D.

Beber, Neena

Adaptive ruse.

Poet has encounter with cleaning woman in motel room. 1m 1w 1 interior

In HB Playwrights short play festival 1997

Afterthought.

Actors attempt to portray love story on set for funeral parlor. 4m 1w 1 interior

In HB Playwrights short play festival 2000

Departures.

Two sisters wait to board plane to visit ill father. 2w 2 interiors 1 exterior

In HB Playwrights short play festival 1999

Misreadings.

Conversation between teacher and cynical student. 2w

In 30 ten-minute plays for 2 actors from Actors Theatre of Louisville's National Ten-minute Play Contest

—Same

In Actors Theatre of Louisville. Ten-minute plays: v4

—Same

In The Best American short plays, 1996-1997

Beber, Neena—*Continued*
Sensation(s).

Drama set in art gallery. Reactions to controversial painting of British murderer Myra Hindley. 2m 1w 1 interior
  In HB Playwrights short play festival 1998
Because I want to say. O'Donnell, S.
BecauseHeCan. Kopit, A. L.
Becque, Henry, 1837-1899
  La Parisienne (adaptation) See Marowitz, C. La Parisienne
Bed & breakfast. Dresser, R.
A **bed** for the knight. Ardito, C.
The **bee,** the harp, the mouse, and the bum-clock. Barchers, S. I.
Beethoven, Ludwig von
                    about
  Kennedy, A. She talks to Beethoven

Beevers, Geoffrey
  George Eliot's Silas Marner. French (London) 1999 84p
    ISBN 0-573-01912-6

Dramatization of George Eliot's 19th century novel about reclusive miser transformed by arrival in his life of young girl. 2 acts 38 scenes Variable cast 23 characters extras
The **beggar**. Sorge, R.
The **beggar's** opera. Havel, V.
The **beginning** of August. Donaghy, T.
Behave, my sorrow. Tait, L.
Behn, Aphra, 1640-1689
  Oroonoko (dramatization) See Bandele, 'Biyi Aphra Behn's Oroonoko
Being friends. Holman, R.
Beirut. Bowne, A.

Beissel, Henry
  Inuk and the sun.

Fantasy about boy's journey to manhood through acceptance of change and destiny. Prologue 10 episodes epilogue 18 characters 1 setting
  In Staging the North; ed. by S. Grace, E. D'Aeth and L. Chalykoff
Bel canto. Scheffer, W.

Belasco, David
  The heart of Maryland.

Melodrama set in Maryland during Civil War. Southern woman saves lover caught spying for the North. 4 acts 6 scenes 26m 4w extras 3 interiors

1 exterior 1 setting
  In Fateful lightning; ed. by W. J. Meserve and M. A. Meserve

Belbel, Sergi
  Fourplay.

A couple try to maneuver two friends into trying out their gigantic new bed. Odd-numbered scenes go forward in time; even-numbered scenes go backward. 1 act 38 scenes 4 characters 2m 2w 1 interior
  In Modern Catalan plays; ed. by J. London and D. George

Belber, Stephen
  Tape. Dramatists 2002
    ISBN 0-8222-1862-3

Jon, an aspiring filmaker, hooks up for the weekend with his best friend from high school, Vince. Questions of motive, memory, truth, and perception are examined. 2m 1w 1 interior setting

Belfast (Northern Ireland)
  Charabanc Theatre Company. Somewhere over the balcony
  Devlin, A. Ourselves alone
  Mitchell, G. In a little world of our own
  Parker, S. Spokesong; or, The common wheel

Belgrade (Serbia)
  Stanley, J. Tesla's letters
Belinsky, Vissarion Grigoryevich, 1811-1848
                    about
  Stoppard, T. Shipwreck

Belke, David
  Blackpool and Parrish. French 82p
    ISBN 0-573-627-39-4

The fate of humanity will be determined by a chess game played between agents of Good and Evil. 2 acts 4 scenes 3m 2w 1 setting

  The Maltese bodkin.

Opening monologue in a parody of the hard-boiled detective genre, set in Shakespeare's London. 1 scene 1m 1 setting
  In Short spells: scenes & monologues; ed. by V. Shantz

  That darn plot. French 2002 85p
    ISBN 0-573-62779-7

Belke, David—*Continued*

Comedy about fathers and sons, playwriting, and reality. Prominent Canadian dramatist must write play overnight to fulfill contractual obligations. 2 acts epilogue 4m 2w 1 interior

Bell, Neal

McTeague: a tale of San Francisco.

Dramatization of Frank Norris novel. Cautionary tale set in 1890s San Francisco. Downward slide of miner turned dentist. 3 acts 39 scenes 5m 4w settings

In Bell, N. Plays

Ragged Dick.

Study of sex, politics, and poverty set in 1890s New York City. 2 acts 23 scenes 2b 5m 5w extras settings

In Bell, N. Plays

Thérèse Raquin. Broadway Play Pub. 1998 88p

ISBN 0-88145-136-3

Expressionistic dramatization of Émile Zola novel about infidelity, murder, madness, and suicide. Set in Paris in the late 1800s. 2 acts 5 scenes 5m 3w settings

—Same

In Bell, N. Plays

Belle. Gibson, F.

Belle Lamar. Boucicault, D.

Bellies, knees and ankles. Hamilton, W. A.

Bellusci, Mark

Born to be blue.

Comedy about parents who want son to underachieve. 3 scenes 3m 2w settings

In Off-Off Broadway Festival plays, 27th series

Belluso, John

The technology project: voice properties.

A paralyzed man and his date, recently divorced from a "robot," talk via a computerized voice system until a moment of spontaneity occurs. Music. 1 act 1m 1w 1 interior

In Humana Festival 2002

Bellyfruit. Bernhard, M., and others

Belonging. Deverell, R.

A **bench** in the sun. Clark, R.

Benet i Jornet, Josep Maria

Desire.

Enigmatic drama involving two couples, the connections between them unclear. Music. 1 act 5 scenes 2m 2w 2 interiors 1 exterior

In Modern Catalan plays; ed. by J. London and D. George

Legacy; tr. by Janet Decesaris. Estreno 2000 45p (Contemporary Spanish Plays, 17)

ISBN 1-888463-09-0

An elderly professor who does not have long to live attempts to create a legacy. Prologue. 1 act 6 scenes 3m 3 interiors

Benfield, Derek

In at the deep end. French (London) 2003 94p

ISBN 0-573-01982-7

Comedy about high class health farm disrupted by wealthy businessman's trio of ladies. 2 acts 3m 3w 1 setting

Second time around. French (London) 2000 91p

ISBN 0-573-01887-1

Romantic comedy about a couple who meet each other after 22 years, relive memories of love and family. 2 acts 1m 1w 1 setting

Two and two together. French (London) 1999 89p

ISBN 0-573-01947-9

Comedy about a couple both committing adultery and the resulting lies and misunderstandings. 2 acts 4m 3w

Benjamin, Keith Alan

Mary Macgregor.

Spirit of dead husband listens to unsuspecting widow. 1m 1w 1 setting

In 3 more by E.S.T. '98

—Same

In EST marathon '98: the one-act plays; ed. by M. Smith

Bennett, Alan

c Kenneth Grahame's The wind in the willows. French (London) 1996 76p

ISBN 0-573-01930-4

An adaptation of Kenneth Grahame's classic animal tale. Music, singing. 2 parts 1b 2g 19m 4w extras settings

Bennett, Simon

Drummers. Hern Bks. 1999 68p
ISBN 1-85459-457-5
A small gang of professional burglars undermined by drug use, double dealing, and brotherly hatreds. 2 acts 7 scenes 4m 1w 2 interiors

Benson, E. F. (Edward Frederic), 1867-1940

Make way for Lucia: the complete Lucia (dramatization) See Van Druten, J. Make way for Lucia

Bent. Sherman, M.

The **bequest**. Wasserman, D.

Berger, Glen

I will go. . . I will go. . .
Drama inspired by true story of Henry Sullivan who in 1923 becomes first American to swim English Channel. Variable cast 14 characters 1 exterior
In The Best American short plays, 2000-2001

Berman, Brooke

Dancing with a devil.
Young woman's story of rape in New York City. 1m 2w
In 30 ten-minute plays for 3 actors from Actors Theatre of Louisville's National Ten-minute Play Contest
—Same
In Actors Theatre of Louisville. Ten-minute plays; v5

Bermuda Avenue triangle. Taylor, R., and Bologna, J.

Bernard, Kenneth

The magic show of Dr. Ma-Gico.
Experimental drama in which magician acts as master of ceremonies in series of violent encounters based on fairy-tale and romance themes. Background music, dancing. 9m 10w 1 interior
In Theatre of the ridiculous; ed. by B. Marranca and G. Dasgupta

Bernard, Lawrence

The bear. French (London) 2000 15p
ISBN 0-573-12016-1

Romantic comedy. Bearish landowner meets his match when he tries to collect a debt from a pretty widow. This adaptation is set in Victorian Scotland. 1 act 2m 1w 1 interior

Bernhard, Maria, and others

Bellyfruit.
Women from different backgrounds discuss teenage sex, pregnancy, and motherhood. 1g 2m 8w
In The Best American Short plays, 1997-1998

Bernstein, Leonard

about
Bogart, A. Score

Best beware my sting. Christiansen, A.

The **best** daddy. Silverstein, S.

The **best** little whorehouse goes public. Hall, C.

The **best** man. Vidal, G.

Bestiality

Owens, R. Futz

Betrayal

Baker, E. A. Up, down, strange, charmed, beauty, and truth
Bandele, 'Biyi. Aphra Behn's Oroonoko
Bullock, M. Sokotra
Field, B. Monsieur de Molière
Foley, D. Sad hotel
Guare, J. Greenwich mean
Manzoni, A. The Count of Carmagnola: a tragedy
Margulies, D. Collected stories
Mullins, B. Click
Nigro, D. The Irish girl kissed in the rain
Scheffer, W. Alien boy

Betsy Philadelphia. Tait, L.

Bette and me. Wasserstein, W.

Bettenbender, Benjamin

The siren song of Stephen Jay Gould.
Black comedy. Man attempts suicide by throwing himself off bridge but lands on woman instead. 1m 1w 1 exterior
In The Best American short plays, 2000-2001

Better half dead. Torres, J.

Better living. Walker, G. F.

Betts, Jim
Colour in the storm. Playwrights Canada 2000 194p
ISBN 0-88754-587-4
Play with songs about life and mysterious death of Canadian painter Tom Thomson Music, singing. 2 acts 32 scenes Variable cast 13 characters 1 setting
Betty's garage. Rivera, C.
Betty's summer vacation. Durang, C.
Between blessings. Feliciano, G.
Between worlds. Schmitt, E.-E.
Beulah and the feast. Art, S. S.
Bevan, Aneurin, 1897-1960
about
Griffiths, T. Food for ravens
Beynon, Francis Marion
about
Lill, W. The fighting days
Beyond the horizon. O'Neill, E.
Beyond therapy. Durang, C.

Bhagat, Datta
Routes and escape routes.
Social turmoil in India over the rights of Untouchables. Student radical clashes with veteran of the movement and with gradualist professor. 2 acts 5 scenes 9m 2w 1 interior
In DramaContemporary: India; ed. by E. B. Mee

Bhuchar, Sudha, and Landon-Smith, Kristine
A tainted dawn. Hern Bks. 1999 48p
ISBN 1-85459-451-6
Vignettes about violence and dislocations that resulted from the partition of British India. 1 act 19 scenes 1b 6m 2w extras settings
Bible
Long, A. The Bible: the complete word of God (abridged)
Bible. N.T. Matthew
c Vogel, L. Surfin' Galilay
Bible. O.T. Daniel
c McCullough, L. E. Dare to be a Daniel!
Bible. O.T. Esther
c Vogel, L. A test for Esther
Bible. O.T. Exodus
c Vogel, L. Fearless Pharaoh FooFoo
c Vogel, L. Wilderness wandering

Bible. O.T. Genesis
c McCullough, L. E. What is a brother?
Van Itallie, J.-C. The serpent: a ceremony
c Vogel, L. The fall into sin
c Vogel, L. The flood
c Vogel, L. Joseph
c Vogel, L. The patriarchs
Bible. O.T. Jonah
c McCullough, L. E. Jonah and the whale
Bible. O.T. Judges
c McCullough, L. E. Samson and Delilah
c Vogel, L. Judges—again
c Vogel, L. Samson
Bible. O.T. Kings
c Vogel, L. An Ahab headache and a Jezebelly ache
c Vogel, L. The B-I-B-L-E is L-O-S-T
Vogel, L. Elijah's no good, horrible, very bad job
c Vogel, L. Everything's falling
c Vogel, L. Nay, nay, Naaman
c Vogel, L. Rehoboam rubs 'em wrong
c Vogel, L. Ring around Jerusalem
c Vogel, L. Solomon—wise for a while
Bible. O.T. Ruth
c Vogel, L. Ruth
Bible. O.T. Samuel
c Vogel, L. Big little man
c Vogel, L. From cool to fool
c Vogel, L. What's up, rock?
The **Bible:** the complete word of God (abridged). Long, A., and others
A **bicycle** country. Cruz, N.
Bierce, Ambrose, 1842-1914?
about
Bosakowski, P. Bierce takes on the railroad!
Bierce takes on the railroad! Bosakowski, P.
The **big** bang. Feuer, J., and Boyd, G.
Big boys don't cry. Harden, V.
Big little man. Vogel, L.
Big night. Powell, D.
The **big** one. Anderson, S. J.
The **big** picture. Compton, J.
The **big** scoop (newspaper reporter). McCullough, L. E.
Big tush, little tush. Hutter, R.

Bigamy

Cooney, R. Caught in the net

Hall, L. Two's company

Miller, A. The ride down Mt. Morgan

Bilingual plays

Spanish-English

Boomer, L. Bocón

Bill Erophon and his horse Peggy Sue. McBride-Smith, B.

Bill W. and Dr. Bob. Shem, S., and Surrey, J. L.

Bingham, Sallie

Throwaway.

Young woman turns to grandmother for help in healing broken family. 5 scenes 3m 4w 1 interior 1 exterior

In Women's Project & productions; ed. by J. Miles

Bingo babes. Duarte, I.

Birch, Michael

Pratt of the Argus. French (London) 2002 79p

ISBN 0-573-01967-3

Dramatization of David Nobbs' novel about British journalist in 1950s Yorkshire. Sequel to: Second from last in the sack race (1992). 2 acts 21 scenes variable cast settings

The **bird** of happiness. McCullough, L. E.

The **bird** of paradise. Cavacchioli, E.

A **bird** of prey. Grimsley, J.

Birds. Aristophanes

Birmingham (England)

Woods, S. Trips

Birney, David

The diaries of Adam & Eve. French (London) 2003 42p

ISBN 0-573-69172-X

Adapted from Mark Twain's The Diaries of Adam and Eve. Comedy about the famous couple set in Victorian garden where Eve's curiosity annoys Adam. 1m 1w 1 exterior

Birth marks. Caputo, L.

The **birth** of Casper G. Schmidt. Gilbert, S.

The **birthday**. Merrill, J.

The **birthday** gifts. Rowland, B. T.

Birthdays

Chinn, J. The garden party

Hedges, P. Cake

c Rowland, B. T. The birthday gifts

c Wood, D. Spot's birthday party

The **birthmark**. London, J.

Birthright. Murray, T. C.

Bisexuality

Durang, C. Beyond therapy

Bishop, Conrad, and Fuller, Elizabeth

Dividing lines.

Twelve micro-plays about breaking through barriers of cultural difference, of self-willed isolation, and of personal defenses. Variable cast

In Bishop, C. and Fuller, E. Seismic stages

Family snapshots.

Sixty-four 90-second micro-dramas about the absurdities, traumas and tiny ecstasies that make up family life. Variable cast

In Bishop, C. and Fuller, E. Seismic stages

A friend from high school.

Young mother confronts issue of AIDS when an acquaintance from high school contracts the disease. 2m 2w 1 interior

In Bishop, C. and Fuller, E. Seismic stages

Get happy.

Young girl tries to deal with boyfriend's drinking problem. 1g 4m 3w

In Bishop, C. and Fuller, E. Seismic stages

Success.

Three high school friends get together to catch up, and talk about what they've been doing with their lives. 2m 1w extra

In Bishop, C. and Fuller, E. Seismic stages

Bishop, Elizabeth, 1911-1979

about

Smyth, D. E. Sole survivors

Bitter homes and gardens. Alfaro, L.

Bitter sauce. Bogosian, E.

Bittergirl. Griffiths, A., and others

Bitterman, Shem

The job. French 2001 64p

Black comedy. Former con artist, who wants to marry, applies for a job, only to discover he was hired to carry out a murder. 2 acts 4m 1w 1 setting

Bitterman, Shem—*Continued*

—Same

In New Playwrights: the best plays of 1998

The price.

Two people seeking friendship meet and talk on a park bench. 1m 1w 1 setting

In Actors Theatre of Louisville. Ten-minute plays: v5

The **black** crook. Barras, C. M.

Black mass. Constable, J.

Black nativity. Hughes, L.

Black water. Oates, J. C.

Blackden. McLean, D.

The **blackmailers**. Gray, J., and Raffalovich, M.-A.

Blackpool and Parrish. Belke, D.

Blacks

Borden, W. M. Tightrope time: ain't nuthin' more than some itty bitty madness between twilight & dawn

Boyd, G. E. Consecrated ground

Brown, C. The Negro of Peter the Great

Carter, L. Gulliver

Carter, L. Gulliver redux

Carter, L. Lemuel

Césaire, A. A tempest

Clarke, A. When he was free and young and he used to wear silks

Clarke, G. E. Whylah Falls: the play

Mandiela, A. Z. Dark diaspora . . . in dub

Moodie, A. A common man's guide to loving women

Moodie, A. Riot

Norman, M. Third and Oak

Philip, M. N. Coups and calypsos

River, S. B. Moor masterpieces

Sears, D. Harlem duet

Walker, G. F. Love and anger

Canada

Anthony, T. 'Da kink in my hair

Sears, D. The adventures of a black girl in search of God

Ward, F. Somebody somebody's returning

Young, D. Yagayah: two.black.womyn. griots

Great Britain

Keeffe, B. Barbarians: abide with me

Keeffe, B. Barbarians: in the city

Keeffe, B. Barbarians: killing time

Jamaica

Young, D. Yagayah: two.black.womyn. griots

Blais, Marie-Claire

A couple.

Conversation between two people, the parents of a child, who have radically different goals in life. First performed as a radio play. Music. 1 act 1m 1w settings

In Blais, M.-C. Wintersleep

Exile.

Husband and wife, foreign residents in an unnamed country, speak of frightening rumors, surveillance, and police violence. First performed as a radio play. Music. 1 act 2m 1w 1 setting

In Blais, M.-C. Wintersleep

Fever.

Tourist couple; wife becomes ill while visiting North Africa and begins to see husband through the eyes of the impoverished people around them. First performed as a radio play. Music. 1 act 1m 1w 1 setting

In Blais, M.-C. Wintersleep

Ghost of a voice.

A singer fears she has lost her own voice in serving as muse to her composer-husband. First performed as a radio play. Music. 1 act 1m 1w 1 setting

In Blais, M.-C. Wintersleep

Wintersleep.

Symbolist theater piece on themes of isolation, death, and wasted life. Music. 1 act 3 scenes 5m 7w 1 setting

In Blais, M.-C. Wintersleep

Blake, William D., and Blake, Cynthia H.

Jesus our brother is alive!.

Worship program about Jesus' four brothers on morning following crucifixion. 1 act 4m 3w 1 interior

In The drama of Easter; ed. by R. Wray

Blakeman, Helen

Caravan. French (London) 1998 81p

ISBN 0-573-01770-0

Blakeman, Helen—*Continued*

Comedy set in Wales about a mother and her two daughters from Liverpool living in a trailer park. 2 acts 9 scenes 3w 2m 1 setting

Bland, Joellen K.

y A tale of two cities. Pioneer Drama Service 1998 52p

Dramatization of Dickens's classic novel of the French Revolution. 2 acts Variable cast settings

Blasted. Kane, S.

Blessing, Lee

Chesapeake.

Tragicomedy about abducted retriever, vengeful performance artist, and scheme against a right-wing politician. 2 acts 1m

In Blessing, L. Chesapeake

Reproduction.

Four young people, including two pregnant seventeen-year-olds, discuss abortion and single motherhood. 2m 2w

In Blessing, L. Chesapeake

Snapshot: Tyler poked Taylor.

Monologue by a young man with a perverse fixation on US presidents. 1 act 1m 1 setting

In Humana Festival 2002

Thief river. Dramatists 2002

ISBN 0-8222-1839-9

The story of two men and their fifty-three-year relationship. They struggle with their feelings for each other in a society that doesn't understand. 6m 1 interior

Blessings. Surface, M. H.

Blind

Lewis, C. W. The one-eyed man is king

c Martini, C. The field

Nigro, D. The Babel of circular labyrinths

Plowman, G. There's none so blind

Blind Willie and the talking dog. Silverstein, S.

Blink of an eye. Dobrish, J.

Blithe spirit. Coward, N.

Blitzstein, Marc

about

Sherman, J. It's all true

Blok, Alexander

The unknown woman.

Symbolist drama based on Blok's poem Neznakomka. Poet sees star fall to earth and discovers it is beautiful woman of his vision. 3 parts Variable cast 1 interior 2 exteriors

In Eight twentieth-century Russian plays; ed. by T. Langen and J. Weir

Blomquist, Erica

Reality.

Woman washing dishes reflects on her abusive husband. 1w 1 setting

In Blast from the future; ed. by D. Yeaton

Blood brothers. Russell, W.

Blood lines. McClelland, J.

The **blood** of the Bambergs. Osborne, J.

Blowfish. Thiessen, V.

Blowjob. Wilson, S.

Blown sideways through life. Shear, C.

The **blue** and the grey. Harrigan, E.

Blue kettle. Churchill, C.

The **blue** light and other stories. Sills, P.

The **blue** room. Baron, C.

The **blue** room. Hare, D.

Blue suede blues. Raffle, D.

Blue surge. Gilman, R.

Bluebeard. Ludlam, C.

Bluebeard. Reakes, P.

Blues (Music)

Taylor, R. It ain't nothin' but the blues

Tidler, C. Red mango

Blues for an Alabama sky. Cleage, P.

Bly, Nellie

about

c McCullough, L. E. Around the world with Nellie Bly

The **boardinghouse**. Harden, V.

Bobby Supreme. Miller, J. B.

Bobrauschenbergamerica. Mee, C. L.

Bobrick, Sam

Death in England. French 2003 57p

ISBN 0-573-69373-0

Comedy murder mystery about someone who is posing as death in an English household. 2 acts 2 scenes 5m 3w 1 setting

Remember me? French 2001 59p

ISBN 0-573-62780-0

Bobrick, Sam—*Continued*

Comedy about an old college boyfriend visiting ex-girlfriend, who had the perfect marriage, until his visit. 2 acts 4 scenes 2m 2w 1 interior

Boccioni, Umberto

Genius and culture; tr. by Victoria Nes Kirby.

Futurist theater piece featuring artist and critic. 1w 2m

   In Theater of the avant-garde, 1890-1950; ed. by B. Cardullo and R. Knopf

Bocón. Boomer, L.

Body, Jerry Jr.

The Indian draft spirit. American Literary Press, Inc. 1998 58p

   ISBN 1-56167-416-8

Murder mystery about a Native American whose spirit returns in the form of a doll seeking revenge upon an unsuspecting community. 2 acts 6 scenes Variable cast 1 setting

The **body**. Darke, N.

Body and soul. Francis, S.

The **body-builder's** book of love. Arrabal, F.

The **body** guards. Yellow Robe, W. S.

Body Indian. Geiogamah, H.

Body language. Ayckbourn, A.

Body talk. Palmer, T.

Boettcher-Tate, Karen

c Rapunzel. Pioneer Drama Service 1998 32p

Comic fairy tale. Young beauty held captive in tower by witch is rescued in unusual fashion. 5 scenes Variable cast 2 interior 1 exterior

Bogart, Anne, and Clarke, Jocelyn

Score.

Monologue by Leonard Bernstein, about music and the joy of life. Largely assembled from his writings and from interviews. 1 act 1m 1 setting

   In Humana Festival 2002

Bogdan, Koca

Annette and Annette.

Second play in author's Triptych trilogy. Sexual and emotional exploitation forces two women to engage in crisis of identity. Music. 9 scenes 2w

   In Bogdan, K. My name is such and such and other plays

Gunter's wife.

Concluding play in author's Triptych trilogy. Woman discovers that the usual rules of communication must be rewritten during first days of her most unusual marriage. Music. 7 scenes 1m 1w

   In Bogdan, K. My name is such and such and other plays

My name is such and such.

Two estranged lovers, a composer and violinist, struggle to reconnect. 4 scenes 1m 1w

   In Bogdan, K. My name is such and such and other plays

Sparring partner.

First play in author's Triptych trilogy. Drama about issues of identity centers on a reclusive chess master who hires someone because he wants to practice his skills. 4 scenes 2m

   In Bogdan, K. My name is such and such and other plays

Bogosian, Eric

Bitter sauce.

Inspired by Shakespeare's Sonnet 118. Farce of sexual jealousy and obsession. 1 act 2m 1w 1 interior

   In Love's fire

Wake up and smell the coffee. Theatre Comunications Group 2002 112p

   ISBN 1-55936-202-2

Black comedy. Series of satiric monologues on contemporary society. 1m

Bohemianism

Akalaitis, J. Ti Jean blues

Osborne, J. Watch it come down

Bohjalian, Christopher A.

Midwives (dramatization) See Yeaton, D. Midwives

Bohr, Niels Henrik David, 1885-1962

about

Frayn, M. Copenhagen

Boid & Oskar. Wong, E.

Boker, George Henry

Francesca da Rimini.

Tragedy set in medieval Italy. Noblewoman falls in love with her deformed husband's handsome brother. Inspired by a passage in Dante's Inferno. Music, singing. 5 acts 14 scenes 7m 2w extras settings

   In Nineteenth century American plays; ed. by M. Matlaw

Bolero. Ives, D.

Bolger, Dermot

The passion of Jerome. Methuen 1999 89p

ISBN 0-413-73880-9

The story of an ordinary man suddenly forced to confront both his own demons and the trapped poltergeist spirit of a dead boy. 2 acts 16 scenes 9m 3w 1 interior setting

Bollocks. Hall, L.

Bond, Edward

Early morning.

Surrealistic horror farce depicting evil and corruption of man. Setting is Queen Victoria's entourage, a nest of intriguers and murderers who end up in cannibalistic feast in heaven. 21 scenes 12m 3w 1 setting

In The Methuen book of sixties drama

y Eleven vests.

Drama about authority and personal responsibility. Depicts how person reacts to similar events, first as teenager, then as adult. 7 scenes 2m 1w

In Bond, E. Eleven vests & Tuesday

y Eleven vests & Tuesday. Methuen 1997 117p

ISBN 0-413-72120-5

Drama about authority and personal responsibility. Depicts how person reacts to similar events first as teenager, then as adult. 7 scenes 2m 1w

y Tuesday.

Young girl's attitude toward father, war, and violence changes when boyfriend arrives unexpectedly from active service abroad. 1 act 3 scenes 1 interior 8m 3w

In Bond, E. Eleven vests & Tuesday

Bondage. Hwang, D. H.

Bonel, Wilma

Good grief, Lolita.

Lively child dies after a long hospital stay, is mourned by mother and friends with a musical party. One actress plays all roles. Music, singing. 1 scene 1w settings

In Puro teatro; ed. by A. Sandoval-Sánchez and N. S. Sternbach

Bones. Straughan, P.

Book of days. Wilson, L.

The **book** of Ruth. Frockt, D. L.

Books and reading

Weldon, F. The reading group

The **boom** box. Lucas, C.

Boom town. Daniels, J.

Boomer, Lisa

Bocón.

Play about opposition to dictatorial power incorporates Latin folkloric characters. Dialogue in English and Spanish. Singing. Prologue 6 scenes Variable cast 25 characters

In Theatre for young audiences; ed. by C. A. Jennings

Boone, Daniel

about

Norman, M. Loving Daniel Boone

The **boor** hug. Feydeau, G.

Booth, Edwin, 1833-1893

about

Tait, L. Edwin Booth

Borden, Walter M.

Tightrope time: ain't nuthin' more than some itty bitty madness between twilight & dawn.

Explores one black man's polyphonous consciousness. Incorporates material by James Baldwin, Langston Hughes, Lorraine Hansberry and James Weldon Johnson. 2 acts 23 scenes 1m 1 setting

In Testifyin' v1; ed. by D. Sears

The **borderland**. Grimsley, J.

Bordertown. Culture Clash (Group)

Borges, Jorge Luis, 1899-1986

about

Nigro, D. The Babel of circular labyrinths

Born to be blue. Bellusci, M.

Bornstein, Kate

Virtually yours.

Transgendered artist uses computer game to help deal with her fears. 1w

In O Solo homo; ed. by H. Hughes and D. Román

Bosakowski, Phil

Bierce takes on the railroad!.

Journalist Ambrose Bierce looks into political chicanery in the late 19th century. Theodore Roosevelt, William Randolph Hearst, and Pancho Villa are among the characters. 2 acts 8m 2w extras

In Bosakowski, P. Plays

Bosakowski, Phil—*Continued*

Chopin in space.

Series of surreal blackout scenes examine passion, inspiration, and Polish nationalism. 8m 3w 1 setting

   In Bosakowski, P. Plays

Nixon apologizes to the nation.

Political satire. In ten takes before television camera, Richard Nixon tries to tape apology to country. 2 acts 13m 4w extras 1 interior

   In Bosakowski, P. Plays

Bosnia

  Ensler, E. Necessary targets

  O'Malley, G. Concertina's rainbow

Boston massacre, 1770

  Nigro, D. Horrid massacre in Boston

Botánica. Prida, D.

Bouchard, Michel Marc

Down Dangerous Passes Road. Talonbooks 2000 95p

  ISBN 0-88922-440-4

Three brothers in an accident on a forest road, very close to the spot where their despised father drowned years ago, and where he still exerts a hold on them. 1 act 3m 1 exterior

Boucicault, Dion

Belle Lamar.

Melodrama set during Civil War. Three officers, two Northern and one Confederate, appear at Southern heroine's trial for espionage. 3 acts 4 scenes 11m 1w 1 interior 2 exteriors

   In Fateful lightning; ed. by W. J. Meserve and M. A. Meserve

The octoroon; or, Life in Louisiana.

Melodrama set in pre–Civil War South. Octoroon daughter of bankrupt planter commits suicide when she is bought by scheming overseer. 5 acts 8 scenes 14m 6w extras 3 interiors 4 exteriors

   In Nineteenth century American plays; ed. by M. Matlaw

Bouncers. Godber, J.

Bound east for Cardiff. O'Neill, E.

Boundary County, Idaho. Topor, T.

Bourbon at the border. Cleage, P.

The **bourgeois** gentleman. Molière

Bourke, Ken

The hunt for Red Willie.

The Irish countryside in the 1820s. A landowner drops dead and a moonshiner is suspected of murder. Comic pursuit follows. 2 parts 15 scenes 3m 2w settings

   In Down the line; The hunt for Red Willie

Bovell, Andrew

Speaking in tongues. Currency Press 1998 68p

  ISBN 0-86819-419-0   LC 99-487664

Interlinked scenes follow two couples in mystery of infidelity and deceit. 3 parts Variable cast 9 characters

—Same. Dramatists 2003

  ISBN 0-8222-1903-4

Bowen, John

After the rain.

Fantasy. Set two hundred years after the Great Rain of 1969. A paraphrasing of the Bible commencing with Noah and the flood, ending with the sacrifice of the God-figure. 2 acts 9m 3w

   In Bowen, J. Plays: one

Cold salmon. French (London) 1998 26, [10]p

  ISBN 0-573-12032-3   LC 00-703028

Dark comedy set in church graveyard, where a deceased man tries to communicate with his living wife through a teenage medium and a cold salmon. 4m 6w 1 setting

The disorderly women.

Version of Euripides' Bacchae reflecting 20th-century concerns. Music. 2 acts 6m 7w 1 setting

   In Bowen, J. Plays: one

Little boxes: the coffee lace.

Group of elderly theatrical folk start life anew when one of their circle dies. 4m 5w 1 interior

   In Bowen, J. Plays: one

Little boxes: Trevor.

Farce. Two female roommates try to conceal their relationship from parents by inventing a mythical male suitor. 4m 4w 1 interior

   In Bowen, J. Plays: one

Singles.

Young woman advertises in London newspaper for volunteer willing to impregnate her. 2m 3w 1 interior

   In Bowen, J. Plays: one

Bower, Humphrey

Natural life. Currency Press 1998 32p

ISBN 0-86819-555-3

Dramatization of Marcus Clarke's classic nineteenth century Australian novel, For the term of his natural life. It tells of the life of the convict Rufus Dawes, condemned to suffer endlessly at the hands of the brutal ruling elite of Australia's early penal colonies. 22 scenes 6m 1w extras settings

A **bowl** of beings. Culture Clash (Group)

A **bowl** of soup. Lane, E.

A **bowl** of soup, a piece of bread. Fredericks, A. D.

Bowne, Alan

Beirut.

Drama set in near future on New York's Lower East Side. Young woman crosses quarantine line to be with boyfriend who has tested positive for devastating disease. 1 act 2m 1w 1 interior

In Bowne, A. Plays

Forty-deuce.

Drama set in environs of Times Square. Portrays world of homosexual prostitution. 1 act 4 scenes 7m 1 interior

In Bowne, A. Plays

Sharon and Billy.

Drama about brother-sister incest set in 1950s suburban southern California. 1 act 7 scenes 2m 2w 1 interior

In Bowne, A. Plays

Box, Muriel

Angels of war.

Feminist anti-war play about all-woman ambulance corps on the Western Front in 1918. 3 acts 4 scenes 10w 2 interiors

In War plays by women; ed. by C. M. Tylee, E. Turner, and A. Cardinal

Box. Francis, J.

Boxcar. Gonzalez, S. S.

Boxers

Osborne, A. Bull, rock, and nut

Boy gets girl. Gilman, R.

The **boy** in the treehouse. Taylor, D. H.

Boy meets girl. Wasserstein, W.

The **boy** who left home to find out about the shivers. Bush, M.

Boyband. Quilter, P.

Boyd, George Elroy

Consecrated ground. Blizzard Pub. 1999 69p

ISBN 0-921368-91-7

Plans to demolish an historic black settlement in Halifax, Nova Scotia, to make way for waterfront development have tragic consequences for the residents and their minister, and for the social worker sent to oversee their relocation. Based on an actual event. 2 acts 22 scenes 4m 3w settings

—Same

In Testifyin' v2; ed. by D. Sears

Boyd, Graham. See Feuer, J. jt. auth.

Boyfriend riff. Lucas, C.

Boys

c Beattie, A. The looking-glass alchemist

c DeTurk, S. The musical adventures of Oliver Twist

Francis, M. The adventures of Huckleberry Finn

c Grauer, R. Mark Twain's Huckleberry Finn

Gurney, A. R. Ancestral voices: a family story

Herrick, J. Kudzu

c Houston, V. H. Hula heart

Lathrop, M. The visible horse

c Mason, T. The adventures of Huckleberry Finn

c Mason, T. The adventures of Tom Sawyer

Taylor, D. H. The boy in the treehouse

c Weller, M. Dogbrain

Bozzone, Bill

War.

Son of too-loving antiwar mom makes a break for it. Music. 1 act 2m 1w 1 interior

In Ensemble Studio Theatre marathon '99: the one-act plays

Bradbeer, Suzanne

Full bloom.

Adolescent copes with parents' divorce and society's emphasis on personal beauty. 2 acts 10 scenes 1b 1g 1m 2w 1 interior 1 exterior

In Women playwrights: the best plays of 2000

Bradley, Jyll

Digging for ladies.

Story of four women's journey from innocence to experience told through the lore and language of gardening. 3 acts 4 scenes Variable cast 1 exterior

In Mythic women/Real women

Bran nue dae. Chi, J.

Brandl, Dave

y Too wrapped up for Christmas. Pioneer Drama Service 1999 32p

Christmas play set in busy shopping mall. High school students try to raise money for homeless shelter. 1 act Variable cast 25 characters extras 1 interior

Brandt, Alan

2 1/2 Jews. Broadway Play Pub. 2000 67p

ISBN 0-88145-167-3

Tragicomedy about famous lawyer's bitter relationships with his immigrant father and Yale-educated son. 2 acts 3m

Braun, Eva, 1912-1945

about

Schenkar, J. The last of Hitler

Brave hearts. Rintoul, H.

Brave smiles . . . another lesbian tragedy. Five Lesbian Brothers (Theater company)

Bread. Hunt, M.

Breakfast for one. Foxton, D.

Breakfast serial. Terry, M.

Breaking the chain. Smith, V.

Breaking up. Cristofer, M.

Breast cancer

Green, A. For tiger lilies out of season

The **breath** of life. Hare, D.

Brecht, Bertolt

Baal. Arcade Pub. 1998 86p

ISBN 1-55970-419-5

Downhill progress of a magnetic, dissolute poet who does whatever he wants. Singing. Prologue 1 act 22 scenes 18m 12w extras 7 interiors 8 exteriors

about

Kleberg, L. The Aquarians

Brel, Jacques

Jacques Brel is alive and well & living in Paris; production conception, English lyrics, additional material by Eric Blau and Mort Shuman. Dramatists 2003

ISBN 0-8222-1905-0

Cabaret musical based on lyrics and commentary by Jacques Brel. 2m 2w 1 setting

Brennan, Kit

Magpie.

A woman about to be discharged from an insane asylum swings back and forth between grim realities and vivid fantasies. Dancing. 1 scene 2m 1w 1 setting

In Short spells: scenes & monologues; ed. by V. Shantz

Breslin, Jimmy

Contract with Jackie.

Short satirical piece on politics and politicians. Congressman visits wife in Atlanta hospital, 1980. 1m 1w 1 interior

In Actors Theatre of Louisville. Ten-minute plays: v4

Brett, Simon

Putting the kettle on. French (London) 2002 24p

ISBN 0-573-03391-X

Monologue by thirty-something woman who has just been dumped by boyfriend for being "shallow" and environmentally unaware. 1w 1 interior

Silhouette. French (London) 1999 78p

ISBN 0-573-01877-4   LC 00-502899

Mystery thriller about actress wife, her journalist lover, and the murder of her husband. 2 acts 5m 3w 1 setting

Brett, Simon, and Travis, Sarah

c Sleeping beauty. French (London) 1999 74p

ISBN 0-573-08110-7

A pantomime update of the classic fairy tale, with a time machine, an ecological message, and an unromantic view of monarchy. Music, singing, dancing. 2 acts 13 scenes 4m 4w extras 4 interiors 3 exteriors

Brevoort, Deborah Baley

Into the fire. French 2000 71p

ISBN 0-573-62721-5

Brevoort, Deborah Baley—*Continued*

Tragicomedy about Alaskan fishing village scandalized by the mayor's wife's behavior. 3 acts 2 scenes 6m 4m extras settings

The women of Lockerbie.

Seven years after the destruction of Pan Am Flight 103, grieving American couple and women of Lockerbie, Scotland, struggle to come to terms with their losses and to recover victims' personal effects from the U.S. authorities. 2m 5w 1 exterior

In New dramatists: best plays by the graduating class of 2001

Bricusse, Leslie

Scrooge. French 1998 97p

ISBN 0-573-08092-5

Musical version of Dickens's classic Christmas tale. Miser reforms after being visited by three spirits. 2 acts 23 scenes Large mixed cast 10 interiors 5 exteriors

The **bridegroom** of Blowing Rock. Trieschmann, C.

Brides of the moon. Five Lesbian Brothers (Theater company)

Bridge head. Mayne, R.

Bridgeman, Laura

Maison Splendide.

Comedy. Explores relationship of lesbian petty criminals house-sitting for big time gangster. Music. 1 act 2w 1 interior

In Best of the Fest; ed. by Phil Setren

Brief candle. Ardito, C.

Brief lives. Garland, P.

The **briery** gap. Murray, T. C.

Brigands and robbers

Orton, J. Loot

Briggs, Stephen

Terry Pratchett's Maskerade. French (London) 1998 99p

ISBN 0-573-01829-4

Dark comedy dramatization of Pratchett's Discworld novel about ghost stalking the corridors of the Ankh-Morpork Opera House. 2 acts 31 scenes Large mixed cast 1 setting

Bright angel. Radano, L.-M.

Bright interval. Vooght, C.

Brights. Smilow, D.

British

Singapore

Wood, C. Jingo

Brittney, Lynn

Pickwick papers; book by Charles Dickens. French (London) 1999 99p

ISBN 0-573-01860-X

Dramatization of the posthumous papers of the Pickwick Club by Charles Dickens. Wealthy and learned Mr. Pickwick takes his fellow club members on comic journey through early 19th century England. 2 acts 21 scenes 12m 10w extras 14 interiors 7 exteriors

Briusov, Valery

The wayfarer; tr. by Daniel Gerould.

Symbolist play about woman's desire to connect with another. 1 act 1m 1w 1 setting

In Theater of the avant-garde, 1890-1950; ed. by B. Cardullo and R. Knopf

Broadway macabre. Nigro, D.

Brofsky, Kevin

Strawberry fields.

In a small, hostile Florida town, the mother of a murdered gay is interviewed by a network celebrity in preparation for an appearance on her show. Unexpected solidarity. 1 act 3w 1 interior

In Off-Off Broadway Festival plays, 25th ser.

Broken hearts. McLeod, K. R.

The **broken** jug. Kleist, H. von

Broken rainbows. Surface, M. H.

Brontë, Charlotte, 1816-1855

Jane Eyre (dramatization) See Teale, P. Jane Eyre

about

Gough, L. The red room

Bronx express. Dymov, O.

Brooks, Jeremy, and Mitchell, Adrian

c A child's Christmas in Wales.

Based on Dylan Thomas' story of his memories of Christmas day. 4b 2g 7m 4w extras 1 setting

In The twelve plays of Christmas; ed. by L. Swortzell

Brooks, Vanessa

Swan song. French (London) 2003 29p

ISBN 0-573-023581

Bittersweet comedy about a retiring chartered surveyor, his devoted secretary and his bored wife. 5 scenes 1m 2w 1 setting

Brossa, Joan

The quarrelsome party.

An absurdist comedy of non sequiturs and class paralysis, set in Barcelona in the early 1960s. 3 acts 5m 4w 3 settings

   In Modern Catalan plays; ed. by J. London and D. George

Brother. Gallagher, M.

Brother Andre's heart. Griffiths, L.

Brother Fire. Wilder, T.

Brother Rabbit sells corn. Winther, B.

Brothers

   Bennett, S. Drummers

   Boker, G. H. Francesca da Rimini

   Bouchard, M. M. Down Dangerous Passes Road

   Clarvoe, A. The brothers Karamazov

   Coen, L. Epic proportions

   Dresser, R. Wonderful world

   Enright, N. Spurboard

   Gadea, W. Brothers

   Hoffman, J. Francis Brick needs no introduction

   Jacker, C. A new life

   Jeffries, B. Pastimes

   Keane, J. B. The highest house on the mountain

   Lane, E. A bowl of soup

c McCullough, L. E. What is a brother?

   McDonagh, M. The lonesome West

y Medoff, M. Showdown on Rio Road

   Meyer, M. The mystery of attraction

   Nielson, K. A true fool's folly

   O'Neill, E. Beyond the horizon

   Orloff, R. I didn't know you could cook

   Plautus, T. M. Double bind (Menaechmi)

   Straughan, P. Bones

   Tasca, J. Deus-X

   Terence. The brothers (Adelphoe)

   Terence. The mother-in-law (Hecyra)

   Vinaver, M. Nina, that's something else

   Warmflash, S. Six inch adjustable

   Woudstra, K. Burying the dog

Brothers. Gadea, W.

The **brothers** (Adelphoe). Terence

Brothers and sisters

   Bowne, A. Sharon and Billy

   Chinn, J. A different way home

   De Matteo, D. The obit

   Flacks, D. Sib

Forde, M. X-stacy

Gallagher, M. Brother

Goldberg, J. The hologram theory

Hedges, P. Andy and Claire

Henley, B. Control freaks

Kennedy, A. A rat's mass

Kops, B. Playing Sinatra

Kramer, S. David's redhaired death

Kramer, S. Things that break

y Lazarus, J. Night light

Mamet, D. Jolly

Margulies, D. Misadventure

Martin, J. The deal

Menander. Closely cropped locks

Mitchell, D. The hour of lamps

Oliver, K. Swollen tongues

Rapp, A. Nocturne

Rivera, J. Flowers

Sophocles. Electra

Tibbetts, M. LittleBro morning and BigSis afternoon

Williams, T. Kingdom of earth

Williams, T. Out cry

Yellow Robe, W. S. The independence of Eddie Rose

The **brothers** Karamazov. Clarvoe, A.

Brown, Bertha

It's okay, honey.

Clueless mother attempts to have a heart-to-heart talk with her daughter about sexual preferences. 1 act 2w 1 interior

   In Off-Off Broadway Festival plays, 23rd ser.

Brown, Carlyle

The Negro of Peter the Great.

Historical drama based on story by Pushkin about African-born godson of Tsar Peter the Great. Music. 2 acts 12m 6w 5 interiors 2 exteriors

   In New dramatists: best plays by the graduating class of 2001

Brown, Jason Robert

Parade (condensation); Book by Alfred Uhry; music and lyrics by Jason Robert Brown; co-conceived by Harold Prince.

   In The Best Plays of 1998-1999; ed. by Otis L. Guernsey, Jr.

Brown, John, 1800-1859
about
Swayze, J. C. Ossawattomie Brown

Brown, Stewart
Toshie. Playwrights Canada 2002 90p
ISBN 1-873130-22-8
Drama with music based on life of Dundee whaler James McIntosh. "Toshi" is visited by Captain Robert Scott to find out how he survived in open boat without food in freezing South Atlantic seas. Music, singing. 2 acts 8m 4w extras 1 setting

Brown, Stuart R.
Slice of life.
Tentative human contact between two lonely, mistrustful men. Set in a luncheonette on a wintry day. 1 act 2m 1 interior
  In EST marathon '96: the one-act plays; ed. by M. Smith

Brown, Victoria Norman
Roadtrip.
Young man and woman driving down highway discuss their relationship. 1m 1w 1 setting
  In Actors Theatre of Louisville. Ten-minute plays: v5

Brown, Wesley
Life during wartime.
Drama about African American graffiti artist's questionable death in police custody. Music. 2 acts 27 scenes 3m 6w 1 interior 1 exterior
  In Action; ed. by M. Algarin and L. Griffith

Brown, William Wells
The escape.
A hyprocritical physician, abolitionists, and runaway slaves are portrayed in this drama about slavery in the United States. Singing. 5 acts 20 scenes Large mixed cast 9 interiors 4 exteriors
  In Fateful lightning; ed. by W. J. Meserve and M. A. Meserve
—Same; edited, with an introduction by John Ernest. University of Tenn. Press 2001 54p
ISBN 1-572-33105-4; 1-572-33106-2 (pa)
LC 00-9484

Browne, Sir Thomas
about
Kushner, T. Hydriotaphia; or, The death of Dr. Browne

Bruchac, Joseph
The cannibal monster.
Based on Tlingit Indian legend. When people fail to heed Raven's advice they are menaced by mosquitoes. 3 scenes Variable cast 10 characters 1 exterior
  In Bruchac, J. Pushing up the sky
Gluskabe and Old Man Winter.
Based on Indian legend. Battle of wits between Abenaki hero and ruler of Winter Land. Singing, dancing. 4 scenes 2m 1w extras 2 interiors 1 exterior
  In Bruchac, J. Pushing up the sky
Possum's tail.
Based on Cherokee Indian legend. Other animals tire of possum's boasting about his bushy tail. 3 scenes Unidentified cast 8 characters 1 exterior
  In Bruchac, J. Pushing up the sky
Pushing up the sky.
Based on legend of Snohomish Indians of Northwest. By working together seven tribes use poles to push sky higher. 3 scenes 1b 1g 8m 1w 1 exterior
  In Bruchac, J. Pushing up the sky
Star sisters.
Based on Ojibwa Indian legend about sisters who marry star people. 4 scenes Variable cast 3 exteriors
  In Bruchac, J. Pushing up the sky
Wihio's duck dance.
Based on Cheyenne Indian legend. Young brave catches ducks for dinner but loses them with his foolishness. 3 scenes Unidentified cast 8 characters extras 1 interior 2 exteriors
  In Bruchac, J. Pushing up the sky

Bruckner, Ferdinand, 1891-1958
Race (adaptation) See Edelstein, Barry Race

Bruno. Giordano
about
Wilson, S. More light

Brustein, Robert
Enrico IV; [by] Luigi Pirandello; in a new adaptation by Robert Brustein; based on a translation by Gloria Pastorino. Dee, I. R. 2002 78p
ISBN 1-56663-447-4; 1-56663-446-6
LC 2002-22960
Wealthy aristocrat falls into fantasy in which he is embattled medieval emperor. 3 acts 9m 2w 2 interiors 2 exteriors

Brustein, Robert—*Continued*

Nobody dies on Friday.

Drama about impact of Marilyn Monroe on family of acting coach Lee Strasberg. Portrays emotional and intellectual tensions among family members. 2 acts 3 scenes 2m 2w extras 1 interior

In New Playwrights: the best plays of 1998

Six characters in search of an author; in a new adaptation by Robert Brustein and The American Repertory Theatre Company. Dee, I. R. 1998 83p

ISBN 0-929587-62-6; 0-929587-58-8

LC 97-24711

Play within a play. Director attempts rehearsal staging story of characters from unwritten play. Each character tells story from own viewpoint, complains that actors and director/author misrepresent them. Singing. 1b 7m 4w extras 1 interior

Bubba the cowboy prince. McBride-Smith, B.

Bubble trouble. Fredericks, A. D.

Büchner, Georg, 1813-1837

Woyzeck (adaptation) See Iizuka, N. Skin

Woyzeck; in a new translation and adaptation by Nicholas Rudall. Dee, I. R. 2002 51p

ISBN 1-566-63449-0   LC 2002-73497

Series of related incidents portray simple soldier's inner torment and disintegration leading to murder of his faithless common-law wife. 27 scenes 1b 10m 3w 1 setting

The **Buddha** of Ceylon. De Boer, L.

Buddhism

c McCullough, L. E. The Monkey King

Van Itallie, J.-C. The Tibetan book of the dead; or, How not to do it again

Buero-Vallejo, Antonio

The sleep of reason. Estreno 1998 65p (Contemporary Spanish Plays, 14)

ISBN 1-888463-04-X

Old age of the painter Goya. A target for royalist reprisals, he has moved to a provincial town and is further isolated by his deafness and nightmare visions. Projections 2 parts 7 scenes 10m 2w 2 interiors

The **bug.** Strand, R.

Building Jerusalem. Redhill, M.

Bulgakov, Mikhail

A cabal of hypocrites (adaptation) See Field, B. Monsieur de Molière

Flight; tr. and adapted by Ron Hutchinson. Hern Bks. 1998 94p

ISBN 1-85459-379-X

Comedy satire set in 1920 during Russian civil war and played out through eight dreams. 8 parts 14m 6w extras

Bull, rock, and nut. Osborne, A.

Bullock, Michael

Sokotra. Rainbird Press 1997 58p

ISBN 0-9690504-7-X

Surrealist drama about dreams, betrayal, and murder. 3 acts 3 scenes 2m 2w 2 settings

El **bully** (El valenton). Espinosa, R.

The **bungler.** Molière

Bunin, Keith

Credeaux canvas. Dramatists 2002

ISBN 0-8222-1838-0

Winston, a young painter, shares an East Village apartment with Jamie, the son of a prominent art dealer. After his father dies, disinheriting him, Jamie comes up with an idea to forge a Credeaux painting. 2m 2w 1 setting

Bunker, Chang, 1811-1874

about

Gregg, S. A private moment

Bunker, Eng, 1811-1874

about

Gregg, S. A private moment

Bunyan, H. Jay

Prodigals in a promised land.

Drama about racism and cultural identity. Jamaican couple move to Canada with dream of bettering themselves. Prologue 2 acts 13 scenes 1g 2m 3w 1 interior

In Testifyin' v1; ed. by D. Sears

Bureaucracy

Fo, D. Archangels don't play pinball

Burgoyne, John

about

Shaw, B. The devil's disciple

The **burial** society. Sandler, S.

Buried treasure

c Mason, T. Treasure Island

Buried treasure—*Continued*

c Reakes, P. Robinson Crusoe and the pirates

Burke, Kelley Jo

Charming & Rose: true love.

Fairy tale of woman reared by wolves who believes she is princess destined for "true love." Music. 1m 2w 1 interior

In Prerogatives

Comfort and joy.

In a monologue addressed to her children, a mother remembers her own infatuation, as a teenager, with the crucified Christ. 1 scene 1w extras 1 interior

In Short spells: scenes & monologues; ed. by V. Shantz

Burn. Goldstein, D. L.

Burnett, Frances Hodgson, 1849-1924

A little princess (dramatization) See Vreeke, J. A little princess

The secret garden (dramatization) See Duffield, N. The secret garden; Sterling, P. The secret garden

The **burning** bush. Kokoschka, O.

Burning desires. Schenkar, J.

Burroughs, John

about

Metcalf, P. The players

Burying the dog. Woudstra, K.

Bus stop. Gao Xingjian

Bus stop. Silverstein, S.

Busch, Charles

The lady in question.

Comedy set in the Bavarian Alps, 1940. Concert pianist becomes embroiled in underground activities. Background music. Prologue 2 acts 8 scenes Variable cast 13 characters

In Busch, C. The tale of the allergist's wife and other plays

Psycho beach party.

Parody of 1960s beach party movies. Surfing teenagers go crazy in Malibu. Background music. 10 scenes 5m 6w 3 interiors 1 exterior

In Busch, C. The tale of the allergist's wife and other plays

Queen Amarantha; a romantic adventure. French 1998 93p

ISBN 0-573-62642-1

Tragicomedy. Queen dresses as man with interesting romantic results. Prologue 2 acts 18 scenes 2m 2w 1 setting

Red scare on Sunset.

Farce set in Hollywood during the 1950s. Musical comedy star discovers communist plot to take over movie industry. Prologue 2 acts 12 scenes 5m 3w extras

In Busch, C. The tale of the allergist's wife and other plays

Shanghai moon. French 2000 61p

ISBN 0-573-62728-2   LC 00-711143

Spoofing 1930s film melodrama, elderly British diplomat and beautiful wife visit Shanghai, China, where their adventures begin. 8 scenes Variable cast 9 characters 1 interior

The tale of the allergist's wife.

Satire on Jewish foibles and midlife malaise set on New York's Upper West Side. 2 acts 7 scenes 2m 3w 1 interior

In Busch, C. The tale of the allergist's wife and other plays

Vampire lesbians of Sodom.

Comedy about revenge. Encounters between two female vampires in ancient Sodom, 1920s Hollywood, and 1980s Las Vegas. 3 scenes 6m 2w 1 setting

In Busch, C. The tale of the allergist's wife and other plays

Bush, Duncan

Sailing to America.

Drama about two women in hospital ward who have intense conversation about life. 1 act 2w 1 setting

In Act one Wales; ed. by P. Clark

Bush, Max

c The boy who left home to find out about the shivers. Anchorage Press 1999 61p

ISBN 0-87602-372-3

Fairy tale adventure. Boy's journey to self-awareness. Music, singing. 11 scenes Variable cast 17 characters 3 interiors 2 exteriors

Ezigbo, the spirit child. Anchorage Press 2001 69p

ISBN 0-87602-403-7

River Goddess grants a barren woman a daughter, but she is a spirit child, and despite the best efforts of the village she is lured back to the spirit world when her mother breaks a magical prohibition. Adapted from an Igbo tale related by Adaora Nzelibe Schmiedl. Music, singing, dancing. 1 act 1b 2g 3w extras settings

Bush, Max—*Continued*

—Same

In Multicultural theatre II; ed. by R. Ellis

c Wildboy. Dramatic Publishing 2003 59p

Drama. As fifteen-year-old boy relates dream he had to mother and sister the characters in his dream begin to appear in the flesh. Variable cast 1 exterior

Bushveld bibble babble. Woolfson, M.

Business

Chapman, J. Business affairs

Gore, C. Lords and commons

Henkel, M. Corporate handbook line 11

Nottage, L. Snapshot: becoming American

Tait, L. East play

Vinaver, M. Overboard

Vinaver, M. A smile on the end of the line

Williamson, D. Corporate vibes

Unscrupulous methods

Elton, B. Gasping

Williams, C. Just be frank

Business affairs. Chapman, J., and Lloyd, J.

Businessmen

Anderson, Roger. Shine!: the Horatio Alger musical

Bailey, L. Baby doll

Baitz, J. R. Mizlansky/Zilinsky

Carley, S. The edge

DeLillo, D. Valparaiso

DiPietro, J. Executive dance

Hochwälder, F. Thursday

Ives, D. The red address

May, A. Rising fish prayer

Sagal, P. Game theory

Schisgal, M. Playtime

Stratton, A. The Phoenix lottery

Wong, E. Let the big dog eat

Young, D. Clout

Businesswomen

De Angelis, A. Ironmistress

Smith, V. Meow

Buster Keaton takes a walk. García Lorca, F.

But there are fires. Svich, C.

Butler, Caroline. See Goold, R. jt. auth.

Butler, Dan

The only thing worse you could have told me—. Dramatists 1997 48p

ISBN 0-8222-1613-2   LC 99-200359

One-man show portrays 10 predominantly gay characters in 14 vignettes. 1m 1 setting

The **butterfly** collection. Rebeck, T.

Butterworth, Jez

Mojo. Dramatists 1999 79p

ISBN 0-8222-1661-2   LC 99-462448

Black comedy set in 1958 Soho club about British rock and roll scene. 2 acts 4 scenes 6m 2 interiors

Buttonholes in silk. Fricker, G.

Buttram, Jan

The Parker family circus. French 2003 79p

ISBN 0-573-62914-5

Comic drama about five members of dysfunctional Texas family. 2 acts 2m 4w 1 interior

Buy one, get one free. Silverstein, S.

Buying time. Weller, M.

By the Bog of Cats. . . Carr, M.

By the name of Kensington. Toddie, J. L.

Byerrum, Eliot

Deja rendezvous.

Two private investigators become partners in a new office with interesting consequences. 2m 2w 1 setting

In Byerrum, E. Gumshoe Rendezvous

Remedial surveillance.

Would-be private investigator uncovers some strange facts about her private investigator teacher. 2m 2w 1 setting

In Byerrum, E. Gumshoe Rendezvous

Byron, George Gordon Byron, 6th Baron, 1788-1824

about

Grimm, D. Sheridan; or, Schooled in scandal

Williams, T. Lord Byron's love letter

C

Cabal, Fermin

Passage. Estreno 1998 57p
    ISBN 1-888463-03-1
On voyage to Africa, physician becomes third party in failing marriage. 2m 1w 1 interior
El **caballito** of seven colors. Winther, B.
Cabin fever. Dunn, M.
Cabin fever. Schenkar, J.
El **cabron**. Pietri, E. R. P.
Cactus Pass. Woodford, K.
Caesar and Cleopatra. Shaw, B.

Caesar, Caius Julius
                    about
Shaw, B. Caesar and Cleopatra

Cahill, Laura

Home.
    Divorced woman returns home to live with widowed mother. 1 act 2w 1 interior
    In 3 by EST
—Same
    In The Best American short plays 1998-1999
—Same
    In EST marathon '96: the one-act plays; ed. by M. Smith

Cairns, Glen

Danceland. Playwrights Canada 2002 77p
    ISBN 0-88754-637-4
Expatriot Canadian jazz singer returns to her Saskatchewan town in 1934 in search of santuary and lost innocence. Music, singing. 2 acts 6 scenes 2m 2w 1 setting

Cajal, Oana-Maria

Exchange at Cafe Mimosa.
    Satire. Representatives from two huge and divergent cultures are meeting on tropical island (neutral territory) to exchange the two identical boxes they carry with them. The fate of the whole world may rest on the success of this exchange. 18 scenes 1b 8m 4w settings
    In New dramatists: best plays by the graduating class of 2000
Cake. Hedges, P.
Cake-walk. Curran, C.
Cakewalk. Feibleman, P. S.

Calarco, Joe

Shakespeare's R & J. Dramatists 1999 77p
    ISBN 0-8222-1679-5
Four boys at a rigid prep school get hold of a copy of Romeo and Juliet and begin to act it out, becoming more and more absorbed in their roles and in the play. 2 acts 2 scenes 4m 1 setting

Calderón de la Barca, Pedro

Life is a dream; tr. by Gwynne Edwards.
    17th century Spanish verse play. King of Poland tests son, imprisoned from birth because of prophecy, to see if he will become tyrant. Savage at first, Prince later shows true nobility. 3 acts 5m 2w extras 3 interiors 2 exteriors
    In Calderon de la Barca, P. Plays: one
The surgeon of honour; tr. by Gwynne Edwards.
    17th century Spanish tragedy in verse. Man suspecting wife of infidelity has her murdered. 3 acts 9m 5w extras 1 interior 2 exteriors
    In Calderon de la Barca, P. Plays: one
Three judgements in one; tr. by Gwynne Edwards.
    17th century Spanish tragedy in verse. Exaggerated sense of justice implicates father in son's death. 3 acts 6m 4w extras 3 exteriors
    In Calderon de la Barca, P. Plays: one

Caleb, J. Rufus

The rehearsal.
    Jimi Hendrix and Little Richard play back tape of previous night's concert and reassess their relationship. Music. 2m 1 interior
    In The Best American short plays, 1996-1997

Calendars

c McCullough, L. E. Marking time: clocks and calendars through the centuries
Call of the wild (park ranger). McCullough, L. E.
Call waiting. Claff, R.

Cambodia

Filloux, C. Photographs from S-21
Camera, woman. Vaughan, R. M.

Cameron, Matt

Tear from a glass eye. Currency Press 1998 66p il
    ISBN 0-86819-559-6

Cameron, Matt—*Continued*
Psychological mystery about airplane accident investigator, who becomes an amnesiac after surviving an airplane explosion. 2 acts 13 scenes 3m 2w extras

Cameron, Susan
Flights.
Man and woman bump into one another at airport, recounting humorous feelings. 1m 1w 1 interior
In Off-Off Broadway Festival plays, 27th series
Camille. Field, B.
Camille. Ludlam, C.
Camino Real. Williams, T.
Campaign capers at Taft High. Cook, P.
Can Mrs. Claus save Christmas? Pattee, R. A.

Canada
Griffiths, L. Maggie & Pierre
Healey, M. Plan B
Nelson, G. Speak
Nelson, G. Spirit
Wood, T. Claptrap

     Race relations
Bunyan, H. J. Prodigals in a promised land

Cancer
Bailey, M. Sistahs
Barry, S. Our lady of Sligo
Edson, M. Wit
Miller, S. My left breast
Pelfrey, M. Drive angry
Pomerance, B. Superhighway

Cangiullo, Francesco
Detonation: synthesis of all modern theater; tr. by Victoria Nes Kirby.
Futurist performance piece. Gun is fired.
In Theater of the avant-garde, 1890-1950; ed. by B. Cardullo and R. Knopf

Canino, Frank
The Angelina project. Guernica 2000 137p
ISBN 1-55071-109-1   LC 00-101693

Historical facts and conjecture depict next three generations of daughters of Angelina Napolitano, a pregnant immigrant who axed her abusive husband to death in 1911 Sault Ste. Marie, Ontario. 2 acts 2m 6w extras 1 setting
The **cannibal** monster. Bruchac, J.
Cannibals. Dundas, H.
The **Canterville** ghost. Miller, C.
The **Canterville** ghost. Vreeke, J.
Cape Enrage. Chiasson, H.

Capital punishment
Caplan, P. J. The test
Cooper, C. L. Sentences and words
Graham, B. Coyote on a fence
Neilson, A. Normal

Capitalism
Kushner, T. Hydriotaphia; or, The death of Dr. Browne
Robinson, M. Downsizing democracy: a polemic

Capitalists and financiers
Darke, N. Ting Tang mine
Huxley, A. Now more than ever

Caplan, Paula J.
The test.
A mentally handicapped murderer faces a test that may save him from the death penalty. 1 act 2m 1 interior
In Off-Off Broadway Festival plays, 26th ser.
Capone, Al, 1899-1947
     about
Nigro, D. Capone
Capone. Nigro, D.
Captain Brassbound's conversion. Shaw, B.
Captains courageous. Barchers, S. I., and Kroll, J. L.
The **captain's** tiger. Fugard, A.
Captive audience. Ives, D.

Caputo, Leslie
Birth marks.
In the maternity ward, a new mother, apparently abandoned by her Puerto Rican husband, gets conflicting reactions from her family and from his. 1 act 2m 2w 1 interior
In Ensemble Studio Theatre marathon 2000: the one-act plays

Caramba's revenge. Norfolk, W.

Caravan. Blakeman, H.

Caribbean region

Césaire, A. A tempest

y Hippolyte, K. The song of one; or, The journey of Ti Marie

Carine; or, The young woman who was crazy about her soul. Crommelynck, F.

Carley, Dave

Two ships passing. Simon & Pierre 1999 88p
ISBN 0-88924-282-8

Sequel to Midnight madness (1988). Old friends, woman judge and minister, reunited after ten years. 2 acts 2m 1w 2 interiors

A view from the roof. Playwrights Canada 1997 82p
ISBN 0-88754-525-4

Based on stories of Helen Weinzweig. Drama about memory loss and love amid terror. Pieces together tale of young woman who flees Germany in 1938 with lover. 4 parts 2m 3w 3 exteriors

Carley, Steve

The edge. French (London) 1998 28p
ISBN 0-573-12151-6   LC 00-703033

Drama. Stockbroker who can see into the near future confesses to psychiatrist. 3m 1 setting

Carlin, Aviva Jane

Jodie's body.

One-woman play. Protagonist poses nude before an art class, while discussing everything from Apartheid to her childhood and her body. 1 act 1 interior 1w
In Women playwrights: the best plays of 1998

Carlisle, Barbara

c The crane wife.

Man rewarded for helping wounded crane. Music, dancing. Puppets. Prologue 1 act 3m 1w extras
In Theatre for young audiences; ed. by C. A. Jennings

Carlton, Bob

Return to the forbidden planet. French 1998 72p
ISBN 0-573-69599-7

Sci-fi version of The tempest set to rock and roll. 2 acts 7m 4w 1 interior

Carmichael, Fred

Decisions, decisions. French 1999 21p
ISBN 0-573-62648-0

Comedy about an indecisive single woman living alone in New York, who meets an intriguing, yet tramp-like stranger in a park. 1 act 3m 1w

Murder-go-round. French 2003 60p
ISBN 0-573-62903-x

Comedy about a witness in a murder trial and her witness protection program representative staying in an off-season summer cottage. 2 acts 2 scenes 3m 5w 1 interior

The trouble with Trent. French 1998 63p
ISBN 0-573-62655-3   LC 99-205950

Comedy about three mystery buffs, mistaken identity, e-mail, and blackmail. 2 acts 2m 6w 1 interior

What if...? French 2000 79p
ISBN 0-573-62724-x

Mystery-comedy. Woman returns to her New England town and discovers town council involved in some underhanded affairs. 2 acts 4m 4w 1 interior

Carnality. Loewenstern, M.

Carpe jugulum. Pratchett, T.

Carpenter, Bridget

Fall.

Comedy about family that, much to the dismay of 14-year-old daughter, goes to ballroom dancing camp. Music, dancing. 2 acts 35 scenes 3m 1w extras
In Women playwrights: the best plays of 1999

The **carpenter** and the cross. Thum, N.

Carr, Marina

By the bog of cats. Dramatists 2002
ISBN 0-8222-1856-9

Loosely based on Euripides' tragedy Medea, this is the prophetic tale of an Irish traveler who attempts to come to terms with a lifetime of abandonment in a world where everyone she has loved has discarded her. 6m 5w 1 setting

—Same
In Carr, M. Plays: one

—Same
In New plays from the Abbey Theatre v2

Carr, Marina—*Continued*

Low in the dark.

Black comedy about mothers and daughters, sex roles, and pregnancy. 2 acts 16 scenes 2m 3w 1 setting

In Carr, M. Plays: one

The Mai. Dramatists 2003

ISBN 0-8222-1853-4

This is an epic tale of love and loss, of elusive dreams shattered by vulgar but inescapable reality. 1m 7w 1 interior setting

—Same

In Carr, M. Plays: one

On Raftery's hill. Dramatists 2002

ISBN 0-8222-1855-0

Set on a remote hill farm. Removed from the civilized world, farmer lives by his own rules, where natural order is inverted and humanity is brutalized. 4m 3w settings

Portia Coughlan. Dramatists 2003

ISBN 0-8222-1854-2

Beautiful and blessed, Portia Coughlan seems to have it all, but grief over the drowning of her twin brother fifteen years ago continues to torment her. 5m 6w 1 setting

—Same

In Carr, M. Plays: one

Carroll, Lewis

Parodies, imitations, etc.

c DeVita, J. Looking glass land

c Francoeur, B. Wonderland!

Carry the tiger to the mountain. Lee, C.

Carter, Lonnie

Gulliver.

Second play in author's Gulliver trilogy. Satirical look at American politics. 2 acts 2m 1w extras settings

In Carter, L. Plays: the Gulliver trilogy

Gulliver redux.

Third play in Gulliver trilogy finds hero of Swift's satire in deepest, darkest Africa. 2 acts 4m 4w settings

In Carter, L. Plays: the Gulliver trilogy

Lemuel.

First play in the author's Gulliver trilogy. Experimental drama about the first forty-five years of a 20th century black Everyman. Prologue 2 acts 25 scenes 4m 4w settings

In Carter, L. Plays: the Gulliver trilogy

Carter, Ruth

Women of the dust. Hern Bks. 1999 60p

ISBN 1-85459-448-6

Drama about all-female workforce on Delhi construction site. 2 acts 1g 4m 8w 1 interior 2 exteriors

A yearning. Hern Bks. 1999 54p

ISBN 1-85459-450-8

Adaptation of García Lorca's Yerma set in Punjabi community of Britain. Focuses on plight of married woman who longs for a child. 3 acts 5 scenes 4m 4w 3 interiors 2 exteriors

Cartesian dreams. O'Connell, S.

Cartwright, Jim

I liked a slag's deodorant. Methuen 1996 18p

ISBN 0-413-71540-X

A crack-addicted streetwalker and a vulnerable, broken man try to salvage an awkward intimacy away from harsh and ugly streets. 2 acts 1m 1w 1 setting

Carvajal's family (La famille de Carvajal). Mérimée, P.

The **case** of the entry room. Ardov, V.

The **case** of the purple pen (crime lab technician). McCullough, L. E.

Casey, Gene, and Casey, Jan

Hubba hubba; book, music and lyrics by Gene Casey and Jan Casey. Pioneer Drama Service 2001 48p

Musical satirizing Hollywood stars, plots, and songs of swing era. Prologue 2 acts 18 scenes Variable cast 14 characters 1 setting

Cashin, Carl C.

Mail-order Annie.

Mail-order bride arrives at barren harvest station in rural Saskatchewan in 1923. 2m 1w 1 setting

In Seven short plays from Theatre Ontario

Cashmore, Bill, and Powrie, Andy

Trip of a lifetime. French (London) 2003 44p

ISBN 0-573-02363-8

Recently divorced man takes trip around the world with his parents. 11 scenes 2m 1w

Casimir and Caroline. Horváth, Ö. von

Casina. Plautus, T. M.

Castle, Gerald V.

c The Jungle Book: the musical; book by Vera Morris; music by Gerald V. Castle; lyrics by Michael C. Vigilant. Pioneer Drama Service 1997 44p

Musical adaptation of Kipling's tales of Mowgli, a boy raised by wolves in the jungle. 2 acts 9 scenes Variable cast 20 characters extras 1 exterior

Welcome to Bedside Manor; book by Tim Kelly; lyrics by Michael Vigilant; music by Gerry Castle. Pioneer Drama Service 1992 47p

Musical comedy set in hospital. Physician faints at sight of blood and nursing staff is obsessed with soap opera. Variable cast 25 characters extras 1 interior

Cat-skins. McBride-Smith, B.

Catch a falling star. Murphy, L.

Catchpenny twist. Parker, S.

Cather, Willa, 1873-1947

The song of the lark (dramatization) See Linney, R. Lark

Catherine and her destiny. Barchers, S. I.

Catholic faith

Curran, C. Sacred hearts

Griffiths, L. Brother Andre's heart

Wolff, R. The abdication

Catholics

Durang, C. The marriage of Bette and Boo

Skarstedt, S. A. Saint Francis of Esplanade

Ireland

O'Casey, S. Red roses for me

Cathy's kitchen. Howes, L.

Cats and dogs. Vogelstein, C.

Cat's-paw. Wellman, M.

Caught in the net. Cooney, R.

Caught on a train. Poliakoff, S.

Caught with his trance down. Feydeau, G.

Cavacchioli, Enrico

The bird of paradise; tr. by Michael Vena.

Abstract personage controls world of ornithologist husband and estranged wife via his powers of suggestion. 3 acts 11m 7w 1 setting

In Italian grotesque theater

Ceauşescu, Nicolae

about

Leight, W. The final interrogation of Ceauşescu's dog

Cecilia. Tarses, J.

Cedar (John of the Cross). Ehn, E.

Celaine. Parker, Matt

Celebrating ladies. Aristophanes

Celebration. Pinter, H.

Celesia, Cathy

Anything for you.

Two women meet in cafe and discuss men, life and having lesbian affair. 2w 1 setting

In take ten; ed. by E. Lane and N. Shengold

Cellini, Benvenuto, 1500-1571

Autobiography (dramatization) See Shanley, J. P. Cellini

Cellophane. Wellman, M.

Celts

y McClelland, J. Blood lines

Cemeteries

Bowen, J. Cold salmon

McDonagh, M. A skull in Connemara

The **censor**. Neilson, A.

Censorship

Field, B. Monsieur de Molière

Neilson, A. The censor

Centaurs. Wilder, T.

Ceremonies

Martin, J. Middle-aged white guys

Certain arrangements. McClelland, C. E.

Cervantes Saavedra, Miguel de, 1547-1616

Don Quixote de La Mancha (dramatization) See Barchers, S. I., and Kroll, J. L. Episodes from Don Quixote

Parodies, imitations, etc.

c Espinosa, R. Don Quijote in America (Don Quijote en America)

Césaire, Aimé

A tempest; based on Shakespeare's The tempest, adaptation for a Black theatre; translated from the French by Richard Miller. TCG Translations 2002 xv, 69p

ISBN 1-559-36210-3   LC 2002-7439

Césaire, Aimé—*Continued*

Based on Shakespeare's The tempest and adapted for a black theater. Draws on Caribbean society and African-American experience. 3 acts 10 scenes 11m 3w

Chad Curtiss, lost again. Kopit, A. L.

Chaim's love song. Chernoff, M.

Chain. Cleage, P.

Chairmaker: the musical. MacDonald, A.

Challenger (Space shuttle)

Anderson, J. Defying gravity

Chambers, Ron

Dirt.

Comic murder mystery. Eccentric cops attempt to pry truth from cruel, cantakerous murder suspect. 2 acts 10 scenes 3m 2w 1 interior

In Chambers, R. Three nasty plays

Marg Szkaluba (Pissy's wife).

Woman escaping abusive marriage starts new life as country singer in small town bars. Music, singing. 2 acts 1m 1w 1 interior

In Chambers, R. Three nasty plays

Pretty blue.

Welfare recipient becomes catalyst in lives of lawyer and his professor wife. 2 acts 33 scenes 2m 1w 4 interiors 1 exterior

In Chambers, R. Three nasty plays

Champagne, Lenora

Coaticook.

Tragedy set in French Canadian countryside. Mother and daughter vie for affection of Eskimo boy. Household unravels when baby is born to one of them. 20 scenes 1g 2m 1w extras 1 interior

In New dramatists: best plays by the graduating class of 2000

The **champion** of Paribanou. Ayckbourn, A.

Chan, Marty

Maggie's last dance.

Monologue. At a high school dance, a would-be ladies' man gets cold feet. Music, dancing. 1 scene 1m extras 1 interior

In Short spells: scenes & monologues; ed. by V. Shantz

Mom, Dad, I'm living with a white girl. Playwrights Canada 2001 85p

ISBN 0-88754-614-5

Comedy. Chinese son must tell parents he is living with white girlfriend. Asian stereotypes explored in B-movie spoof counter-narrative. 2 acts 2m 2w 1 setting

The **change** in Mame Fadden. Keane, J. B.

The **changeling.** Middleton, T., and Rowley, W.

Changes. Tunooniq Theatre

Changes of heart. Marivaux, P. C. de C. de

Chanukah: come light the menorah! McCullough, L. E.

Chapman, John

Nil by mouth. French (London) 2003 67p

ISBN 0-573-01983-5

Comedy about a chaotic weekend at an English hospital. 2 acts 6m 7w 1 setting

Chapman, John, and Davidson, Ian

Late flowering. French 1999 92p

ISBN 0-573-62659-6

Comedy about a computer system installed in marriage agency in London. 2 acts 5 scenes 1m 4w 1 interior

Chapman, John, and Lloyd, Jeremy

Business affairs. Weinberger, J. 2001 101p

ISBN 0-85676-258-X

Two British businessmen, looking to sell their firm, arrange for an "escort service" to entertain the prospective buyers. When the businessmen's wives unexpectedly show up at the same hotel, they are mistaken for the escort girls, and decide to play along and help their husbands close the deal. 2 acts 4m 4w 1 interior

Chappell, Eric

Cut and dried.

Companion piece to We don't want to lose you. Office mates, threatened with termination, respond to new management ploy. 1 act 5 scenes 5m 2w 1 interior

In Chappell, E. Fiddlers three

Double vision. French (London) 2002 72p

ISBN 0-573-01976-2

A rundown ex-boxer pretends to have won the lottery and enjoys the world's sudden attention. When two different women show interest, a question arises: who's fooling whom? 2 acts 6 scenes 2m 1w 1 interior

Haywire. French (London) 1998 61p

ISBN 0-573-01798-0

Chappell, Eric—*Continued*

Comedy. Bookseller having an affair with his assistant plans what he thinks is the perfect holiday, until family members get in the way. 2 acts 4 scenes 2m 4w 1 interior

Heatstroke. French (London) 1999 69p
  ISBN 0-573-01800-6

Comedy about couple whose Spanish holiday in rent-free villa turns out to be less than perfect. 2 acts 6m 3w 1 setting

Something's burning. French (London) 2001 71p
  ISBN 0-573-01890-1

Comedy about a woman, deserted by her husband, who has an affair with a married man. 2 acts 6 scenes 2m 3w 1 setting

Up and coming. French (London) 2001 73p
  ISBN 0-573-09153-3

Drama about political chicanery. British Deputy Prime Minister's campaign for power in danger of collapse. 2 acts 4 scenes 5m 2w 1 interior

We don't want to lose you.

Comedy about office politics set in three-man department that management would like to downsize. Can be performed together with Cut and dried as Fiddlers three. 1 act 3 scenes 4m 2w 1 interior
  In Chappell, E. Fiddlers three

Chapter & verse. Rux, C. H.

Charabanc Theatre Company

Somewhere over the balcony.

Political drama about Catholics living in apartment complex in Belfast, Northern Ireland. 2 acts 3w 1 setting
  In Postcolonial plays; ed. by H. Gilbert

Charleston!. Francoeur, B.

Charlotte's web. Robinette, J.

Charming & Rose: true love. Burke, K. J.

Charnas, Suzy McKee

Vampire dreams. Broadway Play Pub. 2001 69p
  ISBN 0-88145-190-8

Psychoanalyst falls in love with a patient, who thinks he is a vampire. 2 acts 2m 2w 1 setting

Chasing the money. Foon, D.

A **chaste** maid in Cheapside. Middleton, T.

Chateau La Roach. Wilson, L.

Chaurette, Normand

All the Verdis of Venice; translated by Linda Gaboriau. Talonbooks 2000 111p
  ISBN 0-88922-442-0

Farce about opera world focusing on Giuseppi Verdi. 4 scenes 4m 1w 1 setting

The queens; translated by Linda Gaboriau. 2. ed. Talonbooks 1998 94p
  ISBN 0-88922-403-X   LC 99-176483

Drama set in 1483 London. Depicts shifting passions and ambitions of six historical women drawn from Shakespeare's Richard III. 6w 1 setting

Cheaper than roses. Mahomed, I.

Cheasebro, Margaret

The empty tomb.

Easter worship program explores hopes and fears of Mary Magdalene and Mary the mother of Jesus. 2w extra 1 exterior
  In Jubilation: dramas for Easter

Cheever, John, 1912-1982
          Parodies, imitations, etc.

Gurney, A. R. A Cheever evening

A **Cheever** evening. Gurney, A. R.

Chekhov, Anton Paulovich

The man in a case (dramatization) See Wasserstein, W. The man in a case

Chekhov, Anton Pavlovich, 1860-1904

The bear (adaptation) See Bernard, L. The bear

A joke (dramatization) See Guare, J. The talking dog

The lady with the lapdog (dramatization) See Friel, B. The Yalta game

The seagull (adaptation) See Williams, T. The notebook of Trigorin

Three sisters (adaptation) See Friel, B. Three sisters

Three years (dramatization) See Dunai, F. The parasol

The bear.

Romantic comedy. Landowner tries to collect debt from neighbor but collects young widow instead. 1 act 11 scenes 2m 1w 1 interior
  In Chekhov, A. P. 7 short farces

—Same; tr. by Carol Rocamora
  In Chekhov, A. P. The vaudevilles and other short works

Chekhov, Anton Pavlovich, 1860-1904—*Continued*

The dangers of tobacco.

Variant title: On the harmful effects of tobacco. Satirical lecture by henpecked husband. 1 act 1m

In Chekhov, A. 7 short farces

The festivities.

Farce. Variant title: The jubilee. Bank chairman's jubilee celebration disrupted by raving woman demanding money. 1 act 2m 2w extras 1 interior

In Chekhov, A. 7 short farces

In Moscow; tr. by Carol Rocamora.

Feuilleton that may be performed as dramatic monologue. Intellectual suffering from ennui dissatisfied with cultural life of Moscow. Variable cast

In Chekhov, A. P. The vaudevilles and other short works

Ivanov; a new translation by Paul Schmidt. Dramatists 1999 65p

ISBN 0-8222-1646-9

Social tragedy. Idealistic, intellectual landowner in czarist Russia, depressed by failure to realize his youthful ambitions, commits suicide. 4 acts 40 scenes 8m 10w extras 3 interiors 1 exterior

—Same; in a new translation and adaptation by Yasen Peyankov and Peter Christensen. Dee, I. R. 2001 87p

ISBN 1-56663-409-1; 1-56663-408-3 (pa)

—Same; tr. by Carol Rocamora

In Chekhov, A. Chekhov: the early plays

The jubilee; tr. by Carol Rocamora.

Farce. Variant title: The festivities. Bank chairman's jubilee celebration disrupted by raving woman demanding money. 1 act 3m 2w extras 1 interior

In Chekhov, A. P. The vaudevilles and other short works

The night before the trial; tr. by Carol Rocamora.

Farce. Unfinished dramatized adaptation of the author's short story with same title. 3m 1w 1 interior

In Chekhov, A. P. The vaudevilles and other short works

On the harmful effects of tobacco; tr. by Carol Rocamora.

Variant title: The dangers of tobacco. Satirical lecture by henpecked husband. Male cast

In Chekhov, A. P. The vaudevilles and other short works

On the high road; tr. by Carol Rocamora.

Dramatized adaptation of the author's short story, in Autumn. Chance encounter of ruined landowner and his faithless wife. 1 act 5 scenes 8m 3w extras 1 interior

In Chekhov, A. P. The vaudevilles and other short works

Platonov; tr. by Carol Rocamora.

Variant title: A country scandal. Romantic farce about fickle schoolmaster in 19th century Russia. 4 acts 83 scenes 15m 5w extras 3 interiors 2 exteriors

In Chekhov, A. Chekhov: the early plays

The proposal.

Farce. Hypochondriacal suitor quarrels with the girl he wants to marry, but she accepts him. 1 act 7 scenes 2m 1w 1 interior

In Chekhov, A. 7 short farces

—Same; tr. by Carol Rocamora

In Chekhov, A. P. The vaudevilles and other short works

The sea gull; translated by Nicholas Saunders and Frank Dwyer. Smith & Kraus 1994 97p

ISBN 1-88039-953-9   LC 94-7990

Tragic outcome of young actress's love for selfish playwright. 4 acts 7m 5w 2 interiors 1 exterior

The seagull; a new version by Tom Stoppard. Faber & Faber 1997 71p

ISBN 0-571-19270-X

Tragic outcome of young actress's love for selfish playwright. 4 acts 7m 5w 2 interiors 1 exterior

Swan song.

Dramatized adaptation of the author's short story, Calchas. Study of a life broken by old age. 1 act 2 scenes 2m 1 interior

In Chekhov, A. 7 short farces

—Same; tr. by Carol Rocamora

In Chekhov, A. P. The vaudevilles and other short works

Tatyana Repina.

A dramatic postscript to Suvorin's play of the same title, which ended with Tatyana's suicide. Shows the Orthodox wedding of her former lover,

Chekhov, Anton Pavlovich, 1860-1904—*Continued*

with the comments of the crowd and the bridegroom's terror at the presence of a woman in black. Music, singing. 1 act 1 scene 14m 4w extras 1 interior

In Tatyana Repina; ed. by J. Racin

—Same; tr. by Carol Rocamora

In Chekhov, A. P. The vaudevilles and other short works

Three sisters; tr. by Samuel Adamson. French (London) 2000 75p
ISBN 0-573-01949-5

Plight of the intelligentsia in 19th century Russia reflected in the unhappy lives of a Moscow family stranded (financially) in a provincial garrison town. Music, singing, dancing. 4 acts 9m 5w extras 2 interiors 1 exterior

Uncle Vanya; in a new translation by Curt Columbus. Dee, I. R. 2002 78p
ISBN 1-56663-443-1; 1-56663-442-3 pb

Life on a failing country estate in 19th-century Russia. 4 acts 5m 4w 3 interiors 1 exterior

Uncle Vanya; scenes from country life; translated by Mike Poulton. French (London) 2001 49p
ISBN 0-573-01958-4

Life on a failing country estate in 19th-century Russia. 4 acts 5m 4w 3 interiors 1 exterior

The wedding; tr. by Carol Rocamora.

Farce based on author's short story. Satirical portrayal of guests at wedding reception. 1 act 7m 3w extras 1 interior

In Chekhov, A. P. The vaudevilles and other short works

The wedding reception.

Farce based on author's short story. Satirical portrayal of guests at wedding reception. 1 act 7m 3w extras 1 interior

In Chekhov, A. 7 short farces

The wood demon; tr. by Carol Rocamora.

Tragicomedy. Life of the upper middle class in a late nineteenth century Russian village. 4 acts 47 scenes 9m 4w 2 interiors 2 exteriors

In Chekhov, A. Chekhov: the early plays

about

Martin, J. Anton in show business
Rocamora, C. "I take your hand in mine. . ."

Chen, Kitty

Rowing to America.

Two sisters row to the United States dreaming of a better life. Singing. 2 scenes 2w

In Women's Project & productions; ed. by J. Miles

Chen Zidu, and others

Sangshuping chronicles.

Drama about life in 1968-1969 Chinese village. Based on series of stories by Zhu Xiaoping. Prologue 3 acts 19 scenes epilogue 1b 1g 17m 7w

In Theater & society; ed. by Haiping Yan

Cheng, Kipp Erante

The China crisis.

Satiric "film noir" set in restaurant in New York's Chinatown. Examines issues of Asian-American identity. Music. 2m 2w 1 interior

In Multicultural theatre II; ed. by R. Ellis

Chepiga, Michael J.

Getting and spending. French 1999 91p

Investment banker persuades a famous retired trial lawyer living in a monastery to come to her defense in an insider trading trial. 2 acts 4m 3w 2 settings

Chernoff, Marvin

Chaim's love song. French 2000 67p
ISBN 0-573-62755-X

Tragicomedy. Retired Brooklyn mailman meets a teacher from Iowa and transforms her life through his stories. 2 acts 6 scenes 3m 4w 1 exterior

Cherokee Indians

Bruchac, J. Possum's tail
Cherry and Little Banjo. Levi, S.
Chesapeake. Blessing, L.

Chess

Belke, D. Blackpool and Parrish
Bogdan, K. Sparring partner

Cheyenne Indians

Bruchac, J. Wihio's duck dance

Chi, Jimmy

Bran nue dae.

Musical about Aboriginal life in Australia. Music, singing, dancing. 2 acts Variable cast

In Postcolonial plays; ed. by H. Gilbert

Chiarelli, Luigi

The mask and the face; tr. by Michael Vena.

Ironical comedy about infidelity. Betrayed husband, to avenge his honor, pretends he has killed wife. 3 acts 7m 6w 1 interior

In Italian grotesque theater

Chiasson, Herménégilde

Alienor.

Lyrical drama about father who removed himself and daughter from modern society to live deep in woods. Violent encounter with hunters has him answering to charges of having sexually abused his daughter. Music. 1 act 14 scenes 3m 4w 3 interiors 1 exterior

In Angels and anger; ed. by G. Nichols

Cape Enrage.

Canadian teen accused of murder and his girlfriend are interrogated by detective assigned to case. Includes alternate versions of some scenes. Prologue 11 scenes 2m 1w 3 interiors

In Angels and anger; ed. by G. Nichols

Chicago (Ill.)

Kern, W. Hellcab

Sherman, J. Romance in D

Chicken potential. Hedges, P.

Chicken soup with barley. Wesker, A.

Chicken wings. Pritchard, E.

Chickenheart. Sodaro, C.

Chikamatsu, Monzaemon

The battles of Coxinga.

Japanese puppet play. Half Chinese, half Japanese hero attempts to restore rightful emperor to Chinese throne. 5 acts 12 scenes 2b 14m 6w extras 3 interiors 9 exteriors

In Chikamatsu, M. Four major plays of Chikamatsu

The love suicides at Amijima.

Tragedy. Wife nobly tries to help husband buy his mistress out of bondage. Interfering father-in-law drives husband and prostitute to suicide. Singing. Puppets. 3 acts 6 scenes 7m 4w extras 2 interiors 4 exteriors

In Chikamatsu, M. Four major plays of Chikamatsu

The love suicides at Sonezaki.

Tragedy. Cheated by money-lender and unable to pay his own debts, man is joined by his mistress in suicide pact of honor. Japanese puppet-play.

Singing. 1 act 3 scenes 4m 1w extras 1 interior 2 exteriors

In Chikamatsu, M. Four major plays of Chikamatsu

The uprooted pine.

Japanese puppet-play. Impressed by the love of a courtesan for her lover, young man tries to buy her contract and unite the two. 3 acts 5 scenes 8m 4w extras 1 setting

In Chikamatsu, M. Four major plays of Chikamatsu

Child abuse

Crimp, M. Getting attention

Crow, A. G. A roomful of men

Cullen, M. Anna Weiss

y Harden, V. Big boys don't cry

Harrison, J. Stolen

Lodato, V. Snapshot: the great father

Martin, J. Mr. Bundy

Nelson, J. L. Somebody call 911

Osborne, A. In sunshine and in shadow

Thompson, J. Perfect pie

Townsend, J. Terms of abuse

Child of our time: child of the snow. Hall, L.

Child of our time: children of the rain. Hall, L.

Childbirth

Oates, J. C. Good to know you

Childe Roland to the dark tower came. Wilder, T.

Childe Rowland to the dark tower came. Nigro, D.

The **childish** lovers. Crommelynck, F.

Childlessness

Jensen, J. Old wives tale

Laxdal, V. Cyber:/womb

Lewis, D. Misconceptions

Children

Bonel, W. Good grief, Lolita

c Clark, A. The red balloon

Cruz, N. Night train to Bolina

Duffield, N. The secret garden

Dundas, H. Cannibals

c Espinosa, R. El bully (El valenton)

Glancy, D. Jump kiss

Hall, L. Child of our time: child of the snow

Hall, L. Child of our time: children of the rain

Children—*Continued*
Hall, L. I love you, Jimmy Spud
Hall, L. Spoonface Steinberg
c Harris, A. The orphan train
Harrison, J. Stolen
Kennedy, A. A rat's mass
Margulies, D. Nocturne
Miller, T. Fruit cocktail
Sterling, P. The secret garden
Tibbetts, M. LittleBro morning and BigSis afternoon
c Warburton, N. Domby-Dom
Children of Heracles. Euripides
Children of neon lights. Grassmann, B.

Childress, Alice
Wedding band: a love/hate story in black and white.
Drama exploring race relations in South Carolina during World War I focuses on black girl's long-standing affair with white baker. 2 acts 4 scenes 2g 3m 6w 1 setting
In Plays of provocation; ed. by F. P. Richmond
A **child's** Christmas in Wales. Brooks, J., and Mitchell, A.
Chilling and killing my Annabel Lee. Fennessy, A.
Chimera. García Lorca, F.

China
Chen Zidu. Sangshuping chronicles
Gao Xingjian. Bus stop
Glancy, D. The toad (another name for the moon) should have a bite
Hare, D. Fanshen
Hwang, D. H. The dance and the railroad
c Mason, T. The nightingale
Neipris, J. A small delegation
Tait, L. East play
Wang Peigong. WM
Wei Minglun. Pan Jinlian: the history of a fallen woman
Wong, E. Letters to a student revolutionary
Yew, C. Red
The **China** crisis. Cheng, K. E.

Chinese Americans
Cheng, K. E. The China crisis
Eng, A. The Goong Hay Kid

Hwang, D. H. Family devotions
Hwang, D. H. Fob
Hwang, D. H. Trying to find Chinatown
Wong, E. Letters to a student revolutionary
Yew, C. Wonderland
The **Chinese** art of placement. Rutherford, S.

Chinn, Jimmie
A different way home. French (London) 1999 33p
Drama. Two monologues by a brother and sister who reflect on their lives after their mother's death. 2 acts Variable cast 2 characters 1 setting

Chinn, Jimmie, and Wyld, Hazel
The garden party. French (London) 2000 77p
ISBN 0-573-01879-0
Drama about a man's 70th birthday on the Isle of Wight. His sons and his wife's first husband arrive and the scene is set for a very emotional experience. 2 acts 5m 4w 1 exterior

Chislett, Anne
y Flippin' in.
Teenage girl encounters dissension when she attempts to organize fellow fast-food workers. 1m 4w 1 setting
In Chislett, A. Flippin' in & Then and now
y Then and now.
Anglophone father and daughter and francophone father and daughter transported via video game to past where they witness beginnings of French-English conflict. 2m 2w extras 1 setting
In Chislett, A. Flippin' in & Then and now
Choephori. Aeschylus
Chopin, Frédéric, 1810-1849
about
Bosakowski, P. Chopin in space

Chopin, K. M.
Double take.
Man and woman spend uncomfortable "morning after" together. 2m 2w 1 interior
In 30 ten-minute plays for 4, 5 & 6 actors from Actors Theatre of Louisville's National Ten-minute Play Contest

Chopin in space. Bosakowski, P.
The Chopin playoffs. Horovitz, I.
The chosen. Posner, A.

Christenson, Jonathan, and Tremblay, Joey

Elephant wake.

Monologue telling how drunken revelers destroyed a papier-maché elephant that, to the speaker, symbolized the spirit of his French-Canadian village. Singing. 1m 1 setting

In Short spells: scenes & monologues; ed. by V. Shantz

A Christian turned Turk. Daborne, R.

Christianity

Juana Inés de la Cruz. The divine Narcissus (El divino Narciso)

The Christians and the Moors (Los moros y los cristianos); tr. by Larry Torres.

Muslims steal the Holy Cross and hold it for ransom. Christian knights go to war, regain Cross, and convert Muslims. Rhymed folk drama; bilingual edition. Singing. 15 scenes 7m chorus settings

In Six nuevomexicano folk dramas for Advent season

Christiansen, Arne

Best beware my sting; book by Paul T. Nolan; music by Arne Christiansen; lyrics by Ole Kittleson. Pioneer Drama Service 1999 48p

Musical adaptation of Shakespeare's The taming of the shrew about man's courtship and marriage to headstrong woman. 2 acts 8 scenes 8m 7w extras settings

The masked canary; book by Tim Kelly; music by Arne Christiansen; lyrics by Ole Kittleson. Pioneer Drama Service 2000 56p

Musical comedy set in Old West. Former society belle blackmailed when she is discovered singing in Tombstone, Arizona. 4m 8w extras 1 interior

Christina, Queen of Sweden, 1626-1689

about

Wolff, R. The abdication

Christmas

Anderson, S. J. Echoes of Christmas
Anderson, S. J. Hanging on the tree
Anderson, S. J. The night before pageant
Anderson, S. J. Now a shepherd, no longer a sheep

Anderson, S. J. Oh, come on, Emmanuel
Anderson, S. J. Tidings of comfort and joy
Anderson, S. J. While you were out
Armstrong, D. A Christmas Twist
y Barchers, S. I. A Christmas carol
y Brandl, D. Too wrapped up for Christmas
Bricusse, L. Scrooge
c Brooks, J. A child's Christmas in Wales
c A Christmas pageant
Cook, P. The ghost of Christmas presents
Cook, P. Last stop till Christmas
Field, B. A Christmas carol
Filippo, E. de. Christmas in Naples
Foster, N. Ethan Claymore
c Francoeur, B. Babes in Toyland
c Francoeur, B. Bah, humbug!
c Gollobin, L. B. The match girl's gift: A Christmas story
c Hamlett, C. It's an okie-dokie life
Harding, M. Comfort and joy
c Harris, A. The second shepherd's play
c Hoffman, E. T. A. The nutcracker and the mouse-king
c Horovitz, I. A Christmas carol: Scrooge and Marley
y Hughes, L. Black nativity
c Ingram, S. L. Christmas? Bah humbug!
c Ingram, S. L. Everywhere, everywhere, Christmas tonight
y Jones, E. Y. Not on this night
c Kee, A. Joseph and the holly
c Lebow, B. Tiny Tim is dead
Mantello, J. The Santaland diaries
McPherson, C. Dublin carol
c Medoff, M. Kringle's window
c Menotti, G.-C. Amahl and the night visitors
Neilson, A. The night before Christmas
No room at the inn (Las posadas)
c Pattee, R. A. Can Mrs. Claus save Christmas?
c Roman, J. Papa's angels: a Christmas story
c Rosenberg, N. The gifts of Obidiah Oak
c Rowland, B. T. The birthday gifts
c Rowland, B. T. Christmas hide and seek
The second shepherd's play (Los pastores)

Christmas—*Continued*
c Sigley, M. Saint George and the dragon at Christmas tide
Sills, P. A Christmas carol
c Smith, J. G. What the animals made known
Snyder, P. D. B. Miracle on 34th Street
c Swortzell, L. A partridge in a pear tree
y Swortzell, L. The shepherds of Saint Francis
c Swortzell, L. A visit from St. Nicholas; or, The night before Christmas
Thomas, B. The crumple zone
The Three Kings (Los tres Reyes Magos)
Whelan, P. Nativity
Wilder, T. The long Christmas dinner
c Wood, D. Mother Goose's golden Christmas
Christmas at the Ivanovs'. Vvedensky, A.
Christmas? Bah humbug! Ingram, S. L.
A **Christmas** carol. Barchers, S. I., and Kroll, J. L.
A **Christmas** carol. Field, B.
A **Christmas** carol. Sills, P.
A **Christmas** carol: Scrooge and Marley. Horovitz, I.
Christmas hide and seek. Rowland, B. T.
Christmas in Naples. Filippo, E. de

c A **Christmas** pageant.
Story of Nativity told in a series of tableaux. Music, singing. 5 scenes Variable cast
In The twelve plays of Christmas; ed. by L. Swortzell
A **Christmas** Twist. Armstrong, D., and others
Christopher, Saint, 3rd cent.?
         about
Ehn, E. Dashboard (Christopher)
Christopher Marlowe's Doctor Faustus. Morgan, E.
Christus. Spitz, A.

Christy, James
Creep.
Man and woman meet at party. 1m 1w 1 interior
In 30 ten-minute plays for 2 actors from Actors Theatre of Louisville's National Ten-minute Play Contest

Chronicles. Nigro, D.
Chucky's hunch. Owens, R.

Churchill, Caryl
Blue kettle.
Young con man poses as the long-lost son of various elderly women. As the play progresses, the words "blue" and "kettle" invade the dialogue like a spreading illness. 1 act 11 scenes 2m 6w settings
In Churchill, C. Blue heart
Far away. Theatre Communications Group 2000 44p
ISBN 1-55936-199-9
Woman witnesses violence and brutality from childhood through adulthood. 3 acts 1m 2w settings
Heart's desire.
Father, mother, aunt, and brother await the return of the couple's grown daughter from Australia. The parents' marriage is unstable. 1 act 3m 4w 1 interior
In Churchill, C. Blue heart
A number. Theatre Communications Group 2002 62p
ISBN 1-55936-225-1
Father meets son and two clones of his son to better understand morality behind cloning. 5 parts 5m 1 interior
This is a chair; Caryl Churchill. Theatre Communications Group 1999 32p
ISBN 1-559-36177-8   LC 99-44744
Eight scenes dealing with increasing surreality of modern existence. 8 scenes 8m 7w settings
Top girls.
Plight of independent women focusing on head of Top Girls Employment Agency. 2 acts 5 scenes 16w 3 interiors 1 exterior
In The Methuen book of modern drama; ed. by G. Whybrow
Chutes. Paterson, D. L.

Chye, Kee Thuan
Here and now.
Social drama based on Malaysian tiger dance, using Chinese, Indian and Malay elements. Music, singing, dancing. 19 scenes Variable cast
In Postcolonial plays; ed. by H. Gilbert

Cibber, Colley
Love makes a man; or, The fop's fortune.
Romantic 18th century English comedy adapted from Beaumont and Fletcher's The elder brother and The custom of the country. Two gentlemen

Cibber, Colley—*Continued*

agree that if daughter of one marries one of the other's two sons, the latter will inherit his father's fortune. 5 acts 14 scenes epilogue 9m 4w extras 9 interiors 2 exteriors

In Cibber, C. The plays of Colley Cibber v 1

Love's last shift; or, The fool in fashion.

Restoration comedy. Man vows to reform when he is tricked into affair with wife he abandoned eight years ago. Music, singing. Chorus. Prologue 5 acts 12 scenes epilogue 7m 6w extras 4 interiors 2 exteriors

In Cibber, C. The plays of Colley Cibber v 1

The rival queans.

Restoration parody in verse of Nathaniel Lee's heroic tragedy: The rival queens; or, the rivalry of two great ladies for the attentions of Alexander the Great. 5 acts 6 scenes 9m 4w extras 1 setting

In Cibber, C. The plays of Colley Cibber v 1

The tragical history of King Richard III.

Restoration historical drama derived from Shakespeare's Richard III. 4 acts 16 scenes 11m 3w 2 interiors 6 exteriors

In Cibber, C. The plays of Colley Cibber v 1

Woman's wit; or, The lady in fashion.

Restoration comedy follows romantic adventures of coquette. Prologue 5 acts 9 scenes epilogue 6m 5w extras 6 interiors

In Cibber, C. The plays of Colley Cibber v 1

Xerxes.

Restoration historical drama about machinations of Persian court. Prologue epilogue 5 acts 9 scenes 7m 1w extras 4 interiors 2 exteriors

In Cibber, C. The plays of Colley Cibber v 1

The **cicadas**. Bachmann, I.

The **cider** house rules: part 1. Parnell, P.

The **cider** house rules: part 2. Parnell, P.

Cinderella

Parodies, imitations, etc.

y Hoogland, C. Salmonberry: a West Coast fairy tale

y St. John, B. Cindy Ella's going to the ball, baby!

Cinderella. Cornett, E.

Cinderella. Green, M.

Cinderella in modern times (Cenicienta en tiempos modernos). Espinosa, R.

Cinderella: the true story. Ahlin, L.

Cinderella's glass slipper. Francoeur, B.

Cindie Ellis. Art, S. S.

Cindy Ella's going to the ball, baby! St. John, B.

Circus

c Abela, D. Circus caravan

y Cook, P. Stop sending in the clowns

Krieger, H. Side show

Norman, M. Circus Valentine

The **circus** animals desertion. Nigro, D.

Circus caravan. Abela, D.

Circus Valentine. Norman, M.

City and town life

Barry, P. J. Jump the train at Riverpoint

Wesker, A. Chicken soup with barley

City of gold. Smith, C.

Claff, Rachel

Call waiting.

Monologue. Woman expresses love in phone call. 1w

In Humana Festival 2001

Claire. Silver, N.

Clam. Levy, D.

Claptrap. Wood, T.

Clara S. Jelinek, E.

Clark, Anthony

c The red balloon. Oberon Bks. 1999 111p
ISBN 1-84002-079-2

A friendless boy acquires a companion in the form of a mischievous red balloon, the envy of his schoolmates. Musical adaptation of Albert Lamorisse's 1956 film. Music, singing. Puppets. Prologue 2 acts 16 scenes 1b 1g 9m 2w extras 2 interiors 3 exteriors 5 settings

Clark, Brian

In pursuit of Eve. Amber Lane Press 2001 80p
ISBN 1-872868-31-2

Sonnet sequence for performance. Sexual predator is forced to face his problem and the damage he has done in the past when he falls in love with a sensitive and intelligent woman. 1m

Clark, Ron

A bench in the sun. French 2002 71p
ISBN 0-573-62818-1

Clark, Ron—*Continued*

Comedy. Two longtime friends and once-famous actress join forces to prevent sale of retirement home. 2 acts 5 scenes 2m 1w 1 exterior

The incomparable LouLou. French 2002 85p

ISBN 0-573-62875-0

Romantic comedy. Forgotten chanteuse thinks of rekindling old flame but instead restarts her career. Adapted from a work by Pierre Barillet and Jean-Pierre Grédy. Music, singing. 2 acts 5 scenes 4m 3w 1 interior

Pierre and Marie. French 2002 87p

ISBN 0-573-62919-6

A high-spirited account of the Curies' discovery of radium, with much comic byplay and sharp detail about the difficulties attendant on pure science. Adapted from a play by Jean-Noël Fenwick. 2 acts 10 scenes 3m 2w 1 interior

Clarke, Austin

When he was free and young and he used to wear silks.

Drama about Canadian blacks set at wedding reception in Toronto. Based on the author's collection of short stories. 2 acts 6m 3w 1 setting

In Testifyin' v1; ed. by D. Sears

Clarke, George Elliott

Beatrice Chancy. Polestar 1999 157p il, map

ISBN 1-89609-594-1   LC 99-61831

Verse drama about slavery, rape, miscegenation, incest, and patricide set in 1801 Nova Scotia. 5 acts 27 scenes 9m 2w extras

Whylah Falls: the play. Playwrights Canada 1999 111p

ISBN 0-88754-565-3

Drama set in 1930 in rural African-American community in Nova Scotia, about events that ensue when wayward poet returns home. Music, singing. 2 acts 35 scenes 4m 4w extras

—Same

In Testifyin' v1; ed. by D. Sears

Clarke, Marcus, 1846-1881

For the term of his natural life (dramatization) See Bower, H. Natural life

Clarvoe, Anthony

The brothers Karamazov. Broadway Play Pub. 1997 110p

ISBN 0-88145-125-8

Dramatization of Dostoyevsky's novel about lust, patricide and redemption, revolving around three brothers in 19th century Russia. 3 acts 19 scenes 7m 3w 1 setting

Walking on the roof. Broadway Play Pub. 1999 62p

ISBN 0-88145-162-2

Drama about two couples, one married, the other boyfriend/girlfriend, committing adultery. 2 acts 8 scenes 2m 2w 1 setting

Class distinction

Grimsley, J. The borderland

McGuinness, F. Miss Julie

Mérimée, P. Inès Mendo; or, The defeat of prejudice (Inès Mendo; ou, Le préjugé vaincu)

Mérimée, P. Inès Mendo; or, The triumph of prejudice (Inès Mendo; ou, Le triomphe du préjugé)

Russell, W. Blood brothers

Strindberg, A. Lady Julie

Strindberg, A. Miss Julie

   Great Britain

Godber, J. On a night like this

   Great Britain

Edgar, D. That summer

Field, B. Great expectations

Godber, J. Perfect pitch

Gore, C. Lords and commons

Gore, C. Quid pro quo; or, The day of the dupes

Keeffe, B. Gimme shelter: Gem

Keeffe, B. Gimme shelter: Gotcha

Larbey, B. Sand castles

Valenti, M. Bashville in love

   India

Bhagat, D. Routes and escape routes

Karnad, G. The fire and the rain

   United States

Gilroy, F. D. Getting in

Jennings, C. S. Classyass

Wilder, T. The marriage we deplore

Classyass. Jennings, C. S.

Claudia meets Fulano Colorado. Farias, J.

Cleage, Pearl

Blues for an Alabama sky. Dramatists 1999 81p

ISBN 0-8222-1634-5   LC 99-215184

Cleage, Pearl—*Continued*
Drama about friends living in 1930 Harlem, New York during the Harlem Renaissance. 2 acts 10 scenes 3m 2w Unit set

—Same

In Cleage, P. Flyin' west and other plays

Bourbon at the border.

Middle-aged black couple in mid-1990s Detroit copes with memory of their experience as civil rights activists in Mississippi during "Freedom Summer" of 1964. 2 acts 8 scenes 2m 2w 1 interior

In Cleage, P. Flyin' west and other plays

Chain.

One-woman play. Crack-addicted daughter kept chained to radiator by parents. 1w 1 interior

In The Best American short plays 1999-2000

—Same

In Cleage, P. Flyin' west and other plays

Flyin' west.

Historical drama set in 1898. Story of African American women pioneers who left the South and settled in all-black town of Nicodemus, Kansas. 2 acts 11 scenes 2m 4w 1 setting

In Cleage, P. Flyin' west and other plays

Late bus to Mecca.

Drama set in 1970 Detroit bus station. Two young black women form bond while waiting for bus. Slide projections. 13 scenes 2w 1 setting

In Cleage, P. Flyin' west and other plays

Clean. Sánchez, E.

Cleaning woman

Mckee, J. The daffodils

Cleansed. Kane, S.

Clements, Marie

Now look what you made me do.

Drama explores responses of women to their sexuality within the context of domestic violence. Variable cast 8 characters 1 setting

In Prerogatives

Cleopatra

about

Shaw, B. Caesar and Cleopatra

Clergy

Carley, D. Two ships passing
Mamet, D. A sermon
Rambo, D. God's man in Texas
Wilder, T. Fanny Otcott

Cleveland, Rick

Jerry and Tom. French 2002 56p
ISBN 0-573-62782-7

Two hitmen go about their work, with unsettling normalcy. Black comedy. 16 scenes 2m settings

Cleveland. Wellman, M.
The **clever** daughter. Barchers, S. I.
Click. Mullins, B.
Click. Silverstein, S.
Clit notes. Hughes, H.

Clocks and watches

c McCullough, L. E. Marking time: clocks and calendars through the centuries

Closely cropped locks. Menander
Closer. Marber, P.
Closer (condensation). Marber, P.
A **closer** look. Hutton, A.
Clothes do not make the man (El habito no hace al monje). Espinosa, R.
Cloud tectonics. Rivera, J.
Clouds. Aristophanes
Cloudstreet. Enright, N., and Monjo, J.
Clout. Young, D.

Clubs

Ardito, C. St. James's blues
y Medoff, M. Showdown on Rio Road
Sutton, M. Over my dead body

Coal mines and mining

Godber, J. Salt of the earth
Lill, W. The Glace Bay Miners' Museum

Coaticook. Champagne, L.
Cock-a-doodle dandy. O'Casey, S.

Cockroaches

Al-Hakim, T. Fate of a cockroach

Cocks, Harvey. See Frost, H. jt. auth.
The **cocktail** hour. Gurney, A. R.
Cocktails at Pam's. Lemoine, S.

Coen, Larry, and Crane, David

Epic proportions. Dramatists 2000 47p
ISBN 0-8222-1741-4   LC 2002-278984

Coen, Larry, and Crane, David—*Continued*

Set in 1930s Arizona desert. Two brothers in a biblical film, one a director, one an actor, both fall in love with the same woman. 3m 1w extras 1 setting

A **coffin** in Egypt. Foote, H.

Cohen, Douglas J.

No way to treat a lady. French 1999 102p
ISBN 0-573-62633-2

Musical comedy thriller based on novel by William Goldman. New York theater manager and serial killer plays taunting mind-games with dogged police detective on his trail. 2 acts 19 scenes 2m 2w 1 setting

Cohen, Frumi

Amy Crockett: M.V.P. Anchorage Press 2002 57p
ISBN 0-87602-405-3

Teenage girl athlete confined to wheelchair seeks solace in computer games. Music, singing. Prologue 2 acts 9 scenes Variable cast

Cohn, Roy, 1927-1986
about

Kushner, T. G. David Schine in Hell
Vawter, R. Roy Cohn/Jack Smith

Cold salmon. Bowen, J.

Coleman, Elizabeth

Secret bridesmaids' business. Currency Press 1999 93p
ISBN 84-8121-676-3   LC 99-487919

On night before wedding bride-to-be learns of groom's infidelity. 2 acts 20 scenes 1m 5w extras 1 interior

Collected stories. Margulies, D.

College students

Aronson, B. Light years
Dee, P. English is a foreign language
Dixcy, M. Pyramid effect
Galton, F. Nothing in the world like it
Gilman, R. Spinning into butter
Gilroy, F. D. Getting in
Godber, J. It started with a kiss
Gurney, A. R. Another Antigone
Jennings, C. S. Classyass
Jory, J. Heads
Levin, K. Just one night
Megna, K. An evening crossword

Moses, B. P. This is how it is
y Murray, S. This old house
Russell, W. Educating Rita
Ryan, J. Warm love
Wilner, S. Joan of Arkansas

College teachers

Benet i Jornet, J. M. Legacy
Edgar, D. That summer
Gurney, A. R. Another Antigone
Gurney, A. R. Human events
Kennedy, A. Ohio State murders
MacDonald, A.-M. Goodnight Desdemona (good morning Juliet)
Reich, J. Proof
Russell, W. Educating Rita
Williamson, D. Dead white males

Collision of altars. Gabre-Medhin, T.

Collodi, Carlo, 1826-1890

The adventures of Pinocchio (dramatization) See Katz, L. Pinocchio
Pinocchio (dramatization) See Hall, L. The adventures of Pinocchio; Mason, T. Pinocchio; Nelson, R. The return of Pinocchio

Collyer, Homer, 1881-1947
about

Greenberg, R. The dazzle

Collyer, Langley, 1885-1947
about

Greenberg, R. The dazzle

Colonial tongues. Robinson, M.

Colonialism

Fusco, C. Stuff

The **color** of August. Pedrero, P.

Colour in the storm. Betts, J.

The **colour** of justice. Norton-Taylor, R.

A **Coloured** place. Conning, L.

Coloureds (South Africa)

Conning, L. A Coloured place
Mahomed, I. Cheaper than roses

Columbus, Christopher
about

c Fredericks, A. D. Columbus pleads his case
y Smith, C. City of gold
Walcott, D. Drums and colours

Columbus pleads his case. Fredericks, A. D.

Comedy—*Continued*

Dobrish, J. The handless maiden
Dobrish, J. Notions in motion
Downing, M. Frankenstein's guests
Dozer, D. The milling crowd dies
Dresser, R. Wonderful world
Duarte, I. Bingo babes
Dunbar, P. L. Herrick
Durang, C. Baby with the bathwater
Durang, C. Beyond therapy
Dyer, C. R. Time, murderer, please
Elton, B. Popcorn
Esson, L. Australia felix
Esson, L. Mates
Esson, L. Vagabond camp
Evans, A. Pageant
Farias, J. Claudia meets Fulano Colorado
Field, B. Marriage
Filippo, E. de. Christmas in Naples
Filippo, E. de. Filumena—a marriage
  Italian style
Filippo, E. de. Those damned ghosts
Five Lesbian Brothers (Theater compa-
  ny). Brave smiles . . . another lesbian
  tragedy
Five Lesbian Brothers (Theater compa-
  ny). Voyage to Lesbos
Fosbrook, M. Figuring things
Fosbrook, M. Remembering things
Foster, N. Office hours
Francoeur, B. Charleston!
Francoeur, B. Flapper!
y Francoeur, B. Going. . .going. . .gone
  with the breeze
y Francoeur, B. Kokonut Island
y Francoeur, B. Kokonut kapers
c Frankel, R. Jurassic Park and Wreck
Frankel, R. WhoDunit. . .and to whom?
Frankel, R. WhoDunit. . .and who's the
  big idea anyway?
Frayn, M. Now you know
Fréchette, C. Seven days in the life of
  Simon Labrosse
Gardner, H. The goodbye people
Gardner, H. I'm not Rappaport
Gardner, H. A thousand clowns
Gates, T. Ladies who lunch
Gilroy, F. D. Fore
Gilroy, F. D. Give the bishop my faint
  regards
Gilroy, F. D. Real to reel

Gilroy, F. D. 'Twas brillig
c Glennon, W. The trial of the Arkansas
  bear
Godber, J. Shakers
y Godber, J. Teechers
Godber, J. Up 'n' under
Goldoni, C. The Venetian twins
Gomolvilas, P. Donut holes in orbit
Gomolvilas, P. The theory of everything
Gore, C. King O'Neil; or, The Irish Bri-
  gade
Gore, C. The school for coquettes
Gore, C. The tale of a tub
Gould, H. M. Diva
Grant, D. M. Snakebit
Graybill, C. Eye to eye
Greenberg, R. The author's voice
Greenberg, R. Hurrah at last
Greenhorn, S. Passing places
Grimm, D. Sheridan; or, Schooled in
  scandal
Gromelski, B. Position available
Guare, J. Chaucer in Rome
Gurney, A. R. The cocktail hour
Gurney, A. R. Darlene
Gurney, A. R. The fourth wall
Gurney, A. R. Sylvia
Hall, L. Cooking with Elvis
Hall, L. Two's company
c Hamlett, C. Author! Author!
c Hamlett, C. Eat, drink, and be scary
c Hamlett, C. The ghost of Hemstead
  House
c Hamlett, C. It's an okie-dokie life
c Hamlett, C. Once upon a fairy tale
c Hamlett, C. Picture perfect
c Hamlett, C. The prince's dilemma
c Hamlett, C. Secret agents in disguise
c Hamlett, C. Where there's a Will, there's
  a play
Hanes, M. Doin' time at the Alamo
y Harden, V. The boardinghouse
Harding, M. Comfort and joy
Harrison, N. Whodidit?
Harvey, J. Beautiful thing
Hawdon, R. Perfect wedding
Haywood, E. F. A wife to be lett: a
  comedy.
c Heard, D. B. The love for three oranges
Hedges, P. The age of pie
Hedges, P. Good as new

Comedy—*Continued*

Marivaux, P. C. de C. de. Changes of heart

Martin, J. Anton in show business

Martin, J. Beauty

Martin, J. Flaming guns of the purple sage

Martin, J. Making the call

Martin, J. Middle-aged white guys

Martin, S. Guillotine

Martin, S. Wasp

Matthews, S. Who wins

May, E. Taller than a dwarf

May, E. The way of all fish

Mayer, O. Ragged time

Mayne, R. The drone

Mayne, R. Peter

McConnell, J. Cruise missile

McConnell, J. Cupboard love

McConnell, J. Day trippers

McConnell, J. Theatrical digs

McCormack, Thomas. Endpapers

McKay, G. In order of appearance

McKay, R. Seeing the light

McLean, D. Rug comes to Shuv

McPherson, E. Divine Stella Devine

y McPherson, E. Legend of Sammy's Swamp

y Medoff, M. Showdown on Rio Road

Meyer, M. The mystery of attraction

Middleton, T. A chaste maid in Cheapside

Miller, C. The Canterville ghost

c Miller, K. S. The Mark Twain show

Miller, T. Naked breath

Milligan, J. Any friend of Percy D'Angelino is a friend of mine

Milligan, J. Exodus from McDonaldland

Milligan, J. Family values

Milligan, J. Getting even

Milligan, J. Less said, the better

Milligan, J. Rivals

Mode, B. Fully committed

Molière. The bungler

Molière. Those learned ladies

Molloy, M. J. The bachelor's daughter

Molloy, M. J. Daughter from over the water

Mori, B. Adult fiction

Morley, M. The glass mendacity

Murphy, L. Catch a falling star

y Murray, S. Inspector Incognito and the Kansas City Kid

Murray, S. Rocky of the rainforest

Napier, E. The English teachers

Neilson, A. The night before Christmas

Neilson, A. Year of the family

Newmeir, J. H. Babysitting Calvin

Nigro, D. Deflores

Nigro, D. Higgs field

Nigro, D. Lucy and the mystery of the vine-encrusted mansion

Nigro, D. November

Nigro, D. Uncle Clete's toad

Nigro, D. Warburton's Cook

Norman, M. Loving Daniel Boone

Nottage, L. Mud, river, stone

O'Donnell, M. Marred bliss

Ogden, A. Johnny, don't jump

Ogilvy, I. A slight hangover

Orloff, R. Oedi

y Ott, G. Minor leagues

Ouellette, J. The marriage counselor

Overmyer, E. On the verge; or, The geography of yearning

Palacios, M. Describe your work

Palacios, M. Greetings from a queer señorita

Palmieri, M. Carl the Second

Panych, M. Earshot

Parker, M. Hotbed Hotel

Parker, M. Whose wives are they anyway?

Parnell, P. QED

Pedrero, P. A night in the subway

Pelfrey, M. Jerry Springer is God

Pielmeier, J. Pillow talk

Pietri, E. R. P. El cabron

Powell, D. Women at four o'clock

Power, D. Tales of the undead

Quilter, P. Respecting your piers

Rachilde. The prowler (Le Rôdeur)

Racine, J. The suitors

Raffle, D. Blue suede blues

Rambo, D. God's man in Texas

Raznovich, D. Inner gardens (Jardín de otoño)

Raznovich, D. Rear entry (De atrás para adelante)

Rebeck, T. Does this woman have a name?

Rebeck, T. Loose knit

Comedy—*Continued*

Turlish, S. Lafferty's wake

Uyehara, D. Hello (sex) kitty: mad Asian bitch on wheels

Valcq, J. Zombies from the beyond

Valentine, P. Day of reckoning

Van Druten, J. Make way for Lucia

Van Zandt, B. Confessions of a dirty blonde

Vickery, F. Pullin' the wool

Vogel, P. The Mineola twins

Vogelstein, C. All about Al

Vooght, C. Bright interval

Vreeke, J. The Canterville ghost

Vvedensky, A. Christmas at the Ivanovs'

Walker, G. F. The art of war

Walker, G. F. Beautiful city

Walker, G. F. Filthy rich

Walker, G. F. Gossip

Warburton, N. Garlic and lavender

Warburton, N. Office song

Wasserstein, W. An American daughter

Wasserstein, W. Bette and me

Wasserstein, W. Old money

Wasserstein, W. Waiting for Philip Glass

Wasserstein, W. Workout

Wein, G. Grandma Sylvia's funeral

Weiner, W. Give me shelter

Weisman, A. Snapshot: thrift of the Magi

Welch, S. M. Earl the vampire

Weller, M. The heart of art

West, Cheryl. Jar the floor

Wilder, T. The drunken sisters

Wilhelm, L. A pink Cadillac nightmare

Williams, B. C. Token to the moon

Williams, C. Just be frank

Williams, S. Laying the ghost

Williams, S. Nobody's perfect

Williams, T. Stairs to the roof

Wilner, S. Bake off

Wilner, S. Relative strangers

Wilson, D. H. How to make your theater pay

Wilson, J. Kilt

Wilson, S. The grass widow

Wiltse, D. Otis proposes

Wiltse, D. Triangles for two

Woldin, J. Murder in Baker Street

Wong, E. Let the big dog eat

Wood, T. Claptrap

Woodford, K. Cactus Pass

Woods, S. Trips

Woolley, J. You can't be serious

Worsley, V. Lift and separate

Wymark, O. Mothering Sunday

Black humor

Alfaro, L. Bitter homes and gardens

Alvarez, L. The reincarnation of Jaime Brown

Auburn, D. Skyscraper

Bettenbender, B. The siren song of Stephen Jay Gould

Bitterman, S. The job

Bogosian, E. Wake up and smell the coffee

Bowen, J. Cold salmon

Briggs, S. Terry Pratchett's Maskerade

Butterworth, J. Mojo

Carr, M. Low in the dark

Cleveland, R. Jerry and Tom

Constable, J. The false hairpiece

Constable, J. Iceman

Cram, C. West of stupid

Cruz, M. Fur

Culture Clash (Group). The mission

Durang, C. Betty's summer vacation

Farquhar, R. God's official

Finlayson, A. Winding the ball

Fishelson, D. The castle

Five Lesbian Brothers (Theater company). The secretaries

Gilroy, F. D. Match point

Głowacki, J. The fourth sister

Godber, J. Perfect pitch

Graham, B. Desperate affection

Guyer, M. World of mirth

Henley, B. The debutante ball

Henley, B. Sisters of the winter madrigal

Hughes, D. Digging for fire

Hutton, A. The price you pay

Kushner, T. Reverse transcription

Letts, T. Killer Joe

Lindsay-Abaire, D. A devil inside

Lindsay-Abaire, D. Fuddy meers

Long, Q. The joy of going somewhere definite

Lowe, M. The smell of the kill

MacDonald, A. Eat me

Martin, J. Tattoo

McDonagh, M. A skull in Connemara

Comedy—Romantic—*Continued*

Ryan, J. The young girl and the monsoon

Schulner, D. An infinite ache

Shaw, B. Man and superman

Shaw, B. The philanderer

Silver, N. The maiden's prayer

Smith, E. The uneasy chair

Son, D. Stop kiss

Tattersall, C. The last dance

Social

Aristophanes. Acharnians

Aristophanes. Birds

Armstrong, D. Of grapes and nuts

Bean, R. Pride at Southanger Park

Beane, D. C. The country club

Blakeman, H. Caravan

Coward, N. After the ball

Geiogamah, H. Body Indian

Gilroy, F. D. Dreams of glory

Gore, C. Quid pro quo; or, The day of the dupes

Gurney, A. R. The perfect party

Halliwell, D. Little Malcolm and his struggle against the eunuchs

Henley, B. Impossible marriage

Kelly, G. The show-off

Levy, D. Clam

McGuinness, F. The stronger

Molière. The affected damsels

Molière. The bourgeois gentleman

Molière. The hypochondriac

Molière. The misanthrope

Molière. The miser

Molière. The miser (short edition)

Molière. Such foolish affected ladies

Molière. Tartuffe

Molière. The would-be gentleman

Mowatt, A. C. Fashion; or, Life in New York

Nelson, G. Speak

Nelson, R. An American comedy

Osborne, R. Seeing stars in Dixie

Powell, D. Jig saw

Shaw, B. Mrs. Warren's profession

Strand, R. The guest of honor

Strindberg, A. Playing with fire

Strindberg, A. The stronger

Thorne, J. V. The exact center of the universe

Wilde, O. An ideal husband

Wilde, O. The importance of being Earnest

Wilde, O. Lady Windermere's fan

Wilde, O. A woman of no importance

Wilder, T. The marriage we deplore

Williams, J. L. Why marry?

Comenius, Johann Amos, 1592-1670
about
Kokoschka, O. Comenius

Comenius. Kokoschka, O.

Comfort and joy. Burke, K. J.

Comfort and joy. Harding, M.

Comic potential. Ayckbourn, A.

Coming around. Jensen, L., and Wing, P.

Coming in to land. Poliakoff, S.

The **coming** of winter (La llegada del invierno). Espinosa, R.

A **common** man's guide to loving women. Moodie, A.

Communicating doors. Ayckbourn, A.

Communication. Weil, V. C.

Compatible. Li, A.

Composers

Finn, W. A new brain

Jelinek, E. Clara S.

Parker, S. Catchpenny twist

Compton, Jennifer

The big picture. Currency Press 1999 82p
ISBN 0-86819-594-4   LC 99-487925
Three single mothers rely on each other to get through tough times in Australian country town. 2 acts 14 scenes 1m 3w 1 interior

Computers

Cohen, F. Amy Crockett: M.V.P.

c Fredericks, A. D. The masters of all

Kopit, A. L. BecauseHeCan

Strand, R. The bug

Concertina's rainbow. O'Malley, G.

Conditions. Hackenbrook, W. J.

Conduct of life

Blais, M.-C. A couple

Gore, C. Lords and commons

Gore, C. The school for coquettes

Margulies, D. Zimmer

Sherman, J. Patience

Sportiello, A. Tickets, please!

Wilder, T. Fanny Otcott

Coney Island (New York, N.Y.)

Gardner, H. The goodbye people

The **confession** of many strangers. Mueller, L.

Confessions of a dirty blonde. Van Zandt, B., and Milmore, J.

Confessions of Zeno. Ardito, C.

Confidence. Upton, J.

The **confidence** man. Metcalf, P.

Confidentially yours. Rubenstein, D.

Conflict of generations

Benet i Jornet, J. M. Legacy

Dike, F. So what's new?

Glancy, D. The woman who was a red deer dressed for the deer dance

y Godber, J. Happy families

Hutton, A. A closer look

Prida, D. Botánica

Sorge, R. The beggar

Wilder, T. The marriage we deplore

Wilson, L. Talley & son

Zorin, L. The guests

Congdon, Constance

The automata pieta.

Drama about teen fashion doll who grows to human proportions after being abandoned in desert. 3 parts 3g 3m 3w 2 settings

In New plays; ed. by C. Slaight

c Beauty and the beast.

Adaptation of French fairy tale about young maiden and enchanted prince. 19 scenes 3m 7w extras 1 setting

In Eight plays for children; ed. by C. A. Jennings

Dog opera. French 1998 100p

ISBN 0-573-69574-1   LC 00-704065

Comedy. Intimate friendship between gay man and straight woman. 2 acts 5m 2w 1 setting

Lips. Broadway Play Pub. 2000 91p

ISBN 0-88145-170-3

Tragicomedy about first woman president who makes gay rights a priority issue for her political platform. 2 acts 24 scenes 1m 2w extras

The servant of two masters; [by] Carlo Goldoni; adapted by Constance Congdon; from a translation by Christina Sibul. Broadway Play Pub. 2000 89p

ISBN 0-88145-147-9

Adaptation of Goldoni's romantic comedy. Young woman, disguised as her dead brother, travels to Venice in seach of her fiance. Servant secretly serves her and man she is looking for at same time. 3 acts 55 scenes 1g 8m 2w settings

Under Lubianka Square.

Set in Moscow. American student encounters impoverished woman in subway station. 1m 2w 1 interior

In 30 ten-minute plays for 3 actors from Actors Theatre of Louisville's National Ten-minute Play Contest

—Same

In Actors Theatre of Louisville. Ten-minute plays: v4

Conjuring an event. Nelson, R.

Conning, Lueen

A Coloured place.

Vignettes of Coloured life in South Africa. Slide projections. 1 act 7 scenes Variable cast settings

In Black South African women; ed. by K. A. Perkins

Connolly, James, 1868-1916

about

Eagleton, T. The white, the gold and the gangrene

Conquest, Ned

For they shall see God.

The death of a saintly butler reveals a grisly secret. 1 act 1 scene 5m 2w 1 interior

In Conquest N. The widow's might: three plays

A modern romance.

Whirlwind courtship succeeds, with a little deception. 1 act 1 scene 2m 2w 1 interior

In Conquest, N. The widow's might: three plays

The widow's might.

Set during the Civil War. A widow cannot believe her sons are dead; a mortally wounded Confederate chaplain helps break the spell. 3 acts 5 scenes 5m 2w 2 interiors 1 exterior

In Conquest, N. The widow's might: three plays

Conscience

McIntyre, D. Split second: a play in two acts

Consecrated ground. Boyd, G. E.

Conspiracies

Stockwell, R. Killing time
The **conspiracy** of silence. Rudolph, K.

Constable, John

Black mass.

Drama set during Carnival in Trinidad. White singer and her lover-manager find themselves mixed up in deadly game between hotelier, masquerading as Anancy the spider, and wealthy white man dressed as Death. 4m 1w 1 setting

In Constable, J. Sha-manic plays

Dead man's handle.

Man in coma visited by distraught lover. 3m 1w 1 interior

In Constable, J. Sha-manic plays

The false hairpiece.

Black comedy version of Jacob and Esau story. Mother conspires with one son to cheat elder brother out of inheritance. 2 acts 3m 2w 1 interior 1 exterior

In Constable, J. Sha-manic plays

Iceman.

Farce about war on drugs. Undercover cop sacrifices his identify, moral authority, and sanity in drug-fueled bid to crack his own case. 2 acts 2m 1w extras 1 interior

In Constable, J. Sha-manic plays

The Southwark Mysteries. Oberon Bks. 1999 343p

ISBN 1-84002-099-7

Urban cycle of plays loosely based on medieval mysteries fusing traditional Christian and pagan elements with local folklore and contemporary humor. Large mixed cast

"Constellations then arise": astronomy in the age of Copernicus. McCullough, L. E.

Construction workers

Carter, R. Women of the dust
c McCullough, L. E. Yankee Doodle had a brick (brick mason)
Contact (condensation). Weidman, J.
Contact with the enemy. Gilroy, F. D.
Contemplacion (Mary and Martha). Ehn, E.
The **contest**. Lauro, S.
The **contest** for Athens. McBride-Smith, B.
The **contract**. Rebeck, T.
Contract with Jackie. Breslin, J.
Control freaks. Henley, B.

Conversation after a burial. Reza, Y.
A **conversation** with Thomas Jefferson. Fredericks, A. D.
Conversations with my father. Gardner, H.
Conversations with my neighbour's pit bull. Martini, C.

Conversion, Religious

Daborne, R. A Christian turned Turk
The **conversion** of Ka'ahumanu. Kneubuhl, V. N.
Convivencia. Sandberg, R. N.

Cook, Pat

Ax of murder. Pioneer Drama Service 2000 54p

Murder mystery. Theater troupe horrified as events in haunted play mirror reality. 2 acts 9m 12w extras 1 interior

y Campaign capers at Taft High. Pioneer Drama Service 1999 56p

Comedy about high school elections. 2 acts 6 scenes 11m 17w 1 interior

The ghost of Christmas presents. Pioneer Drama Service 2002 23p

Mysterious woman infuses department store with Christmas spirit. 7m 13w extras 1 setting

Hillbilly hankerin'. Pioneer Drama Service 1999 56p

Comedy set in Ozarks about five husband-hunting sisters. 2 acts 5 scenes 9m 17w 1 interior

y Last one to survive is a rotten egg. Pioneer Drama Service 2000 56p

Two high schools compete in series of survival contests. 2 acts 9 scenes 8m 18w extras 1 setting

Last stop till Christmas. Pioneer Drama Service 2001 22p

Girl spreads spirit of Christmas at bus stop. 1 act Variable cast 20 characters extras 1 exterior

The saga of the golden horseshoe; or, That was no lady, that was my filly. Pioneer Drama Service 2000 49p

Western spoof. Blacksmith's plan to nab horse thieves backfires. 2 acts 5 scenes 10m 12w extras 1 interior

y Stop sending in the clowns. Pioneer Drama Service 2001 48p

Comedy. Circus performers scramble to avoid foreclosure. 2 acts 8m 13w 1 interior

Cook, Pat—*Continued*

y Switching principals. Pioneer Drama Service 2002 52p

Con artist on run from law mistaken for high schools' new principal. 2 acts 4 scenes 7m 14w 1 interior

We the people. Pioneer Drama Service 2001 36p

Committee discusses staging patriotic show. 10 scenes Variable cast 1 setting

Who's dying to be a millionaire? Pioneer Drama Service 2000 59p

Comedy about greed and television. Contestants die after winning money on popular quiz show. 2 acts 6 scenes 7m 18 women extras 1 interior

Cooking

McConnell, J. Cupboard love
Mena, A. Las nuevas tamaleras
Romero, E. The fat-free Chicana and the Snow Cap queen
Wilner, S. Bake off

Cooking with Elvis. Hall, L.

Cooney, Ray

Caught in the net. French (London) 2002 120p

ISBN 0-573-01975-4

Sequel to Run for your wife (1984). Comedy set in Wimbledon, England. Bigamist tries to keep his teenage children from meeting each other. 2 acts 4m 3w 1 interior

Cooper, Cynthia L.

Sentences and words.

Defense attorney of man accused of murder pleads with victim's family not to seek death penalty. 2w 1 exterior

In Women's Project & productions; ed. by J. Miles

Cooper, Keith. See Armstrong, D. jt. auth.
Copenhagen. Frayn, M.
Copenhagen (condensation). Frayn, M.
Copernicus, Nicolaus, 1473-1543

about

c McCullough, L. E. "Constellations then arise": astronomy in the age of Copernicus

Corbett, Bill

The big slam. Dramatists 1999 73p

ISBN 0-8222-1692-2   LC 99-224321

Satirical look at get-rich-quick schemes. Four yuppies join forces to market bizarre new product. 2 acts 2m 2w 1 setting

Corey, Irene Lockridge

c The magic garden. Anchorage Press 2000 65p

ISBN 0-87602-402-9

Fantasy about a conflict between the vegetable kingdom and candy kingdom. Music, singing. 2 acts 5 scenes Variable cast 18 characters

Cornett, Ewel

c Cinderella; script and lyrics by Moses Goldberg; music by Ewel Cornell. Anchorage Press 1998 68p

ISBN 0-87602-357-X

A musical version of the Grimm Brothers' Cinderella, with a hazel tree serving as fairy godmother. Singing, dancing. 2 acts 14 scenes 4m 6w 1 interior 2 exteriors

Cornwall (England)

Darke, N. The King of Prussia
Darke, N. Ting Tang mine

Corporate handbook line 11. Henkel, M.
Corporate vibes. Williamson, D.
Corpus Christi. McNally, T.
The **correction**. Müller, H.

Corruption (in politics)

Bosakowski, P. Bierce takes on the railroad!
Ibsen, H. An enemy of the people
London, J. Theft
Odets, C. Waiting for Lefty
Santander, F. Mexico, USA
Santander, F. The unwritten law
Thomson, K. Navigating
Walker, G. F. Filthy rich
Warren, R. P. All the king's men
Warren, R. P. Proud flesh
Warren, R. P. Willie Stark

Cortese, Raimondo

St. Kilda tales. Currency Press 2001 81p

ISBN 0-86819-641-X

Drama about subculture and urban mix of St. Kilda, suburb of Melbourne, Australia. 5m 5w 1 setting

Corthron, Kia

Breath, boom. Dramatists 2002

ISBN 0-8222-1849-6

Corthron, Kia—*Continued*

Fourteen years in the life of Prix, a Bronx native, from her ruthless girl-gang leadership at sixteen to her maturity at thirty. 1m 9w 1 setting

Force continuum. Dramatists 2002
ISBN 0-8222-1817-8

Three generations of African-American New York City police officers. 6m 2w 1 setting

Seeking the genesis. Dramatists 2002
ISBN 0-8222-1818-6

Sixteen-year-old son attempts to move out of the gangs and is startled to realize his mother thinks his activities were the result of some brain malfunction. 4m 3w 1 setting

Splash hatch on the E going down. Dramatists 2002 60p
ISBN 0-8222-1819-4

Drama about a pregnant teenager and her husband living with her parents in a Harlem, New York apartment. 2 acts 20 scenes 2g 1b 1m 2w 1 setting

A **cosmic** bouquet: sun, moon and stars. McCullough, L. E.

The **cosmonaut's** last message to the woman he once loved in the former Soviet Union. Greig, D.

The **cotton** blend horse. Art, S. S.

The **council**. Yellow Robe, W. S.

The **Count** of Carmagnola: a tragedy. Manzoni, A.

The **countess**. Murphy, G.

Counting, from quipu to googol. McCullough, L. E.

The **country** club. Beane, D. C.

A **country** doctor. Jenkin, L.

Country life

Curran, C. Sacred hearts
Henley, B. The Miss Firecracker contest
Simpson, E. A point of order
Wilson, L. Book of days

France

Gore, C. The maid of Croissey; or, Theresa's vow

Great Britain

Wesker, A. I'm talking about Jerusalem

A **couple**. Blais, M.-C.

Coups and calypsos. Philip, M. N.

Courtesans

Chikamatsu, M. The love suicides at Amijima

Chikamatsu, M. The uprooted pine

Courting Prometheus. Forbes, C.

Courtney, Erin

Owls.

Runaway girl calls her father, lying about her location. 1m 1w

In Humana Festival 2001

Courtship

Bernard, L. The bear
Chan, M. Maggie's last dance
Chekhov, A. P. The bear
Chekhov, A. P. The proposal
Conquest, N. A modern romance
Field, B. Marriage
Melski, M. Hockey mom, hockey dad
Molière. The school for wives
Shanley, J. P. Psychopathia sexualis
Smith, E. The uneasy chair
Wilson, L. Talley's folly
Wiltse, D. Otis proposes

Couturier, Gracia

My husband's an angel.

Monologue by pregnant man. 6 scenes 1m 1 setting

In Angels and anger; ed. by G. Nichols

Cover. Sweet, J.

Coward, Noel

After the ball. French 2002 77p
ISBN 0-573-62820-3

A Noël Coward musical based on Lady Windermere's fan (1892), a comedy of manners by Oscar Wilde. Barry Day, the editor of this concert version, has restored material that Coward was forced to cut from the original performance in 1954. Music, singing. 2 acts 7 scenes 3m 3w extras settings

Blithe spirit.

Farce. Spirit of writer's former wife materializes during seance causing endless misunderstandings and complications. 3 acts 7 scenes 2m 5w 1 interior

In Coward, N. Three Plays

Hay fever.

Domestic comedy. Antics of eccentric household drive away weekend guests. 3 acts 4m 4w 1 interior

In Coward, N. Three Plays

Crimp, Martin

Dealing with Clair.

Drama set in London. Woman estate agent becomes target of vendor's greed and sexual object to buyer and seller alike. 2 acts 12 scenes 5m 3w 2 interiors 1 exterior

In Crimp, M. Plays: one

Getting attention.

Dramatic portrayal of the brutality and emotional scars inflicted upon family by acts of child abuse. 2 acts 13 scenes 3m 2w 1 setting

In Crimp, M. Plays: one

Play with repeats.

Psychological drama set in London. Man's dismal life of drab routine gradually leads him to bitterness and violence. 2 acts 7 scenes 3m 2w 1 setting

In Crimp, M. Plays: one

The treatment.

Black comedy set in Manhattan. Woman on run from brutal husband exploited by two sleazy film producers. 4 acts 15 scenes 5m 3w extras 1 setting

In Crimp, M. Plays: one

Crip, N. J.

That good night. French (London) 1999 67p

ISBN 0-573-01913-4

Terminally ill screenwriter attempts reconciliation with his son and plans to die by euthanasia. 2 acts 6 scenes 3m 2w 1 setting

The **cripple** of Inishmaan. McDonagh, M.

Cristofer, Michael

Amazing grace. French 2002 85p

A woman reflects on life, love, and her sad past, while awaiting her execution for murders she can not recollect. 2 acts 3m 5w 1 setting

Breaking up. French 1999 56p

ISBN 0-573-62683-9   LC 00-266355

Comedy. Couple tries hard to break up with unusual results. Prologue 12 scenes epilogue 1m 1w 1 interior

A **critic** and his wife. Noonan, J. F.

Croft, David. See Lloyd, J. jt. auth.

Cromelin, Caroline

Man in the flying lawn chair.

Tragicomedy about stunt performer and motivational speaker Larry Walters, who achieves his dream of aviating in an aluminum lawn chair. Mu-sic, singing. 1 act 14 scenes 2g 2m 2w extras 5 interiors 2 exteriors

In New playwrights: the best plays of 2000

Crommelynck, Fernand

Carine; or, The young woman who was crazy about her soul; tr. from the French by Alain Piette.

Boulevard play. On morning after her marriage sheltered young girl learns shocking truths about husband, friends, and family. 1 act 4m 7w extras 1 interior

In Crommelynck, F. The theater of Fernand Crommelynck

The childish lovers; tr. from the French by Alain Piette.

Surreal examination of peculiar love affair. 3 acts 4m 6w extras 1 interior

In Crommelynck, F. The theater of Fernand Crommelynck

Golden guts; tr. from the French by Alain Piette.

Surreal farce. Gold is inherited, coveted, eaten, and excreted. 3 acts 9m 3w extras 1 interior

In Crommelynck, F. The theater of Fernand Crommelynck

Hot and cold; or, Mr. Dom's idea; tr. from the French by Alain Piette.

Comedic farce about mythmaking. Upon death of drab cuckold rumor spreads that upon his deathbed he had marvelous idea. 3 acts 4m 4w 1 interior

In Crommelynck, F. The theater of Fernand Crommelynck

The magnanimous cuckold; tr. from the French by Jan-Albert Goris.

Tragicomedy. Jealous husband forces faithful wife to prostitute herself to satisfy his doubts. 3 acts 7m 4w extras 1 interior

In Crommelynck, F. The theater of Fernand Crommelynck

The merchant of regrets; tr. from the French by Alain Piette.

Surreal tale of cuckold. Young wife seeks to extricate herself from unhappy marriage. 1 act 4m 3w extras 1 interior

In Crommelynck, F. The theater of Fernand Crommelynck

Crommelynck, Fernand—*Continued*
The sculptor of masks; tr. from the French by Nadine Dormoy-Savage.

Exaggerated gestures, silences, and sound effects relate story of maskmaker whose wife dies of broken heart. 3 acts 7m 3w extras 1 interior
In Crommelynck, F. The theater of Fernand Crommelynck

A small-hearted woman; tr. from the French by Xavier Lizin.

Satire about virtuous prude who alienates everyone around her. 3 acts 4m 5w 1 interior
In Crommelynck, F. The theater of Fernand Crommelynck

The **crooked** cross. Rivera, J.

Crookes, Sir William, 1832-1919
about
Nigro, D. Seance

Cross, Gillain
The demon headmaster (dramatization) See Angus, Eric, and Shostak, Cathy The demon headmaster

Crossing. De Wet, R.

Crossing the bar. Gough, L.

Crothers, Rachel
A man's world.

Woman writer in early 1900s discovers man she loves is father of her adopted son. 4 acts 1b 4m 3w 2 interiors
In American plays of the new woman; ed. by K. Newlin

Crow, Amparo García
A roomful of men.

Performance piece in which a woman begins to free herself from a traumatic childhood. Music. 2 acts 2 scenes 1w 1 setting
In Puro teatro; ed. by A. Sandoval-Sánchez and N. S. Sternbach

Crow & Weasel. Leonard, J.

Crowther, Colin
Footprints in the sand. French (London) 2001 33p

Drama about terminally ill man who meets mysterious woman and fifth century maid-in-waiting to the queen on deserted beach. 1m 3w 1 setting

Tryst. French (London) 1999 35p
ISBN 0-573-12311-X

Drama about man with heart disease who commissions an artist to paint his picture to leave to his wife. 2m 1w

Crowther, Colin, and Crowther, Mary
c Noah's ark. French (London) 2001 15p
ISBN 0-573-06255-2

Dramatization of biblical tale of the flood. 4b 4g extras 1 setting

Till we meet again. French (London) 2003 46p
ISBN 0-573-02360-3

Drama. On his deathbed man revisits himself as teenager, disgruntled middle-aged husband, and finally as newborn child and old man he will never be. 3m 3w 1 interior

Crowther, Mary. See Crowther, C. jt. auth.

Cruise missile. McConnell, J.

Crumley, George W.
Death day/life day.

Worship program. Contemporary sunrise service for Easter Sunday. Variable cast
In The drama of Easter; ed. by R. Wray

The **crumple** zone. Thomas, B.

Crunch time. Medoff, M. H., and Treon, P.

Crusades
The Christians and the Moors (Los moros y los cristianos)

Cruz, Migdalia
Fur.

Beneath a pet shop in the California desert, the owner keeps a feral woman in a cage. Singing. Prologue 1 act 19 scenes 1m 2w 1 interior
In Out of the fringe; ed. by C. Svich and M. T. Marrero

Cruz, Migdalia, and Blecher, Hilary
Frida: the story of Frida Kahlo.

An opera-like dramatization of the life of the Mexican artist Frida Kahlo, with particular emphasis on her stormy relationship with Diego Rivera. Slide projections. Music, singing, dancing. Puppets. 2 acts 13 scenes 3m 3w extras settings
In Puro teatro; ed. by A. Sandoval-Sánchez and N. S. Sternbach

Cruz, Nilo

A bicycle country.

Elderly Cuban heart patient and his caretakers attempt to reach United States by raft. Music, singing. 4 acts 11 scenes 2m 1w 1 interior 1 exterior

In New dramatists: best plays by the graduating class of 2001

Night train to Bolina.

Latin American children dream of traveling to U.S. to start new life with new freedoms. 2 acts 18 scenes 1b 2g 1m 1w extras 1 setting

In Multicultural theatre II; ed. by R. Ellis

—Same

In Out of the fringe; ed. by C. Svich and M. T. Marrero

Cuba

Cruz, N. A bicycle country

Machado, E. When the sea drowns in sand

Martinez, R. Illuminating Veronica

Monge-Rafuls, P. R. Trash

Tropicana, C. Milk of amnesia (Leche de amnesia)

Tropicana, C. Memorias de la revolución

Cullen, Countee, 1903-1946

about

Smith, C. Knock me a kiss

Cullen, Mike

Anna Weiss. Hern Bks. 1997 69p

ISBN 1-85459-388-9

Drama about phenomena of False Memory Syndrome. Hypnotherapist helps young woman recall childhood abuse by father. 2 acts 1m 2w 1 interior

Culture Clash (Group)

Anthems.

Comic collage of culture conflict in the nation's capitol. Variable cast

In Culture Clash. Culture Clash in America

Bordertown.

Comedy, Explores political and psychological borders and boundaries facing Mexican Americans in the San Diego/Tijuana region. Variable cast

In Culture Clash. Culture Clash in America

A bowl of beings.

A comic trip through Chicano history, with an assortment of heros and pop-culture icons. Music, singing, dancing. epilogue 1 act 6 scenes 4m 1w settings

In Culture Clash. Culture Clash: life, death and revolutionary comedy

The mission.

Satirical comedy about three Chicano actors, the descendants of a long line of exploited peoples, who kidnap Jose Iglesias and demand a share of the limelight. Music, singing, dancing. epilogue 2 acts 12 scenes 3m settings

In Culture Clash. Culture Clash: life, death and revolutionary comedy

Mission magic mystery tour.

Interview based collage about San Francisco's Mission District. Variable cast

In Culture Clash. Culture Clash in America

Nuyorican stories.

Comedy about Puerto Rican poetry movement of the 1970s in New York City. Variable cast

In Culture Clash. Culture Clash in America

Radio mambo.

Sharp sketches of a fragmented, multicultural city (Miami). Characters include Cubans, Jews, Haitians, African Americans, gays, environmentalists, and developers. Based on interviews. Music, singing, dancing. 1 act 21 scenes 3m settings

In Culture Clash. Culture Clash: life, death and revolutionary comedy

Culture conflict

Aidoo, A. A. The dilemma of a ghost

Caputo, L. Birth marks

Culture Clash (Group). Anthems

Culture Clash (Group). Radio mambo

c Houston, V. H. Hula heart

Hwang, D. H. Family devotions

Ibsen, H. Emperor and Galilean: a world historical drama

Posner, A. The chosen

Prida, D. Botánica

Romero, E. The fat-free Chicana and the Snow Cap queen

Taylor, D. H. alterNatives

Taylor, D. H. Only drunks and children tell the truth

Cumming, Peter

Ti-Jean.

Participation play based on French-Canadian folk figure. Clever boy is asked by King to find long-lost daughter. Music. 1 act 4m 1w 1 setting

In TYA5: theatre for young audience

Cunninghan, Laura

Flop cop.

Tragicomedy about police officer who encounters a depressed playwright. 2m 1 setting

In take ten; ed. by E. Lane and N. Shengold

Cupboard love. McConnell, J.

¡Curanderas! serpents of the clouds. Romero, E.

Curie, Marie, 1867-1934

about

Clark, R. Pierre and Marie

Curie, Pierre

about

Clark, R. Pierre and Marie

Curino, Laura

Passion.

Autobiographical one-woman show. Author reflects on her childhood in newly industrialized Northern Italy. 1w

In Mythic women/Real women

The **curious** quest for the sandman's sand. Toksvig, J., and Perkins, D.

Curran, Colleen

Cake-walk. Playwrights Canada 2000 100p

ISBN 0-88754-586-6   LC 00-456866

Comedy about a cake-baking contest held on Canada Day in a small town in Ontario. 2 acts 2m 5w 1 setting

Maple Lodge. French (London) 1999 77p

ISBN 0-573-62702-9

Comedy. Brother and his two sisters open their cottage for the summer and await the arrival of their formidable mother. 2 acts 5 scenes 2m 3w 1 setting

Sacred hearts. Playwrights Canada 1990 122p

ISBN 0-88754-484-3

A woman witnesses a miracle that may heal her secret grief, if she can pick her way through an assortment of believers and debunkers. Singing. 2 acts 3m 3w 4 interiors 4 exteriors 1 setting

Currie, Sheldon

The Glace Bay Miner's Museum (dramatization) See Lill, W. The Glace Bay Miners' Museum '

Curtain call. Manktelow, B.

Curtain up on murder. Manktelow, B.

Curtis, Doug

Mesa. Playwrights Canada 2000 60p

ISBN 0-88754-639-0

Man drives his wife's 93-year-old grandfather from Calgary to his retirement trailer in Mesa, Arizona. Music. 2m extras 1 setting

Cut and dried. Chappell, E.

Cut and run. Horsler, P.

The **cuttlefish;** or, The Hyrcanian worldview. Witkiewicz, S. I.

Cyber:/womb. Laxdal, V.

Cyclops. Euripides

Cyrano. Roets, J.

D

'Da kink in my hair. Anthony, T.

Da Ponte, Lorenzo, 1749-1838

about

Ardito, C. Da Ponte's last stand

Da Ponte's last stand. Ardito, C.

Daborne, Robert

A Christian turned Turk.

Jacobean drama. Two notorious Barbary pirates accept Ottoman protection, the better to prey on Christian shipping. One converts to Islam at a woman's behest and dies horribly; the other repents but also perishes. Prologue 16 scenes epilogue 22m 3w extras settings

In Three Turk plays from early modern England; ed. by D. J. Vitkus

Dadaism

Tzara, T. The gas heart

The **dadshuttle.** Donaghy, T.

Daedalus and Icarus. Barchers, S. I.

The **daffodils.** Mckee, J.

Dafydd, Gwenno

No regrets.

Monologue. Life of Edith Piaf through speech and song. Music. singing. 1w

In One woman, one voice; ed. by H. W. Davies

Dahl, Roald

The Twits (dramatization) See Wood, D. The Twits

Dalí, Salvador, 1904-1989

about

Johnson, T. Hysteria; or, Fragments of an analysis of an obsessional neurosis

Obolensky, K. Lobster Alice

Damage control. Auburn, D.

Damages to Tony. Southworth, M.

Danae (Greek mythology)

Aeschylus. The suppliants

The **dance** and the railroad. Hwang, D. H.

Dance halls

Martin, M. Once upon a time in Wigan

Danceland. Cairns, G.

Dancers

Carpenter, B. Fall

Kander, J. Steel pier

King, D. Stepping Out

Nigro, D. Ballerinas

y Surface, M. H. Dancing solo

Wilder, T. The penny that beauty spent

Dancing by myself. Slaight, B.

Dancing solo. Surface, M. H.

Dancing with a devil. Berman, B.

The **dandy** of the Savoy. Olmos, C.

The **dangerous** precaution. Kuzmin, M.

The **dangers** of tobacco. Chekhov, A. P.

Daniel (Biblical figure)

c McCullough, L. E. Dare to be a Daniel!

Daniels, Jeff

Apartment 3A. Dramatists 2000 69p

ISBN 0-8222-1759-7

Romantic comedy. Thirty-something female media professional develops feelings for artist neighbor. 2 acts 4m 1w 1 setting

Boom town. Dramatists 2000 48p

ISBN 0-8222-1760-0

Drama about a woman with a failing marriage and a failing business, who dreams of running away with her lover. 2 acts 2m 1w 1 setting

Escanaba in da moonlight. Dramatists 2000 60p

ISBN 0-8222-1761-9

Tragicomedy about a family gathering on the opening day of hunting season near Escanaba in the upper Peninsula in Michigan. 2 acts 5m 1w 1 setting

Daniels, Sarah

Dust.

Story of female gladiators in ancient Roman London. 13 scenes Large mixed cast

In New Plays; ed. by C. Slaight

Purple side coasters.

Accidental reunion in department store two women who met years ago in mental institution. Music. 33 scenes 7m 6w settings

In Mythic women/Real women

The **Danish** Play. Mills, S.

Danz, Cassandra, and others

Fame takes a holiday. Dramatists 2002

ISBN 0-8222-1796-1

A four-girl cabaret, known as the High-Heeled Women, experience their two worst nights of their show biz lives. 4w 1 interior setting

Dare to be a Daniel! McCullough, L. E.

The **dark**. Holloway, J.

Dark diaspora . . . in dub. Mandiela, A. Z.

Dark owl; or, The renegade angel. Goupil, L.

Dark rapture. Overmyer, E.

Darke, Nick

The body.

Cornish seaside village and nearby American airbase setting for symbolic look of philosophical questions about evidence, rationality and responsibility in a nuclear age. Music. Prologue 2 parts 12m 3w extras 1 setting

In Darke, N. Plays: 1

The dead monkey.

Black comedy. California couple celebrate death of their pet and through startling revelations reveal crumbling marriage. 2 acts 9 scenes 2m 1w 1 interior

In Darke, N. Plays: 1

The King of Prussia.

Drama about smuggling and Cornish identity set in 1787. 4m 2w

In Darke, N. Plays: 1

Darke, Nick—*Continued*

Ting Tang mine.

Drama set in 1815 Cornish mining village follows disastrous consequences of young entrepreneur's behavior. 2 acts 18m 8w 1 setting

In Darke, N. Plays: 1

Darkness like a dream. Nigro, D.

Darlene. Gurney, A. R.

The **Darling** family. Griffiths, L.

Darrow, Clarence, 1857-1938

about

Logan, J. Never the sinner

Darwin, Charles, 1809-1882

about

Wertenbaker, T. After Darwin

Wilson, S. Darwin's flood

Darwin's flood. Wilson, S.

Dashboard (Christopher). Ehn, E.

Dating (Social customs)

Belluso, J. The technology project: voice properties

Gilman, R. Boy gets girl

Graybill, C. Eye to eye

Real, C. The battle of Bull Run always makes me cry

Robson, J. Mr Wonderful

Dattani, Mahesh

Tara.

Family tragedy ensues after conjoined twins are separated in a way that favors the boy. Music. 2 acts 2 scenes 4m 3w settings

In DramaContemporary: India; ed. by E. B. Mee

Daughter from over the water. Molloy, M. J.

Daughters of Troy. Euripides

Davey, Shaun

James Joyce's The dead; book by Richard Nelson; music by Shaun Davey; lyrics conceived and adapted by Richard Nelson and Shaun Dewey. French 2001 64p

ISBN 0-573-62783-5

Musical about two spinsters and their niece who hold Yuletide party in turn-of-the-century Dublin. 3 scenes 5m 8w 1 interior

James Joyce's The dead (condensation); book by Richard Nelson; lyrics by Richard Nelson and Shaun Davey; music by Shaun Davey.

In The Best plays of 1999-2000; ed. by Otis L. Guernsey, Jr.

David, King of Israel

about

c McCullough, L. E. King David's harp

c Vogel, L. Big little man

c Vogel, L. What's up, rock?

David Copperfield. Francis, M.

David Mamet fan club. Tait, L.

David's redhaired death. Kramer, S.

Davidson, Conrad E.

Mosquito dirigible aerosol deodorant. French 2003 23p

ISBN 0-573-62893-9

Farce. Psychiatrist's patient keeps changing identity. 1 act 2m 2w 1 interior

Davidson, Ian. See Chapman, J. jt. auth.

Davidson, Rachel

y The Pony Express. Pioneer Drama Service 2000 38p

Melodrama. Hero saves struggling coffee shop and finds true love. 4m 7w 1 setting

y The vile veterinarian; or, How much is that doggie with the widow? Pioneer Drama Service 2002 43p

Melodrama set in Old West. Hoping to steal hidden gold, devious duo pose as veterinarian and assistant. 2 scenes 4m 11w 1 interior

Davies, Cynthia, and Fendrich, Steven

y Tongue twisted. Pioneer Drama Service 1999 36p

Farce about high school tongue-twisting tournament. 1 act 5 scenes 9m 18w 1 interior

Davies, Valentine, 1905-1961

Miracle on 34th Street (dramatization) See Snyder, P. D. B. Miracle on 34th Street

Davis, Bill C.

Avow. Dramatists 2001 70p

ISBN 0-8222-1783-X   LC 2001-275576

Liberal priest refuses to marry homosexual couple. Prologue 2 acts 26 scenes 4m 3w 1 setting

Davis, Katie

The sure-success twelve-step program to self-affirmation and esteem.

Secretary driving in her car listens to self-help tape. 2m 1w

In Blast from the future; ed. by D. Yeaton

Davis, Michelle R.

Mystery at Shady Acres; or, Carats and crumpets. Pioneer Drama Service 1999 39p

Audience participation mystery-comedy. Theft at cozy hotel in English countryside in late 1920s. 2 acts 6 scenes 12m 14w

Davis, Thad

Lawyers, guns, & money.

Young man and his two friends discuss the merits of security, opportunity, and power. 2m 1w 1 interior

In 30 ten-minute plays for 3 actors from Actors Theatre of Louisville's National Ten-minute Play Contest

—Same

In Actors Theatre of Louisville. Ten-minute plays: v5

Davis, Thulani

Everybody's Ruby. French 2000 79p

Drama about 1952 Florida murder trial of Ruby McCollum. Writer Zora Neal Hurston covers the trial and discovers how race, sex and class are important factors in this case. Prologue 2 acts 27 scenes 10m 4w Unit set

Day, Barry

Aspects of Oscar. French 2001 35p
ISBN 0-573-62772

Comic drama. Oscar Wilde appears on talk show. 4m 2w 1 setting

The **day** Emily married. Foote, H.

The **day** I stood still. Elyot, K.

A **day** in Mesa Verde. Fredericks, A. D.

Day of reckoning. Valentine, P.

Day trippers. McConnell, J.

The **dazzle**. Greenberg, R.

De Angelis, April

Hush.

Explores madness, mysticism, nihilism and pessimism as responses to world without compassionate ideology. Family and friends confront their personal demons on anniversary of woman's death by drowning. 2 parts 3m 3w 1 setting

In De Angelis, A. Plays: one

Ironmistress.

Drama set in 1840s England. Business woman and her free-spirited daughter clash on eve of daughter's money-based marriage. 2w 1 setting

In De Angelis, A. Plays: one

Playhouse creatures.

Examines lives of English actresses during Restoration. Prologue 2 acts 18 scenes 5w 1 setting

In De Angelis, A. Plays: one

The positive hour.

Satirical look at lives of forty-somethings who emerged from radicalized late 1960s. Social worker, with problems of her own, faces issues of gender and sexuality. 2 acts 16 scenes 2m 5w 4 interiors 2 exteriors

In De Angelis, A. Plays: one

De Boer, Lodewijk

The Buddha of Ceylon; tr. by Della Couling.

Drama set in South American Dutch colony in 1943. Colonial governor, ambivalent about Nazism, entertains Jewish violinist and mysterious German agent. Music. 3 acts 8 scenes 3m 3w 1 interior

In Dutch and Flemish plays, ed. by D. Couling

De Groen, Alma

The woman in the window. Currency Press 1999 57p
ISBN 0-86819-593-6

Imprisonment of Russian poet Anna Akhmatova juxtaposed with futuristic Australian society obsessed with virtual reality. 2 acts 37 scenes 4m 6w 2 settings

De Matteo, Donna

The heart transplant.

Strained relationship between mother and daughter. 2w 1 interior

In HB Playwrights short play festival 1997

De Matteo, Donna—*Continued*
The obit.
Father's sudden death gives birth to new relationship between daughters and illegitimate brother. 1m 1w 1 interior
In HB Playwrights short play festival 2000

De Wet, Reza
Crossing.
Drama about restless spirits and incestuous obsessions. Twin sisters recall their encounter with itinerant hypnotist and his assistant. Set in South Africa in 1930. 1 act 1m 3w 1 interior
In Drama for a new South Africa; ed. by D. Graver
Dead certain. Lloyd, M.
Dead funny. Johnson, T.
Dead man's handle. Constable, J.
The **dead** monkey. Darke, N.
Dead timber. Esson, L.
Dead white males. Williamson, D.
The **dead** wife. Nigro, D.

Deaf
Ayvazian, L. Deaf day
Buero-Vallejo, A. The sleep of reason
Margulies, D. Louie
O'Malley, G. Concertina's rainbow
y Zeder, S. The taste of sunrise
Deaf day. Ayvazian, L.
The **deal**. Martin, J.
A **deal** in dreams. Bachmann, I.
Dealer's choice. Marber, P.
Dealing with Clair. Crimp, M.

Dean, Philip
48 shades of brown. Currency Press 2001 112p
ISBN 0-86819-652-5
Teenage boy moves in with young musician aunt and develops crush on her friend. Dramatization of novel by Nick Earls. 2 acts 2b 4g 2m 2w settings
After January. Currency Press 2000 113p
ISBN 0-86819-636-3
Adapted from the novel by Nick Earls. Young Australian man falls in love during summer at the shore between high school and university. Singing. 2 acts 4m 3w 2 interiors 1 exterior
Dearborn Heights. Medley, C.

Death
Ackermann, J. The batting cage

Angeles, T. Tightwad
Benet i Jornet, J. M. Legacy
Benjamin, K. A. Mary MacGregor
Blais, M.-C. Wintersleep
Bobrick, S. Death in England
Bonel, W. Good grief, Lolita
Bouchard, M. M. Down Dangerous Passes Road
c Bush, M. The boy who left home to find out about the shivers
Constable, J. Dead man's handle
Crowther, C. Till we meet again
Enoch, W. The 7 stages of grieving
Farquhar, R. Dust to dust
Fill, S. Night visits
García Lorca, F. As five years pass
Glore, J. The Morpheus quartet
Griffin, H. The ark
Hairston, J. Forty-minute finish
Hall, L. Spoonface Steinberg
c Harris, A. The Arkansaw bear
Kramer, L. The normal heart
Kushner, T. Hydriotaphia; or, The death of Dr. Browne
Lambert, A. Very heaven
Lathrop, M. The visible horse
Lavery, B. Nothing compares to you
Lavery, B. Two Marias
c Laxdal, V. Ruby and the rock
Levi, S. The gulf of crimson
Lhota, B. Strangers
Linney, R. Goodbye, Oscar
Linney, R. A lesson before dying
Lucas, C. The boom box
Lucas, C. If Columbus does not figure in your travel plans
McLean, D. One sure thing
Murphy, C. Beating heart cadaver
Napier, E. Gone missing
Norman, M. Traveler in the dark
O'Neill, E. Bound east for Cardiff
Parker, S. Nightshade
Parnell, P. QED
Pomerance, B. Superhighway
Rachilde. Madame La Mort
Rachilde. Pleasure (Volupté)
Radano, L.-M. Bright angel
Ruskin, A. L. The art of remembering
Schmitt, E.-E. Between worlds
Sears, D. The adventures of a black girl in search of God

Death—*Continued*

Sorge, R. The beggar

Sportiello, A. Tickets, please!

Strindberg, A. The ghost sonata

Van Itallie, J.-C. The Tibetan book of the dead; or, How not to do it again

Wallace, N. In the fields of Aceldama

Wilder, T. Childe Roland to the dark tower came

Wilder, T. Mozart and the gray steward

Williams, T. I rise in flame, cried the phoenix

Williams, T. The milk train doesn't stop here anymore

Yellow Robe, W. S. Sneaky

Yourgrau, T. Peanuts

Death and dancing. Dowie, C.

Death and devil. Wedekind, F.

Death and the king's horseman. Soyinka, W.

Death day/life day. Crumley, G. W.

Death in England. Bobrick, S.

Death in the family. Margulies, D.

Death is catching. McConnell, J., and Tripp, M.

Death of a salesman. Miller, A.

The **death** of cool. Pollock, A.

Death penalty

Graham, B. Coyote on a fence

Kushner, T. Hydriotaphia; or, The death of Dr. Browne

Robinson, M. Downsizing democracy: a polemic

The **debutante** ball. Henley, B.

December 1, 1955: Montgomery, Alabama. Fredericks, A. D.

December 7, 1941: aboard the USS Arizona. Fredericks, A. D.

DeChristopher, Dave

Fifteen minutes.

Woman confronts husband and mistress. 1m 4w

In The Best American short plays 1998-1999

Decisions, decisions. Carmichael, F.

Dee, Peter

English is a foreign language. French 1999 78p

Drama. Community college invites playwright to write a drama based on interviews with dyslexic students, enabling the school to confront problems of learning disabilities. 2 acts 6m 7w 1 setting

Deeny. Mamet, D.

The **deer** and the antelope play. Dunn, M.

The **deer** dance. Winther, B.

Defiled; or, The convenience of a shorthaired dog. Kalcheim, L.

Deflores. Nigro, D.

Defying gravity. Anderson, J.

Degas, Edgar, 1834-1917

about

Ives, D. Degas, c'est moi

Degas, c'est moi. Ives, D.

Degeneration

Williams, T. 27 wagons full of cotton

Williams, T. Camino Real

Deja rendezvous. Byerrum, E.

Dekker, Thomas

The magnificent entertainment.

Pageant given for King James I, Queen Anne, his wife, and Henry Frederick, Prince of Wales, on day of their triumphant passage through London. March 15, 1603. Large mixed cast

In Renaissance drama; ed. by A. F. Kinney

The shoemaker's holiday.

Elizabethan romantic comedy in verse. Success story of Simon Eyre, 15th century craftsman who became Lord Mayor of London. Singing, dancing. Prologue 5 acts 21 scenes 18m 4w extras

In Renaissance drama; ed. by A. F. Kinney

—Same; adaptation by Bernard Shalins. Dee, I. R. 2003 89p

ISBN 1-56663-543-8

del Valle, Janis Astor

Fuchsia.

A latina lesbian whose uncle is dying of AIDS needs support from her gay friends. Music. 1 act 5 scenes 5m 1w settings

In Puro teatro; ed. by A. Sandoval-Sánchez and N. S. Sternbach

The **delegates** speak out. Fredericks, A. D.

Delilah (Biblical figure)

c McCullough, L. E. Samson and Delilah
c Vogel, L. Samson

DeLillo, Don

Valparaiso. Scribner 1999 110p
  ISBN 0-684-86421-5   LC 99-10488
American businessman becomes media curiosity
when he "mistakenly" boards flight to Valparaiso,
Chile instead of Valparaiso, Indiana. Speaking
chorus 2 acts 9 scenes 2m 2w 2 interiors

Demeter (Greek mythology)

c Barchers, S. I. Demeter and Persephone
c McBride-Smith, B. Demeter and Per-
    sephone
c Thistle, L. The myth of Demeter and
    Persephone; or, The origin of the sea-
    sons

Demeter and Persephone. Barchers, S. I.
Demeter and Persephone. McBride-Smith,
  B.

The **demon** headmaster. Angus, Eric, and
  Shostak, Cathy

Dempsey, Sandra

Armagideon.
Set in a dystopian future as war approaches. A
young man tries to prepare his two old aunts for
life on the run from a cruel government. 1 scene
1m 2w 1 setting
  In Short spells: scenes & monologues;
    ed. by V. Shantz

Dempsey, Shawna, and Millan, Lorri

Mary Medusa.
Monologue traces girl's journey to self-
fulfillment. 1w
  In Mythic women/Real women
Plastic bride.
Monologue about women and fashion, by an ac-
tress swathed in a transparent bridal gown. 1 scene
1w 1 setting
  In Short spells: scenes & monologues;
    ed. by V. Shantz

Denial is a river. Sher, E.

Dentists

Bell, N. McTeague: a tale of San Fran-
  cisco
May, E. In and out of the light
The **departure** of Brian O'Callahan.
  Palmieri, M.

Departures. Beber, N.

Depression, Mental

y Harden, V. Nobody heard mercy
Derailed. Sher, E.

Derrett, Bridget

A light lunch. French (London) 2001 27p
  ISBN 0-573-12314-4
Comedy about a couple commemorating their divorce by booking a table for lunch at their favorite
restaurant. 3m 1w 1 setting

Descartes, René, 1596-1650

about

O'Connell, S. Cartesian dreams
Describe your work. Palacios, M.

Desertion, Military

Arden, J. Serjeant Musgrave's dance

Desertion and non-support

Glaspell, S. The outside
Keane, J. B. The year of the hiker
The **designated** mourner (condensation).
  Shawn, W.
Desire. Benet i Jornet, J. M.
Desire. Lan, D.
Desperate affection. Graham, B.
Desperately seeking justice. Menander

Dessalines, Jean Jacques, Emperor of
  Haiti, 1758-1806

about

Walcott, D. Henri Christophe
The **destiny** of me. Kramer, L.
Details cannot body wants. Ping, C. W.

Detectives

Belke, D. The Maltese bodkin
Byerrum, E. Deja rendezvous
Byerrum, E. Remedial surveillance
Cohen, D. J. No way to treat a lady
Dobrish, J. Blink of an eye
c Hamlett, C. Mother Goose gumshoe
Lange, E. Sherlock's secret life
Stern, N. Murder at Cafe Noir
Detonation: synthesis of all modern the-
  ater. Cangiullo, F.

DeTurk, Scott

c Let your hair down, Rapunzel; book by Karen Boettcher-Tate; music and lyrics by Scott DeTurk. Pioneer Drama Service 2000 44p

Musical version of Karen Boettcher-Tate's Rapunzel. Girl with long hair is imprisoned in tower by witch. 5 scenes Variable cast 1 setting

c The mad adventures of Mr. Toad; book by Vera Morris; music and lyrics by Scott DeTurk. Pioneer Drama Service 2002 56p

Musical version of Vera Morris' play based on The wind in the willows about the adventures of eccentric Mr. Toad. Prologue 2 acts 14 scenes epilogue variable cast settings

c The musical adventures of Oliver Twist; book by Joellen Bland; Music and Lyrics by Scott DeTurk. Pioneer Drama Service 1999 60p

Musical adaptation of Dickens's classic tale of orphan boy in 1830s London. 2 acts 6 scenes 1b 8m 10w extras settings

c Pocahontas; book by Vera Morris; Music by Scott DeTurk. Pioneer Drama Service 1998 54p

Musical version of legend of Pocahontas, daughter of Chief Powhaton, friend of English settlers of Jamestown. 2 acts 12 scenes Variable cast 21 characters 1 setting

y Summer's in the air; book by Tim Kelly; music & lyrics by Scott DeTurk. Pioneer Drama Service 1997 72p

Musical comedy. High school students become entangled with jewel thieves. 2 acts 11m 21w extras 1 setting

y Yearbook reflections; book by Steven Fendrich; music and lyrics by Scott DeTurk. Pioneer Drama Service 2000 54p

Musical version of the Steven Fendrich play. Portrays positive attributes of contemporary high school students. 2 acts 10 scenes epilogue variable cast 1 setting

Deucalion and Pyrrha. Barchers, S. I.

Deus-X. Tasca, J.

Deux marriages: Romola and Nijinsky. Alvarez, L.

Deverell, Rex

c Belonging.

Classmates laugh at girl with gift for poetry. 2m 2w 1 setting

In Deverell, R. Plays of belonging

c Video wars.

Refugee child struggles to explain why video war game is not simply entertainment. 2m 2w 1 interior

In Deverell, R. Plays of belonging

c Weird kid.

Group of young people track down vandal and are surprised by what they find. 2m 2w 1 interior

In Deverell, R. Plays of belonging

Devil

Andrews, T. The admissions officers

Giancoli, E. The devil's parole

Gordin, J. God, man, and devil (got, mentsh, un tayvl)

Harrison, T. Doomsday

Holloway, J. The dark

Marlowe, C. The tragical history of Dr. Faustus

Medoff, M. H. Crunch time

Morgan, E. Christopher Marlowe's Doctor Faustus

Nigro, D. Doctor Faustus

Pattison, J. A word from our sponsor

Strand, J. Tom Walker

Wilder, T. Hast thou considered my servant Job?

Wilder, T. Proserpina and the devil: a play for marionettes

A **devil** inside. Lindsay-Abaire, D.

The **devils**. Egloff, E.

The **devil's** disciple. Shaw, B.

The **devil's** parole. Giancoli, E.

DeVita, James

c Looking glass land. Pioneer Drama Service 2000 56p

Wild interpretation of Lewis Carroll's Through the looking glass. Among new characters added are a baseball team, a gospel group and light saber wielding knights. 2 acts 8 scenes variable cast 1 setting

Devlin, Anne

After Easter. Dramatists 1999 82p

ISBN 0-8222-1671-X   LC 99-462451

Devlin, Anne—*Continued*

Comic drama. Woman returns to Northern Ireland after living years in England and confronts aspects of identity she has willfully excluded. 8 scenes 6m 6w 5 interiors 2 exteriors

Ourselves alone. Dramatists 1999 84p

   ISBN 0-8222-1672-8   LC 00-503097

Three women are caught between family loyalties and the politics of Belfast, Northern Ireland, in their relationships with men. 2 acts 15 scenes 7m 3w

Dewberry, Elizabeth

Happy mug.

Two sisters talk about the joys and hardships of having children. 2 w 1 interior

In 30 ten-minute plays for 2 actors from Actors Theatre of Louisville's National Ten-minute Play Contest

Head on.

Comedy about therapist and her patient waiting in the Greenroom of the Oprah Winfrey show. 2w 1 setting

In Actors Theatre of Louisville. Ten-minute plays: v4

The **diaries** of Adam & Eve. Birney, D.

Dick Whittington and his cat. Barchers, S. I.

Dickens, Charles, 1812-1870

A Christmas carol (dramatization) See Barchers, S. I., and Kroll, J. L. A Christmas carol; Bricusse, L. Scrooge; Field, B. A Christmas carol; Francoeur, B. Bah, humbug! Horovitz, I. A Christmas carol: Scrooge and Marley; Sills, P. A Christmas carol; Sills, P. A Christmas carol

David Copperfield (dramatization) See Francis, M. David Copperfield

Great expectations (dramatization) See Field, B. Great expectations; Field, B. Great expectations; Leonard, H. Great expectations

Hard times (dramatization) See Barchers, S. I., and Kroll, J. L. Hard times

Oliver Twist (dramatization) See DeTurk, S. The musical adventures of Oliver Twist

The Pickwick papers (dramatization) See Brittney, L. Pickwick papers

A tale of two cities (dramatization) See Bland, J. K. A tale of two cities

about

Gearing, N. Dickens in America

Walker, J. M. Inventing Montana

Parodies, imitations, etc.

Armstrong, D. A Christmas Twist

Dictators

Leight, W. The final interrogation of Ceauşescu's dog

O'Neill, E. The Emperor Jones

Dietrich, Marlene, 1901-1992

about

Gems, P. Marlene

Dietz, Steven

After you.

Ex-lovers meet year after break-up. 1m 1w 1 interior

In 30 ten-minute plays for 2 actors from Actors Theatre of Louisville's National Ten-minute Play Contest

Force of nature. Dramatists 2003

   ISBN 0-8222-1890-9

Freely adapted from Goethe's Elective affinities, this romance brings together the perfect couple with two persons from their past. 5m 4w 1 setting

The Nina variations. Dramatists 2003

   ISBN 0-8222-1891-7

In this funny, fierce, and heartbreaking homage to The seagull, Dietz puts Anton Chekhov's star-crossed lovers in a room and doesn't let them out. 1m 1w 1 interior setting

Private eyes. Dramatists 1998 71p

   ISBN 0-8222-1619-1

Comedy. Man suspects wife of having an affair with a British theater director, but it turns out to be part of play rehearsal. 2 acts Variable cast 5 characters 1 setting

Rocket man. Dramatists 2003

   ISBN 0-8222-1889-5

A serious comedy about the road not taken. Donny Rowan believes somewhere in the universe is a place where all the roads we never chose converge. 2m 3w 1 setting

Dietz, Steven—*Continued*

y Still life with Iris.

In fantasy land of Nocturno girl regains memory and parents. Background music. 2 acts 5m 4w 1 setting

In Seattle Children's theatre v2

A **different** way home. Chinn, J.

Digging for fire. Hughes, D.

Digging for ladies. Bradley, J.

Diggs, Elizabeth

How to plant a rose.

Monologue by a gardener, whose planting instructions are mixed with family history. 1 act 1w 1 setting

In EST marathon '98: the one-act plays; ed. by M. Smith

Dike, Fatima

So what's new?

Interactions between three older South African women, longtime friends, who run their own legal and illegal businesses, and a sweetly idealistic daughter who is becoming a social activist. Singing. 2 acts 11 scenes 4w 1 interior

In Black South African women; ed. by K. A. Perkins

The **dilemma** of a ghost. Aidoo, A. A.

Diminished capacity. Dulack, T.

Dimly perceived threats to the system. Klein, J.

Dingo. Wood, C.

Dinner at eight. Kaufman, G. S., and Ferber, E.

The **dinner** party. Simon, N.

Dinner with friends. Margulies, D.

Dinner with friends (condensation). Margulies, D.

Dinosaurs

c Dodge, A. Joshua's egg

Dionysus (Greek mythology)

c Barchers, S. I. Dionysus

Euripides. Bacchae

Dionysus. Barchers, S. I.

DiPietro, Joe

Executive dance.

Men discuss how to get promoted in corporate world. Music. 2m 1 interior

In 30 ten-minute plays for 2 actors

from Actors Theatre of Louisville's National Ten-minute Play Contest

Dirt. Chambers, R.

Dirty blonde. Shear, C.

The **disappearance** of the Jews. Mamet, D.

Disappearances. Eagleton, T.

Disasters

Guare, J. Greenwich mean

Disco pigs. Walsh, E.

DiscoKnights. Francoeur, B.

Disconcerted (El disconcierto). Raznovich, D.

Disguises

Christiansen, A. The masked canary

Congdon, C. The servant of two masters

Gore, C. King O'Neil; or, The Irish Brigade

Gore, C. The king's seal

Gore, C. The tale of a tub

Jennings, C. S. Classyass

Jonson, B. Bartholomew Fair

London, J. The birthmark

Louise, D. The servant of two masters

Marivaux, P. C. de C. de. The game of love and chance

Molière. The bungler

c Sodaro, C. Chickenheart

The **disorderly** women. Bowen, J.

Disposing of the body. Whitemore, H.

Dissident, goes without saying. Vinaver, M.

Ditch. Kavanagh, G.

Diva. Gould, H. M.

Dividing lines. Bishop, C., and Fuller, E.

The **divine** child. Radano, L.-M.

The **divine** fallacy. Howe, T.

The **divine** Narcissus (El divino Narciso). Juana Inés de la Cruz

Divine Stella Devine. McPherson, E.

Divorce

Andersen, D. R. Yes, sir, that's my baby

Aron, G. My brilliant divorce

Bradbeer, S. Full bloom

Derrett, Bridget. A light lunch

Foote, H. Getting Frankie married—and afterwards

Gilroy, F. D. A way with words

Divorce—*Continued*

Loewenstern, M. Carnality

Margulies, D. Dinner with friends

Mee, C. L. Limonade tous les jours

Neipris, J. The agreement

Owens, R. Chucky's hunch

Pedrero, P. The voucher

Robinson, R. No love lost

Divulgence at Damarak 18. Reitz, D.

Dixcy, Marcia

Eating out.

Three women talk about their eating disorders. 3w

> *In* 30 ten-minute plays for 3 actors from Actors Theatre of Louisville's National Ten-minute Play Contest

Pyramid effect.

Group of college kids try to set Guinness world record. 3m 3w

> *In* 30 ten-minute plays for 4, 5 & 6 actors from Actors Theatre of Louisville's National Ten-minute Play Contest

Dixon, Michael Bigelow, and Smith, Val

The problem solver.

Friends try to get away for relaxing weekend. 3m 2w 1 exterior

> *In* 30 ten-minute plays for 4, 5 & 6 actors from Actors Theatre of Louisville's National Ten-minute Play Contest

Snapshot: little Pezidents.

Stranded in the middle of nowhere, woman tries to placate fed-up boyfriend with kitschy souvenirs. 1 act 1m 1w 1 setting

> *In* Humana Festival 2002

Dixon, Michael E.

Into the light.

Lenten drama. Nicodemus, member of Sanhedrin, on trial for blasphemy following disappearance of Christ's body. 3m 2w 1 setting

> *In* The drama of Easter; ed. by R. Wray

Dmitri. Tait, L.

Do it yourself! Fredericks, A. D.

Do not feed the animal. Silverstein, S.

Dobrish, Jeremy

Blink of an eye.

Gumshoe's Chandleresque search for billionaire's missing brother. 9m 1w

> *In* Dobrish, J. Plays

The handless maiden.

Comedy with fairy-tale elements set in New York City. Man plans his own wedding and woman is made partner in law firm before husband. Music. 2 acts 19 scenes 5m 3w 1 setting

> *In* Dobrish, J. Plays

Notions in motion.

Comedy inspired by Pirandello's Each in his own way. Tale of love and revenge reset in world of small-time New York gangsters. 7m 3w

> *In* Dobrish, J. Plays

Orpheus and Eurydice. Broadway Play Pub. 2001 74p

ISBN 0-88145-194-0

In this send-up of Greek mythology, Orpheus is a rock star and Eurydice the shy nymph who could break up the band. Music, singing, dancing. Prologue 2 acts 28 scenes 9m 6w extras 9 interiors 4 exteriors

The **doctor** despite himself. Molière

Doctor! Doctor! a medical musical comedy revue. Ekstrom, P., and DeBoy, D.

Doctor Faustus. Nigro, D.

Doctor Faustus lights the lights. Stein, G.

The **doctor** in spite of himself. Molière

A **doctor's** visit. Loewenstern, M.

Dodge, Andrew

c Joshua's egg; book by Jacqui Shapiro; music by Andrew Dodge. French (London) 1999 34p

ISBN 0-573-05119-4

Story of boy who discovers a dinosaur egg and travels back in time to deliver the egg to its mother. Music, singing. 1b 1g 2m 3w

Does this woman have a name? Rebeck, T.

Dog opera. Congdon, C.

The **dog** problem. Rabe, D.

Dogbrain. Weller, M.

Dogs

Andersen, D. R. Yes, sir, that's my baby

Blessing, L. Chesapeake

Gurney, A. R. Sylvia

Leight, W. The final interrogation of Ceauşescu's dog

Lipkin, D. I am Laika

Dogs—*Continued*

Martini, C. Conversations with my neighbour's pit bull

O'Neill, T. The dogs play

Pedrero, P. The voucher

Valentine, P. A dog's life

c Wood, D. Spot's birthday party

A **dog's** life. Valentine, P.

The **dogs** play. O'Neill, T.

Doin' time at the Alamo. Hanes, M.

Dolls

Congdon, C. The automata pieta

A **doll's** house. Ibsen, H.

A **doll's** house. McGuinness, F.

Dolly West's kitchen. McGuinness, F.

Domby-Dom. Warburton, N.

Don Juan (Legendary character)

Molière. Don Juan

Pushkin, A. The stone guest

Schmitt, E.-E. Don Juan on trial

Shaw, B. Man and superman

Don Juan. Molière

Don Juan of Austria. Gore, C.

Don Juan of Seville. Alvarez, L.

Don Juan on trial. Schmitt, E.-E.

Don Quijote in America (Don Quijote en America). Espinosa, R.

Donaghy, Tom

The beginning of August. Dramatists 2001 56p

ISBN 0-8222-1786-4   LC 2002-276384

Social satire. Man, abandoned by wife, cobbles together unique extended family to help care for infant daughter. 2 acts 3m 2w 1 exterior

—Same

In Donaghy, T. The beginning of August and other plays

The dadshuttle.

Drama about AIDS. Father and homosexual son speak at cross purposes during drive to train station. 2m

In Donaghy, T. The beginning of August and other plays

From above. Dramatists 1999 55p

ISBN 0-8222-1689-2   LC 00-503396

Middle-aged hotel housekeeping supervisor visited by young man claiming to be her late husband. 3 acts 3m 3w 1 setting

Minutes from the blue route.

Tempers flare and truths emerge as suburban family in the throes of change, spend long Labor Day weekend together. 2 acts 2m 2w 1 interior

In Donaghy, T. The beginning of August and other plays

Northeast local.

Depicts working-class marriage from 1963 to its dissolution thirty years later. 3m 1w 1 setting

In Donaghy, T. The beginning of August and other plays

Donkeys

Wilder, T. The flight into Egypt

Donnellan, Declan

Vanity fair. French 2002 53p

ISBN 0-573-01974-6

Dramatization of the novel by William Makepeace Thackeray. Interwoven fortunes of two women, one wellborn and passive, the other ambitious and essentially amoral. 2 acts 32 scenes Laarge mixed cast settings

Donut holes in orbit. Gomolvilas, P.

The **doomed** prince. Barchers, S. I.

Doomsday. Harrison, T.

Dora. McAvera, B.

Dostoyevsky, Fyodor, 1821-1881

The brothers Karamazov (dramatization) See Clarvoe, A. The brothers Karamazov

The devils (dramatization) See Egloff, E. The devils

Parodies, imitations, etc.

Durang, C. The idiots Karamazov

Dottie and Richie. Reingold, J.

Double bind (Menaechmi). Plautus, T. M.

Double take. Chopin, K. M.

Double vision. Chappell, E.

Douglas, Alfred Bruce, Lord, 1870-1945

about

Kilroy, T. The secret fall of Constance Wilde

Dove, Rita

The darker face of the earth; a play; by Rita Dove. 3rd ed, new & rev ed. Story Line Press 2000 173p

ISBN 1-88526-694-4   LC 00-59573

Tragedy in blank verse based on Oedipus story set on plantation in antebellum South Carolina. Prologue 2 acts 16 scenes 10m 7w extras

Dowie, Claire

Adult child/dead child.

Monologue. Exploration of a personality under siege. 1w 1 setting

In Dowie, C. Why is John Lennon wearing a skirt? and other stand-up theatre plays

Death and dancing.

Monologue exploring issues of sex and gender. 2 acts 1m 1w 1 interior 1 setting

In Dowie, C. Why is John Lennon wearing a skirt? and other stand-up theatre plays

Drag act.

Monologue. Butch dyke comments on gay culture. 1 act 1w 1 interior 1 setting

In Dowie, C. Why is John Lennon wearing a skirt? and other stand-up theatre plays

Leaking from every orifice.

Monologue. Lesbian has sexual relationship with gay man and ends up pregnant. 2 acts 1w 1 setting

In Dowie, C. Why is John Lennon wearing a skirt? and other stand-up theatre plays

Why is John Lennon wearing a skirt?

Monologue by young woman who hates being a girl. 2 acts 1w 1 setting

In Dowie, C. Why is John Lennon wearing a skirt? and other stand-up theatre plays

Down Dangerous Passes Road. Bouchard, M. M.

Down the line. Mercier, P.

Downing, Martin

Frankenstein's guests. French (London) 1998 54p il

ISBN 0-573-12150-8   LC 00-703032

Comedy parody of Frankenstein films. Baron Frankenstein invites a group of monsters to his castle. 3 scenes 5m 4w 1 interior

Downsizing democracy: a polemic. Robinson, M.

Downtown. Alfaro, L.

Downtown. Hatcher, J.

Doyle, Sir Arthur Conan, 1859-1930

Parodies, imitations, etc.

y Sodaro, C. Hound of the Clackervilles

Woldin, J. Murder in Baker Street

Dozer, David

The milling crowd dies.

Drama about young married Manhattan couple who adopt old man from Welfare department. 4 scenes 3m 1w extras 2 interiors 1 exterior

In The Best American short plays 1999-2000

Dr. Fritz; or, The forces of light. Ives, D.

Dr. Jekyll and Mr. Hyde. Barchers, S. I., and Kroll, J. L.

Dracula. Norman, M.

Drader, Brian

The fruit machine.

Monologue by a gay man disappointed in love. Music. 1 scene 1m 1 setting

In Short spells: scenes & monologues; ed. by V. Shantz

Drag act. Dowie, C.

The **drag** factor. Vickery, F.

The **dragonfly** of Chicoutimi. Tremblay, L.

The **dramatic** attitudes of Miss Fanny Kemble. Luckham, C.

Dramatic circle. Kennedy, A.

Dramatists

Belke, D. That darn plot

Chekhov, A. P. The sea gull

Chekhov, A. P. The seagull

Cunninghan, L. Flop cop

Dee, P. English is a foreign language

Gems, P. The snow palace

Grimm, D. Sheridan; or, Schooled in scandal

Gurney, A. R. Labor Day

Hughes, D. Love and a bottle

Kushner, T. Reverse transcription

Margulies, D. Pitching to the star

McGuire, M. Helen's play

McKay, G. In order of appearance

Nelson, R. An American comedy

Noonan, J. F. What drove me back to reconsidering my father

Sharland, E. Love from Shakespeare to Coward

Slaight, B. Dancing by myself

Stoppard, T. The real thing

Tremblay, M. For the pleasure of seeing her again

Weller, M. The heart of art

The **drawer** boy. Healey, M.
Dream. Aronson, B.
Dream lovers. Dunbar, P. L.
A **dream** play. Strindberg, A.
Dreamers. Silverstein, S.
Dreaming of Aloysius. Lippa, L.

Dreams

Aronson, B. Dream
Bachmann, I. A deal in dreams
Buero-Vallejo, A. The sleep of reason
Bulgakov, M. Flight
c Bush, M. Wildboy
Margulies, D. Luna Park
Margulies, D. Nocturne
Mayne, R. Peter
Murray-Smith, J. Nightfall
O'Brien, D. The Last Supper restoration
Wellman, M. Cleveland
Williams, T. Camino Real
Dreams of Anne Frank. Kops, B.
Dreams of glory. Gilroy, F. D.
Dreamtime for Alice. Kim, S.

Dresser, Richard

Bed & breakfast.
Wife slips pill into husband's coffee while on honeymoon. 2m 3w
  In 30 ten-minute plays for 4, 5 & 6 actors from Actors Theatre of Louisville's National Ten-minute Play Contest
The road to ruin.
Thirty-something couple with car trouble spend evening at service station in menacing Jersey City neighborhood. 3m 1w 1 interior
  In 30 ten-minute plays for 4, 5 & 6 actors from Actors Theatre of Louisville's National Ten-minute Play Contest
Something in the air. Dramatic Publishing 2003 60p
Noir drama set in shadowy urban landscape. Desperate man involved in insurance scam. 2 acts 3m 2w 1 setting
What are you afraid of?
Play performed in a parked car. Man picks up woman hitchhiker for some romance. 1m 1w 1 interior
  In Actors Theatre of Louisville. Ten-minute plays; v5

Wonderful world. Dramatic Publishing 2003 72p
Comedy about escalating family misunderstandings that involve two brothers and three women in their lives. 2 acts 2m 3w 1 setting
—Same
  In Humana Festival 2001
Drive angry. Pelfrey, M.
Driving the final spike. Fredericks, A. D.
The **drone**. Mayne, R.
Drop. Madden, D.
The **drovers**. Esson, L.

Drowning

De Angelis, A. Hush
Oates, J. C. Black water
Drowning sorrows. Post, D.

Drugs

Alexander, R. A preface to the alien garden
Bennett, S. Drummers
Constable, J. Iceman
Harvey, J. Hushabye Mountain
Lucie, D. Gaucho
Macadaeg, R. Woozey woo!
Margolin, D. Snapshot: rock scissors paper
Osborne, A. In sunshine and in shadow
Osborne, A. The redemption song
Piñero, M. Playland blues
Rapp, A. Finer noble gases
Ravenhill, M. Shopping and fucking
Reed, I. Hubba city
Santander, F. The unwritten law
Walsh, E. Sucking Dublin
Drummers. Bennett, S.
Drummers. Sierens, A.
Drums and colours. Walcott, D.
The **drunken** sisters. Wilder, T.
Du Bois, W. E. B. (William Edward Burghardt), 1868-1963
about
Smith, C. Knock me a kiss

Duarte, Isabel

Bingo babes. French 2002 86p
ISBN 0-573-62809-2
Comedy. Two female bingo players under pressure to improve themselves. 2 acts 19 scenes 2m 3w 1 interior

Dublin (Ireland)

Barry, S. Our lady of Sligo
Johnston, A. Melon farmer
McPherson, C. Dublin carol
McPherson, C. Port Authority
Mercier, P. Down the line
Walsh, E. Sucking Dublin

Dublin carol. McPherson, C.

The **Duchess**, a.k.a. Wallis Simpson. Griffiths, L.

The **Duchess** of Malfi. Webster, J.

Duck. Silverstein, S.

Dueling

Brown, C. The Negro of Peter the Great

Duet. Jackson, G., and Purcell, E. Q.

Duet. Oates, J. C.

Duet for bear and dog. Rosen, S.

Duffield, Neil

The secret garden. French (London) 1999 54p
ISBN 0-573-05120-8
Dramatization of Frances Hodgson Burnett's children's classic. Orphan girl and invalid cousin are restored to health and happiness as they tend secret garden. 2 acts 3 scenes 2b 2g 6m 3w 3 interiors 1 exterior

c Skin and bones.
Fantasy about prejudice based on folktales from around the world. Background music. Puppets. 1m 2w 1 setting
In International plays for young people

Duke Kahanamoku vs. the surfnappers. Overmyer, E.

Dulack, Tom

Diminished capacity. Dramatists 1999 63p
ISBN 0-8222-1686-8
Drama about a burned-out New York State Supreme Court Judge who confronts personal problems, bureaucracy, corruption, and a hostage situation. 2 acts 5m 1w 1 setting

Dumas, Alexandre, 1824-1895
The lady of the camellias (dramatization) See Field, B. Camille

Dumas, Alexandre, 1802-1870
about
Smith, C. Les trois Dumas
Parodies, imitations, etc.
Lloyd, R. The three musketeers—le panteau!

Dumas, Alexandre, 1824-1895
about
Smith, C. Les trois Dumas
Parodies, imitations, etc.
Ludlam, C. Camille

Dumas, Thomas
about
Smith, C. Les trois Dumas

Dunai, Frank

The parasol. Amber Lane Press 1998 89p
ISBN 1-872868-24-X
Dramatization of Chekhov's novel Three years about young woman who makes loveless marriage to older man to escape father. 2 acts 4 scenes 8m 2w 3 interiors

Dunbar, Paul Laurence

Dream lovers.
Musical. Mulatto prince from Madagascar and his friend search for perfect mates. 2m 2w 1 interior
In Dunbar, P. L. In his own voice

Herrick.
Comedy of manners based loosely on life of poet Robert Herrick. 3 acts Variable cast 1 interior 2 exteriors
In Dunbar, P. L. In his own voice

Jes lak white fo'ks.
Musical comedy of manners. Social aspirations of African American man used to satirize aspirations of white society. Variable cast 1 setting
In Dunbar, P. L. In his own voice

Uncle Eph's Christmas.
Musical set during Christmas season. Young African American woman with college degree wooed by hometown suitors. 1 acts 6m 3w extras 1 interior
In In His Own Voice; ed. by H.W. Martin and R. Primeau

Dunbar-Nelson, Alice

Mine eyes have seen.
Young black man is drafted into World War I army but doesn't want to serve a nation in which he is a victim of racial prejudice. 1 act 4m 4w 1 interior
In War plays by women; ed. by C. M. Tylee, E. Turner, and A. Cardinal

Dundas, Heather

Cannibals.

The joys of motherhood, as experienced in the car pool. Child roles are played by adults. 1 act 1 scene 1m 4w settings

In Ensemble Studio Theatre marathon 2000: the one-act plays

Dunn, Mark

Cabin fever. French 2000 79p

ISBN 0-573-62746-0   LC 2001-278086

Tragicomedy about misadventures of family who gather at their cabin in Texas. 2 acts 5m 2w 1 interior

The deer and the antelope play. Dramatists 2001 61p

ISBN 0-8222-1794-5   LC 2001-281052

Tragicomedy of an East Texas family who face problems head-on with the help of a young woman who comes to live with them. 2 acts 4w 1 setting

Gendermat. French 1999 22p

ISBN 0-573-62689-8

Story of two people who meet in an apartment house laundry room having both just ended relationships. 1 act 2m 2w 1 interior

Durang, Christopher

Baby with the bathwater.

Satiric look at parenthood and sex roles in contemporary society. 2 acts 9 scenes 2m 3w 1 setting

In Durang, C. Complete full-length plays 1975-1995

—Same

In Plays of provocation; ed. by F. P. Richmond

Betty's summer vacation. Grove Press 1999 89p

ISBN 0-8021-3661-3   LC 99-51709

Absurdist comedy set in New Jersey beach cottage lampoons voyeuristic culture, postmodernism, and reality television. 2 acts 65 scenes epilogue 3m 3w extras 1 setting

Beyond therapy.

Satirical look at psychotherapy and its ineffectiveness in dealing with contemporary relationships. 2 acts 9 scenes 4m 2w 1 setting

In Durang, C. Complete full-length plays 1975-1995

A history of the American film; book & lyrics by Christopher Durang; music by Mel Marvin.

Musical comedy. Take-off on American films. Parodies various Hollywood genres and types of actors. 2 acts 35 scenes 9m 6w 1 setting

In Durang, C. Complete full-length plays 1975-1959

The idiots Karamazov.

Filled with numerous literary illusions and intellectual gamesmanship, this parody of Dostoyevsky is narrated by famed translator Constance Garnett. 2 acts 19 scenes 7m 6w extras 1 setting

In Durang, C. Complete full-length plays 1975-1995

Laughing wild.

Satirical sketches on comtemporary life. 2 acts 1m 1w 1 setting

In Durang, C. Complete full-length plays 1975-1995

The marriage of Bette and Boo.

Black comedy. Marriage between two Catholic Americans reflects uncertainties of modern life. 2 acts 11 scenes 5m 5w 1 setting

In Durang, C. Complete full-length plays 1975-1995

Mrs. Sorken.

Humorous monologue about theater. 1w 1 setting

In The Best American short plays, 1996-1997

—Same

In take ten; ed. by E. Lane and N. Shengold

The Vietnamization of New Jersey.

Satiric view of post-Vietnam American incorporating suicide, adultery and homosexuality. Eccentric New Jersey family awaits return of Vietnam veteran son and his native wife. 2 acts 8 scenes 6m 2w 1 setting

In Durang, C. Complete full-length plays 1975-1995

Dust. Daniels, S.

Dust to dust. Farquhar, R.

Dutch

Indonesia

Nowra, L. The language of the gods

Dutchman. Baraka, A.

A **dybbuk,** or between two worlds. Kushner, T.

Dyer, Charles Raymond

Time, murderer, please. Weinberger, J. 2001 115p

ISBN 0-85676-038-2

Comedy thriller. Stranger who arrives at north London public house claiming to have amnesia closely resembles man wanted for questioning in gruesome murder. 3 acts 4 scenes 5m 5w extras 1 setting

The **dying** Gaul. Lucas, C.

Dymov, Osip

Bronx express; tr. by Nahma Sandrow.

The experience of Jewish immigrants in the United States and their difficulty in choosing between the values of the old country and the New World. Music. Prologue 3 acts epilogue 1b 4m 2w extras 3 interiors 1 exterior

In God, man and devil; ed. by N. Sandrow

Dyskolos. Menander

E

Eagleton, Terry

Disappearances.

Internationally fêted African poet living in drunken, self-imposed exile in London faces no-win conflict of loyalties between country and family. 2 acts 6m 2w 1 interior

In Eagleton, T. Saint Oscar and other plays

God's locusts.

Radio play commemorates Great Famine. British officialdom mismanages relief efforts. 6m 2w

In Eagleton, T. Saint Oscar and other plays

Saint Oscar.

Drama. Conflicts within Oscar Wilde reflect contradictory nature of Irish society. Singing. 2 acts 6m 1w extras 1 setting

In Eagleton, T. Saint Oscar and other plays

The white, the gold and the gangrene.

Postmodern drama based on life of Irish socialist leader James Connolly who was executed for his part in the 1916 Easter Rising. 2 acts 4m 1 setting

In Eagleton, T. Saint Oscar and other plays

Earl the vampire. Welch, S. M.

Earls, Nick, 1963-

48 shades of brown (dramatization) See Dean, P. 48 shades of brown

After January (dramatization) See Dean, P. After January

Early morning. Bond, E.

The **early** years. Morgan, E.

Earshot. Panych, M.

Earth spirit. Wedekind, F.

East coast ode to Howard Jarvis: a little teleplay in tiny monologues. Kushner, T.

East Indians

Canada

Kuruvilla, S. Rice boy

England

Carter, R. A yearning

East of the sun and west of the moon. Handy, P.

East of the sun and west of the moon. Howe, T.

East of the sun, west of the moon. McCullough, L. E.

East play. Tait, L.

Easter

Anderson, S. J. Tidings of comfort and joy

Bass, A. The redeemer of minutes

Bass, A. Shattering word

Bass, T. Inventory

Bass, T. Letting Mikey go

Cheasebro, M. The empty tomb

Crumley, G. W. Death day/life day

c Forsten, M. L. The sycamore cross

Gillies, J. Give us a sign

Goens, L. M. Resurrection on trial

Younger, M. Making the rain stop

c Zapel, A. L. All things are bright and beautiful

c Zapel, A. L. Three gifts from gentle Jesus

c Zapel, A. L. Who am I?

Easter. Scheffer, W.

Easy Lenny Lazmon and the great western ascension. Piatigorsky, A.

Eat cake. Van Itallie, J.-C.

Eat, drink, and be scary. Hamlett, C.

Eat me. MacDonald, A.

Eating disorders

Dixcy, M. Eating out

Eating out. Dixcy, M.

Ebb, Fred. See Kander, J. jt. auth.
The **eccentric.** Abse, D.
The **eccentricities** of a nightingale. Williams, T.

Eccentrics and eccentricities

Barnes, P. The ruling class
Greenberg, R. The dazzle
Henley, B. The debutante ball
Henley, B. The Lucky Spot
Echoes of Christmas. Anderson, S. J.

Ecology

Ellenbogen, N. Horn of sorrow
c Fredericks, A. D. Air to breathe, water to drink
c Wood, D. The see-saw tree
York, Y. The snowflake avalanche
Eddie Mundo Edmundo. Alvarez, L.

Edelstein, Barry

Race. Dramatists 2002
ISBN 0-82232-1830-5
An adaptation of Bruckner's Race set in 1933 German university town. Two young medical students, Karlanner and Tessow, debate the future of their country and that of Karlanner's relationship with his Jewish girlfriend. 13m 3w 1 setting

Edgar, David

Maydays.
Interconnecting stories of three political agitators give panoramic view of public events, private concerns, and political life since 1945. 3 acts 21 scenes Large mixed cast 1 setting
In Edgar, D. Plays: 3

Our own people.
Political drama. Racial prejudice and discrimination against women are at heart of British industrial dispute. 2 acts 24 scenes 4m 4w 1 setting
In Edgar, D. Plays: 3

That summer.
Drama set in England, summer 1984. Oxford don, his current lover, and his son from first marriage host teenage daughters of striking Welsh miners at their holiday home. 2 acts 6 scenes 4m 3w 1 setting
In Edgar, D. Plays: 3

Edgar, David, and Todd, Susan

Teendreams.
Two friends cope with their maturing feminist consciousness in England, 1961-1978. One abandons her conventional marriage while other examines relationship with sympathetic male radical. Music. 24 scenes 7m 11w 15 interiors 2 exteriors
In Edgar, D. Plays: 3
The **edge.** Carley, S.

Edson, Margaret

Wit. Dramatists 1999 68p
ISBN 0-8222-1704-X
Drama about English literature professor and Donne scholar hospitalized with advanced ovarian cancer. 3m 3w 1 setting

—Same. Faber & Faber 1999 85p
ISBN 0-571-19877-5

Wit (condensation).
In The Best Plays of 1998-1999; ed. by Otis L. Guernsey, Jr.
Educating Rita. Russell, W.
Edward II

about

Marlowe, C. The troublesome reign and lamentable death of Edward the Second
Edward Jenner and the gossip of milkmaids. McCullough, L. E.

Edwards, Gus

Four walls.
Husband and wife assemble cheap facsimile of life. 3 scenes 1m 2w 1 interior
In The Best American short plays, 1996-1997
Edwin Booth. Tait, L.

Egloff, Elizabeth

The devils. Dramatists 1999 219p
ISBN 0-8222-1656-6
Based on The devils by Fyodor Dostoyevsky. Set in 1870s Russia. Group of provincial friends join national movement for socialist revolution. 3 acts 50 scenes 9m 6w 1 setting

Egoism

Wedekind, F. The Marquis of Keith
Wedekind, F. The tenor

Ehn, Erik

16670 (Maximilian Mary Kolbe).

Poetic theater piece about priest who took another's place at Auschwitz. Music. 1 act 6 scenes 4m 1w extras settings

In Ehn, E. The saint plays

Cedar (John of the Cross).

Meditation on life and poems of Saint John of the Cross. Singing. 1 act 12 scenes 1g 2m 2w settings

In Ehn, E. The saint plays

Contemplacion (Mary and Martha).

Theater piece revolving around an innocent housemaid accused of murders by her employer. Prologue. 1 act 3 scenes 1b 1m 3w settings

In Ehn, E. The saint plays

Dashboard (Christopher).

Theater piece about a fragmented family and a car accident, and bridges to the dead. Music, singing. 1 act 2 scenes 1g 2m 1w settings

In Ehn, E. The saint plays

The freak (George).

To make a name for himself, a second-rate knight cuts off the wings of a flying girl, but she lives to encourage other "freaks." 1 act 6 scenes 1g 1m extra settings

In Ehn, E. The saint plays

The imp of simplicity (Thomas à Kempis).

Sisters in a convent input the works of Thomas à Kempis for posting on the Internet. Comic synchronization. 1 act 23 scenes 16w extras settings

In Ehn, E. The saint plays

Incide (Judas Iscariot).

A playlet suggesting that Judas is the archetypal human being. 1 act 3 scenes 3m 3w settings

In Ehn, E. The saint plays

Locus (John the Baptist).

The death of John the Baptist in a quasi-contemporary setting, with references to others whose promise was cut short. Music, dancing. 1 act 3 scenes 8m 4w extra settings

In Ehn, E. The saint plays

Pain (Eulalia).

The martyrdom of Saint Eulalia and the agony of modern parents searching for a murdered child. Singing. 2g 2m 1w extras settings

In Ehn, E. The saint plays

Radio elephant (Barbara).

Fairy tale-like piece about Saint Barbara, conflated with adventurous modern girl. Music. 1 act 3m 2w extras settings

In Ehn, E. The saint plays

Song for the end.

Song concluding a series of experimental plays based on Catholic saints and biblical figures. Music, singing. 1 scene Variable cast 1 setting

In Ehn, E. The saint plays

Thistle.

A massacre of villagers in El Salvador. Music, dancing. 3 acts 16 scenes 1g 2w 3m extras settings

In Ehn, E. The saint plays

Tree of hope, keep firm (Mary, the Annunciation).

Poetic meditation on the Annunciation. Music, dancing. Puppets. 1 act 1b 1g 2m 2w extras 1 setting

In Ehn, E. The saint plays

Una carroña (Rose of Lima).

Theater piece interweaves stories of Saint Rose of Lima with accounts of a massacre in El Salvador. 1 act 1g 3w 1 setting

In Ehn, E. The saint plays

Wholly Joan's (Joan of Arc).

A timeless Joan of Arc keeps her faith, is visited in prison by an angel composed of three actresses. Singing. 1 act 2 scenes 2m 4w 1 setting

In Ehn, E. The saint plays

Eight days, three hours, and eighteen minutes. Fredericks, A. D.

Eisenstein, Sergei, 1898-1948

about

Kleberg, L. The Aquarians
Kleberg, L. Ash Wednesday

Ekstrom, Peter, and DeBoy, David

Doctor! Doctor! a medical musical comedy revue; book by Peter Ekstrom; music and lyrics by Peter Ekstrom; additional lyrics and material by David DeBoy. French 1998 72p

ISBN 0-573-66233-9

Musical revue about doctors, patients and medicine. Music, singing. 2 acts 2m 2w 1 setting

El Salvador

Ehn, E. Thistle
Ehn, E. Una carroña (Rose of Lima)

Eldridge, David

Under the blue sky. Methuen 2000 84p
ISBN 0-413-75860-5

Single teachers, three relationships, hopes and failed dreams. 3 acts 3m 3w settings

The **election** machine warehouse. Baraka, A.

Electra (Greek mythology)

Aeschylus. Libation bearers
Euripides. Electra
Euripides. Orestes
Sophocles. Electra
Sophocles. Elektra

Electra. Euripides

Electra. Sophocles

Electra (Euripides). Kennedy, A.

Electric roses. Howard, D.

Electricity

Ehn, E. Radio elephant (Barbara)

Elegy for a lady. Miller, A.

Elektra. Sophocles

Elephant wake. Christenson, J., and Tremblay, J.

Eleven vests. Bond, E.

Eleven vests & Tuesday. Bond, E.

Elijah (Biblical figure)

c McCullough, L. E. The prophet and the rabbi
Vogel, L. Elijah's no good, horrible, very bad job

Elijah's no good, horrible, very bad job. Vogel, L.

Eliot, George, 1819-1880

Silas Marner (dramatization) See Beevers, G. George Eliot's Silas Marner

Elisa's skin. Fréchette, C.

Elisha, Ron

The Goldberg variations. Currency Press 2000 78p
ISBN 0-86819-622-3

Drama about a blind piano player who is asked to write a speech about his family, releasing a torrent of emotions. 2 acts 3m 2w 1 setting

Two.

Set in post-war Germany. Encounters between rabbi and woman eager to learn Hebrew vehicle for exploration of Jewish identity, Holocaust, and

good and evil in humankind. 2 acts 1m 1w 1 interior

In Contemporary Australian plays; ed. by R. Vandenbroucke

Elizabeth: almost by chance a woman. Fo, D.

Elizabeth I, Queen of England
about

Fo, D. Elizabeth: almost by chance a woman

Elizaveta Bam. Kharms, D.

Ellenbogen, Nicholas

Horn of sorrow.

Political drama explores environmental impact of apartheid. Depicts plight of black rhino. 1 act 6m 1 setting

In Drama for a new South Africa; ed. by D. Graver

Elliot, Tom

Feed. French (London) 2000 76p
ISBN 0-573-01760-3

Drama about retired music-hall comedian confined to nursing home struggling to revive his memories. Music, singing. 2 acts 1m 2w 1 setting

Ellis, David

c The three little pigs out west; book and lyrics by R. Eugene Jackson; music by David Ellis. Pioneer Drama Service 1998 45p

Three little pigs visit dude ranch. 2 scenes Variable cast 17 characters extras 2 extrior

Ellis, Havelock, 1859-1939
about

Power, D. Tales of the undead

Ellison, Les

c Space junk. French (London) 1999 39p
ISBN 0-573-05121-6

Fairy tale about bad rats and good rats. Good rats propel themselves into space and crash on a derelict Russian space station. Music, singing. Unidentified cast 16 characters 2 settings

Elton, Ben

Gasping.

Satire on big business. Marketing of "designer air" depletes oxygen supply. 2 acts 17 scenes 3m 3w extras settings

In Elton, B. Plays: 1

Elton, Ben—*Continued*

Popcorn. French (London) 1998 58p
  ISBN 0-573-01869-3   LC 97-23024
Satirical comedy set in Beverly Hills. Two killers intend to use film director's "art" as justification for murder. 2 acts 5 scenes 4m 5w 1 setting
—Same
  In Elton, B. Plays: 1

Silly cow. French (London) 1998 46p
  ISBN 0-573-01875-8   LC 99-214715
Satirical look at British tabloid press. Venomous TV columnist tries to keep her past secret. 2 acts 3 scenes 3m 2w 1 interior
—Same
  In Elton, B. Plays: 1

Elwell, Jeffery Scott

Evening education.
Overbearing college professor gets a lesson from canny black janitor. 1 act 2m 1 interior
  In Off-Off Broadway Festival plays, 25th ser.

Elyot, Kevin

The day I stood still. Hern Bks. 1998 96p
  ISBN 1-85459-334-X
Drama about three friends spanning 30 years from the 1960s, one friend is dead, another is in love, and the third friend is gay and has personal problems until he receives a surprise visitor. 3 scenes 5m 1w 1 setting

Emergency exit. Santanelli, M.

Emergency medical technicians

c McCullough, L. E. It's an emergency! (emergency medical technician)

Emigration and immigration

Arizmendi, Y. Nostalgia maldita: 1-900-MEXICO, a Stairmaster piece
Boomer, L. Bocón
Cruz, N. A bicycle country
c Fredericks, A. D. The Shapiros' new adventure
Gonzalez, S. S. Boxcar
Hwang, D. H. Fob
Lipkin, D. Skitaletz (The wanderer)
Machado, E. When the sea drowns in sand
Magona, S. House-hunting unlike Soweto
c McCullough, L. E. Di goldineh medineh (The golden land)

Monge-Rafuls, P. R. Trash
Poliakoff, S. Coming in to land
Svich, C. Prodigal kiss
Emily. Norman, M.
The **emotionalists**. Gilbert, S.
Emperor and Galilean: a world historical drama. Ibsen, H.
The **Emperor** Jones. O'Neill, E.
The **emperor's** new clothes. Miller, K. S.

Employment agencies

Churchill, C. Top girls
The **Emporium**. Wilder, T.
The **empty** tomb. Cheasebro, M.
The **Encanto** file. Lowinger, R.
Enchanted Sleeping Beauty. Francoeur, B.
The **enchantress** of Ipswich. Sturgill, B.
End dream. Pollock, S.
The **end** of civilization. Walker, G. F.
The **end** of the affair. Goold, R., and Butler, C.
The **end** of the earth. Lan, D.

End of the world

Lipkin, D. I am Laika
Wilder, T. And the sea shall give up its dead
The **endless** adventure of MCKAY; or, How they got from A to B. Jones, J. M.
An **enemy** of the people. Ibsen, H.

Eng, Alvin

The Goong Hay Kid.
Musical epic about ethnic identity and assimilation set in 1980s in New York City's Chinatown. Music. 8 scenes 5m 4w settings
  In Action; ed. by M. Algarin and L. Griffith

Engineers

c McCullough, L. E. Robots are everywhere (robotics engineer)

English drama

Early modern and Elizabethan

Arden of Faversham. Arden of Faversham
Dekker, T. The shoemaker's holiday
Greene, R. Selimus, emperor of the Turks
Kyd, T. The Spanish tragedy
Marlowe, C. The tragical history of Dr. Faustus

English drama—Early modern and Elizabethan—*Continued*

Marlowe, C. The troublesome reign and lamentable death of Edward the Second

Sidney, Sir P. The Lady of May

17th century

Beaumont, F. The knight of the burning pestle

Daborne, R. A Christian turned Turk

Dekker, T. The magnificent entertainment

Dekker, T. The shoemaker's holiday

Ford, J. 'Tis pity she's a whore

Heywood, T. A woman killed with kindness

Jonson, B. The alchemist

Jonson, B. Bartholomew Fair

Jonson, B. Epicoene

Jonson, B. The masque of blackness

Jonson, B. Mercury vindicated from the alchemists at court

Jonson, B. Pleasure reconciled to Virtue

Jonson, B. The queen's masques: the first, of blackness

Jonson, B. Volpone

Massinger, P. The renegado

Middleton, T. A chaste maid in Cheapside

Middleton, T. The changeling

Webster, J. The Duchess of Malfi

18th century

Cibber, C. Love makes a man; or, The fop's fortune

Cibber, C. Love's last shift; or, The fool in fashion

Cibber, C. The rival queans

Cibber, C. The tragical history of King Richard III

Cibber, C. Woman's wit; or, The lady in fashion

Cibber, C. Xerxes

Haywood, E. F. The opera of operas; or, Tom Thumb the Great

Haywood, E. F. A wife to be lett: a comedy.

English is a foreign language. Dee, P.

English (it's where the words are). Basch, P.

The **English** teachers. Napier, E.

Enigma variations. Ives, D.
Enigma variations. Schmitt, E.-E.

Enoch, Wesley, and Mailman, Deborah

The 7 stages of grieving.

Grief at death of grandmother is catalyst for Australian Aboriginal woman to consider family and friends who have died young and under unnatural circumstances. Slide projections. Music. 1w

In Contemporary Australian plays; ed. by R. Vandenbroucke

Enrico IV. Brustein, R.

Enright, Nick

Spurboard. Currency Press 2001 102p
ISBN 0-86819-643-6

Drama about two brothers, with little in common, and two friends, with very different ambitions. 2 acts 7m 8w 1 setting

Enright, Nick, and Monjo, Justin

Cloudstreet. Currency Press 1999 122p
ISBN 0-86819-589-8

Sprawling saga of two families who share a run-down house in a working-class neighborhood of Perth, Australia. Touches of magic realism. Adapted from a novel by Tim Winton. Music, singing, dancing. 3 parts 102 scenes 18m 16w extras 17 interiors 10 exteriors

Ensler, Eve

Necessary targets. Villard Bks. 2001 122p
ISBN 0-375-75603-5

Two American women, one a Park Avenue psychiatrist the other a human rights worker, minister to five Bosnian women in refugee camp. 17 scenes 7w

The Vagina monologues. Villard Bks. 2001 185p
ISBN 0-375-75698-1

Celebration of female sexuality based on over 200 interviews with diverse group of women from around the globe. Explores the humor, power, pain, wisdom, outrage, mystery and excitement hidden in vaginas. Variable cast

Entertainers

Bowen, J. Little boxes: the coffee lace

c Espinosa, R. Clothes do not make the man (El habito no hace al monje)

Gems, P. Marlene

Hanan, S. M. Jolson & company

Hindman, J. Pete 'n' Keely

Entertainers—*Continued*
Swingtime Canteen
Eos, Selene, and Helios. Barchers, S. I.
Epic proportions. Coen, L., and Crane, D.
Epicoene. Jonson, B.
Epiphany
Anderson, S. J. Epiphany mosaic
Epiphany mosaic. Anderson, S. J.
Episodes from Don Quixote. Barchers, S.
I., and Kroll, J. L.

Epstein, David
Exact change. Dramatists 2000 51p
ISBN 0-8222-1739-2   LC 00-703195
Dark comedy about three Vietnam vet buddies
who, as result of bad investment, are forced to resort to desperate measures to pay off local heavy
and retain their bar and grill. 2 acts 3m 2 settings

Equal Rights Amendment
c Fredericks, A. D. Equal Rights Amendment
Equal Rights Amendment. Fredericks, A.
D.

Erdman, Nikolai
The suicide. Broadway Play Pub. 2000
90p
ISBN 0-88145-173-8
Satirical comedy from the Soviet Union (1931).
Man without a job threatens suicide and finds himself suddenly popular. All sorts of people wish to
use his death to further their various causes and
are outraged when he remains alive. 5 acts 5
scenes 2b 13m 9w settings

Ernst, Pete
The most perfect day.
Romantic comedy about a man who takes his
beloved on a picnic to prove how beautiful she is.
3m 1w 1 setting
In Off-Off Broadway Festival plays,
22nd ser.
Eros and Psyche. Barchers, S. I.
The **Eros** trilogy. Silver, N.
Escanaba in da moonlight. Daniels, J.
The **escape**. Brown, W. W.
Escape from happiness. Walker, G. F.
Escape from paradise. Taylor, R.
Escobedo de la Aixa
about
Linney, R. Madmen

Esker Mike & his wife, Agiluk. Hardin,
H.

Espinosa, Resurrección
c Ay, Carmelo! (Ay, Carmelo!).
Town storyteller on Caribbean island learns lesson about listening. Spanish and English versions.
4m 3w
In Espinosa, R. Don Quijote in
America
c El bully (El valenton).
Children deal with bully on playground. Spanish
and English versions. 6 scenes 3b 3g 1w extras 1
interior 1 exterior
In Espinosa, R. Don Quijote in
America
c Cinderella in modern times (Cenicienta
en tiempos modernos).
Updating of Cinderella story. Spanish and English versions. 5 scenes Variable cast 10 characters
In Espinosa, R. Don Quijote in
America
c Clothes do not make the man (El habito
no hace al monje).
Court entertainers perform for prince's birthday.
Spanish and English versions. 4 scenes Variable
cast
In Espinosa, R. Don Quijote in
America
c The coming of winter (La llegada del
invierno).
Old man and woman, cat, mouse and pigeons
prepare for winter. Spanish and English versions.
3 scenes Variable cast 7 characters extras
In Espinosa, R. Don Quijote in
America
c Don Quijote in America (Don Quijote en
America).
Don Quijote's exploits in New York City. Span-
ish and English versions. 4 scenes Variable cast
In Espinosa, R. Don Quijote in
America
c The farmer finds his true friends (El
granjero descubre a sus verdaderos
amigos).
Animals help farmer. Spanish and English ver-
sions. 4 scenes Variable cast 10 characters extras
In Espinosa, R. Don Quijote in
America

Espinosa, Resurrección—*Continued*

c The princess is sad (La princesa esta
    triste).

Friends of princess try to make her feel better.
Spanish and English versions. 5 scenes Variable
cast 10 characters

> *In* Espinosa, R. Don Quijote In
> America

c What happened in the garden this sum-
    mer? (Que paso en el jardin este
    verano?).

Inhabitants of garden work to be good neighbors.
Spanish and English versions. 3 scenes Variable
cast

> *In* Espinosa, R. Don Quijote in
> America

c Where did they go? Where did I put
    them? (A donde se fueron? Donde las
    puse yo?).

Boy, with help of his conscience, learns about
friendship. Spanish and English versions. 4 scenes
6m 2w extra

> *In* Espinosa, R. Don Quijote in
> America

Esson, Louis

Andeganora.

Australian aborigine moves to prevent white man
from stealing his woman. 1b 3m 1w 1 exterior

> *In* Esson, L. Plays 1: Terra Australis

Australia felix.

Comedy. Friends discuss Australian politics as
they wait for election results. 1 scene 4m 1w 1 exterior

> *In* Esson, L. Plays 1: Terra Australis

Dead timber.

Unmarried daughter's pregnancy devastates father. 3m 2w 1 exterior

> *In* Esson, L. Plays 1: Terra Australis

The drovers.

Drama set in Australian aboriginal drovers camp.
1 act 1b 6m 1 exterior

> *In* Esson, L. Plays 1: Terra Australis

Mates.

Comedy set in Australian outback. To repay
debt, man was barmaid on friend's behalf. 3m 1w
1 interior

> *In* Esson, L. Plays 1: Terra Australis

Mother and son.

Youngest son causes heartache for family in
Australian bush. 3 acts 1b 4m 3w 1 interior 1 exterior

> *In* Esson, L. Plays 1: Terra Australis

The quest.

Spaniard explores Peru in 1600. 6 scenes 12m
5w extras 2 interiors 3 exteriors

> *In* Esson, L. Plays 1: Terra Australis

Shipwreck.

Drama set in Australian bush. Young girl is
forced to marry much older man. 4 acts 6 scenes
5m 2w 5 interiors 1 extrior

> *In* Esson, L. Plays 1: Terra Australis

Terra Australis.

Fragments of conversation about Australia's past.
Variable cast 3 characters 1 interior

> *In* Esson, L. Plays 1: Terra Australis

Vagabond camp.

Man decides to leave his wife for another woman, but other woman deceives him and he is left
alone. 1 act 4m 2w 1 exterior

> *In* Esson, L. Plays 1: Terra Australis

Esther (Biblical figure)

c McCullough, L. E. Hail, Queen Esther!

c Vogel, L. A test for Esther

Esthetics

Jonson, B. The masque of blackness

Jonson, B. The queen's masques: the
    first, of blackness

Estorias del barrio: special people of international character. Perez, F.

Estorias del barrio: un ghost. Rodriguez,
    E.

Esu and the vagabond minstrels. Osofisan,
    F.

Ethan Claymore. Foster, N.

Ethiopia

Gabre-Medhin, T. Collision of altars

Eulalia, of Merida, Saint

about

Ehn, E. Pain (Eulalia)

The **Eumenides**. Aeschylus

Euripides, ca. 485-ca. 406 B.C.

Alcestis (adaptation) See Hughes, T. Eu-
    ripides' Alcestis

Electra (adaptation) See Kennedy, A.
    Electra (Euripides)

Iphigenia in Aulis (adaptation) See
    Teevan, C. Iph. . .

Euripides, ca. 485-ca. 406 B.C.—*Continued*

Orestes (adaptation) See Kennedy, A. Orestes (Euripides)

Alcestis; tr. by Fred Chappell.

Greek classical drama. Psychological fantasy, based on the legend of a sacrificing wife who agrees to die so that husband may live. Speaking chorus

In Euripides. Euripides, 3

The Alcestis of Euripides; with introduction, translation, and commentary by John E. Thorburn, Jr. Edwin Mellen Press 2002 203p (Studies in Classics, 16)

ISBN 0-7734-7396-3

Greek classical drama. Psychological fantasy, based on the legend of sacrificing wife who agrees to die so that husband may live. Speaking chorus 1 act 1 scene 7m 2w 1 exterior

Alkestis; trans. by J. Michael Walton.

Greek classical drama. Psychological fantasy, based on legend of sacrificing wife who agrees to die so that husband may live. Speaking chorus

In Six Greek comedies

Andromache; tr. by Donald Junkins.

Greek classical tragedy in verse. Legend relating how Andromache and her son were saved from a death plot instigated by Hermione and Menelaus.

In Euripides. Euripides, 1

Bacchae; tr. by Daniel Mark Epstein.

Greek classical tragedy in verse. Punishment of Pentheus, King of Thebes, by Dionysus, god of wine, for his refusal to permit Bacchanaeian revels in Thebes. Speaking chorus

In Euripides. Euripides, 1

—Same; tr. by James Morwood

In Euripides. Iphigenia among the Taurians, Bacchae, Iphigenia at Aulis, Rhesus

Children of Heracles; tr. J. T. Barbarese.

Variant title: Heracleidae. Greek classical verse tragedy. Legendary account of war resulting from refusal of Demophon, King of Athens, to surrender the children of Heracles to their enemy. Eursytheus, King of Argos. Speaking chorus

In Euripides. Euripides, 4

Cyclops; tr. by Palmer Bovie.

Greek satyr play in verse. Based on Homer's story of Odysseus' escape from the cave of the Cyclops Polyphemus. Speaking chorus

In Euripides. Euripides, 2

—Same; trans. by J. Michael Walton

In Six Greek comedies

Daughters of Troy; tr. by Mark Rudman and Katharine Washburn.

Variant title: The Trojan women. Greek classical tragedy. Fate of the women of Troy after city was captured by Greeks in Trojan War.

In Euripides. Euripides, 3

Electra; tr. by Elizabeth Seydel Morgan.

Greek classical tragedy in verse. Legend of Orestes and Electra, son and daughter of Agamemnon, telling how they avenged their father's murder.

In Euripides. Euripides, 2

Hecuba; tr. by Marilyn Nelson.

Greek tragedy in verse based on legend. Hecuba, formerly Queen of Troy, avenges son's murder committed by King of Thrace. Speaking chorus

In Euripides. Euripides, 1

Helen; tr. by Rachel Hada.

Greek classical tragicomedy in verse. Based on legend that only wraith of Helen of Troy had caused Trojan War, Helen herself being in Egypt.

In Euripides. Euripides, 2

Hippolytus; tr. by Richard Moore.

Verse play. Greek tragedy based on legend. Phaedra, scorned by chaste stepson Hippolytus, arranges his destruction by falsely accusing him to his father Theseus. Speaking chorus

In Euripides. Euripides, 2

Ion; tr. by Deborah H. Roberts.

Skeptical drama treating legend of Ion, sone of Creusa and Apollo, who ultimately becomes King of Athens and ancestor of Ionian race. Questions sanctity of Apollo and honesty of his Delphie Oracle. Speaking chorus

In Euripides. Euripides, 4

Iphigenia among the Taurians; tr. by James Morwood.

Variant title: Iphigenia in Tauris. Greek classical tragedy in verse. Legend relating how Iphigenia, while serving as priestess of Artemis, plots to save her brother, Orestes, from being sacrificed to the goddess.

In Euripides. Iphigenia among the Taurians, Bacchae, Iphigenia at Aulis, Rhesus

Iphigenia at Aulis; tr. by Elaine Terranova.

Greek classical tragedy in verse. Based on legend of Medea's revenge against husband Jason for deserting her. Speaking chorus

In Euripides. Euripides, 3

Euripides, ca. 485-ca. 406 B.C.—_Continued_

—Same; tr. by James Morwood

  _In_ Euripides. Iphigenia among the Taurians, Bacchae, Iphigenia at Aulis, Rhesus

Iphigenia in Tauris; tr. by Carolyn Kizer.

Variant title: Iphigenia among the Taurians. Greek classical tragedy in verse. Legend relating how Iphigenia, while serving as priestess of Artemis, plots to save her brother, Orestes, from being sacrificed to the goddess.

  _In_ Euripides. Euripides, 4

The madness of Heracles; tr. by Katharine Washburn and David Curzon.

Variant title: Heracles. Greek classical tragedy in verse. Based on legend about Herakles who in a fit of temporary insanity kills his wife and children, whom he has come to save from the tyrant Lycus.

  _In_ Euripides. Euripides, 4

Medea; in a new translation by Nicholas Rudall. Dee, I. R. 2000 59p

  ISBN 1-56663-320-6; 1-56663-321-4 (pa)

Greek classical tragedy in verse. Based on legend of Medea's revenge against husband Jason for deserting her. Speaking chorus.

—Same; tr. by Eleanor Wilner with Ines Azar

  _In_ Euripides. Euripides, 1

Orestes; tr. by Greg Delanty.

Greek classical tragedy in verse. Apollo intervenes to save Orestes and Electra after they had been condemned to death for revenge slaying of their mother.

  _In_ Euripides. Euripides, 4

The Phoenician women; tr. by Richard Elman.

Variant title: The Phoenician maidens. Greek classical tragedy. Eteokles and Polyneikes, sons of Oedipus, King of Thebes, kill each other in battle over Theban sovereignty. Verse play. Speaking chorus

  _In_ Euripides. Euripides, 3

Rhesus; tr. by George Economou.

Greek classical tragedy in verse. Based on legend of Trojan War, concerning the slaying by Greek spies of Rehesus, King of Thrace and an ally of the Trojans.

  _In_ Euripides. Euripides, 3

—Same; tr. by James Morwood

  _In_ Euripides. Iphigenia among the Taurians, Bacchae, Iphigenia at Aulis, Rhesus

Suppliant women; tr. by John Frederick Nims.

Greek classical tragey in verse. Based on legend of Argive women who invoked aid of the gods in recovering from the Thebans bodies of the Argive warriors slain in battle against Thebes.

  _In_ Euripides. Euripides, 2

The Trojan women; in a new translation by Nicholas Rudall. Dee, I. R. 1999 61p

  ISBN 1-566-63223-4; 1-566-63224-2 (pa)

                          LC 99-21034

Variant title: Daughters of Troy. Classical Greek tragedy showing brutality of war relates events immediately after fall of Troy.

           about

Aristophanes. Frogs

    Parodies, imitations, etc.

Aristophanes. Celebrating ladies

Europe. Greig, D.

Eurydice (Greek mythology)

Kokoschka, O. Orpheus and Eurydice

Eva. McAvera, B.

Evans, Albert, and others

Pageant; book & lyrics by Bill Russell and Frank Kelly; music by Albert Evans; conceived by Robert Longbottom. French 1998 61p

  ISBN 0-573-69655-1   LC 98-222978

Musical comedy about six beauty queens participating in the Miss Glamouresse pageant. 7m 1 interior

Evans, Sally

_y_ Jesus loved them.

Nine biblical personalities who knew Jesus tell their stories. Music, singing. Variable cast 10 characters

  _In_ The drama of Easter; ed. by R. Wray

Evans, Sian

Little sister.

Portrait of 16-year-old homeless girl in Cardiff, Wales. 17 scenes 2m 2w 1 setting

  _In_ New Welsh Drama II; ed. by J. Teare

Farces—*Continued*

Bowen, J. Little boxes: Trevor
Busch, C. Red scare on Sunset
Chekhov, A. P. The bear
Chekhov, A. P. The festivities
Chekhov, A. P. The jubilee
Chekhov, A. P. The night before the trial
Chekhov, A. P. Platonov
Chekhov, A. P. The proposal
Chekhov, A. P. The wedding
Chekhov, A. P. The wedding reception
Coward, N. Blithe spirit
Crommelynck, F. Golden guts
Crommelynck, F. Hot and cold; or, Mr. Dom's idea
Davidson, C. E. Mosquito dirigible aerosol deodorant
Feydeau, G. The boor hug
Feydeau, G. Caught with his trance down
Feydeau, G. Fit to be tried; or, Stepbrothers in crime
Feydeau, G. Going to pot (On purge Bébé)
Feydeau, G. Ladies' man
Feydeau, G. Romance in a flat
Feydeau, G. Tooth and consequences; or, Hortense said: "No skin off my ass!"
Feydeau, G. Winner takes all
Feydeau, G. Wooed and viewed
Feydeau, G. Mixed doubles
Fo, D. About face
Fo, D. Elizabeth: almost by chance a woman
Fo, D. We won't pay! We won't pay
Foxton, D. Breakfast for one
García Lorca, F. The love of Don Perlimplin for Belisa in the garden
Gore, C. A good night's rest; or, Two in the morning
Hackenbrook, W. J. Conditions
Hall, L. Wittgenstein on Tyne
Hatcher, J. To fool the eye
Hennequin, M. Anything to declare?
Huie, K. Yasuko and the young s-s-samurai
Irwin, B. Scapin
Jarry, A. King Ubu
Jonson, B. Bartholomew Fair
Jonson, B. Epicoene
y Kelly, T. Sundown Alley

Kokoschka, O. Job
Kramer, S. The wall of water
Laurence, C. The Ring sisters
Macpherson, R. The terrible false deception
Marowitz, C. La Parisienne
Marowitz, C. Quack
Marowitz, C. Stark naked
May, E. In and out of the light
Milligan, J. Juris prudence
Molière. The doctor despite himself
O'Casey, S. Cock-a-doodle dandy
O'Casey, S. Hall of healing
Orton, J. Loot
Orton, J. What the butler saw
Parker, M. The Lone Star love potion
Parker, M. The sensuous senator
Plautus, T. M. Double bind (Menaechmi)
Plautus, T. M. Major Blowhard (Miles gloriosus)
Quilter, P. Respecting your piers
Rodriguez, E. S. Soldiers will be soldiers
Wilson, L. Chateau La Roach
Woolf, B. E. Off to the war

fareWel. Ross, I.

Farias, Joann

Claudia meets Fulano Colorado.

Comedy set in small Texas town in 1950s, where Mexican-American community of eccentric characters examine facts of life, love and death. 23 scenes 1g 4m 4w extra 1 exterior

   In Latino plays from South Coast Repertory

Farley and Betsy. Foote, D.

Farley, Keythe, and Flemming, Brian

Bat boy; the musical; book by Keythe Farley and Brian Flemming; music and lyrics by Laurence O'Keefe. Dramatists 2002

ISBN 0-8222-1834-8

Based on a story in the Weekly World News, this is a musical comedy/horror show about a half boy/half bat creature who is found and brought to live in a small town in West Virginia. 6m 4w 1 exterior

Farm life

c Espinosa, R. The farmer finds his true friends (El granjero descubre a sus verdaderos amigos)

Farm life—*Continued*

Gallagher, M. Windshook

Healey, M. The drawer boy

Miller, Jesse. Onionheads

O'Neill, E. Beyond the horizon

Sapergia, B. Roundup

Wiltse, D. Temporary

The **farmer** and the animals. Barchers, S. I.

The **farmer** finds his true friends (El granjero descubre a sus verdaderos amigos). Espinosa, R.

Farquhar, George, 1677?-1707

Love and a bottle (adaptation) See Hughes, D. Love and a bottle

Farquhar, Robert

Dust to dust. Weinberger, J. 2002 77p

ISBN 0-85676-270-9

After a man's death, two of his drinking buddies and his ex-wife clean out his apartment, arrange for a cremation, quarrel, reminisce, and finally take his ashes to the sea. Music. 1 act 2m 1w 1 setting

God's official. Weinberger, J. 2002 95p

ISBN 0-85676-265-2

Black comedy. Two disappointed soccer fans kidnap offending referee. 3m 1 setting

Kissing Sid James. Weinberger, J. 2003 2003p

ISBN 0-85676-266-0

Romantic weekend doesn't live up to expectations. Music, singing. 2 acts 13 scenes 1m 1w settings

Farquhar, Simon

I do solemnly declare. French (London) 2001 21p

ISBN 0-573-12282-2

Suburban family's idyllic existence shattered when wife discovers husband is having an affair. 1b 1g 1m 1w 1 interior

Farrell, Christine

The once attractive woman.

Woman professor, fifty years old, is suddenly turned on by the opportunities for adultery. 1 act 8 scenes 2m 3w settings

In Ensemble Studio Theatre marathon '99: the one-act plays

Fascism

Wilson, S. The glad hand

Fashion. Lucie, D.

Fashion; or, Life in New York. Mowatt, A. C.

The **fat-free** Chicana and the Snow Cap queen. Romero, E.

Fate

Wilder, T. The drunken sisters

Wilder, T. Nascuntur poetae . . .

Fate of a cockroach. Al-Hakim, T.

The **father**. Strindberg, A.

Father and son. Margulies, D.

Fathers

Martin, J. Good boys

Fathers and daughters

Beber, N. Departures

y Bond, E. Tuesday

Chiasson, H. Alienor

Churchill, C. Heart's desire

Clarke, G. E. Beatrice Chancy

Cullen, M. Anna Weiss

Donaghy, T. The beginning of August

Ehn, E. Radio elephant (Barbara)

Esson, L. Dead timber

Filloux, C. The lessons of my father

Hedges, P. Good as new

Junyent, S. Packing up the past

Korder, H. Geliebteh

Kramer, S. World without memory

Lan, D. The end of the earth

Laxdal, V. Karla and Grif

Levi, S. The gulf of crimson

Martini, C. Conversations with my neighbour's pit bull

Mattern, J. Scrapple

McPherson, C. Dublin carol

Mérimée, P. Carvajal's family (La famille de Carvajal)

Noonan, J. F. What drove me back to reconsidering my father

O'Neill, E. Anna Christie

Parker, Matt. Celaine

Rebeck, T. Abstract expression

Redgrave, L. Shakespeare for my father

Ruskin, A. L. The art of remembering

Ryan, J. The young girl and the monsoon

Sher, E. Mourning dove

Smith, C. Knock me a kiss

Solis, O. El otro

Fathers and daughters—*Continued*
Tasca, J. Judah's daughter
Wasserstein, W. Tender offer
Women's Theatre Group. Lear's daughters
Yew, C. Red

Fathers and sons
Bouchard, M. M. Down Dangerous Passes Road
Brandt, A. 2 1/2 Jews
Churchill, C. A number
Clarvoe, A. The brothers Karamazov
Crip, N. J. That good night
Donaghy, T. The dadshuttle
Gardner, H. Conversations with my father
Gilroy, F. D. Last licks
Gilroy, F. D. That summer—that fall
Gonzalez, S. S. The migrant farmworker's son
Gorden, C. Guarding the bridge
Gurney, A. R. The cocktail hour
Hannah, D. Fathers and sons
y Harden, V. Big boys don't cry
Hoffman, J. Francis Brick needs no introduction
Horovitz, I. Our father's failing
Horovitz, I. A Rosen by any other name
Keane, J. B. The highest house on the mountain
Leight, W. Side man
Maloney, P. Accident
Margulies, D. Father and son
Miller, A. Death of a salesman
Mouawad, W. Tideline (Littoral)
Murray, T. C. Autumn fire
Murray, T. C. Birthright
O'Neill, E. The rope
Palmer, J. Singapore
Parnell, P. The cider house rules: part 1
Parnell, P. The cider house rules: part 2
Paterson, D. L. Shades of autumn
Piatigorsky, A. The offering
Posner, A. The chosen
Pushkin, A. The miserly knight
Raznovich, D. Rear entry (De atrás para adelante)
Rebeck, T. The butterfly collection
Rodriguez, E. Estorias del barrio: un ghost

Rudolph, K. The conspiracy of silence
c Surface, M. H. Prodigy
Walker, G. F. Criminal genius
Wells, M. L. Real real gone
Williams, R. Starstruck
Wilson, L. Talley & son
Fathers and sons. Hannah, D.
Faulkner, William, 1897-1962
Tomorrow (dramatization) See Foote, H. Tomorrow

Faust (Legendary character)
Marlowe, C. The tragical history of Dr. Faustus
Faust (Faust is dead). Ravenhill, M.
Fawkes, Guy, 1570-1606
about
Poskitt, K. Fawkes—the quiet guy
Fawkes—the quiet guy. Poskitt, K.

Fear
c Bush, M. The boy who left home to find out about the shivers
c Martini, C. Mouse
Mastrosimone, W. Precipice
Nigro, D. Darkness like a dream
Nigro, D. Things that go bump in the night
Pielmeier, J. Voices in the dark
Pritchard, E. Chicken wings
Rachilde. The prowler (Le Rôdeur)
Rivera, J. A tiger in Central Park
Sater, S. Phone sex and a dumb show
Fearless Pharaoh FooFoo. Vogel, L.
A **feast** during the plague. Pushkin, A.
Featuring Loretta. Walker, G. F.

Fechter, Steven
The last cigarette.
Woman with a past and lonely man meet in last smoking bar in Santa Monica. 1 act 1m 1w 1 interior
In Off-Off Broadway festival plays, 24th ser.
Feed. Elliot, T.
Feet. Marinetti, F.

Feffer, Steve

Little airplanes of the heart.

Young boy obsessed with building own plane and flying same route as pilot uncle's fatal flight. 1b 1g 2m 2w extras 1 interior

In The Best American Short plays, 1997-1998

—Same

In Ensemble Studio Theatre marathon 2000: the one-act plays

Feibleman, Peter S.

Cakewalk; original music by Carly Simon. Dramatists 1998 71p

ISBN 0-8222-1593-4   LC 98-231836

Romantic comedy about Lillian Hellman and her relationship with lover twenty years her junior. Music 2 acts 2m 2w 1 setting

Felder, Louis

Flight of fancy.

Young MBA and middle-aged salesman meet in airport lounge in Portland, Oregon. 1 act 1m 1w 1 interior

In Off-Off Broadway festival plays, 24th ser.

The magic kingdom.

Drama set in bus depot. Interracial couple about to get married and honeymoon in Disneyland. 1m 1w 1 interior

In Multicultural theatre II; ed. by R. Ellis

Feliciano, Gloria

Between blessings.

With help of priest, twenty-eight-year-old Puerto Rican man tells father he is gay. 2 acts 8 scenes 4m 4 interiors 2 exteriors

In Action; ed. by M. Algarin and L. Griffith

Feminism

Ardito, C. St. James's blues

Edgar, D. Teendreams

Martinez, R. Illuminating Veronica

Plata, M. C. Justice for whom?

Reed, I. Savage wilds

Schenkar, J. The universal wolf

Fendrich, Steven

y Yearbook. Pioneer Drama Service 1999 42p

Vingettes about positive attributes of high school students. Prologue 2 acts 10 scenes epilogue variable cast 1 setting

See also Davies, C. jt. auth.

Fennessy, Aidan

Chilling and killing my Annabel Lee. Currency Press 1999 69p

ISBN 0-86819-584-7

Surreal tale of murder, intrigue, creativity and lost love. An author manipulates story of his past. 2 acts 35 scenes 4m 4w extra

Fenton, Elizabeth

From dream to ash.

Elderly Jewish composer living in Nazi Germany tries to complete musical composition. 4m 1 setting

In Blast from the future; ed. by D. Yeaton

Fenwick, Jean-Nöel

Le palmes de M. Schutz (adaptation) See Clark, R. Pierre and Marie

Fernande. McAvera, B.

Ferris wheel. Miller, M.

Festivals

Ayckbourn, A. Garden

Valentine, P. Day of reckoning

Wood, T. Claptrap

The **festivities**. Chekhov, A. P.

Feuds

c Art, S. S. The Hatfields and the McCoys

Feuer, Jed, and Boyd, Graham

The big bang; book and lyrics by Boyd Graham; music by Jed Feuer. French 2001 55p

ISBN 0-573-62754-1

Comic revue. Backer's audition for 83.5 million-dollar twelve-hour stage history of the world. Music, singing. 2m 1 interior

Fever. Blais, M.-C.

A **few** roos loose in the top paddock. O'Neill, T.

A **few** stout individuals. Guare, J.

Feydeau, Georges, 1862-1921

A qui ma femme? (adaptation) See Shapiro, N. R. Take her, she's yours! or, Til divorce do us part

Stark naked (adaptation) See Marowitz, C. Stark naked

The boor hug.
Early 20th century French farce. 1 act 2m 2w 1 interior
   In Feydeau, G. Feydeau, first to last

Caught with his trance down.
Early 20th century French farce. 1 act 4m 2w 1 interior
   In Feydeau, G. Feydeau, first to last

Fit to be tried; or, Stepbrothers in crime.
Farce revolves around husband suspicious of actress wife's admirer and mistaken identity of visitor. 1 act 5m 3w 1 interior
   In Feydeau, G. Feydeau, first to last

Going to pot (On purge Bébé).
Farce. Bickering parents and their imperious brat reduce a luncheon party to chaos. 1 act 1b 3m 3w 1 interior
   In Feydeau, G. Four farces

Ladies' man.
Farce. Young woman gives advice about men to another young woman. 1 act 2w 1 setting
   In Feydeau, G. Feydeau, first to last

Not by bed alone (Un fil à la patte).
Farce. Man-about-town must dump temperamental mistress before he can marry sweet young thing. Singing. 3 acts 10m 6w extras 3 interiors
   In Feydeau, G. Four farces

Romance in a flat.
Parisian society lady meets her rather odd new piano teacher. 1 act 2m 1w
   In Feydeau, G. Feydeau, first to last

Tooth and consequences; or, Hortense said: "No skin off my ass!".
Early 20th century French farce. 1 act 5m 4w 1 interior
   In Feydeau, G. Feydeau, first to last

Winner takes all; tr. by Reggie Oliver.
French (London) 2001 94p
   ISBN 0-573-01950-9
Farce. Complications multiply after a phonograph accidentally records the voices of a wife and her lover. 2 acts 4 scenes 10m 3w 3 interiors

Wooed and viewed.
Farce. Husband alone while his wife visits her mother, is approached by neighbor to make love in front of her jealous husband. 1 act 1m 1w 1 interior
   In Feydeau, G. Feydeau, first to last
—Same
   In Feydeau, G. Four farces

Feydeau, Georges, and Desvallières, Maurice

Mixed doubles.
Farce. Infidelity, romantic intrigue and divorce among Parisian society. 1 act 3m 3w 1 interior
   In Feydeau, G. Feydeau, first to last

On the marry-go-wrong (Le mariage de Barillon).
Farce. Mistakes at the marriage bureau leave groom hitched to mother-in-law, for starters. Singing. 3 acts 1b 7m 3w extras 3 interiors
   In Feydeau, G. Four farces

Feynmann, Richard
about
   Parnell, P. QED

Fidrych, Mark, 1954-
about
   Metcalf, P. The players

Field, Barbara

Camille.
Dramatization of Dumas fils' romantic tale of a beautiful courtesan in love with a young aristocrat in 19th century Paris. Music, singing, dancing. 2 acts 12 scenes 13m 8w extras settings
   In Field, B. New classics from the Guthrie Theater

A Christmas carol.
A dramatization of Dicken's classic holiday story. Music, singing, dancing. 2 acts 5 scenes 1b 13m 9w settings
   In Field, B. New classics from the Guthrie Theater

Great expectations.
Dramatization of Dickens's novel about a poor orphan who is educated as a gentleman, thanks to a mysterious benefactor. Set in 19th century England. 2 acts 7m 4w settings
   In Field, B. New classics from the Guthrie Theater

Field, Barbara—*Continued*

—Same

In Seattle Children's Theatre v2

Marriage.

Comedy adapted from a play by Nikolai Gogol. A confirmed bachelor is almost hustled into marriage. 2 acts 3 scenes epilogue 6m 4w 2 interiors

In Field, B. New classics from the Guthrie Theater

Monsieur de Molière.

Molière's enemies use his friends and relatives to destroy him. Adapted from a 1932 play by Mikhail Bulgakov. Music. 1 act 7 scenes 15m 4w extras 5 interiors

In Field, B. New classics from the Guthrie Theater

Pantagleize.

Satirical farce. A cheerful nobody unwittingly gives the signal for a revolution and is mistaken for its long-awaited leader. Adapted from a play by Michel de Ghelderode. Music, singing. 1 act 9 scenes epilogue 16m 3w extras settings

In Field, B. New classics from the Guthrie Theater

Playing with fire.

A dialogue between Dr. Frankenstein and his Creature, with flashbacks. Based on the Mary Shelley classic. Singing. 1 act 5m 1w settings

In Field, B. New classics from the Guthrie Theater

The **field**. Martini, C.

Fifteen minutes. DeChristopher, D.

Fifth of July. Wilson, L.

The **fifth** planet. Auburn, D.

Fifty years ago. Schisgal, M.

The **fighting** days. Lill, W.

Figuring things. Fosbrook, M.

Filippo, Eduardo de

Christmas in Naples; tr. by Maria Tucci.

Comedy set in Naples. Father insists on maintaining Christmas spirit even though family behaves horribly. 3 acts 7m 3w extras 1 setting

In Filippo, E. D. Four Plays

Filumena—a marriage Italian style; tr. by Maria Tucci.

Comedy set in Naples. Former prostitute assures financial future of her three illegitimate sons by tricking lover into marriage. 3 acts 8m 5w 1 interior

In Filippo, E. D. Four Plays

Naples gets rich; tr. by Maria Tucci.

Moral corruption of family involved in war-time black market activities. 3 acts Large mixed cast settings

In Filippo, E. D. Four Plays

Those damned ghosts; tr. by Maria Tucci.

Comedy. Good-hearted but pathetic man tries to overlook ghosts in apartment he and new wife (and her lover, the "ghost") are living in. 3 acts 1b 1g 4m 4w extras 1 interior

In Filippo, E. D. Four Plays

Fill, Simon

Night visits.

Doctor shaken by wife's death. 1m 2w 1 interior

In 30 ten-minute plays for 3 actors from Actors Theatre of Louisville's National Ten-minute Play Contest

Filloux, Catherine

The lessons of my father.

Woman deals with father's death by remembering things he taught her when she was young. 1g 1m 1w

In HB Playwrights short play festival 2000

Photographs from S-21.

Cambodian man and woman, former prisoners of Khmer Rouge, visit photography exhibit. 1m 1w 1 interior

In HB Playwrights short play festival 1998

Storks.

Woman spends time at airport during grandmother's lay over. 1m 2w 1interior

In HB Playwrights short play festival 1999

The **film** club (a monologue by Suzanne Alexander). Kennedy, A.

Film society. Baitz, J. R.

Filthy rich. Walker, G. F.

Filumena—a marriage Italian style. Filippo, E. de

The **final** interrogation of Ceauşescu's dog. Leight, W.

Finding the foolish. Barchers, S. I.

Finer noble gases. Rapp, A.

Finland

Hall, L. Child of our time: child of the snow

Finlayson, Alex

Misfits.

Drama explores dissolution of Marilyn Monroe's marriage to Arthur Miller during filming of 1960s movie The misfits. 2 acts 20 scenes 1g 17m 6w extras 9 interiors 4 exteriors

In Finlayson, A. Plays

Winding the ball.

Black comedy set in farm co-op store in Appalachian Mountains of southwestern Virginia. Lurid tale of desperate ambition leading to senseless violence. 2 acts 5m 4w 1 interior

In Finlayson, A. Plays

Finn, William

A new brain; book by William Finn & James Lapine; music and lyrics by William Finn. French 1999 76p

ISBN 0-573-62713-4

Musical. Jewish composer-lyricist diagnosed and treated for brain tumor. Prologue 3m 4w 1 interior

Painting you.

Inspired by Shakespeare's Sonnet 102. Artist struggles to paint his lover. 1 act 2m extras

In Love's fire

Finn M'Coul. McBride-Smith, B.

Fionn in search of his youth. McCullough, L. E.

The **fire** and the rain. Karnad, G.

Firebird. Scollard, R.

First love. Schisgal, M.

The **first** poet. London, J.

First star (Una estrella). Pedrero, P.

Firth, Tim

The safari party. French (London) 2003 84p

ISBN 0-573-01981-9

Revelations lead to violence when three households in Cheshire, England agree to hold dinner party where each course is served in different house. 3 acts 3m 3w 3 interiors

Fish, Robert L., 1912-

Murder league (dramatization) See Sutton, M., and Fingleton, A. Over my dead body

Fishelson, David

The golem; tr. by Landis, Joseph C. Dramatists 2003

ISBN 0-8222-1889-2

Retells the legend of the sixteenth century Prague Rabbi who molds and animates a huge clay figure to protect the Jewish community. 11m 2w 1 setting

Fishelson, David, and Leichter, Aaron

The castle; adaptation by David Fishelson and Aaron Leicher from a dramatization by Max Brod. Dramatists 2003

ISBN 0-8222-1900-X

This adaptation of Kafka's classic work tells the story of a man who decides to fight a monstrous bureaucracy rather than give in to it. 8m 3w 1 exterior setting

Fishermen

Beattie, A. The story of Peter Grimes

Horovitz, I. Barking sharks

Romeril, J. Miss Tanaka

Simpson, B. King Mackerel & the blues are running

Fit to be tried; or, Stepbrothers in crime. Feydeau, G.

Fitzgerald, F. Scott (Francis Scott), 1896-1940

about

Pollock, S. Angel's trumpet

Fitzgerald, Zelda, 1900-1948

about

Pollock, S. Angel's trumpet

Fitzroy, Robert, 1805-1865

about

Wertenbaker, T. After Darwin

Fitzsimmons, Robert Prometheus, 1862 or 3-1917

about

London, J. The birthmark

Five Lesbian Brothers (Theater company)

Brave smiles . . . another lesbian tragedy.

Comedic look at lesbian life. 2 acts 11 scenes 5w 1 setting

In Five Lesbian Brothers. The Five Lesbian Brothers: four plays

Brides of the moon.

Comedy about sex set in 2069. All-women team of astronauts overtaken by technological lust. 2 acts 31 scenes 5w 2 settings

In Five Lesbian Brothers. The Five Lesbian Brothers: four plays

Five Lesbian Brothers (Theater company)—*Continued*

The secretaries.

Black comedy about American images of womanhood focuses on five man-hating lesbian office workers. Prologue 20 scenes 5w 1 setting

In Five Lesbian Brothers. The Five Lesbian Brothers: four plays

Voyage to Lesbos.

Social comedy. Lesbian view of marriage. Music, singing. 20 scenes 5w 1 setting

In Five Lesbian Brothers. The Five Lesbian Brothers: four plays

Flacks, Diane, and Greenblatt, Richard

Sib. Playwrights Canada 2000 75p

ISBN 0-88754-623-4

Expressionistic exploration of relationship between brothers and sisters. Adult siblings deal with parent's estate. Music. 1m 1w 1 interior

Flaming guns of the purple sage. Martin, J.

Flapper!. Francoeur, B.

The **flatted** fifth. Rosenfeld, S. Z.

Flewitt, L.

Is there anybody there? French (London) 1999 34p

ISBN 0-573-12315-2

Murder mystery set in Victorian London about a clairvoyant whose aristocratic client thinks she is possessed by murdered prostitute. 4m 4w settings

"**Flickering** images". Rudolph, K.

Flight. Bulgakov, M.

Flight. Giron, A.

Flight. Lan, D.

Flight from the Mahabarath. Naidoo, M.

The **flight** into Egypt. Wilder, T.

Flight of fancy. Felder, L.

The **flight** of Icarus. McCullough, L. E.

The **flight** of the last Calhoon. Long, Q.

Flights. Cameron, S.

Flippin' in. Chislett, A.

Flirtation. Schnitzler, A.

The **floating** light bulb. Allen, W.

The **flood**. Vogel, L.

Flood warning. Weldon, F.

Floods

Toddie, J. L. And send forth a raven

Floorshow: Doña Sol and her trained dog. Sánchez, E.

Flop cop. Cunninghan, L.

Florence (Italy)

Wilde, O. A Florentine tragedy

A **Florentine** tragedy. Wilde, O.

Flowers. Rivera, J.

Flyer. Aspengren, K.

Flyin' west. Cleage, P.

Fnu Lnu. Wellman, M.

Fo, Dario

About face.

Political farce. Following an accident, Italian business executive has surgery that make him dead ringer for communist worker. Prologue. 2 acts 4 scenes 8m 2w 2 interiors 1 exterior

In Fo, D. We won't pay! We won't pay! and other plays

Archangels don't play pinball.

Satire on govenent bureaucracy. Petty thief mistakenly registered as dog is due to be imprisoned in kennel. 3 acts 12 scenes 7m 3w settings

In Fo, D. We won't pay! We won't pay! and other plays

Elizabeth: almost by chance a woman.

Political farce offering radical interpretation of reign of Elizabeth I. 2 acts 4m 2w 1 setting

In Fo, D. We won't pay! We won't pay! and other plays

We won't pay! We won't pay.

Political farce set in working class suburb of Milan where housewives struggle with inflation and their communist trade unionist husbands. 2 acts 3m 2w 1 interior

In Fo, D. We Won't Pay! We Won't Pay! and other plays

Fob. Hwang, D. H.

Foley, David

Sad hotel. Oberon Bks. 1998 88p

ISBN 1-84002-085-7

Drama about Tennessee Williams, set in his Florida beach house after his career has peaked and focusing on his wrenching breakup with his long-time companion. Variable cast

Folk drama

The Christians and the Moors (Los moros y los cristianos)

The four apparitions of Guadalupe (Las cuatro apariciones de Guadalupe)

Los Matachines unmasked (Los Matachines desenmascarados)

Folk drama—*Continued*

No room at the inn (Las posadas)
The second shepherd's play (Los pastores)
The Three Kings (Los tres Reyes Magos)

Folk medicine

Romero, E. ¡Curanderas! serpents of the clouds
Folk tales for fun. Perez, C.

Folklore

Asher, S. F. The wolf and its shadows
c Barchers, S. I. The white-haired old woman
c Kacmar, K. The oldest story ever told
c McBride-Smith, B. Aaron Kelly is dead!
c McBride-Smith, B. Henny Penny
c McCullough, L. E. A cosmic bouquet: sun, moon and stars
c McCullough, L. E. Squeak and maiow!
c Perez, C. Folk tales for fun
Sills, P. The blue light and other stories
c Swortzell, L. The mischief makers

African

c Barchers, S. I. Why ants carry burdens
Bush, M. Ezigbo, the spirit child
c Mason, T. African tales: Kalulu and his monkey farm and Rumpelstiltskin
Smith, C. Takunda
c Woolfson, M. Bushveld bibble babble

American

c Barchers, S. I. Polly Ann and John Henry
c Barchers, S. I. Sally Ann Thunder and Davey Crockett
c Barchers, S. I. Los tres ratoncitos: a chiste
Jefferson, J. Rip Van Winkle
c McBride-Smith, B. Sody Salleratus
Svich, C. Alchemy of desire/dead-man's blues
c Zeder, S. Wiley and the Hairy Man

Arabian

Francoeur, B. The stories of Scheherazade

Egyptian

c Barchers, S. I. The doomed prince

English

c Barchers, S. I. Dick Whittington and his cat
c Hamlett, C. The magic mermaid
Nigro, D. The sin-eater

Finnish

c Barchers, S. I. The farmer and the animals
c McCullough, L. E. Young Olli and the trolls

French

c Barchers, S. I. Fortunée

French Canadian

Cumming, P. Ti-Jean

German

c Barchers, S. I. The magic table
c McBride-Smith, B. Cat-skins
c McBride-Smith, B. The wolf and the seven kids
c McCullough, L. E. The six swans
c Wolfman, J. The golden goose

Hungarian

c Barchers, S. I. The three wishes

Icelandic

c Barchers, S. I. The shepherd and the troll

Indic

c Barchers, S. I. Princess Sivatra
c Gavin, J. Monkey in the stars
Karnad, G. Hayavadana

Indonesian

c McCullough, L. E. Aruman, hero of Java

Irish

c Barchers, S. I. The bee, the harp, the mouse, and the bum-clock
Conquest, N. The widow's might
MacLiammóir, M. Ill met by moonlight
c McBride-Smith, B. Finn M'Coul
c McCullough, L. E. Una and the goblin king
c Wing, P. The King of Ireland's son

Islamic

Sills, P. Rumi

Italian

c Barchers, S. I. Catherine and her destiny
c Barchers, S. I. The clever daughter
c McCullough, L. E. The magic ring

Japanese

c Barchers, S. I. The peach boy

Folklore—Japanese—*Continued*
c Carlisle, B. The crane wife
Hwang, D. H. The sound of a voice
Liebman, S. The tale of the Mandarin ducks
c Schutzman, S. Round the world tales
Jewish
c Asher, S. F. The wise men of Chelm
Kushner, T. A dybbuk, or between two worlds
c McBride-Smith, B. Hershel and the Hanukkah goblins
c McCullough, L. E. The bird of happiness
c McCullough, L. E. The Golem of Belmont Boulevard
c McCullough, L. E. Nitwits and numskulls: outwitting the oppressor
c McCullough, L. E. Rachel the clever
c McCullough, L. E. Two goats, two sisters, and a beggar king
c McCullough, L. E. The wise men and women of Chelm
Kenyan
c Barchers, S. I. Water, water will be mine
Korean
c Barchers, S. I. Gifts of love
Liberian
c Barchers, S. I. Spider flies to the feast
Maori
c Barchers, S. I. The young chief who played the flute
Micronesian
c Barchers, S. I. The tree that bled fish
Nicaraguan
c Schutzman, S. Round the world tales
Norwegian
c Barchers, S. I. The master-maid
c McBride-Smith, B. The squire's bride
c McBride-Smith, B. Three billy goats gruff: poetry-style
c McCullough, L. E. East of the sun, west of the moon
Russian
c Barchers, S. I. Baba Yaga
c Korty, C. Baba Yaga and the black sunflower
c Lander, A. Vasilisa the fair
c McCullough, L. E. The great flying ship of Ivan the Impossible

c Palmer, G. The falcon
c Paxton, K. Tatyana's golden doe
Scandinavian
Overmyer, E. Alki
Scottish
c Barchers, S. I. Finding the foolish
c Barchers, S. I. The giant in the garden
c Barchers, S. I. Molly Whuppie
y Gollobin, L. B. Selkie
Slovakian
c McCullough, L. E. The twelve months
Spanish
c Barchers, S. I. To the sun, moon, and wind
Swedish
c Schutzman, S. Round the world tales
Ukrainian
c Mason, T. Ukrainian tales
West African
Bush, M. Ezigbo, the spirit child
c McCullough, L. E. The lost spear
West Indian
c Miller, K. S. Island son
Yiddish
c Barchers, S. I. It could always be worse
Zulu
c Scholtz, P. Tokoloshe
Follies. Sondheim, S.

Foon, Dennis
y Chasing the money. Blizzard Pub. 2000 56p
ISBN 0-921368-93-3
High school student addicted to gambling. 1 act 2m 1w settings

Foote, Daisy
Farley and Betsy.
Explores bizzare relationship between brother and sister. 1m 1w 1 interior
In Women's Project & productions; ed. by J. Miles
y When they speak of Rita.
Mother is discontented with her life and can't seem to figure out what is missing. 2 acts 9 scenes 3m 2w 1 interior
In New Plays from A.C.T.'s young conservatory v3

Foote, Horton

The actor.

Set in the depression, young man from Texas decides to become an actor. 5m 5w 1 setting

In New plays; ed. by C. Slaight

The carpetbagger's children. Dramatists 2002

ISBN 0-8222-1843-7

In monologues, three sisters spin a tale of their family and an era. 3w 1 setting

A coffin in Egypt.

Memory play set in 1966 in small Texas town. Ninety-year-old widow looks back on her marriage to wealthy adulterer. 1 act 2w extra 1 interior

In Foote, H. Getting Frankie married—
and afterwards, and other plays

The day Emily married.

Portrait of woman's doomed second marriage in 1956 Texas town. 3 acts 5 scenes 2m 7w 1 interior

In Foote, H. Getting Frankie married—
and afterwards, and other plays

Getting Frankie married—and afterwards.

Domestic drama set in small Texas town in 1990 about illegitimacy, divorce, and land ownership. 2 acts 4 scenes 6m 8w 1 interior

In Foote, H. Getting Frankie married—
and afterwards, and other plays

Laura Dennis.

High school senior in 1938 small Texas town confronts truth about her family's sordid past as she contends with her burgeoning sexuality. 1 act 5m 8w 1 setting

In Foote, H. Getting Frankie married—
and afterwards, and other plays

Tomorrow.

Tragedy. Television play adapted from William Faulkner's short story about shooting in rural area of Deep South. 2 acts 15m 3w extras settings

In Foote, H. Getting Frankie married—
and afterwards, and other plays

Vernon Early. Dramatists 2003 49p

ISBN 0-8222-1691-4

Drama about small town physician and his family in 1950s Texas. 1 act 1b 1g 5m 7w 1 interior

—Same

In Foote, H. Getting Frankie married—
and afterwards, and other plays

Footprints in the sand. Crowther, C.

For the pleasure of seeing her again. Tremblay, M.

For they shall see God. Conquest, N.

For tiger lilies out of season. Green, A.

Forbes, Charles

Courting Prometheus.

Two office workers converse in their cubicles after a night of sex. 1m 1w 1 setting

In Actors Theatre of Louisville. Ten-minute plays: v4

Ford, John

'Tis pity she's a whore.

Jacobean tragedy in verse set in Renaissance Italy. Disastrous consequences follow when young man's incestuous love for his sister is revealed. 5 acts 27 scenes 11m 4w extras

In Renaissance drama; ed. by A. F. Kinney

Forde, Margery

X-stacy. Currency Press 1999 120p il

Brother and sister's involvement in rave scene leads to tragedy. 20 scenes 3m 4w 1 setting

Fore. Gilroy, F. D.

Foreplay; or, The art of the fugue. Ives, D.

Forever is a long time. Fredericks, A. D.

Forgiveness

Foley, D. Sad hotel

Forsten, Myrtle L.

c The sycamore cross.

Easter worship program based on traditional folk tale. Stump of sycamore tree used for cross miraculously sprouts new shoot following Christ's resurrection. 1 act Variable cast 9 characters extras

In The drama of Easter; ed. by R. Wray

Fortunée. Barchers, S. I.

Fortune's fool. Poulton, M.

Forty-deuce. Bowne, A.

Forty-minute finish. Hairston, J.

Fosbrook, Michael

Figuring things. French (London) 1999 32p

ISBN 0-573-12205-9

Comedy. Man endangers his marriage when he befriends first female member of his cricket statisticians circle. 2m 2w 3 interiors

Fosbrook, Michael—*Continued*

Remembering things. French (London) 2001 25p

ISBN 0-573-12252-0

Comedy about forgetful elderly lady who thinks she has been robbed. 1m 2w 1 setting

Foster, Norm

Ethan Claymore. Playwrights Canada 1998 96p

ISBN 0-88754-581-5

Christmas drama. Reclusive Canadian egg farmer is visted by recently deceased older brother and meets woman who could turn his life around. 2 acts 7 scenes 1b 4m 1w 1 interior

The foursome. Playwrights Canada 1998 128p

ISBN 0-88754-582-3   LC 00-456850

Comedy about four former college friends who play a round of golf at their fifteen year reunion. 2 acts 19 scenes 4m 1 setting

Office hours. Playwrights Canada 1996 88p

ISBN 0-88754-541-6

Comedy. Six different stories unfold in six different offices at same time. 6 scenes Variable cast 17 characters

Foster children

Beevers, G. George Eliot's Silas Marner

The **four** apparitions of Guadalupe (Las cuatro apariciones de Guadalupe); tr. by Larry Torres.

Folk drama in rhyme about a Mexican Indian and his encounters with the Virgin Mary (Our Lady of Guadalupe) and the local archbishop. Bilingual edition. Music. 12 scenes 2b 3m 1w settings

In Six nuevomexicano folk dramas for Advent season

The **four** lives of Marie. Fréchette, C.

Four-play. Smith, C.

Four portraits—of mothers. Wesker, A.

Four walls. Edwards, G.

Fourplay. Belbel, S.

The **foursome**. Foster, N.

The **fourth** sister. Głowacki, J.

The **fourth** wall. Gurney, A. R.

Fox, Amy

Summer cyclone. Dramatists 2002

ISBN 0-8222-1835-6

A woman artist in her thirties joins a clinical drug study where an idealistic medical student awakens her to a romance she finds both exciting and frightening. 3m 3w 1 setting

Foxton, David

Breakfast for one. French (London) 2002 24p

ISBN 0-573-02356-5

A comedy of mistaken identities, set in Paris in 1895. Singing, dancing. 1 act 3m 2w 1 interior

Francesca da Rimini. Boker, G. H.

Francis, of Assisi, Saint

about

Wilder, T. Brother Fire

Francis, Juliana

Box.

Young woman working in porn booth performs for customers. 1w extras 1 interior

In Women's Project & productions; ed. J. Miles

Francis, Matthew

The adventures of Huckleberry Finn. French (London) 1998 94p

ISBN 0-573-01779-4

Dramatization of Twain's classic adventure tale set along the Mississippi River. Music. 2 acts 45 scenes Prologue 22m 8w settings

y David Copperfield. French (London) 1999 110p

ISBN 0-573-01775-1

Based on Charles Dicken's semi-autobiographical novel, follows adventure of young man over span of three decades. 2 acts 52 scenes Large mixed cast

Francis, Saxon

y Body and soul; [by] Richard Tolloch; music by Saxon Francis. Currency Press 1998 104p

ISBN 0-26819-558-8

Musical comedy about young athletes from all over Australia training at Challenge C for shot at 2000 Olympics. 7b 6g 1m 2w extras 1 setting

Francis Brick needs no introduction. Hoffman, J.

Francoeur, Bill

c Babes in Toyland; book by R. J. Ryland; music and lyrics by Bill Francoeur. Pioneer Drama Service 2002 59p

Christmas musical set in Mother Goose Land and Toyland. 2 acts 3 scenes Variable cast 19 characters 1 interior

c Bah, humbug!; Scrooge's Christmas carol; book by Rebecca Ryland; music and lyrics by Bill Francoeur. Pioneer Drama Service 2000 47p

Musical version of Dickens's holiday classic. Variable cast 27 characters 1 interior

Charleston!; book by Tim Kelly, music and lyrics by Bill Francoeur. Pioneer Drama Service 1999 55p

Musical comedy of the 1920s. Shorter version of Flapper! Prologue 10 scenes 11m 21w settings

c Cinderella's glass slipper; book by Vera Morris; music and lyrics by Bill Francoeur. Pioneer Drama Service 2001 52p

Musical version of Perrault's fairy tale. 2 acts 3 scenes Variable cast 2 interiors

y DiscoKnights; book by Rachel Davidson; music and lyrics by Bill Francoeur. Pioneer Drama Service 2001 45p

Disco musical set in 1970s, originally produced with title Friday knight fever. High school students gather at roller rink for results of principal of the year contest. 5 scenes Large mixed cast 1 interior

c Enchanted Sleeping Beauty; the legend of Briar-Rose; book by Vera Morris; music and lyrics by Bill Francoeur. Pioneer Drama Service 1999 56p

Prince must fight wall of thorns and the Dark Knight to rescue princess from enchantment. Prologue 2 acts 7 scenes 7m 18w 1 setting

Flapper!; A madcap musical comedy tribute to the 1920s; book by Tim Kelly; music and lyrics by Bill Francoeur. Pioneer Drama Service 1999 72p

Musical comedy set in Southampton, Long Island in 1920s. Young girl thwarts jewel thieves, saves aunt from confidence scheme and becomes star of Ziegfeld Follies. 2 acts 14 scenes 11m 21w 1 setting

y Friday night fever; book by Rachael Davidson; music and lyrics by Bill Francoeur. Pioneer Drama Service 2001 60p

Musical adaptation of Rachel Davidson's comedy tribute to 1970s 2 acts 6 scenes 13m 19w extras 1 interior

y Going. . .going. . .gone with the breeze; book by Tim Kelly; music & lyrics by Bill Francoeur. Pioneer Drama Service 1994 47p

First produced as two-act musical 1994 with title: Gone with the breeze. Musical comedy. Complications arise as studio prepares to film bestselling novel. 10 scenes 8m 19w extras 1 setting

y Groovy!; book by Tim Kelly; music and lyrics by Bill Francoeur. Pioneer Drama Service 1998 64p

Musical celebrating the hippies and flower children attending 1960s music festival. Prologue 2 acts 11m 16w extras 1 exterior

y Kokonut Island; book by Tim Kelly; music and lyrics by Bill Francoeur. Pioneer Drama Service 2000 56p

Shorter version of Kokonut kapers. Musical comedy set on island about private high school, a crime syndicate, and ghost of Captain Kidd. Prologue 9 scenes 10m 19w extras 1 exterior

y Kokonut kapers; book by Tim Kelly; music and lyrics by Bill Francoeur. Pioneer Drama Service 2000 80p

Musical comedy set on island off Florida's coast. To raise money islanders open private high school. Prologue 2 acts 10 scenes 11m 20w extras 1 exterior

y Oh, horrors! It's murder!; book by Billy St. John; music and lyrics by Bill Francoeur. Pioneer Drama Service 1999 68p

Musical audience participation. Noted Egyptologist murdered during museum lecture. 2 acts 12 scenes 7m 8w extras 1 interior

y Rock around the block; book by Tim Kelly; music and lyrics by Bill Francoeur. Pioneer Drama Service 1997 56p

First produced with title The Nifty Fifties. High school girl pledges to deliver rock star for school dance. 8 scenes 9m 10w extra 1 interior

Francoeur, Bill—*Continued*

c Sleepy Hollow; book by Vera Morris; music and lyrics by Bill Francoeur. Pioneer Drama Service 67 67p

Musical version of Washington Irving's ghostly tale of superstitious schoolmaster. 2 acts 11 scenes 8m 10w extras 1 setting

The stories of Scheherazade; book by Susan Pargman; music and lyrics by Bill Francoeur. Pioneer Drama Service 2001 54p

Musical based on legend of greatest storyteller of ancient Arabian world. 2 acts 7 scenes 6m 17w extras 1 interior 1 exterior

c The story of Hansel and Gretel; book by Vera Morris; music and lyrics by Bill Francoeur. Pioneer Drama Service 1998 59p

Musical version of Grimm Fairy tale. Girl outsmarts witch and releases brother and other children from spell. 2 acts 6 scenes Variable cast 18 characters extras settings

Sunset trail; or, Norma's desperate to get back to the boulevard; music and lyrics by Bill Francoeur. Pioneer Drama Service 1998 63p

Spoof of Sunset Boulevard set in Old West. Eccentric actress runs hotel and dreams of comeback. Prologue 2 acts 5 scenes 7m 11w extras 1 interior

c Tiny Thumbelina; book by Vera Morris; music and lyrics by Bill Francoeur. Pioneer Drama Service 1999 56p

Musical dramatization of Hans Christian Andersen tale about tiny girl and her animal friends. Prologue 2 acts 9 scenes Variable cast 20 characters extras 1 setting

y Way out west in a dress; or, Life's a hurdle when you're wearing a girdle; book by Billy St. John; music and lyrics by Bill Francoeur. Pioneer Drama Service 2002 69p

Musical version of Billy St. John melodrama. Adventures of acting troupe in old west. 2 acts 12 scenes 11m 10m extras settings

c Wonderland!; book by James Devita; music and lyrics by Bill Francoeur. Pioneer Drama Service 2002 68p

Musical version of James Devita's Looking Glass Land. Loosely based on Lewis Carroll's Through the looking glass. Young girl' adventures in fantastic land. 2 acts Variable cast 1 setting

Françoise. McAvera, B.

Frank, Anne, 1929-1945

about

Hochwälder, F. Orders
Kops, B. Dreams of Anne Frank
Frank Langella's Cyrano. Langella, F.

Frankel, Robert

c Jurassic Park and Wreck. Pioneer Drama Service 2001 46p

Comedy about princess who hides out at tottering auto parts business. 2 acts 5m 14w extras 1 exterior

Strange happenings. Pioneer Drama Service 1998 38p

Four Twilight zone type tales of extraterrestrials and supernatural phenomena. Music. 2 preludes 2 acts 4 scenes Variable cast 28 characters 2 interiors

WhoDunit. . .and to whom? Pioneer Drama Service 1999 52p

As third rate mystery author writes novel his characters appear on stage. 2 acts Variable cast 19 characters 1 interior

WhoDunit. . .and who's the big idea anyway? Pioneer Drama Service 2000 63p

Spoof of classic gumshoe story. Plodding mystery author's characters appear as thought forms on stage. 2 acts 6m 8w extras 1 interior

Frankenstein. Barchers, S. I., and Kroll, J. L.

Franklin, Benjamin

about

c McCullough, L. E. Everyday science in Ben Franklin's America

Franklin, John, 1786-1847

about

MacEwen, G. Terror and Erebus

Frankonis, W.A.

The killings tale. French 2002 91p
ISBN 0-573-62790-8

Mystery about murders at the Globe theater in London, England in 1606 with multiple suspects, including William Shakespeare. 2 acts 16 scenes 1b 12m 3w settings

c A tale of Cinderella. French 2002 71p
ISBN 0-573-62798-3

Frankonis, W.A.—*Continued*

A musical version of the Grimm Brothers' tale, set in Venice and featuring a spirited young heroine. Songs by Will Severin and George David Weiss. Music, singing, dancing. 2 acts 1g 5m 6w extras 1 interior 2 exterior

Fraser, Brad

Poor Superman.

A bitter quarrel between a gay man and his straight woman friend. 1 scene 1m 1w 1 setting

In Short spells: scenes & monologues; ed. by V. Shantz

Snake in fridge. NeWest Press 2001 153p
ISBN 1-896300-27-8

Drama set in large rooming house about group of twenty-somethings on the edge of porn industry. 2 acts 85 scenes 5m 4w 1 setting

Fraud

Baitz, J. R. Mizlansky/Zilinsky
Davis, T. Lawyers, guns, & money
Gates, T. Ladies who lunch
Gore, C. Modern honor; or, The sharper in high life
Kushner, T. East coast ode to Howard Jarvis: a little teleplay in tiny monologues
McConnell, J. The guilt card
McConnell, J. Last post
Nigro, D. Seance

Frayn, Michael

Alarms & excursions. French (London) 2000 131p
ISBN 0-573-01808-1

Four old friends sit down for a quiet evening together. But they are harassed by various bells, sirens, buzzers, warblers, beepers and cheepers, all trying to warn them of something. 2 acts 8 scenes 2m 2w 1 interior

—Same. Methuen 1998 130p
ISBN 0-413-73280-0

Copenhagen. Anchor Bks. 2000 132p
ISBN 0-385-72079-3   LC 00-55814

Drama about the 1941 meeting in Copenhagen, Denmark between physicists Niels Bohr and Werner Heisenberg. 2 acts 2m 1w 1 interior

—Same. French 2000 113p
ISBN 0-573-62752-5   LC 00-55814

Copenhagen (condensation).

In The Best Plays of 1999-2000; ed. by Otis L. Guernsey, Jr.

Here.

Drama about responsibility and decision-making. Two people move into empty room and began to construct life together. 2 acts 5 scenes 1m 2w 1 interior

In Frayn, M. Plays: 3

Now you know.

Everyone has something to hide in comedy based on author's novel about London freedom-of-information pressure group. 2 acts 4 scenes 4m 4w 1 setting

In Frayn, M. Plays: 3

The **freak** (George). Ehn, E.
Freakish times. Morizono, L.-J.

Fréchette, Carole

Elisa's skin.

Young woman tells delicate tales of love. 1 act 1w 1 setting

In Frechette, C. Three plays

The four lives of Marie.

Account of woman's life, from age 11 to death, told in four elliptical Tableaux. Prologue 4 scenes Variable cast 9 characters

In Frechette, C. Three plays

Seven days in the life of Simon Labrosse.

Comedy. Play within a play. Earnest, unemployed young man invites public to witness scenes from his life. 2m 1w

In Frechette, C. Three plays

Fred and Madge. Orton, J.

Fredericks, Anthony D.

c Across the new frontier.

Fourth year that group of travelers is journeying across new frontier. Variable cast 8 characters

In Fredericks, A. D. Science Fiction Readers theatre

c Air to breathe, water to drink.

Explanation of ecological issues. Variable cast 6 characters

In Fredericks, A. D. Readers theatre for American history

c Alien teacher.

Teacher from another world. Variable cast 8 characters

In Fredericks, A. D. Science Fiction Readers theatre

Fredericks, Anthony D.—*Continued*

c All the knowledge in the universe.

One small pill contains all knowledge in the universe. Variable cast 5 characters

In Fredericks, A. D. Science Fiction Readers theatre

c Artifact.

Scientists on distant planet discover ancient artifact. Variable cast 8 characters

In Fredericks, A. D. Science Fiction Readers theatre

c A bowl of soup, a piece of bread.

Scene in 1933 Chicago soup kitchen. Variable cast 7 characters

In Fredericks, A. D. Readers theatre for American history

c Bubble trouble.

Communication between humans and aliens. Variable cast 7 characters

In Fredericks, A. D. Science Fiction Readers theatre

c Columbus pleads his case.

Columbus tries to convince King Ferdinand and Queen Isabel to finance his voyage. Variable cast 4 characters

In Fredericks, A. D. Readers theatre for American history

c A conversation with Thomas Jefferson.

Reporters conduct interview with America's third president. Variable cast 5 characters

In Fredericks, A. D. Readers theatre for American history

c A day in Mesa Verde.

Portrays Anasazi family in 13 A.D. Variable cast 5 characters

In Fredericks, A. D. Readers theatre for American history

c December 1, 1955: Montgomery, Alabama.

Rosa Parks refuses to move to back of bus in 1955 Montgomery. Variable cast 10 characters

In Fredericks, A. D. Readers theatre for American history

c December 7, 1941: aboard the USS Arizona.

Japanese surprise attack on Pearl Harbor. Variable cast 8 characters

In Fredericks, A. D. Readers theatre for American history

c The delegates speak out.

The constitutional convention of 1787. Variable cast 7 characters

In Fredericks, A. D. Readers theatre for American history

c Do it yourself!.

Play designed to allow students to create their own science fiction script. Variable cast 6 characters

In Fredericks, A. D. Science Fiction Readers theatre

c Driving the final spike.

Two railroad lines meet at Promontory Point, Utah on May 10, 1869. Variable cast 7 characters

In Fredericks, A. D. Readers theatre for American history

c Eight days, three hours, and eighteen minutes.

Apollo 11 lands on moon. Variable cast 5 characters

In Fredericks, A. D. Readers theatre for American history

c Equal Rights Amendment.

Debate over adding Equal Rights Amendment to U. S. constitution. Variable cast 10 characters

In Fredericks, A. D. Readers theatre for American history

c Forever is a long time.

Price must be paid for immortality. Variable cast 8 characters

In Fredericks, A. D. Science Fiction Readers theatre

c Heads/tails.

Scientists examine samples gathered by explorers of mysterious planet. Variable cast 4 characters

In Fredericks, A. D. Science Fiction Readers theatre

c I am Slime.

Individual characteristics are isolated and converted to slime. Variable cast 4 characters

In Fredericks, A. D. Science Fiction Readers theatre

c I scream, you scream, we all scream for ice cream.

Ice cream is something quite different to interplanatory visitors. Variable cast 6 characters

In Fredericks, A. D. Science Fiction Readers theatre

Fredericks, Anthony D.—*Continued*

c An imaginary discussion.

Explorers of North America discuss their voyages and explorations. Variable cast 10 characters

In Fredericks, A. D. Readers theatre for American history

c Into, beyond, and back again.

Future travel measured in microseconds. Variable cast 6 characters

In Fredericks, A. D. Science Fiction Readers theatre

c It's in the bag.

Strange life form found in bag. Variable cast 4 characters

In Fredericks, A. D. Science Fiction Readers t5eatre

c The Jovian pact.

Colonists about to land on Jupiter establish form of government. Variable cast 9 characters

In Fredericks, A. D. Science Fiction Readers theatre

c Just a thought.

Machine has ability to read subconscious thoughts. Variable cast 8 characters

In Fredericks, A. D. Science Fiction Readers theatre

c The last decision.

Earth is dying and an important decision must be made. Who will go to a distant world to begin a new colony? Variable cast 10 characters extra

In Fredericks, A. D. Science Fiction Readers theatre

c Leif Eriksson discovers Vinland.

Viking explorer Leif Eriksson visits North American continent around 1000 A.D. Variable cast 6 characters

In Fredericks, A. D. Readers theatre for American history

c Long hours, long days.

Drama about Industrial Revolution of late 1800s. Variable cast 5 characters

In Fredericks, A. D. Readers theatre for American history

c A long, long time.

Future utopia. Variable cast 7 characters

In Fredericks, A. D. Science Fiction Readers theatre

c March 1917: in a coffee shop.

Five characters discuss America's entry into World War I. Variable cast 7 characters

In Fredericks, A. D. Readers theatre for American history

c The masters of all.

Computers vs. human brain. Variable cast 6 characters

In Fredericks, A. D. Science Fiction Readers theatre

c A matter of survival.

Group of nomads is attempting to eke out an existence in harsh and bitter land. Variable cast 7 characters

In Fredericks, A. D. Science Fiction Readers theatre

c The Mayflower Compact.

Group of 101 men and women set sail for Virginia in 1620. Variable cast 8 characters

In Fredericks, A. D. Readers theatre for American history

c Me, myself, and I.

Play set in future when clones are a reality. Variable cast 4 characters

In Fredericks, A. D. Science Fiction Readers theatre

c Mission San Juan Capistrano.

In 1776 Roman Catholic missionary Junipero Serra establishes mission in California. Variable cast 6 characters

In Fredericks, A. D. Readers theatre for American history

c Once upon a time.

Martians land on Earth. Variable cast 4 characters extra

In Fredericks, A. D. Science Fiction Readers theatre

c One day in Gettysburg.

Lincoln delivers his famous address at consecration of cemetery. Variable cast 20 characters

In Fredericks, A. D. Readers theatre for American history

c A right to vote.

Drama about woman's suffrage movement. Variable cast 5 characters

In Fredericks, A. D. Readers theatre for American history

Fredericks, Anthony D.—*Continued*

c The Shapiros' new adventure.

Family of Russian Jews emigrates to America in 1892. Variable cast 5 characters

In Fredericks, A. D. Readers theatre for American history

c Two soldiers: talking, dying.

Drama about American participation in Vietnam War. 3 scenes Variable cast 5 characters

In Fredericks, A. D. Readers theatre for American history

c With the McMillans on the Oregon Trail.

Pioneer family on journey west. Variable cast 7 characters

In Fredericks, A. D. Readers theatre for American history

Freed, Amy

The psychic life of savages.

Drama about transformative power of art loosely based on lives and writings of several major poets. 3 acts 22 scenes 3m 4w settings

In Plays from Woolly Mammoth; ed. by R. alexander and M. Kyrioglou

Free's point. Adams, P.

French, David

y That summer. Talon 2000 128p

ISBN 0-88922-439-0

Drama set in rural Ontario cottage. Woman watches her younger self relive innocence and beauty of earlier enchanted summer. 3g 2m 2w settings

French Canadians

y Chislett, A. Then and now

Christenson, J. Elephant wake

French drama

17th century

Marowitz, C. Quack

Molière. The affected damsels

Molière. The bourgeois gentleman

Molière. The bungler

Molière. The doctor despite himself

Molière. Don Juan

Molière. The hypochondriac

Molière. The misanthrope

Molière. The miser

Molière. The miser (short edition)

Molière. Such foolish affected ladies

Molière. Tartuffe

Molière. Those learned ladies

Racine, J. The suitors

18th century

Marivaux, P. C. de C. de. Changes of heart

Marivaux, P. C. de C. de. The game of love and chance

Marivaux, P. C. de C. de. The triumph of love

Freud, Sigmund, 1856-1939

about

Johnson, T. Hysteria; or, Fragments of an analysis of an obsessional neurosis

Schmitt, E.-E. The visitor

Wilson, S. Sabina

Freya's golden necklace. McCullough, L. E.

Fricker, Gail

Buttonholes in silk.

Woman enlists grandmother's help when she returns to England from Canada hoping to end estrangement from mother. Slide projections. 3 scenes 3w 1 setting

In Seven short plays from Theatre Ontario

Frida: the story of Frida Kahlo. Cruz, M., and Blecher, H.

Friday night fever. Francoeur, B.

Friedman, Gary William

The last supper; a musical enactment; music and vocal arrangements by Gary William Friedman; book and lyrics by Thomas Mitz; based on an original concept by Andy Krey. French 1999 31p

ISBN 0-573-62708-8

Inspirational musical. Angel/muse inspires Leonardo Da Vinci to invoke the Apostles so he can paint their last meal with Jesus. 14m 3w extras

Friel, Brian

Give me your answer, do. Dramatists 2002

ISBN 0-8222-1748-1

The play is set in the home of an impoverished Irish novelist and his wife whose lives are overshadowed by their permanently hospitalized daughter. 4m 5w 1 exterior setting

Friel, Brian—*Continued*

Three sisters. Dramatists 2000 92p
  ISBN 0-8222-1749-X

Life of the intelligentsia in 19th century Russia reflected in unhappy lives of a Moscow family stranded (financially) in a small provincial city. 4 acts 9m 5w 2 interiors 1 exterior

The Yalta game. Gallery Press 2001 36p
  ISBN 1-85235-302-3; 1-85235-301-5

Based on a theme in Chekhov's Lady with the lapdog. Two lonely people meet in Yalta, and fantasize about lives of other holiday-makers. 1m 1w 1 setting

A **friend** from high school. Bishop, C., and Fuller, E.

Friendship

Badlam, R. Slop-culture
Baker, J. Male bondage
Barry, P. J. Jump the train at Riverpoint
Benfield, D. Second time around
Bishop, C. Success
Bitterman, S. The price
Brown, V. N. Roadtrip
Cameron, S. Flights
Celesia, C. Anything for you
Chernoff, M. Chaim's love song
c Clark, A. The red balloon
Cleage, P. Blues for an Alabama sky
Congdon, C. Dog opera
Cruz, N. Night train to Bolina
Davis, T. Lawyers, guns, & money
del Valle, J. A. Fuchsia
Elyot, K. The day I stood still
Enright, N. Spurboard
Epstein, D. Exact change
c Espinosa, R. Where did they go? Where did I put them? (A donde se fueron? Donde las puse yo?)
Foster, N. The foursome
Fraser, B. Poor Superman
Ganguli, U. Rudali
Gilbert, S. The birth of Casper G. Schmidt
Gilroy, F. D. Dreams of glory
Gilroy, F. D. A way with words
Gilroy, F. D. Who'll save the plowboy?
Godber, J. It started with a kiss
Goldberg, J. Stuck
Grant, D. M. Snakebit
Hedges, P. Chicken potential
Henley, B. Am I blue

Hewett, R. Goodbye Mrs. Blore
Jordan, J. Mpls., St. Paul
Katims, J. The man who couldn't dance
Keeffe, B. Barbarians: killing time
Kramer, S. Hold for three
Kyle, C. Plunge
Levi, S. Cherry and Little Banjo
Linney, R. Stars
Lochhead, L. Perfect days
Margulies, D. Dinner with friends
Margulies, D. Joey
Margulies, D. Women in motion
c Martini, C. The field
McLean, L. Riddance
Miller, M. Ferris wheel
Mori, B. Adult fiction
Nelson, G. Speak
O'Donnell, S. Because I want to say
Pelfrey, M. Drive angry
Penhall, J. Love and Understanding
Posner, A. The chosen
Real, C. The battle of Bull Run always makes me cry
Reynolds, J. Physical therapy
Reza, Y. Art
Rivera, J. 187
c Robinette, J. Charlotte's web
Rosenfeld, S. Z. The flatted fifth
Ross, B. Little by little
Shanley, J. P. Welcome to the moon
Shearer, J. Georgia
Sheppard, J. Whatever
Sherman, J. The League of Nathans
Smith, V. Meow
Son, D. Stop kiss
Stamos, D. G. The unintended video
Stinson, J. Median
Tattersall, C. The last dance
Thatcher, K. Among friends
Thompson, J. Perfect pie
Tricker, G. Life support
Vogelstein, C. All about Al
Washburn, A. The intervention
Wells, M. L. Real real gone
White, E. N. Millennium 7
Wilhelm, L. The parrot
Wilhelm, L. Tremulous
Williams, R. Lift off
Williams, R. The No Boys Cricket Club
Williamson, D. Money and friends
Wilner, S. Labor Day

Friendship—*Continued*
  Wilson, L. Your everyday ghost story
  Wiltse, D. Otis proposes
c Wood, D. Tom's midnight garden
  Woods, S. Trips
  Yew, C. Scissors

Frisby, Terence
  Funny about love. French (London) 2002
    74p
    ISBN 0-573-01961-4
  Comedy set in London. Romance blossoms when
  woman and the husband of her ex-husband's mistress plot revenge. 2 acts 5 scenes 2m 2w 1 interi-
  or

Frockt, Deborah Lynn
y The book of Ruth.
  Teenager in Terezin concentration camp is com-
  forted by grandmother's recipes. 2 acts 3m 2w 1
  setting
    In Seattle Children's Theatre v2
  Hard-boiled.
  Male co-workers react to woman's promotion.
  2m 1w 1 interior
    In 30 ten-minute plays for 3 actors
        from Actors Theatre of
        Louisville's National Ten-minute
        Play Contest
The **frog** in all of us. Adamson-Klein, T.
The **frog** princess. Howard, C.
Frogs. Aristophanes
From above. Donaghy, T.
From both hips. O'Rowe, M.
From cool to fool. Vogel, L.
From dream to ash. Fenton, E.
Fronteras Americanas (American borders).
    Verdecchia, G.

Frontier and pioneer life
y Barchers, S. I. The luck of Roaring
    Camp
  Cleage, P. Flyin' west
  Cook, P. The saga of the golden horse-
    shoe
y Davidson, R. The Pony Express
y Davidson, R. The vile veterinarian
c Ellis, D. The three little pigs out west
y Francoeur, B. Way out west in a dress
c Fredericks, A. D. With the McMillans on
    the Oregon Trail
y Gieschen, C. How the West was Dun

  Henley, B. Abundance
y Kelly, T. The snake in the grass
y Kelly, T. Sundown Alley
  Kopit, A. L. Indians
  London, J. Scorn of women
y Murray, S. Inspector Incognito and the
    Kansas City Kid
  Norman, M. The holdup
  Scott, G. A town called Shame
y St. John, B. Holder Posey, the felonious
    photographer
y St. John, B. Taming the wild, wild West
    in a dress
  Woodford, K. Cactus Pass

Frost, Helen, and Cocks, Harvey
y Why darkness seems so light; by Helen
    Frost and Harvey Cocks. Pioneer
    Drama Service 1999 36p
  Drama based on writings of Fort Wayne, Indiana
  high school students. Scenes depict effects of violence on teens and their families. Prologue 9
  scenes 5 segues Variable cast
Fruit cocktail. Miller, T.
The **fruit** machine. Drader, B.

Fry, Christopher
  A ringing of bells. French (London) 2000
    13p
    ISBN 0-573-12207-5
  Fantasy about a couple, Adam and Eve, who
  come upon a hotel on the Millennium New Year's
  Eve, located in Elstow, birthplace of author John
  Bunyan. 4m 2w 1 setting
  A yard of sun. Dramatists 1999 100p
    ISBN 0-8222-1641-8
  Set in Siena, Italy in 1946. Drama about two
  families before and during the Palio horse race. 2
  acts 9m 3w 1 setting

Fry, Garry
c Lockie Leonard, scumbuster. Currency
    Press 2000 77p
    ISBN 0-86819-608-8
  Dramatization of Tim Winton's novel. When
  Australian Lockie wipes out on huge wave he be-
  friends head banger who joins him in his crusade
  to clean up pollution and make it safe to surf
  again. 20 scenes 3m 2w 1 setting
Fuchsia. del Valle, J. A.
Fucking A. Parks, S.-L.
Fuddy meers. Lindsay-Abaire, D.

Fugard, Athol

The captain's tiger. French 1999 64p
ISBN 1-55936-164-6

Drama. A mother's portrait come to life and an illiterate ship's mechanic both help a young sailor write his first novel and understand his emotions. 15 scenes 2m 1w 1 setting

—Same. Theatre Communications Group 1999 64p
ISBN 1-55936-164-6

Sorrows and rejoicings. French 2002 42p
ISBN 0-573-629919-9   LC 2001-45683

Allegorical drama set in South Africa. After Afikaner poet's funeral, his white academic wife confronts black servant who bore him a daughter. 1m 3w 1 interior

Fugard, Athol, and others

Sizwe Bansi is dead.

Set in Port Elizabeth, South Africa. Man assumes identity of dead man in order to earn a living. 3m 1 setting

In Modern African drama; ed. by B. Jeyifo

Fugitive kind. Williams, T.

Fulfilling Koch's postulate. Schenkar, J.

Fulford, R. W.

Gulag.

Sequel to Steel kiss. Four gay bashers qualify for parole but when they return to community things end violently. 38 scenes 4m 1w

In Fulford, R. Faggot!

Steel kiss.

Play about 1985 Toronto murder of gay librarian by group of drunken high school students. 36 scences 4m

In Fulford, R. Faggot!

Full bloom. Bradbeer, S.

The **full** Monty. Yazbek, D.

Fuller, Henry Blake

At Saint Judas's.

Symbolist one-act play of unrequited love set in church. Best man confesses his love for groom. 2m extras 1 interior

In Lovesick; ed. by L. Senelick

Fully committed. Mode, B.

Funeral home. Long, Q.

The **funeral** play. Rebeck, T.

Funeral rites and ceremonies

Bonel, W. Good grief, Lolita

Farquhar, R. Dust to dust
Ganguli, U. Rudali
Gersten-Vassilaros, A. Rescue at the moment of death
Henley, B. The wake of Jamey Foster
Hodges, A. Life goes on
Hoffman, J. Francis Brick needs no introduction
Kushner, T. Reverse transcription
c McCullough, L. E. Isaac Newton's poetry of the rainbow
McKee, J. Invitation to a funeral
Nigro, D. The sin-eater
Palmieri, M. Makin' sense of nothin'
Radano, L.-M. The divine child
Rebeck, T. The funeral play
Reingold, J. Dottie and Richie
Reitz, D. Mathematics
Reza, Y. Conversation after a burial
Roth, A. Jeffrey Slugworth: ex-embalmer
Sagal, P. Milton Bradley
Sandler, S. The burial society
Turlish, S. Lafferty's wake
Wein, G. Grandma Sylvia's funeral
Williamson, D. The great man
Yellow Robe, W. S. Sneaky
Yourgrau, T. Cries from the cockpit

Funny about love. Frisby, T.

A **funny** thing happened on the way to the forum. Sondheim, S.

Funnyhouse of a Negro. Kennedy, A.

Fur. Cruz, M.

Furies

Aeschylus. The Eumenides

Fusco, Coco, and Bustamante, María Teresa

Stuff.

Satirical revue about Latin women, food, and sex—cultural consumption, as practiced by North Americans and Europeans. Audience participation. Music, singing, dancing. Prologue 1 act 2 scenes 1m 2w extras 1 setting

In Out of the fringe; ed. by C. Svich and M. T. Marrero

Fuson, Deni

y All the king's horses. French 1999 56p
ISBN 0-573-62706-1

Fuson, Deni—*Continued*
Drama. Four idealistic high school girls set out to inspire hope by writing poetry on restroom walls. 3 acts 5 scenes 6m 7w 2 interiors

Futcher, Michael, and Howard, Helen
A beautiful life; Michael Futcher and Helen Howard. Currency Press 2000 102p il
ISBN 0-86819-605-3   LC 00-421095
Political drama about totalitarianism and prejudices. Iranian immigrants in Canberra, Australia arrested on terrorism charges. 6m 2w extras

Future
Ayckbourn, A. Comic potential
De Groen, A. The woman in the window
Dempsey, S. Armagideon
Henley, B. Signature
Morizono, L.-J. Freakish times
Overmyer, E. On the verge; or, The geography of yearning
Rogers, A. The life before/reconstruction/ reconstructing whiteness
c Thwaite, E. Future perfect
Future perfect. Thwaite, E., and Sanderson, B.
Futz. Owens, R.

G

G. David Schine in Hell. Kushner, T.

Gabre-Medhin, Tsegaye
Collision of altars.
Four religions compete for control of an ancient Ethiopian kingdom, hastening its decline. Speaking chorus. 3 acts 8 scenes 12m 3w extras 1 setting
    In Modern African drama; ed. by B. Jeyifo
Gaby. McAvera, B.

Gadea, William
Brothers.
Comedy about man who meets woman through personals, but takes her home to date his brother. 2m 1w 1 setting
    In Off-Off Broadway Festival plays, 22nd ser.

Gage, Carolyn
Harriet Tubman visits a therapist.
Therapist tries to dissuade the slave Harriet Tubman from attempting escape but ultimately provides advice on how to do it. Singing. 1 act 2w 1 interior
    In Off-Off Broadway Festival plays, 23rd ser.
Gaines, Ernest J., 1933-
A lesson before dying (dramatization) See Linney, R. A lesson before dying
Galas. Ludlam, C.

Gale, Lorena
Angélique. Playwrights Canada 2000 76p
ISBN 0-88754-585-8   LC 00-340060
Drama about slavery set in 1700s Montreal. 2 acts 42 scenes 4m 3w 1 setting
—Same
    In Testifyin' v2; ed. by D. Sears

Gallagher, Dick
Howard Crabtree's when pigs fly; the side splitting musical extravaganza; conceived by Howard Crabtree and Mark Waldrop; sketches and lyrics by Mark Waldrop; music by Dick Gallagher with Stanley Bojarski (et al.). French 1999 66p
ISBN 0-573-62331-7
Musical about a man who stages a gay revue. Prologue 2 acts 5m 1 interior

Gallagher, Mary
Brother.
Brother and sister meet after long separation. 1m 1w 1 setting
    In take ten; ed. by E. Lane and N. Shengold

Windshook. Dramatists 1998 59p
ISBN 0-8222-1596-9   LC 98-158686
Catskills farm family faces consequences from sale of family farm. 5m 4w 1 setting

Galton, Frances

Nothing in the world like it.

Drama about pregnant college junior, her senior boyfriend, and sympathetic cafeteria worker. 1 act 1 m 2w 1 interior

   In Off-Off Broadway festival plays, 24th ser.

Gambling

y Foon, D. Chasing the money

Gilroy, F. D. The golf ball

Gilroy, F. D. The only game in town

Gore, C. Modern honor; or, The sharper in high life

Meyer, M. The mystery of attraction

A **game** of inches. Griffiths, L.

The **game** of love and chance. Marivaux, P. C. de C. de

Game theory. Sagal, P.

Gangs

Alexander, R. A preface to the alien garden

Prichard, R. Yard gal

y Romer, M. Rumble fish

Upton, J. Ashes and sand

Ganguli, Usha

Rudali.

After a lifetime of toil for others, a poor woman, left alone in old age, becomes a professional mourner. Music, singing. 1 act 12 scenes Large mixed cast settings

   In DramaContemporary: India; ed. by E. B. Mee

Gao Xingjian

Bus stop.

Symbolic drama with realistic characterization-Group of people in China have been waiting ten years for bus. 1 act 5m 3w 1 setting

   In Theater & society; ed. by Haiping Yan

Garbage bags. Silverstein, S.

García Lorca, Federico, 1898-1936

The house of Bernarda Alba (adaptation) See Mann, S. The house of Bernarda Alba

Yerma (adaptation) See Carter, R. A yearning

As five years pass; tr. Caridad Svich.

Surrealistic drama depicting subconscious thoughts of young man about to die.

   In Federico Garcia Lorca: impossible theater

Blood wedding; tr. by Lillian Groag. Dramatists 2002

   ISBN 0-8222-1816-X

Two families in a semi-mythical, rural Spain are bound in an unbreakable circle of murder and revenge. 6m 10w 1 setting

Buster Keaton takes a walk; tr. Caridad Svich.

Surrealist playlet employing variations on themes from Keaton's films. 1m 1w extras

   In Federico Garcia Lorca: impossible theater

Chimera; tr. Caridad Svich.

Experimental sketch. Man takes leave of wife and children. 1g 2m 1w

   In Federico Garcia Lorca: impossible theater

The house of Bernarda Alba; adapted in English by Emily Mann. Dramatists 1999 49p

   ISBN 0-8222-1653-1

Tragedy. Realistic portrayal of sexual repression among women in villages of rural Spain. 3 acts 10w 1 setting

The love of Don Perlimplin for Belisa in the garden; tr. Caridad Svich.

Farce. Love as conflict of flesh and spirit. Man married to much younger woman poses as her lover. Prologue 3 scenes 1m 3w extras 3 interiors 1 exterior

   In Federico Garcia Lorca: impossible theater

The maiden, the sailor, and the student; tr. Caridad Svich.

Experimental theater piece. 1g 2m 1w

   In Federico Garcia Lorca: impossible theater

Garden. Ayckbourn, A.

The **garden** party. Chinn, J., and Wyld, H.

Gardens and gardening

Bradley, J. Digging for ladies

c Espinosa, R. What happened in the garden this summer? (Que paso en el jardin este verano?)

Norman, M. Larry's party

Gardner, Herb

Conversations with my father.

Drama set in Lower East Side bar about father-son relationships and the assimilation of New York Jews into American culture. 2 acts 4 scenes 4m 3w 1 exterior

In Gardner, H. The collected plays

The goodbye people.

Nostalgic comedy. Would-be actress daughter and struggling sculptor help her elderly Jewish father reopen his Coney Island hot dog stand. 2 acts 5m 1w 1 exterior

In Gardner, H. The collected plays

I'm not Rappaport.

Comedy about relationship between two octogenarians, one a lifelong radical, the other, a black apartment super. Both men are fighting attempts to put them out to pasture. 2 acts 4 scenes 4m 3w 1 exterior

In Gardner, H. The collected plays

I'm with ya, Duke.

Physician helps bitter patient face truths about himself. 2m extras 1 interior

In The Best American short plays, 1996-1997

Thieves.

Comedy set on Manhattan's Upper East Side. Two schoolteachers work to revive their failing marriage. 2 acts 12m 3w 1 interior

In Gardner, H. The collected plays

A thousand clowns.

Comedy. Pretty New York social worker investigates unemployed television writer who is raising precocious nephew. 3 acts 5 scenes 5m 1w 2 interiors

In Gardner, H. The collected plays

Garland, Patrick

Brief lives. French (London) 2000 37p

ISBN 0-573-04022-2

Adapted from writings of John Aubrey. Reclusive antiquarian John Aubrey reflects on personalities of 1690s England. 2 acts 1m extras 1 setting

Garlic and lavender. Warburton, N.

Garner, Julian

c A giant's giant pizza. French (London) 2001 35p

ISBN 0-573-05126-7

Story of a giant, a kidnapped princess, and an unlikely hero who saves her. Music, singing. Prologue 11 scenes Variable cast

Gary Grinkle's battles with wrinkles and other troubles in Mudgeville. Lanfer, S. G.

Gas. Rivera, J.

The **gas** heart. Tzara, T.

Gasping. Elton, B.

Gasteazoro, Eva

Amor de mis amores.

One woman performance piece with video preset. Juxtaposes story of upper class Nicaraguan beauty of the fifties and her independent daughter. 2 acts 1w

In Action; ed. by M. Algarin and L. Griffith

Gates, Tudor

Ladies who lunch. French (London) 1999 70p

ISBN 0-573-01853-7

Comedy about three wives of the world's richest men who scheme to raise money for their favorite charity. Prologue 2 acts 13 scenes 5m 8w 3 settings

Gaucho. Lucie, D.

Gault, Connie

Otherwise Bob.

Using tin foil and candles, Bob tries to suggest that egotism has its limits, a conclusion his audience may not be ready for. 1 scene 2m 2w 1 setting

In Short spells: scenes & monologues; ed. by V. Shantz

Sky.

Drama set in 1920s prairie village. Sixteen-year-old, impregnated by father, tells her dimwitted new husband that the baby is the Second Coming. 2 acts 16 scenes 1m 3w 1 setting

In 7 cannons

Gave her the eye. Sheehy, J.

Gavin, Jamila

c Monkey in the stars. French (London) 2001 55p

ISBN 0-573-05128-7

Adapted by Jamila Gavin from her book The Monkey in the stars. Story about Rama and Sita from Indian epic poem The Ramayana. 2 acts 8 scenes Variable cast 15 characters extras 1 setting

Gawain and the Green Knight. Barchers, S. I.

Gay, John, 1685-1732

The beggar's opera (adaptation) See Havel, V. The beggar's opera

Gay, Noel

Radio times; music by Noel Gay; book by Abi Grant; book devised by Robin Miller; original conception by Alex Armitage; additional material and book revision by Paul Alexander and Alex Armitage. French (London) 2002 91p
ISBN 0-573-08108-5
Set in London's Criterion theatre in the spring of 1941. Traces struggles of cast of Variety Bandwagon, a BBC light entertainment show, broadcasting for the first time live to America. 2 acts 21 scenes 8m 5w settings

Gazooka. Thomas, G.

Gearing, Nigel

Dickens in America. Oberon Bks. 1998 55p
ISBN 1-84002-066-0
Imaginary lecture given by Charles Dickens on his travels in the United States. 2 parts 1m 1 setting

Geegaws and doohickeys: indispensible inventions and their forgotten inventors. McCullough, L. E.

Geiogamah, Hanay

Body Indian.
Native American play. When crippled Bobby Lee passes out at heavy drinking scene, his friends and relatives roll him for money he plans to use for AA program, then steal his artificial leg to trade for more wine. Singing, dancing, 5 scenes 4m 7w 1 interior
In Seventh generation; ed. by M. G. D'Aponte

Geliebteh. Korder, H.

Gems, Pam

Marlene. Oberon Bks. 1998 56p
ISBN 1-84003-074-4
Story based on an evening performance by Marlene Dietrich in 1970s Paris. 2 acts 2m 1w extras 1 setting

The snow palace. Oberon Bks. 1998 71p
ISBN 1-84002-065-2
Set in 1920s Poland, drama about Stanislawa Przybyszewska, author of the play about the French Revolution, Danton. 2 acts 3m 3w 1 setting

Gendermat. Dunn, M.

The **gene** pool. Stewart-Brown, C.

The **general** from America. Nelson, R.

The **general** of hot desire. Guare, J.

Genie. Hall, L.

Genius

Pushkin, A. Mozart and Salieri

Genius and culture. Boccioni, U.

The **gentleman** of the chrysanthemums. Armory

The **genuine** article. Milligan, J.

George, Saint

about

Ehn, E. The freak (George)

c Sigley, M. Saint George and the dragon at Christmas tide

George, Madeleine

The most massive woman wins.
Four women exchange confidences while sitting in waiting room of liposuction clinic. 4w 1 interior
In The Best American Short plays, 1997-1998

George Eliot's Silas Marner. Beevers, G.

Georgia. Shearer, J.

Gerald's good idea. York, Y.

Germania 3 ghosts at dead man. Müller, H.

Germann, Greg

The observatory.
Man and woman who shared one-night stand reunited after many years. 1 act 1m 1w 1 setting
In 3 by EST

—Same
In EST marathon '96: the one-act plays; ed. by M. Smith

Germany

Busch, C. The lady in question
Elisha, R. Two
Horváth, Ö. von. The Italian evening
Mühsam, E. Thunderation! (Alle Wetter!)
Müller, H. Germania 3 ghosts at dead man
Sherman, M. Bent

Germany. Tait, L.

Gersten-Vassilaros, Alexandra

The airport play.

Stranger strikes up conversation with woman at airport about author of book she's reading. 1m 1w 1 interior

In HB Playwrights short play festival 1999

Motel story.

Woman recruits old friend to rough up her husband. 1m 1w 1 interior

In HB Playwrights short play festival 1997

Rescue at the moment of death.

Woman's therapist attends her father's funeral to present her with past due bill. 1m 1w 1 interior

In HB Playwrights short play festival 2000

Two Jewish men in their seventies.

Two Jewish concentration camp survivors reminisce about their experience after leaving Holocaust memorial. 2m 1 exterior

In HB Playwrights short play festival 1998

Gerstenberg, Alice

Overtones.

Two cultured fashionable women conduct polite conversation while their alter egos reveal jealousy and backbiting one-upmanship. 1 act 4w 1 interior

In American plays of the new woman; ed. by K. Newlin

Get happy. Bishop, C., and Fuller, E.

Getting and spending. Chepiga, M. J.

Getting attention. Crimp, M.

Getting even. Milligan, J.

Getting Frankie married—and afterwards. Foote, H.

Getting in. Gilroy, F. D.

Getting out. Norman, M.

Getting the picture. Pownall, D.

Ghana

Aidoo, A. A. Anowa

Aidoo, A. A. The dilemma of a ghost

Ghelderode, Michel de, 1898-1962

Pantagleize (adaptation) See Field, B. Pantagleize

The **ghost** dance. Walcott, D.

Ghost of a chance. Kobler, F., and Marcus, C.

Ghost of a voice. Blais, M.-C.

The **ghost** of Christmas presents. Cook, P.

The **ghost** of El Castillo. Winther, B.

The **ghost** of Hemstead House. Hamlett, C.

Ghost on fire. Weller, M.

The **ghost** sonata. Strindberg, A.

Ghosts

Arnault, M. The legend of Sleepy Hollow

y Barchers, S. I. A Christmas carol

y Barchers, S. I. The legend of Sleepy Hollow

Benjamin, K. A. Mary MacGregor

Carr, M. Portia Coughlan

Farquhar, R. Dust to dust

Field, B. A Christmas carol

Foster, N. Ethan Claymore

c Francoeur, B. Sleepy Hollow

c Hamlett, C. The ghost of Hemstead House

y Hollingsworth, M. B. Johnny Brooke

Kobler, F. Ghost of a chance

Kyd, T. The Spanish tragedy

Levi, S. Hearts 'n kisses 'n Miss Vickers

Mena, A. Las nuevas tamaleras

Miller, C. The Canterville ghost

Molloy, M. J. The bachelor's daughter

Nigro, D. The dead wife

Nigro, D. Quint and Miss Jessel at Bly

Rodriguez, E. Estorias del barrio: un ghost

Scheffer, W. Tennessee and me

Sills, P. A Christmas carol

Svich, C. Alchemy of desire/dead-man's blues

Thompson, J. Lion in the street

Toddie, J. L. The juice of wild strawberries

Vreeke, J. The Canterville ghost

c Winther, B. The ghost of El Castillo

Ghosts. Harris, R.

Giancoli, Eric

The devil's parole.

Comedy about devil's parole hearing in front of God. 2m 1 setting

In Off-Off Broadway Festival plays, 27th series

The **giant** in the garden. Barchers, S. I.

Giant steps. Smith, O.

A **giant's** giant pizza. Garner, J.

Gibson, Florence

Belle. Playwrights Canada 2000 87p
   ISBN 0-88754-592-0   LC 00-340064
   Drama about post Civil War America. Two recently freed slaves, husband and wife, encounter
white suffragette. 2 acts 23 scenes 3m 2w 1 setting

Gien, Pamela

The syringa tree. Dramatists 2002
   ISBN 0-8222-1792-9
   Story of an abiding love between two families,
one white, one black, and the two children that are
born into their shared houshold in early sixties
South Africa. Story spans four generations. One
actress can play all 24 roles or a company of actors can perform a variety of roles. 1w 1 setting
—Same
      In Women playwrights: the best plays
         of 2001

Gieschen, Christopher

y How the West was Dun. Pioneer Drama
   Service 2000 68p
   Comic melodrama spoofing western film conven-
tions. 2 acts 17 scenes 10m 6w extras
A **gift** for Pachacuti Inca. Winther, B.
Gifts of love. Barchers, S. I.
The **gifts** of Obidiah Oak. Rosenberg, N.

Gilbert, Sky

The birth of Casper G. Schmidt.
   Interactions between heterosexual couple and
their ailing homosexual friend. 1 act 2m 1w 1 interior
      In Gilbert, S. Avoidance tactics
The emotionalists. Blizzard Pub. 2000
   63p
   ISBN 1-553-31001-2   LC 2001-334764
   Drama about novelist Ayn Rand, her lover and
her husband. 2 acts 4m 2w 1 setting
Independence.
   Experimental drama about repressed homosexual
content of plays by William Inge. 4 scenes 2m 2w
3 interiors
      In Gilbert, S. Avoidance tactics
Schubert lied.
   Drama about composer Franz Schubert, who at-
tracts and exploits would-be lovers but remains
evasive about his own desires. Prologue 3 scenes
2m 1w 1 interior
      In Gilbert, S. Avoidance tactics

The **gilded** coach (Le carrosse du Saint-
   Sacrement). Mérimée, P.
Gilgamesh and the rose of eternal youth.
   McCullough, L. E.

Gillette, William

Secret service.
   Affairs of Northern spy and his Southern sweetheart in Richmond, when Union forces were be-
sieging city. 4 acts 13m 4w extras 2 interiors
      In Fateful lightning; ed. by W. J.
         Meserve and M. A. Meserve

Gillian, Plowman

Two fat men. French (London) 1999 26p
   ISBN 0-573-12313-6
   Tragicomedy about two obese men and the
woman they meet at a health club. 3m 5w 1 setting

Gillies, John

Give us a sign.
   Worship program. Roman soldier gives order to
old Jewish sign painter to paint sign for head of
cross on which Jesus is to be crucified. 1 act 2m
1 setting
      In The drama of Easter; ed. by R.
         Wray

Gilman, Rebecca

Blue surge. Faber & Faber 2001 115p
   ISBN 0-571-21107-0
   Social realism. Small-town midwestern cop at-
tempts to help nineteen-year-old prostitute. 2 acts
15 scenes 2m 3w 4 interiors
Boy gets girl. Faber & Faber 2000 119p
   ISBN 0-571-19983-6   LC 99-89185
   Drama about a New York magazine journalist
stalked by a blind date she rejected. 2 acts 18
scenes 4m 3w 1 setting
The glory of living. Dramatic Publishing
   2003 66p
   Young woman married to ex-con twice her age,
coerced into helping him commit crimes, including
murder. 2 acts 5m 5w 3 interiors
—Same. Faber & Faber 2001 83p
   ISBN 0-571-19998-4   LC 2001-42898
Spinning into butter. Faber & Faber 2000
   105p
   ISBN 0-571-19984-4   LC 99-89186
   Drama about liberal-minded dean of students
who must confront racism on the campus of Vermont college. 2 acts 13 scenes 5m 2w 1 setting

Gilot, Françoise, 1921-

about

McAvera, B. Françoise

Gilroy, Frank Daniel

Any given day.

Prelude to the author's The subject was roses. Depicts tensions in middle-class Bronx family from 1941 to 1943. 2 acts 3 scenes 6m 3w 1 interior

In Gilroy, F. D. Complete full-length plays, 1962-1999

Come next Tuesday.

On eve of eighteenth anniversary wife receives conclusive proof of husband's indiscretions. 1 act 1m 1w 1 interior

In Gilroy, F. D. 15 one-act plays

Contact with the enemy.

Two American soldiers who witnessed the liberation of the first concentration camp in April, 1945, meet by chance years later at the Holocaust museum in Washington, D.C. 6 scenes 3m 2w extras 1 setting

In Gilroy, F. Getting in and Contact with the enemy

Dreams of glory.

At country-club summer dance, middle-aged man celebrating business promotion nostalgically looks back on youthful desire to become a musician. Music. 1 act 2m 2w 1 exterior

In Gilroy, F. D. 15 one-act plays

Far Rockaway.

Television drama. Man who killed murderer is haunted by deed. 13 scenes 7m 3w

In Gilroy, F. D. 15 one-act plays

Fore.

Comedy. Two Hollywood writers and secretary share bungalow at major movie studio. 1 act 3m 1w 1 setting

In Gilroy, F. D. 15 one-act plays

Getting in.

Young World War II veteran, not the Ivy League type, gains admission to Dartmouth College. 1 act 1 scene 5m 2w settings

In Gilroy, F. D. 15 one-act plays

—Same

In Gilroy, F. Getting in and Contact with the enemy

Give the bishop my faint regards.

Comedy. Tensions rise as young woman interviews legendary Hollywood screenwriting team. 1 act 2m 1w 1 interior

In Gilroy, F. D. 15 one-act plays

The golf ball.

Bored to death with retirement, a man gingers up his life with an unlikely bet—which may cost him his marriage. 1 act 8 scenes 2m 1w settings

In Ensemble Studio Theatre marathon '99: the one-act plays

—Same

In Gilroy, F. D. 15 one-act plays

Last licks.

Domestic drama set in Brooklyn. Son resents widowed father's involvement with woman. 2 acts 2m 1w 1 interior

In Gilroy, F. D. Complete full-length plays, 1962-1999

Match point.

Black comedy set at desert resort. Woman drives husband's lover to suicide. 1 act 2 scenes 1m 2w 1 exterior

In Gilroy, F. D. 15 one-act plays

The next contestant.

Humorous spoof of radio game shows. Soon-to-be-married contestant must arrange date with old girlfriend on phone in order to win the Big Challenge. 1 act 2m 1w 1 setting

In Gilroy, F. D. 15 one-act plays

The only game in town.

Las Vegas is scene for compulsive gambling piano player's romance with chorine. 2 acts 2m 1w 1 setting

In Gilroy, F. D. Complete full-length plays, 1962-1999

Present tense.

Allusive dialogue between husband and wife, parents of grown son, during Vietnam War. 1 act 1m 1w 1 interior

In Gilroy, F. D. 15 one-act plays

Real to reel.

Comedy. Intellectual film critic saved from Central Park mugging by filmmaker/actor she loathes. 1 act 2 scenes 1m 1w 1 interior 1 exterior

In Gilroy, F. D. 15 one-act plays

So please be kind.

Adulterous tryst derailed by movie trivia game. 1 act 2 scenes 2m 1w 1 interior

In Gilroy, F. D. 15 one-act plays

Gilroy, Frank Daniel—*Continued*
The subject was roses.
Emotional weekend of adjustment for parents and 21-year-old son, who comes home after three years in Army during World War II. 2 acts 7 scenes 2m 1w 1 interior
In Gilroy, F. D. Complete full-length plays, 1962-1999
That summer—that fall.
Tragedy based on the Phaedra-Hippolytus myth, transposed to 1960, New York. 2 acts 13 scenes 2m 2w 1 exterior 1 setting
In Gilroy, F. D. Complete full-length plays, 1962-1999
'Twas brillig.
Writer arrives on Hollywood studio lot and encounters puzzling eccentric. 1 act 2 scenes 2m 2w 1 interior
In Gilroy, F. D. 15 one-act plays
The viewing.
American unit entering Germany in World War II comes across booby-trapped body of enemy soldier. 1 act 2 scenes 25m 1 setting
In Gilroy, F. D. 15 one-act plays
A way with words.
Man hopes friend will help him get his wife back. 1 act 3 scenes 2m 1w 1 interior 1 exterior
In Gilroy, F. D. 15 one-act plays
Who'll save the plowboy?
Middle-aged failure visited by dying wartime buddy who saved his life. 2 acts 3 scenes 1b 4m 2w 1 interior
In Gilroy, F. D. Complete full-length plays, 1962-1999
Gimme shelter: Gem. Keeffe, B.
Gimme shelter: Getaway. Keeffe, B.
Gimme shelter: Gotcha. Keeffe, B.
The **gimmick**. Orlandersmith, D.
The **gingerbread** man. Wood, D.
Gint. Linney, R.

Gippius, Zinaida
Sacred blood.
Symbolic discourse on Christianity and paganism employing hermits, mermaids and witch. 3 scenes Variable cast 1 setting
In Eight twentieth-century Russian plays; ed. by T. Langen and J. Weir
Girl. Kincaid, J.
Girl gone. Wellman, M.
The **girl** who lost her voice. Lipkin, J.

Girl who loved her horses. Taylor, D. H.
Girls
  Cohen, F. Amy Crockett: M.V.P.
  Kennedy, A. A lesson in a dead language
y Kral, B. Paper lanterns, paper cranes
y Lazarus, J. Schoolyard games
  Ledoux, P. Anne
  Martini, C. House of glass
  Mérimée, P. The opportunity (L'Occasion)
  Mhlophe, G. Have you seen Zandile?
c Pargman, S. Pollyanna
  Taylor, D. H. Girl who loved her horses
  Upton, J. Ashes and sand
  Warburton, N. Garlic and lavender
  Williams, R. The No Boys Cricket Club
The **girls** from Samos. Menander

Giron, Arthur
Flight. French 1998 87p
Comic drama. Looks at the lives of the dysfunctional family of Orville and Wilbur Wright. 2 acts 4m 1w Unit set
Give me shelter. Weiner, W.
Give the bishop my faint regards. Gilroy, F. D.
Give us a sign. Gillies, J.
Gizmo. Ayckbourn, A.
The **Glace** Bay Miners' Museum. Lill, W.
The **glad** hand. Wilson, S.

Glancy, Diane
American gypsy.
Interactions between a husband and wife, her younger sister, who is touched in the head, and their friends in an Oklahoma Indian community. A freak accident leads to decisions. 14 scenes 4m 2w 3 interiors 3 exteriors
In Glancy, D. American gypsy: six Native American plays
Jump kiss.
A collection of fragments and monologues about childhood, motherhood, family life, and mystical perceptions, plus several dialogues between family members. 7 sections 49 scenes 2m 2w 1 setting
In Glancy, D. American gypsy: six Native American plays
The lesser wars.
A man and a woman, apparent opposites, meet at a dance hall and gradually begin to trust one another. Each bears the scars of previous affairs.

Glancy, Diane—*Continued*
Music, dancing. 12 scenes 1m 1w 1 setting

In Glancy, D. American gypsy: six Native American plays

The toad (another name for the moon) should have a bite.

Monologue about a woman's trip to China, the modern cities and the relics of antiquity, including the custom of foot-binding. 1 scene 1w 1 setting

In Glancy, D. American gypsy: six Native American plays

The woman who was a red deer dressed for the deer dance.

Dialogue between young Native American woman who lives in world of honky-tonks and soup kitchens, and her grandmother, who lives in world of spirits. 1 act 2w 1 setting

In Glancy, D. American gypsy: six Native American plays

—Same

In Seventh generation; ed. by M. G. D'Aponte

The women who loved house trailers.

With lyrical indirection, three Native American craftswomen invoke the traditions of their people to move past grim personal histories toward more creative lives. 5 scenes 3w 1 setting

In Glancy, D. American gypsy: six Native American plays

Glaspell, Susan

The outside.

Meditation on meaning of life by two reclusive women, one widowed, the other abandoned by husband. 1 act 3m 2w 1 setting

In American plays of the new woman; ed. by K. Newlin

Trifles.

Two Iowa housewives contemplate reasons for man's murder, while their husbands remain baffled. 3m 2w 1 setting

In Political stages; ed. by E. Mann and D. Roessel

Glass, Joanna McClelland

Play memory. Playwrights Canada 1999 69p

ISBN 0-88754-575-0

Canadian salesman, scapegoated in WWII gas-ration scandal, unable to pick up pieces of his shattered life. 2 acts 8m 3w 1 interior

—Same

In Short spells: scenes & monologues; ed. by V. Shantz

Yesteryear. Playwrights Canada 1998 103p

ISBN 0-88754-573-4

Romantic comedy set in small Saskatchewan prairie town in 1948. Irish Sweepstakes ticket alters lives in close-knit community. Music. 2 acts 5 scenes 7m 3w 1 interior

The **glass** ceiling. Tait, L.

The **glass** menagerie. Williams, T.

The **glass** mendacity. Morley, M., and Willmorth, T.

Glenn. Young, D.

Glennon, William

c The trial of the Arkansas bear. Dramatic Publishing 2003 52p

Comedy inspired by Albert Bigelow Paine's book about talking, fiddle-playing bear. 2 acts 7m 2w extras 1 interior

Glimmer, glimmer and shine. Leight, W.

Glore, John

The Morpheus quartet.

Drama in form of string quartet. Attempt to come to terms with brother's death. Music. 2m 2w

In 30 ten-minute plays for 4, 5 & 6 actors from Actors Theatre of Louisville's National Ten-minute Play Contest

Glory box. Miller, T.

The **glory** of living. Gilman, R.

Głowacki, Janusz

The fourth sister; tr. by Eva Nagurski and Janusz Głowacki. French (London) 2003 104p

ISBN 0-573-62844-0

Dark comedy about modern Moscow's greedy gangsters. 2 acts 30 scenes Variable cast 14 characters 1 setting

Gluskabe and Old Man Winter. Bruchac, J.

God

Guare, J. The general of hot desire

Schmitt, E.-E. The visitor

God and Stephen Hawking. Hawdon, R.

God, man, and devil (got, mentsh, un tayvl). Gordin, J.

God only knows. Whitemore, H.

Goda, Billy

No crime.

Young lawyer is interviewed for position in prestigious law firm. 2m 1 interior

In The Best American short plays 1998-1999

Godber, John

April in Paris.

Comedy. English couple wins holiday in Paris. 2 acts 1m 1w 1 setting

In Godber, J. Plays: 3

Bouncers.

Comedy set in British club scene. Singing. 4m 1 setting

In Godber, J. Plays: 1

y Happy families.

Drama set in West Yorkshire. On his graduation day young man looks back over his teenage years. 2 acts 1g 3m 5w 1 interior

In Godber, J. Plays: 1

Happy Jack.

Love story set in 1930s Yorkshire. Fragmentary look at miner's long marriage. 2 acts 1m 1w 1 setting

In Godber, J. Plays: 2

It started with a kiss. French (London) 2001 80p

ISBN 0-573-01859-6

College drama students in the 1970s discover love, sex, drugs, and rock 'n' roll. 3 acts 2m 4w 1 setting

On a night like this. Weinberger, J. 2002 145p

ISBN 0-85676-260-1

A well-to-do artist in Yorkshire has a wild night on the town with the contractors who are working on his house, plus their uninhibited wives. Music, dancing. Puppets. 2 acts 13 scenes 3m 5w settings

Perfect pitch. French (London) 2002 85p

ISBN 0-573-01966-5

Black comedy. Middle-class British couple mix with working-class couple at camper vacation site. 2 acts 23 scenes 2m 2w 1 setting

—Same

In Godber, J. Plays: 3

Salt of the earth.

Portrayal of life in West Yorkshire coal fields from 1947 to 1980s. 2 acts Variable cast 11 characters 1 setting

In Godber, J. Plays: 2

September in the rain.

Yorkshire couple stumble through silly rows and inarticulate frustration of ordinary marriage. Singing. 2 acts 1m 1w 1 setting

In Godber, J. Plays: 2

Shakers.

Four long-suffering waitresses offer their views of patrons at trendy lounge. 2 acts 4w 1 interior

In Godber, J. Plays: 1

y Teechers.

Teenage students write sketch about new drama teacher for end-of-term play. 2 acts Variable cast 21 characters 1 interior

In Godber, J. Plays: 2

Unleashed. French (London) 2002 80p

ISBN 0-573-01927-4

Play-within-a-play. Married British businessman becomes enamored of Amsterdam's club scene. 2 acts 3m 2w 1 setting

Up 'n' under.

Comedy set in North of England. Amateur rugby team's pride lies in their unbroken record of defeat. 2 acts 6m 1w

In Godber, J. Plays: 3

Weekend breaks. French (London) 1998 56p

ISBN 0-573-01940-1

Drama explores relationship between theater studies teacher and his elderly parents. 2 acts 2m 1w

Godiva, Lady

Tavel, R. The life of Lady Godiva

God's heart. Lucas, C.

God's locusts. Eagleton, T.

God's man in Texas. Rambo, D.

God's official. Farquhar, R.

Goens, Linda M.

Resurrection on trial.

Worship program. Trial to judge veracity of resurrection of Christ. Variable cast 15 characters extras

In The drama of Easter; ed. by R. Wray

Goethe, Johann Wolfgang von, 1749-1832

Elective Affinities (dramatization) See Dietz, S. Force of nature

about

Warner, F. Goethe's Weimar

Goethe's Weimar. Warner, F.

Gogol, Nikolai

Marriage: an absolutely incredible event in two acts (adaptation) See Field, B. Marriage

about

Nigro, D. Gogol

Gogol. Nigro, D.

Going. . .going. . .gone with the breeze. Francoeur, B.

Going nowhere apace. Merzer, G.

Going once. Silverstein, S.

Going to pot (On purge Bébé). Feydeau, G.

Goldberg, Jessica

Good thing. Dramatists 2002
ISBN 0-8222-1869-0

The relationships between two couples: forty-something guidance counselors whose marriage is on the rocks, and recent graduates struggling to make their way in life. 2m 3w 1 setting

The hologram theory. Dramatists 2001 76p
ISBN 0-8222-1776-7

Trinidadian artist travels to New York to unravel mystery of her brother's murder. Prologue 4 parts epilogue 6m 4w settings

Refuge. Dramatists 2000 46p
ISBN 0-8222-1777-5

Tragicomedy. Young woman forced to care for ill younger brother and drug addicted younger sister when abandoned by parents. 14 scenes 2m 2w 1 setting

—Same

In Women playwrights: the best plays of 1998

Stuck. Dramatists 2001 61p
ISBN 0-8222-1778-3   LC 2002-275596

Tragicomedy tells of disintegrating friendship between two twenty-something women in backwater town. Prologue 16 scenes 2m 3w 1 setting

The **Goldberg** variations. Elisha, R.

The **golden** age. Gurney, A. R.

Golden child. Hwang, D. H.

The **golden** goose. Wolfman, J.

Golden guts. Crommelynck, F.

Di **goldineh** medineh (The golden land). McCullough, L. E.

Goldoni, Carlo, 1707-1793

The servant of two masters (adaptation) See Congdon, C. The servant of two masters

The Venetian twins; tr. by Michael Feingold. French 2002 104p
ISBN 0-573-62763-0

Comedy of intrigue, love, and mistaken identity, set in 18th century Verona. Music, singing. 3 acts 6 scenes 10m 3w extras 2 interiors 3 exteriors

Goldstein, Baruch, d. 1994

about

Sherman, J. Reading Hebron

Goldstein, Dana Leslie

Burn.

Husband and wife discuss feeling of guilt, frustration, and anger following three-year-old daughter's accident. 1m 1w 1 interior

In Women's Project & productions; ed. by J. Miles

The **Golem** of Belmont Boulevard. McCullough, L. E.

Golf

Foster, N. The foursome

Gilroy, F. D. The golf ball

Healey, M. Yodellers

Wong, E. Let the big dog eat

The **golf** ball. Gilroy, F. D.

Goliath (Biblical figure)

c Vogel, L. Big little man

Gollobin, Laurie Brooks

c The match girl's gift: A Christmas story.

Based on Hans Christian Andersen's The Little Match Girl. Set in New York in early 1900s, homeless girl is taken in by wealthy family. 2b 1g 1m 2w settings

In The twelve plays of Christmas; ed. by L. Swortzell

y Selkie.

Drama based on Scottish folklore about sealfolk able to assume human form on land. Background music, singing, dancing. 1 act 3m 4w 1 setting

In Theatre for young audiences; ed. by C. A. Jennings

Goluboff, Bryan

In-betweens. Dramatists 2000 52p

ISBN 0-8222-1758-9

Two criminals compete for the affections of a transvestite in Bronx, N. Y., apartment. 2 acts 8 scenes 3m 1w 1 setting

Gomolvilas, Prince

Donut holes in orbit.

Chinese American mother interferes with her daughter's life. 1 act 16 scenes 2m 2w 2 interiors 2 exteriors

   In EST marathon '98: the one-act plays; ed. by M. Smith

The theory of everything. Dramatic Publishing 2003 72p

Comedy about race, identity and faith. Seven Asian Americans gather atop a Las Vegas wedding chapel every week for a UFO watch. 2 acts 3m 4w 1 setting

Gone missing. Napier, E.

Gone to take a . . . Silverstein, S.

Gonzalez, Silvia S.

Boxcar.

Illegal immigrants from Mexico and El Salvador, hunted by the Border Patrol, die in boxcar in the desert. Singing. Prologue 2 acts 17 scenes 10m 1w extras 1 interior

   In New dramatists: best plays by the graduating class of 2001

The migrant farmworker's son.

Father-son conflict between values of old Mexico and pop culture of '90s America threatens to tear migrant farmworker's family apart. 2 acts 22 scenes 1g 3m 1w extras settings

   In Multicultural theatre II; ed. by R. Ellis

Good and evil

Belke, D. Blackpool and Parrish

Elisha, R. Two

Field, B. Playing with fire

Los Matachines unmasked (Los Matachines desenmascarados)

Neilson, A. Normal

Schmitt, E.-E. The visitor

Wilder, T. Hast thou considered my servant Job?

Good as new. Hedges, P.

Good boys. Martin, J.

The **good** god of Manhattan. Bachmann, I.

Good grief. Waterhouse, K.

Good grief, Lolita. Bonel, W.

A **good** night's rest; or, Two in the morning. Gore, C.

The **good** thief. McPherson, C.

Good to know you. Oates, J. C.

Goodbye, Iphigenia. Green, G. M.

Goodbye, Oscar. Linney, R.

The **goodbye** people. Gardner, H.

Goodden, Herman

Suffering fools.

Memory play. In aftermath of failed suicide attempt friend helps man exorcise his demons. 5m 4w 1 setting

   In Seven short plays from Theatre Ontario

Goodnight Desdemona (good morning Juliet). MacDonald, A.-M.

Goold, Rupert, and Butler, Caroline

The end of the affair; [by] Graham Greene; adapted for the stage by Rupert Goold and Caroline Butler. French (London) 2001 71p

ISBN 0-573-01886-3   LC 2001-24847

Drama based on Graham Greene novel, set in 1946 London, about marital duplicity and Catholic faith. Civil servant suspects his wife of having affair and asks friend for help, unaware that friend was once wife's lover. 2 acts 28 scenes 6m 1w 1 setting

The **Goong** Hay Kid. Eng, A.

Gorden, Chuck

Guarding the bridge. French 1999 21p

ISBN 0-573-64235-4   LC 99-218309

Son discovers that his father's prejudices are embedded in his subconscious. 1 act 2m extras 1 setting

Gordin, Jacob

God, man, and devil (got, mentsh, un tayvl); tr. by Nahma Sandrow.

Pious Torah scribe is seduced by Satan and transformed into dishonest factory owner who destroys the religious and communal fabric. Music. Prologue 4 acts 6 scenes 1g 7m 3w extras 3 interiors 2 exteriors

   In God, man and devil; ed. by N. Sandrow

Gordon, George William, 1820-1865

about

Walcott, D. Drums and colours

Gore, Catherine

Don Juan of Austria.

Melodramatic love tragedy. Juan, ignorant of his parentage, loves Florinda, who is secretly a Jew; the jealous king of Spain (Juan's half brother) uses the Inquisition to seize Florinda, but she escapes by suicide. Music. 3 acts 6 scenes 14m 2w extras 4 interiors 1 exterior

In Gore, C. Gore on stage

A good night's rest; or, Two in the morning.

Farce. Timid fusspot offers a stranger lodging for the night and soon regrets it. 1 act 1 scene 2m 1 interior

In Gore, C. Gore on stage

King O'Neil; or, The Irish Brigade.

High jinks in the French king's Irish Brigade, culminating in a happily drunken soldier assuming the throne and sorting out various problems. Music, singing. 2 acts 8 scenes 9m 3w extras 5 interiors 2 exteriors

In Gore, C. Gore on stage

The king's seal.

Romantic comedy set in Renaissance Paris. Intrigues at the court of Henry IV are finally resolved by the king, with the help of an honest old engraver and his comic assistant. Music. 2 acts 9 scenes 11m 3w extras 7 interiors

In Gore, C. Gore on stage

Lords and commons.

Satirical comedy. Good-hearted young man learns the hard way that his upper-crust friends are merely using him. Music. 3 acts 11 scenes 11m 6w extras interior settings

In Gore, C. Gore on stage

The maid of Croissey; or, Theresa's vow.

Melodrama set in Napoleonic France. Village girl promises to marry any man who will take her brother's place in the army. Adapted from an unknown French play. Music, singing. 2 acts 2 scenes 5m 2w 1 exterior

In Gore, C. Gore on stage

Modern honor; or, The sharper in high life.

Drama. Young man discovers that his father cheats at cards to maintain the family's income. 3 acts 3 scenes 8m 3w extras 3 interiors

In Gore, C. Gore on stage

The queen's champion.

Historical melodrama. A country nobleman goes mad for love of Marie Antoinette, but later uses his madness to help the queen flee from revolutionaries. Adapted from a play by Scribe; this was the second, more idiomatic version. Music. 2 acts 4 scenes 5m 3w extras 2 interiors

In Gore, C. Gore on stage

Quid pro quo; or, The day of the dupes.

19th century English comedy. Amateur theatricals provide the occasion for romantic entanglements; satire of social and political mores. Music, singing. Prologue 5 acts 9 scenes epilogue 10m 5w 6 interiors 2 exteriors

In Gore, C. Gore on stage

Salvoisy; or, The queen's lover.

An earlier version of The Queen's Champion, identical in plot. 2 acts 2 scenes 5m 3w extras 2 interiors

In Gore, C. Gore on stage

The school for coquettes.

Comedy. A fashionable flirt sows confusion as she tries to win proof of her husband's love and protect a cousin's secret. Prologue 5 acts 13 scenes epilogue 11m 6w 6 interiors

In Gore, C. Gore on stage

The tale of a tub.

Period comedy, set in France of Louis XV. Laundress cousin teaches Madame du Barry a lesson in manners and family feeling. Music. 2 acts 2 scenes 8m 3w extras 1 interior 1 exterior

In Gore, C. Gore on stage

Gorisch, Anna K.

The individuality of streetlamps.

Ex-couple revisits failed relationship. 1m 1w 1 exterior

In 30 ten-minute plays for 2 actors from Actors Theatre of Louisville's National Ten-minute Play Contest

Gossip. Walker, G. F.

Gotanda, Philip Kan

Yankee dawg you die.

Asian American actors face discrimination and stereotyping. 2 acts 14 scenes 2m 1 setting

In Plays of provocation; ed. by F. P. Richmond

Gouel, Eva, d. 1915

about

McAvera, B. Eva

Gough, Lucy

Crossing the bar.

Two suicides—a modern delinquent and a medieval nun—are imprisoned in a place called Dread, between death and life. 2 acts 13 scenes 2m 1w 1 setting

In Gough, L. Crossing the bar; Head; Our lady of shadows

Head.

Like Keats's Isabella, a woman digs up her murdered lover and stores his head in a pot of basil; however, the head is quite talkative and the lady is not inclined to pine away. Originally performed on radio. 1 act 10 scenes 3m 1w 3 interiors 1 exterior

In Gough, L. Crossing the bar; Head; Our lady of shadows

Our lady of shadows.

A revisionist version of Tennyson's The Lady of Shalott. Gough's heroine is not resigned to her tower prison but converts it into an alchemist's laboratory until she can escape in a knight's armor. Radio play. Singing, dancing. 1 act 18 scenes 3w extras 1 setting

In Gough, L. Crossing the bar; Head; Our lady of shadows

The red room.

Monologue. Story of Charlotte Bronte's imagination during the writing of Jane. Eyre. 1m 1w 1 setting

In One woman, one voice; ed. by H. W. Davies

The tail.

Monologue. Young woman fantasizes on becoming a mermaid and reflects upon her insecurities. 1w 1 setting

In One woman, one voice; ed. by H. W. Davies

Gould, Glenn, 1932-1982

about

Young, D. Glenn

Gould, Howard M.

Diva. French 2000 82p

ISBN 0-573-62836-x

Comedy. Behind the scenes look at hit television sitcom. 2 acts 9 scenes 5m 1w 5 interiors

Goupil, Laval

Dark owl; or, The renegade angel.

Revenge tragedy set in New Brunswick, Canada. Stranger's arrival in village forces dysfunctional family to confront their involvement in rape. Pro-

logue 2 acts 24 scenes 3m 4w 1 setting

In Angels and anger; ed. by G. Nichols

Government, Resistance to

Anouilh, J. Antigone

Dempsey, S. Armagideon

Kushner, T. East coast ode to Howard Jarvis: a little teleplay in tiny monologues

Lodato, V. Snapshot: the great father

Nanus, S. The survivor

Nolan, Y. Annie Mae's movement

Wright, C. Snapshot: bomb squad

Gow, David

Bea's niece. Playwrights Canada 2000 94p

ISBN 0-88754-589-0   LC 00-363715

Exploration into mind of female novelist secluded in mental hospital. 2 acts 10 scenes afterword 1m 3w settings

Goya, Francisco de

about

Buero-Vallejo, A. The sleep of reason

Goyette, Alison

Marc and Marie.

Man and woman sitting in an apartment discuss how the man killed a D.A., who was about to arrest the woman's gangster father. 1m 1w 1 setting

In Blast from the future; ed. by D. Yeaton

Gozzi, Carlo, conte, 1722-1806

Amore delle tre melarance (adaptation) See Heard, D. B. The love for three oranges

Grace. Lucie, D.

Grace-Smith, Briar

Nag pou wahine.

Drama about Maori life in New Zealand incorporates elements of traditional ritual. Music, singing. 8 scenes 1w

In Postcolonial plays; ed. by H. Gilbert

Gracious goodness, great tongues of fire. Vogel, L.

Graham, Andy. See Parsley, R. jt. auth.

Graham, Bruce

Coyote on a fence. Dramatists 2000 57p

ISBN 0-8222-1738-4

Graham, Bruce—*Continued*

Drama set on death row. White supremacist mass murderer and liberal political activist strike up unusual friendship. 3m 1w 1 setting

Desperate affection. Dramatists 1998 59p il

ISBN 0-8222-1578-0　　　　LC 98-146941

Dark comedy about an actress who finally meets the perfect man, but the perfect man turns out to be a professional assassin. 2 acts Variable cast 3 characters 1 interior

Graham, Nadine

The basement at the bottom at the end of the world.

Drama about racial conflict. Young black and white man trapped in basement. 9 scenes interlude 1m 1w 1 interior

In Multicultural theatre II; ed. by R. Ellis

Grahame, Kenneth, 1859-1932

The wind in the willows (dramatization) See Bennett, A. Kenneth Grahame's The wind in the willows; DeTurk, S. The mad adventures of Mr. Toad; Morris, V. Mr. Toad's mad adventures

Grain. Kirshon, V.

Grandfathers

Miller, E. Last will and testament

Grandma Sylvia's funeral. Wein, G., and Blumsack, A. L.

Grandmothers

Filloux, C. Storks

y Frockt, D. L. The book of Ruth

Gurney, A. R. The golden age

Howe, T. Pride's Crossing

Leonard, H. Love in the title

Mhlophe, G. Have you seen Zandile?

Townsend, J. Angels and saints

Wein, G. Grandma Sylvia's funeral

Grant, David Marshall

Snakebit. Dramatists 2000 69p

ISBN 0-8222-1724-4

Study of modern friendship set in Los Angeles. Couple stays with husband's gay friend when he lands audition for film role. 3 acts 2 scenes 3m 1w 1 setting

—Same

In New Playwrights: the best plays of 1998

Grant, Ulysses S. (Ulysses Simpson), 1822-1885

about

Guare, J. A few stout individuals

The **grass** widow. Wilson, S.

Grassmann, Bettina

Children of neon lights.

A young man in a psychiatric ward describes the moment his breakdown began. 1 scene 1m 1 interior

In Short spells: scenes & monologues; ed. by V. Shantz

Grateful women. Kreidl, M.

Grauer, Rita, and Urquhart, John

c Mark Twain's Huckleberry Finn. Anchorage Press 1979-80 66p

ISBN 0-87602-371-5

Dramatization of Twain's classic about boy's adventures on Mississippi River. Music. 3m 1w extra 1 setting

Gray, John, and Raffalovich, Marc-André

The blackmailers.

Explores homoerotic relationship between two extortionists in fin-de-siècle London. 4 acts 6m 7w extras 3 interiors

In Lovesick; ed. by L. Senelick

Gray, Simon

The late middle classes. Hern Bks. 1999 88p

ISBN 1-85459-433-8

Satire set in early 1950s on England's south coast. Twelve-year-old boy, whose snobbish mother fills her day with tennis and gin and whose father is having an affair, must also contend with piano tutor whose interest in him is more than musical. 2 acts 7 scenes 1b 2m 3w 2 interiors

Graybill, Christopher

Eye to eye.

Man and woman on date have staring contest to see who will pay the check. 2m 1w 1 interior

In 30 ten-minutes plays for 3 actors from Actors Theatre of Louisville's National Ten-minute Play Contest

Grazia, Edward de

The vacuum cleaner.

Satirical "opera". Family spouts robolic platitudes as machines gain power with their lifetime warranties. Music, singing. 1b 1g 1m 2w extras 1 interior

In The Best American short plays, 1996-1997

Graziano, David

Acorn.

An unemployed carpenter and high school graduate share a clothesline and fall in love. 1m 1w 1 setting

In Actors Theatre of Louisville. Ten-minute plays: v5

Great Britain

History

Chaurette, N. The queens

Cibber, C. The tragical history of King Richard III

Fo, D. Elizabeth: almost by chance a woman

Griffiths, L. The Duchess, a.k.a. Wallis Simpson

Griffiths, T. Food for ravens

Grimm, D. Sheridan; or, Schooled in scandal

Luckham, C. The seduction of Anne Boleyn

Marlowe, C. The troublesome reign and lamentable death of Edward the Second

Nicholson, W. Katherine Howard

Poliakoff, S. Talk of the city

Poskitt, K. Fawkes—the quiet guy

Poskitt, K. Nell's belles

Schiller, F. Mary Stuart

Slover, T. Joyful noise

Politics and government

Edgar, D. Teendreams

Grimm, D. Kit Marlow

Wesker, A. Whatever happened to Betty Lemon?

Race relations

Edgar, D. Our own people

Keeffe, B. Barbarians: in the city

Social conditions

Darke, N. Ting Tang mine

Edgar, D. That summer

Edgar, D. Teendreams

Godber, J. Bouncers

Hall, L. Child of our time: children of the rain

Keeffe, B. Barbarians: abide with me

Keeffe, B. Barbarians: in the city

Keeffe, B. Barbarians: killing time

Shaw, B. Heartbreak House

Shaw, B. Mrs. Warren's profession

Shaw, B. Widowers' houses

Wesker, A. Chicken soup with barley

Social life and customs

y Barchers, S. I. Hard times

Brittney, L. Pickwick papers

Duffield, N. The secret garden

y Field, B. Great expectations

Garland, P. Brief lives

Godber, J. Salt of the earth

Haywood, E. F. A wife to be lett: a comedy.

Horsler, P. Cut and run

Leonard, H. Great expectations

Levy, D. Honey, baby

Lucie, D. Progress

Sterling, P. The secret garden

Teale, P. Jane Eyre

Valentine, P. Day of reckoning

Van Druten, J. Make way for Lucia

Whelan, P. The herbal bed

Wilde, O. An ideal husband

Great day in the morning. Babe, T.

The **great** Denver railroad scam; or, If aunt May leaves, who'll weed the 'tunias? Kotwica, D.

The **Great** Divide. Moody, W. V.

Great expectations. Field, B.

Great expectations. Leonard, H.

The **great** flying ship of Ivan the Impossible. McCullough, L. E.

The **great** Gilly Hopkins. Paterson, D. L., and Liebman, S.

The **great** Gromboolian plain. Nigro, D.

The **great** hurricane. Winther, B.

The **great** man. Williamson, D.

Great to see you. Rebeck, T.

Grédy, Jean-Pierre

The incomparable LouLou (adaptation) See Clark, R. The incomparable LouLou

Greek drama (Comedy)

Aristophanes. Acharnians
Aristophanes. Birds
Aristophanes. Celebrating ladies
Aristophanes. Clouds
Aristophanes. Frogs
Aristophanes. Lysistrata
Aristophanes. Peace
Aristophanes. The sexual congress
Aristophanes. The suits
Aristophanes. Wasps
Aristophanes. Wealth
Aristophanes. Women in power
Menander. Closely cropped locks
Menander. Desperately seeking justice
Menander. Dyskolos
Menander. The girls from Samos
Menander. The grouch
Menander. The shield
Menander. The woman from Samos

Greek drama (Satyr play)

Euripides. Cyclops

Greek drama (Tragedy)

Aeschylus. Agamemnon
Aeschylus. Choephori
Aeschylus. The Eumenides
Aeschylus. Libation bearers
Aeschylus. The Persians
Aeschylus. Prometheus bound
Aeschylus. Seven against Thebes
Aeschylus. The suppliants
Euripides. Alcestis
Euripides. The Alcestis of Euripides
Euripides. Alkestis
Euripides. Andromache
Euripides. Bacchae
Euripides. Children of Heracles
Euripides. Daughters of Troy
Euripides. Electra
Euripides. Hecuba
Euripides. Ion
Euripides. Iphigenia among the Taurians
Euripides. Iphigenia at Aulis
Euripides. Iphigenia in Tauris
Euripides. The madness of Heracles
Euripides. Medea
Euripides. Orestes
Euripides. The Phoenician women
Euripides. Rhesus
Euripides. Suppliant women

Euripides. The Trojan women
Sophocles. Aias
Sophocles. Ajax
Sophocles. Antigone
Sophocles. Electra
Sophocles. Elektra
Sophocles. King Oedipus
Sophocles. Oedipus at Colonus
Sophocles. Oedipus at Kolonos
Sophocles. Oedipus the King
Sophocles. Oedipus Tyrannos
Sophocles. Philoctetes
Sophocles. Philoktetes
Sophocles. The women of Trachis
Greeks and centaurs. Adams, L. D.

Green, Andrea

For tiger lilies out of season.

Drama about woman who interacts with family, support group and doctors, in order to cope with breast cancer. 10 scenes 1m 5w

In Off-Off Broadway Festival plays, 22nd ser.

Green, George MacEwan

Goodbye, Iphigenia. French (London) 1998 31p

ISBN 0-573-12097-8

Legend of Iphigenia sacrificed by her father Agamemnon to goddess Artemis in order to free Greek fleet. Eyewitness account by soldier guarding royal tent. 3m 3w 1 setting

Green, Michael

Cinderella.

A traditional English pantomime goes badly wrong. Music, singing. 1 act 4 scenes 3m 6w 2 interiors

In Coarse acting strikes back; ed. by M. Green

Oedipus, King of Thebes.

A mock Greek tragedy, with over-the-top horrors and an under-rehearsed chorus. 1 act 5 scenes 2m 4w extras 1 setting

In Coarse acting strikes back; ed. by M. Green

Trapped.

Parody of a traditional English murder mystery, as performed by a hopelessly unlucky amateur troupe. 1 act 4m 5w 1 interior

In Coarse acting strikes back; ed. by M. Green

Green, Paul

Hymn to the rising sun: a drama of man's waste.

Depiction of cruel conditions in racially mixed Southern prison. 1 act 13m extras 1 setting

In Green, P. A Paul Green reader

In Abraham's bosom: the tragedy of a southern Negro.

Mulatto son of Southern plantation owner struggles to rise above his station. Music, singing. 1 act 7 scenes 1b 8m 3w 3 interiors 2 exteriors

In Green, P. A Paul Green reader

The lost colony; a symphonic drama of American history; edited, with an introduction and a note on the text, by Laurence G. Avery. University of N.C. Press 2001 152p

ISBN 0-8078-4970-7   LC 2001-25339

Dramatic retelling of founding and mysterious disappearance of Roanoke Island colony. Prologue 2 acts 11 scenes Large mixed cast 1 setting

The **green** cockatoo. Schnitzler, A.

Green fields. Hirschbein, P.

The **green** heart. Magee, R.

The **green** hill. Ives, D.

Greenberg, Richard

The American plan.

Drama about loneliness, homosexuality and class distinction set in 1960s Catskill resort. Jewish widow discourages disturbed daughter's romance with young social climber. 2 acts 13 scenes 3m 2w 1 setting

In Greenberg, R. Three days of rain and other plays

The author's voice.

Satirical look at publishing world. Editor discovers that her latest protege is taking credit for work of misshapen creature whose physical ugliness forces him to remain in closet. 9 scenes 2m 1w 1 interior

In Greenberg, R. Three days of rain and other plays

The dazzle.

Drama about obsession based on lives of the Collyer brothers, New York's legendary recluses. 2 acts 10 scenes 2m 1w 1 interior

In Greenberg, R. The dazzle and Everett Beekin

Everett Beekin.

Drama set in tenement apartment on New York's Lower East Side, 1947. Relationships of two sets of Jewish sisters. 2 parts 2m 4w 1 interior

In Greenberg, R. The dazzle and Everett Beekin

Hurrah at last.

Comedy about effects of desiring and having money. Struggling highbrow writer annoyed by playwright friend whose trash makes millions. 2 acts 3 scenes epilogue 5m 3w interiors

In Greenberg, R. Three days of rain and other plays

Take me out. Faber & Faber 2003 115p

ISBN 0-571-21118-6

Tragicomedy about baseball and bigotry. Star center fielder for New York team announces he is gay. 3 acts 11m

Three days of rain. Dramatists 1999 70p

ISBN 0-8222-1676-0

Drama set in Manhattan loft. Following his death, brother and sister struggle to reconcile troubling childhood memories with their architect father's journal account of past. 2 acts 2m 1w 1 interior

—Same

In Greenberg, R. Three days of rain and other Plays

Greenblatt, Richard. See Flacks, D. jt. auth.

Greene, Graham

The end of the affair (dramatization) See Goold, R., and Butler, C. The end of the affair

Greene, Robert

Selimus, emperor of the Turks.

Elizabethan play about the rise to power of Selim I, sultan of the Turks, portrayed as a godless and murderous villain. Music. Prologue 29 scenes epilogue 21m 3w extras settings

In Three Turk plays from early modern England; ed. by D. J. Vitkus

Greenhorn, Stephen

Passing places. Hern Bks. 1998 84p

ISBN 1-85459-349-8

Pursued by mad gangster, two young Scots make unplanned road trip through the Highlands. 54 scenes 8m 3w extras 1 setting

Greenwich mean. Guare, J.

Greetings from a queer señorita. Palacios, M.

Gregg, Stephen

A private moment.

Drama set in mid-nineteenth-century North Carolina. Siamese twin Chang Bunker attempts to have private moment with young woman. 2m 2w 1 interior

In 30 ten-minute plays for 4, 5 & 6 actors from Actors Theatre of Louisville's National Ten-minute Play Contest

Greig, David

The architect.

Portrait of once idealistic architect whose buildings and family crumble in light of harsh reality. 2 acts 49 scenes 4m 3w 1 setting

In Greig, D. Plays: 1

The cosmonaut's last message to the woman he once loved in the former Soviet Union.

Drama about language, space and love. Stranded cosmonaut attempts to contact lover. 2 acts 40 scenes 4m 2w settings

In Greig, D. Plays: 1

Europe.

Drama about love, loss and longing. Old and new Europeans interact in railway station in unnamed border town. 2 acts 20 scenes 6m 2w 1 setting

In Greig, D. Plays: 1

The **grey** zone. Nelson, T. B.

Grief. Lucas, C.

Griffin, Helen

The ark.

Drama about grieving family of woman, after death of father. 1 act 3w 1 setting

In Act one Wales; ed. by P. Clark

Griffith, Lois Elaine

White sirens.

One woman show. Monologues by various women of color. 1 act 1w

In Action; ed. by M. Algarin and L. Griffith

Griffiths, Annabel, and others

Bittergirl.

Comedy about abandonment and resilience. Three women go from shock and grief to anger and vengeance after being dumped by generic man. 26 scenes 1m 3w 1 setting

In Seven short plays from Theatre Ontario

Griffiths, Linda

Alien creature. Playwrights Canada 2000 58p

ISBN 0-88754-598-X   LC 00-421191

Monologue supposedly spoken by the Canadian poet Gwendolyn MacEwen, who died of alcoholism in 1987; draws on her writings to tell her life story. 1w 1 interior

Brother Andre's heart.

Montreal misfits steal holy relic. 2 acts 2m 2w 1 interior

In Griffiths, L. Sheer nerve

The Darling family.

Conflict between man and woman who disagree over what to do about unplanned pregnancy. 1 act 1m 1w 1 setting

In 7 cannons

—Same

In Griffiths, L. Sheer nerve

The Duchess, a.k.a. Wallis Simpson.

Radio play based on life of Wallis Simpson, who became Duchess of Windsor when King Edward VIII abdicated the throne to marry her. Background music. 13 scenes 6m 4w

In Griffiths, L. Sheer nerve

A game of inches.

Woman reflects on Zen, baseball and sex. 1w 1 interior

In Griffiths, L. Sheer nerve

Jessica.

Charts a Metis woman's search for personal identity. 2 acts 3m 3w 2 interiors

In Griffiths, L. Sheer nerve

Maggie & Pierre.

One woman show in which an actress portrays Canadian Prime Minister Elliott Trudeau and wife Margaret through their turbulent marriage. The media is represented by Henry, a reporter, also played by same actress. Background music. 2 acts 19 scenes 1w 1 setting

In Griffiths, L. Sheer nerve

Griffiths, Linda—*Continued*

O.D. on paradise.

Three couples vacationing in Jamaica face harsh truth about themselves and each other. 2 acts 14 scenes 4m 4w 1 setting

In Griffiths, L. Sheer nerve

Griffiths, Trevor

Food for ravens. Oberon Bks. 1997 83p

ISBN 1-8400-2028-8   LC 2002-523041

Television play about the life of Aneurin Bevan, British Labour politician and architect of the National Health Service. 1b 7m 4w

Grimm, David

Kit Marlow. Dramatists 2001 76p

ISBN 0-8222-1802-X

Drama about Christopher Marlowe's work as spy for dark wing of the Tudor government. 2 acts 12m extras 1 interior 1 exterior

Sheridan; or, Schooled in scandal. Dramatists 2001 75p il

ISBN 0-8222-1803-8   LC 2001-277839

Follows the lives of playwright Richard Brinsley Sheridan and poet Lord Byron in London, England, during the reign of King George III. 2 acts 7 scenes 6m 3w 1 setting

Grimm, Brothers

The boy who left home to find out about the shivers (dramatization) See Bush, M. The boy who left home to find out about the shivers

Cinderella (dramatization) See Cornett, E. Cinderella; Frankonis, W. A. A tale of Cinderella

Hansel and Gretel (dramatization) See Francoeur, B. The story of Hansel and Gretel

Rumpelstiltskin (dramatization) See Mason, T. African tales: Kalulu and his monkey farm and Rumpelstiltskin

The six swans (dramatization) See McCullough, L. E. The six swans

Sleeping Beauty (dramatization) See Francoeur, B. Enchanted Sleeping Beauty

The wolf and the seven kids (dramatization) See McBride-Smith, B. The wolf and the seven kids

Grimsley, Jim

y A bird of prey.

Story behind young man's murder and its effect on his classmates. 4m 4w extras

In New Plays from A.C.T.'s young conservatory v3

The borderland.

Neighboring families of distinctly different social backgrounds are brought together by storm. 2 acts 2m 2w 1 interior

In Grimsley, J. Mr. Universe and other plays

The lizard of Tarsus.

Paul of Tarsus interrogates an imprisoned Jesus. 2m 1w 1 interior

In Grimsley, J. Mr. Universe and other plays

Math and aftermath.

During film shoot on beach at Bikini Atoll in 1954 worlds of pornography and nuclear testing collide. 5m 2w extra 1 exterior

In Grimsley, J. Mr. Universe and other plays

Mr. Universe.

Portrays sexual obsessions and fetishes of marginal characters in underbelly of New Orleans. 2 acts 5 scenes 4m 3w 1 exterior 1 interior

In Grimsley, J. Mr. Universe and other plays

Gromelski, Brad

Position available. French 1998 31p

ISBN 0-573-62622-7   LC 98-211978

Comedy which develops into a mystery resulting from a classified ad. 2m 1w

Gross indecency: the three trials of Oscar Wilde. Kaufman, M.

Gross indecency: the three trials of Oscar Wilde (condensation). Kaufman, M.

The **grouch**. Menander

Growing up

Norman, M. Emily

Parnell, P. The cider house rules: part 1

Parnell, P. The cider house rules: part 2

Posner, A. The chosen

Guardian and ward

Molière. The school for wives

Guarding the bridge. Gorden, C.

Guare, John

Chaucer in Rome. Dramatists 2002
ISBN 0-8222-1840-2

Matt has learned that his painting has given him cancer. In return for survival, he must abandon paint for a new artistic medium. 8m 4w 1 setting

A few stout individuals. Grove Press 2003 121p
ISBN 0-8021-4002-5

Drama set in 1885. Ulysses Grant, dying of throat cancer, struggles to complete memoirs. 2 acts 9m 4w

The general of hot desire.

Inspired by Shakespeare's sonnets 153 and 154 and The golden legend by Jacobus de Voragine. Troupe of actors stage wild version of the expulsion from Eden, featuring a cranky, indifferent God and human beings who are compelled to love and create art if they desire solace. Singing. 1 act 1 scene 5m 4w 1 setting

In Guare, J. The general of hot desire and other plays

—Same

In Love's fire

Greenwich mean.

Two people are in the process of joining households when an earthquake destroys the trust between them. 1 act Variable cast 2 characters 1 setting

Guare, J. The general of hot desire and other plays

Lake Hollywood. Dramatists 2000 87p
ISBN 0-8222-1737-6

Tragicomedy that spans 50 years in the lives of a couple who once dreamt of a lake retreat for Hollywood stars, now face the reality of love and friendship. Prologue 2 acts 9 scenes 4m 4w 2 settings

New York actor.

Satirical look at New York theater community. 1 act 5m 3w 1 interior

In Guare, J. The general of hot desire and other plays

—Same

In Take ten; ed. by E. Lane and N. Shengold

The talking dog.

Adapted from a Chekhov story, but set among hang-gliders. A man whispers inspiring, tantalizing phrases to a woman but never acknowledges that he spoke. 1 act 1m 1w extras 1 setting

In Guare, J. The general of hot desire and other plays

Guatemala

y McIntyre, H. Hunger

The **guerrillas**. McCabe, J. D. J.

The **guest** lecturer. Gurney, A. R.

The **guest** of honor. Strand, R.

The **guests**. Zorin, L.

Guevara, Che

about

Culture Clash (Group). A bowl of beings

A **guide** to mourning. Stickland, E.

Guiding star. Harvey, J.

Guillotine. Martin, S.

Guilt

Chekhov, A. P. Tatyana Repina

Dattani, M. Tara

Ehn, E. Incide (Judas Iscariot)

Harvey, J. Guiding star

Herbert, K. Hit and run

Holman, R. Bad weather

Ibsen, H. Little Eyolf

Kennedy, A. Orestes (Euripides)

Kennedy, A. A rat's mass

Lan, D. The end of the earth

Lucas, C. Throwing your voice

Nigro, D. Creatures lurking in the churchyard

Nigro, D. The sin-eater

Pirandello, L. Naked

Rachilde. The painted woman (La Femme peinte)

Strindberg, A. The ghost sonata

Wilhelm, L. Meridian, Mississippi redux

The **guilt** card. McConnell, J.

Guirgis, Stephen Adly

In Arabia we'd all be kings. Dramatists 2002
ISBN 0-8222-1800-3

At a seedy bar in pre-Giuliani Times Square, various characters meet, unaware that the owner wants to sell the place. 8m 4w 1 interior setting

Jesus hopped the 'A' train. Dramatists 2002
ISBN 0-8222-1799-6

Guirgis, Stephen Adly—*Continued*

Angel Cruz is a thirty-year-old bike messenger in Riker's Island prison, awaiting trial for shooting a religious cult leader who later dies. Put in protective custody, his only human contact is another prisoner, who is a sociopathic serial killer who has found God. 4m 1w 1 interior setting

—Same

In New playwrights: the best plays of 2000

The **guitarrón**. Alvarez, L.

Gulag. Fulford, R. W.

The **gulf** of crimson. Levi, S.

Gulliver. Carter, L.

Gulliver redux. Carter, L.

Gum. Hartman, K.

Gunpowder Plot, 1605

Poskitt, K. Fawkes—the quiet guy

Gunter's wife. Bogdan, K.

Gurney, A. R. (Albert Ramsdell)

Ancestral voices: a family story. Broadway Play Pub. 2000 52p

ISBN 0-88145-171-1

Family drama staged as concert work with five performers sitting in front of music stands. Grandfather, grandmother, mother, father and son of wealthy WASP family in Buffalo, New York between 1935 and 1942. 1b 2m 2w 1 setting

—Same

In Gurney, A. R. Collected plays, 1992-1999

Another Antigone.

Classics professor at small Boston college clashes with student over adaptation of Antigone raising issues of anti-Semitism and academic freedom. 1 act 2m 2w settings

In Gurney, A. R. Collected plays, 1984-1991

A Cheever evening.

Episodes from seventeen of John Cheever's stories interwoven to portray WASP life in 1950s and 1960s. Music. 2 acts 3m 3w 1 setting

In Gurney, A. R. Collected plays, 1991-1995

The cocktail hour.

Set in 1970s upstate New York. Playwright comes in conflict with elderly father when he writes play about his family. 2 acts 2m 2w 1 interior

In Gurney, A. R. Collected plays, 1984-1991

Darlene.

Comedy about suburban couple with mixed reactions to explicit letter left on their windshield. 1 act 1m 1w 1 interior

In Gurney, A. R. Collected plays, 1992-1999

—Same

In Gurney, A. R. Darlene and The guest lecturer

Far East. Broadway Play Pub. 1999 85p

ISBN 0-88145-161-4

Drama about young U.S. naval officer on tour of duty in mid-1950s Japan, who falls in love with Japanese woman. 2 acts 3m 2w extra 1 setting

—Same

In Gurney, A. R. Collected plays, 1992-1999

The fourth wall. Dramatists 2003

ISBN 0-8222-1349-4

Comedy set in Buffalo, New York. Wife decides to redecorate living room as if it were a stage set. Music, singing. 2m 2w 1 interior

—Same

In Gurney, A. R. Collected plays, 1991-1995

The golden age.

Contemporary comedy suggested by Henry James' The Aspern papers. Ambitious young academic seeks out reclusive New York dowager who he is convinced possesses unpublished chapter of The great Gatsby. 2 acts 1m 2w 1 setting

In Gurney, A. R. Collected plays, 1984-1991

The guest lecturer.

Down on its luck, a theater resorts to guest speakers for income. Music, singing. 1 act 2m 2w 1 interior

In Gurney, A. R. Collected plays, 1992-1999

—Same

In Gurney, A. R. Darlene and The guest lecturer

Human events. Broadway Play Pub. 2001 88p

ISBN 0-88145-201-7

Comedy of manners. Associate professor at esteemed Boston college watches as his protégé surpasses him in the department hierarchy and takes an interest in his wife. 2 acts 3m 2w extras 1 setting

Gurney, A. R. (Albert Ramsdell)—*Continued*

Labor Day. Dramatists 1999 71p
ISBN 0-8222-1685-X

Tragicomedy set in Connecticut country home over Labor Day weekend. Cancer-stricken playwright wrestles with recent script based on his own family. 2 acts 3m 2w 1 setting

—Same

In Gurney, A. R. Collected plays, 1992-1999

Later life.

Romantic comedy. Boston cocktail party setting for divorced middle-aged banker's encounter with woman he nearly had an affair with in his youth. Background music. 2m 2w 1 exterior

In Gurney, A. R. Collected plays, 1991-1995

Love letters.

Traces epistolary romance from grade school through middle age. 2 parts 1m 1w

In Gurney, A. R. Collected plays, 1984-1991

The old boy.

Drama. Politician's return to prep-school to dedicate building to friend dead of AIDS forces crisis of conscience. 2 acts 3m 3w 1 setting

In Gurney, A. R. Collected plays, 1984-1991

Overtime.

Modern sequel to The merchant of Venice set in contemporary America. 6m 3w 1 setting

In Gurney, A. R. Collected plays, 1991-1995

The perfect party.

Comedy. Urbane college professor quits job and tries to climb social ladder by hosting the perfect party. 2 acts 2m 3w 1 interior

In Gurney, A. R. Collected plays, 1984-1991

The snow ball.

Drama depicting middle-aged WASP men attempting to relive their youth by staging midwinter charity ball. Dancing. 2 acts 5m 5w extras 1 interior

In Gurney, A. R. Collected plays, 1991-1995

Sweet Sue.

Comedy. Two actresses and two actors portray different aspects of same two characters who become romantically involved—a middle-aged divorcee and her son's college roommate. 2 acts 2m 2w 1 interior

In Gurney, A. R. Collected plays, 1984-1991

Sylvia.

Comedy. Middle-aged New York couple's marriage put in jeopardy when husband becomes overly attached to stray dog (portrayed by actress) he found in park. Music. 2 acts 2 scenes 2m 2w 1 setting

In Gurney, A. R. Collected plays, 1992-1999

Gurr, Michael

Crazy brave. Currency Press 2000 53p
ISBN 0-868-19-615-0

Drama about urban guerilla group in Melbourne, Australia. 19 scenes 4m 2w 1 setting

Guyer, Murphy

Loyalties.

Men have heated discussion about cowardice and patriotism as wives attempt to keep them calm. 2m 2w 1 interior

In 30 ten-minute plays for 4, 5 & 6 actors from Actors Theatre of Louisville's National Ten-minute Play Contest

World of mirth. Dramatists 2002
ISBN 0-8222-1845-3

When the self-described "family" of the World of Mirth carnival hits astreak of bad weather and bad luck, their response is fearfully un-family-like. 7m 2w 1 setting

Guys. Badlam, R.

Gwyn, Nell, 1650-1687

about

Poskitt, K. Nell's belles

Gypsies

O'Malley, G. Concertina's rainbow

H

H; or, Monologues at front of burning cities. Wood, C.

Habitat. Thompson, J.

Hackenbrook, William J.

Conditions. French 2001 103p
ISBN 0-573-62777-0

Hackenbrook, William J.—*Continued*

Farce. Grandson will inherit 10 million dollars if he marries his grandmother's assistant and they remain faithful to each other for one year. 3 acts 5m 3w 1 setting

Haere mai ki aotearoa. McKee, J.

Hail, Queen Esther! McCullough, L. E.

Hairston, Jerome

a.m. Sunday.

Black father, white mother, and their two sons. A family in quiet crisis, with many secrets. 1 act 6 scenes 1b 2m 2w 3 interiors 2 exteriors

In Humana Festival 2002

Forty-minute finish.

Two young grocery clerks have to clean up after man dies in store. 2m 1 interior

In 30 ten-minute plays for 2 actors from Actors Theatre of Louisville's National Ten-minute Play Contest

—Same

In Actors Theatre of Louisville: Ten-minute plays; v5

The **hairy** ape. O'Neill, E.

Haiti

Walcott, D. Drums and colours
Walcott, D. The Haitian earth
Walcott, D. Henri Christophe

The **Haitian** earth. Walcott, D.

Hall, Carol

The best little whorehouse goes public; book by Larry L. King and Peter Masterson; music and lyrics by Carol Hall. French 1999 80p

ISBN 0-573-62660-X

Satirical musical. The famous Texas brothel reopens as a publicly owned corporation. Prologue. 2 acts 15 scenes 11m 3w settings

See also Hall, C. jt. auth.

Hall, Lee

c The adventures of Pinocchio. Methuen 2000 81p

ISBN 0-413-76720-5

Adaptation of Collodi's classic. Singing. 2 acts 24 scenes 21m 1w settings

Bollocks.

Inspired by Toller's novel, Hinkeman, this is a stage adaptation of the radio play, Gristle. It examines the impotence of lives ruined by war. 1 act 27 scenes 4m 2w settings

In Hall, L. Cooking with Elvis & Bollocks

—Same

In Hall, L. Plays: 1

Child of our time: child of the snow.

Monologue by a Sami (Lapp) boy, about his people and their reindeer and life on the tundra. Juxtaposes ancient and modern elements. Music. 1 act 1b 1 setting

In Hall, L. Plays: 1

Child of our time: children of the rain.

Radio play created from fictional material and interviews with English children. Questioned about the world and themselves, they answer with comic ignorance, idealism, cynicism, and pathos. Music. 1 act Variable cast 1 setting

In Hall, L. Plays: 1

Cooking with Elvis.

Stage adaptation of the radio play, Blood sugar. When an Elvis impersonator is paralyzed in a car crash, his wife and daughter are forced to cope with the aftermath. 1 act 23 scenes 3m 3w 1 setting

In Hall, L. Cooking with Elvis & Bollocks

—Same

In Hall, L. Plays: 1

Genie.

Short play about a girl brought up in isolation to see if she will spontaneously develop language. Music. 1 act 7 scenes 1g 1w 1 setting

In Hall, L. Plays: 1

I love you, Jimmy Spud.

A boy who is constantly teased by schoolmates and criticized by his dying father becomes an apprentice angel and sets out to save lives. Music. 1 act 2b 3m 1w extras settings

In Hall, L. Plays: 1

Spoonface Steinberg.

Monologue by a quirky autistic child who is dying of cancer. Tragicomedy inspired in part by Hasidic writings. 1 act 1g 1 interior

In Hall, L. Plays: 1

Two's company.

Comic monologue by an earnest bigamist. 1 act 1m 1 setting

In Hall, L. Plays: 1

Hall, Lee—*Continued*

Wittgenstein on Tyne.

Farce set in World War II England. The philosopher Wittgenstein, surprised in a compromising position, discusses the meaning of meaning with some ineffably British neighbors during an airraid. 1 act 2m 2w 1 setting

In Hall, L. Plays: 1

Hall, Rodney

A return to the brink. Currency Press 1999 64p

ISBN 0-86819-590-1   LC 2001-334396

Drama examines personal courage and political drama behind 1838 court investigation into notorius Myall Creek massacre. 2 acts 6m 1w 2 interiors

Hall, Tony

Jean and Dinah who have been locked away in a world famous calypso since 1956 speak their minds publicly.

Retake on popular calypso that won 1956 Calypso Crown for Mighty Sparrow. Two elderly, dying Trinidadian women look back at past through shared memory. Prologue 2 acts epilogue

In Testifyin' v2; ed. by D. Sears

Hall of healing. O'Casey, S.

Halliwell, David

Little Malcolm and his struggle against the eunuchs. French (London) 1998 76p

ISBN 0-573-01544-9

Dark comedy about a failed art student who forms neo-fascist type party against the headmaster and uncreative students. 2 acts 2 scenes 4m 1w 1 setting

Halloween night. Hughes, D.

Halvorson, Kristina

One hundred women.

Young woman yearns for female companionship. 1m 2w 1 interior

In 30 ten-minute plays for 3 actors from Actors Theatre of Louisville's National Ten-minute Play Contest

Hamilton, Richard

The slaves of solitude (dramatization) See Kane, R. Miss Roach's war

Hamilton, W. A.

Bellies, knees and ankles.

Conversations between waitress and three female customers uncover secrets. 4w 1 interior

In Seven short plays from Theatre Ontario

Hamlet. Nielsen, K.

The **hamlet** of Stepney Green. Kops, B.

Hamlett, Christina

c Author! Author!.

Comedy. Fairy-tale characters promote their books on television talk show. 1 act 2m 2w 1 interior

In Hamlett, C. Lively plays for young actors

c Eat, drink, and be scary.

Comedy. Witch restauranteur tries not to scare off daughter's new beau. 1 act 5m 8w 1 interior

In Hamlett, C. Lively plays for young actors

c The ghost of Hemstead House.

Comedy. Sheriff receives reports of ghostly activity. 1 act 4m 2w 1 interior

In Hamlett, C. Lively plays for young actors

c It's an okie-dokie life.

Parody of motion picture It's a wonderful life set in the Old West. 1 act 3m 5w 1 setting

In Hamlett, C. Lively plays for young actors

c The magic mermaid.

Verse play for round-the-table reading based on English folktale about mermaid. 1 act Variable cast 9 characters

In Hamlett, C. Lively plays for young actors

c Mother Goose gumshoe.

Comedy. Detective searches for missing nursery rhyme characters. 1 act 1m 4w 1 interior

In Hamlett, C. Lively plays for young actors

c Once upon a fairy tale.

Comedy. Three fairy-tale witches escape from book and lose powers. 1 act 2 scenes 1b 6m 8w 1 interior 2 exteriors

In Hamlett, C. Lively plays for young actors

Hamlett, Christina—*Continued*

c Picture perfect.

Parody of Oscar Wilde's The picture of Dorian Gray. 1 act 2 scenes 4m 5w 1 interior 1 exterior

In Hamlett, C. Lively plays for young actors

c The prince's dilemma.

Arabian nights parody. 1 act 4m 2w 1 interior

In Hamlett, C. Lively plays for young actors

c Secret agents in disguise.

Comedy. Spies use quiet career woman's house to hide government witness. 1 act 2 scenes 3m 4w 2 interiors

In Hamlett, C. Lively plays for young actors

c The wedding bell blues.

Romantic comedy. Wedding planner copes with difficult client. 1 act 2m 4w 1 interior

In Hamlett, C. Lively plays for young actors

c Where there's a Will, there's a play.

Comedy. William Shakespeare struggles with writer's block. 1 act 3m 4w 1 interior

In Hamlett, C. Lively plays for young actors

Hanan, Stephen Mo

Jolson & company.

Biography of Al Jolson, framed as radio interview with flashbacks. 2 acts Variable cast 17 characters settings

In New playwrights: the best plays of 2000

Handel, George Frederick

about

Slover, T. Joyful noise

The **handless** maiden. Dobrish, J.

Hands of light. Pomerance, B.

Handy, Peter

East of the sun and west of the moon.

A life-altering correspondence between an English nurse and a Native American soldier, stemming from their meeting at a field hospital in Flanders during World War I. Music. 1 act 1m 1w 1 setting

In Off-Off Broadway Festival plays, 25th ser.

Hanes, Mary

The crimson thread. French 1998 76p

ISBN 0-573-63220-0   LC 98-213914

Drama set 1869 to 1911. Follows Irish sisters from their homeland to New York. 3 acts 6w 1 interior

Doin' time at the Alamo. French 1999 72p

ISBN 0-573-62657-X

Comedy about seven people who stay in a Texas motel located across from a federal penitentiary where their loved ones are imprisoned. 2 acts 10 scenes 2m 5w 1 interior

Hanging on the tree. Anderson, S. J.

Hangnail. Silverstein, S.

Hannah, Don

Fathers and sons.

Succession of reflective monologues performed by two actors, one portraying boy from infancy to maturity, the other portraying man from youthful parenthood to death. Music. 4 acts 31 scenes 2m 1w

In Hannah, D. Shoreline

Rubber Dolly.

Portrait of illiterate, unemployed, sometimes abused, single welfare mother. 22 scenes 1b 1g 1m 2w 1 setting

In Hannah, D. Shoreline

Running far back.

Drama spans three generations of New Brunswick family. Examines tensions between anglophone and francophone communities. 2 acts 28 scenes 1b 3m 3w 1 exterior

In Hannah, D. Shoreline

Hansell, Susan

My Medea.

Makeover of Medea myth set in 1990s Los Angeles. 4m 1w extras 1 setting

In The Best American short plays, 1996-1997

Hanukkah

c McCullough, L. E. Chanukah: come light the menorah!

Hapgood. Stoppard, T.

Happenstance. Sagal, P.

Happy families. Godber, J.

Happy Jack. Godber, J.

Happy mug. Dewberry, E.

The **happy** prince. Wong, E.

Hard-boiled. Frockt, D. L.

Hard hat area. Silverstein, S.

Hard times. Barchers, S. I., and Kroll, J. L.

Harden, Vern

y Big boys don't cry. Pioneer Drama Service 1998 52p

Drama portrays devastation of child abuse and poverty. Courtroom stunned when 15-year-old boy is released from hospital to testify at father's trial. 2 acts Variable cast 17 characters settings

y The boardinghouse. Pioneer Drama Service 2000 64p

Comedy about eccentric residents of lodging house. 2 acts 3m 7w 1 interior

y HIV positive. Pioneer Drama Service 1998 30p

While in hospital for simple procedure, 18-year-old man learns he is HIV positive. 4m 5w 1 interior

y Jessica and Jolene. Pioneer Drama Service 2000 22p

Portrays struggle of teenage twin sisters to establish own identities while still retaining links to friends and family. 1 act 3 scenes 3m 7w 1 setting

y Nobody heard mercy. Pioneer Drama Service 1999 34p

Follows teenage boy suffering from depression. 6m 6w 1 interior

Hardin, Herschel

Esker Mike & his wife, Agiluk.

Social satire. After bearing fourteen children, Inuit woman refuses to have any more until her lover can provide for them. 14 scenes 9m 6w 4 interiors 7 exteriors

In Staging the North; ed. by S. Grace, E. D'Aeth and L. Chalykoff

Harding, Michael P.

Sour grapes.

Drama exploring taboos of seminary life including pedophilia and homosexuality. 2 acts 35 scenes 8m 1 setting

In New plays from the Abbey Theatre v2

Harding, Mike

Comfort and joy. French (London) 1998 78p

ISBN 0-573-01772-7   LC 98-229011

Comedy about family gathering at Christmas which turns into series of small disasters. 2 acts 6 scenes 6m 6w 1 interior

Hardy, Carey Jane

Let it be me. French (London) 2003 63p

ISBN 0-573-01986-X

Woman falls in love with bookseller while caring for aunt with Alzheimer's. 2 acts 5 scenes 2m 4w 1 setting

Hardy, Thomas

Far from the madding crowd (dramatization) See White, M. Far from the madding crowd

Hare, David

Amy's view. Faber & Faber 1997 127p

ISBN 0-571-19179-7

Drama set in England between 1979 and 1995. Struggle for separation between famous actress and dutiful daughter. 4 acts 3m 3w 2 interiors

—Same. French 1999 117p

The bay at Nice.

Drama set in 1956 Leningrad about attempt to authenticate a painting. 2m 2w 1 interior

In Hare, D. The secret rapture and other plays

The blue room. French 1999 75p

ISBN 0-573-62705-3

Freely adapted from Arthur Schnitzler's La ronde. Five different couples form inadvertent sexual daisy chain that traverses lines of social class and money. 10 scenes 1m 1w 1 setting

—Same. Grove Press 1998 85p

ISBN 0-8021-3596-X

The breath of life. Faber & Faber 2002 93p

ISBN 0-571-21593-9

Drama set on Isle of Wight about two women in their sixties who have been abandoned by London barrister in favor of young girl. Confrontation between wife, now a popular novelist, and mistress, a retired museum curator. 4 scenes 2w 1 setting

Fanshen.

Dramatization of William Hinton's book detailing effect of Chinese revolution on inhabitants of village of Long Bow. 2 acts 12 sections 7m 2w

In Hare, D. The secret rapture and other plays

The Judas kiss. French 1999 104p

ISBN 0-573-62665-0   LC 99-219507

Hare, David—*Continued*

Drama about Oscar Wilde, his lover, Lord Alfred Douglas, and the consequences of facing imprisonment. 2 acts 4 scenes 6m 1w 2 settings

A map of the world.

Set in Bombay during UNESCO conference on world poverty. Relationship of the West to Third World reflected in ideological and emotional clashes between cynical Indian novelist and idealistic British journalist. 2 acts 10 scenes 6m 4w extras 1 setting

In Hare, D. The secret rapture and other plays

My zinc bed. Faber & Faber 2000 130p

ISBN 0-571-20574-7   LC 2001-334131

Internet businessman hires alcoholic poet as copywriter, and the poet falls in love with the businessman's cocaine-addicted ex-wife. 2 acts 12 scenes 2m 1w

Saigon: year of the cat.

Drama focusing on emotional turmoil endured by individuals during United States's withdrawal from Vietnam. 11m 1w extras

In Hare, D. The secret rapture and other plays

The secret rapture.

Political allegory set in Margaret Thatcher's England. Following father's death, "good" sister's life is destroyed by ambitious MP sister, her born-again Christian husband, and father's destructive young alcoholic widow. 2 acts 8 scenes 2m 4w settings

In Hare, D. The secret rapture and other plays

Via Dolorosa. Samuel French 2000 38p

ISBN 0-573-62733-9

Monologue based on author's visits to Middle East in 1990s. Examines personalities of actual figures on both sides of Arab-Israeli conflict. 1m 1 setting

—Same

In Hare, D. Via Dolorosa & When shall we live?

Harelik, Mark

The legacy. Broadway Play Pub. 1997 87p

ISBN 0-88145-1320

Drama about the on-going story of the Estanitskys, a Jewish family living in West Texas. 2 acts 4 scenes 1b 3m 3w 1 setting

Harlem duet. Sears, D.

Harper, Lisa

An' push da wind down. French 1998 86p

ISBN 0-573-69665-0

Drama set in rural Georgia from 1828 to 1838. Follows runaway slave as she heads north to freedom. 2 acts 25 scenes 3m 5w 1 setting

Harpers Ferry (W. Va.)

John Brown's Raid, 1859

Swayze, J. C. Ossawattomie Brown

The **harps** of God. Stetson, K.

Harriet Tubman visits a therapist. Gage, C.

Harrigan, Edward

The blue and the grey.

Two Irish immigrant brothers fight on opposing sides in Civil War. Singing. 2 scenes 2m 1w extras 1 interior 1 exterior

In Fateful lightning; ed. by W. J. Meserve and M. A. Meserve

Harris, Aurand

c The Arkansaw bear.

Metaphorical play about coping with death featuring young girl whose grandfather is dying and a dancing bear. 1 act Variable cast 5 characters extras 1 setting

In Theatre for young audiences; ed. by C. A. Jennings

c The orphan train. Anchorage Press 1998 59p

ISBN 0-87602-360-X

Set in 1914. Dramatizes the experiences of city children who were sent to the country for adoption. Music, singing, dancing. Prologue 1 act 8 scenes Variable cast 1 setting

c The second shepherd's play.

Adaptation of early modern miracle play. Music, singing. Variable cast

In The twelve plays of Christmas; ed. by L. Swortzell

Harris, Richard

Ghosts; from a translation by J. Basil Cowlishaw. French (London) 2002 50p

ISBN 0-573-01969-X

Adaptation of play by Henrik Ibsen. Tragedy about effects of suppressing disturbing truths. Widow finally faces husband's dissipation and adultery and realizes her son is suffering from hereditary syphilis. 2 acts 3m 2w 1 interior

Harris, Richard—*Continued*

In two minds. French (London) 2002 87p

ISBN 0-573-01968-1

Unmarried couple move into old house, and man gradually comes to suspect their next-door neighbor of murder. 2 acts 15 scenes 2m 2w 2 interiors

Harris, Zinnie

Further than the furthest thing. Dramatists 2003

ISBN 0-8222-1874-7

On a remote island in the middle of the Atlantic, secrets are buried. 3m 2w 1 setting

Harrison, Jane

Stolen. rev ed. Currency Press 2000 36p

ISBN 0-86819-637-1   LC 2001-326038

Drama about five Aboriginal children forcibly removed from their parents, put in a children's home, and trained for domestic service. Variable cast 5 characters 1 setting

Harrison, Neil

Whodidit? French (London) 2001 50p

ISBN 0-573-12316-0

Spoof on country house murder mystery. 1b 9m 5w

Harrison, Tony

Doomsday.

Verse drama based on medieval mystery play cycles about Christ's descent into hell. Large mixed cast 1 setting

In Harrison, T. Plays: one: The mysteries

The Nativity.

Combines aspects of various mystery play cycles into depiction of Christ's birth. Variable cast 33 characters 1 setting

In Harrison, T. Plays: one: The mysteries

The passion.

This account of the crucifixion and burial of Christ incorporates material from York, Chester, Wakefield and Coventry cycles. 18m 5w extras 1 setting

In Harrison, T. Pays: one: The mysteries

Harrower, David

Kill the old torture their young. Methuen 1998 72p

ISBN 0-413-73510-9

A documentary maker returns to the city of his birth. He films his impressions. People tells stories, but who will listen? 4 acts 18 scenes 5m 2w settings

Harte, Bret, 1836-1902

The luck of Roaring Camp (dramatization) See Barchers, S. I., and Kroll, J. L. The luck of Roaring Camp

Hartman, Karen

Gum.

Two sisters in fictitious country, veiled and secluded in garden, share a piece of forbidden "gum." 10 scenes 2m 3w

In Hartman K. Gum

The mother of modern censorship.

In a fictional country, the job of the chief music censor is challenged by ambitious new girl. 1 act 1m 3w settings

In Hartman, K. Gum

Harvest. Hughes, L.

Harvest. Padmanabhan, M.

Harvey, Jonathan

Beautiful thing; an urban fairytale. Methuen 2002 86p

ISBN 00-413-71030-0

A portrait of adolescent self-discovery. 2 acts 10 scenes 3m 2w settings

Guiding star. Methuen 1998 114p

ISBN 0-413-73610-5

Drama set in Liverpool, Tenby, and London, 1998. Nine years after surviving Hillsborough stadium disaster middle-aged father and husband is haunted by survivor's guilt. 2 acts 14 scenes 5m 4w 3 interiors 5 exteriors

—Same

In Harvey, J. Plays: 2

Hushabye Mountain. Methuen 1999 104p

ISBN 0-413-72960-5

Drama about love, pain, friendship and drugs in world that has learned how to live with AIDS. 6m 7w extras

—Same

In Harvey, J. Plays: 2

Out in the open. Methuen 2001 113p

ISBN 0-413-76250-5

Comedy about love triangle set in London. Gay "widower" and young Mancunian turn out to have partner in common. 2 acts 6 scenes 3m 3w 1 exterior

Harvey, Jonathan—*Continued*
—Same
   In Harvey, J. Plays: 2

Hasidism
   Kushner, T. A dybbuk, or between two worlds
   c McCullough, L. E. Tale of the Baal Shem Tov
Hast thou considered my servant Job? Wilder, T.

Hatcher, Jeffrey
Downtown.
   Three wanna-be writers meet in bar. 2m 1w 1 interior
      In 30 ten-minute plays for 3 actors from Actors Theatre of Louisville's National Ten-minute Play Contest
Tango Delta.
   Agents on rooftop await presidential motorcade. 3m extras 1 exterior
      In 30 ten-minute plays for 3 Actors from Actors Theatre of Louisville's National Ten-minute Play Contest
To fool the eye; tr. by Stephenie L. Debner. Dramatists 2003
   ISBN 0-8222-1846-1
New adaptation of Anouilh's 1940 romantic comedy. A poor hatmaker is invited to a chateau by an eccentric duchess to try to make her suicidal nephew forget about the death of his great love. 7m 2w settings
What Corbin knew.
   Social comedy satirizes two middle classes: suburban yuppies and urban hipsters clash. 4 prologues 2 acts 7 scenes 3m 2w 1 interior
      In New playwrights: the best plays of 1999
The **Hatfields** and the McCoys. Art, S. S.
Hauptmann. Logan, J.
Have a nice day. Silverstein, S.
Have you seen Zandile? Mhlophe, G.

Havel, Václav
The beggar's opera. Cornell University Press 2001 84p
   ISBN 0-8014-3833-0

Free-wheeling, politicized adaptation of John Gay's 18th century play. Uses underworld milieu to explore intermingled themes of love, loyalty and treachery. 14 scenes 8m 8w extras

Hawaii
   c Overmyer, E. Duke Kahanamoku vs. the surfnappers

Hawdon, Robin
God and Stephen Hawking. Weinberger, J. 2000 92p
   ISBN 0-85676-242-3
Life and thought of astrophysicist Stephen Hawking, presented as an ongoing debate between Hawking and God, who appears in many guises. 2 acts 2m 2w 1 setting
The mating game. French 2002 95p
   ISBN 0-573-61288-9
Comedy. Dashing talk show host who has no luck with women enlists the help of his wordly brother. 2 acts 4 scenes 2m 3w 1 interior
Perfect wedding. French 2001 103p
   ISBN 0-573-62727-4
Comedy about a man who wakes up on his wedding morning with a complete stranger, while his future bride is about to arrive. 2 acts 2m 4w 1 interior

Hawking, Stephen
   about
   Hawdon, R. God and Stephen Hawking

Hawthorne, Nathaniel, 1804-1864
The House of the Seven Gables (dramatization) See Morreale, V. J. House of the Seven Gables
Rappaccini's daughter (dramatization) See Barchers, S. I., and Kroll, J. L. Rappaccini's daughter
The scarlet letter (dramatization) See Abbott, G. W. The scarlet letter
Hay fever. Coward, N.
Hayavadana. Karnad, G.

Hayes, Sebastian
   c The pomegranate seeds; a play for children. French (London) 2000 40p
      ISBN 0-573-15228-4
Play based on Greek myth of Persephone's descent into the underworld. Music. Prologue 8 scenes 4m 12w 1 setting
Haywire. Chappell, E.

Haywood, Eliza Fowler

The opera of operas; or, Tom Thumb the Great.

Drama set in 18th century London with music based on Henry Fielding's text for The tragedy of tragedies. Comic lament about how diminished the English court is compared to time of King Arthur. 11m 5w extras

In Haywood, E. F. Selected fiction and drama of Eliza Haywood

A wife to be lett: a comedy.

Comedy set in 18th century London about forced marriages, an eager-to-be married widow, and scheme to make man an ideal husband. Prologue 5 acts epilogue 18m 12w

In Haywood, E. F. Selected fiction and drama of Eliza Haywood

Hazing the monkey. Hennessy, M. A.

Head. Gough, L.

Head on. Dewberry, E.

Heads/tails. Fredericks, A. D.

Heads. Jory, J.

Healey, Michael

The drawer boy. Playwrights Canada 1999 66p

ISBN 0-88754-568-8   LC 00-274247

Tragicomedy about an actor doing hands-on research for a role by living with two middle-aged farmers, resulting in rural/urban culture clash. 2 acts 10 scenes 3m 1 setting

Plan B. Playwrights Canada 2002 110p

ISBN 0-88754-641-2

Political satire. High-level meetings to negotiate Quebec's departure from Canada sabotaged by seduction and betrayal. Prologue 2 acts 18 scenes 3m 1w 2 interiors

Healey, Michael, and Lynch, Kate

Kreskinned.

Romantic comedy. Awkward couple of thirtysomethings use hypnosis on each other. 1 act Prologue 12 scenes 1m 1w 1 setting

In Healey, M. and Lynch, K. The road to hell

Yodellers.

Comedy. Male golf reporter falls in love with lesbian professional golfer. 1 act 18 scenes 1m 1w 1 setting

In Healey, M. and Lynch, K. The road to hell

Healy, Ann Marie

Kat and Eliza.

Two sisters discuss their relationship and being parents. 2w 1 interior

In 30 ten-minute plays for 2 actors from Actors Theatre of Louisville's National Ten-minute Play Contest

Lonely.

Young woman causes rift between sister and brother-in-law. 1m 2w 1 interior

In 30 ten-minute plays for 3 actors from Actors Theatre of Louisville's National Ten-minute Play Contest

—Same

In Actors Theatre of Louisville. Ten-minute plays: v5

Heard, Doreen B.

c The love for three oranges. Anchorage Press 2000 31p

ISBN 0-87602-407-X

A bewitched prince accomplishes an impossible task and wins happiness and a beautiful princess. Adapted from a 1761 scenario created for the Venetian commedia dell'arte by Count Carlo Gozzi. Music, dancing. Prologue 1 act 5m 4w extras settings

The **heart** as it lived. Robinson, M.

The **heart** of art. Weller, M.

The **heart** of Maryland. Belasco, D.

Heart of the earth: a Popol Vuh story. Moraga, C.

The **heart** transplant. De Matteo, D.

Heartbreak House. Shaw, B.

Hearts. Holtzman, W.

Heart's desire. Churchill, C.

Hearts 'n kisses 'n Miss Vickers. Levi, S.

Heather Brothers

Love bites; book and lyrics by the Heather Brothers. French 2000 79p

ISBN 0-573-62709-6

Rock and roll musical about an American actress in London who gets involved with music copyist. Music. Singing. Prologue 2 acts 27 scenes 1g 2m 2w 2 settings

Heatstroke. Chappell, E.

Heave away, haul away! (tugboat captain). McCullough, L. E.

Heaven and hell (on earth): a divine comedy. Alexander, R. and others

Hebrew language

c McCullough, L. E. The alphabet

Hecuba. Euripides

Hedda Gabler. Baitz, J. R.

Hedda Gabler. Ibsen, H.

Hedges, Peter

The age of pie.

Comedy about people in a support group ending up throwing and using cream pies on one another. 4m 4w 1 interior

In Hedges, P. Oregon and other short plays

Andy and Claire.

A sister and brother with close relationship have problems when the sister brings home a boyfriend. 6 scenes 2m 1w 1 setting

In Hedges, P. Oregon and other short plays

Baby anger. Dramatists 1999 67p

ISBN 0-8222-1637-x

Absurdist satire on exploitation of children by parents. 2 acts 27 scenes 2b 3m 2w 1 setting

Cake.

Couple become better acquainted over a birthday cake. 1m 1w

In Hedges, P. Oregon and other short plays

Chicken potential.

Two friends talk about women while making scrambled eggs. 2m

In Hedges, P. Oregon and other short plays

Good as new. Dramatists 1999 65p

ISBN 0-8222-1638-8   LC 99-205427

Dark comedy about Chicago family. Teenage daughter becomes embroiled in middle-aged parents' disintegrating marriage. 1m 2w

Noodles and peas.

During a restaurant dinner, woman informs man that she is not pregnant. 1m 1w

In Hedges, P. Oregon and other short plays

Oregon.

Born-again Christian on his way to Bible college in Oregon is picked up by two punk rockers. 12 scenes 2m 1w

In Hedges, P. Oregon and other short plays

Scene with celery.

Couple discuss sex while man eats celery. 1m 1w

In Hedges, P. Oregon and other short plays

Two and an orange.

Woman peels orange while listening to a man describe an operation. 2m 1w

In Hedges, P. Oregon and other short plays

Heisenberg, Werner, 1901-1976

about

Frayn, M. Copenhagen

Helen. Barchers, S. I.

Helen. Euripides

Helen at risk. Yeaton, D.

Helen of Troy (Greek mythology)

Euripides. Helen

Yeaton, D. Helen at risk

Helen's play. McGuire, M.

Hell

Kushner, T. G. David Schine in Hell

Nigro, D. Doctor Faustus

Hellcab. Kern, W.

Hellman, Lillian, 1906-1984

about

Feibleman, P. S. Cakewalk

Hello (sex) kitty: mad Asian bitch on wheels. Uyehara, D.

Hemophilia

c Saar, D. The yellow boat

Hendrix, Jimi

about

Caleb, J. R. The rehearsal

Henkel, Matt

Corporate handbook line 11.

Story of two ambitious executives and autistic mailroom employee. 2m 1w 1 setting

In Blast from the future; ed. by D. Yeaton

Henley, Beth

Abundance.

Drama set in late 1860s Wyoming Territory. Two mail-order brides meet the men they are fated to call their husbands. 2 acts 19 scenes 3m 2w 1 setting

In Henley, B. Collected plays v2, 1990-1999

Henley, Beth—*Continued*

Am I blue.

Comedy. Precocious teenage girl lures timid college freshman to her apartment where both, although unsure and apprehensive, learn lesson in coping with life. 1 act 3m 4w 1 setting

In Henley, B. Collected plays v1, 1980-1989

Control freaks.

Woman with multiple personalities avenges herself on brother who forced sex on her years ago. 1 act 2m 2w 1 setting

In Henley, B. Collected plays v2, 1990-1999

—Same

In Henley B. Three plays by Beth Henley

Crimes of the heart.

Shared memories and forgotten dreams revealed at reunion of three young sisters in Mississippi home. Present family crises involves youngest sister who has just shot her politically prominent husband. 3 acts 2m 4w 1 interior

In Henley, B. Collected plays v1, 1980-1989

The debutante ball. Dramatists 1997 63p

ISBN 0-8222-1583-7   LC 98-115340

Tragicomedy set in Hattiesburg, Mississippi. Socialite mother, accused and acquitted of murdering her wealthy husband, uses her daughter's debutante ball to revive the family reputation. 2 acts 5 scenes 2m 5w 1 setting

—Same

In Henley, B. Collected plays v1, 1980-1989

Impossible marriage. Dramatists 1999 45p

ISBN 0-8222-1697-3   LC 00-502422

Comedy about young woman about to be wed to worldly artist twice her age. 3 parts 4m 3w 1 setting

—Same

In Henley, B. Collected plays v2, 1990-1999

L-play.

Series of 12 playlets examines the human condition, each scene focusing on a different dramatic or comedic "L" theme. 12 scenes 3m 3w settings

In Henley, B. Collected plays v2, 1990-1999

—Same

In Henley B. Three plays by Beth Henley

The Lucky Spot.

Comedy. Follows fortunes of low-life Louisianian and group of eccentric misfits as they struggle to make success of rural dance hall in midst of the Depression. Music. 2 acts 4m 3w 1 interior

In Henley, B. Collected plays v1, 1980-1989

The Miss Firecracker contest.

Comedy. Small-town beauty contestant hoping to salvage tarnished reputation must cope with eccentric relatives. Dancing. 2 acts 5 scenes 2m 4w 2 exteriors

In Henley, B. Collected plays v1, 1980-1989

Revelers. Dramatists 2002

ISBN 0-8222-1877-1

On the shore of Lake Michigan devotees of Dash Grey, the charismatic artistic director of the Red Lantern Theatre, come to commemorate his death. 5m 2w settings

—Same

In Henley, B. Collected plays v2, 1990-1999

Signature. Dramatists 2002

ISBN 0-8222-1876-3

Two brothers, Boswell and Maxwell, are living in Los Angeles in 2052. Boswell is seriously ill and wants to revive his fame. Maxwell becomes so distraught when his wife divorces him that he seeks euthanasia. 5m 4w settings

—Same

In Henley, B. Collected plays v2, 1990-1999

Sisters of the winter madrigal.

Calaih and Taretta, two orphaned daughters, live together in a hut outside a medieval village. Fortune changes for the two sisters when the high lord proclaims he will marry Calaih, and Taretta's arm is afflicted by a menacing disease. 1 act 5m 4w

In Henley B. Three plays by Beth Henley

The wake of Jamey Foster.

Comic study of eccentric members of small town Mississippi family reunited for wake. 3 acts 5 scenes 3m 4w 1 setting

In Henley, B. Collected plays v1, 1980-1989

Hennequin, Maurice, and Veber, Pierre
Anything to declare? Broadway Play Pub.
   1997
   ISBN 0-88145-133-9
A classic French farce from 1906. A count is traumatized on his wedding night by an intrusive customs inspector. 3 acts 7m 5w extras 2 interiors

Hennessy, Marcus A.
Hazing the monkey. French 2000 85p
Comedy. Young worker in a tractor factory assembly line applies for junior management training program and discovers an unusual interviewing process. Music, singing. 2 acts 6 scenes 5m 6w 2 interiors
Henny Penny. McBride-Smith, B.
Henri Christophe, King of Haiti, 1767-1820
                    about
Walcott, D. Henri Christophe
Henri Christophe. Walcott, D.
Henry IV, 1553-1610
                    about
Gore, C. The king's seal
Henry VIII, King of England, 1491-1547
                    about
Luckham, C. The seduction of Anne Boleyn
Henry, O., 1862-1910
A retrieved reformation (dramatization) See Barchers, S. I., and Kroll, J. L. A retrieved reformation
Henry IV (Enrico IV). Pirandello, L.
Henry VIII, King of England
                    about
Nicholson, W. Katherine Howard
Her aching heart. Lavery, B.
Hera (Greek mythology)
c Barchers, S. I. Zeus and Hera
Heracles (Greek mythology)
c Banks, J. Hercules—The panto!!
c Barchers, S. I. Heracles
   Euripides. The madness of Heracles
   Jonson, B. Pleasure reconciled to Virtue
c McBride-Smith, B. The twelve labors of Hercules
   Sophocles. Women of Trachis
c Thistle, L. The labors of Hercules
   Wilder, T. The Alcestiad

Heracles. Barchers, S. I.
Heracles 5. Müller, H.
The herbal bed. Whelan, P.

Herbert, Kate
Hit and run. Currency Press 2001 46p
   ISBN 0-86819-654-1
Psychological portrait of woman keeping terrible secret about circumstances of hit and run accident that killed her son. Music, singing. 2m 2w 1 setting
Herbert, Xavier, 1901-1984
Miss Tanaka (dramatization) See Romeril, J. Miss Tanaka
Hercules—The panto!! Banks, J.
Here. Frayn, M.
Here and now. Chye, K. T.
Here I am. Oates, J. C.
Hermes
Jonson, B. Mercury vindicated from the alchemists at court
Hermes. Barchers, S. I.

Herne, James A.
Margaret Fleming.
Loving wife discovers husband's adultery and its dire consequences. Music, singing. 4 acts 5 scenes 2b 5m 5w 3 settings
   In Nineteenth century American plays; ed. by M. Matlaw
Herod I, the Great, King of Judea, 73 B.C.-4 B.C.
                    about
The Three Kings (Los tres Reyes Magos)

Herrick, Jack, and others
Kudzu; book, music and lyrics by Jack Herrick, Doug Marlette and Bland Simpson. French 1999 90p
   ISBN 0-573-62688-X
Musical based on the comic strip by Doug Marlette. Story of a boy growing up in the changing American South. Music, singing. Prologue 2 acts 16 scenes 11m 3w extra
Herrick. Dunbar, P. L.
Hershel and the Hanukkah goblins. McBride-Smith, B.
Hershey: a space odyssey. Baron, J.

Herzberg, Judith
The wedding party.
Members of Dutch wedding party share a common involvement in fate of the Jews. 7m 7w 1 setting
In Dutch and Flemish plays, ed. by D. Couling

Herzen, Aleksandr, 1812-1870
                    about
Stoppard, T. Salvage

Herzl, Theodor, 1860-1904
                    about
c McCullough, L. E. Next year in Jerusalem

He's so vain. Vogel, L.

Hewett, Dorothy
The man from Mukinupin.
Musical memory play set in Western Australia 1912-1920 fousing on Great War horrors of Gallipoli and the Somme. Singing, dancing. 2 acts 7m 7w 1 setting
In War plays by women; ed. by C. M. Tylee, E. Turner, and A. Cardinal

Hewett, Robert
Goodbye Mrs. Blore. Currency Press 2000 70p
ISBN 0-86819-626-6   LC 2001-326039
Comedy about two very mismatched women who develop special friendship based on trust, respect, and love. 2 acts 20 scenes 2w 1 setting

Heywood, Thomas
A woman killed with kindness.
Play in verse. Elizabethan domesic tragedy. Husband forgives wife's infidelity before her death. Prologue 18 scenes epilogue 18m 6w extras
In Renaissance drama; ed. by A. F. Kinney

Hickman, Craig
Skin & ornaments.
Monologue by African American homosexual. Music. 1m
In O Solo homo; ed. by H. hughes and D. Román

Hidden parts. Alvarez, L.
Higgs field. Nigro, D.
High places. Vinaver, M.
High school dropouts from outer space. Jackson, K.

High schools
Chan, M. Maggie's last dance
y Cook, P. Campaign capers at Taft High
y Cook, P. Last one to survive is a rotten egg
y Cook, P. Switching principals
y DeTurk, S. Yearbook reflections
y Fendrich, S. Yearbook
y Francoeur, B. DiscoKnights
y Francoeur, B. Kokonut Island
y Francoeur, B. Kokonut kapers
y Francoeur, B. Rock around the block
y Fuson, D. All the king's horses
y Jackson, K. High school dropouts from outer space
y Jackson, R. E. Bad hair day
y Kelly, T. Kokonut High
LaDue, T. Prom night
Milligan, J. Rivals
Murray, S. Tales of terror from Nightmare High School
y Murray, S. A twist of the tongue
y Slaight, B. Second class
St. John, B. The reunion
The **highest** house on the mountain. Keane, J. B.

Highsmith, Patricia, 1921-1995
Strangers on a train (dramatization) See Warner, C. Strangers on a train
The talented Mr Ripley (dramatization) See Nagy, P. The talented Mr. Ripley

Highway, Tomson
The Rez sisters.
Drama about fictionalized Native-American community in Canada. 2 acts 7w 1 setting
In Postcolonial plays; ed. by H. Gilbert

Hill, Ronnie
Faces of the cross.
Worship program. The crucifixion story in six monologues. 5m 1w
In The drama of Easter; ed. by R. Wray

Hillbilly hankerin'. Cook, P.

Hindley, Myra, 1942-2002
                    about
Beber, N. Sensation(s)

Hindman, James

Pete 'n' Keely; book by James Hindman; lyrics by Mark Waldrop; music by Patrick Brady. French 1995 68p
ISBN 0-573-62920-X

Musical. Attempt to reconcile estranged husband-and-wife team on live telecast. Singing. 2 acts 1m 1w extras 1 interior

Hinduism

Joshi, A. A shaft of sunlight
Karnad, G. The fire and the rain
Viswananthan, P. House of sacred cows

Hines, Kim

c Home on the mornin' train.

Parallel stories set in 1839 and 1939 about American runaway slaves and German-Jewish refugees from the Holocaust. Singing. 9 scenes 6m 8w extras 1 setting

    In Theatre for young audiences; ed. by C. A. Jennings

Hinton, S. E.

Rumble Fish (dramatization) See Romer, M. Rumble fish

Hippies

y Francoeur, B. Groovy!

Hippolyte, Kendel

y The song of one; or, The journey of Ti Marie.

Allegory set on Caribbean island of St. Lucia. Young girl faces trials to save humankind from evil. Singing. 7 scenes Variable cast 1 setting

    In International plays for young people

Hippolytus (Greek mythology)

Euripides. Hippolytus
Hippolytus. Euripides
Hiraeth. Thomas, E.

Hiroshima (Japan)

y Kral, B. Paper lanterns, paper cranes
c Miller, K. S. A thousand cranes

Hirschbein, Peretz

Green fields; tr. by Nahma Sandrow.

When orphaned Lithuanian scholar leaves the yeshiva to find "true Jews" he learns some unexpected lessons from Jewish peasants who take him in as boarder and tutor for their children. 3 acts 1b 4m 4w 1 interior 2 exteriors

    In God, man and devil; ed. by N. Sandrow

Hirschberg, Herbert

"Mistakes".

Tragedy set in 1906 Berlin. Young homosexual lawyer who marries to save father from bankruptcy is blackmailed by former lover. 3 acts 4m 1w extras 1 interior

    In Lovesick; ed. by L. Senelick

Hirson, David

Wrong mountain. French 2001 144p
ISBN 0-573-62967-6

Lampoon of contemporary theater. Poet enters playwriting contest to win bet with ex-wife's fiancee. 2 acts 25 scenes 7m 5w settings

Hischak, Thomas

Molière's Tartuffe. Pioneer Drama Service 2001 38p

Adaptation of Moliere's 17th century comedy. Impostor worms his way into good graces of wealthy, imprudent man. 5 scenes 7m 6w 1 interior

Hispanic Americans

Alfaro, L. Bitter homes and gardens
Arizmendi, Y. Nostalgia maldita: 1-900-MEXICO, a Stairmaster piece
Caputo, L. Birth marks
Culture Clash (Group). A bowl of beings
Culture Clash (Group). The mission
Culture Clash (Group). Radio mambo
Mena, A. Las nuevas tamaleras
Palacios, M. Describe your work
Perez, F. Estorias del barrio: special people of international character
Prida, D. Botánica
Rivera, J. Gas
Romero, E. The fat-free Chicana and the Snow Cap queen
Wood, S. And where was Pancho Villa when you really needed him?

Hiss. Parsley, J.

A **history** of the American film. Durang, C.

Hit and run. Herbert, K.

Hitler, Adolf

           about

Schenkar, J. The last of Hitler

HIV positive. Harden, V.

Hoaxes

Filippo, E. de. Filumena—a marriage Italian style

Hoaxes—*Continued*

Plautus, T. M. The wild, wild women (Bacchides)

Hoben, Ginna

Telephone.

Couple on verge of break-up neither one wants. 3m 2w 1 interior

In 30 ten-minute plays for 4, 5 & 6 actors from Actors Theatre of Louisville's Ten-Minute Play Contest

Hoch, Danny

Jails, hospitals and hip-hop.

Series of monologues lampooning individual vanities, ethnic stereotypes and hypocrisy. 1m

In Hoch, D. Jails, hospitals & hip-hop and Some people

Some people.

Series of monologues about racial and ethnic prejudice in New York City. 1m

In Hoch, D. Jails, hospitals & hip-hop and Some people

Hochwälder, Fritz

1003; or, Don Giovanni's back in town; translated by Todd C. Hanlin.

Sequel to: Thursday. Satire with hallucinatory overtones about author with divided soul. 2 acts 2m 1 interior

In Hochwälder, F. The holy experiment and other plays

The holy experiment; translated by Heidi L. Hutchinson.

Set in an 18th century Jesuit state of South America. Communal and amicable working conditions, fostered by Jesuit priests for the converted Indians, is regarded jealously by neighboring Spanish colonists, who eventually succeed in destroying the holy experiment. 5 acts 37 scenes 17m

In Hochwälder, F. The holy experiment and other plays

Orders; translated by Todd C. Hanlin.

Television play about man who arrested Anne Frank. 9m 4w extras

In Hochwälder, F. The holy experiment and other plays

Thursday; translated by Todd C. Hanlin.

Businessman makes Faustian pact with the devil. 3 acts 8m 2w 1 setting

In Hochwälder, F. The holy experiment and other plays

Hockey

Melski, M. Hockey mom, hockey dad

Hockey mom, hockey dad. Melski, M.

Hodges, Adrian

Life goes on; a play. French 1999 85p

ISBN 0-573-01809-X   LC 00-712936

Comedy about the drastic events following a funeral, including a catering mix-up, a philandering younger brother, and a ghost's appearance. 2 acts 7 scenes 2m 4w 1 setting

Hoffman, E. T. A.

c The nutcracker and the mouse-king.

Based on the E.T.A. Hoffman fantasy of the enchanted Nutcracker who fights a mouse king. Variable cast

In The twelve plays of Christmas; ed. by L. Swortzell

Hoffman, Jeff

Francis Brick needs no introduction.

Four competitive brothers at father's wake; revelations about the old man. 1 act 4m 1 interior

In Off-Off Broadway Festival plays, 23rd ser.

Hoffman, Stephen

Splendora; book by Peter Webb; music by Stephen Hoffman; lyrics by Mark Campbell. Dramatists 1998 89p

ISBN 0-8222-1557-8

Musical fable of sexual identity set in small east Texas town. Based on novel by Edward Swift. 2 acts 7 scenes 2m 6w 1 setting

Hoffower, Kate

The office.

Idle chatter among office workers. 3w 1 interior

In 30 ten-minute plays for 3 actors from Actors Theatre of Louisville's National Ten-minute Play Contest

Hold for three. Kramer, S.

Hold me. McGuire, M.

Holder Posey, the felonious photographer. St. John, B.

The **holdup**. Norman, M.

Holland, Norman

To meet Oscar Wilde. French (London) 1999 59p
ISBN 0-573-01948-7

Drama about Wilde's dissertation on his life given at a Parisian lecture in 1899. 2 acts Variable cast 4 characters 2 settings

Hollinger, Michael

An empty plate in the Café du Grand Boeuf. Dramatists 2003
ISBN 0-8222-1790-2

No menu is necessary at the world's greatest restaurant, as they have everything. 4m 2w 1 interior setting

Incorruptible; a dark comedy about the dark ages. Dramatists 2002 84p
ISBN 0-8222-1787-2

Comedy set in 1250 A.D. France, about the chaotic conditions in a monastery desperate for some miracles. 2 acts 2 scenes 5m 3w 1 setting

Red herring. Dramatists 2002
ISBN 0-8222-1788-0

Three love stories, a murder mystery, and a nuclear espionage plot converge in this 1952 noir comedy about marriage and other explosive devices. 3m 3w settings

Tiny island. Dramatists 2001 85p il
ISBN 0-8222-1789-9   LC 2002-278646

Drama about aging, estranged sisters whose family operates classic movie cinema in Philadelphia. 2 acts 5 scenes 1m 3w 1 setting

—Same

In New playwrights: the best plays of 1999

Hollingsworth, Marian Blair

y Johnny Brooke; a ghost story. Pioneer Drama Service 1999 60p

Ghost of teenager helps girl adjust to new town, new job and new school. 3 acts 7 scenes 6m 8w 1 interior

Hollmann, Mark

Urinetown the musical; book and lyrics by Greg Kotis; music and lyrics by Mark Hollmann. Faber & Faber 2003 103p
ISBN 0-571-21182-8

Musical satire about world wracked by ecological disaster and run by corporate greed. 10m 9w extras 1 setting

Holloway, Jonathan

The dark.

Successful novelist, who wants more success, meets his Mephistopheles and a sinister fate. 2 scenes 3m 1w 1 setting

In Holloway, J. Darkness falls

Les miserables. French (London) 2001 85p
ISBN 0-573-01880-4

Based on Victor Hugo's novel. Story of love, class conflict, revolt, and social injustice in 19th century France. 2 acts 36 scenes 10m 5w settings

The monkey's paw.

Three wishes are granted to working-class family. All come true in a strange way. 5 scenes 4m 1w 1 setting

In Holloway, J. Darkness falls

Hollywood (Calif.)

Baitz, J. R. Mizlansky/Zilinsky
Busch, C. Red scare on Sunset
Hanan, S. M. Jolson & company
Margulies, D. Pitching to the star
Mastrosimone, W. Like totally weird
Vaughan, R. M. Camera, woman

Holman, Robert

Bad weather. Hern Bks. 1998 104p
ISBN 1-85459-324-2

Drama set in Middlesborough, England, and rural France. Youth wrongfully locked up for crime committed by best friend. 2 acts 12 scenes 3m 3w 5 exteriors 3 interiors

Being friends.

In 1944, as V2s whizz overhead, two young men meet in Kent meadow. 2m 1 setting

In Holman, R. Making noise quietly

Lost.

Mother who has not seen son for five years learns he has been killed in Falkland Islands War. 1m 1w 1 setting

In Holman, R. Making noise quietly

Making noise quietly.

In 1986, in the Black Forest, German businesswoman takes into her home fugitive British Private and his disturbed stepson. 2 scenes 1b 1m 1w 1 setting

In Holman, R. Making noise quietly

Holocaust, Jewish (1933-1945)

Elisha, R. Two
Fenton, E. From dream to ash
y Frockt, D. L. The book of Ruth
Gilroy, F. D. Contact with the enemy
c Hines, K. Home on the mornin' train
Kops, B. Dreams of Anne Frank
Kron, L. 2.5 minute ride
Mann, A. Judgment at Nuremberg
c McCullough, L. E. Three Holocaust tales
Nanus, S. The survivor
Nelson, T. B. The grey zone

Holocaust survivors

Gersten-Vassilaros, A. Two Jewish men
in their seventies
Margulies, D. Lola
Slotboom, C. The train
The **hologram** theory. Goldberg, J.

Holtzman, Willy

Hearts.
Retirement-aged Jew from St. Louis suffers from post-traumatic stress disorder as result of his experiences as forward observer in Western Europe in WW II. Music. Prologue 1 act 4m 1w settings
   In New playwrights: the best plays of
   1999
The **holy** experiment. Hochwälder, F.

Holy Week

Smith, J. M. This is my story
Home. Cahill, L.
Home on the mornin' train. Hines, K.

Homecoming

Horovitz, I. Alfred the Great
Horovitz, I. Barking sharks
Keane, J. B. The year of the hiker
Pape, R. Hearts beating faster
Thomas, D. Return journey

Homeless

Evans, S. Little sister
c Lebow, B. Tiny Tim is dead
Parks, S.-L. In the blood
Plowman, G. Touching tomorrow

Homer

The Odyssey (dramatization) See Thistle,
   L. The Odyssey
Homesick. Oates, J. C.

Homesickness

Arizmendi, Y. Nostalgia maldita: 1-900-
   MEXICO, a Stairmaster piece

Homosexuality

Adams, G. Something blue
Alfaro, L. Downtown
Armory. The gentleman of the chrysan-
   themums
Baron, J. Visiting Mr. Green
Benet i Jornet, J. M. Legacy
Bowne, A. Forty-deuce
Brofsky, K. Strawberry fields
Butler, D. The only thing worse you
   could have told me—
Congdon, C. Dog opera
Davis, B. C. Avow
del Valle, J. A. Fuchsia
Donaghy, T. The dadshuttle
Drader, B. The fruit machine
Eagleton, T. Saint Oscar
Elyot, K. The day I stood still
Feliciano, G. Between blessings
Foley, D. Sad hotel
Fraser, B. Poor Superman
Fulford, R. W. Gulag
Fulford, R. W. Steel kiss
Fuller, H. B. At Saint Judas's
Gallagher, D. Howard Crabtree's when
   pigs fly
Gilbert, S. The birth of Casper G.
   Schmidt
Gilbert, S. Independence
Gilbert, S. Schubert lied
Gray, J. The blackmailers
Greenberg, R. The American plan
Greenberg, R. Take me out
Grimsley, J. Mr. Universe
Gurney, A. R. The old boy
Hall, L. Wittgenstein on Tyne
Harding, M. P. Sour grapes
Hare, D. The Judas kiss
Harvey, J. Out in the open
Hickman, C. Skin & ornaments
Hirschberg, H. "Mistakes"
Holman, R. Being friends
Kaplan, B. J. Landscape of desire
Kaufman, M. Gross indecency: the three
   trials of Oscar Wilde
Kaufman, M. The Laramie Project
Kramer, L. The destiny of me

Homosexuality—*Continued*

Kramer, L. The normal heart

Kushner, T. G. David Schine in Hell

Kushner, T. Terminating

Kuzmin, M. The dangerous precaution

Lucas, C. Bad dream

Lucas, C. The boom box

Lucas, C. Boyfriend riff

Lucas, C. The dying Gaul

Lucas, C. If Columbus does not figure in your travel plans

Lucas, C. What I meant was

Machado, E. When the sea drowns in sand

MacLennan, M. L. Beat the sunset

Mann, K. Ania and Esther

Manzi, W. The award

Mapa, A. I remember Mapa

McNally, T. Corpus Christi

Mendez Rodriguez, J. M. Autumn flower

Miller, T. Fruit cocktail

Miller, T. Glory box

Miller, T. My queer body

Miller, T. Naked breath

Miller, T. Some golden states

Miller, T. Stretch marks

Orloff, R. I didn't know you could cook

Osment, P. The undertaking

Ravenhill, M. Mother Clap's Molly house

Reitz, D. And that's how people burn to death in motel rooms

Rintoul, H. Brave hearts

Sánchez, E. Clean

Scheffer, W. Alien boy

Scheffer, W. Tennessee and me

Sherman, M. Bent

Skarstedt, S. A. Saint Francis of Esplanade

Smith, C. Knock me a kiss

Spencer, S. Sudden devotion

Stoppard, T. The invention of love

Thomas, B. The crumple zone

Vawter, R. Roy Cohn/Jack Smith

Wallace, N. In the heart of America

Williams, T. And tell sad stories of the death of queens

Williams, T. Vieux Carré

Wilson, J. Kilt

Wilson, L. Your everyday ghost story

Wolf, M. Another American: asking and telling

Yew, C. Wonderland

Honey, baby. Levy, D.

Hong Kong

Johnston, S. Running dog, paper tiger

Honky-tonk highway. Nassif, R. L.

Honor

Calderón de la Barca, P. The surgeon of honour

Calderón de la Barca, P. Three judgements in one

Hoodless, Adelaide, 1858-1910

about

Redhill, M. Building Jerusalem

Hoogland, Cornelia

y Salmonberry: a West Coast fairy tale.

Version of Cinderella set in Pacific Northwest. Audience participation. Puppets. 19 scenes Variable cast 8 characters extras 1 setting

In International plays for young people

Hope is the thing with feathers. Pugliese, F.

The **hope** slide. MacLeod, J.

Hoppe, Gip

Jackie, an American life. French 1998 81p

ISBN 0-573-63262-6   LC 99-213836

Comedy about the life of Jackie Kennedy. 2 acts Variable cast 8 characters

Horn of sorrow. Ellenbogen, N.

Horovitz, Israel

Alfred dies.

Third play in The Alfred trilogy. Man is held hostage by his wife, her mother, and an old friend, who accuse him of murder, incest, and ruining their lives. 3 acts 7 scenes 2m 2w 1 interior

In Horovitz, I. Two trilogies

Alfred the Great.

First play of The Alfred trilogy. Successful man, followed by wife, returns to hometown and visits former sweetheart and her husband. Revelations of adultery, murder, and sexual impotence emerge from conflicting statements of the characters. 3 acts 5 scenes 2m 2w 1 interior

In Horovitz, I. Two trilogies

Barking sharks. French 2003 90p

ISBN 0-573-62810-4

Horovitz, Israel—*Continued*

New York ad agency director returns to his hometown of Gloucester, Massachusetts, to become a fisherman. 2 acts 23 scenes 4m 3w settings

The Chopin playoffs.

Concluding play in trilogy based on stories by Morley Torgov. Two Jewish families in Ontario find themselves in conflict when their sons, both piano prodigies, vie with each other in piano competition and for the favors of lovely Protestant girl. 5m 3w 1 setting

In Horovitz, I. Two trilogies

c A Christmas carol: Scrooge and Marley.

Adaptation of Dickens's classic Christmas story. 2 acts 10 scenes Large mixed cast

In The twelve plays of Christmas; ed. by L. Swortzell

Lebensraum. French 1999 67p

Drama set at start of 21st century. Family accepts Germany's offer of work and citizenship to 6,000,000 Jews. 2m 1w 1 setting

Our father's failing.

Second play in The Alfred trilogy. Man visiting his aged father in insane asylum learns that as a boy he killed his mother and her lover and that his father confessed to the crime to protect him. 3 acts 5 scenes 2m 2w 1 setting

In Horovitz, I. Two trilogies

A Rosen by any other name.

Second play of trilogy about Jewish family life in Canada inspired by Morley Torgov's book A good place to come from. Focuses on approaching bar mitzvah of young boy and his father's growing sensitivity to anti-Semitism. 4m 2w 1 setting

In Horovitz, I. Two trilogies

Today, I am a fountain pen.

Play based on stories by Morley Torgov. First of trilogy dealing with Jewish home life in Sault Ste. Marie, Ontario, in the 1940s. Traces coming of age of precocious, musically gifted pre-teenager. 2 acts 1b 4m 3w 1 setting

In Horovitz, I. Two trilogies

Horrid massacre in Boston. Nigro, D.

Horror plays

y Barchers, S. I. Dr. Jekyll and Mr. Hyde
y Barchers, S. I. Frankenstein
Bolger, D. The passion of Jerome
Moore, S. Misery
Ohm, A. Night of the living dead
Williams, S. Kiss of death

Horse racing

Fry, C. A yard of sun

Horsler, Peter

Cut and run. French (London) 1999 57p
   ISBN 0-573-01768-9   LC 00-703043

Comedy about National Health Service Clinic in England where two doctors practice, one naive and altruistic, the other devious and without scruples. 2 acts 4 scenes 4m 5w 1 setting

Horváth, Ödön von

Casimir and Caroline.

Drama set in Munich amusement park during Octoberfest. Disillusion of two young people whose relationship is doomed by their desperate economic plight. Music. 117 scenes Variable cast 1 setting

In Horváth, O. von. Tales from the Vienna woods and other plays

Faith, love, hope.

Drama set in Munich based on true story of petty crime and punishment. Music. 5 acts 66 scenes 13m 5w

In Horváth, O. von. Tales from the Vienna woods and other plays

The Italian evening.

Satirizes smug obtuseness of complacent Germans as Nazis rise to power. 7 scenes Variable cast 1 interior 3 exteriors

In Horváth, O. von. Tales from the Vienna woods and other plays

Tales from the Vienna woods.

Satirical melodrama set in Vienna about hypocritical piety of complacent townspeople who stand idly by as Nazi forces rise to power. Episodes mockingly underscored by lilting strains of Strauss waltzes. 7 scenes 10m 10w extras settings

In Horváth, O. von. Tales from the Vienna woods and other plays

Hospitals

Ayckbourn, A. Body language
Ayckbourn, A. Gizmo
Barry, S. Our lady of Sligo
Bush, D. Sailing to America
Castle, G. V. Welcome to Bedside Manor
Chapman, J. Nil by mouth
Constable, J. Dead man's handle
y Kral, B. Paper lanterns, paper cranes
Maponya, M. Umongikazi (The nurse)

Hospitals—*Continued*
Odato, A. The profoundness of events
Orton, J. The visitors
Río, M. del. On the way to the concert
Southworth, M. Damages to Tony
Tricker, G. Life support

Hostages
Laxdal, V. Karla and Grif
Hostages in the barrio. Alonso de Santos, J. L.
Hot and cold; or, Mr. Dom's idea. Crommelynck, F.
The **Hot** L Baltimore. Wilson, L.
Hot Rod. Kareken, J.
A **hotel** on Marvin Gardens. Jackson, N.
Hotel Sorrento. Rayson, H.

Hotels, taverns, etc.
Benfield, D. In at the deep end
Chambers, R. Marg Szkaluba (Pissy's wife)
Chekhov, A. P. On the high road
Fechter, S. The last cigarette
Fry, C. A ringing of bells
Godber, J. Shakers
Hanes, M. Doin' time at the Alamo
Hatcher, J. Downtown
Linklater, L. Sixty below
Lucas, C. If Columbus does not figure in your travel plans
McPherson, C. The weir
Nigro, D. Horrid massacre in Boston
Nottage, L. Mud, river, stone
O'Neill, A. What I came for
Palmieri, M. Poor fellas
Parker, M. Hotbed Hotel
Pedrero, P. First star (Una estrella)
Rebeck, T. The bar plays
Shanley, J. P. Welcome to the moon
Walcott, D. Pantomime
Williams, T. The night of the iguana
Williams, T. Small craft warnings
Wilson, L. The Hot L Baltimore
Wilson, L. Chateau La Roach
Hot'n' throbbing. Vogel, P.
Hound of the Clackervilles. Sodaro, C.
The **hour** of lamps. Mitchell, D.
House. Ayckbourn, A.
House-hunting unlike Soweto. Magona, S.
The **house** of Bernarda Alba. García Lorca, F.

The **house** of Bernarda Alba. Mann, S.
House of glass. Martini, C.
House of sacred cows. Viswananthan, P.
The **house** of sleeping beauties. Hwang, D. H.
House of the Seven Gables. Morreale, V. J.

Houseman, John
about
Sherman, J. It's all true

Housman, Alfred Edward
about
Stoppard, T. The invention of love

Houston, Sterling
Message sent.
Telephone messages delineate the final days of an AIDS patient. Variable cast 11 characters
In Humana Festival 2001

Houston, Velina Hasu
c Hula heart.
Drama about retaining one's roots. Multiethnic seven-year-old boy from Hawaii moves to Southern California. 7 scenes 3b 1w settings
In Eight plays for children; ed. by C A. Jennings
How Fisher went to the skyland. Barchers, S. I.
How his bride came to Abraham. Sunde, K.
How I learned to drive. Vogel, P.
How Quentzalcoatl found the sun. McCullough, L. E.
How the West was Dun. Gieschen, C.
How to make your theater pay. Wilson, D. H.
How to plant a rose. Diggs, E.

Howard, Bronson
Shenandoah.
Sentimental drama of Northern officer and his Southern sweetheart during Civil War. 4 acts 14m 7w 2 interiors 1 exterior
In Fateful lightning; ed. by W. J. Meserve and M. A. Meserve
—Same
In Nineteenth century American plays; ed. by M. Matlaw

Howard, Cathy

c The frog princess. Pioneer Drama
  Service 2001 38p

Adaptation of Russian folktale about queen who
sends her three sons off to find wives. One marries a frog. 3 scenes Variable cast 1 interior

Howard, David

Electric roses.

Drama about domestic abuse. 2m 1w 1 interior
  In 30 ten-minute plays for 3 actors
    from Actors Theatre of
    Louisville's National Ten-minute
    Play Contest

Howard, Katherine

about

Nicholson, W. Katherine Howard
Howard Crabtree's when pigs fly.
  Gallagher, D.

Howe, LeAnne, and Gordon, Roxy

Indian radio days.

Farce and melodrama abound in stereotypical
"history" of Native Americans. Music. Large
mixed cast
  In Seventh generation; ed. by M. G.
    D'Aponte

Howe, Tina

The divine fallacy.

Writer goes to see photographer about taking her
picture for jacket of her new book. 1m 1w 1 interior
  In 30 ten-minute plays for 2 actors
    from Actors Theatre of
    Louisville's National Ten-minute
    Play Contest

c East of the sun and west of the moon.

Young girl embarks on epic journey with polar
bear in order to help her poor family. Prologue 2
acts 10 scenes 1b 1g 9m 8w extras 4 interiors 5
exteriors
  In Eight plays for children; ed. C. A.
    Jennings

Pride's Crossing. French 1998 117p
  ISBN 0-573-62656-1

Drama about grandmother who reflects on her
life during a croquet party attended by her
grandaughter. 2 acts 12 scenes 4m 3w extras 1 setting

—Same. Theatre Communications Group
  1998 111p
    ISBN 1-559-36153-0   LC 98-14964

Pride's Crossing (condensation).
  In The Best Plays of 1997-1998; ed.
    by. Otis L. Guernsey, Jr.

Rembrandt's gift.

The painter Rembrandt magically appears in the
cluttered loft of a Soho couple who are about to
be evicted. Music, dancing. 1 act 2m 1w extras 1
interior
  In Humana Festival 2002

Howes, Lynn

Cathy's kitchen. Playwrights Pub 48p
  ISBN 1-873130-23-6

Story about the dialogue between three women
in a bakery. 2 acts 3w 1 setting

Howie, Betsy. See Murfitt, M. jt. auth.
Howie the rookie. O'Rowe, M.
Howya doin' Franky Banana? Spiro, P.
Hubba city. Reed, I.
Hubba hubba. Casey, Gene, and Casey,
  Jan

Hughes, Declan

Digging for fire.

Black comedy set in Dublin bar about disastrous,
beer-soaked college reunion. 4 acts 6 scenes 5m
2w 2 interiors
  In Hughes, D. Plays: 1

Halloween night.

Dark comedy with supernatural overtones. Group
of friends hold reunion in old holiday house on
coast of Ireland. 2 acts 13 scenes 7m 3w 1 setting
  In Hughes, D. Plays: 1

Love and a bottle.

Play-within-a-play about creation and rewriting
of George Farquhar's Love and a bottle. Impecunious Irish rake cuts sexual swath through London
society in 1697. 2 acts 7 scenes 4m 4w 2 interiors
2 exteriors
  In Hughes, D. Plays: 1

New morning.

Family drama about guilt and redemption. Two
sisters seek reconciliation with one another and
their past. 3 acts 3 scenes 1m 2w 1 interior
  In Hughes, D. Plays: 1

Hughes, Holly

Clit notes.

Comic one woman show that looks at life, family, coming out, first love, homophobia, county fairs and the art of making out at a luau. 1w

In O Solo homo; ed. by H. Hughes and D. Román

Hughes, Langston

Angelo Herndon Jones.

Political drama set in 1930s. Dramatizes squalor, despair, lack of opportunity, and personal and financial victimization of urban African Americans. 1 act 2m 4w extras 1 interior

In Hughes, L. The political plays of Langston Hughes

y Black nativity.

Gospel version of the Nativity. Music, singing, dancing. 2 acts Variable cast

In The twelve plays of Christmas; ed. by L. Swortzell

Harvest.

Docudrama with audience participation about Carmel, California, farm workers strike of 1933. Singing. 3 acts 8 scenes Large mixed cast 3 interiors 5 exteriors

In Hughes, L. The political plays of Langston Hughes

Mulatto: a tragedy of the Deep South.

Tragedy about race relations set in Georgia. Problems and attitudes of children of white landowner and African American housekeeper-mistress. 2 acts 3 scenes 1b 10m 2w extras 1 interior

In Political stages; ed. by E. Mann and D. Roessel

De organizer.

Blues opera about blacks and organized labor. Singing. 1 act 5m 2w 1 interior

In Hughes, L. The political plays of Langston Hughes

Scottsboro, limited.

Leftist political play with audience participation based on notorious Scottsboro trial of 1931, in which nine African American boys were charged with raping two white women on a train. 1 act 19 scenes 8b 2g 1m 2w extras 3 interiors 1 exterior

In Hughes, L. The political plays of Langston Hughes

Hughes, Ted

Euripides' Alcestis; translated and adapted by Ted Hughes. Farrar Straus Giroux 1999 103p

ISBN 0-374-14920-8   LC 99-42757

Adaptation of Greek classical drama that tells of king's grief for his wife, who has given her young life so that he may live. Variable cast 1 setting

Hugo, Victor, 1802-1885

Les miserables (dramatization) See Holloway, J. Les miserables

Huie, Karen

Yasuko and the young s-s-samurai.

Farce about reluctant samurai trying to convince dewy-eyed maiden that gutlessness is next to godlessness in country rife with honor, hara-kiri and hondas. 1 act 1m 1w 1 setting

In Multicultural theatre II; ed. by R. Ellis

Hula heart. Houston, V. H.

Human events. Gurney, A. R.

Humbertson, Lisa L.

The nature of things.

Stormy relationship between woman and adolescent daughter. 1g 1w 1 interior

In Women's Project & productions; ed. by J. Miles

Humble boy. Jones, C.

Humpty-Dumpty is missing. Robinette, J.

The **hundred** penny box. Sundstrom, B.

Hunger. McIntyre, H.

Hunger. Wilner, S.

The **hungry** earth. Maponya, M.

The **hungry** woman: a Mexican Medea. Moraga, C.

Hunt, Lisa

A night under canvas.

While touring National Museum of Wales Art Gallery, two woman are accidentally locked inside. 1 act 2w 1 setting

In Act one Wales; ed. by P. Clark

Hunt, Margaret

Bread.

Woman struggles to maintain her sanity. 1g 2w 1 interior

In Women's Project & productions; ed. by J. Miles

Hunt, Stephen

The white guy.

Monologue about race and ethnicity. 1m

In The Best American Short plays,
1997-1998

The **hunt** for Red Willie. Bourke, K.

Hunter, Dan

Un tango en la noche. French 2000 24p

ISBN 0-573-62772-3

Drama about love and memory set in poor Mexican village. Old man makes bargain with the Devil. 1 act 2m 2w 2 interiors 1 exterior

Hunter, Maureen

Atlantis.

Monologue. A self-exiled Canadian on a Greek island has a sudden, piercing memory of home. 1 scene 1m 1 setting

In Short spells: scenes & monologues;
ed. by V. Shantz

Transit of Venus.

Historical drama set in France 1760-1771 loosely based on life of Guillaume Le Gentil. Astronomer's obsessive attempts to chart the transits of Venus cost him true love. 3 acts 8 scenes 2m 3w 1 interior

In 7 cannons

Hurrah at last. Greenberg, R.

Hurricane. Wilson, C.

Husband and wife

Ayvazian, L. Twenty-four years

Baker, E. A. The seventeenth of June

Benjamin, K. A. Mary MacGregor

Blais, M.-C. A couple

Blais, M.-C. Fever

Chambers, R. Pretty blue

Cibber, C. Love's last shift; or, The fool in fashion

Clark, R. Pierre and Marie

Cleage, P. Bourbon at the border

Crommelynck, F. The magnanimous cuckold

Dozer, D. The milling crowd dies

Dresser, R. Bed & breakfast

Edwards, G. Four walls

Feydeau, G. Going to pot (On purge Bébé)

Feydeau, G. Wooed and viewed

Filippo, E. de. Those damned ghosts

García Lorca, F. The love of Don Perlimplin for Belisa in the garden

Gates, T. Ladies who lunch

Gilroy, F. D. Come next Tuesday

Gilroy, F. D. Present tense

Gilroy, F. D. The subject was roses

Gilroy, F. D. That summer—that fall

Glass, J. M. Play memory

Godber, J. Happy Jack

Godber, J. September in the rain

Heywood, T. A woman killed with kindness

Howe, T. Rembrandt's gift

Ibsen, H. A doll's house

Ibsen, H. Little Eyolf

Kennedy, A. Dramatic circle

Kennedy, A. The film club (a monologue by Suzanne Alexander)

Kennedy, A. She talks to Beethoven

Kopit, A. L. BecauseHeCan

Kushner, T. Homebody/Kabul

Lawrence, D. H. The widowing of Mrs. Holroyd

Levy, D. Macbeth—false memories

Lhota, B. Strangers

MacDonald, R. D. The ice house

c McBride-Smith, B. Aaron Kelly is dead!

McGuinness, F. A doll's house

Murray-Smith, J. Nightfall

Noonan, J. F. A critic and his wife

Orton, J. Fred and Madge

Owens, R. Three front

Parker, M. Whose wives are they anyway?

Parsley, J. Hiss

Rayson, H. Life after George

Rebeck, T. Katie and Frank

Scheffer, W. Easter

Schisgal, M. Fifty years ago

Schisgal, M. The man who couldn't stop crying

Steele, D. The way to Miami

Strindberg, A. Playing with fire

Sturner, L. Look what you made me do

Svich, C. But there are fires

Upton, J. Everlasting rose

Walker, G. F. Problem child

Wallace, N. In the fields of Aceldama

Wiltse, D. To wit and to whom

Yew, C. Snapshot: here and now

Hush. De Angelis, A.

Hush: an interview with America. Still, J.
Hushabye Mountain. Harvey, J.

Hutter, Robyn

c Big tush, little tush; Book and lyrics by Jeffrey lantos; music and lyrics by Robyn Hutter; additional music by Jeffrey Lantos and Bill Augustine. Dramatic Publishing 2003 45p

Musical fantasy adventure based on book by LeeAn and Jeffrey Lantos. Five-year-old girl convinced that all her problems in life stem from the fact that her tush is too small. Variable cast 1 setting

Hutton, Arlene

As it is in heaven. Dramatists 2003
　ISBN 0-8222-1860-7
An 1830 Shaker community in Kentucky is changed when a non-believer has an ecstatic experience. 9w 1 setting

A closer look.
Frantic action behind the scenes at a reality TV show, as the on-screen hostess is prepared for the next round of schlock. 1 act 1 scene 5w 1 interior
　In Off-Off Broadway Festival plays, 26th ser.

I dream before I take the stand.
Young woman discusses being attacked in park. 1m 1w 1 setting
　In The Best American short plays 1998-1999

Last train to Nibroc. Dramatists 2000 57p il
　ISBN 0-8222-1753-8
Romantic comedy set in December, 1940, on New York bound train. Young flyer and missionary fall in love. 3 scenes 1m 1w settings
—Same
　In Women playwrights: the best plays of 1999

The price you pay.
Dark comedy about two boastful women, whose world is turned upside down by stranger. 1 act 3w 1 setting
　In Off-Off Broadway festival plays, 24th ser.

Studio portrait.
Woman having her picture taken reveals that she met the photographer years ago; rueful acknowledgment of missed opportunities. 1 act 1 scene 1m

1w 1 interior
　In Off-Off Broadway Festival plays, 23rd ser.

Huxley, Aldous

Now more than ever. University of Texas Press 2000 95p
　ISBN 0-292-73122-1
Idealistic financier's scheme for industrial renewal drives him to swindling and finally suicide. 3 acts 5 scenes epilogue 7m 2w extras 2 interiors 1 exterior

Hwang, David Henry

Bondage.
　A look at race and sexual attraction set in Los Angeles S & M parlor. 1 act 1m 1w 1 interior
　In Hwang, D. H. Trying to find Chinatown

The dance and the railroad.
　While on strike two Chinese railroad workers express their feelings in Chinese dance, song and playacting. 1 act 2m 1 exterior
　In Hwang, D. H. Trying to find Chinatown

Family devotions.
　Confrontation between Chinese American family and their visiting relative from mainland China. 2 acts 4m 5w 1 setting
　In Hwang, D. H,. Trying to find Chinatown

Fob.
　In back room of small Chinese restaurant in California three young people interact tensely—a second-generation Chinese-American youth, his female first-generation cousin, and her friend from UCLA, a youth newly arrived from Hong Kong. Prologue 2 acts 3 scenes coda 2m 1w 1 setting
　In Hwang, D. H. Trying to find Chinatown

Golden child. Dramatists 1999 53p
　ISBN 0-8222-1682-5　　　　LC 00-709429
Drama about collision of cultures set in 1918 China. Depicts incursion of renegade Christian ideas into traditional Confucian family. 2 acts 2m 4w extras 1 setting
—Same. Theatre Communications Group 1998 62p
　ISBN 1-55936-158-1　　　　LC 00-709429

The house of sleeping beauties.
　Loosely based on autobiographical story by Yasunari Kawabata. Author's visits to bizarre brothel in search of material for story ends tragi-

Hwang, David Henry—*Continued*
cally. 4 scenes 1m 1w 1 interior

In Hwang, D. H. Trying to find Chinatown

The sound of a voice.

Stylized tale with folkloric nuances of young samurai's encounter with mysterious woman. 9 scenes 1m 1w 1 setting

In Hwang, D. H. Trying to find Chinatown

Trying to find Chinatown.

Lower East Side confrontation between two men explores questions of race, ethnicity and identity. 2m 1 exterior

In 30 ten-minute plays for 2 actors from Actors Theatre of Louisville's National Ten-minute Play Contest

—Same

In Hwang, D. H. Trying to find Chinatown

Hydraulics phat like mean. Shange, N.

Hydriotaphia; or, The death of Dr. Browne. Kushner, T.

Hymn to the rising sun: a drama of man's waste. Green, P.

Hypatia, ca. 370-415

about

Wellman, M. Hypatia; or, The divine algebra

Hypatia; or, The divine algebra. Wellman, M.

Hype-r-connectivity. Bayiates, A.

Hypochondria

Molière. The hypochondriac

The **hypochondriac.** Molière

Hypocrisy

Molière. Don Juan

Molière. The misanthrope

Hyronomous A. Frog. Weiss, E.

Hysteria; or, Fragments of an analysis of an obsessional neurosis. Johnson, T.

I

I am Angela Brazil. Coxon, L.

I am Laika. Lipkin, D.

I am Slime. Fredericks, A. D.

I didn't know you could cook. Orloff, R.

I do solemnly declare. Farquhar, S.

I don't know what I'm doing. Margulies, D.

I dream before I take the stand. Hutton, A.

I hate you on Mondays. Miles, K.

I live in music. Shange, N.

I love you, Jimmy Spud. Hall, L.

I remember Mapa. Mapa, A.

I rise in flame, cried the phoenix. Williams, T.

I scream, you scream, we all scream for ice cream. Fredericks, A. D.

"**I** take your hand in mine. . .". Rocamora, C.

I will go. . . I will go. . . Berger, G.

I will marry when I want. Thiong'o, N. W., and Mirii, N. W.

The "**I**" word: interns. Wells, M. L.

Ibsen, Henrik, 1828-1906

Ghosts (adaptation) See Harris, R. Ghosts

Hedda Gabler (adaptation) See Baitz, J. R. Hedda Gabler; Baitz, J. R. Hedda Gabler

Peer Gynt (adaptation) See Overmyer, E. Alki

A doll's house; translation by Nicholas Rudall. Dee, I. R. 1999 119p
ISBN 1-56663-225-0; 1-56663-226-9 (pa)
LC 99-52239

Social drama. Woman comes to realization that her married life is a farce and decides to leave family to pursue personal freedom. 3 acts 2b 1g 4m 4w 1 interior

Emperor and Galilean: a world historical drama. Smith & Kraus 1999 203p
ISBN 1-57525-194-9

Written in 1873. Historical drama about the career of Julian the Apostate (331-363), the Roman emperor who tried to re-establish paganism. Music, singing, dancing. 2 parts 10 acts 10 scenes Large mixed cast 4 interiors 6 exteriors

An enemy of the people; translator Christopher Hampton. French 2001 122p
ISBN 0-573-62764-X

Social drama set in 19th century Norway. Idealistic doctor who advocates community water purification is considered hostile to town's financial interests. 5 acts 8m 2w extras 4 interiors

Ibsen, Henrik, 1828-1906—*Continued*
Hedda Gabler; English version by Doug
Hughes. Dramatists 2001 78p
ISBN 0-8222-1784-8
Tragedy of clever, sophisticated woman bored
with dull marriage and social conventions. Her
role in lover's death discovered, she shoots herself.
4 acts 3m 4w 1 interior
John Gabriel Borkman; tr. by Brian John-
ston with Rick Davis.
Borkman realizes his error in having sacrificed
love for ambition; his bid for power led him to
break engagement and misappropriate bank funds.
4 acts 3m 5w 2 interiors 1 exterior
In Ibsen, H. Ibsen: four plays v3
The lady from the sea; tr. by Brian John-
ston with Rick Davis.
Wife is haunted by memory of mysterious sailor.
When he returns, her husband grants her freedom.
Only then does she realize the value of her mar-
riage. 5 acts 5m 3w extras 1 interior 3 exteriors
In Ibsen, H. Ibsen: four plays v3
Little Eyolf; tr. by Brian Johnston with
Rick Davis.
Psychological study of relations between hus-
band and wife after death of their child. 3 acts 1b
2m 3w 1 interior 2 exteriors
In Ibsen, H. Ibsen: four plays v3
When we dead awaken; tr. by Brian
Johnston with Rick Davis.
Symbolic play of life versus mission. In 19th
century Norway, sculptor is reunited with foreign
woman who had been the inspiration for his mas-
terpiece many years earlier. 3 acts 3m 3w extras
3 interiors
In Ibsen, H. Ibsen: four plays v3
Parodies, imitations, etc.
Linney, R. Gint
Icarus. Sánchez, E.
The **ice** house. MacDonald, R. D.
The **ice** wolf. Kraus, J. H.
Iceland
Ardal, M. Midnight sun
Iceman. Constable, J.
I'd rather go blind. McLean, D.
The **ideal** gnome expedition. Wood, D.
An **ideal** husband. Wilde, O.
Identity (Psychology)
Kennedy, A. Funnyhouse of a Negro
Kennedy, A. The owl answers
c Korty, C. Baba Yaga and the black sun-
flower

Kushner, T. Terminating
Margulies, D. Zimmer
Marnich, M. Quake
Martin, J. Beauty
Martin, J. The deal
Nigro, D. Ballerinas
Nigro, D. The lost girl
Prida, D. Botánica
Vogelstein, C. Cats and dogs
Wilder, T. And the sea shall give up its
dead
The **idiots** Karamazov. Durang, C.
If Columbus does not figure in your travel
plans. Lucas, C.
If it was easy. . . Lane, S. F., and
Morehouse, W.
If memory serves. Tolins, J.
If Susan Smith could talk. Romero, E.
If the shoe fits. Woodford, K.

Ihimaera, Witi
Woman far walking. Huia 2000 100p
ISBN 1-877241-51-2   LC 00-691141
One-hundred-sixty-year-old Maori woman remi-
nisces on her birthday. Prologue 4 acts 16 scenes
2w 1 setting

Iizuka, Naomi
Skin.
Poverty, social injustice, and the prostitution of
his lover drive a man to madness and murder.
Adapted from Büchner's Woyzeck but set in the
U.S. near the Mexican border. Music, dancing. 1
act 33 scenes 1g 4m 2w extras 6 interiors 6 exteri-
ors
In Out of the fringe; ed. by C. Svich
and M. T. Marrero

Ikoli, Tunde
Scrape off the black. Oberon Bks. 1998
103p
ISBN 1-84002-084-9
Domestic drama about racially mixed family in
1970s London. 2 acts 2m 2w 1 interior
Ile. O'Neill, E.
Ill met by moonlight. MacLiammóir, M.
I'll take Manhattan. Andersen, D. R.
Illegal entry. Martini, C.
Illness
Argall, T. G. A year in the death of Ed-
die Jester

Illness—*Continued*
Ayckbourn, A. Gizmo
Beber, N. Departures
Bonel, W. Good grief, Lolita
Crip, N. J. That good night
Crowther, C. Footprints in the sand
Crowther, C. Tryst
Finn, W. A new brain
Hall, L. I love you, Jimmy Spud
Hedges, P. Two and an orange
y Kral, B. Paper lanterns, paper cranes
Lindsay-Abaire, D. Fuddy meers
McConnell, J. The guilt card
McLeod, K. R. Broken hearts
O'Brien, D. The Last Supper restoration
Schmitt, E.-E. Enigma variations
Sewell, S. The sick room
Sherborne, C. Look at everything twice, for me
Tricker, G. Life support
Weller, M. Ghost on fire
Illuminating Veronica. Martinez, R.
I'm not Rappaport. Gardner, H.
I'm talking about Jerusalem. Wesker, A.
I'm with ya, Duke. Gardner, H.
An **imaginary** discussion. Fredericks, A. D.
Imagine drowning. Johnson, T.
The **immortal** husband. Merrill, J.

Immortality
c Fredericks, A. D. Forever is a long time
Merrill, J. The immortal husband
The **imp** of simplicity (Thomas à Kempis). Ehn, E.

Impersonation
Churchill, C. Blue kettle
Ives, D. Degas, c'est moi
Kleist, H. von. Amphitryon
Langella, F. Frank Langella's Cyrano
Molière. The doctor despite himself
Nottage, L. Snapshot: becoming American
The **importance** of being Earnest. Wilde, O.
Impossible marriage. Henley, B.

Impostors and imposture
Fugard, A. Sizwe Bansi is dead
Hischak, T. Molière's Tartuffe
Jonson, B. Volpone

Marowitz, C. Quack
Schmitt, E.-E. Enigma variations
In a kingdom by the Sea. Sunde, K.
In a little world of our own. Mitchell, G.
In Abraham's bosom: the tragedy of a southern Negro. Green, P.
In and out of the light. May, E.
In at the deep end. Benfield, D.
In-betweens. Goluboff, B.
In Moscow. Chekhov, A. P.
In order of appearance. McKay, G.
In other words. Andersen, D. R.
In perpetuity throughout the universe. Overmyer, E.
In pursuit of Eve. Clark, B.
In search of a friend. Tunooniq Theatre
In sunshine and in shadow. Osborne, A.
In the blood. Parks, S.-L.
In the fields of Aceldama. Wallace, N.
In the green room. Paolucci, A.
In the heart of America. Wallace, N.
In the western garden. Spencer, S.
In the zone. O'Neill, E.
In two minds. Harris, R.

Incest
Bowne, A. Sharon and Billy
Ford, J. 'Tis pity she's a whore
Gault, C. Sky
Henley, B. Control freaks
Horovitz, I. Alfred dies
Kane, S. Phaedra's love
Osborne, J. Under plain cover
Sophocles. King Oedipus
Sophocles. Oedipus Tyrannos
Incide (Judas Iscariot). Ehn, E.
The **incomparable** LouLou. Clark, R.
Incorruptible. Hollinger, M.
Independence. Gilbert, S.
The **independence** of Eddie Rose. Yellow Robe, W. S.

India
Bhagat, D. Routes and escape routes
Bhuchar, S. A tainted dawn
Ganguli, U. Rudali
Joshi, A. A shaft of sunlight
Kuruvilla, S. Rice boy
Padmanabhan, M. Harvest
Sharma, T. The wooden cart
Stoppard, T. Indian ink
The **Indian** draft spirit. Body, J. J.

Indian ink. Stoppard, T.

Indian radio days. Howe, L., and Gordon, R.

Indians. Kopit, A. L.

Indians of North America

Body, J. J. The Indian draft spirit

c DeTurk, S. Pocahontas

Geiogamah, H. Body Indian

Glancy, D. American gypsy

Glancy, D. Jump kiss

Glancy, D. The lesser wars

Glancy, D. The woman who was a red deer dressed for the deer dance

Glancy, D. The women who loved house trailers

Handy, P. East of the sun and west of the moon

Howe, L. Indian radio days

Kopit, A. L. Indians

Lodato, V. Snapshot: the great father

Nolan, Y. Annie Mae's movement

Pomerance, B. Melons

Spiderwoman Theater. Power pipes

Walcott, D. The ghost dance

Yellow Robe, W. S. The body guards

Yellow Robe, W. S. The council

Yellow Robe, W. S. The independence of Eddie Rose

Yellow Robe, W. S. Rez politics

Yellow Robe, W. S. Sneaky

Yellow Robe, W. S. The star quilter

York, Y. The snowflake avalanche

Legends

c Barchers, S. I. How Fisher went to the skyland

Bruchac, J. The cannibal monster

Bruchac, J. Gluskabe and Old Man Winter

Bruchac, J. Possum's tail

Bruchac, J. Pushing up the sky

Bruchac, J. Star sisters

Bruchac, J. Wihio's duck dance

Kauffman, J. According to Coyote

c Leonard, J. Crow & Weasel

c Miller, K. S. Young Cherokee

Canada

Highway, T. The Rez sisters

Lill, W. The occupation of Heather Rose

Ross, I. fareWel

Taylor, D. H. alterNatives

Taylor, D. H. The baby blues

Taylor, D. H. The boy in the treehouse

Taylor, D. H. Girl who loved her horses

Taylor, D. H. Only drunks and children tell the truth

The **individuality** of streetlamps. Gorisch, A. K.

Inès Mendo; or, The defeat of prejudice (Inès Mendo; ou, Le préjugé vaincu). Mérimée, P.

Inès Mendo; or, The triumph of prejudice (Inès Mendo; ou, Le triomphe du préjugé). Mérimée, P.

Infants

Durang, C. Baby with the bathwater

LeFevre, A. Waterbabies

Newmeir, J. H. Babysitting Calvin

Inge, William, 1913-1973

about

Gilbert, S. Independence

Ingram, Shirley Lockhart

c Christmas? Bah humbug!.

A chorus of children use carols, a spelling game, Bible readings, and a manger tableau to explain the meaning of Christmas to Scrooge Jr. Music, singing. 1 act Variable cast 11 characters extras 1 setting

In 5 Christmas plays for children

c Everywhere, everywhere, Christmas to-night.

Costumed children present Christmas customs of many lands. Music, singing. 1 act Variable cast 10 charcters extras 1 setting

In 5 Christmas plays for children

Inheritance. Woods, J.

Inheritance and succession

Cibber, C. Love makes a man; or, The fop's fortune

Constable, J. The false hairpiece

Hackenbrook, W. J. Conditions

Parker, M. The Lone Star love potion

Wasserman, D. The bequest

Williams, T. Kingdom of earth

Williams, T. Suddenly last summer

Injuries

Ayvazian, L. Twenty-four years

Maloney, P. Accident

Inner gardens (Jardín de otoño). Raznovich, D.

Ireland—*Continued*

Eagleton, T. God's locusts

Jones, M. Stones in his pockets

Keane, J. B. The highest house on the mountain

Keane, J. B. The year of the hiker

MacLiammóir, M. Ill met by moonlight

Mayne, R. Bridge head

Mayne, R. The drone

Mayne, R. The troth

Mayne, R. The turn of the road

y McClelland, J. Blood lines

McDonagh, M. The cripple of Inishmaan

McDonagh, M. The lonesome West

McDonagh, M. A skull in Connemara

McGuinness, F. Dolly West's kitchen

Mitchell, G. Tearing the loom

Molloy, M. J. The bachelor's daughter

Molloy, M. J. Daughter from over the water

Molloy, M. J. The king of Friday's men

Molloy, M. J. Petticoat loose

Molloy, M. J. The wood of the whispering

Murray, T. C. Birthright

Murray, T. C. Maurice Harte

Noone, R. The lepers of Baile Baiste

O'Casey, S. Cock-a-doodle dandy

O'Casey, S. Juno and the paycock

O'Casey, S. The plough and the stars

O'Casey, S. Purple dust

O'Casey, S. Red roses for me

O'Casey, S. The shadow of a gunman

Turlish, S. Lafferty's wake

Walsh, E. Disco pigs

Irish

Gore, C. King O'Neil; or, The Irish Brigade

United States

Hanes, M. The crimson thread

Pownall, D. Getting the picture

The **Irish** girl kissed in the rain. Nigro, D.

Irish Republican Army

O'Callaghan, J. Some mother's son

Ironmistress. De Angelis, A.

Irving, John

The cider house rules (dramatization) See Parnell, P. The cider house rules: part 1; Parnell, P. The cider house rules: part 2

Irving, Washington, 1783-1859

The legend of Sleepy Hollow (dramatization) See Arnault, M., and Arnault, A. The legend of Sleepy Hollow; Barchers, S. I., and Kroll, J. L. The legend of Sleepy Hollow; Francoeur, B. Sleepy Hollow

Rip Van Winkle (dramatization) See Jefferson, J., and Boucicault, D. Rip Van Winkle

Irwin, Bill, and O'Donnell, Mark

Scapin; adapted from Molière; by Bill Irwin and Mark O'Donnell. Dramatists 1997 52p il

ISBN 0-8222-1603-5   LC 98-168535

Romantic farce set in 17th century Naples. Rogue Scapin tricks two wealthy avaricious fathers into financing their children's marriage. 2 acts 24 scenes 9m 3w extras 1 interior 1 exterior

Is there anybody there? Flewitt, L.

Isaac Newton's poetry of the rainbow. McCullough, L. E.

Islam

Sills, P. Rumi

Island son. Miller, K. S.

Israel

Hare, D. Via Dolorosa

Margulies, D. New Year's Eve and Kibbutz

c McCullough, L. E. Israel reborn

c McCullough, L. E. Next year in Jerusalem

Rosenfeld, S. Z. The flatted fifth

Israel reborn. McCullough, L. E.

It ain't nothin' but the blues. Taylor, R.

It could always be worse. Barchers, S. I.

It could be any one of us. Ayckbourn, A.

It is finished. Koopman, L.

It started with a kiss. Godber, J.

Italian Americans

McClelland, C. E. Certain arrangements

The **Italian** evening. Horváth, Ö. von

Italy

Brustein, R. Enrico IV
Fo, D. We won't pay! We won't pay
Ford, J. 'Tis pity she's a whore
Fry, C. A yard of sun
Louise, D. The servant of two masters
Manzoni, A. Adelchi: a tragedy
Manzoni, A. The Count of Carmagnola:
  a tragedy
Pirandello, L. Henry IV (Enrico IV)
y Swortzell, L. The shepherds of Saint
  Francis
Webster, J. The Duchess of Malfi

It's all true. Sherman, J.
It's an emergency! (emergency medical
  technician). McCullough, L. E.
It's an okie-dokie life. Hamlett, C.
It's in the bag. Fredericks, A. D.
It's okay, honey. Brown, B.
Ivanov. Chekhov, A. P.

Ives, David

Arabian nights.

Comedy. Shop owner visited by prince and inter-
preter. Variable cast 3 characters 1 interior

In 30 ten-minute plays for 3 actors
  from Actors Theatre of
  Louisville's National Ten-minute
  Play Contest

—Same

In Ives, D. Lives of the saints

Babel's in arms.

In Mesopotamia, two construction workers are
handed the task of building Tower of Babel. 1 act
3m 2w 1 setting

In Ives, D. Lives of the saints

Bolero.

In middle of the night couple disagree about nature of sounds coming from apartment next door.
1 act 1m 1w 1 interior

In Ives, D. Time flies and other short
  plays

Captive audience.

Couple is threatened by man-eating talking television. 2m 2w

In Ives, D. Lives of the saints

Degas, c'est moi.

Unemployed man passes the day imagining he is
Edgar Degas, which has its rewards. 1 act 1 scene
2m 2w 1 setting

In EST marathon '96: the one-act
  plays; ed. by M. Smith

—Same

In Ives, D. Mere mortals

Dr. Fritz; or, The forces of light.

Comedy. American tourist seeks medical help
from wacky souvenir seller. 1 act 1m 1w 1 interior

In Ives, D. Mere mortals

Enigma variations.

Comedy about pair of look-alikes who solve
identity crisis with help of physician and nurse.
3m 2w 1 interior

In Ives, D. Lives of the saints

Foreplay; or, The art of the fugue.

Comedy. Young man and two older manifestations of himself play at miniature golf and seduction. 1 act 3m 3w 1 setting

In Ives, D. Mere mortals

The green hill.

Man spends years chasing an elusive fantasy. 1
act 1m 1w

In Ives, D. Time flies and other short
  plays

Lives of the saints.

Two elderly ladies with thick Polish accents put-
ter around the church basement, preparing a funeral breakfast for a friend whose husband just died.
Music. 1 act 2w 1 interior

In Ensemble Studio Theatre marathon
  2000: the one-act plays

—Same

In Ives, D. Lives of the saints

Mere mortals.

Comedy. Three construction workers on lunch
break share amazing confidences. 1 act 3m 1 setting

In Ives, D. Mere mortals

The mystery at Twicknam Vicarage.

Comedy murder mystery featuring bumbling detective. 3m 2w 1 setting

In Ives, D. Lives of the saints

The Philadelphia.

Comedy. Man in Twilight Zone-like state must
ask for opposite of what he truly wants. 2m 1w 1
interior

In take ten; ed. by E. Lane and N.
  Shengold

Ives, David—*Continued*

The red address. Dramatists 1998 58p
   ISBN 0-8222-1606-X   LC 98-222977
Drama about middle-American businessman
whose company and life are ruined by rival. 8
scenes 4m 2w 1 setting

Soap opera.
Repairman falls in love with perfect washing
machine. 3m 2w 1 setting
   In Ives, D. Lives of the saints

Speed-the-play.
Comic condensations of David Mamet's
American buffalo, Speed-the-plow, Sexual perver-
sity in Chicago, and Glengarry Glen Ross. 1 act
13m 3w 4 interiors
   In Ives, D. Mere mortals

Time flies.
Comedy. Two mayflies react to news of their
short lifespan. 2m 1w extras 1 exterior
   In The Best American Short plays,
      1997-1998

—Same
   In Ives, D. Mere mortals

J

Jabiru. Johnson, M.
Jack and Jill. Robbins, N.
Jack and Jill: a romance. Martin, J.
Jack and the beanstalk. Miller, K. S.

Jacker, Corinne

A new life.
Two brothers argue over family, work, religion,
and life. 2m 1 setting
   In Actors Theatre of Louisville.
      Ten-minute plays: v4

Jackson, Andrew
                about
Pownall, D. Getting the picture

**Jackson, Gregory, and Purcell, Erin
   Quinn**

Duet. Broadway Play Pub. 2000 55p
   ISBN 0-88145-164-9
Comedy with music satirizing entertainment,
from musicals to B-movies. Music, singing. Puppets. 18 scenes Variable cast 18 characters

Jackson, Keith

y High school dropouts from outer space.
   Pioneer Drama Service 1998 32p
Comedy. Aliens invade bodies of high school
students. 6m 12w extras 1 interior

Jackson, Mahalia, 1911-1972
                about
Stolz, T. Mahalia

Jackson, Nagle

A hotel on Marvin Gardens. Dramatists
   2000 62p
   ISBN 0-8222-1763-5
Comedy about competitive greed set on island
off coast of Connecticut. Magazine diva orches-
trates her annual game of Monopoly. 2 acts 4
scenes 2m 3w 1 interior

—Same
   In New playwrights: the best plays of
      1999

Jackson, R. Eugene

y Bad hair day. Pioneer Drama Service
   2002 61p
Comedy. High school students tricked into using
shampoo that causes hair loss. 2 acts Variable cast
18 characters extras 1 interior 1 exterior

y Touched by an angle. Pioneer Drama
   Service 2000 60p
Comedy. Two angels help motherless teen girl
and town's clumsiest boy. 2 acts 3 scenes 7m 15w
1 interior

**Jacobs, W. W. (William Wymark), 1863-
   1943**

The Monkey's Paw (adaptation) See
   Holloway, J. The monkey's paw
Jacqueline. McAvera, B.
Jacques Brel is alive and well & living in
   Paris. Brel, J.
The **jade** mountain. Mamet, D.
Jails, hospitals and hip-hop. Hoch, D.

Jamaica

Griffiths, L. O.D. on paradise
Sistren Theatre Collective. QPH
Williams, R. Starstruck
Young, D. Yagayah: two.black.womyn.
   griots

Jamaicans

Bunyan, H. J. Prodigals in a promised
   land

James, Alice

about

Schenkar, J. Signs of life

James, Henry

about

Schenkar, J. Signs of life

James, Henry, 1843-1916

Parodies, imitations, etc.

Nigro, D. Quint and Miss Jessel at Bly

James Joyce's The dead. Davey, S.

James Joyce's The dead (condensation). Davey, S.

Janaczewska, Noëlle

y Madagascar lily.

Drama about history of Pacific island region. Background music. Singing. 10 scenes 6m 4w extras 1 setting

In International plays for young people

Jane Eyre. Teale, P.

Janes, Hugh

The perfect murder. French (London) 2001 69p

ISBN 0-573-01954-1

Mystery adapted from a story by Jeffrey Archer. Husband and wife collude to save him from suspicion when his mistress is found murdered. Background music. 2 acts 9m 3w extras 4 interiors

The **janitor**. Wilson, A.

Jannuzzi, Luigi

Night of the foolish moon. French 1999 85p

ISBN 0-573-62692-8

Romantic comedy about a man obsessed with Don Quixote, who falls in love with a murder witness. Sancho Panza breaks through the time warp. 2 acts 6 scenes 4m 2w 1 interior

Japan

Chikamatsu, M. The battles of Coxinga

Chikamatsu, M. The love suicides at Amijima

Chikamatsu, M. The love suicides at Sonezaki

Chikamatsu, M. The uprooted pine

Gurney, A. R. Far East

Huie, K. Yasuko and the young s-s-samurai

Hwang, D. H. The house of sleeping beauties

Jarry, Alfred

King Ubu; tr. by Michael Benedikt and George E. Wellworth.

Variant titles: Ubu Rex; Ubu Roi; Ubu the King. Satirical farce. Pere Ubu makes himself King of Poland. Pokes fun at middle class conservatism and human stupidity. Characters can also be enacted by marionettes. 5 acts 33 scenes Large mixed cast

In Theater of the avant-garde, 1890-1950; ed. by B. Cardullo and R. Knopf

Jason and the golden fleece. Barchers, S. I.

Jazz music

Baraka, A. Primitive world: an antinuclear jazz musical

Leight, W. Side man

Smith, C. The Sutherland

Jealousy

Bobrick, S. Remember me?

Feydeau, G. Wooed and viewed

Keyes, S. Moonlight cocktail

Jean and Dinah who have been locked away in a world famous calypso since 1956 speak their minds publicly. Hall, T.

Jefferson, Joseph, and Boucicault, Dion

Rip Van Winkle.

Amiable sot wanders off into Catskills, drinks magic brew, and wakes up twenty years later to find the world much changed and his wife and daughter in need of rescue. Based on a story by Washington Irving. 4 acts 8 scenes 1b 1g 7m 3w extras settings

In Nineteenth century American plays; ed. by M. Matlaw

Jefferson, Thomas

about

c Fredericks, A. D. A conversation with Thomas Jefferson

Jeffery, Lawrence

Who look in stove.

Final days of three prospectors who starved to death when they misjudged migratory patterns of caribou in 1920s Northwest Territories. 3m 1 setting

In Staging the North; ed. by S. Grace, E. D'Aeth and L. Chalykoff

Jeffrey Slugworth: ex-embalmer. Roth, A.

Jeffries, Brian

Pastimes. French (London) 1998 76p

    ISBN 0-573-01870-7   LC 00-703041

Comedy. In between filling orders at their cafe, two brothers take in runaways and face wives they abandoned forty years ago. 2 acts 5 scenes 2m 3w 1 interior

Jelinek, Elfriede

Clara S.

Drama centers on the figure of Clara Schumann wife of the composer Robert Schumann, who was forced to forgo her own artistic creativity for the sake of her husband's genius and ambitions. 2 parts 3 scenes epilogue 1g 3m 4w extras 2 interiors

    In Women's words, women's work; ed. by U. H. G. Borgert

Jenkin, Len

A country doctor.

Dramatization of short story by Franz Kafka. Physician travels through raging blizzard to treat dying patient. 21 scenes Variable cast 1 setting

    In Jenkin, L. Plays

c The invisible man.

Suspense tale based on story by H. G. Wells. Stranger with bandaged face checks into motel near nuclear power plant and befriends caretaker's son. 1b 1g 4m 2w extras 2 interiors 4 exteriors

    In Eight plays for children; ed. by C. A. Jennings

Like I say.

Experimental comedy about peculiar group of travelers at seaside hotel. 2 acts 22 scenes Large mixed cast settings

    In Jenkin, L. Plays

Pilgrims of the night.

Experimental play. Characters relate stories of headless woman, zombies, psychopathic neurosurgeon, sexually frustrated fry cook, and silver fairy. 2 acts 4m 3w

    In Jenkin, L. Plays

Jenkins, Mark

Strindberg knew my father.

Comedy. August Strindberg loses control over his characters while writing Miss Julie. 2 acts 11 scenes 2m 3w 2 interiors

    In Best of the Fest; ed. by Phil Setren

Jenkins, Mark F.

All powers necessary and convenient. University of Washington Press 2000 146p

    ISBN 0-295-97939-9   LC 99-055768

Docudrama depicting 1948 legislative hearings called to investigate communism in Washington State. Prelude 3 acts Large mixed cast 1 setting

Jenner, Edward, 1749-1823

about

c McCullough, L. E. Edward Jenner and the gossip of milkmaids

Jennings, Caleen Sinnette

Classyass.

Street person sweeps into campus radio station, teaches music snob a lesson. 1 act 2m 1w 1 interior

    In Humana Festival 2002

Jensen, Julie

Old wives tale.

Childless older woman in rural Utah develops relationship with new neighbor and her deformed children. 6 scenes 1g 3w 1 interior

    In Women's Project & productions; ed. by J. Miles

Snapshot: on Lincoln's head.

Park ranger at Mount Rushmore persuades rowdy woman that Lincoln's statue is sentient and will be disturbed by cherry bombs. Music. 1 act 2w 1 exterior

    In Humana Festival 2002

Two-headed. Dramatic Publishing 2003 58p

Lives of two 19th century women overshadowed by polygamy and the Mountain Meadows Massacre of 127 California-bound pioneers by Mormon zealots. 5 scenes 2w 1 exterior

—Same

    In Women playwrights: the best plays of 2000

Jensen, Lorre, and Wing, Paula

c Coming around.

Animal characters from legend help brother, sister and uncle deal with adversity. 1g 1b 1m 1 setting

    In TYA5: theatre for young audience

Jerry and Tom. Cleveland, R.

Jerry Springer is God. Pelfrey, M.

Jews—*Continued*
Eastern Europe
Kushner, T. A dybbuk, or between two worlds
England
Kops, B. The hamlet of Stepney Green
Marber, P. Howard Katz
Straughan, P. Bones
Germany
c Hines, K. Home on the mornin' train
Horovitz, I. Lebensraum
Italy
c McCullough, L. E. Hail, Queen Esther!
Tasca, J. Judah's daughter
Netherlands
Apstein, T. The likeness
Kops, B. Dreams of Anne Frank
New York (N.Y.)
Gardner, H. Conversations with my father
Greenberg, R. Everett Beekin
Korder, H. Geliebteh
Kramer, L. The destiny of me
c McCullough, L. E. Di goldineh medineh (The golden land)
Poland
c McCullough, L. E. Tale of the Baal Shem Tov
c McCullough, L. E. The wise men and women of Chelm
Nanus, S. The survivor
Queens (N.Y.)
May, E. Taller than a dwarf
Russia
Joselovitz, E. Vilna's got a golem
Spain
Gore, C. Don Juan of Austria
Sandberg, R. N. Convivencia
United States
Brandt, A. 2 1/2 Jews
Dymov, O. Bronx express
Harelik, M. The legacy
Kushner, T. Notes on Akiba
Lauro, S. The contest
Mamet, D. The disappearance of the Jews
Margulies, D. Lola

Margulies, D. New Year's Eve and Kibbutz
Margulies, D. Zimmer
Posner, A. The chosen
y Rabin, A. The man-child
Rosenfeld, S. Z. The flatted fifth
y Surface, M. H. Broken rainbows

Jezebel (Biblical figure)
c Vogel, L. An Ahab headache and a Jezebelly ache
Jig saw. Powell, D.
Jill on a recliner, reading. McKee, J.
"Jingle bells" revisited. Anderson, S. J.
Jingo. Wood, C.
Jitney. Wilson, A.
Jitney (condensation). Wilson, A.
Jitterbugging: scenes of sex in a new society. Nelson, R.
Joan, of Arc, Saint
about
Ehn, E. Wholly Joan's (Joan of Arc)
Nigro, D. Joan of Arc in the autumn
Schenkar, J. Burning desires
Joan of Arc in the autumn. Nigro, D.
Joan of Arkansas. Wilner, S.
The **job**. Bitterman, S.
Job. Kokoschka, O.
Job, the patriarch
about
Kokoschka, O. Job
Jodie's body. Carlin, A. J.
Joe and Stew's Theatre of Brotherly Love and Financial Success. Reingold, J.
Joe Knight and the seven serfs. Art, S. S.
Joey. Margulies, D.
John, of the Cross, Saint
about
Ehn, E. Cedar (John of the Cross)
John, the Baptist, Saint
about
Ehn, E. Locus (John the Baptist)
Wilde, O. Salome
John Gabriel Borkman. Ibsen, H.
Johnny Appleseed. Snyder, G. A.
Johnny Brooke. Hollingsworth, M. B.
Johnny, don't jump. Ogden, A.

Johnson, Margaret

Jabiru. French (London) 2002 23p
ISBN 0-573-02355-7

On a birdwatching holiday, a romantic couple revisit the Caribbean island where each of them vacationed when single; the tour guide both of them slept with is still there, still hoping to make enough money to leave the island. 1 act 5 scenes 2m 1w 1 setting

Johnson, Terry

Dead funny.

Comedy about impotence, sex therapy and English sense of humor. 2 acts 4 scenes 3m 2w 1 interior
In Johnson, T. Plays: 2

Hysteria; or, Fragments of an analysis of an obsessional neurosis.

Comedy set in 1939 London. Sigmund Freud, in state of near hysteria, burns latest publication and is berated by surrealist Salvador Dali. 2 acts 3 scenes 3m 1w 1 interior
In Johnson, T. Plays: 2
—Same
In The Methuen book of modern drama; ed. by G. Whybrow

Imagine drowning.

Thriller set on Cumbrian coast. Woman's search for journalist husband who has disappeared, brings her to boarding house populated by radical dwarf in wheelchair, an ex-astronaut and a landlady with horrific secret in her past. Prologue 2 acts 9 scenes 4m 2w 1 setting
In Johnson, T. Plays: 2

Johnston, Alex

Melon farmer.

Drama set in Dublin. Interlocking lives of eight morally adrift young men and women. 4m 4w extras
In New plays from the Abbey Theatre v2

Johnston, Simon

Running dog, paper tiger. Playwrights Canada 1998 114p
ISBN 0-88754-556-4

Drama set in 1967 Hong Kong. Communist Chinese riots force mixed-race family to choose between loyalty to British roots and their race. 2 acts 5m 2w 2 interiors

Johnston, Bob, and Hochhauser, Jeff

Theda Bara and the Frontier Rabbi. Dramatists 2002
ISBN 0-8222-1837-2

A newly ordained rabbi enjoys Theda Bara's movies. His congregation does not approve. Theda Bara is really Theodosia Goodman, a nice Jewish girl, who would like to meet a nice rabbi. 6m 5w 1 setting

Jolly. Mamet, D.

Jolly Roger. Mitchell, W.

Jolson, Al, d. 1950

about

Hanan, S. M. Jolson & company

Jolson & company. Hanan, S. M.

Jonah (Biblical figure)

c McCullough, L. E. Jonah and the whale

Jonah and the whale. McCullough, L. E.

Jones, Charlotte

Humble boy. Faber & Faber 2001 101p
ISBN 0-571-21287-5

Following sudden death of his father, thirty-five-year-old Cambridge astrophysicist returns to his middle England home and his difficult and demanding mother. Music. 2 acts 5 scenes 3m 3w 1 interior

Jones, E. Y.

y Not on this night. Pioneer Drama Service 2001 18p

Drama set Christmas Eve 1944 in France. Two lost soldiers, one American and one German, meet in remote farmhouse. 2m 1w

Jones, Jeffrey M.

The crazy plays.

Theatrical collage of six plays. Characters appear and disappear randomly and resurface in variety of guises. 3m 2w 1 setting
In Jones, J. M. Plays

The endless adventure of MCKAY; or, How they got from A to B.

Satirical post-modern vaudeville framed by playwright wandering small town in search of characters. 6m 4w 1 setting
In Jones, J. M. Plays

Jones, Jeffrey M.—*Continued*

Tomorrowland.

Verbal collage constructed from 1950 source material. Interweaves plot elements of sci-fi thriller, western and family sitcom. Prologue 50 scenes 3m 3w

In Jones, J. M. Plays

Jones, Marie

Stones in his pockets. Applause 2001 94p
ISBN 1-55783-472-5

Satire. Hollywood film crew sets up shop in rural Irish village to make absurdly plotted 19th-century blockbuster. 2 acts 2m 1 setting

—Same; introduction by Mel Gussow. Applause 2001 94p il
ISBN 1-557-83472-5   LC 2001-88727

Jonson, Ben

The alchemist.

Jacobean satire in verse. Rogues cheat the greedy who seek easy money through alchemy. Prologue 5 acts 27 scenes 10 2w extras 2 interiors 1 exterior

In Jonson, B. Ben Jonson's plays and masques

Bartholomew Fair.

Jacobean satirical comedy set in 17th century London. Events, farcical and romantic, ensue when justice of peace goes to Fair in disguise to seek out criminals. Prologue 5 acts 10 scenes epilogue 23m 7w extras 1 interior 3 exteriors

In Renaissance drama; ed. by A. F. Kinney

Epicoene.

Jacobean farce in verse ridiculing 17th century English society. 2 prologues 5 acts 28 scenes 11m 5w extras 4 interiors 1 exterior

In Jonson, B. Ben Jonson's plays and masques

The masque of blackness.

Masque in verse. Black Ethiopian water nymphs desire fair complexions, which they think more beautiful. Moon goddess will grant wish if they go to Britannia and perform moon rituals. Music, singing, dancing. 2m 1w extras

In Renaissance drama; ed. by A. F. Kinney

Mercury vindicated from the alchemists at court.

Masque with anti-masque. Mercury banishes alchemist Vulcan and his monstrous creations. Music, singing, dancing. 3m 1w extras

In Jonson, B. Ben Jonson's plays and masques

Pleasure reconciled to Virtue.

Allegorical masque in verse. Hercules at crossroads must choose between Virtue and Vice (Pleasure). Music, singing, dancing. 9m 2w extras

In Jonson, B. Ben Jonson's plays and masques

The queen's masques: the first, of blackness.

Masque in verse. Black Ethiopian water nymphs desire fair complexions which they think more beautiful. Moon goddess will grant wish if they go to Britannia and perform moon rituals. Music, singing, dancing. 2m 1w extras

In Jonson, B. Ben Jonson's plays and masques

Volpone.

Jacobean comedy in verse. Servant and master play on greed of master's friends. Prologue 5 acts 39 scenes 20m 2w extras 4 interiors 2 exteriors

In Jonson, B. Ben Jonson's plays and masques

Jordan, Julia

Mpls., St. Paul.

Two teenagers sit on a roof and discuss music, friends, and the sea. 1m 1w 1 setting

In Actors Theatre of Louisville. Ten-minute plays; v5

Nightswim.

Girl tries to convince friend to sneak out of house and go swimming. 2w 1 setting

In 30 ten-minute plays for 2 actors from Actors Theatre of Louisville's National Ten-minute Play Contest

—Same

In Humana Festival 2002

Tatjana in color.

Loosely based on events in the life of Egon Schiele. Young girl drawn to older artist. 2 acts 24 scenes 2g 2m 1w 1 setting

In Women playwrights: the best plays of 1997

Jory, Jon
Heads.
Three female college roommates consider dating wealthy nerd. 3w
In 30 ten-minute plays for 3 actors from Actors Theatre of Louisville's National Ten-minute Play Contest
Scruples.
Three girls waiting to audition for pantyhose commercial. 1m 4w 1 interior
In 30 ten-minute plays for 4, 5 & 6 actors from Actors Theatre of Louisville's National Ten-minute Play Contest

Joselovitz, Ernest
Vilna's got a golem. French 2000 106p
ISBN 0-573-62716-9
Drama set in 1899. Troupe of Jewish actors in imperialist Russia perform version of folktale. Music. 2 acts 6m 2w 1 setting

Joseph (Biblical figure)
c Vogel, L. Joseph
Joseph. Vogel, L.
Joseph and the holly. Kee, A.
Josephus, Flavius
about
Allison, B. Titus at the gates of Syon

Joshi, Abhijat
A shaft of sunlight. Hern Bks. 1999 51p
ISBN 1-85459-449-4
Drama set in 1994 Ahmedabad. Conflict in marriage between Hindu and Muslim reflects divisive politics of India. 1 act 14 scenes 1g 2m 2w extras 2 interiors
Joshua's egg. Dodge, A.

Journalists
Birch, M. Pratt of the Argus
Bosakowski, P. Bierce takes on the railroad!
DeLillo, D. Valparaiso
Elton, B. Silly cow
Gilman, R. Boy gets girl
Hare, D. A map of the world
Johnson, T. Imagine drowning
c McCullough, L. E. Around the world with Nellie Bly
c McCullough, L. E. The big scoop (newspaper reporter)

Townsend, J. Terms of abuse
Williamson, D. Sanctuary
Young, D. Clout
The **Jovian** pact. Fredericks, A. D.
The **joy** of going somewhere definite. Long, Q.
Joyce, James, 1882-1941
The dead (dramatization) See Davey, S. James Joyce's The dead; Davey, S. James Joyce's The dead (condensation)
Joyful noise. Slover, T.

Juana Inés de la Cruz
The divine Narcissus (El divino Narciso); tr. by Patricia Peters and Renée Domeier. Univ. of New Mexico Press 1998 202p
ISBN 0-8263-1888-6
An auto sacramental from 17th century Mexico. Allegorical personages present a Christianized version of the myth of Narcissus to conquered Aztecs, in hopes of converting them. Music, singing, dancing. 3 parts 26 scenes 4m 8w extras settings
The **jubilee**. Chekhov, A. P.
Judah's daughter. Tasca, J.
Judas Iscariot
about
Ehn, E. Incide (Judas Iscariot)
Wilder, T. Hast thou considered my servant Job?
The **Judas** kiss. Hare, D.
Judgement Day
Constable, J. The Southwark Mysteries
Judges
Carley, D. Two ships passing
Dulack, T. Diminished capacity
Kleist, H. von. The broken jug
Shaw, B. Captain Brassbound's conversion
Judges—again. Vogel, L.
Judgment at Nuremberg. Mann, A.
Judgment call. Stroppel, F.
The **juice** of wild strawberries. Toddie, J. L.
Julian the Apostate
about
Ibsen, H. Emperor and Galilean: a world historical drama
Julie Allardyce. McLean, D.

July 7, 1994. Margulies, D.
Jump kiss. Glancy, D.
Jump the train at Riverpoint. Barry, P. J.

Junction Avenue Theatre Company

Sophiatown.

Protest drama set in 1950s South Africa. Vignettes explore relations between races at beginning of apartheid era. 2 acts 14 scenes 3m 4w 1 setting

    In Drama for a new South Africa; ed. by D. Graver

June and Jean in concert (the concert of their lives). Kennedy, A.

Jung, C. G. (Carl Gustave), 1856-1934

about

    Wilson, S. Sabina

Jungalbook. Mast, E.

The **Jungle** Book: the musical. Castle, G. V.

Jungle coup. Nelson, R.

Juno and the paycock. O'Casey, S.

Junyent, Sebastián

Packing up the past; tr. by Ana Mengual. Estreno 2000 46p (Contemporary Spanish Plays, 18)

    ISBN 1-888463-10-4

Two sisters, long estranged, pack up their childhood home and realize how deeply their lives have been affected by their late father, a repressive patriarch. Singing. 1 act 2w 1 interior

Jurassic Park and Wreck. Frankel, R.

Juris prudence. Milligan, J.

Jury

    Tropf, R. Shadow hour

Just a thought. Fredericks, A. D.

Just be frank. Williams, C.

Just one night. Levin, K.

Just say yes! Sharkey, J., and Sharkey, T.

Just the boys. Moritz, D.

Justice for whom? Plata, M. C.

Justices of the peace

    Jonson, B. Bartholomew Fair

Juvenile delinquency

    Walsh, E. Disco pigs

K

Kaahumanu, Queen

about

    Kneubuhl, V. N. The conversion of Ka'ahumanu

The **kabbalistic** psychoanalysis of Adam R. Tzaddik. Piatigorsky, A.

Kacmar, Kenneth

c The oldest story ever told; music by Kenneth Kacmar. Anchorage Press 1994 43p

    ISBN 0-87602-377-4

Drama about storytelling based on Chinese, African, and Indian folklore. Music, singing. 2m 2w 1 setting

Kafka, Fanz

A Country Doctor (dramatization) See Jenkin, L. A country doctor

Kafka, Franz, 1883-1924

The castle (dramatization) See Fishelson, D., and Leichter, A. The castle

Kahanamoku, Duke, 1890-1968

about

c Overmyer, E. Duke Kahanamoku vs. the surfnappers

Kahlo, Frida, 1907-1954

about

    Cruz, M. Frida: the story of Frida Kahlo

Kalcheim, Lee

Defiled; or, The convenience of a shorthaired dog. French 2002

    ISBN 0-573-62835-1

Comic drama about technophobic librarian and harried police negotiator. 2m extras 1 interior

Kander, John, and Ebb, Fred

Steel pier; book by David Thompson; music and lyrics by John Kander and Fred Ebb; conceived by Scott Ellis, Susan Stroman and David Thompson. French 1998 112p

    ISBN 0-573-62335-X

Musical set in 1933 in Atlantic City, New Jersey, about marathon dancing. Music, singing, dancing. 2 acts 24 scenes 7m 8w 1 interior

Kandinsky, Wassily

The yellow sound; tr. by John C. Crawford.

Experimental theatrical piece concerned with movement, sound, and color. Music. 5 scenes Variable cast 1 setting

In Theater of the avant-garde, 1890-1950; ed. by B. Cardullo and R. Knopf

Kane, Arnold

Marriage can be hazardous to your health. French 2001 53p

ISBN 0-573-62776-2

Comedy about man who has mid-life crisis, leaves his perfect family, and sets himself up in bachelor pad. 2 acts 8 scenes 2m 3w 1 interior

Kane, Honour

Snapshot: monument.

Telephone operators at the New York Office of Emergency Management receive and reroute calls after planes hit the World Trade Center; harrowing picture develops. 1 act 1 set Unidentified cast 2 characters 1 setting

In Humana Festival 2002

Kane, Richard

Miss Roach's war. French (London) 1998 81p

ISBN 0-573-01919-3   LC 00-703052

Dramatization of the novel The slaves of solitude by Richard Hamilton. Drama set in 1943 London about boarding house for women and elderly men, all of them single and lonely. 2 acts 19 scenes 4m 4w 2 settings

Kane, Sarah

4.48 psychosis.

Fragmentary episodes explore psychotic mind. Variable cast 3 characters

In Kane, S. Complete Plays

Blasted.

Drama about male carnality and modern warfare. Hotel in civil war ravaged Europe setting for rape, torture and cannibalism. 5 scenes 2m 1w 1 interior

In Kane, S. Complete Plays

—Same

In the Methuen book of modern drama; ed. by G. Whybrow

Cleansed.

Series of poetic images and pared dialogue explore limits of love. Concerns inhabitants of institution under control of sadistic psychiatrist. 20 scenes 4m 3w

In Kane, S. Complete Plays

Crave.

Chamber quartet for four lost voices. Charts disintegration of human under pressures of love, loss and desire. 2m 2w

In Kane, S. Complete Plays

Phaedra's love.

Drama about incest and unrequited love based on Seneca's classical tragedy. 8 scenes 5m 4w extras 1 setting

In Kane, S. Complete Plays

Skin.

Television play about politics of hate and quest for power. 5m 3w

In Kane, S. Complete Plays

Kang, M. J.

Noran bang: the yellow room. Playwrights Canada 1999 62p il

ISBN 0-88754-571-8

Drama about Korean family in Canada, facing realities of their new country, and the difficulties forgetting their homeland. 2 acts 27 scenes 2b 3g 6m 3w 2 settings

Kantor, Tadeusz, 1915-1990

about

Kraszewski, C. S. The archives at Kanonicza 5

Kaplan, Barry Jay

Landscape of desire.

Gay writer uses his personal life to sell himself and his novel. 3 acts 6m 2w 2 interiors 2 exteriors

In New dramatists: best plays by the graduating class of 2000

Karcz, L. R.

y The taming of LaRue. Pioneer Drama Service 1999 18p

Comedy take-off on Shakespeare's The taming of the shrew, set in Wild West. 1 act 2 scenes Variable cast 16 characters 1 exterior

Kareken, Jeremy

Hot Rod.

At the bridal registry in an upscale department store an engaged couple meet a saleswoman who takes a dim view of marriage, especially theirs. 1 act 1m 2w 1 interior

   In Off-Off Broadway Festival plays, 25th ser.

Karla and Grif. Laxdal, V.

Karnad, Girish

The fire and the rain.

Drama set in a mythological past. A play performed during the Brahmin fire sacrifice exposes crimes within the chief priest's family and disrupts the ceremony, but the gods are touched by an outcast's compassion. Music, dancing. Prologue 2 acts epilogue 12m 2w extras settings

   In DramaContemporary: India; ed. by E. B. Mee

Hayavadana.

Based on Sanskrit tales, the god Ganesha Puja ensures completion of any endeavour. 2 acts Variable cast 1 setting.

   In Postcolonial plays; ed. by H. Gilbert

Kash, Marcia, and Hughes, Doug

A party to murder; by Marcia Kash and Douglas E. Hughes. French 1999 85p il

   ISBN 0-573-62675-8   LC 99-475993

Mystery about a writer who stages a murder mystery game on Hallowe'en, but the game turns serious when guests start dying. 2 acts 4 scenes 3m 3w 1 setting

Kat and Eliza. Healy, A. M.

Kataev, Valentin

Squaring the circle.

Farce about Soviet life in 1920s. Two ill-matched newly married couples find amusing solution to their problems. 3 acts 39 scenes 4m 3w extras 1 interior

   In Eight twentieth-century Russian plays; ed. by T. Langen and J. Weir

Katherine Howard. Nicholson, W.

Katie and Frank. Rebeck, T.

Katims, Jason

The man who couldn't dance.

Man visits former girlfriend and discusses old times. 1m 1w 1 setting

   In take ten; ed. by E. Lane and N. Shengold

Katz, Leon

c Pinocchio. Applause 2001 77p

   ISBN 1-55783-462-8

Based on the story by Carlo Collodi about mischievous marionette who becomes real boy. 14 scenes Variable cast settings

Kauffman, John

According to Coyote.

Monologue based on Native American creation myths. Singing. 1 scene Unidentified cast 1 character 1 setting

   In Theatre for young audiences; ed. by C. A. Jennings

Kaufman, George S., and Ferber, Edna

Dinner at eight.

Comedy. Tells overlapping stories of guests invited to dinner. 3 acts 11 scenes settings

   In Kaufman, G. S. and Ferber, E. Three comedies

The royal family.

Satirical look at life in the theater. Portrays dynasty of actors. Thinly veiled parody of Barrymore clan. 3 acts 11m 6w settings

   In Kaufman, G. S. and Ferber, E. Three comedies

Stage door.

Comedy about hopes and ambitions of sixteen aspiring actresses who have come to New York to pursue careers in the theater. 3 acts 6 scenes 15m 17w 2 interiors

   In Kaufman, G. S. and Ferber, E. Three comedies

Kaufman, Moisés

Gross indecency: the three trials of Oscar Wilde. Dramatists 1999 85p

   ISBN 0-8222-1649-2   LC 97-37596

Drama based on the libel suit brought by Oscar Wilde against the Marquess of Queensburg, resulting in two more trials for indecency and Wilde's imprisonment. Prologue 2 acts 9m

—Same. Vintage 1998 143p

   ISBN 0-375-70232-6   LC 97-37596

Kaufman, Moisés—*Continued*

Gross indecency: the three trials of Oscar Wilde (condensation).

In The Best Play of 1997-1998; ed. by Otis L. Guernsey, Jr.

The Laramie Project. Vintage 2001 110p

ISBN 0-375-72719-1

Docudrama based on the murder of gay student, Matthew Shepard, on October 7, 1998, outside Laramie, Wyoming. 3 acts epilogue Large mixed cast

Kavanagh, Geoff

Ditch.

Two sailors in ditch during final days of Sir John Franklin's failed arctic expedition of 1845. 6 scenes 2m 1 exterior

In Staging the North; ed. by S. Grace, E. D'Aeth and L. Chalykoff

Kawabata, Yasunari, 1899-1972

about

Hwang, D. H. The house of sleeping beauties

Keane, John B.

The change in Mame Fadden.

Woman is torn between repairing her disastrous marriage or freedom from family obligations. 2 acts 7 scenes 8m 3w 1 interior 2 exteriors

In Keane, J. B. Three plays

The highest house on the mountain.

Domestic drama set in rural Ireland. Escalating tensions between brothers, fathers and sons. 3 acts 6 scenes 5m 3w 1 interior

In Keane, J. B. Three plays

The year of the hiker.

Drama set in Ireland. Much-hated father who deserted wife and family returns after long absence. 2 acts 5 scenes 4m 3w 1 interior

In Keane, J. B. Three plays

Kearns, Michael

Attachments.

Monologue. Autobiographical piece that spans childhood to fatherhood. 1m

In O Solo homo; ed. by H. hughes and D. Román

Kee, Alice

c Joseph and the holly. Minerva Press 1998 40p

ISBN 0-75410-540-7

Based on Christmas story by Rhoda Power. Joseph attempts to borrow wood from various trees to keep infant Jesus warm, after ignoring noble offer of little holly tree. Music, singing. Prologue 3 scenes variable cast

Keeffe, Barrie

Barbarians: abide with me.

Second play in trilogy. English working-class youth's frustration at inability to obtain soccer finals tickets becomes violent. He turns against black friend who puts pre-army cadet activities before soccer fandom. 3 scenes 3m 1 exterior

In Keeffe, B. Plays: 1

Barbarians: in the city.

Third play in trilogy. White working-class youths plan final fling with black girls before one joins British troops in Northern Ireland. Encounter with black former friend triggers violent racial conflict. 3m 1 setting

In Keeffe, B. Plays: 1

Barbarians: killing time.

First play of trilogy. Unemployed young English school dropouts, two whites and one black, hang about the streets drifting into petty crime. Music. 1 act 3m 1 setting

In Keeffe, B. Plays: 1

Gimme shelter: Gem.

First play of trilogy. Young Englishman avoids contact with management personnel at company outing as gesture of working-class hostility. Music. 3 scenes 3m 1w 1 exterior

In Keeffe, B. Plays: 1

Gimme shelter: Getaway.

Third play of trilogy. Former rebel, now management trainee, encounters youth who has become groundskeeper after reform school, and sees mirror of own failed rebellion. Music. 1 act 3m 1w 1 exterior

In Keeffe, B. Plays: 1

Gimme shelter: Gotcha.

Second play trilogy. Working class English youth leaving school holds teacher and headmaster prisoner to express bitterness over being judged a failure. Music. 3 scenes 3m 1w 1 interior

In Keeffe, B. Plays: 1

Keens-Douglas, Richardo

c The Nutmeg Princess. Playwrights Canada 2000 69p

ISBN 0-88754-599-8

Musical based on Grenadian/Caribbean folklore. Two young children go on quest to determine if legend of Nutmeg Princess is true. 2 acts 15 scenes 5m 5m 1 setting

Keeper. Bailey, F.

Kelly, George

Craig's wife.

Drama. Housewife sacrifices friendships and marriage to maintain her security and reputation. 3 acts 5m 6w 1 interior

In Kelly, G. Three plays

The show-off.

Comedy. Fast-talking braggart finally becomes successful when he sells brother-in-law's invention. 3 acts 6m 3w 1 interior

In Kelly, G. Three plays

The torch-bearers.

Comedy. Satirical look at vanity of Little Theater movement. 3 acts 6m 6w 3 interiors

In Kelly, G. Three plays

Kelly, Tim

y Kokonut High. Pioneer Drama Service 1999 68p

Residents open private high school to raise money on island devastated by hurricane. Also available as musical by Bill Francoeur. 2 acts 10 scenes 11m 20w extras 1 exterior

y The snake in the grass. Pioneer Drama Service 1985 56p

First produced under title Tied to the tracks. Melodrama set in 1880s Dakota territory. Sheriff rescues helpless maiden and defends town from dastardly villain. 2 acts 4 scenes 10m 16w extras 1 interior

y Stop the presses!. Pioneer Drama Service 1997 41p

Melodrama about crusading young newspaper editor in 1880s Colorado. 2 scenes 5m 7w extras 1 interior

y Sundown Alley. Pioneer Drama Service 1998 56p

Farce set in Old West. Faded actress dreaming of comeback falls prey to coniving con man. 2 acts 5 scenes 7m 11w extras 1 interior

Kemble, Fanny, 1809-1893

about

Luckham, C. The dramatic attitudes of Miss Fanny Kemble

Kemnitz, Robert D., and McMaster, Jennifer

Off the rack.

Comedic play about closet organizer. 2w 1 interior

In 30 ten-minute plays for 2 actors from Actors Theatre of Louisville's National Ten-minute Play Contest

—Same

In Actors Theatre of Louisville. Ten-minute plays: v4

The processional .

Comedy about wedding rehearsal. 3m 2w 1 interior

In 30 ten-minute plays for 4, 5 & 6 actors from Actors Theatre of Louisville's National Ten-minute Play Contest

—Same

In Actors Theatre of Louisville. Ten-minute plays: v5

Kennedy, Adrienne

Dramatic circle.

Radio play developed from The film club, set in London in 1961. Black American writer is waiting in London for news of her husband, who has disappeared in West Africa. Music. Sound effects. 1 act 1 scene 3m 2w extras settings

In Kennedy, A. The Adrienne Kennedy reader

Electra (Euripides).

Electra and her long-lost brother Orestes unite to kill their mother and their mother's lover, thus avenging their father's death. Stark, fast-moving adaptation of classical tragedy. 1 act 1 scene 5m 2w 1 setting

In Kennedy, A. The Adrienne Kennedy reader

An evening with dead Essex.

A theater group explores the background of a figure in the news—a black Vietnam veteran who became a sniper and was killed by the police. Based on an actual case. Music, singing. 1 act 3 scenes 5m 1w 1 setting

In Kennedy, A. The Adrienne Kennedy reader

Kennedy, Adrienne—*Continued*

The film club (a monologue by Suzanne Alexander).

Monologue by a black writer waiting in London for some word of her husband, who has disappeared in West Africa while preparing a book on Frantz Fanon. 1 act 1w 1 setting

In Kennedy, A. The Adrienne Kennedy reader

Funnyhouse of a Negro.

A young writer, torn between the polarities of a biracial heritage, is haunted by personifications of her conflicted self and driven to suicide. Interior drama mixing naturalistic and symbolic elements. 1 act 12 movements 3m 5w settings

In Kennedy, A. The Adrienne Kennedy reader

—Same

In Political stages; ed. by E. Mann and D. Roessel

June and Jean in concert (the concert of their lives).

African American family over the years, as remembered by the surviving twin daughter. Music, singing. 2 acts 5 scenes 3m 4w extras settings

In Kennedy, A. The Adrienne Kennedy reader

A lesson in a dead language.

Surrealistic classroom in which girls at the onset of menstruation receive rote instruction from a large white dog. 1 act 7g 1w 1 setting

In Kennedy, A. The Adrienne Kennedy reader

Motherhood 2000.

Revenge fantasy in which woman finds the policeman who beat her son—he is now running a theater group—and kills him as he enacts the part of Christ. 1 act 4m 1w 1 setting

In Kennedy, A. The Adrienne Kennedy reader

A movie star has to star in black and white.

Screen stars posed in scenes from classic films speak lines pertaining to the memories and family history of a young black writer. Music. 1 act 3 scenes 5m 5w 3 settings

In Kennedy, A. The Adrienne Kennedy reader

Ohio State murders.

An established black author revisits Ohio State University and remembers her brief affair, as a student there, with a teacher of English literature,

a man who subsequently stalked her and murdered their children. 1 act 21 scenes 4w 4m settings

In Kennedy, A. The Adrienne Kennedy reader

Orestes (Euripides).

Orestes, maddened by guilt, and his sister Electra are condemned to death for murdering their mother. In desperation they commit fresh crimes, until Apollo appears to stop the cycle of vengeance. Adapted from classical drama. 1 act 1 scene 5m 3w chorus 1 setting

In Kennedy, A. The Adrienne Kennedy reader

The owl answers.

The protagonist of Funnyhouse of a Negro is again the central figure. Tormented by figures representing English history and literature, she takes refuge in an animal identity and casual pick-ups. Music. 1 act 5m 2w settings

In Kennedy, A. The Adrienne Kennedy reader

A rat's mass.

Surrealistic one-act play. Half-rat siblings growing up in atmosphere of wartime menace commit incest at the command of an older child. 1 act 1 scene 1m 2w extras 1 setting

In Kennedy, A. The Adrienne Kennedy reader

She talks to Beethoven.

In Ghana, a black American writer is visited by Beethoven as she waits for news of her husband, who has disappeared. Music. Radio voice. 1 act 1m 1w 1 setting

In Kennedy, A. The Adrienne Kennedy reader

Sun.

Dedicated to Malcolm X. Theater piece about the human body, dreams, and dismemberment. 1 act 1m 1 setting

In Kennedy, A. The Adrienne Kennedy reader

Kenneth Grahame's The wind in the willows. Bennett, A.

Kentucky

Basham, R. Lot's daughters

Wallace, N. The trestle at Pope Lick Creek

Kenya

Thiong'o, N. W. I will marry when I want

Kern, Will

Hellcab. Dramatists 1997 53p

ISBN 0-8222-1604-3   LC 99-205949

Drama about small town cab driver struggling to stay afloat by ferrying Chicagoans around in freezing Christmas season. 26 scenes Variable cast 7 characters 1 setting

Kerouac, Jack, 1922-1969

about

Akalaitis, J. Ti Jean blues

Kerr, Robert

The Potato Creek chair of death.

A man and his mother, on a tour of weird roadside attractions, cross paths with a young killer on the run from the police. Mom likes him; he likes her. Music, singing. 1 act 17 scenes 2m 3w settings

In EST marathon '97: the one-act plays; ed. by M. Smith

The **Kerry** dance. Rushforth, T.

Kessler, Lyle

Robbers. French 1998 111p

ISBN 0-573-62533-3

Tragicomedy about repressed young man hired to infiltrate a canning factory to expose workers stealing merchandise. 2 acts 24 scenes 5m 2w extras

Ketteman, Helen, 1945-

Bubba the cowboy prince (dramatization) See McBride-Smith, B. Bubba the cowboy prince

Keyes, Steven

Moonlight cocktail. French 2000 57p

ISBN 0-573-62725-8   LC 2001-276801

Comedy about a couple living in a trailer. Husband becomes jealous when his actress wife is attracted to her leading man. 2 acts 14 scenes 3m 2w

Khan-Din, Ayub

Last dance at dum dum. Hern Bks. 72p

ISBN 1-85459-456-7

Drama set in Calcutta, 1981. Ancient denizens of Anglo-Indian community cling determinedly to their supposed superiority. 2 acts 4 scenes 4m 4w 1 exterior

Kharms, Daniil

Elizaveta Bam.

Absurdist Russian drama. Two men attempt to arrest woman for undisclosed crime. 4m 2w extras 1 setting

In Eight twentieth-century Russian plays; ed. by T. Langen and J. Weir

Kibbutzim

c McCullough, L. E. Israel reborn

Kicking out. Oliver, C.

Kidnapped in London. Mason, T.

Kidnapping

Culture Clash (Group). The mission

c Mason, T. Kidnapped in London

O'Neill, E. The long voyage home

Raznovich, D. Inner gardens (Jardín de otoño)

St. John, B. The abduction

Sunde, K. In a kingdom by the Sea

Young, D. Clout

Killer Joe. Letts, T.

Killing hand. Zellnik, D.

Killing kangaroos. Williams, R.

The **killing** of Yablonski: scenes of involvement in a current event. Nelson, R.

Killing time. Stockwell, R.

The **killings** tale. Frankonis, W.

Kilroy, Thomas

The secret fall of Constance Wilde.

Portrays doomed marriage of Constance and Oscar Wilde. 2 parts 2m 1w extras 1 setting

In New plays from the Abbey Theatre v2

Kilt. Wilson, J.

Kim, Susan

Dreamtime for Alice.

Monologue. Woman stranded in the Australian desert, an apt metaphor for her life. 1 act 2w 1 exterior

In Ensemble Studio Theatre '99: the one-act plays

—Same

In Four from E. S. T. marathon '99

Kimmel, Eric

Hershel and the Hanukkah Goblins (adaptation) See McBride-Smith, B. Hershel and the Hanukkah goblins

Kincaid, Jamaica

Girl.

Monologue. Young girl's effort to understand coded instructions passed down to her regarding proper feminine decorum. 1w

In Mythic women/Real women

King, Carole

c Really Rosie.

Sassy kid entertains herself and friends by acting out show-biz fantasies. Music, singing. 1 act 5m 2w extras. 1 interior 2 exterior

In Theatre for young audiences; ed. by C. A. Jennings

King, Denis

Stepping Out; book by Richard Harris; lyrics by Mary Stewart-David; music by Denis King. French (London) 2001 104p

ISBN 0-573-08115-8

Based on the original play by Richard Harris. Musical about a group of women and one man attending weekly tap dancing class in church hall. Music, singing, dancing. 2 acts 18 scenes 1m 9w 1 setting

King, Moynan

Bathory. Broken Jaw Press 2000 80p

ISBN 1-89664-736-7   LC 2001-326348

Dark comedy. Life and crimes of infamous "Blood Countess" Erzsebert Bathory of Hungary. 2 acts 34 scenes 3w extras 2 interior

King, Stephen

Misery (dramatization) See Moore, S. Misery

King Artie and the Knights of the Rad Table. Woolf, W.

King David's harp. McCullough, L. E.

King Mackerel & the blues are running. Simpson, B., and Wann, J.

King Midas. Barchers, S. I.

King Midas. McBride-Smith, B.

King Midas and the golden touch. McCullough, L. E.

King Midas and the touch of gold. Morris, V.

King Oedipus. Sophocles

The **king** of Friday's men. Molloy, M. J.

The **King** of Ireland's son. Wing, P.

The **King** of Prussia. Darke, N.

King O'Neil; or, The Irish Brigade. Gore, C.

King Ubu. Jarry, A.

Kingdom of earth. Williams, T.

The **king's** horses. Paterson, D. L.

The **king's** seal. Gore, C.

Kipling, Rudyard, 1865-1936

Captains courageous (dramatization) See Barchers, S. I., and Kroll, J. L. Captains courageous

The jungle book (dramatization) See Castle, G. V. The Jungle Book: the musical; Mast, E. Jungalbook

Kirshon, Vladimir

Grain.

Socialist realist drama. Promotes collectivization of Soviet agriculture. 5 acts 9 scenes Large mixed cast

In Eight twentieth-century Russian plays; ed. by T. Langen and J. Weir

Kiss of death. Williams, S.

Kissing Sid James. Farquhar, R.

Kit Marlow. Grimm, D.

Klavan, Laurence

The summer sublet.

An unexpected affair between a young man and his landlord. 2m 1w extras 2 interiors

In The Best American short plays, 2000-2001

Kleberg, Lars

The Aquarians.

First play in Starfall triptych. Dramatic dialogue between Sergei Eisenstein and Bertolt Brecht. 2m 1 setting

In Kleberg, L. Starfall

Ash Wednesday.

Concluding piece in Starfall triptych. Dramatic dialogue set 1940 in Moscow Planetarium. Sergei Eisenstein and Mikhail Bakhtin discuss German culture, astrology and jazz music. 2m 1 interior

In Kleberg, L. Starfall

The sorcerer's apprentices.

Second play in Starfall triptych. Series of speeches by noted members of Soviet theater and film circles contrasting Russian theater with that of the Chinese, Germans and British. 11m 1 interior

In Kleberg, L. Starfall

Klein, Jon

Dimly perceived threats to the system.
Dramatists 1999 70p
  ISBN 0-8222-1677-9   LC 99-218318
Dark comedy about dysfunctional family. The
wife can't manage the household, the husband is
having an affair, and their daughter torments the
school therapist when she's not channeling the
spirit of her grandmother. 2 acts 2m 4w

Kleist, Heinrich von, 1777-1811

Amphitryon (adaptation) See Banville, J.
God's gift

Amphitryon; translated by Carl R.
Mueller.
Comedy based on Greek mythology. Jupiter
spends night with Alkmene masquerading as her
husband Amphitryon. 3 acts 22 scenes 4m 2w extras 1 exterior
  In Kleist, H. von. Three major plays

The broken jug; translated by Carl R.
Mueller.
Variant title: The broken pitcher. Farce about pa-
rochial justice set in Dutch village. Woman accuses daughter's fiancé of breaking jug while fleeing girl's bedroom. 12 scenes 5m 3w extras 1 interior
  In Kleist, H. von. Three major plays

The Prince of Homburg; translated by
Carl R. Mueller.
Play set in Prussia in 1675. Prince of Homburg
shows courage in war and in accepting consequences of his mistakes. 5 acts 36 scenes 13m 2w
extras 7 interiors 4 exteriors
  In Kleist, H. von. Three major plays

Kluger, Steve

Pilots of the purple twilight; a play; by
Steve Kluger. French 1999 95p il
  ISBN 0-573-62681-2   LC 99-475200
Comedy drama about nine diverse individuals,
including John Jacob Astor and Ida Straus, who
chose to stay on board the sinking Titanic. 2 acts
5m 4w 1 interior

Kneubuhl, Victoria Nalani

The conversion of Ka'ahumanu.
Missionaries come to Hawaiian Islands and convert Queen Kaahumanu. 2 acts 18 scenes 5w 1
setting
  In Postcolonial plays; ed. by H. Gilbert

The story of Susanna.
Feminist drama opens in Babylon with biblical
story of Susanna. Continues as story of woman in
any culture who is victim of powerful oppressors.
Prologue 2 acts 41 scenes 5m 9w 1 setting
  In Seventh generation; ed. by M. G.
    D'Aponte

The **knight** of the burning pestle. Beaumont, F.

Knights and knighthood

c Art, S. S. Joe Knight and the seven serfs
c Barchers, S. I. Gawain and the Green
  Knight
  Wilder, T. Childe Roland to the dark
  tower came
Knock me a kiss. Smith, C.
Know your rights. Upton, J.

Kobler, Flip, and Marcus, Cindy

Ghost of a chance. French 1999 99p
  ISBN 0-573-62710-x
Comedy about a woman who takes her fiancé
and his mother to her cabin in the woods, where
her first husband's ghost still lurks. 2 acts 7 scenes
3m 3w 1 interior
Kokonut High. Kelly, T.
Kokonut Island. Francoeur, B.
Kokonut kapers. Francoeur, B.

Kokoschka, Oskar

The burning bush.
Expressionist drama. Man abandons object of his
desire, concluding that by nature she is faithless.
5 scenes 1m 1w extras 2 interiors 2 exteriors
  In Kokoschka, O. Plays and poems
Comenius.
Historical play focusing on Czech humanist and
educational reformer Johann Amos Comenius. 4
acts 10 scenes Large mixed cast 5 interiors 3 exte-
riors
  In Kokoschka, O. Plays and poems
Job.
The story of Job retold in an expressionistic
form. 3 acts 1b 3m 2w extras 3 interiors 1 exterior
  In Kokoschka, O. Plays and poems
Murderer, hope of women.
German expressionist play in free verse about
the battle between the sexes. In setting of antiquity
invading adventurer conquers woman leader after
deadly struggle and kills off all her maidens and
his warriors. 1 act 4m 4w 1 exterior
  In Kokoschka, O. Plays and poems

Kokoschka, Oskar—*Continued*

—Same

In Kokoschka, O. Plays and poems

Orpheus and Eurydice.

Expressionist version of Orpheus myth. 3 acts 8 scenes epilogue 4m 4w extras settings

In Kokoschka, O. Plays and poems

Sphinx and strawman.

Expressionist drama about cuckold who mourns loss of his wife, who represents the soul of woman. Variable cast 5 characters

In Kokoschka, O. Plays and poems

Kolbe, Maximilian, Saint, 1894-1941

about

Ehn, E. 16670 (Maximilian Mary Kolbe)

Koltès, Bernard-Marie

In the solitude of cotton fields. Methuen 2001 41p

ISBN 0-413-77177-6

Two men pass on the street. What follows is a game of desire and rejection, power and humiliation, as they negotiate a deal that will never be struck. 1 act 2m 1 setting

Kondoleon, Harry

Saved or destroyed. Dramatists 2002

ISBN 0-8222-1798-8

Play about the staging of a play examines the parallels and paradoxes of life and theatre. 3m 3w 1 setting

Kontraption. Owens, R.

Koopman, LeRoy

It is finished.

Verse play about crucifixion of Christ. Variable cast 20 characters extras

In The drama of Easter; ed. by R. Wray

Kopit, Arthur L.

BecauseHeCan. French 2000 55p

ISBN 0-573-62741-x

Suburban couple's world unravels when hacker takes control of computer records of their lives. 4m 1w 1 setting

Chad Curtiss, lost again.

Three episodes in absurdly sensational serial, about young man braving forces of evil to recover final message from God. 3 espisodes 9m 5w settings

In Humana Festival 2001

Indians.

Series of scenes about opening of the West, in which Buffalo Bill Cody expresses and dramatizes his misgivings about various excesses (slaughter of buffalo, cruelty to Indians) committed in the name of progress. 1 act 13 scenes 20m 3w extras

In Kopit, A. L. Three plays

Oh Dad, poor dad, mamma's hung you in the closet and I'm feelin' so sad.

Tragicomedy. Surrealistic farce satirizing relationship between wealthy, possessive mother and pathetic overprotected adolescent son. 3 scenes 2m 2w extras 1 interior

In Kopit, A. L. Three plays

Wings.

Elderly woman, former aviator, suffers stroke and struggles to recover sense of self, world, language and past as hospital surroundings and people gradually penetrate her consciousness. 4 scenes 5m 5w

In Kopit, A. L. Three plays

Kops, Bernard

Dreams of Anne Frank. Methuen 1997 99p

ISBN 0-413-712250-8

Drama set in occupied Holland. Jewish girl and family hide from Nazis. Singing. 2 acts 18 scenes 4m 4w 1 setting

Ezra.

Ezra Pound's incarceration at U.S. Army detention Centre between Pisa and Viareggio in May, 1945. 3m 3w 1 exterior

In Kops, B. Plays: one

The hamlet of Stepney Green.

Comedy about Jewish community in London's East End reverses family relationships depicted in Shakespeare's Hamlet. Music, singing. 3 acts 4 scenes 7m 3w extras 1 setting

In Kops, B. Plays: one

Playing Sinatra.

Psychological drama set in London. Middle-aged brother and sister who share obsession for Frank Sinatra are conned by scheming hippie. 2 acts 4 scenes 2m 1w 1 interior

In Kops, B. Plays: one

Korder, Howard

Geliebteh.

A woman who grew up on the Lower East Side remembers herself as a child and her mystifying father, in a poignant monologue. 1 act 1w 1 set-

Korder, Howard—*Continued*

ting

In EST marathon '96: the one-act plays; ed. by M. Smith

Koreans

Canada

Kang, M. J. Noran bang: the yellow room

Kornhauser, Barry

y Lincoln's log; or Better angels. Anchorage Press 65p

ISBN 0-87602-369-3

Story of Tad Lincoln's memories of his life in the White House. Music. Puppets. 3m 1w

Korty, Carol

c Baba Yaga and the black sunflower. Anchorage Press 2000 83p

ISBN 0-87602-374-X

Orphaned girl meets witch's challenge, saves baby brother from the stewpot, and gains a better understanding of herself. Music, singing. Puppets. Prologue 9 scenes Variable cast 4 exteriors.

Kossman, Nina

Miracles.

Play set in Havana. Two sisters demonstrate early effects of brainwashing in totalitarian state. 2g 1 interior

In Women playwrights: the best plays of 2000

Kotwica, Douglas

y The great Denver railroad scam; or, If aunt May leaves, who'll weed the 'tunias? Pioneer Drama Service 2001 29p

Melodrama. Evil mastermind plots to steal house from group of widows and sell to railroad. 2 acts 6 scenes Variable cast 11 characters

Krakower, Bob

4 AM (open all night).

Lonely man and woman customers at all-night diner. 3m 1w

In 30 ten-minute plays for 4, 5 & 6 actors from Actors Theatre of Louisville's National Ten-minute Play Contest

Mixed emotions.

Man discovers he is in love with woman about to move in with his best friend. 3m 2w 1 exterior

In 30 ten-minute plays for 4, 5 & 6 actors from Actors Theatre of Louisville's National Ten-minute Play Contest

Kral, Brian

y Paper lanterns, paper cranes. Anchorage Press 2002 75p

ISBN 0-87602-404-5

Japanese street orphan is admitted to hospital in mid 1950s Hiroshima where it is discovered she is losing her eyesight, possibly as result of nuclear fallout. 6 scenes 2b 5g 5m 4w 1 setting

Kramer, Aaron

A treasure in a teacup.

Two sisters rummage through grandmother's belongings in an attic. 2w 1 setting

In Blast from the future; ed. by D. Yeaton

Kramer, Larry

The destiny of me.

Autobiographical memory play about author/activist/AIDS victim who submits to experimental treatment and recalls growing up Jewish and gay in the 1930s and 1940s. 3 acts 5m 2w

In Kramer, L. The normal heart and The destiny of me

The normal heart.

Dramatizes onset of AIDs epidemic in New York, the agonizing fight to get political and social recognition of its problems, and the toll exacted on private lives. 2 acts 16 scenes 13m 1 setting

In Kramer, L. The normal heart and The destiny of me

Kramer, Seth

World without memory.

Thirty-something loses her septuagenarian father to Alzheimer's. 3m 1w extra 4 interior 2 exteriors

In The Best American short plays, 2000-2001

Kramer, Sherry

David's redhaired death.

Best friends Jean and Marilyn relive their affairs and struggle to rebuild their world following suicide of Jean's favorite brother. 2 acts 2w extras 1 setting

In Kramer, S. Plays

Kramer, Sherry—*Continued*

Hold for three.

Three young people play games while sitting on beach looking at waves. 1m 2w 1 setting

In take ten; ed. by E. Lane and N. Shengold

Things that break.

Comedy about sibling rivalry, heart surgery and the American dream. Surreal shifts back and forth between worried wife of man undergoing surgery and her grown son and daughter. 2 parts 3m 4w extras 2 settings

In Kramer, S. Plays

The wall of water.

Farce. Four single women share Upper West Side apartment. 2 acts 4m 4w 1 setting

In Kramer, S. Plays

Krapsleaya, Nadezhda Konstantinova

about

Levy, D. Clam

Kraszewski, Charles S.

The archives at Kanonicza 5.

In archive in Krakow devoted to the works of Polish dramatist Tadeusz Kantor, Kantor himself makes an alarming appearance. Audience participation, alternative endings. Music, singing. 6m 5w extras 1 interior

In Kraszewski, C.S. The archives at Kanonicza 5

Iphigenia in Zagreb.

At disorderly rehearsal for Croatian production of Aeschylus's Iphigenia, the cast explore the arguments of the ancient play, confirming its relevance. 12m 2w 1 interior

In Kraszewski, C.S. The archives at Kanonicza 5

Peter the rock.

Apostle Peter denies Christ and later chooses martyrdom. 7 scenes 20m 6w extras 1 interior 2 exteriors

In Kraszewski, C.S. The archives at Kanonicza 5

Kraus, Joanna Halpert

The ice wolf.

Fair-haired girl is rejected by Eskimo tribe into which she was born. Prologue 3 acts 7 scenes 2g 5m 2w extras

In Theatre for young audiences; ed. by C. A. Jennings

Kreidl, Margret

Grateful women.

Three female characters act out set of female rituals, interspersed with memories, fantasies, crises and unresolved desires. 11 scens 3w 2 interiors

In Women's words, women's work; ed. by U. H. G. Borgert

Kreskinned. Healey, M., and Lynch, K.

Krieger, Henry

Side show; book and lyrics by Bill Russell; music by Henry Krieger. French 1999 120p

ISBN 0-573-65141-8

Siamese twin sisters, quite different in personality, fall in love with the promoters who saved them from the side show and are now offering national fame. Music, singing, dancing. Prologue 2 acts 23 scenes 13m 9w extras 10 interiors 5 exteriors

Kringle's window. Medoff, M.

Kron, Lisa

2.5 minute ride.

One woman performance piece about the Holocaust. 1w 1 setting

In Kron, L. 2.5 minute ride and, 101 humiliating stories

101 humiliating stories.

Comic autobiographical performance piece about growing up lesbian. 1w 1 setting

In Kron, L. 2.5 minute ride and, 101 humiliating stories

Kudzu. Herrick, J., and others

Kuruvilla, Sunil

Rice boy. Playwrights Canada 2000 76p

ISBN 0-99754-672-2

Juxtaposes scenes of young girl in India preparing for marriage to man she never met, with scenes of her cousin in Canada trying to make sense of heritage. 3m 4w extras

Snapshot: night out.

At 2:00 in the morning an adulterous couple search frantically for his car keys, so that he will be gone by the time her husband gets home. 1 act 1m 1w 1 exterior

In Humana Festival 2002

Kushner, Tony

A dybbuk, or between two worlds.

Adaptation of S. Ansky's The dybbuk. Recount's tale of wealthy man's daughter possessed by spirit of dead beloved. 4 acts 7 scenes large mixed cast

Kushner, Tony—*Continued*

settings

   In A dybbuk; and, The dybbuk melody and other themes and variations

East coast ode to Howard Jarvis: a little teleplay in tiny monologues.

West-coast tax revolt spreads to New York City, takes root in civil service. Teleplay loosely based on fact; could be performed on stage by one versatile actor. Singing. 1 act 32 scenes 16 men 7 women settings

   In Kushner, T. Death and taxes

G. David Schine in Hell.

Satire. Schine, newly arrived in Hell, meets a number of old acquaintances from the McCarthy era. 1 act 5m 1 setting

   In Kushner, T. Death and taxes

Homebody/Kabul.   Theatre Communications Group 2002 151p

   ISBN 1-559-36209-X   LC 2002-20702

Divided into two stories, the first is a monologue of a woman who runs away from her family, the second is the husband of the runaway woman, who seeks his wife in Kabul. 3 acts 12 scenes 8m 3w 2 1 setting

Hydriotaphia; or, The death of Dr. Browne.

The death of Sir Thomas Browne, coinciding with the birth of modern capitalism. Horror-comedy, gruesome but lyrically inventive. Accents, concocted dialect. Music, singing. 5 acts 5 scenes 6m 8w 1 interior

   In Kushner, T. Death and taxes

Notes on Akiba.

Two gay Jewish men prepare a Passover seder, with tongue-in-cheek rabbinical commentary. 1 act 2m 1 interior

   In Kushner, T. Death and taxes

Reverse transcription.

Dark comedy about the funeral of a writer held on Abel's Hill, Martha's Vineyard, Massachusetts. 4m 2w 1 setting

   In Actors Theatre of Louisville. Ten-minute plays: v4

—Same

   In The Best American short plays 1998-1999

—Same

   In Kushner, T. Death and taxes

Slavs!.

Satirical socio-political exploration of life in Soviet Union during Perestroika and after break-up of the Soviet Union, set in 1985 Moscow and 1992 Siberia. Prologue 3 acts 8 scenes epilogue 1g 5m 6w

   In Political stages; ed. by E. Mann and D. Roessel

Terminating.

Inspired by Shakespeare's sonnet 75. Lesbian psychoanalyst has a final session with a gay patient who has fallen in love with her. 1 act 2m 2w 1 interior

   In Kushner, T. Death and taxes

—Same

   In Love's fire

Kuzmin, Mikhail

The dangerous precaution.

Comedy set in fairy tale kingdom. Prince falls in love with boy whom courtiers believe to be girl in boy's clothing. Music. 7 scenes 6m 1w extras

   In Lovesick; ed. by L. Senelick

Kwa-landlady. Williams, M. N.

Kyd, Thomas

The Spanish tragedy.

Elizabethan tragedy of revenge set in 16th century Spain and Portugal. Verse play. 4 acts 29 scenes 15m 3w extras

   In Renaissance drama; ed. by A. F. Kinney

Kyle, Christopher

Plunge. Dramatists 1997 65p

   ISBN 0-8222-1670-1

Three friends from college, approaching their 30s, meet for a weekend to reflect about their lives with tragicomedic results. 9 scenes 3m 2w 2 settings

L

L.A.. Margulies, D.

L-play. Henley, B.

Labey, Russell

y New boy. Amber Lane Press 2001 75p

   ISBN 1-872868-32-0

Labey, Russell—*Continued*

Based on the novel by William Sutcliffe. Handsome teenager makes quite an impression at his new school. 13 scenes 3b 3g 1m 3w

Labor and laboring classes

Bean, R. Toast

Hairston, J. Forty-minute finish

Kessler, L. Robbers

LaRusso, L. Sweatshop

Great Britain

Keeffe, B. Barbarians: abide with me

Keeffe, B. Barbarians: in the city

Keeffe, B. Barbarians: killing time

Keeffe, B. Gimme shelter: Gem

Wesker, A. Chicken soup with barley

United States

Leivick, H. Shop

Wallace, N. Slaughter City

Labor Day. Gurney, A. R.

Labor Day. Wilner, S.

Labor unions

Hughes, L. De organizer

Schulberg, B. On the waterfront

The **labors** of Hercules. Thistle, L.

LaBute, Neil

The shape of things. Faber & Faber 2001 138p

ISBN 0-571-21246-8

Ambitious young woman artist remakes an ordinary guy, and documents their affair for an art exhibit. 1 act 10 scenes 2m 2w 8 interiors 2 exteriors

Lacan, Jacques, 1901-1981

about

O'Donnell, D. Who shot Jacques Lacan?

Ladies' man. Feydeau, G.

Ladies who lunch. Gates, T.

LaDue, Tim

Prom night.

Principal of high school and rock band leader have argument on prom night. 2m 1w 1 setting

In Blast from the future; ed. by D. Yeaton

The **lady** from the sea. Ibsen, H.

The **lady** in question. Busch, C.

Lady Julie. Strindberg, A.

The **lady** of Larkspur Lotion. Williams, T.

The **Lady** of May. Sidney, Sir P.

"**Lady** of the Lamp": Florence Nightingale, founder of modern nursing. McCullough, L. E.

The **lady,** or the tiger? Barchers, S. I., and Kroll, J. L.

Lady Windermere's fan. Wilde, O.

Laestrygonians. Nigro, D.

Lafferty's wake. Turlish, S.

Lake Hollywood. Guare, J.

Lambert, Ann

Very heaven. Blizzard Pub. 1999 80p

ISBN 0-921368-92-5   LC 00-274260

Family drama set in Quebec's Eastern Townships. Three sisters reunited at ancestral home to settle mother's estate. 2 acts 9 scenes 1m 4w 1 interior

Lamorisse, Albert, 1922-1970

Le ballon rouge (adaptation) See Clark, A. The red balloon

Lan, David

Desire.

Drama set in 1980 Zimbawean village. Residents prepare for future as war of liberation ends. 7 scenes 4m 6w 1 setting

In Lan, D. Plays: 1

The end of the earth.

Drama set in London and war-torn Balkan country. British geologist, suffering mental breakdown, attempts to save ill daughter. 2 acts 9 scenes 1g 5m 2w 1 setting

In Lan, D. Plays: 1

Flight.

After Rhodesia becomes Zimbabwe, Jewish family prepares to flee to Cape Town. This journey parallels their relatives' perilous escape from Lithuania fifty years before. Prologue 2 parts 5 scenes 5m 5w 5 interiors

In Lan, D. Plays: 1

La lupa; translated by Pandolfi, Gwenda. Methuen 2000 48p

ISBN 0-413-75450-2

A new version of Italian classic by Giovanni Verga. A mother, a daughter, and their lover hurtle towards tragedy. 2 acts 4m 6w 1 exterior

Painting a wall.

While three Cape Town Colored men paint public wall they question their lot, consider rebelling, but ultimately return to their task. 1 act 4m 1 exterior

In Lan, D. Plays: 1

Lan, David—*Continued*

Red earth.

Juxtaposes history of South Africa with story of black worker who decides to leave his job in Cape Town docks and seek his family in Transkei. Singing. 5m 1w 1 setting

In Lan, D. Plays: 1

Lander, Alla

c Vasilisa the fair; based on The frog princess and other Russian folk tales by Sophia Prokofieva & Irina Tokmakova; music by Alla Lander; translated by Sabina Modzhalevskaya & Harlow Robinson; adapted by Adrian Mitchell. French 2003 51p

ISBN 0-573-62951-X

Musical based on Russian folktale. Prince agrees to marry frog who is actually charmed princess. 2 acts 7 scenes 11m 7w 1 setting

Landlocked. Cram, C.

Landlord and tenant

Pedrero, P. The railing (El pasamanos)

Landon-Smith, Kristine. See Bhuchar, S. jt. auth.

Landscape of desire. Kaplan, B. J.

Lane, Eric

A bowl of soup.

Younger brother talks to his emotionally disturbed older brother. 2m 1 setting

In take ten; ed. by E. Lane and N. Shengold

Lane, Stewart F., and Morehouse, Ward

If it was easy. . . Performing Bks. 2002 90p

ISBN 1-55783-594-2

Comedy about showbiz columnist who suggests to failing producer that he stage musical about Frank Sinatra. 2 acts 9 scenes 6m 2w

Lanfer, Stefan Graves

c Gary Grinkle's battles with wrinkles and other troubles in Mudgeville. Dramatic Publishing 2003 50p

Comedy about town where people's fears keep them hidden away in their homes. Variable cast 1 setting

Lange, Ed

Sherlock's secret life. French 2002 79p

ISBN 0-573-62929-3

Mystery comedy about Sherlock Holmes's early years with Dr. Watson. 2 acts 4 scenes 5m 3w 1 setting

Langella, Frank

Frank Langella's Cyrano; an adaptation of Edmond Rostand's Cyrano de Bergerac. Broadway Play Pub. 1999 81p

ISBN 0-88145-149-5

A stripped-down adaptation of Edmond Rostand's romantic swashbuckler. Music. 2 acts 5 scenes 10m 3w 2 interiors 2 exteriors

The **language** of the gods. Nowra, L.

The **Laramie** Project. Kaufman, M.

Larbey, Bob

Sand castles. Amber Lane Press 2000 96p

ISBN 1-872868-29-0

The regulars at a seaside resort face challenges to their tidy little preserve but find an unexpected ally in a jovial fish-and-chips magnate. Singing. 2 acts 5 scenes 5m 10w extras 1 exterior

Large as life. Strachan, Keith

Lark. Linney, R.

Larry's party. Norman, M.

LaRusso, Louis

Sweatshop. French 1999 75p il

ISBN 0-573-62682-0   LC 00-502418

Comedy drama about the lives and problems of ten women working in a New Jersey sweatshop in the summer of 1958. 2 acts 2m 10w 1 interior

Las Vegas (Nev.)

Gilroy, F. D. The only game in town

Neipris, J. Almost in Vegas

Lask, Berta

Liberation (Die Befreiung).

Sixteen tableaux depicting lives of German and Russian women, 1914-1920. Prologue 16 tableaux 2 interludes Large mixed cast settings

In War plays by women; ed. by C. M. Tylee, E. Turner, and A. Cardinal

The **last** cigarette. Fechter, S.

The **last** dance. Tattersall, C.

Last dance at dum dum. Khan-Din, A.

The **last** decision. Fredericks, A. D.

Last licks. Gilroy, F. D.

The **last** of Hitler. Schenkar, J.

The **last** of my solid gold watches. Williams, T.

Last one to survive is a rotten egg. Cook, P.

The **last** orbit of Billy Mars. Alexander, R.

Last post. McConnell, J.

The **last** session. Schalchlin, S.

Last stop till Christmas. Cook, P.

The **last** supper. Friedman, G. W.

The **Last** Supper restoration. O'Brien, D.

Last train to Nibroc. Hutton, A.

Last will and testament. Miller, E.

Late bus to Mecca. Cleage, P.

Late flowering. Chapman, J., and Davidson, I.

The **late** middle classes. Gray, S.

Later life. Gurney, A. R.

Lathrop, Mary

The visible horse.

Twelve-year-old boy tries to deal with the death of his father. 1b 1w 1 interior 4 exteriors

In Women playwrights: the best plays of 2001

Latin America

Cruz, N. Night train to Bolina

Latin drama (Comedy)

Plautus, T. M. Casina

Plautus, T. M. The wild, wild women (Bacchides)

Terence. The brothers (Adelphoe)

Terence. The mother-in-law (Hecyra)

Terence. Phormio

Latino trio: Hormiga's lawsuit. Winther, B.

Latino trio: Pedro's holey sombrero. Winther, B.

Latino trio: Senorita Cucaracha finds a husband. Winther, B.

Laughing wild. Durang, C.

Laura Dennis. Foote, H.

Laurence, Charles

About Alice. French 1998 84p

ISBN 0-573-62632-4   LC 98-211962

Drama set in London. Widow of renowned American sculptor confronted by manipulative representative of publishing house intent on compiling husband's biography. 2 acts 4 scenes 2m 2w 1 interior

The Ring sisters. French 1999 88p il

ISBN 0-573-62677-4   LC 99-475996

Farce. A singer uses desperate measures to cover up her real age. 2 acts 6 scenes 4m 3w 1 interior

Lauro, Shirley

The contest. Applause 2000 110p

ISBN 1-55783-368-0

Set in January, 1943, tragicomedy about Jewish family living in small mid-western town. 3 acts 7 scenes 1b 3g 2m 3w settings

Open admissions.

Drama about tensions between African American male college student and white female college professor. 1 act 1m 1w 1 setting

In Political stages; ed. by E. Mann and D. Roessel

Railing it uptown.

Two women, one black and one white, have an unusual encounter on New York subway. 2w 1 setting

In take ten; ed. by E. Lane and N. Shengold

Sunday go to meetin'.

Two Baptist Sunday school girls encounter Jewish girl in 1905 Midwest village. 3w 1 exterior

In 30 ten-minute plays for 3 actors from Actors Theatre of Louisville's National Ten-minute Play Contest

Lavender, William

c The invisible people; a musical play; play and music by William Lavender. Anchorage Press 1995 75p

ISBN 0-87602-400-2

Girl's special invisible friends are a fun-loving pair who keep her entertained, but when they take her to the invisible village, home of all invisible people, she meets trouble. 2 acts 7 scenes 1b 2g 5m extras 1 interior 2 exteriors

Lavery, Bryony

Her aching heart.

An examination of sexuality and gender incorporating the conventions of romantic fiction. Singing. 2 acts 17 scenes 2w 1 setting

In Lavery B. Plays: 1

Nothing compares to you.

Drama about loss, grief and desire. Women react when touched by death. 2 acts 41 scenes 1m 7w 1 setting

In Lavery B. Plays: 1

Lavery, Bryony—*Continued*

Origin of the species.

Allegorical look at male-constructed history. Elderly female archaeologist relates how when she set out to find primitive man, she instead discovered 4-million-year-old woman. 2 parts 25 scenes 2w 1 setting

In Lavery, B. Plays: 1

Two Marias.

Drama set in Andalusia, Spain. An examination of family identity, faith, love and death. 4w 1 setting

In Lavery B. Plays: 1

LaVohn, Robert W.

y A midsummer night's midterm. Pioneer Drama Service 1999 32p

As four high school students gather to cram for midterm on Shakespeare's Midsummer nights' dream, the play literally comes to life before their eyes. 2 acts Variable cast 26 characters 1 interior 1 exterior

Murder at the banquet. Pioneer Drama Service 1998 28p

Comic mystery. Murder occurs at banquet for world's greatest detectives. 3 scenes 4m 4w extras 1 interior

c The smartest woman in the kingdom. Pioneer Drama Service 2001 26p

Comedy. Not-too-bright prince must marry intelligent woman by nightfall or lose control of kingdom. 3 acts 5 scenes 8m 7w 1 setting

Law and lawyers

Brandt, A. 2 1/2 Jews

Chepiga, M. J. Getting and spending

Cooper, C. L. Sentences and words

Dobrish, J. The handless maiden

Goda, B. No crime

c McCullough, L. E. See you in court! (Legal Aid lawyer)

Milligan, J. Juris prudence

Moffat, P. Nabokov's gloves

Neilson, A. Normal

Walker, G. F. Love and anger

Weiss, P. The new trial

Weller, M. Buying time

Lawler, Ray

The Piccadilly bushman. Currency Press 1998 95p

ISBN 0-86819-560-X

Drama. Actor who returns to Australia after working overseas finds that circumstances have changed during his absence and that his past threatens to impact on his future plans. 2 acts 5m 3w 1 setting

Lawrence, D. H. (David Herbert)

The widowing of Mrs. Holroyd. Pine Street Books 2002 93p

ISBN 0-8122-1817-5

Horrible marriage is cut short by a mining accident, followed by guilt. 3 acts 4 scenes 8m 4w 1 interior

about

Williams, T. I rise in flame, cried the phoenix

Lawrence, Jerome, 1915-. See Lee, R. E. jt. auth.

Lawrence, Margaret, 1950-

Stone angel (Dramatization) See Nichol, J. W. The stone angel

Lawyers, guns, & money. Davis, T.

Laxdal, Vivienne

Cyber:/womb.

Play about woman's response to infertility in age of technology. 2 acts 18 scenes 3m 5w 12 interiors

In Prerogatives

Karla and Grif. Playwrights Canada 1991 112p

ISBN 0-88-754-570-X

In grief over death of her father, young woman goes to extremes to win back lesbian ex-lover. 2 acts 1m 2w 4 interiors

c Ruby and the rock.

Magical rock helps young girl through friend's death. 1m 2w

In TYA5: theatre for young audience

Laying the ghost. Williams, S.

Layover. Sutton, J.

Lazarus, John

y Night light.

Boy learns how to overcome bully and help sister master fear of the dark. 2b 1g 1 interior 1 exterior

In Lazarus, J. Not so dumb

y Not so dumb.

Interaction between three different children in classroom for learning-disabled. 2b 1g 1 interior

In Lazarus, J. Not so dumb

Lazarus, John—*Continued*

y Schoolyard games.
Examination of betrayal focusing on three young girls at playground. 3g 1 exterior
In Lazarus, J. Not so dumb

y Secrets.
Drama explores ambiguities of adolescent relationship. 2 acts 2m 2w 2 interior 1 exterior
In Lazarus, J. Not so dumb
The **League** of Nathans. Sherman, J.
The **league** of semi-super heroes. Smith, V., and Dixon, M. B.
Leaking from every orifice. Dowie, C.

Learner, Tobsha
Miracles; Tobsha Learner. Currency Press 1998 82p
ISBN 0-86819-557-X   LC 98-203809
Supermarket cashier's life is changed when she thinks she hears the voice of God through cash register. 3 acts 5 scenes 6m 6w 2 interiors

Learning disabilities
Dee, P. English is a foreign language
y Lazarus, J. Not so dumb
Plowman, G. Touching tomorrow
y Surface, M. H. Blessings
Lear's daughters. Women's Theatre Group

Lebanon
Mouawad, W. Wedding day at the Cro-Magnons' (Journee de noces chez les Cro-Magnons)
Sunde, K. In a kingdom by the Sea
Lebensraum. Horovitz, I.

Lebow, Barbara
c Tiny Tim is dead.
Christmas with makeshift family of homeless people. 2 acts 3m 2w 1 exterior
In The twelve plays of Christmas; ed. by L. Swortzell

Ledoux, Paul
Anne. Playwrights Canada 1999 110p
ISBN 0-88754-567-9
Dramatization of L. M. Montgomery's novel Anne of Green Gables about orphan girl who changes lives of inhabitants of turn-of-the-century Prince Edward Island. 2 acts 27 scenes 2m 6w 5 interiors 3 exteriors

Lee, C. Y.
Flower drum song (dramatization) See Rodgers, R. Flower drum song

Lee, Cherylene
Carry the tiger to the mountain.
Play based on the true-life story of Vincent Chin, killed in Detroit, 1982. His murder became the first Asian-American civil rights case to be prosecuted by the United States Department of Justice. Music. Prologue 2 acts 7m 4w extras
In New dramatists: best plays by the graduating class of 2000

Lee, Robert E., and Lawrence, Jerome
The night Thoreau spent in jail. Hill & Wang 1999 101p
ISBN 0-8090-1223-5
Incidents in Thoreau's life at Walden Pond. 2 acts 11m 4w extras settings

Leeds (England)
Marcus, F. Matchstick dreams

LeFevre, Adam
Waterbabies.
Mother investigates YMCA swimming program for her eleven-month-old son. 2w 1 interior
In 30 ten-minute plays for 2 actors from Actors Theatre of Louisville's National Ten-minute Play Contest
—Same
In Actors Theatre of Louisville. Ten-minute plays: v4
Legacy. Benet i Jornet, J. M.
The **legacy.** Harelik, M.
Legend of Sammy's Swamp. McPherson, E.
The **legend** of Sleepy Hollow. Arnault, M., and Arnault, A.
The **legend** of Sleepy Hollow. Barchers, S. I., and Kroll, J. L.

Legends

Chinese
Glancy, D. The toad (another name for the moon) should have a bite

Native American
Glancy, D. The lesser wars

Lehan, Robert

c Three fables. Pioneer Drama Service 2000 25p

Aesop introduces and comments on three of his fables: The lion and the mouse, Dog in the manger, and The ant and the grasshopper. 3 scenes Variable cast 1 setting

Leif Eriksson discovers Vinland. Fredericks, A. D.

Leight, Warren

The final interrogation of Ceauşescu's dog.

Role reversal. Privileged pet, oblivious to criminal charges and confident of the dictator's return, reduces interrogator to Jell-O. 1 act Variable cast 2 characters 1 interior

In Ensemble Studio Theatre marathon 2000: the one-act plays

Glimmer, glimmer and shine. Dramatists 2003

ISBN 0-8222-1844-4

Twin brothers, Martin and Daniel Glimmer, along with Eddie Shine, formed trumpet section. Daniel leaves. Years later his daughter finds out about her family when she meets Jordan Shine. 3m 1w 1 setting

Side man. Dramatists 2000 69p

ISBN 0-8222-1721-X   LC 98-54092

Drama traces life of son between 1953 to 1985, as he watches the world of his Jazz musician father and alcoholic mother crumble. 2 acts 5m 3w 1 setting

—Same. Grove Press 1998 82p

ISBN 0-8021-3622-2   LC 98-54092

—Same

In The Best Plays of 1998-1999; ed. by Otis L. Guernsey, Jr.

Stray cats. Dramatists 1999 80p

ISBN 0-8222-1614-0   LC 99-231509

Series of nine jazz-influenced monologues by men as they hit bottom, paint themselves into corners, or seek moment of transcendence. 9m

Leivick, H.

Shop; tr. by Nahma Sandrow.

Portrays horrendous working conditions in garment manufacturing sweatshop on Lower East Side of New York. 4 acts 10m 5w 1 interior 1 exterior

In God, man and devil; ed. by N. Sandrow

Lemoine, Stewart

Cocktails at Pam's.

Comedy about disastrous cocktail party. 4m 7w 1 interior

In Lemoine, S. Cocktails at Pam's and Evelyn strange

Evelyn Strange.

Comic mystery. Beautiful amnesiac wanders into world of publishing and high society in 1950s New York. Music. 2 acts 9 scenes 2m 2w 6 interiors 1 exterior

In Lemoine, S. Cocktails at Pam's and Evelyn strange

Lemuel. Carter, L.

Lenéru, Marie

Peace (La paix).

Anti-war drama set in 1918 concerned with need to establish international body to facilitate peaceful resolution of conflict. 4 acts 25 scenes 4m 4w extra 1 interior

In War plays by women; ed. by C. M. Tylee, E. Turner, and A. Cardinal

Lenin, Vladimir

about

Levy, D. Clam

Lent

Dixon, M. E. Into the light

Koopman, L. It is finished

c Zapel, A. L. Who am I?

Leon, Moses de

The Zohar: the book of splendor (dramatization) See McCullough, L. E. The alphabet

Leonard, Hugh

Great expectations. French (London) 1998 79p

ISBN 0-573-01778-6

Dramatization of Dickens's classic coming of age tale set in 19th century England. Prologue 7 acts 55 scenes epilogue 9m 3w

Love in the title. French (London) 2000 52p

ISBN 0-573-01889-8

Woman arrives at famous sight in Ireland to paint a watercolor, accompanied by youthful versions of her mother and grandmother. 2 acts 3w 1 setting

Leonard, Jim

c Crow & Weasel.

Based on Native American folklore. The youngsters Crow and Weasel make an important journey. Backgroung music, dancing. 2 acts 5m 3w extras 1 setting

In Theatre for young audiences; ed. by C. A. Jennings

Leonardo, da Vinci, 1452-1519

about

Friedman, G. W. The last supper
O'Brien, D. The Last Supper restoration

Leopold, Nathan

about

Logan, J. Never the sinner

The **lepers** of Baile Baiste. Noone, R.

Leprosy

Sharma, T. The wooden cart

Lequy, Duong

Meat party. Currency Press 2000 44p il
ISBN 0-80819-617-7

Drama about Australian woman searching for truth about her father's disappearance during Vietnam war. 2 acts 6 scenes 5m 3w 1 setting

LeRoy, Gen

Not waving--. Dramatists 1998 68p il
ISBN 0-8222-1612-4   LC 98-228482

Drama about widow and institutionalized daughter coming together after years of separation, resulting in the mother's transformation by bonding with her daughter. 2 acts 1m 3w 1 setting

Lesbianism

Astor del Valle, J. Transplantations: straight and other jackets para mi
Baker, E. A. Up, down, strange, charmed, beauty, and truth
Barfield, T. Without skin or breathlessness
Basham, R. Lot's daughters
Bowen, J. Little boxes: Trevor
Bridgeman, L. Maison Splendide
Brown, B. It's okay, honey
Celesia, C. Anything for you
del Valle, J. A. Fuchsia
Five Lesbian Brothers (Theater company). Brave smiles . . . another lesbian tragedy
Five Lesbian Brothers (Theater company). Brides of the moon

Five Lesbian Brothers (Theater company). The secretaries
Five Lesbian Brothers (Theater company). Voyage to Lesbos
Healey, M. Yodellers
Hughes, H. Clit notes
Kramer, S. David's redhaired death
Kron, L. 101 humiliating stories
Laxdal, V. Karla and Grif
Moraga, C. The hungry woman: a Mexican Medea
Oliver, K. Swollen tongues
Palacios, M. Describe your work
Palacios, M. Greetings from a queer señorita
Pedrero, P. The color of August
Shaw, P. You're just like my father
Son, D. Stop kiss
Stewart-Brown, C. The gene pool
Sunshine, G. Al takes a bride
Tropicana, C. Milk of amnesia (Leche de amnesia)
Uyehara, D. Hello (sex) kitty: mad Asian bitch on wheels
Wiltse, D. Otis proposes
Wolf, M. Another American: asking and telling

Lespinasse, Gaby

about

McAvera, B. Gaby

Less said, the better. Milligan, J.

The **lesser** wars. Glancy, D.

A **lesson** before dying. Linney, R.

A **lesson** in a dead language. Kennedy, A.

The **lessons** of my father. Filloux, C.

Let it be me. Hardy, C. J.

Let the big dog eat. Wong, E.

Let your hair down, Rapunzel. DeTurk, S.

Leto. Barchers, S. I.

Letter to a daughter. Wesker, A.

Letters

Gurney, A. R. Darlene
Gurney, A. R. Love letters
Owens, R. Chucky's hunch
Stohl, H. A play on letters
Wilkins, J. R. War letters
Williams, T. Lord Byron's love letter
Wong, E. Letters to a student revolutionary

Letters to a student revolutionary. Wong, E.

Letting Mikey go. Bass, T.

Letts, Tracy

Killer Joe. French 1999 72p
  ISBN 0-573-62736-3
Comedy set in trailer home outside Dallas, Texas. Family hires killer to murder their mother for the insurance money. 2 acts 7 scenes 3m 2w 1 interior

—Same
  In New Playwrights: the best plays of
      1998

Levi, Stephen

Cherry and Little Banjo.
Two 14-year-olds meet on the abandoned pier where each goes to escape from family troubles. 1 act 1m 1w 1 setting
  In Levi, S. Cherry soda water

The gulf of crimson.
An Irish sailor visits the prostitute who years ago bore his child; much joyful blarney and some sad truths. A companion piece to the author's Cherry and Little Banjo. 1 act 1m 1w 1 exterior
  In Levi, S. Cherry soda water

Hearts 'n kisses 'n Miss Vickers. French 1999 166p
Comedy. Five present-day teens time-travel back to St. Valentine's day 1921 and encounter a lovesick old maid school teacher ghost with unusual romantic schemes. 2 acts 15 scenes Variable cast 17 characters 2 settings

Red roses for my lady.
A small-time country musician and his drunken wife confront their broken dreams, with fatal results. A companion piece to the author's Cherry and Little Banjo. Music on radio. 1 act 1m 1w 1 exterior
  In Levi, S. Cherry soda water
Leviathan. Wilder, T.

Levin, Kim

Just one night.
College student victim of acquaintance rape. 1m 3w 1 interior
  In 30 ten-minute plays for 4, 5 & 6
      actors from Actors Theatre of
      Louisville's National Ten-minute
      Play Contest

—Same
  In Actors Theatre of Louisville.
      Ten-minute plays: v4

Levy, Deborah

The B file.
Ironic look at loss of cultural identity among young women in postmodernist Europe. 5w
  In Levy, D. Plays: 1

Clam.
Experimental comedy about inevitable nuclear war and its results, with Lenin and Nadia Krupskaya as central characters. 9 scenes 1m 1w 1 interior
  In Levy, D. Plays: 1

Honey, baby.
Ensemble piece about cultural identity in contemporary Britain. Music. 3m 2w
  In Levy, D. Plays: 1

Macbeth—false memories.
Drama based on Shakespeare's Macbeth, ambitious businessman and his wife plot and carry out vicious murder. 2m 2w extras
  In Levy, D. Plays: 1

Pax.
Four archetypal women characters illustrate the sickness afflicting modern Europe and its bleak, nuclear future. 2 acts 17 scenes 4w 1 interior
  In Levy, D. Plays: 1

Pushing the prince into Denmark.
Based on characters in Shakespeare's Hamlet. Surreal confrontation between angry Ophelia and wilfully ignorant Gertude. Music. 2w
  In Levy, D. Plays: 1

Lewis, Carter W.

The one-eyed man is king.
Story of blind thief, loosely based on The country of the blind by H.G. Wells. 2 acts 2m 2w 1 interior
  In New Playwrights: the best plays of
      1998

Soft click of a switch. French 1998 60p
  ISBN 0-573-66020-4
Tragicomedy about a borrowed library book on bomb making used by two violent strangers, results in some madcap adventures. 9 scenes 2m extras 1 interior

Lewis, David

Misconceptions. Weinberger, J. 2002 92p
  ISBN 0-85676-262-8

Lewis, David—*Continued*

Comedy. University biology lecturer and wife, unable to conceive baby, turn to old friend for bit of DIY artificial insemination. 2 acts 6 scenes 2m 2w 1 interior

Lewis, Georgina

Siding 37. Playwrights Pub. Co. 1998 23p
ISBN 1-873139-17-1
Story about a doctor treating an unknown injured woman in a railway siding during 1918 Bolshevik Revolution in Russia. 1 act 1g 4m 1w 1 setting

Lewis, Tim

No vacancy.
Worship program set in Bethlehem inn 33 years after Christ's birth. Innkeeper's son recalls visiting infant Jesus and realizes scriptural prophecies were fulfilled by his crucifixion. 2m 1w
In The drama of Easter; ed. by R. Wray

Lhota, Barbara

Romance.
Companion piece to Strangers. Female college professor and mail carrier meet in chapel. 1m 1w 1 interior
In Women playwrights: the best plays of 2001

Strangers.
Couple uses role-playing as they struggle with child's death. 1m 1w 1 interior
In Women playwrights: the best plays of 2001

Li, Anna

Compatible.
Couple in apartment discuss their feelings and love. 1m 1w 1 interior
In Actors Theatre of Louisville. Ten-minute plays: v4

The **liar**. MacLiammóir, M.

Libation bearers. Aeschylus

Liberation (Die Befreiung). Lask, B.

Libraries

Parker, S. Pratt's fall

Liebman, Steve

The Tale of Jemina Puddle-Duck; Book by Katherine Patterson and Stephanie Tolen; music by Steve Liebman. Dramatists 2002
ISBN 0-8222-1832-1

Musical adaptation of Beatrix Potter's classic tale, Jemima wants to prove that ducks do have the patience to hatch their own eggs. 4m 3w 1 exterior 1 setting

The tale of the Mandarin ducks; a musical play; book and lyrics by Katherine Patterson & Stephanie Tolan; music and lyrics by Steve Liebman. French 1999 39p
ISBN 0-573-62668-5
Based on the book by Katherine Paterson. Musical dramatization of Japanese folktale about a pair of ducks and a samurai and a kitchen maid who help them. Music, singing. Prologue 6 scenes 5m 3w 1 setting

Life after George. Rayson, H.

The **life** and times of young Bob Scallion. Martin, M.

The **life** before/reconstruction/ reconstructing whiteness. Rogers, A.

Life during wartime. Brown, W.

Life goes on. Hodges, A.

Life in refusal. Roth, A.

Life is a dream. Calderón de la Barca, P.

The **life** of Lady Godiva. Tavel, R.

Life support. Tricker, G.

Life X 3. Reza, Y.

The **lifeboat** is sinking. Silverstein, S.

Lift and bang. Myatt, J. M.

Lift and separate. Worsley, V.

Lift off. Williams, R.

A **light** lunch. Derrett, Bridget

Light years. Aronson, B.

Lighting up the two-year-old. Aerenson, B.

Lights, camera, traction! (television director). McCullough, L. E.

Like I say. Jenkin, L.

Like totally weird. Mastrosimone, W.

The **likeness**. Apstein, T.

Lill, Wendy

The fighting days.
Set in 1910s. Canadian journalist Francis Beynon enters the feminist movement, where her beliefs clash with those of other feminists and of her suitor. 2 acts 17 scenes 1m 3w 5 interiors 2 exteriors
In War plays by women; ed. by C. M. Tylee, E. Turner, and A. Cardinal

Lill, Wendy—*Continued*

The Glace Bay Miners' Museum.

Dramatization of novel by Sheldon Currie. Memory play about ill-fated romance between itinerant musician and Cape Breton coal miner's daughter. 2 acts 14 scenes 3m 2w 1 setting

In 7 cannons

The occupation of Heather Rose.

Monologue. Nurse recounts her harrowing experiences on isolated Canadian Indian reservation. 1w 1 interior

In Staging the North; ed. by S. Grace, E. D'Aeth and L. Chalykoff

Lima (Peru)

Mérimée, P. The gilded coach (Le carrosse du Saint-Sacrement)

Limited capacity. Urtusastegui, T.

Limonade tous les jours. Mee, C. L.

Lincoln, Abraham

about

c Fredericks, A. D. One day in Gettysburg

Lincoln, Tad, 1853-1871

about

y Kornhauser, B. Lincoln's log; or Better angels

Lincoln's log; or Better angels. Kornhauser, B.

Lindsay-Abaire, David

A devil inside. Dramatists 2000 64p

ISBN 0-8222-1752-X   LC 2002-279078

Dark comedy set in New York's Lower East Side about obsession and revenge. Young man learns his father was murdered. Satirizes elements of 19th-century Russian novels. 2 acts 21 scenes 3m 3w

Fuddy meers. Dramatists 2001 74p

ISBN 0-8222-1751-1   LC 00-50148

Dark comedy about woman who suffers from rare form of amnesia, is abducted by her brother, and embarks on series of amusingly strange adventures. 2 acts 11 scenes 4m 3w

—Same. Overlook Press 2001 155p

ISBN 1-585-67122-3   LC 00-50148

Snapshot: history lesson.

Monologue. A colorful spiel about the presidents by a park ranger who has just been laid off her job at Mount Rushmore. 1 act 1w 1 setting

In Humana Festival 2002

Linklater, Leonard, and Flather, Patti

Sixty below.

Native denizens of Whitehorse, Yukon Territory, bar over three nights of winter solstice. 2 acts 19 scenes 4m 2w 1 interior

In Staging the North; ed. by S. Grace, E. D'Aeth and L. Chalykoff

Linney, Romulus

Gint.

Re-telling of Ibsen's Peer Gynt set in Appalachian Mountains in 1917. 2 acts 4m 5w

In Linney, R. Nine adaptations for the American stage

Goodbye, Oscar.

Oscar Wilde, dying and hallucinating, has an unexpected visitor. Music. 1 act 2m 1 exterior

In Ensemble Studio Theatre marathon '99: the one-act plays

—Same

In Four from E. S. T. marathon '99

Lark.

Woman who eventually becomes famous opera singer thinks she is on her way to a career as concert pianist. 2 acts 4m 1w

In Linney, R. Nine adaptations for the American stage

A lesson before dying. Dramatists 2001 56p

ISBN 0-8222-1785-6   LC 2001-281548

Drama about an emotional man condemned to death in the backwoods of Louisiana, and the teacher asked to teach him to die like a man. 2 acts 5m 3w 1 setting

—Same

In Linney, R. Nine adaptations for the American stage

Love like fire.

Illicit love is kept at a fever pitch by danger, secrecy, guilt, and frustration. Based on the 17th century novel La Princesse de Clèves, by Madame de La Fayette. Music. 1 act 8 scenes 4m 1w 1 setting

In EST marathon '96: the one-act plays; ed. by M. Smith

Madmen.

Set in 1480, in a Spanish monastery soon to become a target for the Inquisition. Abbot converses with madman who claims to be God. 1 act 2m 1 exterior

In Ensemble Studio Theatre marathon 2000: the one-act plays

Linney, Romulus—*Continued*

Oscar over here.

Drama based on controversial playwright Oscar Wilde. 3m 2w

In Linney, R. Nine adaptations for the American stage

Patronage.

A musician at the home of wealthy patrons gets involved in a heated argument over art, morality, religion, patriotism, etc. Music. 1 act Variable cast 4 characters 1 interior

In EST marathon '97: the one-act plays; ed. by M. Smith

Stars.

Present day Manhattan terrace setting for he-she encounter. 1m 1w 1 exterior

In Actors Theatre of Louisville. Ten-minute plays: v4

Strindberg.

Two-part drama about illicit love affair and revenge based on August Strindberg's Miss Julie and The ghost sonata. 2 acts 3m 5w extras 1 interior

In Linney, R. Nine adaptations for the American stage

True crimes.

Drama based on Leo Tolstoy's The power of darkness. Appalachian family struggles to survive Depression. 4m 4w extras 1 exterior

In Linney, R. Nine adaptations for the American stage

Unchanging love.

Drama set in 1921 North Carolina mill town. Inspired by Chekhov's story In the ravine. Child's tragic death humbles wealthy family. 2 acts 6m 4w

In Linney, R. Nine adaptations for the American stage

The unwritten song.

Family-of-man play based on Willard R. Trask's translations of primitive poetry. 3m 3w

In Linney, R. Nine adaptations for the American stage

A woman without a name.

Woman loses one daughter to bungled abortion, another to a brain tumor, and a son to tuberculosis. Music, singing. 2 acts 5m 4w

In Linney, R. Nine adaptations for the American stage

Lion in the street. Thompson, J.

Lipkin, Dmitry

I am Laika.

Recorded announcement and two dogs in carry-on cages are all that is left at airport after bomb destroys world. Unidentified cast 5 characters

In HB Playwrights short play festival 1999

Pithecus.

Couple tries to imagine story behind prehistoric exhibit at museum. 2m 2w 1 interior

In HB Playwrights short play festival 1998

Skitaletz (The wanderer).

Russian immigrants in Brooklyn pursue American dream through crime. Singing. 2 acts 6m 2w 2 interiors 2 exteriors

In New dramatists: best plays by the graduating class of 2001

Lipkin, Joan

The girl who lost her voice.

Young woman's encounter with performance artist causes her to lose her voice. 1w

In Mythic women/Real women

Lipner, Nara

Pearls.

Drama about widow who confronts her late husband's mistress. 1 act 2w 1 interior

In Off-Off Broadway festival plays, 24th ser.

Lippa, Louis

c Dreaming of Aloysius. Dramatic Publishing 2003 69p

Young boy's adventures as he searches for God to ask for gift of song so he can join grandmother in church choir. Singing. 2 acts 6m 4w 1 setting

c The sorcerer's apprentice. Dramatic Publishing 2003 32p

Comedy. Sorcerer's lazy apprentice learns not to fool with powers he can't control. 2m 1w extras 1 interior

c The true adventures of Pinocchio. Dramatic Publishing 2003 80p

Loosely based on Collodi's story. Puppeteer entertains troupe of actors with story of wooden boy. 2 acts 1b 1g 5m 3w 1 setting

Lips. Congdon, C.

Literary forgeries and mystifications

Williams, T. Lord Byron's love letter

Little airplanes of the heart. Feffer, S.

Little boxes: the coffee lace. Bowen, J.

Little boxes: Trevor. Bowen, J.

Little by little. Ross, B.

Little Eyolf. Ibsen, H.

Little Malcolm and his struggle against the eunuchs. Halliwell, D.

A **little** night music. Sondheim, S.

A **little** princess. Vreeke, J.

Little Red Cowboy Hat. McBride-Smith, B.

Little Red Riding Hood

         Parodies, imitations, etc.

c Reiser, D. The real story of Little Red Riding Hood

c Robbins, N. Red Riding Hood

Schenkar, J. The universal wolf

c Snyder, G. A. Red Riding Hood

Little Red Riding Hood. Reakes, P.

Little Red Riding Hood and The magic dragon. Yordy, M.

Little Richard

         about

Caleb, J. R. The rehearsal

Little sister. Evans, S.

The **little** theater's production of Hamlet. Battlo, J.

Little women. Barchers, S. I., and Kroll, J. L.

LittleBro morning and BigSis afternoon. Tibbetts, M.

Live free or die. Tait, L.

Live from Bethlehem. Anderson, S. J.

Lives of the saints. Ives, D.

Liza and the riddling cave. Urquhart, J.

The **lizard** of Tarsus. Grimsley, J.

Lloyd, Jeremy. See Chapman, J. jt. auth.

Lloyd, Jeremy, and Croft, David

Are you being served? French (London) 2002 66p

     ISBN 0-573-01963-0

Comedy adapted from television program. Staff of department store prepares for big sale then departs en masse for holiday in Spain. 2 acts 8m 4w 2 interiors

Lloyd, Marcus

Dead certain. Samuel 1999 70p

     ISBN 0-8222-1868-2

Psychological thriller. Game of cat and mouse between out-of-work actor and wheelchair-bound theater-obsessed ex-dancer. 2 acts 1m 1w 1 interior

—Same. Weinberger, J. 2000 104p

     ISBN 0-85676-239-3

Lloyd, Richard

c Arabian knights—The panto!. French (London) 2000 66p

     ISBN 0-573-16412-6

Pantomimes with music full of B-movie cliches about mysterious orient. Prologue 2 acts 12 scenes 8m 4w 1 setting

The three musketeers—le panteau!. French (London) 2001 94p

     ISBN 0-573-16416-9

A pantomime burlesque of the Dumas novel, featuring a giant snail and the True Quiche of Lorraine. Music, singing, dancing. Puppets. 2 acts 24 scenes 13m 11w extras settings

Lobster Alice. Obolensky, K.

Lochhead, Liz

Perfect days; a romantic comedy. Hern Bks. 1998 84p

     ISBN 1-85459-419-2   LC 99-487837

Comedy set in Glasgow. Celebrity hairdresser sails into midlife crisis involving friends, family, ex-husband, young lover, and possible baby. 2 acts 10 scenes 3m 3w 1 interior

Lockerbie (Scotland)

Brevoort, D. B. The women of Lockerbie

Lockie Leonard, scumbuster. Fry, G.

Locus (John the Baptist). Ehn, E.

Lodato, Victor

Snapshot: the great father.

Two inmates of a mysterious institution make cautious conversation, uncertain of how safe it is to say that some nightmares are real. 1 act 1m 1w 1 setting

     In Humana Festival 2002

Lodging houses

y Harden, V. The boardinghouse

Johnson, T. Imagine drowning

Kane, R. Miss Roach's war

y Murray, S. This old house

Nigro, D. Beast with two backs

Powell, D. Walking down Broadway

Loneliness—*Continued*
Healy, A. M. Lonely
Henley, B. Am I blue
Kim, S. Dreamtime for Alice
Margulies, D. Father and son
McGee, J. A backward glance
Sater, S. Phone sex and a dumb show
Yew, C. Wonderland
Lonely. Healy, A. M.

Lonergan, Kenneth
Lobby hero. Dramatists 2002
ISBN 0-8222-1829-1
When a luckless security guard is drawn into a murder investigation, loyalties are strained to the breaking point. 3m 1w settings
The Waverly Gallery. French 2001 90p
ISBN 0-573-62750-9
Memory play. Elderly family matriarch runs art gallery in small Greenwich Village hotel. 2 acts 11 scenes 3m 2w 1 setting
—Same. Grove Press 2000 108p
ISBN 0-8021-3756-3
The **lonesome** West. McDonagh, M.

Long, Adam, and others
The Bible: the complete word of God (abridged). Broadway Play Pub. 2000 79p
ISBN 0-88145-182-7
Comedic interpretation of the Bible. Music, singing. 2 acts 3m

Long, Quincy
The flight of the last Calhoon.
Middle aged Irishman in airport security office. Music, singing. 1 act 2m 1w 1 interior
In HB Playwrights short play festival 1999
Funeral home.
Man decides to use his home as funeral parlor. Singing. 3m 1w extras 1 interior
In HB Playwrights short play festival 2000
The joy of going somewhere definite. Dramatists 1999 105p
ISBN 0-8222-1673-6
Dark comedy about three drunken loggers who murder a drunken stranger by accident. 2 acts 4m 2w extra 1 setting

The Sixth Floor museum.
Visitor to Dallas museum speculates about assassination of John F. Kennedy. 2m 2w 1 interior
In HB Playwrights short play festival 1998
Snapshot: scene at Mount Rushmore.
On a visit to Mount Rushmore, a teenager tries to help his older brother come to terms with their mother's death. 1 act 2m 1 setting
In Humana Festival 2002
The **long** Christmas dinner. Wilder, T.
Long hours, long days. Fredericks, A. D.
Long Island
Milligan, J. Any friend of Percy D'Angelino is a friend of mine
A **long,** long time. Fredericks, A. D.
The **long** voyage home. O'Neill, E.
Look at everything twice, for me. Sherborne, C.
Look behind you. Wain, D.
Look what you made me do. Sturner, L.
The **looking-glass** alchemist. Beattie, A.
Looking glass land. DeVita, J.
Looking out to see. Way, C.

Loomer, Lisa
Accelerando. Dramatists 1998 53p
ISBN 0-8222-1595-0
Romantic comedy. Ballet dancer with broken foot determined to find true love on New Year's Eve. Music. 12 scenes 1m 3w 1 setting
The waiting room. Dramatists 1998 79p
ISBN 0-8222-1594-2
Three women from different centuries and cultures wait for doctor to cure maladies they have endured in name of beauty. 2 acts 20 scenes 7m 4w 1 setting
Loon boy. McDonnell, K.
Loose knit. Rebeck, T.
Loot. Orton, J.
Lopez, Barry Holstun, 1945-
Crow & Weasel (dramatization) See Leonard, J. Crow & Weasel

Lopez, Robert
y A sick world. Dramatic Publishing 2003 12p
Falsely accused of crime, 16-year-old runaway shares powerful secret with thirty-something interrogator. 2m 1 setting
Lord Byron's love letter. Williams, T.

Lords and commons. Gore, C.

Los Angeles (Calif.)

Hansell, S. My Medea

Margulies, D. L.A.

Rivera, J. Cloud tectonics

Lost. Holman, R.

The **lost** boys. Thomson, R. H.

The **lost** colony. Green, P.

The **lost** girl. Nigro, D.

The **lost** spear. McCullough, L. E.

Lot 13: the bone violin. Wright, D.

Louie. Margulies, D.

Louise, Dorothy

The servant of two masters; (by) Caarlo Goldoni; in a new adaptation by Dorothy Louise. Dee, I. R. 2003 122p

ISBN 1-56663-536-5   LC 2003-43982

Romantic comedy. Young woman, disguised as her dead brother, travels to Venice in search of her fiance. Servant secretly serves her and man she is searching for at same time. Prologue 1 act 7 scenes 5m 6w 1 interior 1 exterior

Louisiana

Henley, B. The debutante ball

Henley, B. The Lucky Spot

Linney, R. A lesson before dying

Love

Alvarez, L. Analiese

Arrabal, F. The body-builder's book of love

Bachmann, I. The good god of Manhattan

Bandele, 'Biyi. Aphra Behn's Oroonoko

Barry, P. J. Jump the train at Riverpoint

Benfield, D. Second time around

Boker, G. H. Francesca da Rimini

Bowne, A. Beirut

Busch, C. Queen Amarantha

Carley, D. A view from the roof

Chappell, E. Something's burning

Charnas, S. M. Vampire dreams

Claff, R. Call waiting

Clark, B. In pursuit of Eve

Clarke, G. E. Whylah Falls: the play

Clarvoe, A. Walking on the roof

Daniels, J. Boom town

Dean, P. 48 shades of brown

Dean, P. After January

Devlin, A. Ourselves alone

Dresser, R. What are you afraid of?

Dunn, M. Gendermat

Feibleman, P. S. Cakewalk

Fennessy, A. Chilling and killing my Annabel Lee

Field, B. Camille

c Frankonis, W. A. A tale of Cinderella

Fréchette, C. Elisa's skin

Glancy, D. The lesser wars

Glass, J. M. Yesteryear

Goldberg, J. Refuge

Goldoni, C. The Venetian twins

Goluboff, B. In-betweens

Goold, R. The end of the affair

Graham, B. Desperate affection

Graziano, D. Acorn

Guare, J. Greenwich mean

Guare, J. Lake Hollywood

Gurney, A. R. Far East

Gurney, A. R. Love letters

Handy, P. East of the sun and west of the moon

Hardy, C. J. Let it be me

Hare, D. My zinc bed

Heather Brothers. Love bites

Hoben, G. Telephone

Hutton, A. Last train to Nibroc

Kobler, F. Ghost of a chance

Krieger, H. Side show

Kushner, T. Terminating

Langella, F. Frank Langella's Cyrano

Lhota, B. Romance

Li, A. Compatible

Lill, W. The Glace Bay Miners' Museum

Linney, R. Love like fire

Linney, R. Strindberg

Lochhead, L. Perfect days

London, J. A wicked woman

Marber, P. Closer

Margulies, D. I don't know what I'm doing

Margulies, D. Lola

Marivaux, P. C. de C. de. Changes of heart

Martin, J. Jack and Jill: a romance

Massicotte, S. Mary's wedding

McConnell, J. Cupboard love

McManus, B. Selkirk Avenue

Mee, C. L. Limonade tous les jours

y Newsome, M. The perfect night

Love—*Continued*

Nigro, D. Beast with two backs

Nigro, D. The circus animals desertion

Nigro, D. Doctor Faustus

Nigro, D. The Irish girl kissed in the rain

Nigro, D. Tristan

Norman, M. Dracula

Pape, R. Hearts beating faster

Parsley, R. Sense and sensibility

Pedrero, P. A night in the subway

Penhall, J. Love and Understanding

Porter, C. Nymph errant

Redwood, J. H. The old settler

Romeril, J. Miss Tanaka

Schmitt, E.-E. Don Juan on trial

Schnitzler, A. Anatol

Schnitzler, A. Flirtation

Shepard, S. Eyes for Consuela

Sherman, J. Romance in D

Shores, D. Sordid lives

Silver, N. The maiden's prayer

Silverstein, S. The trio

Sleeping around

Sondheim, S. A little night music

Tasca, J. Judah's daughter

Teale, P. Jane Eyre

Trieschmann, C. The bridegroom of Blowing Rock

Vogelstein, C. All about Al

White, M. Far from the madding crowd

Love and a bottle. Hughes, D.

Love and anger. Walker, G. F.

Love and Understanding. Penhall, J.

Love and yearning in the not-for-profits. Roth, A.

Love bites. Heather Brothers

Love child. Murray-Smith, J.

The **love** for three oranges. Heard, D. B.

Love from Shakespeare to Coward. Sharland, E.

Love in the title. Leonard, H.

Love letters. Gurney, A. R.

Love like fire. Linney, R.

Love makes a man; or, The fop's fortune. Cibber, C.

The **love** of Don Perlimplin for Belisa in the garden. García Lorca, F.

The **love** of the nightingale. Wertenbaker, T.

Love poem #98. Taylor, R.

The **love** suicides at Amijima. Chikamatsu, M.

The **love** suicides at Sonezaki. Chikamatsu, M.

Love upon the throne. Barlow, P.

A **lovely** Sunday for Creve Coeur. Williams, T.

Love's last shift; or, The fool in fashion. Cibber, C.

Loving Daniel Boone. Norman, M.

Low in the dark. Carr, M.

Lowe, Michelle

The smell of the kill. Dramatic Publishing 2003 77p

Black comedy. Three wives decide whether or not to save their miserable, unloving husbands mistakenly trapped in meat locker. 3m 3w extras 1 interior

Lowell, Susan, 1950-

Little Red Cowboy Hat (dramatization) See McBride-Smith, B. Little Red Cowboy Hat

Lowinger, Rosa

The Encanto file.

Mystery about a Cuban swindle deal. 1m 2w 1 interior

In Women's Project & productions; ed. J. Miles

Loyalties. Guyer, M.

Lucas, Craig

Bad dream.

Fear of sex and intimacy in age of AIDS. 1 act 2m 1 setting

In Lucas, C. What I meant was

The boom box.

Two dead homosexuals converse in spirit realm. 1 act 2m

In Lucas, C. What I meant was

Boyfriend riff.

Monologue by gay man about his boyfriend. 1m

In Lucas, C. What I meant was

Credo.

Monologue. Woman, having just broken up with boyfriend, reacts to death of her dog. 1w

In Lucas, C. What I meant was

The dying Gaul. French 2002 70p

Drama set in Hollywood. Gay screenwriter caught in love triangle with ruthless film producer and wife. 2 arts 3m 1w 1 setting

Lucas, Craig—*Continued*

—Same

　In Lucas, C. What I meant was

God's heart. French 2002 88p

ISBN 0-573-60323-5

Black youth, pregnant woman, and lesbian meet in shared, shifting dreamscape 2 acts 3m 5w settings

Grief.

Following husband's funeral widow plans to jettison everything from her life that reminds her of her terrible marriage, including her two divorced sons. 2m 1w 1 interior

　In Lucas, C. What I meant was

If Columbus does not figure in your travel plans.

Stranger in gay bar arrives to ease bartenders death. 1 act 2m 1 interior

　In Lucas, C. What I meant was

Missing persons.

Revised version of play first produced 1981. Wealthy, tenured professor/author spends Thanksgiving attempting to hold together her fractured family. 2 acts 3 scenes 1b 3m 3w 1 interior

　In Lucas, C. Prelude to a kiss and other plays

Prelude to a kiss.

After their honeymoon man discovers his wife's soul has migrated to body of an old man dying of cancer. 2 acts 8m 4w extras

　In Lucas, C. Prelude to a kiss and other plays

Stranger. French 2002 63p

ISBN 0-573-60278-6

Psychological thriller. After waiting 15 years, kidnap victim exacts revenge upon her ex-con born-again abuctor. 2 acts 2m 2w 4 interiors

Three postcards; with music and lyrics by Craig Carnelia.

Musical. Three women friends share intimate memories in trendy New York restaurant. Singing 2m 3w 1 interior

　In Lucas, C. Prelude to a kiss and other plays

Throwing your voice.

Two New York couples debate morality of owning diamond which may have been mined in South Africa. 2m 2w 1 interior

　In Lucas, C. What I meant was

Unmemorable.

Couple's lovemaking is reviewed. 1 act 3m 2w

　In Lucas, C. What I meant was

What I meant was.

Family members apologize for past wrongs. 2m 2w 1 interior

　In 30 ten-minute plays for 4, 5 & 6 actors from Actors Theatre of Louisville's National Ten-minute Play Contest

—Same

　In Actors Theatre of Louisville. Ten-minute plays: v4

—Same

　In EST marathon '97: the one-act plays; ed. by M. Smith

—Same

　In Lucas, C. What I meant was

Luce, William

Barrymore. French 1998 56p

ISBN 0-573-64240-0

Memory play. One month before his death John Barrymore prepares for role of Shakespeare's Richard III. 2 acts 1m extras 1 setting

Luciano, Ron, 1937-1995

about

Metcalf, P. The players

Lucie, Doug

Fashion.

Satirical look at political advertising. 2 acts 6 scenes 6m 3w 1 interior

　In Lucie, D. Plays 1

Gaucho.

Drama about tragic waste of potential. Traces career of drug baron. 7 scenes 3m 3w 1 setting

　In Lucie, D. Plays 1

Grace.

Satire set on English country estate about greed and hypocrisy of American evangelists. 8 scenes 4m 4w 1 setting

　In Lucie, D. Plays 1

Progress.

Satire set in working-class London. Trendy leftist household is scene of hostile male encounter group and sexual liberationists. 2 acts 7 scenes 6m 2w 1 interior

　In Lucie, D. Plays 1

The **luck** of Roaring Camp. Barchers, S. I., and Kroll, J. L.

Luck of the draw. Manning, N.

Luckham, Claire

The dramatic attitudes of Miss Fanny Kemble.

Drama set in London's Covent Garden and 1832 Georgia plantation, explores acting profession and slavery through life of English actress. Prologue 2 acts Variable cast 16 characters 2 interiors

In Luckham, C. Plays

The seduction of Anne Boleyn.

Romance between Anne Boleyn and Henry VIII. 2 acts 33 scenes 4m 4w 1 setting

In Luckham, C. Plays

Trafford Tanzi.

Woman's life portrayed as series of wrestling matches. 2 acts 3m 3w 1 interior

In Luckham, C. Plays

Lucky four. Russell-King, C.

The **Lucky** Spot. Henley, B.

Lucy and the mystery of the vine-encrusted mansion. Nigro, D.

Ludlam, Charles

Bluebeard.

Theater of the absurd melodrama. Mad scientist Bluebeard experiments on latest wife and creates third sex. 3 acts 42 scenes 5m 5w 2 interiors

In Ludlam, C. The mystery of Irma Vep and other plays

Camille.

Experimental comedy loosely based on Dumas' novel. Melodrama about tubercular courtesan in 19th century Paris. 3 acts 7m 5w 3 interiors

In Ludlam, C. The mystery of Irma Vep and other plays

Galas.

Comedy. Modern tragedy about demanding artist based on life of Maria Callas. 2 acts 7 scenes 8m 5w extras settings

In Ludlam, C. The mystery of Irma Vep and other plays

The mystery of Irma Vep.

Parody of Gothic melodrama featuring werewolf, vampire and Egyptian princess. 3 acts 6 scenes Variable cast 7 characters settings

In Ludlam, C. The mystery of Irma Vep and other plays

Stage blood.

Comedy about family acting company that continually tours U. S. in Hamlet. 3 acts 5m 2w settings

In Ludlam, C. The mystery of Irma Vep and other plays

—Same

In Theatre of the ridiculous; ed. by B. Marranca and G. Dasgupta

Lulu. Wedekind, F.

Luna Park. Margulies, D.

Lunacy. Turtle, R.

Lunchtime. Marcato, R.

Lynch, Jacqueline

Take two. Dramatic Publishing 2003 25p

Award-winning actress confronts morbid obsession of fan. Variable cast 3 characters 1 interior

Lynette has beautiful skin. Anderson, J.

Lysistrata. Aristophanes

M

Maar, Dora, 1907-1997
about

McAvera, B. Dora

Macadaeg, Robert

Woozey woo!.

Two men discuss date rape drug. 2m

In 30 ten-minute plays for 2 actors from Actors Theatre of Louisville's National Ten-minute Play Contest

Macbeth. Nielsen, K.

Macbeth—false memories. Levy, D.

MacDonald, Addison

Eat me.

Dark comedy about couple eating in cafe, where the owner eyes the couple for the next day's meal. 3m 1w 1 setting

In Blast from the future; ed. by D. Yeaton

MacDonald, Alastair

Chairmaker: the musical.

Musical about young love, growing up and growing old set in chair factory in Nova Scotia. 2 acts 4m 1w 1 setting

In Maiden voyages; ed. by S. Burke

MacDonald, Ann-Marie

Goodnight Desdemona (good morning Juliet). Grove Press 1990 88p
ISBN 0-8021-3577-3

MacDonald, Ann-Marie—*Continued*

Feminist comedy based on Shakespeare's Othello and Romeo and Juliet. Female Shakespeare scholar is transported into plays themselves where she alters their outcomes. Prologue 3 acts 3m 5w 1 interior

MacDonald, Robert David

The ice house. Oberon Bks. 1997 64p
ISBN 1-84002-030-X

Drama about a deteriorating marriage, jealousy, and sexual fantasy. 5 scenes 2m 1w 1 setting

MacEwen, Gwendolyn

Terror and Erebus.

Radio play in verse. Set in Arctic. Account of Rasmussen's search for remains of Franklin's expedition. 4m

In Staging the North; ed. by S. Grace, E. D'Aeth and L. Chalykoff

about

Griffiths, L. Alien creature

Machado, Eduardo

When the sea drowns in sand.

Cuban American airlifted to U.S. as child returns to island in the company of his male lover. Takes place during the Elian Gonzalez affair. 2 acts 5 scenes 3m extras 3 interiors 1 exterior

In Humana Festival 2001

MacIvor, Daniel

Marion Bridge. Talonbooks 1999 127p
ISBN 0-88922-407-2   LC 00-274418

Three women in their thirties come "home" to Cape Breton to be with their dying mother. 2 acts 13 scenes 1m 4w 1 interior 1 exterior

Mack, Carol K.

After.

Reporter investigates what becomes of storybook characters after their tales are told. 2w extras 1 exterior

In 30 ten-minute plays for 2 actors from Actors Theatre of Louisville's National Ten-minute Play Contest

—Same

In Actors Theatre of Louisville. Ten-minute plays; v5

Macklin, Peter

Someplace warm.

Her own guilt-ridden mother and a well-to-do gay couple compete for the chance to raise a rape victim's unborn child, while she considers an abortion. 1 act 3m 2w settings

In Off-Off Broadway Festival plays, 26th ser.

MacLachlan, Angus

Dead eye boy. Dramatists 2002
ISBN 0-8222-1844-5

Twenty-nine-year-old Shirley-Diane meets Billy, a thirty-two-year-old ex-con, at their North Carolina working-class Narcotics Anonymous. Together they strive for a clean life. The dead eye boy is Shirley-Diane's fourteen-year-old son. 2m 1w 1 setting

MacLachlan, Patricia

Sarah, plain and tall (dramatization) See Robinette, J. Sarah, plain and tall

MacLennan, Michael Lewis

Beat the sunset. Playwrights Canada 1998 96p
ISBN 0-88754-549-1   LC 98-194240

Memory play about mothers and sons, homosexuality, AIDS, friendship, and intimacy. 15 scenes 2m 2w extras 1 setting

MacLeod, Joan

The hope slide.

Natural disaster serves as metaphor for AIDS crisis. Actress travels back in memory to Hope, British Columbia, site of 1965 mountain collapse. 1w

In 7 cannons

MacLeod, Wendy

Sin. Dramatists 1998 71p
ISBN 0-8222-1561-6   LC 98-222979

Tragicomedy about female heliocopter pilot set around the time of the San Francisco earthquake of 1989. 2 acts 11 scenes 6m 2w

The water children. Dramatists 1999 56p
ISBN 0-8222-1662-0

Serio-comic exploration of abortion from perspective of pro-lifers, pro-choicers, gays, and straights. 4m 4w 1 setting

—Same

In Women playwrights: the best plays of 1998

MacLiammóir, Micheál

Ill met by moonlight.

Based on Irish folk legend set in Connemara about changeling and the havoc he wreaks. 3 acts 5 scenes 4m 4w 1 interior
> *In* MacLiammóir, M. Selected plays of Micheal MacLiammoir

The liar.

Experimental dialogue with choral interjections. Man's lies about social status of both his wife and mother unravel. 4m 6w settings
> *In* MacLiammóir, M. Selected plays of Micheal MacLiammoir

The mountains look different.

Melodrama. Connemara girl, who emigrated to England and turned to prostitution, returns home as wife of innocent and unsuspecting local man. 3 acts 6m 3w 1 interior 1 exterior
> *In* MacLiammóir, M. Selected plays of Micheal MacLiammoir

Prelude in Kazbek Street.

Autobiographical comedy set in Paris about homosexual couple. Prelude 2 interludes 2 acts 4 scenes 6m 2w 1 interior
> *In* MacLiammóir, M. Selected plays of Micheal MacLiammoir

Where stars walk.

Comedy based on Irish saga of Etain and Midhir set in 1940s Dublin. Romance between maid and houseboy in fashionable residence. Prologue 3 acts 5m 4w 1 interior
> *In* MacLiammóir, M. Selected plays of Micheal MacLiammoir

Macona, the honest warrior. Winther, B.

Macpherson, Rafe

The terrible false deception.

Satiric farce set in Victorian drawing room. Play-within-a-play heaps deception upon deception. 4 acts 2m 2w 1 interior
> *In* Seven short plays from Theatre Ontario

The **mad** adventures of Mr. Toad. DeTurk, S.

Mad cow disease in America. Tait, L.

Mad River rising. Yeaton, D.

Madagascar lily. Janaczewska, N.

Madame La Mort. Rachilde

Madame Melville. Nelson, R.

Madden, Dano

Drop. French 1998 45p
> ISBN 0-573-62256-6   LC 99-200358

Comic drama about language and communication set on planet Gavanuuy. Planet's lone dwellers visited by English-speaking creature. Scripted in Gavanuuyian language. 2m 1w

A **madhouse** in Goa. Sherman, M.

Madmen. Linney, R.

The **madness** of Heracles. Euripides

Mafia

Milligan, J. Any friend of Percy D'Angelino is a friend of mine

Milligan, J. Family values

Milligan, J. Men in suits

Mafia on Prozac. Baker, E. A.

Magee, Rusty

The green heart; book by Charles Busch; music & lyrics by Rusty Magee. French 1999 82p
> ISBN 0-573-62667-7

Based on the short story The green heart by Jack Ritchie. Musical about Ivy League playboy scheming to regain lost fortune. 2 acts 14 scenes 2m 3w

Maggie & Pierre. Griffiths, L.

Maggie's last dance. Chan, M.

Magi

The Three Kings (Los tres Reyes Magos)

Magic

Barras, C. M. The black crook

Bernard, K. The magic show of Dr. Ma-Gico

c Frankonis, W. A. A tale of Cinderella

c Heard, D. B. The love for three oranges

Jefferson, J. Rip Van Winkle

Martin, J. Beauty

Martin, S. Patter for the floating lady

Martin, S. The zig-zag woman

c Miller, K. S. The sword in the stone

Neilson, A. The night before Christmas

Sturgill, B. The enchantress of Ipswich

c Zeder, S. Wiley and the Hairy Man

The **magic** garden. Corey, I. L.

The **magic** kingdom. Felder, L.

The **magic** mermaid. Hamlett, C.

The **magic** ring. McCullough, L. E.

The **magic** show of Dr. Ma-Gico. Bernard, K.

The **magic** table. Barchers, S. I.

Magic threads. Morgan, S.

The **magnanimous** cuckold. Crommelynck, F.

The **magnificent** entertainment. Dekker, T.

Magona, Sindiwe

House-hunting unlike Soweto.

Monologue. An African woman and her family search for an affordable apartment and gradually adjust to life in New York. 1 act 1w 1 setting

In Black South African women; ed. by K. A. Perkins

Magpie. Brennan, K.

Mahalia. Stolz, T.

Maharabata, The

Naidoo, M. Flight from the Mahabarath

Mahomed, Ismail

Cheaper than roses.

Monologue by a light-skinned Coloured woman who left her family to pass for white under South Africa's old Apartheid system, now abolished. 1 act 1w 1 exterior

In Black South African women; ed. by K. A. Perkins

Purdah.

Monologue by eighteen-year-old South African Muslim girl. 1 act 1w 1 interior

In Drama for a new South Africa; ed. by D. Graver

The **Mai.** Carr, M.

The **maid** of Croissey; or, Theresa's vow. Gore, C.

Maiden Lane. Medley, C.

The **maiden,** the sailor, and the student. García Lorca, F.

The **maiden's** prayer. Silver, N.

Mail-order Annie. Cashin, C. C.

Maison Splendide. Bridgeman, L.

Major Blowhard (Miles gloriosus). Plautus, T. M.

Make way for Lucia. Van Druten, J.

Makin' sense of nothin'. Palmieri, M.

Making noise quietly. Holman, R.

Making the call. Martin, J.

Making the rain stop. Younger, M.

Malaysia

Chye, K. T. Here and now

Malcolm X, 1925-1965

about

Kennedy, A. Sun

Male bondage. Baker, J.

The **malefactor's** bloody register. Nigro, D.

Males order brides. St. John, B.

Maloney, Peter

Accident.

Middle-aged man convalesces from a roller-blading accident and fears that his son has supplanted him. Monologue with additional voices and a Shadow on skates, who moves props. 1 act 1m extras settings

In Ensemble Studio Theatre marathon 2000: the one-act plays

The **Maltese** bodkin. Belke, D.

Mamet, David

Boston marriage. Dramatists 2003

ISBN 0-08222-1944-1

A comedy about two women who have long lived together on the fringes of upper-class society. 3w 1 interior setting

Deeny.

Faced with man she once loved, woman finds herself obsessively free-associating on wide range of topics. 1 act 1m 1w 1 setting

In Mamet, D. The old neighborhood

—Same

In Mamet, D. The old neighborhood

The disappearance of the Jews.

Middle-aged man discusses faith and sex with boyhood friend. 1 act 2m 1 interior

In Mamet, D. The old neighborhood

—Same

In Mamet, D. The old neighborhood

The jade mountain.

Drama about dream and myth. Two men overhear echoes from their own far-off lives. 2m

In The Best American short plays 1998-1999

—Same

In EST marathon '98: the one-act plays; ed. by M. Smith

Jolly.

Brother and sister share long litany of recrimination, mostly about their parents. 1 act 3 scenes 2m 1w 1 interior

In Mamet, D. The old neighborhood

Mamet, David—*Continued*

—Same

In Mamet, D. The old neighborhood

A sermon.

Clergyman preaches sermon about love, death, and suffering. 1m

In take ten; ed. by E. Lane and N. Shengold

about

Tait, L. David Mamet fan club

Parodies, imitations, etc.

Ives, D. Speed-the-play

Man and superman. Shaw, B.

The **man-child**. Rabin, A.

A **man** confronts himself. Antonelli, L.

The **man** from Mukinupin. Hewett, D.

The **man** in a case. Wasserstein, W.

Man in the flying lawn chair. Cromelin, C.

The **man** who couldn't dance. Katims, J.

The **man** who couldn't stop crying. Schisgal, M.

Man, woman, dinosaur. Porter, R. M.

Mandell, Jude

A thoroughly modern Rapunzel (adaptation) See McBride-Smith, B. A thoroughly modern Rapunzel

Mandiela, Ahdri Zhina

Dark diaspora . . . in dub.

Verse drama discourse on Black womanhood. Variable cast

In Testifyin' v1; ed. by D. Sears

Manktelow, Bettine

Curtain call. French (London) 2001 56p

ISBN 0-573-01918-5

Comedy about a theater manager and his dealings with a director of an amateur production, town council, and board of trustees. 2 acts 4 scenes 3m 5w 1 setting

Curtain up on murder; a thriller; Bettine Manktelow. French (London) 1998 57p

ISBN 0-573-01769-7   LC 00-503011

Mystery about an amateur theater company located at the end of a pier. When the doors lock shut, the murders begin. 3 acts 6 scenes 3m 5w 1 setting

Mann, Abby

Judgment at Nuremberg. French 2001 87p

ISBN 0-573-62789-4   LC 2002-6990

Adapted for stage from the author's scripts for 1957 television drama and 1961 film of the same title. Dramatic reinactment of Nuremberg trial of Nazi war criminals. Prologue 2 acts 19m 5w 1 setting

—Same. New Directions 2002 110p

ISBN 0-8112-1526-1   LC 2002-6990

Mann, Emily

Execution of justice.

Docudrama portraying trial of Dan White for murders of San Francisco Mayor George Moscone and Harvey Milk, city's first openly gay supervisor. Slide projections. 2 acts Large mixed cast 1 setting

In Plays of provocation; ed. by F. P. Richmond

—Same

In Political stages; ed. by E. Mann and D. Roessel

Mann, Klaus

Ania and Esther.

Homoerotic relationships among residents and director of convalescent home for fallen children. 7 scenes 4m 2w extras 2 interiors

In Lovesick; ed. by L. Senelick

Mann, Sally

The house of Bernarda Alba.

Adaptation of play by Federico Garcia Lorca. Cautionary tale of sexual repression among women in villages of rural Spain. 3 acts 10w extras 1 exterior

In Women playwrights: the best plays of 1997

Manning, Ned

Luck of the draw. Currency Press 2000 89p

ISBN 0-86819-635-5

Drama about aboriginal family in Australia coping with forced separation. 2 acts 26 scenes 3m 3w settings

Manno, Karen

The miracles of May. French 1999 67p

ISBN 0-573-62676-6

Tragicomedy about a daughter who suffers a nervous breakdown, her religious mother, and a sick gay stand-up comic her mother takes in. Music. 2 acts 12 scenes 3m 2w 1 interior

Manny. Margulies, D.

A **man's** world. Crothers, R.

Mantello, Joe

The Santaland diaries.

Comic monologue by writer who becomes Macy's elf during holiday crunch. Adapted from work of David Sedaris. 1m extra

In Manello, J. The Santaland diaries and Season's greetings

Season's greetings.

Monologue adapted from work of David Sedaris. Woman uses holiday newsletter to inform family and friends about husband's illegitimate Vietnamese child. 1w

In Mantello, J. The Santaland diaries and Season's greetings

Manzi, Warren

The audition.

In competitive audition actor is asked to behave as though he had murdered his chief rival. Singing. 1 act 1m extra 1 interior

In Manzi, W. The award and other plays

The award.

Actor fails to win award for performance in role that parallels his life. 1 act 1m 1 interior

In Manzi, W. The award and other plays

Moroccan travel guide.

Events on stage (a slide show, a foul-mouthed comic) alternate with a voice-over of tour guide evoking cave in Morocco. 1 act 1m 1w 1 interior

In Manzi, W. The award and other plays

One for the money.

Monologue. Actor goes to pieces while soliciting contributions for charity. 1 act 1m 1 interior

In Manzi, W. The award and other plays

The queen of the parting shot.

An elderly actress desperately searches for old memory. 1 act 1m 1w 1 interior

In Manzi, W. The award and other plays

Manzoni, Alessandro

Adelchi: a tragedy.

The Lombard king's son, an able and thoughtful prince, is destroyed by his father's rash decisions and the intrigues of treacherous nobles during a war with the Franks (772-774). Includes chorus lamenting the fate of subjugated Italians. 5 acts 37 scenes 20m 2w extras settings

In Manzoni, A. Two plays

The Count of Carmagnola: a tragedy.

A proud captain who has won victories for the Venetian Republic excites the suspicions of the secretive Council of Ten and is trapped and executed for treason. Includes chorus lamenting Italian disunity. 5 acts 23 scenes 17m 2w extras settings

In Manzoni, A. Two plays

Maoris

Ihimaera, W. Woman far walking

A **map** of the world. Hare, D.

Mapa, Alec

I remember Mapa.

Comic monologue by Asian American gay man recounting an outsider's experience in show business from smoky cabarets to Broadway theatres. 1m

In O Solo homo; ed. by H. hughes and D. Román

Maple Lodge. Curran, C.

Maponya, Maishe

The hungry earth.

Theatrical piece about aspirations of South African blacks. Singing. Prologue 6 scenes epilogue Variable cast 1 setting

In Postcolonial plays; ed. by H. Gilbert

Umongikazi (The nurse).

Drama about nurses' struggle to form a union to combat corruption and racial discrimination in South Africa's hospital system. Singing. 1 act 7 scenes 2m 3w settings

In Black South African women; ed. by K. A. Perkins

Marat/Sade. Weiss, P.

Marat, Jean Paul, 1743-1793

about

Weiss, P. Marat/Sade

Marber, Patrick

Closer. Grove Press 1999 123p

ISBN 0-8021-3645-1

Quartet of strangers meet, fall in love, and become caught in web of betrayal and desire. 2 acts 12 scenes 2m 2w 11 interiors 1 exterior

Closer (condensation).

In The Best Plays of 1998-1999; ed. by Otis L. Guernsey, Jr.

Marber, Patrick—*Continued*

Dealer's choice. Dramatists 1998 83p
　ISBN 0-8222-1616-7　　　LC 98-138942
Weekly poker game amongst group of regulars
at London restaurant. 3 acts 6m 3 interiors

Howard Katz. Grove Press 2001 104p
　ISBN 0-8021-3953-1　　　LC 2002-75909
Tragicomedy set in London's East End. Midlife
crisis and near breakdown suffered by Jewish
showbiz agent and family man. 2 acts 1b 5m 3w
1 setting

Marc and Marie. Goyette, A.

Marcato, Rob

Lunchtime.
Women accuse man of eavesdropping on their
conversations. 1m 2w 1 interior
　　In 30 ten-minute plays for 3 actors
　　　　from　　Actors　　Theatre　　of
　　　　Louisville's National Ten-minute
　　　　Play Contest
—Same
　　In Actors Theatre of Louisville.
　　　　Ten-minute plays; v5
March 1917: in a coffee shop. Fredericks,
A. D.

Marcus, Fiz

Matchstick dreams. French (London)
　　1999 27p
　ISBN 0-573-12157-5
Comedy about a man who after forty-five years
of marriage decides to build a model of the Town
Hall of Leeds, England, out of matchsticks. 4
scenes 3m 1w 1 setting

Marcus, Milton F.

The gardens of Frau Hess. Dramatists
　　2002
　ISBN 0-8222-1836-4
Germany, 1944, Isaac Baum is selected over
several candidates to replace Frau Ilse Hess's gardener, who was drafted. This is a true incident. 1m
1w 1 setting

Marg Szkaluba (Pissy's wife). Chambers,
R.
Margaret Fleming. Herne, J. A.

Margolin, Deb

Snapshot: rock scissors paper.
In a monologue addressed to a psychotherapist,
a girl discusses her mother's inability to see what
her brother was up to before he died. 1 act 1w 1
setting
　　In Humana Festival 2002
Marguerite Bonet. Smith, V.

Margulies, Donald

Anthony.
Monologue. A boy describes a real-life drama,
with a woman threatening to leap from a building,
and the crowd that gathered to watch. 1 act 1b 1
setting
　　In Margulies, D. Luna Park

Collected stories. Dramatists 1998 72p
　　ISBN 0-8222-1640-X　　　LC 98-164886
An established woman writer takes on a student
as personal assistant and protegée, who then plun-
ders the teacher's private life for material. 2 acts
6 scenes 2w 1 interior

—Same. Theatre Communications Group
　　1998 85p
　ISBN 1-55936-103-4

Death in the family.
Uncle phones nephew when distant relative dies,
makes clumsy attempt to patch up relationship. 1
act 2m 1 setting
　　In Margulies, D. Luna Park

Dinner with friends. Dramatists 2000 76p
　　ISBN 0-8222-1754-6　　　LC 00-41784
Drama about breakup of one couple's marriage
and its effect on their best friends. 2 acts 7 scenes
2m 2w

—Same. Theatre Communications Group
　　2000 86p
　ISBN 1-55936-194-8

—Same
　　In Humana Festival '98

Dinner with friends (condensation).
　　In The Best Plays of 1999-2000; ed.
　　　　by Otis L. Guernsey, Jr.

Father and son.
Father and grown son after mother's death. 1 act
2m 1 interior
　　In Margulies, D. Luna Park

God of vengeance. Dramatists 2003
　　ISBN 0-8222-1930-1

Margulies, Donald—*Continued*

An adaptation from a literal translation by Jo-achim Neugroschel of Sholem Asch's play, God of vengeance. Set on New York's Lower East Side in 1923. 9m 8w 1 interior settings

I don't know what I'm doing.

Monologue by a woman recalling first love. 1 act 1w 1 setting

In Margulies, D. Luna Park

Joey.

Monologue. Directionless young man has a birthday dinner in a Chinese restaurant and resents a friend's remark. 1 act 1m 1 setting

In Margulies, D. Luna Park

July 7, 1994.

Examination of woman doctor's home life and her work at an inner-city clinic. Slide projections. 1 act 1 scene 2m 4w settings

In Margulies, D. Luna Park

L.A.

Los Angeles bar setting for down-on-his-luck TV star's confidences. 1 act 1m 1w 1 interior

In Margulies, D. Luna Park

Lola.

Monologue. Survivor of Auschwitz tells how she met her husband. 1 act 1w 1 setting

In Margolies, D. Luna Park

Louie.

Monologue. An older man speaks of his deaf-ness. 1 act 1m 1 setting

In Margulies, D. Luna Park

Luna Park.

In a dream, a man observes his parents' court-ship and tries to warn them not to marry. Inspired by a Delmore Schwartz story. Prologue 1 act 8 scenes epilogue 2m 2w settings

In Margulies, D. Luna Park

Manny.

Monologue by a 25-year-old petty criminal. 1 act 1m 1 setting

In Margulies, D. Luna Park

Misadventure.

Sister collects brother from police station, where he has been taken after a drunken amble along a highway. 1 act 1m 1w 1 exterior

In Margulies, D. Luna Park

New Year's Eve and Kibbutz.

Two scenes about American Jewish teenagers, set in Brooklyn at a drunken party (1969) and in Israel on a desert kibbutz (1972). 2 scenes 3m 1w 1 interior 1 exterior

In Margulies, D. Luna Park

Nocturne.

A little boy's dream adventures, enacted without dialogue. Inspired by Max Ernst's collages. 1 act 12 sections 1b 2m 1w extras 1 setting

In Margulies, D. Luna Park

Pitching to the star.

New York writer in California discovers that his script for a TV series won't suit the star. 1 act 2m 2w extras 1 interior

In Margulies, D. Luna Park

Space.

Man relates story of breakup with girlfriend. 1 act 2m 1 interior

In Margulies, D. Luna Park

Women in motion.

Friendship of two women who work and vaca-tion together sours when both show interest in the same man. Music. 1 act 5 scenes 2w settings

In Margulies, D. Luna Park

Zimmer.

Jewish record store clerk relates tales of growing up in the 1960s. One actor plays all parts. Music, singing. 1 act 1m 1 setting

In Margulies, D. Luna Park

Maria. Netto, L.

Maricela de la Luz lights the world. Rive-ra, J.

Marie Antoinette, Queen, consort of Louis XVI, King of France, 1755-1793

about

Gore, C. The queen's champion

Gore, C. Salvoisy; or, The queen's lover

Marie-Therese. McAvera, B.

Marijuana

Wilson, S. The grass widow

Marinetti, Filippo

Feet; tr. by Victoria Nes Kirby.

Futurist drama. Audience sees actors only from waist down. 7 scenes Variable cast 1 setting

In Theater of the avant-garde, 1890-1950; ed. by B. Cardullo and R. Knopf

Marivaux, Pierre Carlet de Chamblain de

Changes of heart; tr. by Stephen Wadsworth.

Variant title: Double inconstancy. Romantic comedy in pastoral setting. Two young aristocrats subvert peasants' attraction for one another and win love for themselves. 3 acts 4m 3w 1 interior

In Marivaux, P. C. de Chamblain de. Three plays

—Same; translated and adapted by Stephen Wadsworth. French 1999 95p

ISBN 0-573-62639-1

The game of love and chance; tr. by Stephen Wadsworth.

Comedy about intrigues of courtship and mistaken identity. Father arranges daughter's courtship, she changes places with maid, and her suitor arrives disguised as his valet. 3 acts 5m 2w 1 interior

In Marivaux, P. C. de Chamblain de. Three plays

—Same; translated and adapted by Stephen Wadsworth. French 1999 91p

ISBN 0-573-62637-5

The triumph of love; tr. by Stephen Wadsworth.

Romantic comedy employing disguises and mistaken identity. Spartan princess is in love with heir to her throne. 3 acts 36 scenes intermezzo 4m 3w 1 exterior

In Marivaux, P. C. de Chamblain de. Three plays

The **Mark** Twain show. Miller, K. S.

Mark Twain's Huckleberry Finn. Grauer, R., and Urquhart, J.

Marking time. Snelgrove, M.

Marking time: clocks and calendars through the centuries. McCullough, L. E.

Marks, Ross. See Medoff, M. jt. auth.

Marlene. Gems, P.

Marlette, Doug, 1949-. See Herrick, J. jt. auth.

Marlowe, Christopher, 1564-1593

Doctor Faustus (adaptation) See Morgan, E. Christopher Marlowe's Doctor Faustus

The tragical history of Dr. Faustus.

Elizabethan tragedy in verse based on Faust legend of man who sold his soul to the Devil. Speaking chorus. Music. Prologue 5 acts 20 scenes epilogue 31m 2w extra 1 setting

In Renaissance drama; ed. by A. F. Kinney

The troublesome reign and lamentable death of Edward the Second.

Elizabethan historical tragedy in verse. Edward II's struggle with English lords in 14th century England and his death plotted by Lord Mortimer and Edward's wife Isabella. 23 scenes 27m 2w extras 1 setting

In Renaissance drama; ed. by A. F. Kinney

about

Grimm, D. Kit Marlow

Marnich, Melanie

Quake.

A woman tries out various roles and partners and becomes obsessed with a glamorous serial killer. 13 scenes. Variable cast 13 characters extras 10 interiors 3 exteriors

In Humana Festival 2001

Marowitz, Charles

La Parisienne.

A Parisian socialite manages her husband, his career, a nosy maid, and several lovers without a hitch. Adapted from Henry Becque's 1885 hit. 3 acts 3 scenes 3m 2w 1 interior

In Marowitz, C. Boulevard comedies

Quack.

Tricked into posing as a doctor, a woodcutter discovers wonderful opportunities for lechery and chicanery in his new profession; also helps out some star-crossed lovers. Musical version of Molière's The physian in spite of himself. Music by Michael Valenti. Music, singing. 1 act 3 scenes 6m 3w extras 2 exteriors

In Marowitz, C. Boulevard comedies

Stage fright. Dramatists 1999 56p

ISBN 0-8222-1702-3   LC 00-503532

Drama about an acting couple who torment a nasty drama critic who has destroyed both their careers. 2 acts 2m 1w 1 interior

Stark naked.

Stuffy bourgeois husband is driven to distraction by his feather-brained wife, an innocent child of nature who likes to run around in her nightie. Ad-

Marriage brokerage—*Continued*
Ouellette, J. The marriage counselor
Marriage can be hazardous to your health.
Kane, A.
The **marriage** counselor. Ouellette, J.
The **marriage** of Bette and Boo. Durang,
C.
The **marriage** we deplore. Wilder, T.
Martha, Saint
about
Ehn, E. Contemplacion (Mary and Mar-
tha)

Martin, Jane
Anton in show business. French 2000 85p
ISBN 0-573-62745-2
Comedy. Three actresses pursue their dream of
performing Chekhov's Three Sisters in Texas. 2
acts 6w 1 setting
—Same
In Martin, J. Collected plays, v 2,
1996-2001
Beauty.
Model and her brainy best friend switch bodies
when friend finds magic lamp on the beach. 2w 1
interior
In 30 ten-minute plays for 2 actors
from Actors Theatre of
Louisville's National Ten-minute
Play Contest
—Same
Martin, J. Collected plays, v 2,
1996-2001
The deal.
Monologue by a woman whose life and career
have been subsumed by her brother's. 1 act 1
scene 1w 1 setting
In Martin, J. Collected plays, v 2,
1996-2001
Flaming guns of the purple sage. French
2001 77p
ISBN 0-573-60152-6
Satire about foreclosure of Wyoming ranch that
rehabilitates injured rodeo cowboys. 2 acts 5
scenes 4m 3w 1 interior
—Same
In Humana Festival 2001
—Same
In Martin, J. Collected plays, v 2,
1996-2001

Good boys. French (London) 2003 47p
ISBN 0-573-62858-0
Drama about two fathers, one white, one black,
who meet in a park and reveal their feelings about
fear, guilt, family and race. 5m 1 exterior
Jack and Jill: a romance.
The life, death, and rebirth of a relationship,
traced in a series of short scenes. 2 acts 1m 1w
extras 1 setting
In Martin, J. Collected plays, v 2,
1996-2001
Making the call.
Comedy about a woman who is asked to have
sex with the President of the United States by a
secret service agent. 1m 1w 1 interior
In Actors Theatre of Louisville.
Ten-minute plays: v4
Middle-aged white guys.
Comedy set at garbage dump in Midwest. Three
brothers toast memory of woman, wife to one and
lover to others, who committed suicide. 1 act 1
scene 4m 3w 1 exterior
In Martin, J. Collected plays, v 2,
1996-2001
Mr. Bundy. French 1999 64p
ISBN 0-573-62673-1
Drama about parents who consider vigilante ac-
tion when they learn their next door neighbor is a
convicted child molester and their daughter's safe-
ty is in doubt. 1g 3m 3w
—Same
In Humana Festival '98
—Same
In Martin, J. Collected plays, v 2,
1996-2001
Shasta Rue.
Comedic monologue relating how middle-aged
black woman and her daughter crash beauty pag-
eant. 1w
In Take ten; ed. by E. Lane and N.
Shengold
Tattoo.
Comedy about three women who want philander-
ing lawyer tattooed. 2m 3w 1 interior
In 30 ten-minute plays for 4, 5 & 6
actors from Actors Theatre of
Louisville's National Ten-minute
Play contest
—Same
In Actors Theatre of Louisville.
Ten-minute plays; v5

Martin, Jane—*Continued*

—Same

    In Martin, J. Collected plays, v 2, 1996-2001

Martin, Maurice

Three questions.

Tragicomedy about man who is about to commit suicide, when a woman calls him to ask three questions about his dry-cleaning habits. 1m 1w 1 interior

    In Off-Off Broadway Festival plays, 27th series

Martin, Mick

The life and times of young Bob Scallion. Weinberger, J. 2003 91p

    ISBN 0-85676-267-9

Comedy of manners set in England from 1970s to 1990s. Young man's hopeless journey through jail cells, brothels, church choirs, porn shops and bookies. 2 acts 18 scenes 3m 2w settings

Once upon a time in Wigan. Weinberger, J. 2003 90p

    ISBN 0-85676-271-7

Drama set at Wigan Casino 1973 to 1981. Two couples come of age in face of England's changing political, social and cultural mores. Music. 2 acts 2m 2w 2 interiors

Martin, Neil

Women on the verge of HRT; [by] Marie Jones; music by Neil Martin. French (London) 1999 44p

    ISBN 0-573-01939-8

Musical exploration of female desire. Two middle-aged Belfast women travel to Donegal to see their singing idol perform. Music, singing. 2 acts 1m 2w 1 interior

Martin, Steve

Guillotine.

Comedy skit revolving around guillotine. 2m 1w 1 interior

    In Martin, S. Wasp and other plays

Patter for the floating lady.

Magician's levitation trick allows assistant to attain her freedom from his suffocating love. 1m 2w 1 setting

    In Martin, S. Wasp and other plays

Wasp.

Comedy set in idealized 1950s suburbia depicting stereotypical middle-class white Anglo-Saxon Protestant family. 5 scenes 3m 3w 4 interiors

    In Martin, S. Wasp and other plays

The zig-zag woman.

Woman uses magic in desperate search for affection. 3m 1w 1 setting

    In Martin, S. Wasp and other plays

Martinez, Rogelio

Illuminating Veronica.

Drama set in Havana, Cuba, 1960-1961. Left alone when her family fled the country, pregnant woman discovers that communism is not necessarily in sync with feminism. 2 acts 6 scenes 3m 3w 1 interior

    In Latino plays from South Coast Repertory

Martini, Clem

Conversations with my neighbour's pit bull.

Philosophy professor tries to befriend local canine while dealing with precocious daughter and obnoxious neighbor. 4m 1w extras 2 exteriors

    In Martini, C. A three martini lunch

c The field.

Drama about friendship and prejudice. Blind girl, new in town, befriends boy whose parents are from India. 3 scenes 2m 1w extra 1 exterior

    In Martini, C. The field mouse collection

House of glass.

12-year-old girl must make amends with neighbor for stealing condoms from her store. 5 scenes 1g 1m 1w 1 exterior

    In Martini, C. A three martini lunch

Illegal entry. Playwrights Canada 1999 79p

    ISBN 0-88754-569-6

Three teens from group home for young offenders go AWOL. 3 acts 3m 1 setting

c Mouse.

Youngest mouse in large family of laboratory mice paralyzed by fear. Music. Variable cast 8 characters 1 setting

    In Martini, C. The field mouse collection

Martini, Clem—*Continued*
Up on the roof.

Three characters stranded on rooftop must come to terms with their disintegrating lives and uncertain future. 2m 1w 1 exterior
In Martini, C. A three martini lunch

Martyrdom
Ehn, E. Locus (John the Baptist)

Marx, Karl, 1818-1883
about
Zinn, H. Marx in Soho
Marx in Soho. Zinn, H.

Mary, of Bethany, Saint
about
Ehn, E. Contemplacion (Mary and Martha)

Mary, Queen of Scots, 1542-1587
about
Schiller, F. Mary Stuart

Mary, Virgin, Saint
about
Ehn, E. Tree of hope, keep firm (Mary, the Annunciation)
The four apparitions of Guadalupe (Las cuatro apariciones de Guadalupe)
Mary MacGregor. Benjamin, K. A.

Mary Magdalene, Saint
about
Wilson, S. Darwin's flood
Mary Medusa. Dempsey, S., and Millan, L.
Mary Stuart. Schiller, F.
Mary's wedding. Massicotte, S.
The **mask** and the face. Chiarelli, L.
Mask of the unicorn warrior. York, Y.
The **masked** canary. Christiansen, A.

Mason, Timothy
c The adventures of Huckleberry Finn.

Dramatization of Twain's classic. Boy helps runaway slave escape down the Mississippi on raft. Background music. Prologue 2 acts 18 scenes 5b 11m 9w 1 setting
In Mason, T. Ten plays for children
c The adventures of Tom Sawyer.

Dramatization of Twain's novel about boy's adventures in 19th century Mississippi river town. Music, singing. 22 scenes 4b 1g 9m 2w extras 1 setting
In Mason, T. Ten plays for children

c African tales: Kalulu and his monkey farm and Rumpelstiltskin.

African folktale and Grimm fairy tale told primarily through use of African masks and dance. Music, dancing. Variable cast 21 characters 1 setting
In Mason, T. Ten plays for children
c Aladdin and the wonderful lamp.

Dramatization of Arabian nights story. Background music. Prologue 2 acts 16 scenes 14m 3w extras 1 setting
In Mason, T. Ten plays for children
c Beauty and the beast.

Fairy tale. Beauty's love breaks spell which turned prince into beast. Background music. 2 acts 14 scenes 6m 4w 2 interiors 1 exterior
In Mason, T. Ten plays for children
c Kidnapped in London.

Suggested by John Bennett's 19th century novel, Master Skylark. Shepherd boy visiting Elizabethan London is kidnapped by group of actors. Singing. 3 acts 13 scenes 1b 7m 1w extras 1 setting
In Mason, T. Ten plays for children
c The nightingale.

Hans Christian Andersen's fairy tale is introduced by dramatization of Chinese proverb. Music. 1b 5m 3w extras 1 setting
In Mason, T. Ten plays for children
c Pinocchio.

Dramatization of Collodi's classic. Background music. 2 acts 15 scenes 6m 3w extras settings
In Mason, T. Ten plays for children
Time on fire.

Drama follows the lives of young New Englanders and young British officer in 1775. 2 acts 22 scenes 7m 5w
In New plays; ed. by C. Slaight
c Treasure Island.

Dramatization of Robert Louis Stevenson's adventure of pirates and buried treasure. Background music. 2 acts 12 scenes 20m 1w extras 1 interior 3 exteriors
In Mason, T. Ten plays for children
c Ukrainian tales.

Two Ukrainian folktales told in narration and dance with ad-lib interjections by dancers speaking Ukrainian. Music. Variable cast 9 characters extras 1 setting
In Mason, T. Ten plays for children
The **masque** of blackness. Jonson, B.

Masques
Jonson, B. The masque of blackness

Masques—*Continued*

Jonson, B. Mercury vindicated from the alchemists at court

Jonson, B. Pleasure reconciled to Virtue

Jonson, B. The queen's masques: the first, of blackness

Massacres

Ehn, E. Thistle

Ehn, E. Una carroña (Rose of Lima)

Massicotte, Stephen

Mary's wedding. Playwrights Canada 2002 66p

ISBN 0-88754-636-6

Drama set in 1914 England. Innocent first love on eve of war. 1m 1w 1 setting

Massinger, Philip

The renegado.

Jacobean romance. Muslim lady falls in love with a Christian who has come to Tunis in disguise to rescue his sister. After many perils, all three escape, aided by a repentant pirate. Music. 5 acts 25 scenes 9m 3w extras settings

In Three Turk plays from early modern England; ed. by D. J. Vitkus

Mast, Edward

c Jungalbook.

Dramatization of Kipling's The jungle book. Adventures of boy raised in jungle by wolves. 1 act Variable cast 13 characters 1 setting

In Theatre for young audiences; ed. by C. A. Jennings

y Wolf child. Anchorage Press 1999 54p

ISBN 0-87602-368-5

Drama about young boy raised by wolves, who later enters civilization and is taught to be a human being. 3m 2w 1 setting

Master and servant

Marivaux, P. C. de C. de. The game of love and chance

The **master-maid**. Barchers, S. I.

The **masters** of all. Fredericks, A. D.

Mastrosimone, William

Like totally weird.

Satirical battle of wits between amateur and professional fantasists. Manipulative Hollywood filmmaker and his wife are held captive by two dangerously demented teenagers. 1 act 3m 1w extras 1 setting

In Humana Festival '98

Precipice.

Climbers face dilemma when confronted by storm on Mount Rainier. 1m 1w 1 exterior

In 30 ten-minute plays for 2 actors from Actors Theatre of Louisville's National Ten-minute Play Contest

—Same

In Actors Theatre of Louisville. Ten-minute plays; v5

Los **Matachines** unmasked (Los Matachines desenmascarados); tr. by Larry Torres.

Directions for a Southwestern ceremonial dance, drawing on Hispanic and Indian traditions to represent the triumph of good over evil. Music, dancing. 1 scene 14m 2w 1 setting

In Six nuevomexicano folk dramas for Advent season

The **match** girl's gift: A Christmas story. Gollobin, L. B.

Match point. Gilroy, F. D.

Matchstick dreams. Marcus, F.

Matera, John

y The mirror of Dori Gray. Pioneer Drama Service 1998 58p

Drama about young girl consumed by vanity and ambition. Loosely based on Oscar Wilde's The picture of Dorian Gray. 2 act 8 scenes 2m 8w extras settings

Mates. Esson, L.

Math and aftermath. Grimsley, J.

Mathematics

Auburn, D. Proof

c McCullough, L. E. Counting, from quipu to googol

Stoppard, T. Arcadia

Mathematics. Reitz, D.

Mathis, Sharol Bell

The hundred penny box (dramatization) See Sundstrom, B. The hundred penny box

The **mating** game. Hawdon, R.

MaTRIX, inc. (Casa matriz). Raznovich, D.

A **matter** of survival. Fredericks, A. D.

Mattern, Jennifer

Scrapple.

A man's relentlessly destructive patter has driven away his wife and is now focused on his unmarried daughter. 1 act 1m 1w 1 interior

In EST marathon '98: the one-act plays; ed. by M. Smith

Matthews, Seymour

Who wins. French (London) 2002 53p
ISBN 0-573-01960-6

Comedy about practical joke at dinner party which turns into a murder thriller. 2 acts 6m 4w 1 setting

Maundy Thursday

Owens, J. To serve one another

Maupassant, Guy de, 1850-1893

The necklace (dramatization) See Barchers, S. I., and Kroll, J. L. The necklace

Maurice Harte. Murray, T. C.

May, Adam

Rising fish prayer. Currency Press 1998 70p il
ISBN 0-86819-445-X

Drama about Australian businessman managing a gold mine in Papua New Guinea. 22 scenes 3m 3w 1 setting

May, Elaine

In and out of the light.

Farce involving lecherous dentist, his sexy nurse, wildly remote patient, and dentist's gay son. 1 act 2m 2w 1 interior

In May, E. & Arkin, A. Power plays

Taller than a dwarf. French 2003 75p
ISBN 0-573-60294-8

Comedy about Jewish man from Queens, New York, who suffers from urban angst. 6m 4w 1 interior

May, Elaine, and Arkin, Alan

The way of all fish.

Wine and take-out dinner lead to power struggle between an imperious socialite and her mousy secretary. 1 act 2w 1 interior

In May, E. & Arkin, A. Power plays

Mayakovsky, Vladimir

Vladimir Mayakovsky.

Autobiographical cubo-futurist verse play about rebellious, anarchistic individual who wishes to remake society. Prologue 2 acts epilogue 9m 4w extras 2 exteriors

In Eight twentieth-century Russian plays; ed. by T. Langen and J. Weir

Mayas

Moraga, C. Heart of the earth: a Popol Vuh story

Maydays. Edgar, D.

Mayer, Oliver

Ragged time.

On the eve of the Spanish-American war, a Mexican boy is sold to a blind black street singer in need of a slave. Music, singing, dancing. 2 acts 4m 4w 1 setting

In Out of the fringe; ed. by C. Svich and M. T. Marrero

Mayflower

c Fredericks, A. D. The Mayflower Compact

The **Mayflower** Compact. Fredericks, A. D.

Mayne, Rutherford

Bridge head.

Drama set in early 1900s western Ireland. Agent of Land Commission grapples with issues of arbitration. 3 acts 10m 2w extras 1 interior

In Mayne, R. Selected plays of Rutherford Mayne

The drone.

Peasant comedy set in 1908 County Down, Ireland. Good-natured, witty youth manages to avoid work. 3 acts 6m 3w 1 interior

In Mayne, R. Selected plays of Rutherford Mayne

Peter.

Comic play about anxious engineering student who dreams he is a gigolo in a posh hotel. Prologue 3 acts epilogue 9m 5w extras 3 interiors

In Mayne, R. Selected plays of Rutherford Mayne

Mayne, Rutherford—_Continued_
Phantoms.
Anti-war play set in Bronze Age in which older generation is depicted as evil for inflicting warfare upon the young. 1 act 4m 2w 1 interior
_In_ Mayne, R. Selected plays of Rutherford Mayne

Red turf.
Tragedy set in 1911 Galway, Ireland, about land hunger and murder. 1 act 4m 1w 1 interior
_In_ Mayne, R. Selected plays of Rutherford Mayne

The troth.
Tragedy set in mid-19th century about Irish land problem. Protestant and Catholic farmers unite in plan to murder oppressive landlord. 1 act 3m 1w 1 interior
_In_ Mayne, R. Selected plays of Rutherford Mayne

The turn of the road.
Young Irish man forced to chose between his love of music and working the family farm. Music. 2 scenes epilogue 7m 3w 3 interiors
_In_ Mayne, R. Selected plays of Rutherford Mayne

The **mayor's** limo. Nassar, M.

McAvera, Brian
Dora.
Monologue by Picasso's lover, the surrealist painter Dora Maar. Music. 1w 1 setting
_In_ McAvera, B. Picasso's women

Eva.
Monologue by Eva Gouel, one of Picasso's lovers. Music. 1w 1 setting
_In_ McAvera, B. Picasso's women

Fernande.
Monologue by Fernande Olivier, one of Picasso's models and mistresses. 1w 1 setting
_In_ McAvera, B. Picasso's women

Françoise.
Monologue by painter Francoise Gilot, one of Picasso's lovers. Music. 1w 1 setting
_In_ McAvera, B. Picasso's women

Gaby.
Monologue by Gaby Lespinasse, one of Picasso's lovers. Music. 1w 1 setting
_In_ McAvera, B. Picasso's women

Jacqueline.
Monologue by troubled wife of Picasso. Music. 1w 1 setting
_In_ McAvera, B. Picasso's women

Marie-Therese.
Monologue by Marie-Therese Walter, one of Picasso's mistresses. Music. 1w 1 setting
_In_ McAvera, B. Picasso's women

Olga.
Monologue by Picasso's first wife Olga. Music. 1w 1 setting
_In_ McAvera, B. Picasso's women

McBride-Smith, Barbara
c Aaron Kelly is dead!.
Folktale about deceased husband returning from the dead to his wife. Variable cast 8 characters
_In_ McBride-Smith, B. Tell it together

c Arachne and Athena.
Based on the Greek myth about warring goddesses. Variable cast 9 characters
_In_ McBride-Smith, B. Tell it together

c Atalanta.
Based on Greek myth about abandoned princess. Variable cast
_In_ McBride-Smith, B. Tell it together

c Bill Erophon and his horse Peggy Sue.
Based on Greek myth about Bellerophon and Pegasus. Variable cast 7 characters
_In_ McBride-Smith, B. Tell it together

c Bubba the cowboy prince.
Based on book by Helen Ketteman. Cowboy falls in love with young lady. Variable cast 8 characters
_In_ McBride-Smith, B. Tell it together

c Cat-skins.
Based on German folktale via Appalachian mountains. Girl in cat-skins ends up marrying wealthy son. Variable cast 7 characters
_In_ McBride-Smith, B. Tell it together

c The contest for Athens.
Based on Greek myth about founding of Athens. Variable cast 14 characters
_In_ McBride-Smith, B. Tell it together

c Demeter and Persephone.
Based on Greek myth of Persephone, who was carried off by Hades and made his queen in the underworld. Variable cast 6 characters
_In_ McBride-Smith, B. Tell it together

c Finn M'Coul.
Folklore about gentle Irish giant. Variable cast 9 characters
_In_ McBride-Smith, B. Tell it together

McBride-Smith, Barbara—*Continued*

c Henny Penny.

Folktale about falling sky and sly fox. Variable cast 8 characters

In McBride-Smith, B. Tell it together

c Hershel and the Hanukkah goblins.

Based on book by Eric Kimmel. Man outwits goblins who keep disrupting Hanukkah. Variable cast 10 characters

In McBride-Smith, B. Tell it together

c King Midas.

Based on the Greek myth about greed. Variable cast 8 characters

In McBride-Smith, B. Tell it together

c Little Red Cowboy Hat.

Based on book by Susan Lowell. Parody of Little Red Riding Hood. Variable cast 7 characters

In McBride-Smith, B. Tell it together

c The miller and his donkey.

Based on Aesop fable. Miller learns lesson when his donkey drowns. Variable cast 10 characters

In McBride-Smith, B. Tell it together

c Santaberry and the Snard.

Based on book by Alice and Joel Schick. Parody of Santa Claus. Variable cast 6 characters

In McBride-Smith, B. Tell it together

c Sody Salleratus.

Folktale about bear who eats family and squirrel who saves family. Variable cast 8 characters

In McBride-Smith, B. Tell it together

c The squire's bride.

Folktale about wealthy Norwegian squire looking for a bride. Variable cast 6 characters

In McBride-Smith, B. Tell it together

c A thoroughly modern Rapunzel.

Based on Jude Mandell's book, parody of Rapunzel fairytale. Variable cast 7 characters

In McBride-Smith, B. Tell it together

c Three billy goats gruff: poetry-style.

Based on Norwegian folktale about troll outsmarted by goat. Variable cast 6 characters

In McBride-Smith, B. Tell it together

c Twelfth night.

Parody based on William Shakespeare's Twelfth Night. Variable cast 13 characters

In McBride-Smith, B. Tell it together

c The twelve labors of Hercules.

Based on the Greek myth of 12 tasks performed by Hercules. Variable cast 15 characters

In McBride-Smith, B. Tell it together

c The wolf and the seven kids.

Based on Brothers Grimm story. Big bad wolf preys on baby goats. Variable cast 12 characters

In McBride-Smith, B. Tell it together

McCabe, James Dabney, Jr.

The guerrillas.

Melodrama about Confederate sympathizers in Western Virginia during the Civil War. 3 acts 18 scenes 14m 4w 5 interiors 5 exteriors

In Fateful lightning; ed. by W. J. Meserve and M. A. Meserve

McCarthy, Joseph, 1908-1957

about

Busch, C. Red scare on Sunset

McClelland, C. E.

Certain arrangements. Anchorage Press 1998 31p

ISBN 0-87602-356-1

Drama about African American teenager in Philadelphia on probation and apprenticed to elderly Italian American woman florist. 4 scenes 2b 1m 1w 1 setting

McClelland, John

y Blood lines.

Drama set in 9th century Ireland. Celts and Vikings attempt to coexist. Singing. 5 scenes 8m 2w 1 setting

In International plays for young people

McClinton, Marion Isaac

Stones and bones.

Couple struggle to communicate with each other. 2m 2w

In 30 ten-minute plays for 4, 5 & 6 actors from Actors Theatre of Louisville's National Ten-minute Play Contest

McConnell, Jean

Cruise missile.

Set on a cruise liner. How to fend off an obnoxious shipmate. 1 act 2w 1 exterior

In McConnell, J. Deckchairs III

Cupboard love.

Two women who are gourmet cooks find out they're being two-timed by their gentleman friend and plot revenge. 1 act 2w 1 exterior

In McConnell, J. Deckchairs III

McConnell, Jean—*Continued*

Day trippers.

On a factory outing to the seashore, two women inadvertently settle their chairs on a nudist beach. Unexpected discoveries about what's really going on at work. 1 act 2w 1 exterior

In McConnell, J. Deckchairs II

The guilt card.

Woman confronts older sister, a professional invalid who has taken ruthless advantage. 1 act 2w 1 setting

In McConnell, J. Deckchairs II

Last post.

Recently widowed matron opens a letter indicating that her husband had a secret affair and fathered a child. Then the child's mother shows up on her doorstep. 1 act 2w 1 setting

In McConnell, J. Deckchairs III

Short changed.

The former headmistress of a girls' school is eager to gain admittance to a posh retirement home; her application is in the hands of an old student with reason to hate her. 1 act 2w 1 exterior

In McConnell, J. Deckchairs II

Theatrical digs.

Two actresses meet and comically compete. 1 act 2w 1 exterior

In McConnell, J. Deckchairs II

McConnell, Jean, and Tripp, Miles

Death is catching. French (London) 2002 58p

ISBN 0-573-01977-0

Based on the novel Kilo forty by Miles Tripp. Murder mystery set in desert near Red sea. Ex-pat French couple, their friend from Cairo, and Armenian businessman on deadly fishing holiday. 2 acts 3 scenes 3m 1w 1 setting

McCormack, Thomas

Endpapers. Dramatists 2003

ISBN 0-8222-1908-5

The old and ailing head of Joshua Maynard Books must name a successor. 7m 4w 1 interior setting

McCulley, Johnston

Zorro!, Or, The Curse of Capistrano (dramatization) See Barchers, S. I., and Kroll, J. L. Zorro!; or, The curse of Capistrano

McCullough, L. E.

c The alphabet.

Based on 13th century Spanish scholar Moses de Leon's The Zohar: the book of splendor. God creates world with help of Hebrew alphabet. Singing. Unidentified cast 25 characters 1 setting

In McCullough, L. E. Plays for learning: Israel reborn

c Anthropology, the science of us.

Anthropology students study girl. Variable cast 5 characters 1 setting

In McCullough, L. E. Plays of discovery and exploration for grades 4-6

c Around the world with Nellie Bly.

Portrayal of pioneering female journalist. Singing. 2g 7m 7w extras 1 setting

In McCullough, L. E. Plays of discovery and exploration for grades 4-6

c Aruman, hero of Java.

Folktale fron Java. Magic gifts enable boy to become hero. 3m 3w extras 1 setting

In McCullough, L. E. Plays from fairy tales: grades k-3

c The big scoop (newspaper reporter).

Newspaper journalist reports on storm and detects reckless driver. 2b 2g 2m 4w 1 setting

In McCullough, L. E. Plays of people at work: grades K-3

c The bird of happiness.

Based on Jewish folklore about Shavout, which commemorates the giving of Ten Commandments. Singing. 1b 1m 2w extras 1 setting

In McCullough, L. E. Plays for learning: Israel reborn

c Call of the wild (park ranger).

Park ranger teaches children about her job. 2b 2g 1m 1w extras 1 exterior

In McCullough, L. E. Plays of people at work: grades K-3

c The case of the purple pen (crime lab technician).

Boy hopes visit to crime lab will help him find his stolen bike. Singing. 2b 2g 1m 2w extras 1 interior

In McCullough, L. E. Plays of people at work: grades K-3

McCullough, L. E.—*Continued*

c Chanukah: come light the menorah!.

Worship program. Boy goes back in time and learns meaning of Hanukkah. Singing. 7b 3g extras 1 setting

In McCullough, L. E. Ancient Israel

c "Constellations then arise": astronomy in the age of Copernicus.

Copernicus explains his heliocentric theory. Unidentified cast 11 characters 1 setting

In McCullough, L. E. Plays of exploration and discovery for grades 4-6

c A cosmic bouquet: sun, moon and stars.

Origin of the universe based on folklore from Japan, Hawaii, and the Wasco Indians of Oregon. Singing. Variable cast 24 characters 1 setting

In McCullough, L. E. Plays from fairy tales: grades k-3

c Counting, from quipu to googol.

Students taught about history of numbers. 3m 2w extras 1 setting

In McCullough, L. E. Plays of exploration and discovery for grades 4-6

c Dare to be a Daniel!.

Worship program. Based on biblical story of the prophet Daniel. Music, singing. Unidentified cast 21 characters

In McCullough, L. E. Ancient Israel

c East of the sun, west of the moon.

Dramatization of Norwegian folktale. Girl saves prince from witch's enchantment. Singing. 2m 9w extras 1 setting

In McCullough, L. E. Plays from fairy tales: grades k-3

c Edward Jenner and the gossip of milkmaids.

Story behind Edward Jenner's smallpox vaccine. 6m 3w extra 1 setting

In McCullough, L. E. Plays of discovery and exploration for grades 4-6

c Everyday science in Ben Franklin's America.

Benjamin Franklin performs experiment for skeptical British visitor. 1b 8m 1w 1 interior

In McCullough, L. E. Plays of discovery and exploration for grades 4-6

c Fionn in search of his youth.

Based on Celtic mythology. Irish boy granted gift of prophecy. Music. 5b 2g extras 1 setting

In McCullough, L. E. Plays from Mythology: grades 4-6

c The flight of Icarus.

Based on Greek mythology. Icarus and Daedalus escape labyrinth on waxed wings. 11b 3g extras 1 setting

In McCullough, L. E. Plays from mythology: grades 4-6

c Freya's golden necklace.

Based on Norse mythology. Thrym and Loki recover Thor's hammer. Singing. 4b 4g extras 1 setting

In McCullough, L. E. Plays from mythology: grades 4-6

c Geegaws and doohickeys: indispensible inventions and their forgotten inventors.

Class explores history of various inventions. 1b 1g 6m 4w 1 interior

In McCullough, L. E. Plays of discovery and exploration for grades 4-6

c Gilgamesh and the rose of eternal youth.

Based on Sumerian mythology. Gilgamesh journeys to seek immortality. 7b 3g extras 1 exterior

In McCullough, L. E. Plays from mythology: grades 4-6

c Di goldineh medineh (The golden land).

Solomon Smulewitz, composer for Yiddish theater in early twentieth century New York, writes song about Jewish immigration. Singing. 6m 2w extras 1 setting

In McCullough, L. E. Plays for learning: Israel reborn

c The Golem of Belmont Boulevard.

Based on legends of the Golem. Young boy learns about heaven-sent, man-made protector of Jews. 1b 1g 6m 2w 1 setting

In McCullough, L. E. Plays for learning: Israel reborn

c The great flying ship of Ivan the Impossible.

Russian folktale. Boy performs impossible feats to win czar's daughter. Singing. Variable cast 17 characters 1 setting

In McCullough, L. E. Plays from fairy tales: grades k-3

McCullough, L. E.—*Continued*

c Hail, Queen Esther!.

Worship program. Actors in 1567 Italy present a purim play about biblical queen Esther. Singing. 6b 5g extras 1 setting

In McCullough, L. E. Ancient Israel

c Heave away, haul away! (tugboat captain).

Children learn about the work of seamen. Singing. 2b 2g 2m 1w extras 1 interior

In McCullough, L. E. Plays of people at work: grades K-3

c How Quentzalcoatl found the sun.

Based on Aztec creation myth. Quentzalcoatl returns sun to sky. Singing. 2b 3g extras 1 setting

In McCullough, L. E. Plays from mythology: grades 4-6

c Isaac Newton's poetry of the rainbow.

Mourners at Sir Isaac Newton's funeral praise his genius. 4m 3w 1 setting

In McCullough, L. E. Plays of discovery and exploration for grades 4-6

c Israel reborn.

American joins kibbutz when Israel is declared a state in 1948. Singing. 2m 3w extras 1 setting

In McCullough, L. E. Plays for learning: Israel reborn

c It's an emergency! (emergency medical technician).

Emergency medical technician rescues elderly woman. 2b 2g 2m 4w 1 setting

In McCullough, L. E. Plays of people at work: grades K-3

c Jonah and the whale.

Worship program. Based on biblical story of prophet rescued from whale. Singing. Variable cast 1 setting

In McCullough, L. E. Ancient Israel

c King David's harp.

Worship program. Hodevah's family searches for harp of King David. Singing. 2b 4g extras 1 setting

In McCullough, L. E. Ancient Israel

c King Midas and the golden touch.

Verse play based on Greek myth of greedy king. 3b 6g extras 1 setting

In McCullough, L. E. Plays from mythology: grades 4-6

c "Lady of the Lamp": Florence Nightingale, founder of modern nursing.

Florence Nightingale's contributions to nursing during Crimean War. 6m 6w 1 interior

In McCullough, L. E. Plays of discovery and exploration for grades 4-6

c Lights, camera, traction! (television director).

Children learn how a television program is produced. Singing. 2b 2g 1m 2w extras 1 interior

In McCullough, L. E. Plays of people at work: grades K-3

c The lost spear.

West African folktale. Son of Sengalese herdsman seeks hand of princess. Music, singing. Variable cast 20 characters 1 setting

In McCullough, L. E. Plays from fairy tales: grades k-3

c The magic ring.

Based on Italian folktale. Boy seeks fortune with help of magic ring. Variable cast 13 characters 1 setting

In McCullough, L. E. Plays from fairy tales: grades k-3

c Marking time: clocks and calendars through the centuries.

Girl dreams about time measurement. Singing. Unidentified cast 7 characters 1 interior

In McCullough, L. E. Plays of discovery and exploration for grades 4-6

c The Monkey King.

Based on Jakata tale. Buddha, as the Monkey King, sacrifices his life to save others. Singing. 3b 2g extras

In McCullough, L. E. Plays from mythology: grades 4-6

c Monster in the basement (animal rescue agent).

Animal rescue agent saves raccoon. Singing. 2b 2g 2m 3w extras 1 interior

In McCullough, L. E. Plays of people at work: grades K-3

c Mothers and daughters of invention: 4,000 years of women in science.

Students explore history of women in science. Singing. 2m 13w 1 setting

In McCullough, L. E. Plays of exploration and discovery for grades 4-6

McCullough, L. E.—*Continued*

c Naming the unnamed: the strange saga of Amerigo Vespucci.

In 1545 Princess Elizabeth of England explains to brother Edward why America was named after Vespucci and not Columbus. 1b 8m 5w 1 interior

In McCullough, L. E. Plays of discovery and exploration for grades 4-6

c Next year in Jerusalem.

Story of Theodor Herzl and his dream of Zionist state. Singing. 8m extras 1 interior

In McCullough, L. E. Plays for learning: Israel reborn

c Nitwits and numskulls: outwitting the oppressor.

Based on three Jewish folk tales in which cleverness overcomes oppression. Singing, music. 5b 4g extras 1 setting

In McCullough, L. E. Plays for learning: Israel reborn

c Noah's ark: falsehood and wickedness hitch a ride.

Worship program. Allegory based on story from midrash. Unidentified cast 13 characters 1 setting

In McCullough, L. E. Ancient Israel

c Opening night at the opera, er, opry (piano tuner).

Piano tuner explains work before concert mix-up. 2b 2g 2m 3w 1 interior

In McCullough, L. E. Plays of people at work: grades K-3

c The prophet and the rabbi.

Worship program. Based on biblical story of Elijah of Gilead. 4b 2g extras 1 setting

In McCullough, L. E. Ancient Israel

c Rachel the clever.

Based on Jewish folk tale. Sassy heroine wins heart of Polish king. 2m 2w extras 1 setting

In McCullough, L. E. Plays for learning: Israel reborn

c Reach for the stars.

Teachers and class summarize occupational field trips. Singing. 2b 2g 1m 1w 1 interior

In McCullough, L. E. Plays of people at work: grades K-3

c Robots are everywhere (robotics engineer).

Children learn about robots. Singing. 2b 2g 2m 2w 1 interior

In McCullough, L. E. Plays of people at work: grades K-3

c Roll 'em up, roll 'em up! (pastry chef).

Pastry chef shows children how he works. Singing. 2b 2g 1m extras 1 interior

In McCullough, L. E. Plays of people at work: grades K-3

c Ruth and Naomi: the healing power of friendship.

Worship program. Based on biblical story. Ruth and Naomi journey to Israel. Singing. Unidentified cast 9 characters 1 setting

In McCullough, L. E. Ancient Israel

c Samson and Delilah.

Worship program. Based on biblical story of Samson, who loses his strength when Delilah cuts his hair. Singing. Variable cast 21 characters 1 interior

In McCullough, L. E. Ancient Israel

c See you in court! (Legal Aid lawyer).

Legal aid lawyer explains work to children. 2b 2g 2m 3w extras 1 setting

In McCullough, L. E. Plays of people at work: grades K-3

c The six swans.

Retelling of Grimm's fairy tale. Princess breaks spell which turned brothers into swans. Variable cast 15 characters 1 setting

In McCullough, L. E. Plays from fairy tales: grades k-3

c Squeak and maiow!.

Exploration of antagonistic relationship between felines and rodents based on Welsh and Congolese folktales and Aesop's The lion and the mouse. Singing. Variable cast 10 characters 1 setting

In McCullough, L. E. Plays from fairy tales: grades k-3

c Tale of the Baal Shem Tov.

Based on legends of 18th century Jewish spiritual leader Israel Ben Eliezar, known as Baal Shem Tov, founder of Hasidism. Singing. 1b 7m 3w extras 1 setting

In McCullough, L. E. Plays for learning: Israel reborn

McCullough, L. E.—*Continued*

c Tales of angels.

Worship program. Based on biblical stories. Angels are introduced to children. 3m Variable cast 21 characters 1 exterior

In McCullough, L. E. Ancient Israel

c Three Holocaust tales.

Visions help two rabbis escape Holocaust and two inmates survive Bergen-Belsen concentration camp. Singing. 7m 5w extras 1 setting

In McCullough, L. E. Plays for learning: Israel reborn

c The throne of Osiris.

Based on ancient Egyptian myth. Goddess Isis regains throne for rightful heir Horus. 7b 6g extras 1 setting

In McCullough, L. E. Plays from mythology: grages 4-6

c Tshai the brickmaker.

Based on Chinese mythology. Brickmaker is punished for pride in defying gods. 3b 3g extras 1 setting

In McCullough, L. E. Plays from mythology: grades 4-6

c The twelve months.

Slovakian variant of Cinderella legend. Variable cast 17 characters 1 setting

In McCullough, L. E. Plays from fairy tales: grades k-3

c Two goats, two sisters, and a beggar king.

Based on three Jewish folktales about the power of faith. Music, singing. 1b 4m 5w extras 1 setting

In McCullough, L. E. Plays for learning: Israel reborn

c Una and the goblin king.

Irish folktale. Girl rescues sister from Goblin King. 2g 4m 1w extras 1 setting

In McCullough, L. E. Plays from fairy tales: grades k-3

c What is a brother?

Worship program. Based on biblical stories of brothers including Cain and Abel, Jacob and Esau, and Joseph and his brothers. 13b 5g extras 1 setting

In McCullough, L. E. Ancient Israel

c When a river cries: the myth of Oba and Oshun.

Based on West african mythology. Second wife of thunder god tricks third wife. Singing, dancing. 5b 2g extras 1 setting

In McCullough, L. E. Plays from mythology: grade 4-6

c Why bears no longer talk.

Based on Native American creation myth. 4b 3g extras 1 setting

In McCullough, L. E. Plays from mythology: grades 4-6

c The wisdom of Solomon.

Worship program. Illustrating King Solomon's wisdom. 6b 9g extras 1 setting

In McCullough, L. E. Ancient Israel

c The wise men and women of Chelm.

Based on Jewish folklore about Polish town of foolish people. Singing. 6m 5w 1 setting

In McCullough, L. E. Plays for learning: Israel reborn

c Yankee Doodle had a brick (brick mason).

Children learn about bricklaying. Singing. 2b 2g 2m 2w extras 1 setting

In McCullough, L. E. Plays of people at work: grades K-3

c Young Olli and the trolls.

Based on Finnish folktale. Boy outsmarts trolls and gets treasure. 5m 5w extras 1 setting

In McCullough, L. E. Plays from fairy tales: grades k-3

McDonagh, Martin

The beauty queen of Leenane. Dramatists 1999 56p

ISBN 0-822-1664-7

Part of Leenane trilogy. Domestic drama set in Connemara County, Galway. Aging mother's interference in middle-aged daughter's romantic life leads to terrifying act of violence. 9 scenes 2m 2w 1 interior

—Same

In The Methuen book of modern drama; ed. by G. Whybrow

The beauty queen of Leenane (condensation).

In The Best Plays of 1997-1998; ed. by Otis L. Guernsey, Jr.

McDonagh, Martin—*Continued*

The cripple of Inishmaan. Dramatists 1999 72p

ISBN 0-8222-1663-9

1930s Ireland. Buoyed by reports of a film in progress, a crippled teenager decides to leave his Irish village and go for a screen test. 2 acts 9 scenes 5m 4w 4 interiors 1 exterior

The lonesome West. Dramatists 1999 60p

ISBN 0-8222-1666-3   LC 00-269764

Part of the Leenane trilogy. Domestic drama set in Galway, Ireland, about two brothers living alone following father's death. Young local priest attempts to reconcile brothers before their petty squabbles erupt in violence. 2 acts 7 scenes 3m 3w 1 interior

A skull in Connemara. Dramatists 1999 55p

ISBN 0-8222-1665-5   LC 00-269763

Part of Leenane trilogy. Man hired to disinter bones in Irish village cemetery is rumored to have played role in wife's sudden death seven years earlier. 4 scenes 3m 1w 1 interior

McDonnell, Kathleen

c Loon boy.

Angry 11-year-old boy sent to live with older woman who is attempting to get loons to breed on lake. 1b 2w

In TYA5: theatre for young audience

McGee, Julie

A backward glance.

Older woman tries to persuade her son's ex-girlfriend to break up his impending marriage; younger woman, still in love with him, backs off in dismay. 1 act 2w 1 exterior

In EST marathon '97: the one-act plays; ed. by M. Smith

McGuinness, Frank

A doll's house. Dramatists 1998 69p

ISBN 0-8222-1636-1

Adaptation of Ibsen's classic drama depicting final revolt of wife who has been treated as plaything by pompous husband. 3 acts 2b 3m 4w extras 1 interior

Dolly West's kitchen. Faber & Faber 1999 85p

ISBN 0-571-20370-1

Drama set in County Donegal during World War II. Arrival of allied troops in Derry transforms lives of family. 3 acts 8 scenes 5m 4w 1 interior 1 exterior

Miss Julie.

Adaptation of Strindberg's drama about power, sex and class. Nobleman's haughty daughter seduced by father's manservant. 1m 3w 1 interior

In McGuinness, F. Miss Julie and The stronger

The stronger.

Adaptation of Strindberg's social comedy. Wife versus "the other woman". 3w 1 interior

In McGuinness, F. Miss Julie and The stronger

McGuire, Michael

Helen's play.

Drama set in Chicago, 1940. Play within a play. Successful playwright pens drama for sister-in-law. 2 acts 8 scenes 4m 3w 1 interior

In McGuire, M. Plays

Hold me.

Young woman being stalked takes action on her own but shoots the wrong man. 2 acts 19 scenes 6m 1w settings

In McGuire, M. Plays

These flowers are for my mother.

Tragicomedy. Husband and wife locked in bitter custody battle for gifted son. 2 acts 22 scenes 1b 2m 1w 1 setting

In McGuire, M. Plays

McIntosh, James

about

Brown, S. Toshie

McIntyre, Dennis

Split second: a play in two acts.

Black cop kills white car thief and struggles with his conscience. 2 acts 9 scenes 5m 1w 1 setting

In Plays of provocation; ed. by F. P. Richmond

McIntyre, Hope

y Hunger.

Based on life of Jesse Carter-Havillard, American human rights lawyer in Guatemala. Dancing, music 1w extra 1 setting

In International plays for young people

McKay, Gardner

In order of appearance. French (London) 2003 80p

ISBN 0-573-62870-X

Comedy about a playwright with a big hit who is presumed dead, but is actually alive in Maine. 2 acts 6 scenes 4m 2w extras

McKay, Gardner—*Continued*

Me. French 1998 79p
ISBN 0-573-69029-4

Tragicomedy about bizarre family where the mother knows everyone's secrets but keeps them to herself so family boat won't rock. 2 acts 4 scenes Variable cast 7 characters 1 interior

McKay, Robert

Seeing the light.

Red light goes on signaling possible attack. Watchmen debate whether to tell anyone. 3m

In 30 ten-minutes plays for 3 actors from Actors Theatre of Louisville's National Ten-minute Play Contest

—Same

In Actors Theatre of Louisville. Ten-minute plays; v5

Mckee, Julie

The daffodils.

Motel cleaning women discuss plans for the future. 2w 1 interior

In HB Playwrights short play festival 1997

Haere mai ki aotearoa.

Newly separated woman returns to New Zealand for parents' 50th anniversary. 1w 1 interior

In HB Playwrights short play festival 1999

Invitation to a funeral.

Two ex-wives pay last respects to former husband. 2w 1 interior

In HB Playwrights short play festival 2000

Jill on a recliner, reading.

Woman travels halfway across world to see painting of herself and get reacquainted with artist. 1m 1w 1 interior

In HB Playwrights short play festival 1998

McLaughlin, Ellen

Tongue of a bird. French 2000 65p
ISBN 0-573-62707-X

Drama about female rescue pilot in search for abducted child, is herself haunted by memories of being abandoned by her mother. 2 acts 25 scenes 5w 1 setting

McLean, Duncan

Blackden.

Series of eight monologues, about strange disappearance of young Scottish man in his plane. 8 scenes 3m 1w

In McLean, D. Plays 1

I'd rather go blind.

Parody of pseudo-therapeutic voyeuristic chat shows. Two lovers, his mother, and her father discuss relationships. Music. 2m 2w 1 setting

In McLean, D. Plays 1

Julie Allardyce.

Drama set in and around Aberdeen, Scotland. Oil industry provides great wealth but upsets traditional social relationships. Singing. 18 scenes 4m 2w 1 setting

In McLean, D. Plays 1

One sure thing.

Monologue. Scottish husband and father reflects on death. Background music. 1m

In McLean, D. Plays 1

Rug comes to Shuv.

Comedy set in Edinburgh. Raunchy conversation between two young men. Music. 2m 1 interior

In McLean, D. Plays 1

McLean, Linda

Riddance. Hern Bks. 1999 75p
ISBN 1-85459-465-6   LC 00-302696

Thriller about three friends from Glasgow, Scotland who are bound together by bad memories of a youth spent living in a tenement. 2m 1w 1 setting

McLeish, Kenneth

Orpheus. Oberon Bks. 1997 75p
ISBN 1-84002-016-4

A divinely gifted musician tries to rescue his wife from the underworld but fails a crucial test of faith. Music, singing, dancing. 1 act 3m 5w extras 1 setting

McLeod, Kevin R.

Broken hearts.

Young girl awaits heart transplant. 3w 1 interior

In 30 ten-minute plays for 3 actors from Actors Theatre of Louisville's National Ten-minute Play Contest

McManus, Bruce

Selkirk Avenue.

An old couple share memories and reaffirm their
love as she lies dying. 1 scene 2m 3w 1 setting
In Short spells: scenes & monologues;
ed. by V. Shantz

McNally, Terrence

Corpus Christi. Dramatists 1999 63p
ISBN 0-8222-1696-5

An unorthodox version of the New Testament
life of Christ, from the Nativity to the Crucifixion.
The modern-day protagonist grows up in Texas, is
called Joshua, and is homosexual. Music, singing,
dancing. 1 act 13m settings
—Same. Grove Press 1998 82p
ISBN 0-8021-3635-4

McNeff, Stephen

c Tom Kitten and his friends; book by
Adrian Mitchell; music by Stephen
McNeff. French (London) 1998 35p
ISBN 0-573-05116-X

Musical adaptation of four Beatrix Potter tales:
The story of Miss Moppet, The tale of two bad
mice, The story of a fierce bad rabbit, The tale of
Tom Kitten 2 acts 4 scenes Variable cast 1 setting

McPherson, Conor

Dublin carol. Theatre Communications
Group 2000 89p
ISBN 1-559-36185-9   LC 00-37757

Drama set in Dublin, Ireland. On Christmas Eve
undertaker is sharing funereal memories with
young assistant when his estranged, grown-up
daughter pays him unexpected visit. 3 parts 2m 1w
1 setting
—Same. Theatre Communications Group
2000 89p
ISBN 1-55936-185-9

The good thief.

Monologue by small-time Irish criminal. 1m
In McPherson, C. Four plays
—Same
In McPherson, C. The weir and other
plays

Port Authority. Theatre Communications
Group 91 91p
ISBN 1-55936-207-3

Three monologues about Dubliners. A man desperate to leave home, a middle-aged alcoholic, and
a widower in a nursing home. 15 parts 3m 1 setting

Rum and vodka.

Monologue. Working class Irish husband loses
his job, fights with wife, and spends drunken night
with young woman. 1m
In McPherson, C. Four plays
—Same
In McPherson, C. The weir and other
plays

St Nicholas.

Black comedy about obsession, seduction and
entrapment. Jaded London theater critic falls for
beautiful actress. 2 parts 1m 1 setting
In McPherson, C. Four plays
—Same
In McPherson, C. The weir and other
plays

This lime tree bower.

Hard-boiled suspense yarn. Three men from
small Irish seaside town tell overlapping tales of
fateful night. 3m 1 setting
In McPherson, C. Four plays
—Same
In McPherson, C. The weir and other
plays

The weir. Dramatists 1998 57p
ISBN 0-8222-1706-6

Drama set in rural Irish bar. Tables are turned
on local men swapping spooky stories in attempt
to impress young woman. 4m 1w 1 interior
—Same
In McPherson, C. The weir and other
plays

McPherson, Eddie

Divine Stella Devine. Pioneer Drama
Service 2001 53p

Comedy. Young starlet plots to take over star-
ring role from legendary leading lady. 2 acts 5
scenes 5m 10w extras 1 setting

y Legend of Sammy's Swamp. Pioneer
Drama Service 2002 59p

Comic mystery about motley crew of guests at
mysterious resort. 2 acts 3 scenes 6m 7m extras 1
interior

McTeague: a tale of San Francisco. Bell,
N.

Mda, Zakes

And the girls in their Sunday dresses.

Political drama set in South Africa. Prostitute and working-class woman share single chair as they wait for subsidized allotments of rice. 4 scenes 2w 1 setting

In Drama for a new South Africa; ed. by D. Graver

Me, myself, and I. Fredericks, A. D.

Meakin, Pete

c The tales of Hans Andersen. French (London) 2003 50p

ISBN 0-573-05131-3

Dramatizes several stories of Hans Christian Andersen. 2 acts Large mixed cast

Meat party. Lequy, D.

Medea (Greek mythology)

Euripides. Medea

Wasserstein, W. Medea

Medea. Euripides

Medea. Wasserstein, W.

Median. Stinson, J.

Medical ethics

Stephenson, S. An experiment with an air pump

Mediums

Coward, N. Blithe spirit

Medley, Cassandra

Dearborn Heights.

Drama set in Michigan diner. Two women discover meaning of racism and friendship. 1 act 2w 1 interior

In 3 by EST

Maiden Lane.

Kate, a light-skinned African American, sees a house for sale in an idyllic but lily-white neighborhood and makes friends with the seller, who assumes that Kate is also white. 1 act 1m 3w settings

In Ensemble Studio Theatre marathon '99: the one-act plays

Medoff, Mark

c Kringle's window.

Homeless woman convinces two sisters about reality of Santa Claus and and magic of Christmas. 2 acts 10 scenes 1b 5g 3m 2w extras 2 interiors 1 exterior

In Eight plays for children; ed. by C. A. Jennings

—Same

In The twelve plays of Christmas; ed. by L. Swortzell

Medoff, Mark, and Marks, Ross

y Showdown on Rio Road. Dramatists 1998 53p

ISBN 0-8222-1620-5

Comedy about teenage conflict. Two brothers' sophisticated fort and neighborhood club threatened by new bully in town. 11 scenes 10b 4g 1m

Medoff, Mark Howard, and Treon, Phil

Crunch time. Dramatists 1998 48p

ISBN 0-8222-1621-3   LC 99-199271

Drama about high school girls' basketball star whose life is a complete mess, until she strikes a Faustian deal with the new coach. 25 scenes 4b 5g 7m 3w 1 setting

Mee, Charles L.

Bobrauschenbergamerica.

Sketches of contemporary American life. Theatrical equivalent of Robert Raushenberg artwork. Music, singing. 1g 6m 3w extras

In Humana Festival 2001

The investigation of the murder in El Salvador.

Experimental play. Group of wealthy people converse languidly about unrelated topics. Slide projections. Background music. 1 act 5m 3w 1 exterior

In Mee, C. L. History plays

Limonade tous les jours.

An older American man and a young French woman, both recovering from divorce, drift into a love affair. Music, singing. 1 act 2m 1w settings

In Humana Festival 2002

Orestes.

Experimental theater piece based on Euripides with texts taken from Apollinire, William Burroughs, Vogue and Soap Opera Digest. 10m 2w extras 1 setting

In Mee, C. L. History plays

Time to burn.

Experimental piece inspired by Gorky's Lower Depths explores clash of cultures in America. 7m 4w extras 1 setting

In Mee, C. L. History plays

Mee, Charles L.—*Continued*
The Trojan women: a love story.
Experimental play based on works of Euripides
and Berlioz told through song and dance. Music,
singing. 4m 6w 1 setting
In Mee, C. L. History plays
Vienna: Lusthaus.
Experimental theater piece about turn-of-the-
century Vienna performed with combination of
dance and mime. Variable cast settings
In Mee, C. L. History plays
The war to end war.
Experimental theater piece in three parts; The
Treaty of Versailles, 1920s Germany, and Los Al-
amos. Music. 15m 1w extras 3 settings
In Mee, C. L. History plays

Meetings
Germann, G. The observatory

Megna, Kimberly
An evening crossword.
College co-ed overhears frat members discussing
plans for wild party. 4w 1 interior
In 30 ten-minute plays for 4, 5 & 6
actors from Actors Theatre of
Louisville's National Ten-minute
Play Contest

Melampus. Barchers, S. I.

Melbourne (Australia)
Cortese, R. St. Kilda tales
Gurr, M. Crazy brave

Melodrama
Belasco, D. The heart of Maryland
Boucicault, D. Belle Lamar
Boucicault, D. The octoroon; or, Life in
Louisiana
Cook, P. The saga of the golden horse-
shoe
y Davidson, R. The Pony Express
y Davidson, R. The vile veterinarian
y Gieschen, C. How the West was Dun
Gillette, W. Secret service
Gore, C. Don Juan of Austria
Gore, C. The maid of Croissey; or, The-
resa's vow
Gore, C. The queen's champion
Gore, C. Salvoisy; or, The queen's lover
Horváth, Ö. von. Tales from the Vienna
woods
Howard, B. Shenandoah

Jefferson, J. Rip Van Winkle
y Kelly, T. The snake in the grass
y Kelly, T. Stop the presses!
Kopit, A. L. Chad Curtiss, lost again
y Kotwica, D. The great Denver railroad
scam; or, If aunt May leaves, who'll
weed the 'tunias?
Ludlam, C. Bluebeard
Ludlam, C. The mystery of Irma Vep
MacLiammóir, M. The mountains look
different
Margulies, D. God of vengeance
McCabe, J. D. J. The guerrillas
c Mitchell, W. Jolly Roger
Moody, W. V. The Great Divide
Rust, J. Saved by the Serendipity Circus
c Sodaro, C. Chickenheart
y St. John, B. Holder Posey, the felonious
photographer
St. John, B. Males order brides
y St. John, B. Someone save my Baby
Ruth!
y St. John, B. Wynn Fairly, champeen
rassler! or, Get a grip on yourself!
Melon farmer. Johnston, A.
Melons. Pomerance, B.

Melski, Michael
Hockey mom, hockey dad. Breton Books
2001 85p
ISBN 1-89541-568-3   LC 2001-431898
Divorced dad courts divorced mom as they
watch their sons play hockey. 2 acts 1m 1w 1 in-
terior
Miles from home.
Story of Nova Scotia's Johnny Miles who won
the Boston Marathon twice in the 1920. Prologue
2 acts 31 scenes 4m 2w
In Maiden voyages; ed. by S. Burke
Melville, Herman, 1819-1891
The confidence man (dramatization) See
Metcalf, P. The confidence man
Memorias de la revolución. Tropicana, C.,
and Parnes, U.

Memory
Ackermann, J. Off the map
Baron, C. The blue room
Barry, S. The steward of Christendom
Benfield, D. Second time around
Cameron, M. Tear from a glass eye

Memory—*Continued*

  Cameron, S. Flights

  Carley, D. A view from the roof

  Cristofer, M. Amazing grace

y Dietz, S. Still life with Iris

  Elliot, T. Feed

  Fosbrook, M. Remembering things

  Fréchette, C. The four lives of Marie

  Fugard, A. The captain's tiger

  Glancy, D. American gypsy

  Greenberg, R. Three days of rain

  Hall, T. Jean and Dinah who have been locked away in a world famous calypso since 1956 speak their minds publicly

  Howe, T. Pride's Crossing

  Hunter, M. Atlantis

  Kang, M. J. Noran bang: the yellow room

y Kornhauser, B. Lincoln's log; or Better angels

  Kramer, A. A treasure in a teacup

  MacLeod, J. The hope slide

  Mamet, D. The jade mountain

  Manzi, W. The queen of the parting shot

  McLaughlin, E. Tongue of a bird

  McLean, L. Riddance

  McManus, B. Selkirk Avenue

  Miller, A. Mr. Peters' connections

  Miller, M. Ferris wheel

  Miyagawa, C. Yesterday's window

  Morgan, S. Magic threads

  Paterson, D. L. Shades of autumn

  Rapp, A. Nocturne

  Ross, L. L. Scent of the roses

  Rushforth, T. The Kerry dance

  Ruskin, A. L. The art of remembering

  Shanley, J. P. Welcome to the moon

  Slotboom, C. The train

  Thompson, J. Perfect pie

Men in suits. Milligan, J.

Mena, Alicia

Las nuevas tamaleras.

Contemporary latinas learn to make tamales from scratch, aided by the bickering ghosts of two formidable old ladies. Music. 1 act 7 scenes 5w 1 setting

    Puro teatro; ed. by A. Sandoval-Sánchez and N. S. Sterbach

Menander

Closely cropped locks; translated by Sheila D'Atri and Palmer Bovie.

Variant title: She who was shorn. Fragmentary Greek classical comedy. Tangled affairs of brother and sister separated at birth lead sister's husband to unjust accusation of infidelity.

In Menander. Menander

Desperately seeking justice; translated by Sheila D'Atri and Palmer Bovie.

Variant title: The arbitration. Fragmentary Greek classical drama. Man accuses wife of unfaithfulness but believes her child was conceived by his own drunken attack during festival.

In Menander. Menander

Dyskolos; translated by S. O'Bryhim.

Variant titles: The grouch; The bad tempered man; The misanthrope; Greek classical comedy. Old misanthrope sees value in fellow man after being rescued from well by stepson and daughter's suitor.

In Greek and Roman Comedy; ed. by S. O'Bryhim

The girls from Samos; translated by Richard Elman.

Variant title: The woman of Samos. Fragmentary Greek classical comedy about mistrust, infidelity and illegitimacy.

In Menander. Menander

The grouch; translated by Sheila D'Atri.

Variant titles: The bad-tempered man; The Dyskolos; The misanthrope. Greek classical comedy. Old misanthrope sees value of fellow man after being rescued from well by stepson and daughter's suitor.

In Menander. Menander

The shield; translated by Sheila D'Atri and Palmer Bovie.

Fragmentary Greek classical comedy. Avaricious old man claims right by Athenian law to marry sister of wealthy nephew supposedly killed in battle.

In Menander. Menander

The woman from Samos; trans. by J. Michael Walton.

Fragmentary Greek classical comdey about mistrust, infidelity, and illegitimacy.

In Six Greek comedies

Mendez Rodriguez, Jose Maria

Autumn flower. Estreno 2001 63p

ISBN 1-888463-12-0

Mendez Rodriguez, Jose Maria—*Continued*

Drama set in 1930s Barcelona based on real life of legendary cabaret drag queen and revolutionary. 2 parts Large mixed cast 2 settings

Menotti, Gian-Carlo

c Amahl and the night visitors.

Opera based on the story of the three kings at the nativity of Jesus. Music, singing, dancing. Variable cast

In The twelve plays of Christmas; ed. by L. Swortzell

Mentally handicapped

Caplan, P. J. The test
Henkel, M. Corporate handbook line 11
Meow. Smith, V.
The **merchant** of regrets. Crommelynck, F.

Mercier, Paul

Down the line.

A family in suburban Dublin, over the course of a decade. Music, singing. 1 act 6 scenes 6m 6w 1 setting

In Down the line; The hunt for Red Willie

Mercury vindicated from the alchemists at court. Jonson, B.

Mere mortals. Ives, D.

Meridian, Mississippi redux. Wilhelm, L.

Mérimée, Prosper

Carvajal's family (La famille de Carvajal); tr. by Oscar Mandel.

Set on remote homestead in Andes. Beautiful young girl stabs her ferocious overlord father to death after he poisoned her mother and attempted to rape her. 8 scenes 6m 2w extras 5 interior

In Mérimée, P. Plays on Hispanic themes

The gilded coach (Le carrosse du Saint-Sacrement); tr. by Oscar Mandel.

Drama set in 17th century Lima. Beautiful actress bamboozles her lover, the Viceroy of Peru. 5m 1w 1 interior

In Mérimée, P. Plays on Hispanic themes

Inès Mendo; or, The defeat of prejudice (Inès Mendo; ou, Le préjugé vaincu); tr. by Oscar Mandel.

Drama set in mid-17th century Galicia, Spain. Nobleman falls in love with executioner's daughter, and it nearly costs him his life. 5m 1w extras

In Mérimée, P. Plays on Hispanic themes

Inès Mendo; or, The triumph of prejudice (Inès Mendo; ou, Le triomphe du préjugé); tr. by Oscar Mandel.

Nobleman's marriage to village girl and their dreams of social equality collide with life's brutal realities in 17th century Spain. 3 acts 6 scenes 6m 3w extras 3 interiors

In Mérimée, P. Plays on Hispanic themes

The opportunity (L'Occasion); tr. by Oscar Mandel.

Tragedy sent in 1829 convent school in Havana. Two adolescent girls fall for their priest with fatal consequences. 4g 1m 1w 1 exterior

In Mérimée, P. Plays on Hispanic themes

Merlin (Legendary character)

c Miller, K. S. The sword in the stone
y Woolf, W. King Artie and the Knights of the Rad Table

Mermaids

Gough, L. The tail
c Hamlett, C. The magic mermaid

Merrill, James

The bait (1953).

Verse play. Comedy of manners. Brother and sister seek to avoid all emotional involvement with other people. 1 act 3m 1w 1 setting

In Merrill, J. Collected novels and plays

The bait (1988).

Revised version of 1953 play. 1 act 3m 1w 1 setting

In Merrill, J. Collected novels and plays

The birthday.

Verse play about unusual party gathering. Prologue. 1 act 1 scene 4m 1w 1 interior

In Merrill, J. Collected novels and plays

Merrill, James—*Continued*

The immortal husband.

Retelling of Greek myth of Tithonus and goddess of dawn. Set in England in 1854, Russia in 1894, and America in 1954. 3 acts 3m 3w settings

In Merrill, J. Collected novels and plays

Merzer, Glen

Going nowhere apace.

Man talks to various women at gym. 1m 3w 1 interior

In 30 ten-minute plays for 4, 5 & 6 actors from Actors Theatre of Louisville's National Ten-minute Play Contest

Mesa. Curtis, D.

The **message** and Jehanne. Wilder, T.

Message sent. Houston, S.

Metcalf, Paul

An American chronicle.

Documentary drama. Scenes of American history from Columbus to Lincoln's assassination. Features portraits of Roger Williams, John Brown, and John Wilkes Booth. 2 acts 16 scenes Variable cast

In Metcalf, P. Collected Works: volume three, 1987-1997

The confidence man.

Dramatization of Melville's novel. Satiric look at satanic trickster. Dance. Prologue 16 acts epilogue 10m 1w extras

In Metcalf, P. Collected Works: volume three, 1987-1997

The players.

Documentary comedy-drama featuring naturalist John Burroughs, poet Walt Whitman, baseball pitcher Mark "The Bird" Fidrych, and umpire Ron Luciano. 6 scenes 4m extra 1 setting

In Metcalf, P. Collected Works: volume three, 1987-1997

Metis

Griffiths, L. Jessica

Meuller, Lavonne

The only woman general.

Drama about general who, for her last tour of duty, must orbit the earth in an Army spacecraft with a full load of plutonium for the next 250,000 years. 1m 2w 1 interior

In Women's Project & productions; ed. by J. Miles

Mexican Americans

Alvarez, L. Eddie Mundo Edmundo

Culture Clash (Group). Bordertown

Farias, J. Claudia meets Fulano Colorado

Gonzalez, S. S. The migrant farmworker's son

Moraga, C. Watsonville: some place not here

Solis, O. El otro

Mexico

Alvarez, L. Eddie Mundo Edmundo

Alvarez, L. The guitarrón

Santander, F. The agronomist (El extensionista)

Santander, F. Mexico, USA

Santander, F. The unwritten law

Shepard, S. Eyes for Consuela

Williams, T. The night of the iguana

Mexico, USA. Santander, F.

Meyer, Marlane

The mystery of attraction.

Black comedy. Brothers try to sort out their messed-up lives, in situations that are always much worse than they seem. 1 act 1 scene 4m 2w 1 interior

In Humana Festival 2002

Mhlophe, Gcina

Have you seen Zandile?

South African girl raised by grandmother in city but reclaimed by mother and returned to a rural black enclave grows up to reconcile traditional and non-traditional aspects of her life. Singing. 1 act 14 scenes 2w settings

In Black South African women; ed. by K. A. Perkins

Miami (Fla.)

Aerenson, B. The possum play

Culture Clash (Group). Radio mambo

Mid-life. Yourgrau, T.

Middle-aged white guys. Martin, J.

Middleton, Thomas

A chaste maid in Cheapside.

Jacobean comedy, partly in verse, about sordid alliances and true love. Music, singing. 5 acts 15 scenes Large mixed cast 1 setting

In Renaissance drama; ed. by A. F. Kinney

Middleton, Thomas, and Rowley, William

The changeling.

Jacobean psychological tragedy in verse. In love with another, fickle woman has fiance murdered by deformed servant who loves her. 5 acts 14 scenes 11m 3w extras 7 interiors 2 exteriors

In Renaissance drama; ed. by A. F. Kinney

Midler, Bette

about

Wasserstein, W. Bette and me

Midnight sun. Ardal, M.

A **midsummer** night's midterm. LaVohn, R. W.

Midwives. Yeaton, D.

The **migrant** farmworker's son. Gonzalez, S. S.

Migrant labor

Miller, Jesse. Onionheads

Moraga, C. Watsonville: some place not here

Miles, Johnny, 1905-2003

about

Melski, M. Miles from home

Miles, Kate

I hate you on Mondays.

Gritty depiction of three young people living in downtown Toronto. 15 scenes 2m 1w 5 interiors 1 exterior

In Prerogatives

Miles from home. Melski, M.

Milk, Harvey

about

Mann, E. Execution of justice

Milk of amnesia (Leche de amnesia). Tropicana, C.

The **milk** train doesn't stop here anymore. Williams, T.

Millais, Sir John Everett, 1829-1896

about

Murphy, G. The countess

Millennium 7. White, E. N.

Miller, Arthur

All my sons; a drama in three acts; with an introduction by Christopher Bigsby. Penguin Bks. 2000 84p

ISBN 0-14-118546-5

Materialism of profiteering American arms manufacturer contrasted with idealism of his soldier sons. 3 acts 1b 5m 4w 1 exterior

Death of a salesman; certain private conversations in two acts and a requiem; with a new preface by Arthur Miller; and an afterword by Christopher Bigsby. 50th anniversary ed. Penguin Bks. 1999 142p

ISBN 0-14-028565-2   LC 99-178528

Tragedy. Mediocre salesman, after life of self deception, realizes failure and commits suicide to leave family insurance money. Background music. 2 acts 8m 5w 1 setting

Elegy for a lady.

A man enters a boutique to find a gift for his young mistress, who may be dying, and has a revealing conversation with the woman behind the counter. 1 act 1m 1w 1 interior

In EST marathon '96: the one-act plays; ed. by M. Smith

Mr. Peters' connections. Dramatists 1999 41p

ISBN 0-8222-1687-6

Drama set in abandoned night club. Retired pilot meets a number of characters from his past. 5m 3w 1 interior

The ride down Mt. Morgan. Dramatists 1999 71p

ISBN 0-8222-1700-7   LC 99-228711

Tragicomedy set in upstate New York hospital. Bigamous life of wealthy middle-aged Jewish insurance entrepreneur unravels after auto accident. 2 acts 6 scenes 4m 3w 1 interior

—Same. Penguin Bks. 1999 116p

ISBN 0-14-048244-X   LC 99-228711

about

Finlayson, A. Misfits

Miller, Charles

The Canterville ghost; book and lyrics by Peter Quilter; music by Charles Miller. French (London) 2002 79p

ISBN 0-573-08119-0

Brash American family flummoxes famous English ghost, until their sensitive daughter releases him from an ancient curse. This musical version of Oscar Wilde's story also includes a retelling of "The happy prince," another Wilde tale. Music, singing. 2 acts 10 scenes 2b 2m 3w extras 3 interiors 2 exteriors

Miller, Ev

Last will and testament. Pioneer Drama Service 1999 14p

Elderly man, estranged from son, dictates his will to granddaughter. 1m 1w 1 interior

Miller, J. B.

Bobby Supreme.

Story of a small-time comedian turned big-time performance artist who begins to self-destruct both onstage and off. 5 scenes 3m 3w 1 setting

In New Playwrights: the best plays of 1998

Miller, Kathryn Schultz

c Aladdin and the magic lamp. Pioneer Drama Service 2000 22p

Man escapes drudgery of his chores by fantasizing about Aladdin. 2m 2w 1 setting

c Beauty and the beast. Pioneer Drama Service 2000 22p

Drama based on classic fairy tale. Beautiful maiden's love releases prince from enchantment. Variable cast 8 characters 1 setting

c The emperor's new clothes. Pioneer Drama Service 2000 34p

Audience participation play. Acting family stages version of classic fairy tale. 1b 1m 1w 1 setting

c Island son. Pioneer Drama Service 2000 28p

Undersea adventure based on Caribbean folk tales. Variable cast 5 characters

c Jack and the beanstalk. Pioneer Drama Service 2000 22p

Four actors perform wacky version of classic tale. 2m 2w 1 setting

c The Mark Twain show. Pioneer Drama Service 2000 26p

Patchwork sampler of Mark Twain's comedic works. 2m 1w 1 setting

y Shakespeare to go!. Pioneer Drama Service 1980 25p

Bumbling, kazoo-tooting troupe of actors frame scenes from A midsummer night's dream, Taming of the shrew, and As you like it. 2m 2w 1 setting

c The sword in the stone. Pioneer Drama Service 2000 30p

Tale of Camelot. In course of his studies with Merlin, Arthur learns meaning of "true magic." 1b 2m 1w 1 setting

c A thousand cranes.

Drama based on life of Sadako Sasaki, girl who died of leukemia as a result of 1945 bombardment of Hiroshima. 1 act 1m 2w 1 setting

In Theatre for young audiences; ed. by C. A. Jennings

c The time machine. Pioneer Drama Service 2000 34p

Two mischievous kids accidentally hitch ride in eccentric scientist's time machine. 2m 1w 1 interior

c Young Cherokee. Pioneer Drama Service 2000 33p

Drama based on Native American folklore set in early 19th century Smoky Mountains. Variable cast 8 characters

Miller, Mary

Ferris wheel.

Two people meet on a ferris wheel, reflect on life, and become friends. 1m 1w 1 setting

In Take ten; ed. by E. Lane and N. Shengold

Miller, Susan

My left breast.

Autobiographical account of breast cancer adventure. 1w

In O Solo homo; ed. by H. hughes and D. Román

Miller, Tim

Fruit cocktail.

Memories of growing up gay. Some audience participation. 1m

In Miller, T. Body blows

Glory box.

Gay man describes troubles he and his foreign lover incur because their relationship cannot be legalized. 1m

In Miller, T. Body blows

My queer body.

Performance piece with some audience participation. Monologue by gay man. 1m

In Miller, T. Body blows

Naked breath.

Monologue about gay sex in the age of AIDS. 1m

In Miller, T. Body blows

—Same

In O solo homo; ed. by H. Hughes and D. Román

Miller, Tim—*Continued*

Some golden states.

Monologue. Gay man remembers leaving home for the first time and finding adventure in San Francisco and New York, circa 1978. 1m

In Miller, T. Body blows

Stretch marks.

Monologue. Young gay man becomes AIDS activist. 1m

In Miller, T. Body blows

The **miller** and his donkey. McBride-Smith, B.

Miller, Jesse

Onionheads. French 2001 79p

ISBN 0-573-62723-1

Drama about poor onion farmers during the 1935 Oklahoma dust bowl, their loss of family, love, hardship, and realities of migration. 2 acts 2m 2w

Milligan, Jason

Any friend of Percy D'Angelino is a friend of mine.

Comedy about mobster and actor selected to portray him in film. 2 acts 8 scenes 2m 1w

In Milligan, J. Men in suits

Exodus from McDonaldland.

Comedy. Quality-control officer's obssession with his job aggravates his fiancee. 1 act 2m 1w 1 interior

In Milligan, J. Here, there & everywhere

Family values.

Comedy. On eve of his official induction into crime family mobster accidentally runs over boss's six-year-old heir. 11 scenes 5m 3w

In Milligan, J. Men in suits

The genuine article.

Satire. Fraudulent faith-healer rehearses his spiel and inadvertently performs miracle. 1 act 2m 1 interior

In Milligan, J. Here, there & everywhere

Getting even.

Two vengeance-seekers have conflicting agendas. 1 act 2m 1 interior

In Milligan, J. Here, there & everywhere

Juris prudence.

Farce about crooked lawsuit. 1 act 1b 2m 2w 1 interior

In Milligan, J. Here, there & everywhere

Less said, the better.

Comedy. Crime lord's hit men bungle their New Year's Eve assignment. 1 act 2m 1w 1 setting

In Milligan, J. Here, there & everywhere

Men in suits.

Tragicomedy. Mafia hit men whack wrong target in Grand Central Terminal and drive to Vermont to confess error to boss. 2 acts 12 scenes 3m

In Milligan, J. Men in suits

Rivals.

Comedy. Man seeks loan from former high school rival, now a bank officer. 1 act 2m 1w 1 interior

In Milligan, J. Here, there & everywhere

Strange as it may seem.

Volunteer in soup kitchen encounters her former French teacher, with all her continental airs intact. 1 act 1m 2w 1 interior

In Milligan, J. Here, there & everywhere

Waiting for Ringo.

Beatles impersonators are ready to quit, but "Paul" finds way to keep band going. 1 act 3m 1 interior

In Milligan, J. Here, there & everywhere

The **milling** crowd dies. Dozer, D.

Mills, Sonja

The Danish Play. Playwrights Canada 2002 110p

ISBN 0-88754-702-8

Drama about Danish resistance during World War II based on life and poetry of Agnete Ottosen. 27 scenes 2m 3w extras settings

Milmore, Jane. See Van Zandt, B. jt. auth.

Milton Bradley. Sagal, P.

Mine eyes have seen. Dunbar-Nelson, A.

The **Mineola** twins. Vogel, P.

Mines and mining

Lawrence, D. H. The widowing of Mrs. Holroyd

Mistaken identity—*Continued*
Williams, S. Nobody's perfect
"Mistakes". Hirschberg, H.
Mister Original Bugg. Wellman, M.
The **mistress**. Wesker, A.
Mistresses. Weller, M.

Mitchell, Debbie
The hour of lamps.
Young man struggles to keep the child within himself alive and tells his sister about trip he took back to their childhood home. 1m 2w 1 interior
In 30 ten-minute plays for 3 actors from Actors Theatre of Louisville's National Ten-minute Play Contest

Mitchell, Gary
In a little world of our own.
Domestic tragedy focusing on family of three brothers living in north Belfast. 4 acts 4m 1w 1 interior
In Michell, G. Tearing the loom and In a little world of our own
Tearing the loom.
Drama set in Weaven's cottage County Armagh. Portrait of small Irish community divided against itself during 1798 Rebellion. Prologue 2 acts 5m 2w 1 interior
In Michell, G. Tearing the loom and In a little world of our own
Trust. Hern Bks. 1999 80p
ISBN 1-85459-443-5
Drama about a man in Northern Ireland who puts community before family. 2 acts 8 scenes 5m 2w

Mitchell, John Cameron, and Trask, Stephen
Hedwig and the angry inch. Dramatists 2003
ISBN 0-8222-1901-8
This tells the story of an East German rock-and-roll goddess who also happens to be the victim of a blotched sex-change operation. 1m 1w 1 interior setting

Mitchell, Wayne
c Jolly Roger; king o' the pirates. Pioneer Drama Service 2001 18p
Melodrama about pirates and mistaken identity. 1 act 4m 3w 1 exterior

Mixed doubles. Feydeau, G., and Desvallières, M.
Mixed emotions. Krakower, B.

Miyagawa, Chiori
Yesterday's window.
Japanese-American woman talks about her memories to young girl and delivery man. 1m 2w
In Take ten; ed. by E. Lane and N. Shengold
Mizlansky/Zilinsky. Baitz, J. R.

Mode, Becky
Fully committed. Dramatists 2001 58p
ISBN 0-8222-1768-6   LC 2001-281053
Comedy about an out-of-work actor who mans the reservation line at a leading Manhattan restaurant. 1 act 1m 1 interior
Modern honor; or, The sharper in high life. Gore, C.
A **modern** romance. Conquest, N.

Moffat, Peter
Iona rain.
Twenty-five years after leaving their African boarding school four friends reunite on small Scottish island. 4m 1w
In Nabokov's gloves and Iona rain
Nabokov's gloves.
Successful barrister, estranged from wife, becomes recklessly involved with young, female client. 2 acts 10 scenes 3m 3w 3 interiors 2 exteriors
In Nabokov's gloves and Iona Rain
Mojo. Butterworth, J.
The **Mojo** and the Sayso. Rahman, A.
Molière, 1622-1673
The doctor in spite of himself (dramatization) See Valenti, M. Quack
The physician in spite of himself (adaptation) See Marowitz, C. Quack
Scapin (adaptation) See Irwin, B., and O'Donnell, M. Scapin
Tartuffe (adaptation) See Hischak, T. Molière's Tartuffe
The affected damsels; tr. by Carl Milo Pergolizzi.
Variant title: Such foolish affected ladies. Comedy. Two cousins rudely spurn wealthy suitors because they are direct and dress simply. Mocks over-refined speech, manners and literary preten-

Molière, 1622-1673—*Continued*

tiousness known as preciosité. 17 scenes 6m 3w extras 1 interior

In Molière. Molière, four plays

The bourgeois gentleman; in a new translation and adaptation by Bernard Sahlins. Dee, I. R. 2000 87p

ISBN 1-56663-303-6; 1-56663-304-4 (pa)

LC 00-52304

Variant titles: The middle-class gentleman; The self-made gentleman; The would-be gentleman. Satirical comedy. 17th century French parvenue has himself tutored in the ways of Parisian society. Music, singing, dancing. 2 acts 12m 4w extras 1 interior

—Same; tr. by Carl Milo Pergolizzi

In Molière. Molière, four plays

The bungler; tr. by Richard Wilbur. Dramatists 2000 89p

ISBN 0-8222-1747-3

Rascally valet helps blundering young man win the girl of his dreams. In verse. Music, singing. 5 acts 47 scenes 8m 2w extras 1 exterior

The doctor despite himself; tr. by John Wood and David Coward.

Variant titles: The reluctant doctor; The physician in spite of himself. Satirical farce. Woodcutter posing as a doctor achieves success. 3 acts 21 scenes 8m 3w 1 interior 2 exteriors

In Moliere. The misanthrope and other plays

The doctor in spite of himself; tr. by Carl Milo Pergolizzi.

In Molière. Molière, four plays

Don Juan.

Satire based on Spanish legend. Profligate nobleman is killed by statue of commander whom he killed after seducing his daughter. 5 acts 27 scenes 11m 3w 2 interiors 3 exteriors

In Molière. The miser and other plays

—Same; translated into English by Richard Wilbur. Dramatists 1998 71p

ISBN 0-8222-1657-4

—Same; translated into English by Richard Wilbur. Harcourt Inc. 2001 146p

The hypochondriac.

Variant title: The imaginary invalid. Satirical comedy set in 17th century Paris. Hypochondriac wants to marry his daughter to a doctor in order to get free medical care. Music, singing, dancing.

Prologues 3 acts 31 scenes 1g 9m 2w 1 interior 2 exteriors

In Molière. The miser and other plays

The misanthrope; tr. by John Wood and David Coward.

Comedy of manners. Satire on 17th century Parisian society in which hypocrisy plays an important role. 29 scenes 8m 3w 1 interior

In Moliere. The misanthrope and other plays

The miser.

Comedy satirizing miserliness. Set in 17th century Paris. 8m 3w 1 interior

In Molière. The miser and other plays

—Same; tr. by Carl Milo Pergolizzi

In Molière. Molière, four plays

The miser (short edition); tr. by Carl Milo Pergolizzi.

Shorter version of Moliere's satire on miserliness. 5 acts 31 scenes 10m 3w extras

In Molière. Molière, four plays

The school for wives.

Romantic comedy translated in rhymed couplets. Aged guardian versus young man as suitor of young woman. Set in 17th century France. 5 acts 32 scenes 7m 2w 1 setting

In Molière. The miser and other plays

The school for wives criticized.

Originally intended to accompany performances of The school for wives. Moliere's play is defended as pleasant comedy in conversation among aristocrats. 1 act 4m 3w 1 interior

In Molière. The miser and other plays

Such foolish affected ladies; tr. by John Wood and David Coward.

Variant title: The affected damsels. Comedy. Two cousins rudely spurn wealthy suitors because they are direct and dress simply. Mocks overrefined speech, manners and literary pretentiousness known as preciosité. 17 scenes 6m 3w extras 1 interior

In Moliere. The misanthrope and other plays

Tartuffe; tr. by John Wood and David Coward.

Satirical comedy portraying religious hypocrisy in 17th century France. 5 acts 31 scenes 7m 5w 1 interior

In Moliere. The misanthrope and other plays

Molière, 1622-1673—*Continued*
Those learned ladies; tr. by John Wood
    and David Coward.
Comedy ridiculing cult of grammar, philosophy,
and astronomy popular in 17th century France.
Follows follies of three female pedants. 5 acts 24
scenes 8m 5w settings
    In Moliere. The misanthrope and other
        plays
The would-be gentleman; tr. by John
    Wood and David Coward.
Variant titles: The bourgeois gentleman; The
middle-class gentleman; The self-made gentleman.
Satirical comedy. 17th century French parvenue
has himself tutored in the ways of Parisian society.
2 acts 12m 4w extras 1 interior
    In Moliere. The misanthrope and other
        plays

about

Field, B. Monsieur de Molière
Molière's Tartuffe. Hischak, T.

Molloy, M. J. (Michael Joseph)
The bachelor's daughter.
Comedy set in 1956 County Galway. Rural fami-
ly interacts with poltergeist. 3 acts 4 scenes 5m
3w 1 interior
    In Molloy, M. J. Selected plays of M.
        J. Molloy
Daughter from over the water.
Light comedy focusing on the emigree returning
to Ireland. 3 acts 4 scenes 7m 4w 1 interior
    In Molloy, M. J. Selected plays of M.
        J. Molloy
The king of Friday's men.
Documents the droit du seigneur and faction-
fighting in pre-famine Ireland. 3 acts 4 scenes 7m
4w 2 interiors 1 exterior
    In Molloy, M. J. Selected plays of M.
        J. Molloy
The Paddy pedlar.
An encounter with pedlar carrying the body of
his dead mother on his back in a sack, brings
about the sudden conversion of a petty thief. 1 act
4m 2w 1 interior
    In Molloy, M. J. Selected plays of M.
        J. Molloy
Petticoat loose.
Set in Galway, Ireland, winter of 1822. Ribald
representation of sexual and religious practices of
pagan world totally untouched by orthodox Roman

Catholicism. 3 acts 4 scenes 5m 4w extras 2 inte-
riors 1 exterior
    In Molloy, M. J. Selected plays of M.
        J. Molloy
The wood of the whispering.
Drama set in 1950 Ireland about marginal life of
landlord's villagers and despoliation of once wood-
ed countryside. 3 acts 7m 3w 1 exterior
    In Molloy, M. J. Selected plays of M.
        J. Molloy
Molly Whuppie. Barchers, S. I.
Mom, Dad, I'm living with a white girl.
    Chan, M.
Money and friends. Williamson, D.

Monge-Rafuls, Pedro R.
Trash.
In this monologue, a Cuban Marielito describes
his struggle to survive in the United States, culminating in a lethal encounter with a homosexual
priest. 1 act 1m 1 setting
    In Out of the fringe; ed. by C. Svich
        and M. T. Marrero

Monjo, Justin. See Enright, N. jt. auth.
Monkey in the stars. Gavin, J.
The **Monkey** King. McCullough, L. E.
Monkeys
c McCullough, L. E. The Monkey King
The **monkey's** paw. Holloway, J.
Monologues
Alfaro, L. Downtown
Allen, G. Subliminable
Arizmendi, Y. Nostalgia maldita: 1-900-
    MEXICO, a Stairmaster piece
Augustine, J. Siobhan
Ayvazian, L. Deaf day
Ayvazian, L. Plan day
Barfield, T. Snapshot: defacing patriotic
    property
Barfield, T. Without skin or
    breathlessness
Bayiates, A. Hype-r-connectivity
Belke, D. The Maltese bodkin
Blessing, L. Snapshot: Tyler poked Tay-
    lor
Bogart, A. Score
Bornstein, K. Virtually yours
Brett, S. Putting the kettle on
Burke, K. J. Comfort and joy
Carlin, A. J. Jodie's body

Monologues—*Continued*
Miller, T. Stretch marks
Monge-Rafuls, P. R. Trash
Mooney, V. Sparrow
Moore, A. Snapshot: American klepto
Moore, R. The pain of pink evenings
Morgan, S. Magic threads
Mueller, L. The confession of many strangers
Mueller, L. Voices from September 11th
Nelson, R. Scooping
Nigro, D. Broadway macabre
Nigro, D. Capone
Nigro, D. Childe Rowland to the dark tower came
Nigro, D. Creatures lurking in the churchyard
Nigro, D. Darkness like a dream
Nigro, D. Higgs field
Nigro, D. The Irish girl kissed in the rain
Nigro, D. Joan of Arc in the autumn
Nigro, D. Uncle Clete's toad
Nigro, D. Wolfsbane
Nolan, Y. Annie Mae's movement
Nottage, L. Snapshot: becoming American
Oates, J. C. Here I am
Oates, J. C. No next of kin
Oates, J. C. When I was a little girl and my mother didn't want me
O'Brien, D. Snapshot: her first screen test
Orlandersmith, D. Beauty's daughter
Owen, Gary. Crazy Gary's mobile disco
Owens, R. Chucky's hunch
Paige, J. L. Notes
Palacios, M. Describe your work
Palacios, M. Greetings from a queer señorita
Rame, F. A woman alone
Rapp, A. Nocturne
Raznovich, D. Disconcerted (El disconcierto)
Redgrave, L. Shakespeare for my father
River, S. B. To Rahtid
Rivera, J. Gas
Robinson, M. Downsizing democracy: a polemic
Russell-King, C. Lucky four

Rutherford, S. The Chinese art of placement
Scheffer, W. Alien boy
Scheffer, W. Tennessee and me
Selig, P. Slide show
Shaw, P. You're just like my father
Shear, C. Blown sideways through life
Silver, N. Claire
Stickland, E. Sitting on paradise
Tait, L. Mad cow disease in America
Thompson, J. Pink
Tidler, C. Red mango
Topor, T. Boundary County, Idaho
Tremblay, L. Anatomy lesson
Tropicana, C. Milk of amnesia (Leche de amnesia)
Uyehara, D. Hello (sex) kitty: mad Asian bitch on wheels
Vawter, R. Roy Cohn/Jack Smith
Watkins, C. Queen of hearts
Watkins, C. Welcome to my world
Weaver, L. Faith and dancing
Wesker, A. Annie Wobbler
Wesker, A. Letter to a daughter
Wesker, A. The mistress
Wesker, A. Whatever happened to Betty Lemon?
Wright, C. Snapshot: a quick tour of the monument
Yew, C. Snapshot: here and now

Monroe, Marilyn, 1926-1962
about
Brustein, R. Nobody dies on Friday
Finlayson, A. Misfits

Monsieur de Molière. Field, B.
Monster. Orlandersmith, D.
Monster in the basement (animal rescue agent). McCullough, L. E.

Monsters
Downing, M. Frankenstein's guests
Field, B. Playing with fire
c Roberts, B. Angelica! . . . and the monstrous monster of the deep

Montgomery, L. M. (Lucy Maud), 1874-1942
Anne of Green Gables (dramatization) See Ledoux, P. Anne
Emily trilogy (dramatization) See Norman, M. Emily

Montreal (Quebec)

Griffiths, L. Brother Andre's heart

The **monument**. Wagner, C.

Moodie, Andrew

A common man's guide to loving women.

Meditation on complicated lives of black thirty-something urban males. 2 acts 4m 1 interior

In Testifyin' v2; ed. by D. Sears

Riot.

Political drama set in 1992 Toronto. Blacks riot in response to LA and the acquittal of police who shoot blacks in Canadian context. 3 acts 4m 2w 1 interior

In Testifyin' v1; ed. by D. Sears

Moody, William Vaughn

The Great Divide.

Melodrama explores cultural myths by contrasting genteel Eastern heroine and life-nurturing Western woman who embodies frontier spirit. 3 acts 11m 3w 3 interiors

In American plays of the new woman; ed. by K. Newlin

Mooi Street moves. Slabolepszy, P.

Moon

Baron, J. Hershey: a space odyssey

The **moon** of the Caribbees. O'Neill, E.

Mooney, Vicki

Sparrow.

Monologue. A country woman of Cherokee ancestry tells how she first learned of the Oklahoma City bombing, and what she did afterwards. 1 act 1w 1 setting

In EST marathon '97: the one-act plays; ed. by M. Smith

Moonlight and Valentino. Simon, E.

Moonlight cocktail. Keyes, S.

The **moons** of Alnyron. Walker, B.

Moor masterpieces. River, S. B.

Moore, Allison

Snapshot: American klepto.

Defensive monologue by a woman who has pinched a piece of petrified wood from a national park. 1 act 1w 1 setting

In Humana Festival 2002

Moore, Clement

A visit from St. Nicholas (dramatization) See Swortzell, L. A visit from St. Nicholas; or, The night before Christmas

Moore, Rosemary

The pain of pink evenings.

Monologue by woman on cusp of middle age clinging to memory of dead husband. 1w 1 interior

In The Best American short plays, 2000-2001

Moore, Simon

Misery. French (London) 1999 68p

ISBN 0-573-01850-2

Mystery thriller about poplar novelist held prisoner in remote farm house by schizophrenic admirer. 2 acts 20 scenes 1m 1w settings

Moraga, Cherríe

Heart of the earth: a Popol Vuh story.

Dramatization of a Mayan creation myth. Language mixes several kinds of English and Spanish with Quiché and other Mayan tongues. Music, singing, dancing. 12 scenes 9m 2w extras 1 setting

In Puro teatro; ed. by A. Sandoval-Sánchez and N. S. Sternbach

The hungry woman: a Mexican Medea.

In a balkanized America of the future, Medea lives in the outcasts' territory with her son and her woman lover, for whose sake she has accepted exile. Music, singing. 2 preludes epilogue. 2 acts 19 scenes 1b 7w 7 interiors 1 exterior

In Out of the fringe; ed. by C. Svich and M. T. Marrero

Watsonville: some place not here.

Drama based on actual events in a California agricultural town, chronicles struggles of Mexican immigrant workers as they fight for their rights. Music. 2 acts 18 scenes 3m 4w extras 1 setting

In Latino plays from South Coast Repertory

Moralities

Margulies, D. God of vengeance

More adventures of Noddy. Wood, D.

More light. Wilson, S.

Morehouse, Ward. See Lane, S. F. jt. auth.

Morgan, Edwin

Christopher Marlowe's Doctor Faustus. Canongate Bks. 1999 87p
ISBN 0-86241-989-1

A new version of Marlowe's play, with science replacing magic as the focus of Faustus's ambitions. Largely in verse. Music, dancing. Prologue epilogue 5 acts 16 scenes 3m 2w extras settings

The early years.

The first play in a blank-verse trilogy reimagining the life of Jesus. Shows Jesus searching out his mission during sojourns in Egypt and hedonistic Sepphoris, and in encounters with John the Baptizer and Satan. Singing. Prologue 5 acts 21 scenes 18m 3w 6 interiors 13 exteriors
In Morgan, E. A.D.

The execution.

Concluding play in the author's trilogy includes the Last Supper, betrayal by Judas, and crucifixion. Resurrection is reported in Epilogue. Singing. 5 acts 23 scenes epilogue 24m 5w exras 9 interiors 10 exteriors
In Morgan, E. A.D.

The ministry.

Second play in trilogy reimagining the life of Jesus. Jesus challenges received wisdom and preaches a new and difficult message in face of gathering danger. Singing. 5 acts 25 scenes 1g 23m 8w 11 interiors 9 exteriors
In Morgan, E. A.D.

Morgan, Sharon

Magic threads.

Monologue. Welsh woman reflects on memory of family history. 1w 1 setting
In One woman, one voice; ed. by H. W. Davies

Mori, Brian

Adult fiction.

Comedy. Washed-up manager of porn shop tries to help young asistant. 2 acts 2m 1 interior
In New playwrights: the best plays of 2000

Moriarty, Jay

c Archie of the Amazon. Pioneer Drama Service 1997 29p

Comedy. Motion picture producer travels to jungle to find lead for his new film. 1 act 8m 12w extras 1 setting

Moritz, Dennis

Just the boys.

Chronicles man's relationship with various women. 1 act 24 scenes 5m 4w 3 interiors
In Action; ed. by M. Algarin and L. Griffith

Morizono, Lesli-Jo

Freakish times.

Mother and daughter reunited after apocalypse. 2w 1 exterior
In Women's Project & productions; ed. by J. Miles

Morley, Jill

True confessions of a go-go girl.

Dancer's lifestyle provides her with incredible power as well as destructive dependency. Music. 2w
In Women playwrights: the best plays of 1998

Morley, Maureen. See Armstrong, D. jt. auth.

Morley, Maureen, and Willmorth, Tom

The glass mendacity; Story by Doug Armstrong, Keith Cooper, Maureen Morley, and Tom Willmorth. Broadway Play Pub. 2000 68p
ISBN 0-88145-175-4

Comedy satirizing Tennessee Williams' plays The glass menagerie, A streetcar named Desire and Cat on a hot tin roof. Prologue 2 acts 2 scenes 5m 3w

Mormons and Mormonism

Jensen, J. Two-headed
The **morning** of the Marys. Westerfield, N. G.
Moroccan travel guide. Manzi, W.
The **Morpheus** quartet. Glore, J.

Morreale, Vin Jr.

y House of the Seven Gables. Dramatic Publishing 2003 100p

Dramatization of the Hawthorne novel. Follows the demise and resurrection of once-properous Puritan family. 3 acts 8m 6w extas 1 interior

Morris, Vera

c King Midas and the touch of gold. Pioneer Drama Service 1994 42p

Dramatization of Greek myth about greed. 2 acts 4 scenes Variable cast 21 characters extras 1 setting

c Mr. Toad's mad adventures. Pioneer Drama Service 1997 44p

Based on Kenneth Grahame's The Wind in the Willows. Adventures of the eccentric Mr. Toad. 14 scenes Variable cast

Moses, Bryan Patrick

This is how it is.

College student tries to impress young lady. 3m 1w 1 interior

In Off-Off Broadway Festival plays, 22nd ser.

Moses (Biblical figure)

c Vogel, L. Wilderness wandering

Mosquito dirigible aerosol deodorant. Davidson, C. E.

The **most** massive woman wins. George, M.

The **most** perfect day. Ernst, P.

Most valuable player. Surface, M. H.

Motel story. Gersten-Vassilaros, A.

Mother and son. Esson, L.

Mother Clap's Molly house. Ravenhill, M.

Mother Goose gumshoe. Hamlett, C.

Mother Goose's golden Christmas. Wood, D.

The **mother-in-law** (Hecyra). Terence

The **mother** of modern censorship. Hartman, K.

Motherhood 2000. Kennedy, A.

Mothering Sunday. Wymark, O.

Mothers

Ayvazian, L. Deaf day

Brofsky, K. Strawberry fields

Compton, J. The big picture

Conquest, N. The widow's might

Curran, C. Sacred hearts

Dundas, H. Cannibals

Filippo, E. de. Filumena—a marriage Italian style

Kennedy, A. Motherhood 2000

Long, Q. Snapshot: scene at Mount Rushmore

Moraga, C. The hungry woman: a Mexican Medea

Mueller, L. The mothers

Parks, S.-L. In the blood

Rachilde. The transparent doll (La poupée transparente)

Wesker, A. Four portraits—of mothers

Williams, T. The glass menagerie

Wilner, S. Relative strangers

The **mothers**. Mueller, L.

Mothers and daughters

Aerenson, B. Paradise Island

Alfaro, L. Bitter homes and gardens

Anderson, J. Defying gravity

Blakeman, H. Caravan

Brown, B. It's okay, honey

Cahill, L. Home

Canino, F. The Angelina project

Carr, M. By the Bog of Cats. . .

Carr, M. Low in the dark

Champagne, L. Coaticook

Crow, A. G. A roomful of men

De Angelis, A. Hush

De Angelis, A. Ironmistress

De Matteo, D. The heart transplant

Fricker, G. Buttonholes in silk

García Lorca, F. The house of Bernarda Alba

Gasteazoro, E. Amor de mis amores

Gomolvilas, P. Donut holes in orbit

Greenberg, R. The American plan

Hare, D. Amy's view

Hedges, P. Good as new

Henley, B. The debutante ball

Humbertson, L. L. The nature of things

Leonard, H. Love in the title

LeRoy, G. Not waving--

MacIvor, D. Marion Bridge

Mann, S. The house of Bernarda Alba

Manno, K. The miracles of May

McDonagh, M. The beauty queen of Leenane

Morizono, L.-J. Freakish times

Murray, P. Salt

Murray-Smith, J. Love child

Oates, J. C. Bad girls

Parker, Matt. Celaine

Radano, L.-M. Bright angel

Raznovich, D. MaTRIX, inc. (Casa matriz)

Motion pictures—*Continued*

Wood, C. Veterans; or, Hairs in the gates of Hellespont

Mouawad, Wajdi

Tideline (Littoral); translated from the French by Shelley Tepperman. Playwrights Canada 1999 166p
ISBN 0-88754-633-1
Drama about fathers and sons. Man seeks place to lay father to rest. 52 scenes 6m 2w extras

Wedding day at the Cro-Magnons' (Journee de noces chez les Cro-Magnons); translated from the French by Shelley Tepperman. Playwrights Canada 99p
ISBN 0-88754-619-6
Eccentric Lebanese family prepares for daughter's wedding while neighborhood is destroyed by bombs. 4 acts 3m 3w 1 interior

Mound-builders

Wilson, L. The mound builders
The **mound** builders. Wilson, L.

Mount Rushmore (S.D.)

Barfield, T. Snapshot: defacing patriotic property
Jensen, J. Snapshot: on Lincoln's head
Lindsay-Abaire, D. Snapshot: history lesson
Long, Q. Snapshot: scene at Mount Rushmore
Margolin, D. Snapshot: rock scissors paper
Wright, C. Snapshot: a quick tour of the monument
Wright, C. Snapshot: bomb squad

Mountaineering

Mastrosimone, W. Precipice
The **mountains** look different. MacLiammóir, M.

Mourning

Steele, D. The way to Miami
Mourning dove. Sher, E.
Mouse. Martini, C.
A **movie** star has to star in black and white. Kennedy, A.
Moving pictures. Pollock, S.

Mowatt, Anna Cora

Fashion; or, Life in New York.
Satire on 19th century New York society. Background music. Prologue 5 acts 8 scenes epilogue 8m 5w extras 6 interiors
In Nineteenth century American plays; ed. by M. Matlaw

Mozart, Wolfgang Amadeus, 1756-1791
about

Ardito, C. Da Ponte's last stand
Pushkin, A. Mozart and Salieri
c Surface, M. H. Prodigy
Wilder, T. Mozart and the gray steward
Mozart and Salieri. Pushkin, A.
Mozart and the gray steward. Wilder, T.
Mpls., St. Paul. Jordan, J.
Mr. Bundy. Martin, J.
Mr. Peters' connections. Miller, A.
Mr. Toad's mad adventures. Morris, V.
Mr. Universe. Grimsley, J.
Mr Wonderful. Robson, J.
Mrs. Sorken. Durang, C.
Mrs. Warren's profession. Shaw, B.

Mtshali, Thulani S.

Weemen.
Woman with drunken, abusive husband supports family by secretly running a candy store. After showdown husband changes his ways. 1 act 12 scenes 2m 3w settings
In Black South African women; ed. by K. A. Perkins

Mueller, Lavonne

The confession of many strangers.
Monologue by pilot of the Enola Gay. 1m extras 1 interior
In The Best American Short plays, 1997-1998

The mothers. Applause 2001 88p
ISBN 1-55783-328-1
Political drama set in Argentina between 1952-1976. Two mothers attempt to locate missing children under cruel regime. 1 act 2m 2w 1 setting

Voices from September 11th. Applause 2002 87p
ISBN 1-55783-590-X
Series of monologues dealing with the trauma and shocking results from September 11, 2001 terrorist attacks. 12 scenes 5m 7w

Mühsam, Erich

Thunderation! (Alle Wetter!); folk play with song and dance (Volksstrück mit Gesang und Tanz); translated and edited by David A. Shepherd. Bucknell Univ. Press 2001 289p

ISBN 0-8387-5416-3

When farm workers discover a way of controlling the weather, the government takes charge and messes up the harmonious cycles of nature. Leftist satire from Weimar Germany. Bilingual edition. Music, singing, dancing. 3 acts 3 scenes epilogue 22m 7w extras settings

Mulatto: a tragedy of the Deep South. Hughes, L.

Müller, Heiner

The correction.

Drama about contradictions caused by the political demand for total cooperation among classes. Variable cast

In Müller, H. A Heiner Müller reader

Germania 3 ghosts at dead man.

Grotesgue depiction of history of German militarism. Variable cast

In Müller, H. A Heiner Müller Reader

Heracles 5.

Satire about humankind's craving for heroes. 3m extras 1 setting

In Müller, H. A Heiner Müller Reader

Mullins, Brighde

Click.

Man makes call from rehabs center. 1m 1w 1 setting

In Humana Festival 2001

Munich (Germany)

Wedekind, F. The Marquis of Keith

Murder

Alexander, R. A preface to the alien garden

Arden of Faversham. Arden of Faversham

Ayckbourn, A. It could be any one of us

Beattie, A. The story of Peter Grimes

Bell, N. McTeague: a tale of San Francisco

Bitterman, S. The job

Body, J. J. The Indian draft spirit

Brett, S. Silhouette

Brofsky, K. Strawberry fields

Bullock, M. Sokotra

Canino, F. The Angelina project

Carmichael, F. Murder-go-round

Chambers, R. Dirt

Chiasson, H. Cape Enrage

Cleveland, R. Jerry and Tom

Cohen, D. J. No way to treat a lady

Cook, P. Ax of murder

Cook, P. Who's dying to be a millionaire?

Cooper, C. L. Sentences and words

Davis, T. Everybody's Ruby

Dyer, C. R. Time, murderer, please

Ehn, E. Contemplacion (Mary and Martha)

Fennessy, A. Chilling and killing my Annabel Lee

Flewitt, L. Is there anybody there?

y Francoeur, B. Oh, horrors! It's murder!

Fulford, R. W. Steel kiss

Glaspell, S. Trifles

Goldberg, J. The hologram theory

Goyette, A. Marc and Marie

y Grimsley, J. A bird of prey

Harrison, N. Whodidit?

Horovitz, I. Alfred the Great

Iizuka, N. Skin

Ives, D. The mystery at Twicknam Vicarage

Janes, H. The perfect murder

Kash, M. A party to murder

Kaufman, M. The Laramie Project

Kennedy, A. Ohio State murders

LaVohn, R. W. Murder at the banquet

Lee, C. Carry the tiger to the mountain

Letts, T. Killer Joe

Levy, D. Macbeth—false memories

Lloyd, M. Dead certain

Logan, J. Hauptmann

Logan, J. Never the sinner

Long, Q. The joy of going somewhere definite

Manktelow, B. Curtain up on murder

Matthews, S. Who wins

Mayne, R. Red turf

McConnell, J. Death is catching

Middleton, T. The changeling

Milligan, J. Men in suits

Monge-Rafuls, P. R. Trash

Neilson, A. Normal

Nigro, D. The dead wife

Murder—*Continued*

Nigro, D. Tainted justice

Norton-Taylor, R. The colour of justice

Oates, J. C. Homesick

Orton, J. Loot

Pollock, A. The death of cool

Robbins, N. Tiptoe through the tombstones

Santander, F. Mexico, USA

Schnitzler, A. The green cockatoo

Sirera, R. The audition

Sodaro, C. Murder by the book

Sodaro, C. Who poisoned his meatball?

Sondheim, S. Sweeney Todd

Sophocles. Electra

St. John, B. The plot, like gravy, thickens

St. John, B. The reunion

Stern, N. Murder at Cafe Noir

Sutton, M. Over my dead body

Torres, J. Better half dead

Vinaver, M. The television programme

Vogel, P. Hot'n' throbbing

Walker, G. F. Adult entertainment

Walker, G. F. The art of war

Walker, G. F. The end of civilization

Walker, G. F. Filthy rich

Wallace, N. In the heart of America

Warner, C. Strangers on a train

Wilson, L. Book of days

Wilson, S. The soul of the white ant

Wiltse, D. Temporary

Wiltse, D. To wit and to whom

Woldin, J. Murder in Baker Street

Murder at Cafe Noir. Stern, N.

Murder at the banquet. LaVohn, R. W.

Murder by the book. Sodaro, C.

Murder can be habit-forming. St. John, B.

Murder-go-round. Carmichael, F.

Murder in Baker Street. Woldin, J.

Murderer, hope of women. Kokoschka, O.

Murfitt, Mary, and Howie, Betsy

Cowgirls; conceived by Mary Murfitt;
book by Betsy Howie; music and lyrics by Mary Murfitt. Dramatists 1999
59p

ISBN 0-8222-1573-X   LC 00-511461

Musical comedy set in small Kansas town.
Woman has twenty-four hours to save father's
country-western saloon from foreclosure. Music,
singing. 2 acts 6w 1 interior

Murphy, Colleen

Beating heart cadaver. Playwrights
Canada 1999 83p

ISBN 0-88754-567-X   LC 00-304936

Grief counselor helps paralyzed man and wife
cope with loss of young daughter in car accident.
12 scenes 2m 4w 1 setting

Murphy, Gregory

The countess. Dramatists 2000 69p

ISBN 0-8222-1736-8

Love triangle between John Ruskin, his wife,
and artist John Everett Millais. Prologue 2 acts 15
scenes epilogue 4m 3w extras 4 interiors

Murphy, Lee

Catch a falling star; a comedy. French
1999 96p

ISBN 0-573-69592-X   LC 99-475992

Comedy. Young women returns home to Dewey,
Texas, to reveal to her parents that she is a recovering drug addict and ex-porno star, before these
secrets appear in People magazine. 2 acts 7 scenes
2m 4w setting

Murray, Peta

Salt. Currency Press 2001 84p

ISBN 0-86819-640-1

Set in various kitchens and shifting between past
and present, the play explores the relationship between a gourmet cook and her glamorous, un-
domestic mother. Prologue 5 scenes 1m 2w 1 setting

Murray, Stephen

y Inspector Incognito and the Kansas City
Kid; book by Tim Kelly; music and
lyrics by Stephen Murray. Pioneer
Drama Service 1999 32p

Musical comedy suggested by Gogol's The Inspector General, set in 1880s Arizona Territory.
Town run by family of incompetents. 2 acts 8m
12w extras 1 interior

Murray, Stephen—*Continued*

Rocky of the rainforest; book by Jay Moriarty; music and lyrics by Stephen Murray. Pioneer Drama Service 2000 36p

Musical version of Jay Moriarty's Archie of the Amazon. Film producer searches for jungle man to star in next film. 9 scenes 8m 12w extras 1 exterior

Tales of terror from Nightmare High School; book by Patrick Rainville Dorn; music and Lyrics by Stephen Murray. Pioneer Drama Service 1998 46p

Musical. High school students confronted by their worst nightmares. 2 acts 5 scenes 7m 7w extras 1 interior

y This old house; book by Tim Kelly; music and lyrics by Stephen Murray. Pioneer Drama Service 1998 68p

Musical comedy about rooming house full of rambunctious college students. 2 acts 3 scenes 10m 20w extras 1 interior

y A twist of the tongue; book by Cynthia Davies and Steven Fendrich; music and lyrics by Stephen Murray. Pioneer Drama Service 2001 47p

Musical version of Tongue twisted by Cynthia Davies and Stephen Fendrich. High school competes in tongue-twisting tournament. 1 act 5 scenes 9m 18w 1 interior

Murray, T. C.

Appendix two: illumination.

Young Irish man destined for career in family firm discovers his vocation to be Trappist monk. 2 acts 3 scenes 5m 3w 1 interior

In Murray, T. C. Selected plays of T. C. Murray

Autumn fire.

Drama set in rural Ireland. Widower marries young woman and after becoming crippled watches as she falls in love with his son. 3 acts 4m 4w 2 interiors

In Murray, T. C. Selected plays of T. C. Murray

Birthright.

Domestic tragedy. Two brothers driven to violent hatred of each other by elderly father. 2 acts 4m 1w 1 interior

In Murray, T. C. Selected plays of T. C. Murray

The briery gap.

Set in rural Ireland. Pregnant unmarried girl hears woman in like condition cruelly denounced by local priest. 1 act 2m 1w 1 exterior

In Murray, T. C. Selected plays of T. C. Murray

Maurice Harte.

Young Irishman is driven mad by family's insistence that he become a priest. 2 acts 4m 2w extras 1 interior

In Murray, T. C. Selected plays of T. C. Murray

The pipe in the fields.

Priest confirms young Irish farmboy's calling as artist. Music, dance. 1 act 3m 2w extras 1 interior

In Murray, T. C. Selected plays of T. C. Murray

Sovereign love.

Comedy originally produced under title The wheel of fortune. Satirical portrayal of arranged marriages and power of money to over-ride feeling. 1 act 6m 3w 1 interior

In Murray, T. C. Selected plays of T. C. Murray

Murray-Smith, Joanna

Love child. Currency Press 1998 44p
  ISBN 0-86819-546-4

Drama explores feelings of young woman seeking natural mother. 2w 1 interior

Nightfall. Currency Press 1999 48p
  ISBN 0-86819-591-X   LC 00-304965

Upper middle class suburban couples' lives unravel when visitor forces them to face reason their teenage daughter ran away seven years ago. 1m 2w 1 setting

Muschell, David

Amelia, once more. Pioneer Drama Service 2000 17p

Satirical drama exploring tension between actress and the character she portrays. 1 act 2m 2w 1 interior

Museums

y Francoeur, B. Oh, horrors! It's murder!
  Gilroy, F. D. Contact with the enemy
  Hunt, L. A night under canvas
  Lipkin, D. Pithecus
  Long, Q. The Sixth Floor museum
  Norman, M. Loving Daniel Boone
  Reitz, D. Divulgence at Damarak 18

Musicals—*Continued*

c Lavender, W. The invisible people

Liebman, S. The Tale of Jemina Puddle-Duck

Liebman, S. The tale of the Mandarin ducks

MacDonald, A. Chairmaker: the musical

Magee, R. The green heart

Marowitz, C. Quack

c McNeff, S. Tom Kitten and his friends

Miller, C. The Canterville ghost

Mitchell, J. C. Hedwig and the angry inch

Mühsam, E. Thunderation! (Alle Wetter!)

Murfitt, M. Cowgirls

y Murray, S. Inspector Incognito and the Kansas City Kid

Murray, S. Rocky of the rainforest

y Murray, S. This old house

y Murray, S. A twist of the tongue

Nassif, R. L. Honky-tonk highway

Norman, M. Dracula

Norman, M. Emily

Norman, M. Larry's party

Paolucci, A. In the green room

Paterson, D. L. The great Gilly Hopkins

Pattison, J. A word from our sponsor

Perkins, D. Pandemonium! (a Greek myth-adventure)

y Perkins, D. Shake, ripple & roll

Porter, C. Nymph errant

Poskitt, K. Nell's belles

Quilter, P. Boyband

Ray, C. Sanders family Christmas

c Reiser, D. The real story of Little Red Riding Hood

Rodgers, R. Flower drum song

c Roman, J. Papa's angels: a Christmas story

c Rosenberg, N. The gifts of Obidiah Oak

Ross, B. Little by little

Russell, W. Blood brothers

Schalchlin, S. The last session

c Simmonds, R. N. The Shamrock road

Simpson, B. King Mackerel & the blues are running

c Snyder, G. A. Johnny Appleseed

c Snyder, G. A. Red Riding Hood

Sondheim, S. Follies

Sondheim, S. A funny thing happened on the way to the forum

Sondheim, S. A little night music

Sondheim, S. Sunday in the park with George

Sondheim, S. Sweeney Todd

Stern, N. Murder at Cafe Noir

Stolz, T. Mahalia

Strachan, Keith. Large as life

Swingtime Canteen

c Swortzell, L. A partridge in a pear tree

Taylor, R. It ain't nothin' but the blues

c Toksvig, J. The curious quest for the sandman's sand

Valcq, J. The Spitfire Grill

Valcq, J. Zombies from the beyond

Valenti, M. Bashville in love

Valenti, M. Quack

Willmott, Phil. Around the world in eighty days

c Wood, D. The gingerbread man

c Wood, D. The ideal gnome expedition

c Wood, D. More adventures of Noddy

c Wood, D. Mother Goose's golden Christmas

c Wood, D. The see-saw tree

y Woolf, W. King Artie and the Knights of the Rad Table

Yazbek, D. The full Monty

Musicians

Andersen, D. R. Everywhere

Blais, M.-C. Ghost of a voice

Bogart, A. Score

Dobrish, J. Orpheus and Eurydice

Linney, R. Patronage

Mayer, O. Ragged time

Mayne, R. The turn of the road

c McCullough, L. E. Di goldineh medineh (The golden land)

McLeish, K. Orpheus

Milligan, J. Waiting for Ringo

Nassif, R. L. Honky-tonk highway

Rapp, A. Finer noble gases

Raznovich, D. Disconcerted (El disconcierto)

Silverstein, S. The trio

Smith, C. The Sutherland

c Surface, M. H. Prodigy

Muslims

Joshi, A. A shaft of sunlight

Mystery—*Continued*

y Sodaro, C. Hound of the Clackervilles

Sodaro, C. Murder by the book

y Sodaro, C. Phantom of the campfire

Sodaro, C. Who poisoned his meatball?

St. John, B. Murder can be habit-forming

St. John, B. The plot, like gravy, thickens

St. John, B. You could die laughing!

Stern, N. Murder at Cafe Noir

Stockwell, R. Killing time

Sutton, M. Over my dead body

Taylor, R. Love poem #98

Thomas, R. Trap for a lonely man

Walker, G. F. Gossip

Whitemore, H. Disposing of the body

Williams, S. Kiss of death

Wilson, L. Book of days

Mystery at Shady Acres. Davis, M. R.

The **mystery** at Twicknam Vicarage. Ives, D.

The **mystery** of attraction. Meyer, M.

The **mystery** of Irma Vep. Ludlam, C.

The **myth** of Demeter and Persephone; or, The origin of the seasons. Thistle, L.

The **myth** of Orpheus and Eurydice; or, Descent into the underworld. Thistle, L.

Mythology, Aztec

Moraga, C. The hungry woman: a Mexican Medea

Mythology, Celtic

c McCullough, L. E. Fionn in search of his youth

Mythology, Chinese

c McCullough, L. E. Tshai the brickmaker

Mythology, Egyptian

c McCullough, L. E. The throne of Osiris

Mythology, Greek

Aeschylus. Agamemnon

Aeschylus. The Eumenides

Aeschylus. Prometheus bound

Aeschylus. The suppliants

c Art, S. S. The cotton blend horse

c Barchers, S. I. Aeolus and the winds

c Barchers, S. I. Ariadne

c Barchers, S. I. Arion and his harp

c Barchers, S. I. Artemis and Niobe

c Barchers, S. I. Atalanta

c Barchers, S. I. Athena

c Barchers, S. I. Daedalus and Icarus

c Barchers, S. I. Demeter and Persephone

c Barchers, S. I. Deucalion and Pyrrha

c Barchers, S. I. Dionysus

c Barchers, S. I. Eos, Selene, and Helios

c Barchers, S. I. Eros and Psyche

c Barchers, S. I. Helen

c Barchers, S. I. Heracles

c Barchers, S. I. Hermes

c Barchers, S. I. King Midas

c Barchers, S. I. Leto

c Barchers, S. I. Melampus

c Barchers, S. I. Oedipus

c Barchers, S. I. Orpheus and Eurydice

c Barchers, S. I. Pan

c Barchers, S. I. Perseus

c Barchers, S. I. Prometheus and Pandora

c Barchers, S. I. Sisyphus

c Barchers, S. I. Zeus and Hera

Euripides. Alcestis

Euripides. The Alcestis of Euripides

Euripides. Alkestis

Euripides. Bacchae

Euripides. Children of Heracles

Euripides. Cyclops

Euripides. Daughters of Troy

Euripides. Electra

Euripides. Hecuba

Euripides. Helen

Euripides. Hippolytus

Euripides. Ion

Euripides. Iphigenia among the Taurians

Euripides. Iphigenia at Aulis

Euripides. Iphigenia in Tauris

Euripides. The madness of Heracles

Euripides. Medea

Euripides. Orestes

Euripides. The Phoenician women

Euripides. The Trojan women

c Hayes, S. The pomegranate seeds

Hughes, T. Euripides' Alcestis

Juana Inés de la Cruz. The divine Narcissus (El divino Narciso)

c McBride-Smith, B. Arachne and Athena

c McBride-Smith, B. Atalanta

c McBride-Smith, B. Bill Erophon and his horse Peggy Sue

c McBride-Smith, B. The contest for Athens

Mythology, Greek—*Continued*

c McBride-Smith, B. Demeter and Persephone

c McBride-Smith, B. King Midas

c McBride-Smith, B. The twelve labors of Hercules

c McCullough, L. E. The flight of Icarus

c McCullough, L. E. King Midas and the golden touch

Moraga, C. The hungry woman: a Mexican Medea

c Morris, V. King Midas and the touch of gold

Perkins, D. Pandemonium! (a Greek myth-adventure)

y Reader, C. The Oedipus plays

Sophocles. Aias

Sophocles. Ajax

Sophocles. Antigone

Sophocles. Electra

Sophocles. Elektra

Sophocles. King Oedipus

Sophocles. Oedipus at Colonus

Sophocles. Oedipus at Kolonos

Sophocles. Philoctetes

Sophocles. Philoktetes

Sophocles. The women of Trachis

c Thistle, L. The labors of Hercules

c Thistle, L. The myth of Demeter and Persephone; or, The origin of the seasons

c Thistle, L. The myth of Orpheus and Eurydice; or, Descent into the underworld

Wertenbaker, T. The love of the nightingale

Wilder, T. The Alcestiad

Wilder, T. The drunken sisters

Wilder, T. Proserpina and the devil: a play for marionettes

Mythology, Indian

Karnad, G. The fire and the rain

c McCullough, L. E. The Monkey King

Panikkar, K. N. Aramba Chekkan

Mythology, Mayan

Moraga, C. Heart of the earth: a Popol Vuh story

Mythology, Mexican

c McCullough, L. E. How Quentzalcoatl found the sun

Mythology, Native American

c McCullough, L. E. Why bears no longer talk

Mythology, Norse

c McCullough, L. E. Freya's golden necklace

Mythology, Sumerian

c McCullough, L. E. Gilgamesh and the rose of eternal youth

Mythology, West African

c McCullough, L. E. When a river cries: the myth of Oba and Oshun

Mythology, Yoruban

Bandele, 'Biyi. Aphra Behn's Oroonoko

Osofisan, F. Esu and the vagabond minstrels

N

Naaman (Biblical figure)

c Vogel, L. Nay, nay, Naaman

Nabokov's gloves. Moffat, P.

Nag pou wahine. Grace-Smith, B.

Nagy, Phyllis

Never land. Methuen 1988 103p

ISBN 0-413-70140-9

Set in a small French village, this play is an exploration of a singular French family whose one dream is to settle in England. 3 acts 7 scenes 4m 3w 1 setting

The talented Mr. Ripley. Methuen 1999 100p

ISBN 0-413-73320-7

Adapted from Patricia Highsmith's novel, it explores the mind of an intelligent, suave, and charming psychopath whose amorality is at the center of a plot about duplicity and murder. 2 acts 5m 2w 1 setting

Naidoo, Muthal

Flight from the Mahabarath.

The women of the Mahabarata, an epic of ancient India, escape from the text to create their own stories, examining preconceptions about men and women in the process. Singing, dancing. 1 act 2m 9w extras 1 setting

In Black South African women; ed. by K. A. Perkins

Naked. Pirandello, L.

Naked breath. Miller, T.

Naming the unnamed: the strange saga of Amerigo Vespucci. McCullough, L. E.

Nanus, Susan

The survivor. French 2002 75p

ISBN 0-573-62939-0

Drama based on teenagers in Warsaw, Poland, ghetto during World War II, who resist Nazis and form nucleus of Warsaw ghetto uprising. 2 acts 9m 3w 1 setting

Naomi (Biblical figure)

c McCullough, L. E. Ruth and Naomi: the healing power of friendship

c Vogel, L. Ruth

Napier, Edward

The English teachers. Dramatists 2000 69p

ISBN 0-8222-1723-6

Serio-comic drama set in 1960 West Virginia about two sisters, both teachers, with wildly divergent interests and tastes. 2 acts 16 scenes 1m 5w 1 setting

Gone missing.

Mother's death brings estranged sisters together. 1m 4w

In HB Playwrights short play festival 2000

Naples (Italy)

Filippo, E. de. Christmas in Naples

Filippo, E. de. Filumena—a marriage Italian style

Filippo, E. de. Naples gets rich

Santanelli, M. Emergency exit

Naples gets rich. Filippo, E. de

Nascuntur poetae . . . Wilder, T.

Nassar, Mark

The mayor's limo. French (London) 2003 103p

ISBN 0-573-62894-7

Tragic comedy about frustrated police in East Village police station who arrest homeless man for urinating on mayor's limousine. 2 acts 4 scenes 7m 3w 1 setting

Nassif, Robert Lindsey

Honky-tonk highway; book by Richard Berg; music, lyrics and additional dialogue by Robert Lindsey Nassif. French 1999 78p

ISBN 0-573-62649-9

The meteoric career of a country-and-western singer-songwriter, as reflected in the music performed at a memorial concert by his reunited band. Music, singing, dancing. 2 acts 4m 1w 1 interior 1 setting

National socialism

De Boer, L. The Buddha of Ceylon

Horváth, Ö. von. The Italian evening

Horváth, Ö. von. Tales from the Vienna woods

Nigro, D. Wolfsbane

Pascal, J. Theresa

Sherman, M. Bent

The **Nativity**. Harrison, T.

Nativity. Whelan, P., and Alexander, B.

Natural life. Bower, H.

Nature

Mühsam, E. Thunderation! (Alle Wetter!)

The **nature** of things. Humbertson, L. L.

Nay, nay, Naaman. Vogel, L.

Ndlovu, Duma

Sheila's day.

Play draws parallels between America in the last days of segregation and South Africa as apartheid began to crumble: racial oppression, protests, and police brutality. English and Zulu. Music, singing. 1 act 10 scenes 12w settings

In Black South African women; ed. by K. A. Perkins

Nebraska

Wiltse, D. Temporary

Necessary targets. Ensler, E.

The **necklace**. Barchers, S. I., and Kroll, J. L.

The **Negro** of Peter the Great. Brown, C.

Neighbor Jackwood. Trowbridge, J. T.

Neighbors

Firth, T. The safari party

Graziano, D. Acorn

Grimsley, J. The borderland

Jensen, J. Old wives tale

Martin, J. Mr. Bundy

Neighbors—*Continued*

Martini, C. Conversations with my neighbour's pit bull

Martini, C. House of glass

The **neighbours**. Vinaver, M.

Neil Simon's 45 seconds from Broadway. Simon, N.

Neil Simon's proposals. Simon, N.

Neilson, Anthony

The censor.

Encounters between a male censor and a female filmmaker who wants him to consider pornography as a liberating art-form. 1 act 14 scenes 1m 1w 1 interior

In Neilson, A. Plays: 1

The night before Christmas.

Black comedy. Two warehousemen and a tart have tied up an intruder who claims to be one of Santa's elves. 1 act 3m 1w 1 interior

In Neilson, A. Plays: 1

Normal.

Lawyer appointed to defend a serial killer in Weimar Germany becomes fascinated by his monstrous client. 1 act 30 scenes 2m 1w settings

In Neilson, A. Plays: 1

Penetrator.

Two horny guys who share an apartment must cope with a very scary visitor: a childhood friend who is now a homophobic paranoid. Singing, dancing. 1 act 6 scenes 3m 1 interior

In Neilson, A. Plays: 1

Year of the family.

Black comedy. Obsessive attempts to recover and/or punish absent parents finally create a parody-family. 2 acts 27 scenes 3m 2w settings

In Neilson, A. Plays: 1

Neipris, Janet

The agreement.

Contemporary divorce agreement is hustled through by lawyers, while couple has second thoughts. 6 scenes 4m 3w

In Neipris, J. Plays

Almost in Vegas.

Dark comedy about women's friendships and American icons. Fans gather in Las Vegas for anticipated performance by Frank Sinatra. 2 scenes 2m 2w 1 interior

In Neipris, J. Plays

A small delegation.

Drama about group of American teachers in China during Summer of 1988. 2 acts 25 scenes 5m 3w settings

In Neipris, J. Plays

—Same

In Women playwrights: the best plays of 1999

Nell's belles. Poskitt, K.

Nelson, Anne

The guys. Dramatists 2003

ISBN 0-8222-1902-6

Based on a true story, the play centers around an editor and her relations with the fire captain who contacts her to help him with the eulogies he must write for the memorials of his men who died on September 11th. Music. 1m 1w 1 interior setting

Nelson, Greg

Speak. Playwrights Canada 1998 94p

ISBN 0-88754-566-1   LC 00-304700

Social comedy about a Canadian couple whose young marriage is floundering thanks to provincial politics. 11 scenes 2m 1w 1 setting

—Same

In Short spells: scenes & monologues; ed. by V. Shantz

Spirit. Coteau Bks. 1998 111p

ISBN 1-55050-126-7

Drama about the spiritual community, the Doukhobors, and their leader in Russia and Canada. 2 acts 23 scenes 6m 2w settings

Nelson, Jennifer L.

Somebody call 911.

Young woman abandoned by her boyfriend takes out her anger on their child. Variable cast 3 characters

In Humana Festival 2001

Nelson, Richard

An American comedy.

Comedy set during transatlantic voyage. Half of popular playwriting team embraces communism and tries to escape demands of partner and agent. 3 acts 7m 2w 1 interior

In Nelson, R. Plays by Richard Nelson, early plays volume 3

Nelson, Richard—*Continued*

Bal.

Experimental play. Destructive young man manipulates those around him and causes two suicides. 10 scenes 9m 5w settings

In Nelson, R. Plays by Richard Nelson, early plays volume 2

Conjuring an event.

Experimental play. Reporter believes he can make things happen from sheer will power. 2 acts 1m 5w 2 interiors

In Nelson, R. Plays by Richard Nelson, early plays volume 1

The general from America.

Historical drama about Benedict Arnold. 12m 5w

In Madame Melville and The general from America

Jitterbugging: scenes of sex in a new society.

Freely adapted from Schnitzler's La ronde. Cycle of brief sexual encounters in 1947 seaside New England town. 2m 2w settings

In Nelson R. Plays by Richard Nelson, early plays volume 3

Jungle coup.

Drama set in African jungle about how journalists can remake history with reporting that virtuality obliterates the truth. 8 scenes 3m 1 setting

In Nelson, R. Plays by Richard Nelson, early plays volume 1

The killing of Yablonski: scenes of involvement in a current event.

Reporter covers murder of labor leader Jock Yablonski. Prologue 5 scenes 10m 5w

In Nelson, R. Plays by Richard Nelson, early plays volume 1

Madame Melville.

Drama set in 1966 Paris about fifteen-year-old American boy and his beautiful teacher. 2m 2w 1 interior

In Madame Melville and The general from America

The return of Pinocchio.

Pinocchio returns home from fame in Hollywood. Old friends quickly crush idealism. 11 scenes 5m 4w 3 interiors 3 exteriors

In Nelson, R. Plays by Richard Nelson, early plays volume 2

Rip Van Winkle; or, "The works".

Rip Van Winkle legend, frames, drama about battles between men and women, parent and child, industry and agriculture. 3 parts Large mixed cast

In Nelson, R. Plays by Richard Nelson, early plays volume 3

Scooping.

Monologue. Reporter becomes the story. 1m 1 setting

In Nelson, R. Plays by Richard Nelson, early plays volume 1

The Vienna notes.

Satire. Politician determined to live his life so that it can become a play. 7 scenes 2m 2w

In Nelson, R. Plays by Richard Nelson, early plays volume 2

Nelson, Tim Blake

The grey zone. Dramatists 1998 53p

    ISBN 0-8222-1574-8   LC 98-146947

Drama about Hunganian Jews in Auschwitz. Tricked into assisting in the killing of other Jewish prisoners, they plan to blow up the crematoria, but are caught and are all put to death except for one. 2 acts 11 scenes 7m 1w 1 setting

Netherlands

History—17th century

Warner, F. Rembrandt's mirror

Colonies

De Boer, L. The Buddha of Ceylon

Netto, Leslie

Maria. Minerva Press 1998 171p

    ISBN 1-86106-922-7

Based on a real-life custody battle in Singapore, over a European child adopted by an Asian. 5 acts 21 scenes Epilogue Variable cast 37 characters extras

Nevada

Ackermann, J. Off the map

Never the sinner. Logan, J.

New boy. Labey, R.

A **new** brain. Finn, W.

New Brunswick

Goupil, L. Dark owl; or, The renegade angel

Hannah, D. Fathers and sons

Hannah, D. Rubber Dolly

Hannah, D. Running far back

A **new** life. Jacker, C.

New morning. Hughes, D.

New Orleans (La.)

Grimsley, J. Mr. Universe
Williams, T. A streetcar named Desire
Williams, T. Vieux Carré
The **new** trial. Weiss, P.
New Year's Eve and Kibbutz. Margulies,
D.

New York (N.Y.)

Anderson, Roger. Shine!: the Horatio Alger musical
Bell, N. Ragged Dick
Carmichael, F. Decisions, decisions
Crimp, M. The treatment
Culture Clash (Group). Nuyorican stories
Gilman, R. Boy gets girl
Guare, J. New York actor
Kane, H. Snapshot: monument
Kramer, L. The normal heart
Kushner, T. East coast ode to Howard Jarvis: a little teleplay in tiny monologues
Rebeck, T. Loose knit
Van Itallie, J.-C. Bag lady
Wasserstein, W. Boy meets girl

Bronx

Gilroy, F. D. Any given day
Goluboff, B. In-betweens

Brooklyn

Allen, W. The floating light bulb
Posner, A. The chosen
Pugliese, F. Aven'u boys

Greenwich Village

Lonergan, K. The Waverly Gallery
Nigro, D. Beast with two backs

Harlem

Cleage, P. Blues for an Alabama sky
Redwood, J. H. The old settler

Lower East Side

Leivick, H. Shop

Manhattan

Dozer, D. The milling crowd dies
Gardner, H. I'm not Rappaport
Gilroy, F. D. A way with words
Gurney, A. R. The golden age
Hwang, D. H. Trying to find Chinatown
Kramer, S. The wall of water
Lemoine, S. Evelyn Strange

Lindsay-Abaire, D. A devil inside
Mode, B. Fully committed
Powell, D. Jig saw
Powell, D. Walking down Broadway
Powell, D. Women at four o'clock
Tait, L. East play
Weiner, W. Give me shelter
New York actor. Guare, J.
New York, New York. Streeruwitz, M.

New Zealand

Grace-Smith, B. Nag pou wahine
McGee, J. A backward glance
McKee, J. Haere mai ki aotearoa

Newmeir, John H.

Babysitting Calvin. French (London) 1999
45p
ISBN 0-573-12152-4
Ten-month-old Calvin, who thinks like an adult (and is played by one), thwarts a lecher's designs on his babysitter with a series of infantile pranks but then, unfortunately, outsmarts himself. Background music. 1 act 2 scenes 2m 3w 1 interior

Semblance of madness!. French (London)
2000 34p
ISBN 0-573-03385-4   LC 2002-279015
Three women in psychiatric hospital meet for therapeutic drama lesson. Music. 1 act 3w 1 interior

Newsome, Meg

y The perfect night. Pioneer Drama Service
2001 22p
Examines conflicting emotions of both male and female teens in love. 3m 4w 1 setting

Newspapers

y Kelly, T. Stop the presses!
Walker, J. M. Tales from the Daily Tabloid

Newton, Sir Isaac, 1642-1727

about

c McCullough, L. E. Isaac Newton's poetry of the rainbow
The **next** contestant. Gilroy, F. D.
Next year in Jerusalem. McCullough, L. E.

Nichol, James W.

The stone angel. Playwrights Canada
2002 118p
ISBN 0-88754-631-5

Nichol, James W.—*Continued*

Memory play based on novel by Margaret Lawrence about 90-year-old Scots Presbyterian woman attempting to come to terms with both her past and her present. 2 acts 5m 4w 1 setting

Nicholson, William

Katherine Howard. French (London) 1999 70p

ISBN 0-573-01811-1

Drama which begins with the marriage of Anne of Cleves, Henry VIII's fourth wife, and ends with execution of his fifth wife, Katherine Howard. 2 acts 7m 4w extras 1 setting

Nick at night. Vogel, L.

Nicodemus (Biblical figure)

Vogel, L. Nick at night

Nielsen, Keith

y Hamlet. Pioneer Drama Service 2002 43p

Adaptation of Shakespeare's tragedy. Brooding Prince of Denmark sets out to avenge father's murder. 5 acts 16 scenes Variable cast 19 characters and extras

y Macbeth. Pioneer Drama Service 2002 39p

Simplified version of Shakespeare's tragedy of ambition, crime and punishment set in 11th century Scotland. 5 acts 19 scenes Variable cast 20 characters extras settings

Nielson, Kari

A true fool's folly.

Comedy about a servant who saves his brother from an angry queen. 2m 1w 1 setting

In Blast from the future; ed. by D. Yeaton

Nietzsche, Friedrich

about

Wilson, S. Darwin's flood

Nigeria

c McCullough, L. E. When a river cries: the myth of Oba and Oshun

Osofisan, F. Once upon four robbers

Soyinka, W. The strong breed

Night and day. Stoppard, T.

The **night** before Christmas. Neilson, A.

The **night** before pageant. Anderson, S. J.

The **night** before the trial. Chekhov, A. P.

A **night** divided. Pedrero, P.

A **night** in the subway. Pedrero, P.

Night light. Lazarus, J.

Night of the foolish moon. Jannuzzi, L.

Night of the living dead. Ohm, A.

The **night** Thoreau spent in jail. Lee, R. E., and Lawrence, J.

Night train to Bolina. Cruz, N.

A **night** under canvas. Hunt, L.

Night visits. Fill, S.

Nightfall. Murray-Smith, J.

Nighthawks. Rosen, L.

Nightingale, Florence, 1820-1910

about

c McCullough, L. E. "Lady of the Lamp": Florence Nightingale, founder of modern nursing

The **nightingale**. Mason, T.

Nightshade. Parker, S.

Nightswim. Jordan, J.

Nigro, Don

Armitage. French 2002 119p

ISBN 0-573-62781-9

One of the Pendragon plays. Gothic tale of Ohio family haunted by murder and madness. 2 acts 30 scenes 6m 6w 1 setting

The Babel of circular labyrinths.

Exchanges between the blind Argentinian writer Borges and a beautiful young woman, echoing Borges's work and providing an entrée into his imaginative life. 1 act 1 scene 1m 1w 1 interior

In Nigro, D. The great Gromboolian plain and other plays

Ballerinas.

Short play set backstage at a performance of Swan Lake. Three ballerinas are sinking too deeply into their roles. Music. 1 act 1 scene 3w 1 interior

In Nigro, D. The great Gromboolian plain and other plays

Beast with two backs. French 2002 85p

ISBN 0-573-62811-4

Drama set in 1920, Greenwich Village rooming house. Artist falls for actress living upstairs with philandering poet boyfriend. 2 acts 5 scenes 3m 2w 1 setting

Broadway macabre.

Monologue by ferociously cynical producer, about his career in show business. 1m 1 interior

In Nigro, D. Deflores and other plays

Nigro, Don—_Continued_

Capone.

Monologue. Ganster Al Capone reflects on his life while suffering from syphillis in nursing home. 1m 1 setting

_In_ Nigro, D. Tales from the Red Rose Inn

Childe Rowland to the dark tower came.

Monologue. Drama professor walks into a theater at night and reveals his evil dislikes. 1 interior

_In_ Nigro, D. Tales from the Red Rose Inn

Chronicles. French (London) 2003 96p

ISBN 0-573-62852-1

Tragicomedy set in Ohio mansion. Family and household crumble while father lies dying. 2 acts 10 scenes 4m 5w 1 setting

The circus animals desertion. French (London) 2002 94p

ISBN 0-573-62851-3

Tragicomedy set in 1940s about confused young woman who becomes pregnant after love affair with circus performer. 2 acts 17 scenes 3m 4w

Creatures lurking in the churchyard.

Monologue by despairing, guilt-ridden murderer. 1m 1 interior

_In_ Nigro, D. Deflores and other plays

Darkness like a dream.

Monologue. Actress invites man to performance and coffee afterwards, only to unleash her fears and anxieties. 1w 1 interior

_In_ Nigro, D. Tales from the Red Rose Inn

The dead wife.

On her wedding night a bride is haunted by the ghost of her new husband's late wife, who claims to have been murdered. 1 act 2w 1 interior

_In_ Nigro, D. The great Gromboolian plain and other plays

Deflores.

Inquisitive young woman becomes entangled with an outrageous family of con artists. Part of the author's Pendragon cycle. 4m 3w 1 exterior

_In_ Nigro, D. Deflores and other plays

Doctor Faustus.

Treatment of Faust legend. Here Mephistopheles is a woman, and Faust is damned because he cannot love. Singing. 8 scenes 2m 2w 2 interiors

_In_ Nigro, D. Deflores and other plays

Gogol.

Hallucinatory trip into mind of Russian author Nikolai Gogol. 2m 1w 1 interior

_In_ Nigro, D. Deflores and other plays

The great Gromboolian plain.

Short play set in an insane asylum, about a woman who claims to time-travel and the detective her sister has hired to ferret out her secret. Music. 1 act 1 scene 1m 2w extras 1 exterior

_In_ Nigro, D. The great Gromboolian plain and other plays

Higgs field.

Monologue. Comedy about young woman who enters a forbidden place while searching for her cat. 1w 1 interior

_In_ Nigro, D. Tales from the Red Rose Inn

Horrid massacre in Boston. French 2000 95p

ISBN 0-573-62719-3

Orphan living in a Boston inn during the American revolution meets a variety of unusual characters. 2 acts 5 scenes 4m 4w 1 interior

The Irish girl kissed in the rain.

Monologue by an actress who enchants but cannot love. 1w 1 setting

_In_ Nigro, D. Deflores and other plays

Joan of Arc in the autumn.

Monologue. Joan of Arc is alive three years after her execution. 1w 1 interior

_In_ Nigro, D. Tales from the Red Rose Inn

Laestrygonians. French (London) 2003 85p

ISBN 0-573-62882-3

Self discovery becomes the norm when Shakespearean actor attempts to prevent suicide of silent film starlet. 2 acts 28 scenes 3m 3w 1 setting

The lost girl.

Short play in which successive tourists become temporary natives. 1 act 1 scene 3w 1 exterior

_In_ Nigro, D. The great Gromboolian plain and other plays

Lucy and the mystery of the vine-encrusted mansion.

Mystery comedy about girl's alter ego who lives in a haunted house with a brother planning a murder. 2m 1w 1 interior

_In_ Nigro, D. Tales from the Red Rose Inn

Nigro, Don—*Continued*

The malefactor's bloody register.

Drama taken from 18th century crime compendium, The Newgate Calendar. Three serving girls beaten and tortured by employers. 1m 3w 1 interior

> *In* Nigro, D. Tales from the Red Rose Inn

November. French 2002 72p

ISBN 0-573-62812-2

Aunt Becky is trapped in a nursing home in east Ohio. Her life is complicated by her memories, her niece and the niece's husband, and assorted other characters. 2 acts 3m 6w Unit set

Quint and Miss Jessel at Bly.

Characters from The Turn of the Screw play out the relationship that will turn Quint and Jessel into the malevolent ghosts of James's story. 2 acts 16 scenes 2m 1w 6 interiors 4 exteriors

> *In* New playwrights: the best plays of 2000

Seance.

Set in 1875. A medium confesses to fraud but cannot convince her scientist client—or the audience. 1 act 1m 2w 1 interior

> *In* Nigro, D. The great Gromboolian plain and other plays

The sin-eater.

Story of Welsh sin-eater who, through ritual eating and drinking, takes on sins of deceased. 1m 2w 1 interior

> *In* 30 ten-minute plays for 3 actors from Actors Theatre of Louisville's National Ten-minute Play Contest

—Same

> *In* Actors Theatre of Louisville. Ten-minute plays: v4

—Same

> *In* Nigro, D. The great Gromboolian plain and other plays

Tainted justice. French 1998 77p

ISBN 0-573-62607-3

Based on a true murder mystery on Cape Breton island, Nova Scotia. Doubts haunt daughter over her father's murder. 2 acts 30 scenes 5m 3w 1 setting

Tales from the Red Rose Inn.

Romantic comedy about a woman and an inn won in a game of chance. 1m 1w 1 interior

> *In* Nigro, D. Tales from the Red Rose Inn

Things that go bump in the night.

Tragicomedy of husband who discovers wife sitting in the dark and fearing someone will rearrange the furniture. 1m 1w 1 interior

> *In* Nigro, D. Tales from the Red Rose Inn

Tristan. French (London) 2003 91p

ISBN 0-573-62952-8

Mystery about young girl who appears at aging Ohio mansion. 2 acts 21 scenes 3m 3w 1 setting

Uncle Clete's toad.

Monologue. Comedy about a man and wife who discover a huge toad in their bathroom. 1m 1 interior

> *In* Nigro, D. Tales from the Red Rose Inn

Warburton's Cook.

Comedy about famous English antiquarian's cook, who used rare Shakespeare manuscripts as pie bottoms. 1m 2w 1 interior

> *In* Nigro, D. Tales from the Red Rose Inn

Wolfsbane.

Old man's monologue reveals his horrific Nazi past. 1m 1 exterior

> *In* Nigro, D. Deflores and other plays

Wonders of the invisible world revealed.

Man swathed in bandages claims to be invisible and to have spied on servant girl in her bedroom. 1 act 1m 1w 1 interior

> *In* Nigro, D. The great Gromboolian plain and other plays

Nihilism

Brecht, B. Baal

Nijinsky, Waslaw, 1890-1950

about

Alvarez, L. Deux marriages: Romola and Nijinsky

Nil by mouth. Chapman, J.

Nina, that's something else. Vinaver, M.

Nine Armenians. Ayvazian, L.

Nitwits and numskulls: outwitting the oppressor. McCullough, L. E.

Nixon, Richard M. (Richard Milhous), 1913-1994

about

Bosakowski, P. Nixon apologizes to the nation

Nixon apologizes to the nation. Bosakowski, P.

The **No** Boys Cricket Club. Williams, R.

No crime. Goda, B.

No dogs allowed. Silverstein, S.

No love lost. Robinson, R.

No next of kin. Oates, J. C.

No regrets. Dafydd, G.

No room at the inn (Las posadas); tr. by Larry Torres.

Rhymed folk drama traditionally performed on 9 nights before Christmas. Mary and Joseph go from house to house until they find shelter; prayers follow. Bilingual edition. Music, singing. 1 scene 2m 1w extras settings

In Six nuevomexicano folk dramas for Advent season

No skronking. Silverstein, S.

No soliciting. Silverstein, S.

No vacancy. Lewis, T.

No way to treat a lady. Cohen, D. J.

Noah (Biblical figure)

c Crowther, C. Noah's ark

c McCullough, L. E. Noah's ark: falsehood and wickedness hitch a ride

Noah's ark. Crowther, C., and Crowther, M.

Noah's ark: falsehood and wickedness hitch a ride. McCullough, L. E.

Nobbs, David

Pratt of the Argus (dramatization) See Birch, M. Pratt of the Argus

Nobody dies on Friday. Brustein, R.

Nobody heard mercy. Harden, V.

Nobody's perfect. Williams, S.

Nocturne. Margulies, D.

Nocturne. Rapp, A.

Nolan, Yvette

Annie Mae's movement.

In two linked monologues, a Native American woman relives the commitment to activism that led to her rape and murder by an FBI agent. 1 scene 1m 1w 1 setting

In Short spells: scenes & monologues; ed. by V. Shantz

Noodles and peas. Hedges, P.

Noonan, John Ford

A critic and his wife. Applause Bks. 2001 95p

ISBN 1-55783-325-7

Drama critic and his wife who is a newspaper essayist embark on a war of words, and in print. 2 acts 7 scenes 1m 1w 1 setting

What drove me back to reconsidering my father.

Middle-aged female playwright wrestles with feelings toward absent father. Singing. 1m 1w 1 interior

In The Best American short plays 1998-1999

Noone, Ronan

The lepers of Baile Baiste. French 2003 85p

ISBN 0-573-62883-1

Drama about sexual abuse by priests in Ireland. 2 acts 5 scenes 8m 1 setting

Noran bang: the yellow room. Kang, M. J.

Norfolk, William

Caramba's revenge. French (London) 1998 76p

ISBN 0-573-01771-9   LC 98-232333

Dark comedy about four elderly ladies who share Violet's rented house, but when Violet dies, and her granddaughter arrives, events take an unusual turn. 2 acts 8 scenes 1m 6w 1 interior

Normal. Neilson, A.

The **normal** heart. Kramer, L.

Norman, Marek

Dracula; a chamber musical based on the novel by Bram Stoker; book and lyrics by Richard Ouzounian; music by Marek Norman. McArthur & Co. 2002 97p

ISBN 1-55278-317-0

Musical treatment of 1897 Stoker novel. Seductively evil vampire is defeated by pure love. 2 acts 19 scenes 5m 2w 8 interiors 3 exteriors

Emily; book by Richard Ouzounian; music by Marek Norman. McArthur & Co. 2000 141p

ISBN 1-55278-139-9

Orphan girl raised by strict relatives on Prince Edward Island grows up to become a writer. Musical adaptation of a trilogy of novels by L. M. Montgomery. Music, singing, dancing. 2 acts 5m 9w extras settings

Larry's party; book & lyrics by Richard Ouzounian; music by Marek Norman. McArthur & Co. 2000 157p

ISBN 1-55278-193-3

Norman, Marek—*Continued*

Musical. A landscape designer who specializes in mazes searches for a pattern in life, in vignettes covering 50 years. Based on the novel by Carol Shields. Music, singing. 2 acts 16 scenes 4m 5w settings

Norman, Marsha

140.

Inspired by Shakespeare's Sonnet 140. Daisy chain of betrayal. 1 act 5m 4w

In Love's fire

Circus Valentine.

Drama about family of circus performers. 2 acts 5m 3w 2 interiors 1 exterior

In Norman, M. Collected plays, v1

Getting out.

Young woman recently released from prison struggles to make fresh start. 2 acts 7m 5w 1 setting

In Norman, M. Collected plays, v1

The holdup.

Picaresque play set in changing West of 1914 about aging gunfighter, two young greenhorns, and former dance hall girl who has gone on to better days. 2 acts 3m 1w 1 setting

In Norman, M. Collected plays, v1

Loving Daniel Boone. French 2002 92p

ISBN 0-573-62885-8

Comedy. Cleaning woman in modern-day museum interacts with people and events on Kentucky frontier of 1778. 2 acts 7m 2w 1 setting

—Same

In Norman, M. Collected plays, v1

Sarah and Abraham.

Improvisational theater company's rehearsals for production of biblical story of Abraham and Sarah mirrors off-stage lives of cast members. 2 acts 13 scenes 4m 3w 1 setting

In Norman, M. Collected plays, v1

Third and Oak.

First produced and published as two one-act plays Third and Oak: The laundromat and Third and Oak: The pool hall. Two lonely women interact at laundromat and aging pool hall owner has tense confrontation with successful young disc jockey. 2 acts 2m 2w 2 interiors

In Norman, M. Collected plays, v1

Traveler in the dark.

Drama. Brilliant surgeon, unable to save life of his devoted nurse, struggles with loss of faith. 2 acts 1b 2m 1w 1 exterior

In Norman, M. Collected plays, v1

Trudy Blue. French 2002 85p

ISBN 0-573-62942-0

Successful female writer embarks on spiritual journey accompanied by main character of her novel, Trudy Blue. Prologue 15 scenes 4m 6w extra 1 setting

Norris, Frank

McTeague (dramatization) See Bell, N. McTeague: a tale of San Francisco

North America

Discovery and exploration

c Fredericks, A. D. An imaginary discussion

c Fredericks, A. D. Leif Eriksson discovers Vinland

Northeast local. Donaghy, T.

Northern Ireland

Devlin, A. After Easter

Mitchell, G. Trust

O'Callaghan, J. Some mother's son

Parker, S. Catchpenny twist

Reid, C. My name, shall I tell you my name

Northmen

y McClelland, J. Blood lines

Norton-Taylor, Richard

The colour of justice. Oberon Bks. 1999 143p

ISBN 1-84002-107-1

Dramatization of a British government inquiry into the murder of Stephen Lawrence (a black teenager stabbed to death by whites) and the London police's handling of the case. Based on official transcripts. 1 act 24m 7w extras 1 setting

Norway

Ibsen, H. An enemy of the people

Nose

y Roets, J. Cyrano

Nostalgia maldita: 1-900-MEXICO, a Stairmaster piece. Arizmendi, Y.

Not about nightingales. Williams, T.

Not about nightingales (condensation). Williams, T.

Not by bed alone (Un fil à la patte). Feydeau, G.

Not on this night. Jones, E. Y.

Not so dumb. Lazarus, J.

Not waving--. LeRoy, G.

The **notebook** of Trigorin. Williams, T.
Notes. Paige, J. L.
Notes on Akiba. Kushner, T.
Nothing compares to you. Lavery, B.
Nothing in the world like it. Galton, F.
Notions in motion. Dobrish, J.

Nottage, Lynn

Mud, river, stone. Dramatists 1999 63p

ISBN 0-8222-1660-4   LC 99-215187

Vacationing African-American couple and others stranded in a run-down African colonial hotel are taken hostage by angry bellhop. 2 acts 6 scenes 4m 3w 1 interior

Snapshot: becoming American.

Monologue by instructor teaching Africans how to interact smoothly with American callers, who will think they have reached corporate headquarters. Music. 1 act 1m 1 setting

In Humana Festival 2002

Nova Scotia

Boyd, G. E. Consecrated ground
Clarke, G. E. Beatrice Chancy
Lill, W. The Glace Bay Miners' Museum
MacDonald, A. Chairmaker: the musical
Nigro, D. Tainted justice
Vanhecke, I. Twelve strands of wool
November. Nigro, D.
Now a shepherd, no longer a sheep. Anderson, S. J.
Now look what you made me do. Clements, M.
Now more than ever. Huxley, A.
Now the servant's name was Malchus. Wilder, T.
Now you know. Frayn, M.

Nowra, Louis

Inside the island.

Drama set in Australia and focusing on colonialization, Aboriginal dispossession, and identity. 2 acts 14 scenes 15m 4w extras 1 setting

In Postcolonial plays; ed. by H. Gilbert

The language of the gods. Currency Press 1999 90p

ISBN 0-86819-588-X

Drama about Dutch family living in Indonesia just prior to independence. 2 acts 17 scenes 1g 6m 4w 1 setting

Nuclear power plants
Accidents
Wilson, L. Angels fall
Las **nuevas** tamaleras. Mena, A.
A **number**. Churchill, C.

Nuns

Ehn, E. The imp of simplicity (Thomas à Kempis)
St. John, B. Murder can be habit-forming

Nuremberg, Trial of Major German War Criminals, Nuremberg, Germany, 1945-1946

Mann, A. Judgment at Nuremberg

Nursemaids

Pollock, S. End dream

Nursery rhymes

c Hamlett, C. Mother Goose gumshoe
c Wood, D. Mother Goose's golden Christmas

Nurses and nursing

Handy, P. East of the sun and west of the moon
Lill, W. The occupation of Heather Rose
Maponya, M. Umongikazi (The nurse)
c McCullough, L. E. "Lady of the Lamp": Florence Nightingale, founder of modern nursing
Orton, J. The visitors
Vvedensky, A. Christmas at the Ivanovs'

Nursing homes

Nigro, D. November
White, E. N. Millennium 7
The **nutcracker** and the mouse-king. Hoffman, E. T. A.
The **Nutmeg** Princess. Keens-Douglas, R.
Nuyorican stories. Culture Clash (Group)
Nymph errant. Porter, C.

O

O.D. on paradise. Griffiths, L.

Oakes, Meredith

Faith. Oberon Bks. 1997 88p

ISBN 1-870259-80-7

Drama of soldiers fighting for a small island, and the question why they are fighting this war. 2 parts 5m 1w 1 setting

Oakland (Calif.)

Reed, I. Hubba city

Oates, Joyce Carol

The adoption.

A childless couple, who have applied to adopt a child, are summoned to a Kafkaesque agency and overwhelmed by a procession of abysmally needy orphans. 1 act Variable cast 5 characters 1 interior

In EST marathon '96: the one-act plays; ed. by M. Smith

—Same

In Oates, J. C. New plays

Bad girls.

Three teenage sisters ruin life of man who comes between them and their single mother. 2 acts 13 scenes epilogue 1m 4w 3 interiors

In Oates, J. C. New plays

Black water.

Dramatization of author's novel. Young woman drowns when senator's car goes off bridge. 2 acts 14 scenes 5m 5w 1 setting

In Oates, J. C. New plays

Duet.

Lovers dialogue. 1m 1w

In Oates, J. C. New plays

Good to know you.

Two unmarried middle-aged couples discuss childbirth. 1 act 2m 2w 1 interior

In Oates, J. C. New plays

Here I am.

Monologue. Woman recalls history of sex abuse.

In Oates, J. C. New plays

Homesick.

Drama about serial killer and his latest victim, a runaway girl. 1 act 1m 1w 1 setting

In Oates, J. C. New plays

No next of kin.

Monologue by young man abandoned by father. 1m

In Oates, J. C. New plays

The passion of Henry David Thoreau.

Historical drama set 1838-1862 in Concord, Massachusetts portrays life of influential nature writer. Prologue 2 acts 19 scenes epilogue 8m 3w extras

In Oates, J. C. New plays

Poor Bibi.

Couple murder creature of ambiguous species in their care. 1 act Variable cast 4 characters

In Oates, J. C. New plays

When I was a little girl and my mother didn't want me.

Monologue. Elderly woman recalls troubled childhood. 1w

In Oates, J. C. New plays

Obermeir, Gerlinde

San Francisco of course.

Series of short episodes depicting fate of woman whose world collapses in face of brutal, norm-setting patriarchal oppression. 10 scenes 3m 3w extras 5 interiors

In Women's words, women's work; ed. by U. H. G. Borgert

Obesity

Gillian, P. Two fat men

The **obit**. De Matteo, D.

The **oblong** box. Barchers, S. I., and Kroll, J. L.

Obolensky, Kira

Lobster Alice.

In 1946 Hollywood to create short animated sur-realist ballet, Salvador Dali spends time with ani-mator working on Alice in Wonderland. 8 scenes 3m 1w 1 interior

In Women playwrights: the best plays of 1999

O'Brien, Dan

The Last Supper restoration. French 1998 66p

ISBN 0-573-62623-5

Drama about a dying shirt designer with dream-like delusions about his art restorer father, Leonardo Da Vinci, Sigmund Freud, and Ezra Pound. Prologue 2 acts epilogue 4m 1w 1 interior

Snapshot: her first screen test.

Monologue, set during the Depression. Vaude-ville waif undresses for screen test. 1 act 1w 1 set-ting

In Humana Festival 2002

The **observatory**. Germann, G.

O'Byrne, Joe

En suite. Methuen 2002 86p

ISBN 0-413-77225-X

In Evelyn Dwyer's madcap B&B, a motley col-lection of characters is bound together by a dark secret from the past. 5 acts 3m 4w settings

O'Callaghan, Jill

Some mother's son. Currency Press 1998
   42p il
   ISBN 0-86819-573-1

Two women travellers from Australia in Northern Ireland stay at a bed and breakfast with IRA connections. 2 acts 13 scenes 2m 3w 1 interior

O'Casey, Sean

Cock-a-doodle dandy.

Farce. Two young Irish women break away from superstition and bigotry in their village. Music, singing. 3 scenes 16m 4w 1 exterior
   In O'Casey, S. Plays: one

Hall of healing.

Satrical farce. Medical care of the poor in Dublin dispensary. Music, singing. 1 act 8m 3w 1 interior
   In O'Casey, S. Plays: two

Juno and the paycock.

Political tragedy. Dublin family's struggle between Free Staters and Republicans in 1922. 3 acts 6m 4w extras 1 interior
   In O'Casey, S. Plays: one

—Same
   In O'Casey, S. Three Dublin plays

The plough and the stars.

Tragic incident in the Sinn Fein Rebellion, 1916. Singing. 4 acts 10m 5w 3 interiors 1 exterior
   In O'Casey, S. Plays: two

—Same
   In O'Casey, S. Three Dublin plays

Purple dust.

Satirical and symbolic farce. Two Englishmen attempt to revive the grace of a bygone age by restoring a Tudor house in Ireland. Singing. 3 acts 10m 3w extras 1 interior
   In O'Casey, S. Plays: two

Red roses for me.

Tragedy set in Dublin during 1913 strike. Singing. 4 acts 16m 5w 1 interior 2 exteriors
   In O'Casey, S. Plays: one

The shadow of a gunman.

Tragedy. Young Irish woman killed by Black and Tans during raid in Anglo-Irish War of 1920. 2 acts 8m 3w 1 interior
   In O'Casey, S. Plays: two

—Same
   In O'Casey, S. Three Dublin plays

The silver tassie.

Tragicomedy. Crippled Irish veteran of World War I, formerly football hero, disillusioned upon return home. Singing, dancing. 4 acts 18m 5w 3 interiors 1 exterior
   In O'Casey, S. Plays: two

Within the gates.

Symbolic exposition of human problems. Chorus. Singing. 4 scenes 14m 6w extras 1 exterior
   In O'Casey, S. Plays: one

The **occupation** of Heather Rose. Lill, W.

Ocean travel

Cabal, F. Passage
Nelson, R. An American comedy

O'Connell, Sean

Cartesian dreams. Phi-Psi Publishers 2000
   109p
   ISBN 0-9686685-0-X

Descartes attempts to teach philosophy to the passionate young queen of Sweden. An exposition and critique of the Cartesian system. Music, dancing. 2 acts 8 scenes 2m 4w 3 interiors

The **octoroon;** or, Life in Louisiana. Boucicault, D.

Odato, Allison

The profoundness of events.

Two men meet in a hospital elevator, one claustrophobic, one with AIDS, and have discussion. 2m 1 setting
   In Blast from the future; ed. by D. Yeaton

Odets, Clifford

Waiting for Lefty.

Drama of trade union corruption. 6 parts 11m 3w extras
   In Political stages; ed. by E. Mann and D. Roessel

about

Ronzoni, M. 610 Bedford Drive

O'Donnell, Darren

Over.

Dark comedy about possibilities of paranormal in ordinary lives. 1m 1w 1 setting
   In O'Donnell, D. Inoculations

O'Donnell, Darren—*Continued*

Radio Rooster says that's bad.

Story about egocentric scientist, and the paranoid and neurotic mouse residing in his mind. 1m 1 setting

In O'Donnell, D. Inoculations

White mice.

Dark comedy about two white-furred mice who came to grips over their whiteness. 2m settings

In O'Donnell, D. Inoculations

Who shot Jacques Lacan?

Drama about theories of French psychoanalyst Jacques Lacan. Prologue 11 scenes 6m 1w 1 setting

In O'Donnell, D. Inoculations

O'Donnell, Mark

Marred bliss.

Comic word play discloses how characters really feel about each other and upcoming wedding. 2m 2w 1 exterior

In 30 ten-minute plays for 4, 5 & 6 actors from Actors Theatre of Louisville's National Ten-minute Play Contest

See also Irwin, B. jt. auth.

O'Donnell, Sean

Because I want to say.

Woman recalls happy and fond memories of her best friend who dies of AIDS. 1m 1w 1 setting

In Off-Off Broadway Festival plays, 22nd ser.

Odysseus (Greek mythology)

Euripides. Rhesus

Sophocles. Aias

Sophocles. Ajax

c Thistle, L. The Odyssey

The **Odyssey**. Thistle, L.

Oedi. Orloff, R.

Oedipus (Greek mythology)

Orloff, R. Oedi

y Reader, C. The Oedipus plays

Sophocles. King Oedipus

Sophocles. Oedipus at Colonus

Sophocles. Oedipus at Kolonos

Sophocles. Oedipus the King

Sophocles. Oedipus Tyrannos

Oedipus. Barchers, S. I.

Oedipus at Colonus. Sophocles

Oedipus at Kolonos. Sophocles

Oedipus, King of Thebes. Green, M.

The **Oedipus** plays. Reader, C.

Oedipus the King. Sophocles

Oedipus Tyrannos. Sophocles

Of grapes and nuts. Armstrong, D., and others

Off the map. Ackermann, J.

Off the rack. Kemnitz, R. D., and McMaster, J.

Off to the war. Woolf, B. E.

The **offering**. Piatigorsky, A.

The **office**. Hoffower, K.

Office hours. Foster, N.

Office song. Warburton, N.

Ogden, Alan

Johnny, don't jump; a satirical comedy. French (London) 2000 33p

ISBN 0-573-12310-1   LC 2002-279012

Satirical comedy about young man contemplating suicide while sitting on the ledge of an office building. 5m 3w 1 setting

Ogilvy, Ian

A slight hangover. French (London) 2002 66p

ISBN 0-573-01964-9

A sequel to Noel Coward's Design for Living, set 50 years later. One member of Coward's menage a trois has died; the other two are enjoying a quietly querulous old age when unexpected visitors stir up the past. Background music. 2 acts 3 scenes 4m 2w 1 interior 1 exterior

The **ogpu** men. Rowlands, I.

Ogre. Tremblay, L.

Oh, come on, Emmanuel. Anderson, S. J.

Oh Dad, poor dad, mamma's hung you in the closet and I'm feelin' so sad. Kopit, A. L.

Oh, horrors! It's murder! Francoeur, B.

O'Hara, Robert

Insurrection; holding history. Theatre Communications Group 1999 103p

ISBN 1-559-36157-3   LC 98-49485

Explores repression of race and sexuality in America. Young African-American graduate student and his 189-year-old great-great-grandfather tranported back through time to Nat Turner's slave rebellion. 5m 4w

Ohio State murders. Kennedy, A.

Ohm, Allen

Night of the living dead. Dramatic Publishing 2003 38p

Based on George Romero and John Russo's film about seven people trapped in isolated farmhouse by flesh-eating zombies. 12m 5w extras 1 setting

Ojibwa Indians

Bruchac, J. Star sisters

O'Keeffe, Georgia

about

Shearer, J. Georgia

Oklahoma

Pape, R. Hearts beating faster

Oklahoma City (Okla.) bombing, 1995

Mooney, V. Sparrow

Old age

Baron, J. Visiting Mr. Green

Bowen, J. Little boxes: the coffee lace

Chekhov, A. P. Swan song

Clark, R. A bench in the sun

Curtis, D. Mesa

Elliot, T. Feed

Gardner, H. I'm not Rappaport

Gilroy, F. D. The golf ball

Hannah, D. Fathers and sons

Howe, T. Pride's Crossing

Hunter, D. Un tango en la noche

Lonergan, K. The Waverly Gallery

Nichol, J. W. The stone angel

Paterson, D. L. Shades of autumn

Pedrero, P. The railing (El pasamanos)

Sherman, M. Rose

Shorty, S. Trickster visits the old folks home

Spencer, S. In the western garden

y Sundstrom, B. The hundred penny box

White, E. N. Millennium 7

Yew, C. Scissors

Old age homes

Elliot, T. Feed

Raffle, D. Blue suede blues

The **old** boy. Gurney, A. R.

Old money. Wasserstein, W.

The **old** petrol station. Rhys, T.

The **old** settler. Redwood, J. H.

Old wives tale. Jensen, J.

Old women

Norfolk, W. Caramba's revenge

The **oldest** story ever told. Kacmar, K.

Olga. McAvera, B.

Oliver, Clifford

Kicking out. Carel Press 1996 65p

ISBN 1-900536-00-5

Drama about five young people trying to organize a soccer team and their racist coach. 21 scenes 3b 2g 1m 1 setting

y Ooh ah Showab Khan. ARC Theatre Pubs. 1998 58p

ISBN 1-900536-02-3

Eighteen-year-old soccer player, the first Pakistani in the English Premier League, must deal with a racist manager, some local skinheads, and a reporter who wants to make him a shining example for Asian youth. A sequel to the author's Kicking out. 1 act 16 scenes 4m 1w 5 interiors 2 exteriors

Oliver, Kathleen

Swollen tongues. Playwrights Canada 1999 71p

ISBN 0-88754-572-6

Verse play in rhyming couplets. Set in Restoration era. Brother and sister in love with same woman use poetry and trickery to win her heart. 2 acts 6 scenes 2m 2w 2 interiors

Olivier, Fernande, 1881-1966

about

McAvera, B. Fernande

Olmos, Carlos

The dandy of the Savoy; tr. by Lorna Scott Fox.

Drama set during Oscar Wilde's imprisonment in Reading Gaol. Fluctuates back and forth between trials and prisoner's ordeal. 2 acts variable cast

In Five plays in translation from Mexican contemporary theater; ed. by S. Rodríguez del Pino

O'Malley, Glyn

Concertina's rainbow. French 2002 78p

ISBN 0-573-62830-0

The interlocking journeys of two women who meet on a plane flight to Vienna. The older woman, who escaped the Holocaust, has gathered up the courage to revisit the scenes of her childhood; the younger intends to adopt a Bosnian orphan. Background music. 2 acts 10 scenes 1g 1m 4w 6 interiors 3 exteriors

One-act plays—*Continued*

Feffer, S. Little airplanes of the heart
Felder, L. Flight of fancy
Feydeau, G. The boor hug
Feydeau, G. Caught with his trance down
Feydeau, G. Fit to be tried; or, Stepbrothers in crime
Feydeau, G. Ladies' man
Feydeau, G. Romance in a flat
Feydeau, G. Tooth and consequences; or, Hortense said: "No skin off my ass!"
Feydeau, G. Wooed and viewed
Feydeau, G. Mixed doubles
Finn, W. Painting you
Foote, H. Vernon Early
c Forsten, M. L. The sycamore cross
Fraser, B. Poor Superman
Fréchette, C. Elisa's skin
Fusco, C. Stuff
Galton, F. Nothing in the world like it
Gao Xingjian. Bus stop
Gault, C. Otherwise Bob
Germann, G. The observatory
Gilbert, S. The birth of Casper G. Schmidt
Gilbert, S. Independence
Gillies, J. Give us a sign
Gilroy, F. D. Come next Tuesday
Gilroy, F. D. Dreams of glory
Gilroy, F. D. Fore
Gilroy, F. D. Getting in
Gilroy, F. D. Give the bishop my faint regards
Gilroy, F. D. The golf ball
Gilroy, F. D. Match point
Gilroy, F. D. The next contestant
Gilroy, F. D. Present tense
Gilroy, F. D. Real to reel
Gilroy, F. D. So please be kind
Gilroy, F. D. 'Twas brillig
Gilroy, F. D. The viewing
Gilroy, F. D. A way with words
Glancy, D. American gypsy
Glancy, D. The lesser wars
Glancy, D. The woman who was a red deer dressed for the deer dance
Glancy, D. The women who loved house trailers
Glass, J. M. Play memory
Gorden, C. Guarding the bridge

Grazia, E. de. The vacuum cleaner
Green, P. Hymn to the rising sun: a drama of man's waste
Green, P. In Abraham's bosom: the tragedy of a southern Negro
Greenberg, R. The author's voice
Griffin, H. The ark
Griffiths, L. The Darling family
Gromelski, B. Position available
c Hamlett, C. Author! Author!
c Hamlett, C. Eat, drink, and be scary
c Hamlett, C. The ghost of Hemstead House
c Hamlett, C. It's an okie-dokie life
c Hamlett, C. The magic mermaid
c Hamlett, C. Mother Goose gumshoe
c Hamlett, C. Once upon a fairy tale
c Hamlett, C. Picture perfect
c Hamlett, C. The prince's dilemma
c Hamlett, C. Secret agents in disguise
c Hamlett, C. The wedding bell blues
c Hamlett, C. Where there's a Will, there's a play
Handy, P. East of the sun and west of the moon
y Harden, V. Jessica and Jolene
Hare, D. The bay at Nice
c Harris, A. The orphan train
Hartman, K. The mother of modern censorship
Healey, M. Kreskinned
Healey, M. Yodellers
Henley, B. Am I blue
Hughes, L. Angelo Herndon Jones
Hughes, L. De organizer
Hughes, L. Scottsboro, limited
Huie, K. Yasuko and the young s-s-samurai
Hunt, L. A night under canvas
Hunter, D. Un tango en la noche
Hutton, A. The price you pay
Hwang, D. H. Bondage
Hwang, D. H. The dance and the railroad
Hwang, D. H. The sound of a voice
Iizuka, N. Skin
c Ingram, S. L. Christmas? Bah humbug!
c Ingram, S. L. Everywhere, everywhere, Christmas tonight
Ives, D. Arabian nights
Ives, D. Babel's in arms

One-act plays—*Continued*

Thum, N. The carpenter and the cross
Toddie, J. L. By the name of Kensington
Toddie, J. L. The juice of wild strawberries
Van Itallie, J.-C. Bag lady
Vickery, F. The drag factor
Viswananthan, P. House of sacred cows
Vogelstein, C. All about Al
Vogelstein, C. Cats and dogs
Vogelstein, C. Sisters
Wallace, N. In the fields of Aceldama
Warmflash, S. Six inch adjustable
Wasserman, D. The bequest
Wasserstein, W. Bette and me
Wasserstein, W. The man in a case
Wasserstein, W. Medea
Wasserstein, W. Tender offer
Wasserstein, W. Waiting for Philip Glass
Wasserstein, W. Workout
Way, C. Looking out to see
Wedekind, F. The tenor
Weller, M. Mistresses
Wells, M. L. The "I" word: interns
Wells, M. L. Real real gone
Wentworth, M. C. War brides
White, E. N. Millennium 7
Wilde, O. Salome
Wilder, T. The unerring instinct
Wilhelm, L. A pink Cadillac nightmare
Wilhelm, L. A significant betrayal
Wilkins, J. R. War letters
Williams, T. 27 wagons full of cotton
Williams, T. Auto-da-fe
Williams, T. I rise in flame, cried the phoenix
Williams, T. The lady of Larkspur Lotion
Williams, T. The last of my solid gold watches
Williams, T. Portrait of a Madonna
Williams, T. This property is condemned
Wilson, L. Talley's folly
Wilson, S. The soul of the white ant
c Winther, B. Brother Rabbit sells corn
c Winther, B. El caballito of seven colors
c Winther, B. The deer dance
c Winther, B. The ghost of El Castillo
c Winther, B. A gift for Pachacuti Inca
c Winther, B. The great hurricane

c Winther, B. Latino trio: Hormiga's lawsuit
c Winther, B. Latino trio: Pedro's holey sombrero
c Winther, B. Macona, the honest warrior
c Winther, B. Pedro de Urdemalas
c Winther, B. The sleeping mountains
c Winther, B. The talking burro
Wood, S. And where was Pancho Villa when you really needed him?
Woolf, B. E. Off to the war
Woolf, C. Treseder's seeds
Wright, G. The crime
Yellow Robe, W. S. The body guards
Yellow Robe, W. S. The council
Yellow Robe, W. S. Rez politics
Zellnik, D. Killing hand
One day in Gettysburg. Fredericks, A. D.
The **one-eyed** man is king. Lewis, C. W.
One flea spare. Wallace, N.
One for the money. Manzi, W.
One hundred women. Halvorson, K.
One sure thing. McLean, D.
One tennis shoe. Silverstein, S.

O'Neill, Alice

What I came for.

Late night talk between tipsy woman and bartender. 1m 1w 1 interior

In 30 ten-minute plays for 2 actors from Actors Theatre of Louisville's National Ten-minute Play Contest

O'Neill, Eugene

Anna Christie.

Drama about ex-prostitute's relationships with her Swedish father and Irish sailor lover. 4 acts 11m 2w 3 interiors

In O'Neill, E. Early plays

—Same

In O'Neill, E. Plays by Eugene O'Neill: early full-length plays

Beyond the horizon.

Tragedy. Restless brother of family remains on farm. Property and marriage degenerate. 3 acts 6 scenes 6m 4w 1 interior 3 exteriors

In O'Neill, E. Early plays

—Same

In O'Neill, E. Plays by Eugene O'Neill: early full-length plays

O'Neill, Eugene—*Continued*

Bound east for Cardiff.

One of the author's S.S. Glencairn plays. Last moments of dying sailor. 1 act 11m 1 interior

In O'Neill, E. Early plays

The Emperor Jones.

Tragedy. Black tyrant in West Indies overthrown by natives. 8 scenes 4m 1w extras 1 interior 5 exteriors

In O'Neill, E. Early plays

—Same

In O'Neill, E. Plays by Eugene O'Neill: early full-length plays

The hairy ape.

Symbolic drama about conflict between artistic and materialistic ambitions of an architect. Prologue 4 acts 11 scenes epilogue 9m 5w extras 5 interiors 1 exterior

In O'Neill, E. Early plays

Ile.

Ship captain's egotism and obsessive quest for whale oil threaten wife's sanity. 1 act 1b 4m 1w extras 1 interior

In O'Neill, E. Early plays

In the zone.

One of the author's S.S. Glencairn plays. Seamen on board British merchant marine vessel in World War I suspect fellow worker of being a spy. 1 act 8m 1 interior

In O'Neill, E. Early plays

The long voyage home.

One of the author's S.S. Glencairn plays. Innocent merchant seaman waylaid on journey home. 1 act 8m 3w 1 interior

In O'Neill, E. Early plays

The moon of the Caribbees.

One of the author's S.S. Glencairn plays. Sailors on tramp steamer celebrate in West Indies port with rum and women. 1 act 17m 4w extras 1 exterior

In O'Neill, E. Early plays

The rope.

Wayward son's return renews hostility between him and his father. 1 act 1g 3m 1w 1 setting

In O'Neill, E. Early plays

The straw.

Hopeless love between two tubercular patients at sanatorium. 3 acts 5 scenes 1b 2g 10m 7w 4 interiors 1 exterior

In O'Neill, E. Early plays

Where the cross is made.

Early version of Gold. Tragedy. Greed for gold results in murder, insanity and family ruin. 1 act 6m 1w 1 interior

In O'Neill, E. Early plays

O'Neill, Tee

The dogs play.

Woman living in city surrounds herself with her pet dogs. Variable cast 1 setting

In O'Neill, T. The dogs play and A few roos loose in the top paddock

A few roos loose in the top paddock.

Visitors shatter suburban couple's blissful lifestyle. 3m 2w 1 setting

In O'Neill, T. The dogs play and A few roos loose in the top paddock

Onionheads. Miller, Jesse

Only drunks and children tell the truth. Taylor, D. H.

The **only** game in town. Gilroy, F. D.

Only in America. Rahman, A.

The **only** thing worse you could have told me—. Butler, D.

The **only** woman general. Meuller, L.

Ono, Yōko

about

Yoon, J. The Yoko Ono project

Ontario

Curran, C. Cake-walk

Healey, M. The drawer boy

Horovitz, I. The Chopin playoffs

Horovitz, I. A Rosen by any other name

Horovitz, I. Today, I am a fountain pen

Robinson, M. Colonial tongues

Ooh ah Showab Khan. Oliver, C.

Open admissions. Lauro, S.

Opening night at the opera, er, opry (piano tuner). McCullough, L. E.

Opera

Chaurette, N. All the Verdis of Venice

c Menotti, G.-C. Amahl and the night visitors

Chinese

Yew, C. Red

The **opera** of operas; or, Tom Thumb the Great. Haywood, E. F.

Ophelia. Sanford, K.

The **opportunity** (L'Occasion). Mérimée, P.

Orders. Hochwälder, F.

Oregon

Hedges, P. Oregon

Oregon. Hedges, P.

Orestes (Greek mythology)

Aeschylus. Eumenides

Aeschylus. Libation bearers

Euripides. Andromache

Euripides. Electra

Euripides. Iphigenia among the Taurians

Euripides. Iphigenia in Tauris

Euripides. Orestes

Kennedy, A. Orestes (Euripides)

Mee, C. L. Orestes

Sophocles. Electra

Sophocles. Elektra

Orestes. Euripides

Orestes. Mee, C. L.

Orestes (Euripides). Kennedy, A.

De **organizer**. Hughes, L.

Origin of the species. Lavery, B.

Orlandersmith, Dael

Beauty's daughter.

Monologue. Tough-talking young woman yearns
to free herself of her ghetto neighborhood. 1w

   In Orlandersmith, D. Beauty's
   daughter, Monster and The
   gimmick

—Same

   In Orlandersmith, D. The gimmick and
   other plays

The gimmick.

Young Harlem woman dreams of becoming writer in Paris like James Baldwin. 1w extra

   In Orlandersmith, D. Beauty's
   daughter, Monster and The
   gimmick

—Same

   In Orlandersmith, D. The gimmick and
   other plays

Monster.

Young Harlem woman imagines life with her
idols in rock'n'roll poetry world of the Lower East
side. Variable cast 8 characters

   In Orlandersmith, D. Beauty's
   daughter, Monster and The
   gimmick

—Same

   In Orlandersmith, D. The gimmick and
   other plays

My red hand, my black hand.

A girl's search for belonging and acceptance in
the two, distinct cultures that make up her heritage—African American and Native American. 1m
2w 1 setting

   In Orlandersmith, D. The gimmick and
   other plays

Yellowman. Dramatists 2003

   ISBN 0-8222-1880-1

A play about an African American woman with
a small-town southern upbringing and a light-
skinned man. It explores the negative associations
surrounding male blackness as well as the effect
these stereotypes have on black women. 1m 1w 1
setting

Orloff, Rich

August afternoon.

Man and woman have encounter in motel room.
1m 1w 1 interior

   In Actors Theatre of Louisville.
   Ten-minute plays: v4

I didn't know you could cook.

Emotionally challenged macho yuppie brother
meets physically challenged younger gay brother
for dinner. 2m 1 interior

   In The Best American short plays,
   1996-1997

Oedi.

Comic version of Oedipus story. 3m 1w extras
1 interior

   In The Best American short plays,
   1997-1998

Prague summer.

Surreal drama set in early 1990s Prague cafe. 2m
1w 1 exterior

   In The Best American short plays
   1999-2000

The **Ornamental** hermit. Beard, J.

Oros, Michael

about

Adams, P. Free's point

O'Rowe, Mark

The aspidistra code.

Young Dublin couple, head over heels in debt, fear arrival of violent and unpredictable loan shark. 1 act 5m 1w 1 interior

In O'Rowe, M. From both hips & The aspidistra code

From both hips.

Black comedy in suburb of Dublin. Policeman apologizes to bitter, self-pitying man he accidentally shot and makes him an extraordinary offer. 2 acts 6 scenes 2m 4w 1 interior

In O'Rowe, M. From both hips & The aspidistra code

Howie the rookie. Dramatists 2002
ISBN 0-8222-1813-5

Young man gets dragged into bizarre feud of honor, which spirals out of control. 2m 1 setting

—Same. Hern Bks. 1999 52p
ISBN 1-85459-422-2

The **orphan** train. Harris, A.

Orphans

y Barchers, S. I. The luck of Roaring Camp

c DeTurk, S. The musical adventures of Oliver Twist

Field, B. Great expectations

c Harris, A. The orphan train

Ledoux, P. Anne

Nigro, D. Horrid massacre in Boston

Norman, M. Emily

c Pargman, S. Pollyanna

Parnell, P. The cider house rules: part 1

Parnell, P. The cider house rules: part 2

Paterson, D. L. The great Gilly Hopkins

c Vreeke, J. A little princess

Wilder, T. The Emporium

c Wood, D. Tom's midnight garden

Orpheus (Greek mythology)

c Barchers, S. I. Orpheus and Eurydice

Kokoschka, O. Orpheus and Eurydice

Orpheus. McLeish, K.

Orpheus and Eurydice. Barchers, S. I.

Orpheus and Eurydice. Dobrish, J.

Orpheus and Eurydice. Kokoschka, O.

Orton, Joe

Fred and Madge.

Absurdist drama. Married couple whose respective jobs are the Sisyphean tasks of rolling boulders uphill and sieving water all day long, finally

discover they are inhabiting a play about themselves. 3 acts 5m 4w extras

In Orton, J. The Visitors and Fred and Madge

Loot.

Satirical farce. Bank robber hides stolen money in mother's coffin as bumbling, dishonest Scotland Yard detective and greedy murderess maneuver to get loot for their own purposes. 2 acts 5m 1w 1 interior

In The Methuen book of sixties drama

The visitors.

Dying man is visited in hospital by his middle-aged daughter, while the attending nurses spend more time fighting than caring for their patients. 3 acts 2m 7w 1 interior 1 exterior

In Orton, J. The Visitors and Fred and Madge

What the butler saw.

Satirical sex farce about lecherous psychiatrist and his philandering wife. 2 acts 4m 2w 1 interior

In Plays of provocation; ed. by F. P. Richmond

Osborne, Alan

Bull, rock, and nut.

First play in author's Merthyr trilogy. Two ex-fighters and their manager meet in cafe on day of Johnny Owen's funeral. 6m 1 interior

In Osborne, A. The Merthyr trilogy

In sunshine and in shadow.

Second play in Merthyr trilogy. Black comedy about child abuse and drug addiction in context of extreme poverty. 2 acts 7 scenes 7m 2w 1 setting

In Osborne, A. The Merthyr trilogy

Redemption song.

Violent story about two craftsmen addicted to drugs, who decide to challenge their dealers. 1 act 4m settings

In Act one Wales; ed. by P. Clark

—Same

In Osborne, A. The Merthyr trilogy

Osborne, John

The blood of the Bambergs.

Satire on pomp of royal weddings. Dead bridegroom replaced by commoner. 2 acts 3 scenes 12m 2w extras 2 interiors

In Osborne, J. Plays for England

Osborne, John—*Continued*
Under plain cover.

Satire. After incestuous relationship is revealed, young couple isolate themselves to continue lives together. 1 act 3m 1w extras

In Osborne, J. Plays for England

Watch it come down.

Man waits in old parcels office of one-time railway station for death while his friends scar and trash each other in the waiting rooms. 2 acts 1 setting 4m 4w

In Osborne, J. Plays for England

Osborne, Ron
Seeing stars in Dixie. French 2001 61p
ISBN 0-573-62786-X

Comedy set in 1956 Natchez, Mississippi during filming of Raintree County. Widowed proprietor of tea room has ambitions of stardom and a secret admirer. 2 acts 8 scenes 1m 4w 1 interior

Oscar over here. Linney, R.

Osment, Philip
The undertaking. Oberon Bks. 1997 122p
ISBN 1-870259-87-4

Five Londoners journey to the Irish countryside to scatter ashes of friend who died of AIDS. 7 scenes 5m 1 interior 5 exteriors

Osofisan, Femi
Esu and the vagabond minstrels.

Yoruban god of mischief grants some poor musicians magic power for a day. Only one of them uses it rightly. 4 parts Variable cast 2 exteriors

In Modern African drama; ed. by B. Jeyifo

Once upon four robbers.

Political drama. Characters mimic and symbolize Nigeria's socio-political classes. Singing. Prologue 3 parts epilogue 12m 5w extras

In Postcolonial plays; ed. by H. Gilbert

Ossawattomie Brown. Swayze, J. C.

Oswald, Debra
Sweet road. Currency Press 2000 84p
ISBN 0-86819-616-9

Tragicomedy set in Australia about group of people who take to the road to fulfill their aspirations. 2 acts 48 scenes 3m 4w 1 setting

Otherwise Bob. Gault, C.
Otis proposes. Wiltse, D.
El **otro**. Solis, O.

Ott, Gustavo
y Minor leagues.

Comedy. Teenager swindles American cardbroker in Latin American hotel. 9 scenes 1m 1w 1 interior

In International plays for young people

Ottoman empire
Greene, R. Selimus, emperor of the Turks

Ottosen, Agnete
about

Mills, S. The Danish Play

Ouellette, Joey
The marriage counselor. French 1999 67p
ISBN 0-573-62670-7

Comedy about a traveling vacuum salesman who wanders into a marriage counselor's office and is mistaken for the counselor. 2 acts 4m 3w 1 interior

Our father's failing. Horovitz, I.
Our lady of shadows. Gough, L.
Our lady of Sligo. Barry, S.
Our own people. Edgar, D.
Ourselves alone. Devlin, A.
Out cry. Williams, T.
Out in the open. Harvey, J.

Outlaws
y Barchers, S. I. Zorro!; or, The curse of Capistrano
Norman, M. The holdup

The **outside**. Glaspell, S.
Over. O'Donnell, D.
Over my dead body. Sutton, M., and Fingleton, A.
Overboard. Vinaver, M.

Overmyer, Eric
Alki. Broadway Play Pub. 1997 120p
ISBN 0-88145-126-6

Freely adapted version of Ibsen's Peer Gynt, transposed to Pacific Northwest in the 19th century. Music, singing. 5 acts 31 scenes Large mixed cast 1 setting

Dark rapture.

Play revolves around morally corrupt characters scheming to get their hands on parcel of cash. 2 acts 16 scenes 6m 3w settings

In Overmyer, E. Plays

Overmyer, Eric—*Continued*

c Duke Kahanamoku vs. the surfnappers.

Fantasy. Statue of legendary Hawaiian athlete comes to life and relates his story to couple of children. 6m 2w extras

In Eight plays for children; ed. by C. A. Jennings

In perpetuity throughout the universe.

Dark comedy looks at paranoid reality created by group of ghost writers. 37 scenes 3m 3w 1 setting

In Overmyer, E. Plays

On the verge; or, The geography of yearning.

Three intrepid Victorian lady explorers become disoriented as the surrounding rainforest reveals artifacts from the future. 2 acts 22 scenes 1m 3w 1 setting

In Overmyer, E. Plays

Overtime. Gurney, A. R.

Overtones. Gerstenberg, A.

Owen, Gary

Crazy Gary's mobile disco. Methuen 2001 87p

ISBN 0-413-76850-3

Saturday night, small town Wales, one pub, one party and three lads who dream of getting out. 3 acts 3m settings

Owens, Joanne

To serve one another.

Worship program. A Maundy Thursday service of holy communion and foot-washing. Music, singing. Variable cast 12 characters extras

In The drama of Easter; ed. by R. Wray

Owens, Rochelle

Chucky's hunch.

Middle-aged failure narrates series of letters written to one of his ex-wives. Background music. 1m 1 interior

In Owens, R. Plays

Futz.

Theater of cruelty and violence. Farmer's sexual love for pig demoralizes amoral neighbors, inciting them to lunacy, incest, and murder. 13 scenes 10m 5w

In Owens, R. Plays

Kontraption.

Experimental theater piece with ritualistic and mythic undertones about paradox of human existence. 10m 4w 1 setting

In Owens, R. Plays

Three front.

Experimental play about living at extremes, focuses on successful businessman, his wife and their lovers. 2 acts 15 scenes 1m 2w 1 setting

In Owens, R. Plays

The **owl** answers. Kennedy, A.

Owls. Courtney, E.

P

Pachino, Jamie

y Race.

Dramatization of book by Studs Terkel about race relations in the United States. Background music. 2m 2w 1 setting

In International plays for young people

Packing up the past. Junyent, S.

The **Paddy** pedlar. Molloy, M. J.

Padmanabhan, Manjula

Harvest.

Drama about modern Indian family's disintegration resulting from societal pressures. 3 acts 9 scenes 5m 4w extras

In Postcolonial plays; ed. by H. Gilbert

Pageant. Evans, A., and others

Pageants

Dekker, T. The magnificent entertainment

Evans, A. Pageant

Paige, Jennifer Laura

Notes.

Monologue. Her personal life intrudes as drama teacher addresses students on opening night. 1w

In Women playwrights: the best plays of 2001

Pain (Eulalia). Ehn, E.

The **pain** of pink evenings. Moore, R.

The **painted** woman (La Femme peinte). Rachilde

Painters

Lan, D. Painting a wall

Painting a wall. Lan, D.

Painting you. Finn, W.

Paintings

Beber, N. Sensation(s)
Crowther, C. Tryst
Hare, D. The bay at Nice
McKee, J. Jill on a recliner, reading
Ross, L. L. Scent of the roses
Sondheim, S. Sunday in the park with George

Pakistan

Bhuchar, S. A tainted dawn
y Shafaat, S. Balcony

Pakistanis

England

y Oliver, C. Ooh ah Showab Khan

Palacios, Monica

Describe your work.

Monologue describing how the speaker became a Latina lesbian stand-up comic. Part of the author's Greetings from a queer senorita. 1 act 1w 1 setting

In Puro teatro; ed. by A. Sandoval-Sánchez and N. S. Sternbach

Greetings from a queer señorita.

Performance piece combining the author's Latin lezbo comic and Confessions . . . a sexplosion of tantalizing tales. Depicts world of lesbian comic. Music, singing. 1 act 1w 1 setting

In Out of the fringe; ed. by C. Svich and M. T. Marrero

Palestinian Arabs

Sunde, K. How his bride came to Abraham

Palm Sunday

Stair, E. R. Parade without a permit

Palmer, Greg

c The falcon.

Dramatization of Russian folk tale Fenist, the bright falcon. Fantastic adventures of young farm girl. Singing. 1 act 3m 3w 1 setting

In Theatre for young audiences; ed. by C. A. Jennings

Palmer, John

Singapore. Broken Jaw Press 2000 88p
ISBN 1-896647-85-5

Father ill with Alzheimer's attempts reconciliation with son against backdrop of greed and sex. 2 acts 9 scenes 5m 2w

Palmer, Tanya

Body talk.

Three women discuss body image. 3w

In 30 ten-minute plays for 3 actors from Actors Theatre of Louisville's National Ten-minute Play Contest

Palmieri, Marc

Carl the Second. Dramatists 2003
ISBN 0-8222-1886-0

Midway through living in the shadow of others, man is threatened by woman, who dares him to be loved. 5m 2w 1 interior setting

The departure of Brian O'Callahan.

Lost soul on brink of suicide. 2m 1w 1 exterior

In Palmieri, M. Poor fellas

Makin' sense of nothin'.

Two construction workers discover horrible truth at friend's funeral. 2m 1 exterior

In Palmieri, M. Poor fellas

Poor fellas.

Two recently jilted buddies commiserate in bar. 2m 1w 1 interior

In Palmieri, M. Poor fellas

Prologue.

High school sophomore relates humiliation of his friend in local cineplex. 1m extras 1 setting

In Palmieri, M. Poor fellas

Rocks.

Young prospect ridicules hopes and superstitions of aging minor league player. 4m 1 setting

In Palmieri, M. Poor fellas

Tough guys.

Two men face fact that they have failed to attain their dreams. 2m 1 interior

In Palmieri, M. Poor fellas

Pan. Barchers, S. I.

Pan Jinlian: the history of a fallen woman. Wei Minglun

Pandemonium! (a Greek myth-adventure). Perkins, D.

Pandora (Greek mythology)

c Barchers, S. I. Prometheus and Pandora

Pandora's box. Wedekind, F.

Panikkar, Kavalam Narayana

Aramba Chekkan.

The Orpheus story transplanted to India, and reimagined as a folkloric parable about man's relationship to nature. Music, singing, dancing. 1 act

Panikkar, Kavalam Narayana—*Continued*

Variable cast settings

In DramaContemporary: India; ed. by E. B. Mee

Pantagleize. Field, B.

Pantomime. Walcott, D.

Pantomimes

c Brett, S. Sleeping beauty

Green, M. Cinderella

Lloyd, R. The three musketeers—le panteau!

Los Matachines unmasked (Los Matachines desenmascarados)

c Winther, B. Latino trio: Senorita Cucaracha finds a husband

Pantomimes with music

c Banks, J. Hercules—The panto!!

c Lloyd, R. Arabian knights—The panto!

y Reakes, P. Bluebeard

c Reakes, P. Little Red Riding Hood

c Reakes, P. Robinson Crusoe and the pirates

c Robbins, N. Jack and Jill

c Robbins, N. Red Riding Hood

c Travis, S. The tale of Little Red Riding Hood

Wain, D. Look behind you

Panych, Morris

Earshot. Talonbooks 2001 64p

ISBN 0-88922-444-7   LC 2001-411606

Comedy about man with hyper-sensitive hearing. He is able to hear the most intimate details of lives of everyone in his apartment building. Prologue 18 scenes 1m

Paolucci, Anne

In the green room; book by Anne Paolucci; lyrics and music by Henry Paolucci. Griffon House Publications 1999 71p

ISBN 0-918680-82-4

Musical about the theater with Pirandellian overtones. Music, singing. Prologue 2 acts 4 scenes 5m 6w singing chorus 1 setting.

Papa's angels: a Christmas story. Roman, J.

Pape, Ralph

Hearts beating faster. Dramatists 1997 69p

ISBN 0-8222-1584-5   LC 97-210566

Volatile emotions are unleashed when idealistic young woman returns to her sister's home in Oklahoma in the company of handsome young stranger. 3 acts 12 scenes 2m 3w 1 setting

Paper lanterns, paper cranes. Kral, B.

Parables

Sills, P. Rumi

Parade (condensation). Brown, J. R.

Parade without a permit. Stair, E. R.

Paradise Island. Aerenson, B.

Paranoia

O'Donnell, D. Radio Rooster says that's bad

The **parasol**. Dunai, F.

Parent and child

Ackermann, J. Off the map

Alvarez, L. Hidden parts

y Barchers, S. I. Hard times

Bellusci, M. Born to be blue

Chinn, J. A different way home

Cleage, P. Chain

c Cornett, E. Cinderella

Dattani, M. Tara

Diggs, E. How to plant a rose

Donaghy, T. Minutes from the blue route

Durang, C. Baby with the bathwater

Ehn, E. Pain (Eulalia)

Feydeau, G. Going to pot (On purge Bébé)

Gilroy, F. D. The subject was roses

Godber, J. Weekend breaks

Goldstein, D. L. Burn

Hedges, P. Baby anger

Herbert, K. Hit and run

Lathrop, M. The visible horse

Lhota, B. Strangers

Lucas, C. What I meant was

Margulies, D. July 7, 1994

Martin, J. Mr. Bundy

McGuire, M. These flowers are for my mother

McLean, D. I'd rather go blind

Melski, M. Hockey mom, hockey dad

Murphy, C. Beating heart cadaver

Murray, T. C. Appendix two: illumination

Parent and child—*Continued*
Murray-Smith, J. Nightfall
Neilson, A. Year of the family
Orton, J. Loot
Parks, S.-L. In the blood
Romero, E. If Susan Smith could talk
Southworth, M. Damages to Tony
Steele, D. The way to Miami
Strindberg, A. The father
Vickery, F. The drag factor
Viswananthan, P. House of sacred cows
Walker, G. F. Problem child
Wallace, N. In the fields of Aceldama
Zindel, P. Every seventeen minutes the crowd goes crazy!

Pargman, Susan

c Pollyanna. Pioneer Drama Service 2001 54p

Classic tale of little girl's faith in father's promise. 2 acts 16 scenes 10m 12w extras 2 interiors 1 exterior

c Scheherazade. Pioneer Drama Service 2000 49p

Greatest storyteller in ancient Arabian world called upon to use her talents to save her people from certain destruction. 2 acts 6 scenes 6m 17w extras 2 exteriors

Paris (France)
Bell, N. Thérèse Raquin
Nelson, R. Madame Melville
Tait, L. The swimming pools of Paris
Vinaver, M. Portrait of a woman
La **Parisienne**. Marowitz, C.

Parker, Charlie
about
Rahman, A. Unfinished women cry in no man's land while a bird dies in a gilded cage

Parker, Michael (Michael E.)

Hotbed Hotel; an American farce. French 2000 100p
  ISBN 0-573-62738-X   LC 2002-283935

Comedy. A couple who own a one-star hotel in Florida Keys try to impress a prospective New York buyer by having staff pose as guests. 2 acts 4m 5w Unit set

The Lone Star love potion. French 1999 109p
  ISBN 0-573-62678-2

Farce. Wealthy Texan rancher dies, his niece inherits everything, while his butler produces a love potion from a safe with comic results. 2 acts 3m 4w 1 interior

The sensuous senator; an American farce. French 1998 103p
  ISBN 0-573-62641-3   LC 2001-523739

Farce. Senator must hide his infidelities when he becomes candidate for presidency. Prologue 2 acts 3 scenes 4m 5w 2 interiors

Whose wives are they anyway? French 2003 101p
  ISBN 0-573-62966-8

Comedy. Corporate executives' golf weekend results in chaos when they unexpectedly encounter their new female boss. 2 acts 3m 5w 1 setting

Parker, Stewart

Catchpenny twist.

Charade. The lives and careers of Irish singer and her songwriting duo inevitably become linked with the politics and violence in Northern Ireland. Music, singing. 2 acts 3m 4m 1 setting
  In Parker, S. Plays: 1

Nightshade.

Mortician, forced by teenage daughter to face reality, disintegrates under grief over wife's death. 2 acts 6m 2w extras 1 setting
  In Parker, S. Plays: 1

Pratt's fall.

Man uses old map, which seems to prove the Irish discovered America, to seduce map curator. 2 parts 5m 2w 1 interior
  In Parker, S. Plays: 1

Spokesong; or, The common wheel.

Metaphor for troubles of Northern Ireland in 1970s. All world's transportation woes can be solved if people would switch to the bicycle. 2 acts 4m 2w 1 setting
  In Parker, S. Plays: 1
The **Parker** family circus. Buttram, J.

Parker, Matt

Celaine. Oberon Bks. 1999 88p
  ISBN 1-84022-111-X

Drama about a couple living in Gravesend, England whose daughter has not left her room in over six years. 2 acts 16 scenes 3m 4w 1 setting

Parks, Rosa, 1913-
about
c Fredericks, A. D. December 1, 1955: Montgomery, Alabama

Parks, Suzan-Lori

Fucking A.

In a Brechtian parable, a woman works as an abortionist to buy her son's release from prison; a plan to avenge his initial arrest goes horribly wrong. Singing. 19 scenes 9m 6w extras 5 interiors 4 exteriors

In Parks, S.-L. The red letter plays

In the blood. Dramatists 2000 73p

ISBN 0-8222-1756-2

Drama about homeless single mother of five children living on inner city streets. Music. 9 scenes 3m 3w

—Same

In Parks, S.-L. The red letter plays

Parks

c McCullough, L. E. Call of the wild (park ranger)

Stamos, D. G. The unintended video

Parnell, Peter

The cider house rules: part 1; here in St. Cloud. Dramatists 2001 92p

ISBN 0-8222-1725-2

Dramatization of the novel by John Irving, set in the early 20th century. Part I deals with the relationship between a doctor who runs an orphanage (and abortion clinic) in Maine and the talented orphan, young Homer Wells, who becomes his protegé but is reluctant to succeed him. Music. 3 acts 3 scenes 15m 17w extras settings

The cider house rules: part 2; in other parts of the world. Dramatists 2001 102p

ISBN 0-8222-1726-0

Dramatization of John Irving novel.Young man explores the world but must finally decide whether to return to the place he was raised and take up his mentor's work. Music. 3 acts 3 scenes Large mixed cast settings

QED. Applause 2002 54p

ISBN 1-55783-592-6

Richard Feynmann, a nuclear physicist with a gift for comedy, talks about his life, his work, and his approaching death. Much of the text is drawn from Feynmann's writings. Music and singing; voices. 2 acts 2 scenes 1m 1w 1 interior

—Same. Dramatists 2003

ISBN 0-8222-1924-7

Parodies

Baker, E. A. Mafia on Prozac

Basch, P. English (it's where the words are)

Bean, R. Pride at Southanger Park

Belke, D. The Maltese bodkin

Busch, C. Psycho beach party

Cibber, C. The rival queans

Green, M. Cinderella

Green, M. Oedipus, King of Thebes

Green, M. Trapped

Kopit, A. L. Chad Curtiss, lost again

Ludlam, C. The mystery of Irma Vep

Martin, J. Flaming guns of the purple sage

c McBride-Smith, B. Santaberry and the Snard

c McBride-Smith, B. A thoroughly modern Rapunzel

c McBride-Smith, B. Twelfth night

Scott, G. A town called Shame

The **parrot**. Wilhelm, L.

Parsley, Jett

Hiss.

Husband and wife find snake in their basement. 1m 1w 1 interior

In 30 ten-minute plays for 2 actors from Actors Theatre of Louisville's National Ten-minute Play Contest

Parsley, Roger, and Graham, Andy

Sense and sensibility. French (London) 2001 69p

ISBN 0-573-01926-6

A dramatization of Jane Austen's novel (1811) about two contrasting sisters and their matrimonial prospects. Music, dancing. 2 acts 15 scenes 3m 4w 4 interiors 1 exterior

Parties

Davey, S. James Joyce's The dead

Godber, J. On a night like this

Kash, M. A party to murder

Ryan, T. Pig

Simon, N. The dinner party

Taylor, D. H. alterNatives

A **partridge** in a pear tree. Swortzell, L.

A **party** to murder. Kash, M., and Hughes, D.

Pascal, Julia

Theresa.

Jewish mother, a music professor in Vienna, is forced to leave her job. She is separated from son, as they seek to become invisible in prelude to Holocaust, and spends rest of her life trying to find him. Variable cast 19 characters extras settings

In Mythic women/Real women

Passage. Cabal, F.

Passing places. Greenhorn, S.

Passion. Curino, L.

The **passion**. Harrison, T.

The **passion** of Henry David Thoreau. Oates, J. C.

Passover

Kushner, T. Notes on Akiba

Past imperfect. Sher, E.

Pastimes. Jeffries, B.

Pastoral drama

Marivaux, P. C. de C. de. Changes of heart

Sidney, Sir P. The Lady of May

Tasso, T. Aminta

Paterson, David L.

Chutes.

Two American paratroopers trapped by their chute strings behind enemy lines discover that they have much in common. 5 scenes 2m

In Paterson, D. L. Shades of autumn and Chutes

The king's horses. French (London) 2003 74p

ISBN 0-573-62877-7

Tragicomedy about carpenter with mysterious past who works for two sisters with emotional issues. 2 acts 6 scenes 1m 3w 1 interior

Shades of autumn.

Drama about a son who moves his elderly father near his home, which then triggers off many memories. 1 act 1 interior

In Paterson, D. L. Shades of autumn and Chutes

Stone the crows. French 2003 72p

ISBN 0-573-62995-1

Successful Manhattan couple trying to balance careers and family have their lives changed with visit from older brother. 2 acts 5 scenes 2m 1w 1 setting

Paterson, David L., and Liebman, Steve

The great Gilly Hopkins. French 2001 54p

ISBN 0-573-62768-1

Musical. Adventures of orphan looking for real mother and love. Music, singing. 7 scenes Variable cast 10 characters extras 1 setting

Patience. Sherman, J.

The **patriarchs**. Vogel, L.

Patronage. Linney, R.

Pattee, Ruth Ann

c Can Mrs. Claus save Christmas? Pioneer Drama Service 2000 20p

When Santa is kidnapped by jealous multimillionaire, it is up to Mrs. Claus and the elves to save Christmas. 7 scenes Variable cast 1 setting

Patter for the floating lady. Martin, S.

Pattison, John

A word from our sponsor; (by) Alan Ayckbourn; music by John Pattison. French (London) 1998 94p

ISBN 0-573-08105-0

In a dystopian future, the inhabitants of a small British town decide to stage a musical Nativity play in the hope of reviving their town's fortunes. 2 acts 4m 5w 1 setting

Paul, the Apostle, Saint

about

Grimsley, J. The lizard of Tarsus

The **pavilion**. Wright, C.

Pax. Levy, D.

Paxton, Kate

c Tatyana's golden doe; book, music, and lyrics by Kate Paxton. Anchorage Press 1999 36p

ISBN 0-87602-363-4

Musical version of Russian fairy tale about young girl and magical deer. 8 scenes 2m 2w 1 setting

Paz, Octavio, 1914-1998

The blue bouquet (dramatization) See Shepard, S. Eyes for Consuela

Peace

Aristophanes. Acharnians

Aristophanes. Lysistrata

Aristophanes. Peace

Peace. Aristophanes

Peace (La paix). Lenéru, M.

The **peach** boy. Barchers, S. I.

Peanuts. Yourgrau, T.

Pearce, Philippa, 1920-

Tom's midnight garden (dramatization)
See Wood, D. Tom's midnight garden

Pearl Harbor

c Fredericks, A. D. December 7, 1941:
aboard the USS Arizona

Pearls. Lipner, N.

Pearson, Karl, 1857-1936

about

Redhill, M. Building Jerusalem

Peditto, Paul

Sounds of silents (The Essanay years).
Dramatic Publishing 2003 106p

Drama about early days of the famous Essanay
silent film studio whose stars included Wallace
Beery, Gloria Swanson and Charlie Chaplin. 2 acts
Variable cast 11 characters 1 setting

Pedrero, Paloma

The color of August.

Two woman artists, long estranged, briefly re-
new sadomasochistic relationship. 2w 1 interior

In Pedrero, P. Parting gestures with A
night in the subway

First star (Una estrella); tr. by Rick Hite.

Woman novelist goes to seedy bar and encounters alcoholic father's old drinking and gambling
partner. 3m 1w 1 interior

In Pedrero, P. First star and The
railing

A night divided.

Actress, feeling rejected by her lover, gets drunk
with lonely Bible salesman. Music, dancing. 2m
1w 1 interior

In Pedrero, P. Parting gestures with A
night in the subway

A night in the subway.

Stranded for night in subway station, two strangers become lovers. 1m 1w 1 interior

In Pedrero, P. Parting gestures with A
night in the subway

The railing (El pasamanos); tr. by Rick
Hite.

Elderly couple, trying to get landlady to install
handrail, becomes subject of popular TV show
which engages social issues. 3 scenes 2m 2w 1

setting

In Pedrero, P. First star and The
railing

The voucher.

Divorcing couple use family pet to hurt each
other. 1m 1w 1 interior

In Pedrero, P. Parting gestures and A
night in the subway

Pedro de Urdemalas. Winther, B.

Pelfrey, Matt

Drive angry.

Two men in their twenties, one with cancer,
drive around Los Angeles planning to commit a
crime. 2m 1 exterior

In 30 ten-minute plays for 2 actors
from Actors Theatre of
Louisville's National Ten-minute
Play Contest

—Same

In Actors Theatre of Louisville.
Ten-minute plays; v5

Jerry Springer is God.

Comedy. Secrets revealed between friends re-
semble episode of Jerry Springer. 3m 3w 1 interior

In 30 ten-minute plays for 4, 5 & 6
actors from Actors Theatre of
Louisville's National Ten-minute
Play Contest

Penetrator. Neilson, A.

Penhall, Joe

Love and Understanding. Dramatists 1999
65p

ISBN 0-8222-1688-4

Two stressed-out doctors, who are also lovers,
have their relationship tested by the manipulations
of a underhanded friend. 2 acts 13 scenes 2m 1w

Wild Turkey.

Two small businessmen in London, England
struggle to keep their flagging hamburger bar
afloat in face of bizzare and savage forces. 2
scenes 4m 1 interior

In Best of the Fest; ed. by Phil Setren

The **penny** that beauty spent. Wilder, T.

People on the river. Upton, J.

Perez, Carlos

c Folk tales for fun. Pioneer Drama
Service 2002 40p

Vignettes based on folktales from Germany,
Egypt, Turkey and Liberia. Variable cast

Perez, Frank

Estorias del barrio: special people of international character.

Satire. Talent agency for Latino actors. 1 act 3m 2w 1 interior

In Action; ed. by M. Algarin and L. Griffith

Perfect days. Lochhead, L.

The **perfect** murder. Janes, H.

The **perfect** night. Newsome, M.

The **perfect** party. Gurney, A. R.

Perfect pie. Thompson, J.

Perfect pitch. Godber, J.

Perfect strangers. Poliakoff, S.

Perfect wedding. Hawdon, R.

Period of adjustment. Williams, T.

Perkins, David

Pandemonium! (a Greek myth-adventure); book & lyrics by Jenifer Toksvig; music by David Perkins. French (London) 2002 75p

ISBN 0-573-08117-4

Musical featuring gods, goddesses, nymphs and mortals of Greek mythology. Prologue 2 acts 18 scenes Variable cast 1 setting

y Shake, ripple & roll; book and lyrics by Jenifer Toksvig; music by David Perkins. French (London) 2000 49p

ISBN 0-573-08112-3

Rock and roll musical. When owner of ice-cream parlor passes away staff tries to save shop from falling into the wrong hands. Large mixed cast 1 interior

See also Toksvig, J. jt. auth.

Perrault, Charles, 1628-1703

Cinderella (dramatization) See Ahlin, L. Cinderella: the true story; Francoeur, B. Cinderella's glass slipper

Persecution

Sandberg, R. N. Convivencia

Persephone (Greek mythology)

c Thistle, L. The myth of Demeter and Persephone; or, The origin of the seasons

Perseus. Barchers, S. I.

Persian Gulf War, 1991

Rivera, J. Gas

The **Persians.** Aeschylus

Pete 'n' Keely. Hindman, J.

Peter. Mayne, R.

Peter I, the Great, Tsar of Russia
about

Brown, C. The Negro of Peter the Great

Peter, the Apostle, Saint
about

Kraszewski, C. S. Peter the rock

Peter the rock. Kraszewski, C. S.

Petroleum industry

McLean, D. Julie Allardyce

Petticoat loose. Molloy, M. J.

Phaedra's love. Kane, S.

Phantom of the campfire. Sodaro, C.

Phantoms. Mayne, R.

Phedre. Racine, J.

The **Philadelphia.** Ives, D.

The **philanderer.** Shaw, B.

Philanthropy

Oates, J. C. The adoption

Wong, E. Let the big dog eat

Philip, M. Nourbese

Coups and calypsos.

Drama set in 1992 Tobago about racial mixing within context of failed marriage. 2 acts 4 scenes 1m 2w 1 interior 1 exterior

In Testifyin' v1; ed. by D. Sears

Philistinism

Linney, R. Patronage

Philoctetes. Sophocles

Philoktetes. Sophocles

Philomela (Greek Mythology)

Wertenbaker, T. The love of the nightingale

Philosophers

Ravenhill, M. Faust (Faust is dead)

Philosophy

Gault, C. Otherwise Bob

Hall, L. Genie

Hall, L. Wittgenstein on Tyne

O'Connell, S. Cartesian dreams

Stoppard, T. Arcadia

Witkiewicz, S. I. The cuttlefish; or, The Hyrcanian worldview

The **Phoenician** women. Euripides

The **Phoenix** lottery. Stratton, A.

Phone sex and a dumb show. Sater, S.

Phormio. Terence

Photographers

Hutton, A. Studio portrait
Myatt, J. M. What he sent
Spencer, S. Sudden devotion
Photographs from S-21. Filloux, C.
Physical therapy. Reynolds, J.

Physically handicapped

Belluso, J. The technology project: voice
    properties
Boker, G. H. Francesca da Rimini
Cohen, F. Amy Crockett: M.V.P.
Cruz, M. Frida: the story of Frida Kahlo
Lloyd, M. Dead certain
McDonagh, M. The cripple of Inishmaan
Orloff, R. I didn't know you could cook
Schenkar, J. Signs of life
Williams, T. The glass menagerie
Wilson, L. Fifth of July

Physicians

Brown, W. W. The escape
Ekstrom, P. Doctor! Doctor! a medical
    musical comedy revue
Fill, S. Night visits
Foote, H. Vernon Early
Gardner, H. I'm with ya, Duke
Horsler, P. Cut and run
Jenkin, L. A country doctor
Margulies, D. July 7, 1994
Marowitz, C. Quack
Molière. The doctor despite himself
Parnell, P. The cider house rules: part 1
Parnell, P. The cider house rules: part 2
Wilder, T. The angel that troubled the
    waters

Physicists

Frayn, M. Copenhagen
Jones, C. Humble boy
Piaf, Édith, 1915-1963
    about
Dafydd, G. No regrets

Pianists

Busch, C. The lady in question
Gilroy, F. D. The only game in town

Piano tuners

c McCullough, L. E. Opening night at the
    opera, er, opry (piano tuner)

Piatigorsky, Anton

Easy Lenny Lazmon and the great west-
    ern ascension. Playwrights Canada
    2000 80p
    ISBN 0-88754-588-2
Drama explores mythology of western expansion,
Jewish history and ancient religious traditions.
Two exiled travellers in desert search for promised
land. 2 acts 3m 1w 1 exterior
The kabbalistic psychoanalysis of Adam
    R. Tzaddik.
Psychoanalysis of young man obssessed with sa-
cred Jewish text. Prelude 10 scenes 2m
    In Piatigorsky, A. The offering & The
        kabbalistic psychoanalysis of
        Adam R. Tzaddik
The offering.
Explores relationships between fathers and sons
by drawing on tales of biblical patriarchs. Follows
four generations of single family. 3 acts 3m 2 inte-
riors 1 exterior
    In Piatigorsky, A. The offering & The
        kabbalistic psychoanalysis of
        Adam R. Tzaddik
Picasso, Jacqueline
    about
McAvera, B. Jacqueline
Picasso, Pablo, 1881-1973
    about
McAvera, B. Dora
McAvera, B. Eva
McAvera, B. Fernande
McAvera, B. Françoise
McAvera, B. Gaby
McAvera, B. Jacqueline
McAvera, B. Marie-Therese
McAvera, B. Olga
Picasso, Olga Khoklova
    about
McAvera, B. Olga
The **Piccadilly** bushman. Lawler, R.
Pickwick papers. Brittney, L.
Picture perfect. Hamlett, C.
Picture perfect. Salinas, P.

Pielmeier, John

Pillow talk.
A marriage counseling session goes awry. 2m
2w 1 interior
    In 30 ten-minute plays for 4, 5 & 6

Pielmeier, John—*Continued*

actors from Actors Theatre of Louisville's National Ten-minute Play Contest

Voices in the dark. Broadway Play Pub. 2000 95p

ISBN 0-88145-154-1

Thriller about New York radio talk show host who is harassed and stalked by a deranged caller while vacationing at a resort cabin. 2 acts 6 scenes 7m 2w 2 settings

Pierre and Marie. Clark, R.

Pietri, El Reverendo Pedro

El cabron.

Ethnic comedy. Puerto Rican businessman, who "became" Italian to get ahead in life, recruits blind messenger to spy on wife. 1 act 3m 1w 3 interiors

In Action; ed. by M. Algarin and L. Griffith

Pig. Ryan, T.

Pignight. Wilson, S.

Pigs

Owens, R. Futz

Pilate, Pontius, 1st cent.

about

c Zapel, A. L. Who am I?

Pilgrims of the night. Jenkin, L.

Pillow talk. Pielmeier, J.

Pilots of the purple twilight. Kluger, S.

Piñero, Miguel

Playland blues.

Lives of youthful hustlers and junkies in Times Square. 2 acts 14m 3w 1 exterior

In Action; ed. by M. Algarin and L. Griffith

Ping, Chin Woon

Details cannot body wants.

Drama about cultural identity and feminism in Singapore, performed through poetic test and dance. Music, singing, dancing. 4 parts Variable cast

In Postcolonial plays; ed. by H. Gilbert

Pink. Thompson, J.

A **pink** Cadillac nightmare. Wilhelm, L.

Pinocchio. Katz, L.

Pinocchio. Mason, T.

Pinski, David

The treasure; tr. by Nahma Sandrow.

Family scrambles for gold while gravedigger's daughter seeks out husband. 4 acts Large mixed cast 1 interior 1 exterior

In God, man and devil; ed. by N. Sandrow

Pintauro, Joe

Two eclairs.

Woman learns younger sister is having affair with husband. Background music. 1m 1w 1 interior

In take ten; ed. by E. Lane and N. Shengold

Pinter, Harold

Celebration. French 2002 38p

ISBN 0-573-62828-9

Satiric look at 1990s greed. Three couples dine in elegant restaurant. 5m 4w 1 interior

—Same

In Pinter, H. Celebration and The room

The room.

Drama of menace. Elderly couple seems likely to be evicted from room they have been living in. 4m 2w 1 interior

In Pinter, H. Celebration and The room

The **pipe** in the fields. Murray, T. C.

Pirandello, Luigi, 1867-1936

Enrico IV (adaptation) See Brustein, R. Enrico IV

Six characters in search of an author (adaptation) See Brustein, R. Six characters in search of an author

Henry IV (Enrico IV); translated by Carl R. Mueller.

Tragedy. Man posing as insane for many years commits crime, compelling him to continue his pretended madness. 3 acts 11m 2w 2 interiors 2 exteriors

In Pirandello, L. Three major plays

Naked; a new version by Nicholas Wright; from a literal translation by Gaynor McFarlane. Hern Bks 1998 63p

ISBN 1-85459-339-0

Tragedy about love, suicide, and the unmasking of lies. 3 acts 4m 3w 1 interior

Pirandello, Luigi, 1867-1936—*Continued*

Right you are (if you think you are) (Cosi è, se ui pare); translated by Carl R. Mueller.

A man and his mother-in-law tell conflicting stories about their respective wife and daughter. Audience has to decide which is illusion and which is reality. 3 acts 24 scenes 9m 7w extras 1 interior

In Pirandello, L. Three major plays

Six characters in search of an author (Sei personaggi in cerca d'autore); translated by Carl R. Mueller.

Play within a play. Director attempts rehearsal staging story of characters from unwritten play. Each character tells story from own viewpoint, complains that actors and director/author misrepresent them. Singing. 1b 7m 4w extras 1 interior

In Pirandello, L. Three major plays

Parodies, imitations, etc.

Dobrish, J. Notions in motion

Pirates

Daborne, R. A Christian turned Turk

c Mason, T. Treasure Island

Massinger, P. The renegado

c Mitchell, W. Jolly Roger

Pitching to the star. Margulies, D.

Pithecus. Lipkin, D.

Pixies, kings, and magical things. Averill, R.

Plague

Pushkin, A. A feast during the plague

Plan B. Healey, M.

Plan day. Ayvazian, L.

Plantation life

Aiken, G. L. Uncle Tom's cabin

Dove, R. The darker face of the earth

Plastic bride. Dempsey, S., and Millan, L.

Plastic surgery

Barfield, T. Snapshot: defacing patriotic property

Plata, María Cristina

Justice for whom? Minerva Press 1997 68p

ISBN 1-86106-111-0

Drama about a mythical state where a feminist who performs an abortion can receive a summary death sentence. 3 scenes 4m 4w 1 interior 1 exterior

Plater, Alan

Peggy for you. Methuen 2000 86p

ISBN 0-413-74810-3

A day in the life of Peggy Ramsay, the most celebrated play agent of her time. 2 acts 4 scenes 3m 2w 1 interior

Platonov. Chekhov, A. P.

Plautus, Titus Maccius

Casina; translated by George Fredric Franko.

Variant titles: A funny thing happened on the way to the wedding; the lot-drawers. Latin comedy. Old gentleman tries to marry off beautiful slave girl to his servant in order to get her for himself, while his son attempts similar scheme.

In Greek and Roman Comedy; ed. by S. O'Bryhim

Double bind (Menaechmi); tr. by Douglass Parker.

The Menaechmus twins. Farcical Latin drama about complication arising from man's search for long lost twin brother.

In Plautus and Terence, five comedies

Major Blowhard (Miles gloriosus); tr. by Deena Berg.

Variant titles: The braggart soldier; Major Bullshot-Gorgeous; The swaggering soldier. Farcical verse play about vain and lecherous Roman soldier.

In Plautus and Terence, five comedies

The wild, wild women (Bacchides); tr. by Douglas Parker.

Comedy set in Athens adapted from Menander's The double deceiver. Two young men slavishly devoted to two courtesans who will do anything for money.

In Plautus and Terence, five comedies

Play memory. Glass, J. M.

A **play** on letters. Stohl, H.

Play with repeats. Crimp, M.

Play within a play

Battlo, J. The little theater's production of Hamlet

Beaumont, F. The knight of the burning pestle

Beber, N. Afterthought

Brustein, R. Six characters in search of an author

Frankel, R. WhoDunit. . .and to whom?

Frankel, R. WhoDunit. . .and who's the big idea anyway?

Play within a play—*Continued*
Fréchette, C. Seven days in the life of Simon Labrosse
y Godber, J. Teechers
Godber, J. Unleashed
Gore, C. Quid pro quo; or, The day of the dupes
Gore, C. The tale of a tub
Guare, J. The general of hot desire
Hughes, D. Love and a bottle
Karnad, G. The fire and the rain
Kennedy, A. Motherhood 2000
Macpherson, R. The terrible false deception
c Mason, T. Ukrainian tales
c McCullough, L. E. Hail, Queen Esther!
McGuire, M. Helen's play
c Miller, K. S. Jack and the beanstalk
Mühsam, E. Thunderation! (Alle Wetter!)
Norman, M. Sarah and Abraham
Pirandello, L. Six characters in search of an author (Sei personaggi in cerca d'autore)
Robinson, K. The popular mechanicals
Schnitzler, A. The green cockatoo
y Smith, C. City of gold
Vinaver, M. Overboard
Wain, D. Look behind you
Walker, J. M. Inventing Montana
Wertenbaker, T. After Darwin
Wilder, T. Proserpina and the devil: a play for marionettes
Williams, T. Out cry
The **players**. Metcalf, P.
Playhouse creatures. De Angelis, A.
Playing Sinatra. Kops, B.
Playing with fire. Field, B.
Playing with fire. Strindberg, A.
Playland blues. Piñero, M.

Plays in verse
Aeschylus. Agamemnon
Aeschylus. Choephori
Aeschylus. The Eumenides
Aeschylus. Libation bearers
Aeschylus. The Persians
Aeschylus. Prometheus bound
Aeschylus. Seven against Thebes
Aeschylus. The suppliants
Anderson, S. J. The night before pageant

Arden of Faversham. Arden of Faversham
Aristophanes. Acharnians
Aristophanes. Birds
Aristophanes. Celebrating ladies
Aristophanes. Clouds
Aristophanes. Frogs
Aristophanes. Lysistrata
Aristophanes. Peace
Aristophanes. The sexual congress
Aristophanes. The suits
Aristophanes. Wasps
Aristophanes. Women in power
Boker, G. H. Francesca da Rimini
Calderón de la Barca, P. Life is a dream
Calderón de la Barca, P. The surgeon of honour
Calderón de la Barca, P. Three judgements in one
Cibber, C. The rival queans
Clarke, G. E. Beatrice Chancy
Daborne, R. A Christian turned Turk
Dekker, T. The magnificent entertainment
Dekker, T. The shoemaker's holiday
Euripides. Alcestis
Euripides. The Alcestis of Euripides
Euripides. Alkestis
Euripides. Andromache
Euripides. Bacchae
Euripides. Children of Heracles
Euripides. Cyclops
Euripides. Daughters of Troy
Euripides. Electra
Euripides. Hecuba
Euripides. Helen
Euripides. Hippolytus
Euripides. Ion
Euripides. Iphigenia among the Taurians
Euripides. Iphigenia at Aulis
Euripides. Iphigenia in Tauris
Euripides. The madness of Heracles
Euripides. Medea
Euripides. Orestes
Euripides. The Phoenician women
Euripides. Rhesus
Euripides. Suppliant women
Euripides. The Trojan women
Ford, J. 'Tis pity she's a whore
Greene, R. Selimus, emperor of the Turks

Plays in verse—*Continued*

c Hamlett, C. The magic mermaid
Harrison, T. Doomsday
Harrison, T. The Nativity
Harrison, T. The passion
Heywood, T. A woman killed with kindness
Hughes, L. De organizer
Hughes, T. Euripides' Alcestis
Jonson, B. The alchemist
Jonson, B. Epicoene
Jonson, B. The masque of blackness
Jonson, B. Pleasure reconciled to Virtue
Jonson, B. The queen's masques: the first, of blackness
Jonson, B. Volpone
Kleist, H. von. The broken jug
Kokoschka, O. Murderer, hope of women
Koopman, L. It is finished
Kyd, T. The Spanish tragedy
MacEwen, G. Terror and Erebus
Mandiela, A. Z. Dark diaspora . . . in dub
Manzoni, A. Adelchi: a tragedy
Manzoni, A. The Count of Carmagnola: a tragedy
Marlowe, C. The tragical history of Dr. Faustus
Marlowe, C. The troublesome reign and lamentable death of Edward the Second
Massinger, P. The renegado
c Mast, E. Jungalbook
Mayakovsky, V. Vladimir Mayakovsky
c McCullough, L. E. King Midas and the golden touch
Menander. Dyskolos
Merrill, J. The bait (1953)
Merrill, J. The bait (1988)
Merrill, J. The birthday
Middleton, T. A chaste maid in Cheapside
Middleton, T. The changeling
Molière. The school for wives
Oliver, K. Swollen tongues
Plautus, T. M. Major Blowhard (Miles gloriosus)
Pushkin, A. The miserly knight
Pushkin, A. Mozart and Salieri
Pushkin, A. The stone guest

Racine, J. Phedre
Racine, J. The suitors
Schiller, F. Mary Stuart
Sophocles. Aias
Sophocles. Ajax
Sophocles. Antigone
Sophocles. Electra
Sophocles. Elektra
Sophocles. King Oedipus
Sophocles. Oedipus at Colonus
Sophocles. Oedipus at Kolonos
Sophocles. Oedipus the King
Sophocles. Oedipus Tyrannos
Sophocles. Philoctetes
Sophocles. Philoktetes
Sophocles. The women of Trachis
Warner, F. Goethe's Weimar
Warner, F. Rembrandt's mirror
Webster, J. The Duchess of Malfi
Wilde, O. A Florentine tragedy

Playtime. Schisgal, M.

Please do not suffer. Stein, G.

Pleasure reconciled to Virtue. Jonson, B.

Pleasure (Volupté). Rachilde

The **plot,** like gravy, thickens. St. John, B.

The **plough** and the stars. O'Casey, S.

Plowman, Gillian

There's none so blind. French (London) 1998 30p
ISBN 0-573-12270-9
Blind reflexologist discovers that his wife is having an affair with a colleague. 1 act 4m 3w 1 setting

Touching tomorrow. French (London) 2002 42p
ISBN 0-573-02357-3
Woman with sole responsibility for her learning disabled brother brings home young homeless woman who claims to have been raped. Music, singing. 1 act 6 scenes 2m 3w 1 interior

Plunge. Kyle, C.

Pocahontas, d. 1617

about

c DeTurk, S. Pocahontas

Pocahontas. DeTurk, S.

Pocono Mountains (Pa.)

Simon, N. Neil Simon's proposals

Poe, Edgar Allan, 1809-1849

The oblong box (dramatization) See Barchers, S. I., and Kroll, J. L. The oblong box

Poets

Brecht, B. Baal
Culture Clash (Group). Nuyorican stories
c Deverell, R. Belonging
Eagleton, T. Disappearances
Freed, A. The psychic life of savages
Gough, L. Head
Griffiths, L. Alien creature
Oliver, K. Swollen tongues
Sorge, R. The beggar
Wilder, T. Nascuntur poetae . . .

A **point** of order. Simpson, E.

Poles

England

Poliakoff, S. Coming in to land

Poliakoff, Stephen

Caught on a train.

Television play. Suspense. Young man in European transcontinental express unsettled by high-handed old lady and hostile passengers. 5m 2w extras

In Poliakoff, S. Plays: 3

Coming in to land.

Boulevard play set in London 1986. Successful English professional target of immigration service when he befriends Polish woman desperate to escape oppression. 2 acts 12 scenes 4m 3w 6 interiors

In Poliakoff, S. Plays: 3

Perfect strangers. Methuen 2001 212p
ISBN 0-413-76430-3

Television play. Elaborately organized reunion, held in London. Couple and son find themselves irresistably drawn into their family tree. Large mixed cast

Remember this. Methuen 1999 118p
ISBN 0-413-74360-8

Drama about intense rivalry between generations and insidious role of technology in modern life. While preparing for his second marriage middle-aged man stumbles across disturbing mystery regarding videotape. 2 acts 10 scenes 5m 3w 1 setting

Talk of the city. Methuen 1998 129p
ISBN 0-413-72870-6

Drama about BBC radio on verge of World War II. Singing, dancing. 2 acts 14 scenes 9m 6w 5 interiors 2 exteriors

Police

Corthron, K. Force continuum
Cunninghan, L. Flop cop
Gilman, R. Blue surge
Kalcheim, L. Defiled; or, The convenience of a shorthaired dog
Kennedy, A. Motherhood 2000
McIntyre, D. Split second: a play in two acts
Nassar, M. The mayor's limo
Norton-Taylor, R. The colour of justice
Orton, J. Loot
Walker, G. F. Adult entertainment

Polish Americans

Ives, D. Lives of the saints

Political conventions

Vidal, G. The best man

Political prisoners

Tait, L. East play

Politics

Anouilh, J. Antigone
Ardito, C. A bed for the knight
Ayckbourn, A. House
Bhagat, D. Routes and escape routes
Chappell, E. Up and coming
Congdon, C. Lips
Edgar, D. Maydays
Fo, D. About face
Gurney, A. R. The old boy
Kushner, T. G. David Schine in Hell
Lucie, D. Fashion
Nelson, R. The Vienna notes
Rebeck, T. View of the dome
Robinson, M. Downsizing democracy: a polemic
Taylor, E. A rise in the market
Vidal, G. The best man
Warren, R. P. All the king's men
Warren, R. P. Proud flesh
Warren, R. P. Willie Stark
Wasserstein, W. An American daughter
Wells, M. L. The "I" word: interns
Williamson, D. The great man

Pollock, Alan

The death of cool. Warner Chappell Plays
1999 84p
ISBN 0-85676-234-2

In bohemian London, the charismatic Switch
uses his hangers-on to steal identities and collect
fraudulent disability payments. Black comedy turns
serious when one of his victims tracks him down.
Music. 2 acts 14 scenes 4m 2w 4 interiors 1 exterior

Pollock, Sharon

Angel's trumpet.

Turbulent relationship between Scott and Zelda
Fitzgerald encapsulated in meeting with Zelda's
psychiatrist. 2m 2w 1 setting

In Pollock, S. Three plays

End dream.

Tragedy strikes in 1924 British Columbia when
Scottish nanny looks into odd dealings of her employer. 2 acts 2m 3w

In Pollock, S. Three plays

Moving pictures.

Portrays life of motion picture actress and producer Nell Shipman. 2m 3w

In Pollock, S. Three plays

Pollution

c Fry, G. Lockie Leonard, scumbuster
Polly Ann and John Henry. Barchers, S. I.
Pollyanna. Pargman, S.
The **pomegranate** seeds. Hayes, S.

Pomerance, Bernard

Hands of light.

Allegory about corruptive power of greed. Contemporary exploration of King Midas story. 1 act
15 scenes interlude Variable cast 24 characters 1
setting

In Pomerance, B. The collected plays
of Bernard Pomerance

Melons.

Drama set in New Mexico melon patch, 1906.
Retired Army major and Indian chief reprise Indian Wars. 2 acts 7 scenes 8m 2w 1 setting

In Pomerance, B. The collected plays
of Bernard Pomerance

Quantrill in Lawrence.

Set in Lawrence, Kansas, and environs in 1863.
Guerilla raider William Quantrill leads townspeople on descent into chaos. 16 scenes 12m 5w extras 1 setting

In Pomerance, B. The collected plays
of Bernard Pomerance

Superhighway.

Family of woman dying with cancer find it difficult to cope with her death. 3 acts 8m 6w 1 setting

In Pomerance, B. The collected plays
of Bernard Pomerance

The **Pony** Express. Davidson, R.
Poodle with guitar and dark glasses. Adams, L. D.
Poor Bibi. Oates, J. C.
Poor fellas. Palmieri, M.
Poor Superman. Fraser, B.
Popcorn. Elton, B.
The **popular** mechanicals. Robinson, K.

Pornography

Francis, J. Box
Fraser, B. Snake in fridge
Grimsley, J. Math and aftermath
Mori, B. Adult fiction
Neilson, A. The censor
Vogel, P. Hot'n' throbbing
Port Authority. McPherson, C.

Porter, Cole

Nymph errant; book by Steve Mackes and
Michael Whaley; music and lyrics by
Cole Porter; based on the novel by
James Laver. French 2001 75p
ISBN 0-573-62773-8

Musical about an innocent young woman who
leaves her Swiss finishing school to embark on a
number of romantic adventures across Europe. 2
acts 12 scenes 1m 7w

Porter, Eleanor H., 1868-1920

Polyanna (dramatization) See Pargman,
S. Pollyanna

Porter, Phil

c Smashed eggs. French (London) 2003
54p
ISBN 0-573-05132-1

Two children run away from home because there
are too many rules to obey. 2 acts 4 scenes 1b 1g
1m 1w

Porter, Regina M.

Man, woman, dinosaur.

Mother and son get more than they bargained for
when they hire woman to help out around the
house. 2 acts 12 scenes 1b 2m 2w 1 interior

In Plays from Woolly Mammoth; ed.
by R. Alexander and M. Kyrioglou

Portia Coughlan. Carr, M.
Portrait of a Madonna. Williams, T.
Portrait of a woman. Vinaver, M.
Position available. Gromelski, B.
The **positive** hour. De Angelis, A.

Poskitt, Kjartan

Fawkes—the quiet guy. French (London) 1998 86p
ISBN 0-573-08107-7

A cabaret-type musical about Guy Fawkes and the Gunpowder Plot (1605) to blow up the king and Parliament. Music, singing. 2 acts 17 scenes 15m 8w extras settings

Nell's belles; the swinging sixteen-sixties show. French (London) 2002 103p
ISBN 0-573-08118-2

History as musical comedy. Nell Gwyn (the mistress of Charles II) and her cohorts save England from scheming rivals and religious fanatics. Music, singing. Choruses. Prologue 2 acts 13 scenes 17m 18w extras settings

Posner, Aaron

The chosen. Dramatists 2000 59p
ISBN 0-8222-1740-6

Two Jewish boys from very different homes make friends and come to terms, in surprising ways, with their respective fathers' expectations. Based on Chaim Potok's 1967 novel. Music. 2 acts 17 scenes 5m 4 interiors 2 exteriors 1 setting

Pospisil, Craig

Months on end. Dramatists 2003
ISBN 0-8222-1892-5

In a series of comic scenes—one for each month—we follow the intertwined worlds of a circle of friends and family whose lives are poised between happiness and heartbreak. 5m 5w 1 setting

The **possum** play. Aerenson, B.
Possum's tail. Bruchac, J.

Post, Douglas

Drowning sorrows. Dramatist 1998 61p
ISBN 0-8222-1629-9

Psychological mystery set on island of St. John. Manhattan heiress thinks bartender is fiancé that disappeared years ago. 5 scenes 3m 2w 1 setting

The **Potato** Creek chair of death. Kerr, R.

Potok, Chaim, 1929-2002

The chosen (dramatization) See Posner, A. The chosen

Potter, Beatrix, 1866-1943

The Tale of Jemima Puddle-Duck (dramatization) See Liebman, S. The Tale of Jemina Puddle-Duck

Tales (dramatization) See McNeff, S. Tom Kitten and his friends

Poulton, Mike

Fortune's fool. French (London) 2002 60p
ISBN 0-573-01971-1

Over lunch and champagne, the guests tease one of the estate's permanent residents, a down-at-heels nobleman, until he blurts out a family secret that must be hushed up at all costs. Adapted from a play by Ivan Turgenev. Singing. 2 acts 10m 3w 2 interiors

Pound, Ezra, 1885-1972

about

Kops, B. Ezra

Poverty

Bell, N. McTeague: a tale of San Francisco
Bell, N. Ragged Dick
Blais, M.-C. Fever
Cruz, N. Night train to Bolina
Ganguli, U. Rudali
Gore, C. Modern honor; or, The sharper in high life
y Harden, V. Big boys don't cry
Hughes, L. Angelo Herndon Jones
Johnson, M. Jabiru
Margulies, D. July 7, 1994
Milligan, J. Strange as it may seem
Mtshali, T. S. Weemen
Osborne, A. In sunshine and in shadow
Parks, S.-L. In the blood
Thiong'o, N. W. I will marry when I want
Wood, S. And where was Pancho Villa when you really needed him?

Powell, Dawn

Big night.

Satire set in 1932 New York City. Advertising saleman, on verge of unemployment, entertains potential client from Chicago. 3 acts 6m 3w extras 1 interior

In Powell, D. Four plays

Powell, Dawn—*Continued*

Jig saw.

Comedic look at world of upper-class New Yorkers in 1934. 3 acts 3m 6w extras 2 interiors

In Powell, D. Four plays

Walking down Broadway.

Youthful adventures of residents of women's rooming house in 1931 New York. 3 acts 4 scenes 3m 5w extras 2 interiors

In Powell, D. Four plays

Women at four o'clock.

Expressionistic comedy follows exploits of two young women in whirlwind of 1929 New York. 3 acts 9 scenes 2m 3w extras 6 interiors 2 exteriors

In Powell, D. Four plays

Power, Dominic

Tales of the undead. Favel & Marsden 1997 89p

ISBN 0-9530587-0-0

Comedy set 15 years after conclusion of Bram Stoker's Dracula. Jonathan Harker is in thrall to voluptuous vampire he met in Transylvania. With his marriage on the rocks he agrees to seek help from pioneering sexologist Havelock Ellis. 2 acts 10 scenes 3m 3w settings

Power pipes. Spiderwoman Theater

Pownall, David

Getting the picture. Oberon Bks. 1998 95p

ISBN 1-84002-007-5

Drama set in 1845 America. Irish woman challenges former President, Andrew Jackson, to support movement to break union with Great Britain. 2 acts 4m 2w 1 setting

Powrie, Andy. See Cashmore, B. jt. auth.

Prague (Czech Republic)

Orloff, R. Prague summer

Prague summer. Orloff, R.

Pratchett, Terry

Maskerade (dramatization) See Briggs, S. Terry Pratchett's Maskerade

Carpe jugulum. French (London) 1999 118p

ISBN 0-573-01776-X

Dramatization of the author's novel of the same title. Witches save tiny kingdom of Lancre from suave and deadly vampires. 2 acts 32 scenes Large mixed cast settings

Pratt of the Argus. Birch, M.

Pratt's fall. Parker, S.

Praying for rain. Vaughan, R. L.

The **preacher** and the rapper. Reed, I.

Precipice. Mastrosimone, W.

A **preface** to the alien garden. Alexander, R.

Pregnancy

Blessing, L. Reproduction

Bowen, J. Singles

Corthron, K. Splash hatch on the E going down

Couturier, G. My husband's an angel

Galton, F. Nothing in the world like it

Gault, C. Sky

Griffiths, L. The Darling family

Murray, T. C. The briery gap

Rivera, J. Cloud tectonics

Strachan, Keith. Large as life

Walker, G. F. Tough!

Prehistoric man

London, J. The first poet

Prejudices and antipathies

Chan, M. Mom, Dad, I'm living with a white girl

c Duffield, N. Skin and bones

Gorden, C. Guarding the bridge

Lee, C. Carry the tiger to the mountain

c Martini, C. The field

Wilder, T. The unerring instinct

Williams, R. Lift off

Prelude in Kazbek Street. MacLiammóir, M.

Prelude to a crisis. Roth, A.

Prelude to a kiss. Lucas, C.

Present tense. Gilroy, F. D.

Presidents

Blessing, L. Snapshot: Tyler poked Taylor

Dixon, M. B. Snapshot: little Pezidents

Pretty blue. Chambers, R.

Price, Mary Sue

That midnight rodeo.

Rodeo couple talk about having abortion. 1m 1w 1 setting

In take ten; ed. by E. Lane and N. Shengold

The **price**. Bitterman, S.

The **price** you pay. Hutton, A.

Prichard, Rebecca

Yard gal. Dramatists 2001 45p
ISBN 0-8222-1775-9

Portrays two female gang members, one black and one white, in inner-city London. 3 acts 2w 1 setting

—Same. Faber & Faber 1998 59p
ISBN 0-571-19591-1

Prida, Dolores

Botánica.

College graduate is eager to move away from Spanish neighborhood and grandmother's shop; ends up staying and modernizing business. Music. 2 acts 3m 6w 1 interior

> *In* Puro teatro; ed. by A. Sandoval-Sánchez and N. S. Sternbach

Pride at Southanger Park. Bean, R.

Pride's Crossing. Howe, T.

Pride's Crossing (condensation). Howe, T.

Priests

Davis, B. C. Avow
Feliciano, G. Between blessings
Harding, M. P. Sour grapes
McDonagh, M. The lonesome West
Mérimée, P. The opportunity (L'Occasion)
Murray, T. C. The briery gap
Murray, T. C. Maurice Harte
Murray, T. C. The pipe in the fields
Noone, R. The lepers of Baile Baiste
Reitz, D. Mathematics
Sánchez, E. Clean

Primitive world: an anti-nuclear jazz musical. Baraka, A.

The **prince** and the pauper. Barchers, S. I., and Kroll, J. L.

Prince Edward Island (Canada)

Ledoux, P. Anne
Norman, M. Emily

The **Prince** of Homburg. Kleist, H. von

Princes

c Espinosa, R. Clothes do not make the man (El habito no hace al monje)
c LaVohn, R. W. The smartest woman in the kingdom
c Woodford, K. If the shoe fits

The **prince's** dilemma. Hamlett, C.

The **princess** is sad (La princesa esta triste). Espinosa, R.

Princess Sivatra. Barchers, S. I.

Princesses

c Espinosa, R. The princess is sad (La princesa esta triste)

Prisoners

Bower, H. Natural life
Caplan, P. J. The test
Ehn, E. Cedar (John of the Cross)
Graham, B. Coyote on a fence
Guirgis, S. A. Jesus hopped the "A" train
Horovitz, I. Alfred dies
Tait, L. Live free or die
Williams, T. Not about nightingales

Prisons

Cristofer, M. Amazing grace
Green, P. Hymn to the rising sun: a drama of man's waste
Terry, M. Babes in the bighouse
Williams, T. Not about nightingales
Yeaton, D. Helen at risk

Pritchard, Emily

Chicken wings.

Comedy about two men who meet on a plane, and one of them is afraid of flying. 2m 1 setting

> *In* Blast from the future; ed. by D. Yeaton

Private eyes. Dietz, S.

Private jokes, public places. Safdie, O.

Private lives. Coward, N.

A **private** moment. Gregg, S.

Problem child. Walker, G. F.

The **problem** solver. Dixon, M. B., and Smith, V.

The **processional**. Kemnitz, R. D., and McMaster, J.

Procne (Greek mythology)

Wertenbaker, T. The love of the nightingale

Prodigal kiss. Svich, C.

Prodigals in a promised land. Bunyan, H. J.

Prodigy. Surface, M. H.

The **profoundness** of events. Odato, A.

Progress. Lucie, D.

Prologue. Palmieri, M.

Prom night. LaDue, T.

Prometheus (Greek mythology)

Aeschylus. Prometheus bound

Prometheus and Pandora. Barchers, S. I.

Prometheus bound. Aeschylus

Promiscuity

Williams, T. The eccentricities of a nightingale

Williams, T. Summer and smoke

Proof. Auburn, D.

Proof. Reich, J.

The **prophet** and the rabbi. McCullough, L. E.

The **proposal**. Chekhov, A. P.

Proserpina and the devil: a play for marionettes. Wilder, T.

Prostitutes

Constable, J. The Southwark Mysteries

Field, B. Camille

Filippo, E. de. Filumena—a marriage Italian style

Gilman, R. Blue surge

Levi, S. The gulf of crimson

Ludlam, C. Camille

Piñero, M. Playland blues

Rebeck, T. Sex with the censor

Tait, L. Read to me

Prostitution

Bowne, A. Forty-deuce

Fusco, C. Stuff

Hall, C. The best little whorehouse goes public

Hwang, D. H. The house of sleeping beauties

Iizuka, N. Skin

O'Neill, E. Anna Christie

Ravenhill, M. Mother Clap's Molly house

Robinson, P. Red hot in Amsterdam

Shaw, B. Mrs. Warren's profession

Wedekind, F. Death and devil

Wedekind, F. Lulu

Wedekind, F. The solar spectrum

Protestants

Ireland

O'Casey, S. Red roses for me

Proud flesh. Warren, R. P.

The **prowler** (Le Rôdeur). Rachilde

Przybyszewska, Stanisława, 1901-1935

about

Gems, P. The snow palace

Psychiatric hospitals

Gow, D. Bea's niece

Newmeir, J. H. Semblance of madness!

Psychiatrists

Andersen, D. R. Everywhere

Andersen, D. R. I'll take Manhattan

Andersen, D. R. In other words

Andersen, D. R. They can't take that away from me

Andersen, D. R. Yes, sir, that's my baby

Andersen, D. R. You oughta be in pictures

Carley, S. The edge

Davidson, C. E. Mosquito dirigible aerosol deodorant

Orton, J. What the butler saw

Pollock, S. Angel's trumpet

Scheffer, W. Alien boy

Walker, B. The moons of Alnyron

The **psychic** life of savages. Freed, A.

Psycho beach party. Busch, C.

Psychoanalysis

Ardito, C. Confessions of Zeno

Kushner, T. Terminating

Piatigorsky, A. The kabbalistic psychoanalysis of Adam R. Tzaddik

Psychopathia sexualis. Shanley, J. P.

Psychotherapy

Durang, C. Beyond therapy

Gage, C. Harriet Tubman visits a therapist

Publishers and publishing

Walker, G. F. Love and anger

Puerto Ricans

Astor del Valle, J. Transplantations: straight and other jackets para mi

Pugliese, Frank

Aven'u boys.

Drama about racial and sexual violence among Italian American urban poor in Brooklyn Bensonhurst. Prologue 2 acts 20 scenes epilogue 3m 3w 1 setting

In Pugliese, F. Plays

Pugliese, Frank—*Continued*

Hope is the thing with feathers.

Drama inspired by Emily Dickinson poem. Elderly doctor's moment of impulse towards young girl forever changes lives of three inter-connected couples from different classes. 1b 1g 2m 2w

In Pugliese, F. Plays

The summer winds.

Drama about second-rate singer in Brooklyn motel lounge. Singing. Variable cast 8 characters 1 interior

In Pugliese, F. Plays

Pullin' the wool. Vickery, F.

Puppets and puppet-plays

Beissel, H. Inuk and the sun

Chikamatsu, M. The battles of Coxinga

Chikamatsu, M. The love suicides at Amijima

Chikamatsu, M. The love suicides at Sonezaki

Chikamatsu, M. The uprooted pine

c Hall, L. The adventures of Pinocchio

c Lippa, L. The true adventures of Pinocchio

c Mason, T. Pinocchio

Tait, L. Behave, my sorrow

Taylor, J. Ubu and the Truth Commission

Wellman, M. Infrared

Wilder, T. Proserpina and the devil: a play for marionettes

Purcell, Erin Quinn. See Jackson, G. jt. auth.

Purdah. Mahomed, I.

Purim

c McCullough, L. E. Hail, Queen Esther!

Puritans

y Morreale, V. J. House of the Seven Gables

c York, Y. The witch of Blackbird Pond

Purple dust. O'Casey, S.

Purple side coasters. Daniels, S.

Pushing the prince into Denmark. Levy, D.

Pushing up the sky. Bruchac, J.

Pushkin, Aleksandr Sergeevich, 1799-1837

The negro of Peter the Great (dramatization) See Brown, C. The Negro of Peter the Great

A feast during the plague; tr. by Nancy K. Anderson.

Verse drama based on scene from John Wilson's tragedy The city of the plague about frightened survivors of the Black Death. Variable cast 1 setting

In Pushkin, A. The little tragedies

The miserly knight; tr. by Nancy K. Anderson.

Verse drama portraying clash between miserly father and impecunious son. 3 scenes 6m 3 interiors

In Pushkin, A. The little tragedies

Mozart and Salieri; tr. by Nancy K. Anderson.

Verse drama depicts how Mozart's unpredictable genius affected Antonio Salieri. 2 scenes 2m 2 interiors

In Pushkin, A. The little tragedies

The stone guest; tr. by Nancy K. Anderson.

Verse drama about Don Juan's return from exile. 4 scenes 4m 2w extras 4 interiors

In Pushkin, A. The little tragedies

Putting the kettle on. Brett, S.

Pyramid effect. Dixcy, M.

Q

QED. Parnell, P.

QPH. Sistren Theatre Collective

Quack. Marowitz, C.

Quake. Marnich, M.

Quantrill, William Clarke, 1837-1865

about

Pomerance, B. Quantrill in Lawrence

Quantrill in Lawrence. Pomerance, B.

The **quarrelsome** party. Brossa, J.

Queen Amarantha. Busch, C.

Queen of hearts. Watkins, C.

The **queen** of the parting shot. Manzi, W.

Queens

Busch, C. Queen Amarantha

Queens—*Continued*

Nielson, K. A true fool's folly

The **queens**. Chaurette, N.

The **queen's** champion. Gore, C.

The **queen's** masques: the first, of blackness. Jonson, B.

The **quest**. Esson, L.

A **question** of mercy. Rabe, D.

Quid pro quo; or, The day of the dupes. Gore, C.

Quilter, Peter

Boyband. French (London) 2001 71p
ISBN 0-573-01955-X
Musical about lives of five members of British pop group. 2 acts 5m 1w extras

Respecting your piers. French (London) 2000 71p
ISBN 0-573-13014-0
Comedy farce about five women who inherit a dilapidated pleasure pier. 2 acts 12 scenes 5w 1 setting

Quinn, Nicole B.

The spirit is willing.
Woman reporter at New age espo meets former classmate, who has had a sex change. 2w 1 setting
In take ten; ed. by E. Lane and N. Shengold

Quint and Miss Jessel at Bly. Nigro, D.

R

R. A. W. ('cause I'm a woman). Son, D.

Rabbis

Elisha, R. Two
Sagal, P. Milton Bradley

Rabe, David

The dog problem. French 2002 110p
ISBN 0-573-62796-7
Dark comedy about men, women, sex, betrayal and psychic power. 2 acts 6m 1w extra 1 setting

A question of mercy. Dramatists 1998 77p
ISBN 0-8222-1643-4
Man suffering with AIDS seeks doctor who will put an end to his suffering. 2 acts 6m 1w

—Same. Grove Press 1998 117p
ISBN 0-8021-3549-8   LC 97-40046

Rabin, Arnold

y The man-child.
Boy prepares for Bar Mitzvah. 3 parts 6m 4w extras 1 setting
In Theatre for young audiences; ed. by C. A. Jennings

Race. Pachino, J.

Race discrimination

Boyd, G. E. Consecrated ground
Conning, L. A Coloured place
Davis, T. Everybody's Ruby
Gilman, R. Spinning into butter
Hairston, J. a.m. Sunday
Maponya, M. Umongikazi (The nurse)
Medley, C. Maiden Lane
Ndlovu, D. Sheila's day
Norton-Taylor, R. The colour of justice
Oliver, C. Kicking out
y Oliver, C. Ooh ah Showab Khan
y Surface, M. H. Most valuable player

Race relations

Elwell, J. S. Evening education
O'Donnell, D. White mice
y Surface, M. H. Broken rainbows

Rachel the clever. McCullough, L. E.

Rachilde

Madame La Mort.
Symbolist drama. Neurotic man falls in love with Death (a veiled woman) and commits suicide. 3 acts 13 scenes 4m 2w 1 interior 1 exterior
In Rachilde. Madame La Mort and other plays

The painted woman (La Femme peinte).
A man is haunted by a wartime execution which distorts his relationship with his mistress. 1 act 1m 1w 1 interior
In Rachilde. Madame La Mort and other plays

Pleasure (Volupté).
Teenage lovers play a rather perverse game until frightened by an image of death. 1 act 1 scene 1m 1w 1 exterior
In Rachilde. Madame La Mort and other plays

The prowler (Le Rôdeur).
Women in an isolated house become convinced that a bad man is after them. 1 act 4m settings
In Rachilde. Madame La Mort and other plays

Rachilde—*Continued*

The transparent doll (La poupée transparente).

Grieving woman keeps stillborn child alive in delusional fantasy. Doctor cannot reach her. 1 act 1 scene 1m 1w 1 interior

In Rachilde. Madame La Mort and other plays

Voice of blood (La voix du sang).

Respectable pair ignore cries of "Murder!" from the street; the victim turns out to be their son. 1 act 3m 2w 1 interior

In Rachilde. Madame La Mort and other plays

Racine, Jean

Phedre. Farrar Straus Giroux 1999 87p
ISBN 0-374-23114-1

Blank verse translation of Racine's tragic tale of queen's obsessive love for her stepson and the fall of family and kingdom that result from it. 5 acts 5 scenes 3m 5w

The suitors; tr. by Richard Wilbur. Dramatists 2001 67p
ISBN 0-8222-1804-6

Translation of Racine's only comedy, written in 1688. Satire of the legal system meshes with romantic intrigue. 3 acts 26 scenes 6m 2w settings

Radano, Lisa-Maria

Bright angel.

Woman tries to come to terms with mother's death. 2w 1 interior

In HB Playwrights short play festival 1997

The divine child.

Grieving mother and daughter meet old woman in funeral parlor. 1g 2w 1 interior

In HB Playwrights short play festival 2000

Radicals and radicalism

Silver, N. The altruists

Radio broadcasting

Baraka, A. The election machine warehouse

Gay, N. Radio times

Gilroy, F. D. The next contestant

Poliakoff, S. Talk of the city

Radio elephant (Barbara). Ehn, E.

Radio mambo. Culture Clash (Group)

Radio plays

Bachmann, I. The cicadas

Bachmann, I. A deal in dreams

Bachmann, I. The good god of Manhattan

Blais, M.-C. A couple

Blais, M.-C. Exile

Blais, M.-C. Fever

Blais, M.-C. Ghost of a voice

Eagleton, T. God's locusts

Gough, L. Head

Gough, L. Our lady of shadows

Griffiths, L. The Duchess, a.k.a. Wallis Simpson

Hall, L. Child of our time: child of the snow

Hall, L. Child of our time: children of the rain

Kennedy, A. Dramatic circle

MacEwen, G. Terror and Erebus

Reid, C. My name, shall I tell you my name

Sher, E. Denial is a river

Sher, E. Mourning dove

Sher, E. Past imperfect

Wesker, A. Yardsale

Radio Rooster says that's bad. O'Donnell, D.

Radio times. Gay, N.

Raffle, Diana

Blue suede blues. French (London) 2003 17p
ISBN 0-573-02362-X

Comedy about two nursing home residents who kidnap a young care assistant with hilarious results. 2m 4w 1 setting

Ragged Dick. Bell, N.

Ragged time. Mayer, O.

Rahman, Aishah

The Mojo and the Sayso.

African American family drama portraying effects of police brutality upon victim's survivors. 2 acts 3 scenes 3m 1w 1 interior

In Rahman, A. Plays

Only in America.

Satire. Synthesizes jazz and vernacular speech to give voice to America's invisible women. 2 acts 1m 3w 1 interior

In Rahman, A. Plays

Rahman, Aishah—*Continued*

Unfinished women cry in no man's land while a bird dies in a gilded cage.

Charlie Parker's final hours in his mistress's boudoir juxtaposed with scenes of pregnant residents of 1950, home for unwed mothers. Music. Overture 12 scenes 2m 7w 2 interiors

In Rahman, A. Plays

The **railing** (El pasamanos). Pedrero, P.

Railing it uptown. Lauro, S.

Railroad construction workers

Hwang, D. H. The dance and the railroad

Railroads

Travel

Poliakoff, S. Caught on a train

Sher, E. Derailed

Raleigh, Sir Walter, 1552?-1618

about

Walcott, D. Drums and colours

Rambo, David

God's man in Texas. Dramatists 2001 67p

ISBN 0-8222-1801-1   LC 2002-278653

Comedy about young minister auditioning to become successor to famous pastor of the Rock Baptist Church of Houston, Texas. 2 acts 20 scenes 3m 1 setting

Rame, Franca, and Fo, Dario

A woman alone.

Monologue. Woman locked in apartment by possessive husband illustrates how women are treated as sexual objects. 1w

In Mythic women/Real women

Ramsay, Peggy, 1908-1991

about

Plater, A. Peggy for you

Rand, Ayn, 1905-1982

about

Gilbert, S. The emotionalists

Rand, Silas Teritus

about

Redhill, M. Building Jerusalem

Rape

Alvarez, L. Hidden parts

Berman, B. Dancing with a devil

Chiasson, H. Alienor

Clarke, G. E. Beatrice Chancy

Goupil, L. Dark owl; or, The renegade angel

Macklin, P. Someplace warm

Mérimée, P. Carvajal's family (La famille de Carvajal)

Plowman, G. Touching tomorrow

Walsh, E. Sucking Dublin

Williams, M. N. Kwa-landlady

Rapp, Adam

Finer noble gases.

Drug-addled encounters in a freezing, squalid apartment, home to a once promising rock band. Music, singing. 1 act 5m 1w 1 interior

In Humana Festival 2002

Nocturne. Faber & Faber 2002 81p

ISBN 0-571-21132-1 (pa)   LC 2001-53151

Monologue by man reflecting on the accidental killing of his sister. 4 parts 1g 2m 2w epilogue

Train story.

Drama set on train travelling from New York to Los Angeles. Encounter between middle-aged female book editor and young woman. 2w 1 interior

In The Best American short plays, 2000-2001

Rappaccini's daughter. Barchers, S. I., and Kroll, J. L.

Rapunzel. Boettcher-Tate, K.

Rats

c Ellison, L. Space junk

A **rat's** mass. Kennedy, A.

Ravenhill, Mark

Faust (Faust is dead). Methuen 1997 38p

ISBN 0-413-71840-9

World famous philosopher is greeted as star in Los Angeles. When he meets young man on the run from his software magnate father they embark on hedonistic cross-country trip. 20 scenes 3m extras settings

Mother Clap's Molly house. Methuen 2001 152p

ISBN 0-413-76930-5

Black comedy with songs set in London. Juxtaposes scenes of whorehouse in 1726 with group of wealthy gay men preparing for party in 2001. Music, singing. 2 acts 11 scenes 15m 6w settings

Ravenhill, Mark—*Continued*
Shopping and fucking.

Satiric look at commodity culture in which money rules. Five young Londoners engulfed by drugs, sex and lack of values. 14 scenes 3m 2w 1 setting
In The Methuen book of modern drama; ed. by G. Whybrow

Ray, Connie

Sanders family Christmas; book by Connie Ray; conceived by Alan Bailey; musical arrangement by John Foley and Gary Fagin. French 1999 62p
ISBN 0-573-62644-8

Sequel to Smoke on the mountain. Family invited to sing gospel music on Christmas Eve, 1941 prior to young men going off to war. 2 acts 3m 3w 1 setting

Rayson, Hannie

Hotel Sorrento.

Drama set in Sorrento, Australia. Three sisters, reunited after ten years in vastly different worlds, again experience stress of family life. 2 acts 45 scenes 4m 4w 1 setting
In Contemporary Australian plays; ed. by R. Vandenbroucke

Life after George. Currency Press 2000 80p
ISBN 0-86819-628-2

Academic dies in plane crash, his wife and two ex-wives attend the funeral, each one reflecting a decade from the 1960s to the 1990s. 2 acts 2m 4w settings

Raznovich, Diana

Disconcerted (El disconcierto); tr. by Victoria Martinez.

Monologue by a pianist who is giving one of her famous "silent concerts," the only kind permitted to her by an oppressive regime. Suddenly the keyboard begins to sound. She is overjoyed, then realizes she can no longer play. Music. 1 act 1w 1 interior
In Raznovich, D. Defiant acts (Actos desafiantes)

Inner gardens (Jardín de otoño); tr. by Nora Glickman and Victoria Martinez.

Comedy. Infatuated with a TV soap opera star, two middle-aged ladies decide to abduct him. 2 acts 8 scenes 3m 3w settings
In Raznovich, D. Defiant acts (Actos desafiantes)

MaTRIX, inc. (Casa matriz); tr. by Victoria Martinez and Lidia Ramirez.

Satirical comedy. The MaTRIX agency enables its clients to play out a full range of ghastly mother-daughter relationships. 1 act 2w 1 interior
In Raznovich, D. Defiant acts (Actos desafiantes)

Rear entry (De atrás para adelante); tr. by Victoria Martinez.

Disowned son returns to save the family business—unrecognized, since he is now she. Background music. 2 acts 3 scenes 3m 3w extras 1 interior
In Raznovich, D. Defiant acts (Actos desafiantes)

Reach for the stars. McCullough, L. E.
Read to me. Tait, L.

Reader, Caroline

y The Oedipus plays. French (London) 2002 46p
ISBN 0-573-05130-5

Adaptation of three of Sophocles' classic tragedies: Oedipus the King, Oedipus at Colonus, and Antigone. Thebes rebuilds itself after being ravaged by plague. Speaking chorus. 2 acts 9m 53 extras 2 exteriors

The **reading** group. Weldon, F.
Reading Hebron. Sherman, J.

Reakes, Paul

y Bluebeard. French (London) 2003
ISBN 0-573-16450-9

Pantomine with music based legend of the sinister Baron Bluebeard. Music, singing. 2 acts 12 scenes Variable cast

c Little Red Riding Hood. French (London) 2002 77p
ISBN 0-573-16434-7

Pantomime with music. Prince, a werewolf, rescues young girl from evil count. 2 acts 12 scenes 6m 4w extras 2 interiors 2 exteriors

c Robinson Crusoe and the pirates. French (London) 2000 81p
ISBN 0-573-16443-6

Pantomime with music. Crusoe boys thwarted in hopes of marrying sweethearts go in search of buried treasure. Singing, dancing. 2 acts 12 scenes 9m 4w extras settings

—Same. French (London) 2000 81p
ISBN 0-573-16443-6

Real, Carole

The battle of Bull Run always makes me cry.

Three women meet in coffee shop and talk about man that the women dated. 1m 3w 1 setting

In take ten; ed. by E. Lane and N. Shengold

Real estate business

Crimp, M. Dealing with Clair

Wright, D. Wildwood Park

Real real gone. Wells, M. L.

The **real** story of Little Red Riding Hood. Reiser, D.

The **real** thing. Stoppard, T.

Real to reel. Gilroy, F. D.

Reality. Blomquist, E.

Really Rosie. King, C.

Rear entry (De atrás para adelante). Raznovich, D.

Rebeck, Theresa

Abstract expression.

Drama about true value of art focuses on uneasy relationship between young woman and her alcoholic artist father. 2 acts 21 scenes 6m 3w 3 interiors

In Women playwrights: the best plays of 1999

The bar plays.

Disillusioned denizens of seedy bar. Background music. 1 act 4m 3w extra 1 interior

In Rebeck, T. Collected plays, 1989-1998

The butterfly collection. French 2002

ISBN 0-573-62794-0

Comic drama. Nobel-winning novelist suffering from writer's block interacts with his family. 2 acts 14 scenes 3m 3w 1 interior

—Same

In Women playwrights: the best plays of 2000

The contract.

Actor discusses career with new agent. 1 act 2m 1 interior

In Rebeck, T. Collected plays, 1989-1998

Does this woman have a name?

Comedy. Woman writer starts telephone sex business with actress friend. 7 scenes 1m 2w 1 interior

In Rebeck, T. Collected plays, 1989-1998

The family of Mann.

Satirical look at television sitcom executives. 2 acts 28 scenes 4m 3w 1 interior

In Rebeck, T. Collected plays, 1989-1998

The funeral play.

Mix-up at funeral parlor. 1 act 2m 1 interior

In HB Playwrights short play festival 2000

Great to see you.

Husband and wife meet his old girlfriend for lunch. 1 act 1m 2w 1 interior

In Rebeck, T. Collected plays, 1989-1998

Katie and Frank.

Troubled wife threatens husband with gun. 1 act 1m 1w 1 interior

In Rebeck, T. Collected plays, 1989-1998

Loose knit.

Set in present-day New York City. Five women in their thirties gather to knit while their lives unravel. 2 acts 9 scenes 2m 5w 1 setting

In Rebeck, T. Collected plays, 1989-1998

Sex with the censor.

Unusual encounter with prostitute. 1 act 1m 1w 1 interior

In Rebeck, T. Collected plays, 1989-1998

Spike heels.

Romantic comedy of manners set in Boston explores contemporary relations between the sexes. 2 acts scenes 2m 2w 2 interiors

In Rebeck, T. Collected plays, 1989-1998

Sunday on the rocks.

Comedy. Female housemates drink, joke, and argue about difficulties of making moral decisions in complex world. 2 acts 5 scenes 4w 1 exterior

In Rebeck, T. Collected plays, 1989-1998

View of the dome. French 1998 83p

ISBN 0-573-62603-0

Rebeck, Theresa—*Continued*

Political satire. Young Washington, D.C. attorney persuades her former law professor to run for Congress. 5m 2w 1 interior

—Same

> *In* Rebeck, T. Collected plays, 1989-1998

What we're up against.

Two young male architects discuss female colleague. 1 act 2m 1 interior

> *In* Rebeck, T. Collected plays, 1989-1998

Recipe for murder. Robins, J. D.

Red. Yew, C.

The **red** address. Ives, D.

The **red** balloon. Clark, A.

Red earth. Lan, D.

Red hot in Amsterdam. Robinson, P.

Red mango. Tidler, C.

Red Riding Hood. Robbins, N.

Red Riding Hood. Snyder, G. A.

The **red** room. Gough, L.

Red roses for me. O'Casey, S.

Red roses for my lady. Levi, S.

Red scare on Sunset. Busch, C.

Red turf. Mayne, R.

The **redeemer** of minutes. Bass, A.

The **redemption** song. Osborne, A.

Redgrave, Lynn

Shakespeare for my father. French 2001 61p

> ISBN 0-573-62758-4   LC 2001-270866

Biographical monologue. Uses scenes from Shakespeare to parallel important moments from Ms. Redgrave's young life and memories of her father, Sir Michael Redgrave. 2 acts 5 scenes epilogue 1w 1 setting

Redgrave, Sir Michael, 1908-1985

about

Redgrave, L. Shakespeare for my father

Redhill, Michael

Building Jerusalem. Playwrights Canada 2000 73p

> ISBN 0-88754-610-2

Domestic scientist Adelaide Hoodless, mathematician Karl Pearson, missionary Silas Rand, and physician/suffragette Augusta Stowe-Gullen spend New Year's eve 1899 together. Music. 2m 3w 1 interior

Redwood, John Henry

No niggers, no Jews, no dogs. Dramatists 2003

> ISBN 0-8222-1828-3

Drama about African American couple set in North Carolina in 1949. Wife is raped by white man when husband goes to work in Alabama. 2m 2w 1 exterior setting

The old settler. Dramatists 1998 67p

> ISBN 0-8222-1642-6

Two elderly sisters in Harlem, 1943, take in a boarder, a naive young man who has come to the city to find his runaway girlfriend. The older, more dignified sister sees a last chance for romantic happiness. Music, singing. 2 acts 8 scenes 1m 3w 1 interior

Reed, Ishmael

Hubba city.

Drama set in African American neighborhood in Oakland, California. Local residents confront drug dealer when police and politicians are slow to act. 2 acts 12m 3w 3 interiors

> *In* Action; ed. by M. Algarin and L. Griffith

The preacher and the rapper.

Drama accuses Christian churches of sexism, misogyny and being out of touch on cultural issues. Prologue 2 acts 6 scenes Variable cast 3 interiors

> *In* Action; ed. by M. Algarin and L. Griffith

Savage wilds.

Satire. Two feminists accused of murder participate in sting operation to bring down the mayor of Washington, D.C. 2 acts 7 scenes 8m 5w 4 interiors

> *In* Action; ed. by M. Algarin and L. Griffith

Reed, Martin. See Long, A. jt. auth.

References to Salvador Dali make me hot. Rivera, J.

Refuge. Goldberg, J.

Refugees

c Deverell, R. Video wars

Ensler, E. Necessary targets

c Hines, K. Home on the mornin' train

Regina (Sask.)

Robinson, M. The heart as it lived

The **rehearsal.** Caleb, J. R.

Rehearsal for the destruction of Atlantis. Smith, J.

Rehoboam (Biblical figure)

c Vogel, L. Rehoboam rubs 'em wrong

Rehoboam rubs 'em wrong. Vogel, L.

Reich, Jeff

Proof.

Academic politics. Disillusioned research assistant tries to escape from his mentor, a cunning old bore with a Nobel Prize in his pocket. Slides. 1 act 2 scenes 2m 2 interiors

In Ensemble Studio Theatre marathon 2000: the one-act plays

Reid, Christina

My name, shall I tell you my name.

Radio play set simultaneously in Derry old people's home and London's Holloway prison. Explores intransigent nature of Protestant patriotism in Northern Ireland. 1m 1w extra

In War plays by women; ed. by C. M. Tylee, E. Turner, and A. Cardinal

The **reincarnation** of Jaime Brown. Alvarez, L.

Reingold, Jacquelyn

Acapulco.

Humorous look at a marriage on the rocks in the 1960s, Acapulco. 2 acts 18 scenes 3m 3w settings

In New dramatists: best plays by the graduating class of 2000

Creative development.

Satire. Goddess poses as playwright and confronts creative director of film company. 1m 1w extras 1 interior

In The Best American Short plays, 1997-1998

Dottie and Richie.

Jewish comedian falls for woman he meets in funeral home. 1m 1w 1 interior

In HB Playwrights short play festival 2000

Joe and Stew's Theatre of Brotherly Love and Financial Success.

Comedy set in off-off Broadway theater. Cockroaches survive atomic warfare. Singing. 2m extras 1 interior

In The Best American short plays 1999-2000

Tunnel of love.

Satirical look at shrinks, physicians, analysts and other experts. Young woman and boyfriend have special problem. 12 scenes 2m 4w settings

In The Best American short plays, 1996-1997

Reiser, David

c The real story of Little Red Riding Hood; book by Judy Wolfman; music and lyrics by David Reiser. Pioneer Drama Service 1998 28p

Musical retelling of fairy tale from wolf's point of view. Variable cast 10 characters 1 setting

Reitz, Daniel

And that's how people burn to death in motel rooms.

Two male lovers in motel room. 2m 1 interior

In HB Playwrights short play festival 1997

Divulgence at Damarak 18.

Two women friends in Amsterdam sex museum reconcile past differences. 2w 1 interior

In HB Playwrights short play festival 1998

Mathematics.

Drama set in Brooklyn funeral home. Adolescent boy attends funeral of priest who sexually abused him. 1b 1m 1 interior

In HB Playwrights short play festival 2000

Where I come from.

Play set in passenger terminal at Kennedy Airport. Young woman and boyfriend wait to board flight to Middle East. 2m 1w 1 interior

In HB Playwrights short play festival 1999

Relative strangers. Wilner, S.

Religion

Burke, K. J. Comfort and joy

Conquest, N. For they shall see God

Gabre-Medhin, T. Collision of altars

Gough, L. Crossing the bar

Guare, J. The general of hot desire

Guirgis, S. A. Jesus hopped the "A" train

Hawdon, R. God and Stephen Hawking

Ibsen, H. Emperor and Galilean: a world historical drama

Lauro, S. Sunday go to meetin'

Revenge—*Continued*

Kyd, T. The Spanish tragedy

Lindsay-Abaire, D. Snapshot: history lesson

Linney, R. Strindberg

Lloyd, M. Dead certain

Lucas, C. Stranger

Martin, J. Mr. Bundy

Martin, J. Tattoo

McConnell, J. Short changed

Milligan, J. Getting even

Milligan, J. Rivals

y Nielsen, K. Hamlet

Nigro, D. The dead wife

Parks, S.-L. Fucking A

Shaw, B. Captain Brassbound's conversion

Sondheim, S. Sweeney Todd

Sophocles. Electra

Tait, L. Germany

Walker, G. F. Criminal genius

Webster, J. The Duchess of Malfi

Reverse transcription. Kushner, T.

Revolution

Alvarez, L. Thin air: tales from a revolution

Field, B. Pantagleize

Reynolds, Jean

Physical therapy.

Comedy about woman who persuades friend to get certain type of physical therapy. 1 act 2w 1 interior

In Off-Off Broadway festival plays, 24th ser.

Reynolds, Jonathan

Stonewall Jackson's house. Broadway Play Pub. 1997 84p

ISBN 0-88145-140-1

Comical tirade against political orthodoxy. Black guide in restored home of Confederate general asks well-to-do white couple if she can be their slave. 2 acts 3 scenes 2m 3w 1 interior

Rez politics. Yellow Robe, W. S.

The **Rez** sisters. Highway, T.

Reza, Yasmina

Art; translated by Christopher Hampton. Faber & Faber 1998 63p

ISBN 0-571-19014-6

Relations between three old friends are sorely strained when one of them buys an expensive avant-garde painting. 1 act 3m 1 setting

Art (condensation).

In The Best Plays of 1997-1998; ed. by Otis L. Guernsey, Jr.

Conversation after a burial; translated by Christopher Hampton. Faber & Faber 2000 75p

ISBN 0-571-20441-4

Comic play about love and betrayal. Brother, a sister, lovers, and inlaws of deceased gather for his funeral. 9 scenes 3m 3w 1 setting

Life X 3; tr. by Christopher Hampton. Faber & Faber 2000 66p

ISBN 0-571-20738-3

Comedy about personal intimacies and private longings. Couple arrives day earlier than expected for dinner party. 3 acts 2m 2w extra 1 interior

The unexpected man; translated by Christopher Hampton. Faber & Faber 1998 71p

ISBN 0-571-19604-7

On a train from Paris to Frankfurt an author and an admirer of his work share a compartment. 1m 1w 1 interior

—Same; translation by Christopher Hampton. Dramatists 1998 35p

ISBN 0-8222-1793-7

Rhesus. Euripides

Rhymes, Beverly Guyton

The way of the cross.

Worship program. Seven readers follow a leader on the path of Jesus' life and ministry. Variable cast 8 characters extras

In The drama of Easter; ed. by R. Wray

Rhys, Tim

The old petrol station.

Dark comedy of two gas station attendants who work near a Welsh ghost town, and help two stranded travellers. 1 act 3m 1w 1 setting

In Act one Wales; ed. by P. Clark

Rice boy. Kuruvilla, S.

Riddance. McLean, L.

The **ride** down Mt. Morgan. Miller, A.

Ridley, Philip

y Sparkleshark. French (London) 1997 39p

ISBN 0-573-05122-4

Ridley, Philip—*Continued*

Drama about storytelling. Geeky teenage boy uses his writing ability to fight off taunts of others. 6b 3g 1 setting

A **right** to vote. Fredericks, A. D.

Right you are (if you think you are) (Cosi è, se ui pare). Pirandello, L.

Rilke, Rainer Maria, 1875-1926

Of God and other matters, told to grownups for children (dramatization) See Sills, P. Stories of God

Ring around Jerusalem. Vogel, L.

The **Ring** sisters. Laurence, C.

A **ringing** of bells. Fry, C.

Rintoul, Harry

Brave hearts.

On the fringes of a raucous party, a man contrives to get a moment alone with the older man who influenced him years ago. 1 scene 2m 1 setting

In Short spells: scenes & monologues; ed. by V. Shantz

Río, Marcela del

On the way to the concert; tr. by Juan Bruce-novoa and Marcela de Rio.

Drama set in intensive care unit of hospital in Mexico City, March 1983. Last moments in life of violinist, injured in car accident on way to concert. 1 act 1m extras

In Five plays in translation from Mexican contemporary theater; ed. by S. Rodríguez del Pino

Riot. Moodie, A.

Rip Van Winkle. Jefferson, J., and Boucicault, D.

Rip Van Winkle; or, "The works". Nelson, R.

A **rise** in the market. Taylor, E.

Rising fish prayer. May, A.

Risk everything. Walker, G. F.

Rites and ceremonies

Karnad, G. The fire and the rain

Soyinka, W. The strong breed

Jewish

y Rabin, A. The man-child

The **rival** queans. Cibber, C.

Rivals. Milligan, J.

River, Sol B.

Moor masterpieces.

Journey through black history. Othello, James Baldwin, Solomon, Duke Ellington and Martin Luther King talk about past, present, slavery, and liberation. 4 acts 5 scenes 5m extras 1 setting

In River, S. B. Plays

To Rahtid.

Monologue written in Jamaica patois. 1m

In River, S. B. Plays

Unbroken.

Brief theatrical piece written for dance company. Variable cast 9 characters 1 setting

In River, S. B. Plays

Rivera, Carmen

Betty's garage.

Underground railroad helps victims of domestic abuse. 1g 1m 3w extras 1 interior

In Women's Project & productions; ed. by J. Miles

Rivera, Diego, 1886-1957

about

Cruz, M. Frida: the story of Frida Kahlo

Rivera, Jose

187.

Man pursues woman co-worker at bus stop. 1m 1w 1 setting

In Actors Theatre of Louisville. Ten-minute plays: v4

Cloud tectonics. Broadway Play Pub. 1997 71p

ISBN 0-88145-137-1

Man picks up pregnant hitchhiker on stormy night in Los Angeles after which time stops and supernatural forces take over. Prologue epilogue 2m 1w 1 interior

The crooked cross.

Young woman alienates her friends when she wears swastika earrings her boyfriend gave her as a birthday gift. 3m 3w 1 setting

In Rivera J. Giants have us in their books

Flowers.

Brother and sister talk about her acne problem, when suddenly sister's acne turns into flowers. 1m 1w 1 setting

In Rivera J. Giants have us in their books

Rivera, Jose—*Continued*

Gas.

Monologue. Latino gas pump attendant talks about his brother fighting in first Persian Gulf war. 1m 1 setting

In Rivera J. Giants have us in their books

Maricela de la Luz lights the world.

While Christmas shopping in San Diego Mall, brother and sister witness battle of Gods from various cultures. 2 acts Variable cast 1 setting

In Multicultural theatre II; ed. by R. Ellis

References to Salvador Dali make me hot.

Surrealistic fable set in Barstow, California. Explores subconsious workings of relationship between career soldier and his romantic wife. 4 acts Variable cast 5 characters 2 interiors 1 exterior

In Latino plays from South Coast Repertory

Tape.

Unidentified visitor in room must listen to tape recordings of past lives. Variable cast 2 characters

In 30 ten-minute plays for 2 actors from Actors Theatre of Louisville's National Ten-minute Play Contest

—Same

In Rivera J. Giants have us in their books

A tiger in Central Park.

Couple build a trap in Central Park for an escaped tiger terrorizing New York. 1m 2w extras 1 setting

In Rivera J. Giants have us in their books

The winged man.

High school student exploring cave discovers wounded man with wings. 1m 3w 1 setting

In Rivera, J. Giants have us in their books

The **road** to ruin. Dresser, R.

Road trips

Kerr, R. The Potato Creek chair of death

Roadtrip. Brown, V. N.

Roanoke Colony (N.C.)

Green, P. The lost colony

Robbers. Kessler, L.

Robbins, Norman

c Jack and Jill. French (London) 2002 74p

ISBN 0-573-16426-6

Pantomime with music about two children who fetch water from magic well. Music, singing. Chorus Prologue 2acts 12 scenes Variable cast

c Red Riding Hood. French (London) 1999 79p

ISBN 0-573-06499-7   LC 00-712165

Musical pantomime version of the famous fairy tale. Prologue 2 acts 12 scenes Variable cast 10 characters

Tiptoe through the tombstones. French (London) 1998 75p

ISBN 0-473-01917-7

Comedy thriller about lawyer who plans to kill the remaining members of the Tomb family to get their inheritance. 2 acts 4 scenes 4m 6w 1 setting

Roberts, Belinda

c Angelica! . . . and the monstrous monster of the deep. French (London) 2000 41p

ISBN 0-573-05124-0

An inventive girl enters a goofy undersea kingdom to save her brother from a giant eel. Singing, dancing. 2 acts 11 scenes 1b 1g 8m 3w extras 1 interior 3 exteriors

Robinette, Joseph

c Charlotte's web.

Dramatization of E. B. White's classic children's tale. 2 acts Unidentified cast 14 characters extras 1 interior 2 exteriors

In Theatre for young audiences; ed. by C. A. Jennings

c Humpty-Dumpty is missing. Dramatic Publishing 2003 46p

Spoof of private eye thrillers of the 1940s and '50s. Variable cast 1 setting

c Sarah, plain and tall. Dramatic Publishing 2003

Dramatization of Patricia MacLachlan's novel set in early 1900s Kansas. Widower with two children advertises for wife. 2 acts 5m 7w 1 setting

Robins, J. D.

Recipe for murder. French (London) 2203 45p

ISBN 0-573-01985-1

Thriller about a sickly scientist, whose wife's grandmother and first husband died mysteriously. 2 acts 5 scenes 2m 2w 1 setting

Robinson, Jackie, 1919-1972

about

y Surface, M. H. Most valuable player

Robinson, Keith

The popular mechanicals.

Comedy based on passage from William Shakespeare's A midsummer night's dream. Rustic players present play about Pyramus and Thisbe. 2 acts 11 scenes 4m 2w

In Contemporary Australian plays; ed. by R. Vandenbroucke

Robinson, Mansel

Colonial tongues.

Drama set in small northern Ontario town in 1967 and 1995. Family confronts social and economic changes. 2 acts 3m 2w 1 setting

In Staging the North; ed. by S. Grace, E. D'Aeth and L. Chalykoff

Downsizing democracy: a polemic.

Monologue that is a critique of the Canadian government's economic policies, in the era of big business. 1 scene Variable cast 1 setting

In Short spells: scenes & monologues; ed. by V. Shantz

The heart as it lived. Playwrights Canada 1998 82p

ISBN 0-88754-554-8

Political drama set in 1996 Regina, Saskatchewan. When grandson of her estranged sister breaks into her home, puritanical spinster forced to confront events surrounding riots of 1935. 2 acts 12 scenes 3m 2w 1 interior

Robinson, Patricia

Red hot in Amsterdam. French (London) 1999 37p

ISBN 0-573-12218-0   LC 00-703189

Comedy about two diamond thieves in Amsterdam who hide stolen diamonds in a brothel. 3 scenes 3m 4w 1 setting

Robinson, Rony

No love lost. French (London) 1999 92p

ISBN 0-573-01810-3

Romantic comedy. Couple tell the story of their marriage break-up in two chronological threads. Prologue 2 acts 16 scenes epilogue 5m 4w 1 setting

Robinson Crusoe and the pirates. Reakes, P.

Robots

c McCullough, L. E. Robots are everywhere (robotics engineer)

Robots are everywhere (robotics engineer). McCullough, L. E.

Robson, James

Mr Wonderful. French (London) 2000 81p

ISBN 0-573-01857-X

Forty-five year old factory worker with bedridden mother seeks romance through dating agency. 2 acts 14 scenes 5m 2w settings

Rocamora, Carol

"I take your hand in mine. . .". Smith & Kraus 2000 59p

ISBN 1-57525-244-9

A play suggested by the love letters of Anton Chekhov and Olga Knipper. 1m 1w

Roche, Billy

Amphibians. Dramatists 2003

ISBN 0-8222-1912-3

Inspired by the biblical story of Isaac, this is a dark, elegiac tale of the sea. 8m 3w 1 setting

The Cavalcaders. Dramatists 2003

ISBN 0-8222-1913-1

Four small-town shoemakers transform themselves nightly into a singing quartet, The Cavalcaders. Singing. 4m 2w 1 interior setting

Rock around the block. Francoeur, B.

Rock music

Butterworth, J. Mojo

Quilter, P. Boyband

Rockball, our natural pastime. Vogel, L.

Rocks. Palmieri, M.

Rocky of the rainforest. Murray, S.

Roderer, Emily

Scheherazade.

Man and young girl meet on ship and start making up stories about other travelers to pass the time. 1m 1w 1 exterior

In 30 ten-minute plays for 2 actors from Actors Theatre of Louisville's National Ten-minute Play Contest

Rodgers, Richard

Flower drum song; music by Richard Rodgers; lyrics by Oscar Hammerstein II; book by David Henry Hwang. Theatre Communications Group 2003 115p

ISBN 1-559-36222-7 LC 2003-4055

Musical about Asian Americans living in San Francisco in 1960. Music, singing, dancing. 2 acts 14 scenes 7m 3w extras 1 setting

Rodin, Toby

The slow eviction of Ruby Rosenholtz.

Drama about denizens of rooming house for drifters and displaced persons in Vancouver, Canada. 13 scenes 2m 2w 3 interiors

In Prerogatives

Rodriguez, Eduardo Solis

Soldiers will be soldiers; tr. by William Bryant.

Absurdist anti-war farce. Soldiers fighting in trenches bring along inflatable dolls to sleep with. Prologue 2 acts 6m 4w 1 setting

In Five plays in translation from Mexican contemporary theater; ed. by S. Rodríguez del Pino

Rodriguez, Eugene

Estorias del barrio: un ghost.

Father's ghost comes to aid of poverty stricken son. 1 act 2m 1w 1 interior

In Action; ed. by M. Algarin and L. Griffith

Roets, Jo

y Cyrano.

Adaptation of Cyrano de Bergerac by Edmond Rostand. French poet of the 17th century handicapped by long nose strives to secure happiness of woman he loves. 5 acts 2m 1w

In Seattle Children's Theatre v2

Rogers, Alva

The life before/reconstruction/ reconstructing whiteness.

Drama about miscegenation set in birthing chamber of the future. 5 scenes 5w 1 interior

In Women's Project & productions; ed. by J. Miles

Rogerson, P. B.

While shepherds watched. Pioneer Drama Service 2000 14p

Drama based on Gospels of Mark and Luke. Roman centurion who witnessed execution of Jesus recalls his unexpected role in Christ's nativity. 4 scenes Variable cast 10 characters 1 exterior

Roll 'em up, roll 'em up! (pastry chef). McCullough, L. E.

Roman, John

c Papa's angels: a Christmas story; by Collin Wilcox Paxton; in collaboration with Charles Jones; music by John Roman with arrangements by Phyllis Dunne. French 2000 79p

ISBN 0-573-62749-5

Musical about children who cheer father up with Christmas morning surprises. Music, singing. 13 scenes Variable cast 15 characters extras 1 setting

Roman empire

Ibsen, H. Emperor and Galilean: a world historical drama

Romance. Lhota, B.

Romance in a flat. Feydeau, G.

Romance in D. Sherman, J.

Romania

Leight, W. The final interrogation of Ceauşescu's dog

Rome

Allison, B. Titus at the gates of Syon

Ardito, C. Waiting for the barbarians

Plautus, T. M. Major Blowhard (Miles gloriosus)

Sondheim, S. A funny thing happened on the way to the forum

Romer, Marcus

y Rumble fish. Dramatic Publishing 2003 62p

Stage version of S. E. Hinton's classic novel explores themes of gang culture and the search for identity. 2 acts 15m 6w 1 setting

Romeril, John

Miss Tanaka. Currency Press 2001 58p

ISBN 0-86819-639-8 LC 2001-411979

Romeril, John—*Continued*

Dramatization of Xavier Herbert's story set in 1930s Broome, Australia. Beautiful and enigmatic niece of pearl diver captures hearts of town's menfolk. Music. Puppets. 19 scenes 4m 1w extras 1 setting

Romero, Elaine

¡Curanderas! serpents of the clouds.

Two women—a physician and a folk healer—discover they have more in common than they thought when they share hotel room en route to Mexico City. 2 acts 2 scenes 6 interiors 1 exterior

In Women playwrights: the best plays of 2000

The fat-free Chicana and the Snow Cap queen.

A young woman tries to inaugurate low-fat cooking at her mother's traditional Mexican cafe; supernatural figures join a struggle over ethnic identity. Music. 2 acts 11 scenes 2m 4w 1 setting

In Puro teatro; ed. by A. Sandoval-Sánchez and N. S. Sternbach

If Susan Smith could talk.

Courtroom drama. Appeal to change Susan Smith's sentence to death. Smith drowned her children in family car. 1m 3w 1 interior

In 30 ten-minute plays for 4, 5 & 6 actors from Actors Theatre of Louisville's National Ten-minute Play Contest

—Same

In Actors Theatre of Louisville. Ten-minute plays: v4

La **Ronde**. Schnitzler, A.

Ronzoni, Michaela

610 Bedford Drive.

Portrays lengthy and bitter dispute between the culturally refined European thinker and writer Franz Werfel and the brash and impatient American dramatist Clifford Odets. Prologue 1 act 6 scenes epilogue 4m 1 interior

In Women's words, women's work; ed. by U. H. G. Borgert

The **room**. Pinter, H.

A **roomful** of men. Crow, A. G.

Roommates

Norfolk, W. Caramba's revenge
Santanelli, M. Emergency exit

Williams, T. A lovely Sunday for Creve Coeur

Roots. Wesker, A.

The **rope**. O'Neill, E.

Rose, of Lima, Saint

about

Ehn, E. Thistle
Ehn, E. Una carroña (Rose of Lima)

Rose. Sherman, M.

The **rose** tattoo. Williams, T.

Rosen, Lynn

Nighthawks. French 2002

ISBN 0-573-62792-4

Comic drama inspired by paintings of Edward Hopper. One night in lives of eight lonely city dwellers. 10 scenes 4m 4w settings

Rosen, Sybil

Duet for bear and dog.

Comedy about bear chased up tree by a lap dog. 2m 3w 1 setting

In take ten; ed. by E. Lane and N. Shengold

A **Rosen** by any other name. Horovitz, I.

Rosenberg, Nancy

c The gifts of Obidiah Oak. Anchorage Press 1997 35p

ISBN 0-87602-406-1

Musical. Wise oak tree teaches little girl to share her toys. Variable cast 11 characters 1 setting

Rosenfeld, Seth Zvi

The flatted fifth. French 1999 71p

ISBN 0-573-62690-1

Drama about a Jewish filmmaker, a Puerto Rican poet, and their girlfriends, all embarked on a B'nai B'rith trip to Israel for artists. 2 acts 16 scenes 2m 2w 1 interior

Rosenthal, Amy

Sitting pretty. French (London) 2001 59p

ISBN 0-573-01921-5

Tragicomedy about two sisters, one employed and confident, the other unemployed and self-conscious until she becomes a life-model for an art class. 2 acts 12 scenes 4m 6w 1 setting

Rosie and the bad, bad apples. Whittington, P.

Ross, Brad

Little by little; music by Brad Ross; lyrics by Ellen Greenfield and Hal Hackady; story by Annette and Ellen Greenfield. French 1999 75p
ISBN 0-573-62646-4
Musical. Story of three friends who have known each other since childhood. 1m 2w

Ross, Ian

fareWel.
A meeting to establish self-government on an Indian reserve in Canada becomes a forum for settling scores and pursuing personal advantage. 1 scene 4m 2w 1 interior
In Short spells: scenes & monologues; ed. by V. Shantz

Ross, Lisette Lecat

Scent of the roses. Dramatists 2001 84p
ISBN 0-8222-1774-0   LC 2002-275588
South African woman is urged to sell a rare painting to an international art dealer by her children, releasing emotional memories. 2 acts 17 scenes 4m 6w 1 setting

Rostand, Edmond, 1868-1918

Cyrano de Bergerac (adaptation) See Langella, F. Frank Langella's Cyrano; Roets, J. Cyrano

Roth, Ari

Jeffrey Slugworth: ex-embalmer.
Embalmer must deal with body of victim he killed while driving drunk. 1m 1 interior
In HB Playwrights short play festival 2000

Life in refusal. French (London) 2003 69p
ISBN 0-573-62871-8
Story of American filmmaker who helps Russian refusnik emigrate to the United States. 11 scenes 6m 3w 1 setting

Love and yearning in the not-for-profits.
Comedy. Two employees responsible for typos on museum invitations 1m 1w
In HB Playwrights short play festival 1998

Prelude to a crisis.
Attractive student tempts married teacher into compromising situation. 1m 1w 1 setting
In 3 more by E.S.T. '98

—Same
In EST marathon '98: the one-act plays; ed. by M. Smith
—Same
In HB Playwrights short play festival 1997

Terminal connection.
Man and woman who met on flight have rough time saying goodbye at airport. 1m 1w 1 interior
In HB Playwrights short play festival 1999

The **Rothko** room. Spencer, S.
Round the world tales. Schutzman, S.
Roundup. Sapergia, B.
Routes and escape routes. Bhagat, D.

Roux, Jean-Louis

about
Sher, E. Past imperfect
Rowing to America. Chen, K.

Rowland, Barbara T.

c The birthday gifts.
Children stage a birthday party for Jesus, with concern over appropriate gifts. Music, singing. 1 act 2b 1g extras 1 setting
In 5 Christmas plays for children

c Christmas hide and seek.
Children search for Christmas among its outward manifestations Music. 1 act 3 scenes 1b 3g 1 setting
In 5 Christmas plays for children

Rowlands, Ian

The ogpu men.
Conversation between two unemployed men sitting in a social services office. 2m 1 setting
In Act one Wales; ed. by P. Clark
Roy Cohn/Jack Smith. Vawter, R.
The **royal** family. Kaufman, G. S., and Ferber, E.
Rubber Dolly. Hannah, D.

Rubenstein, Deidre

Confidentially yours. Currency Press 1998 55p
ISBN 0-86819-553-7
Solo performance work. Collection of portraits exploring various aspects of human condition. 1w
Ruby and the rock. Laxdal, V.
Rudali. Ganguli, U.

Rudolph, Kenny

The conspiracy of silence.

Troubled son struggles with feelings toward father. 1 act 1m 1w 1 setting

    In Rudolph, K. Under Hemingway's Michigan sky

"Flickering images".

Betrayed by youth and beauty, movie theater manager in her late fifties offers advice to timid 16-year-old girl employee. 1 act 1m 2w extra 1 interior

    In Rudolph, K. Under Hemingway's Michigan sky

Rug comes to Shuv. McLean, D.

Rugby football

Godber, J. Up 'n' under

Ruhl, Sarah

The technology project: virtual meditation #1.

Two audience members become protagonists in series of virtual encounters. 1 act 3 scenes 1m 1w 3 settings

    In Humana Festival 2002

The **ruling** class. Barnes, P.

Rum and vodka. McPherson, C.

Rumble fish. Romer, M.

Rumi, Jalal al-Din

Mathnawi (selections) (dramatization) See Sills, P. Rumi

Rumi. Sills, P.

Runaways (Youth)

Baker, E. A. Up, down, strange, charmed, beauty, and truth

Courtney, E. Owls

Gilman, R. The glory of living

Jeffries, B. Pastimes

Oates, J. C. Homesick

Running dog, paper tiger. Johnston, S.

Running far back. Hannah, D.

Rusconi, Paul

These two couples went to Italy. Dramatic Publishing 2003

Comedy about ruthless sport of tourism. Two American couples compete for travel savvy dominance in Italy. 2 acts 3m 2w 1 setting

Rushforth, Tony

The Kerry dance. French (London) 2000 82p

    ISBN 0-573-01814-6

Television actor returns to his hometown in Yorkshire, England, and recalls events ten years earlier that led to his acting career. 2 acts 2 scenes 3m 6w 1 setting

Ruskin, Adina L.

The art of remembering. Dramatists 1998 40p il

    ISBN 0-8222-1607-8   LC 98-222976

Drama. Three actresses portray different facets of woman who returns home to bury father. 3w 1 interior

Ruskin, John, 1819-1900

              about

Murphy, G. The countess

Russell, Willy

Blood brothers. Methuen 2001 101p

    ISBN 0-413-76770-1

Musical. Twin brothers raised on opposite sides of society never realize their fraternity until one inadvertently kills the other. 2 acts 5m 3w extras 1 setting

Educating Rita. Methuen 2001 84p

    ISBN 0-413-76790-6

Comedy set in present-day England. Disillusioned English professor and student examine their feelings about education, life and each other. 2 acts 15 scenes 1m 1w 1 interior

Russell-King, Caroline

Lucky four.

Monologue about eating an orange. 1 scene 1m 1 setting

    In Short spells: scenes & monologues; ed. by V. Shantz

Russia

Brown, C. The Negro of Peter the Great

Clarvoe, A. The brothers Karamazov

Congdon, C. Under Lubianka Square

Egloff, E. The devils

Erdman, N. The suicide

Głowacki, J. The fourth sister

Kataev, V. Squaring the circle

Kirshon, V. Grain

Kushner, T. Slavs!

Lewis, G. Siding 37

Russia—*Continued*

Nelson, G. Spirit

Poulton, M. Fortune's fool

c Travis, S. The tale of Little Red Riding Hood

Wasserstein, W. The man in a case

Zorin, L. The guests

Russians

England

Stoppard, T. Salvage

Rust, Jill

Saved by the Serendipity Circus; or, She was trapped with ease. Pioneer Drama Service 1998 15p

Melodrama. Orphanage owner duped by avaricious circus knife thrower. Music. 2 scenes Variable cast 12 characters extras 1 interior

Ruth (Biblical figure)

c McCullough, L. E. Ruth and Naomi: the healing power of friendship

c Vogel, L. Ruth

Ruth. Vogel, L.

Ruth and Naomi: the healing power of friendship. McCullough, L. E.

Rutherford, Stanley

The Chinese art of placement.

Comedic monologue. Former poet struggles to find perfect position for his chair. 1m 1 interior

In Plays from Woolly Mammoth; ed. by R. Alexander and M. Kyrioglou

Rux, Carl Hancock

Chapter & verse.

Experimental theatrical exercise in movement, language, and a capella vocalization exploring faith and the deviation from tradition. Redemption is the quest of each character. Music, singing. Variable cast 1 setting

In Action; ed. by M. Algarin and L. Griffith

Ryan, James

Warm love.

Affair between thesis advisor and her student ends in motel room. 1m 1w 1 interior

In HB Playwrights short play festival 1997

The young girl and the monsoon. Dramatists 1999 57p

ISBN 0-8222-1650-7

Romantic comedy. Divorced father attempts to find room in his life for both his girlfriend and his 13-year-old daughter. 2 acts 1g 2m 2w 2 settings

Ryan, Tammy

Pig. Dramatists 1998 80p

ISBN 0-8222-1600-0   LC 98-222981

Family Labor Day barbecue in 1990 Queens, New York turns violent when son takes family hostage and forces them at gunpoint to play life and death game of charades. 2 acts 5 scenes 4m 5w 1 setting

Rye, Mark S.

y Turning points. Pioneer Drama Service 2000 31p

First produced 1990 with title: Choices. Drama about teenage alcohol abuse. 1 act 9 scenes 4m 5w 1 setting

S

Saar, David

c The yellow boat.

Drama of boy with hemophilia who contracts AIDS virus. 1 act 4m 3w 1 setting

In Theatre for young audiences; ed. by C. A. Jennings

Sabina. Wilson, S.

Sacco-Vanzetti Trial, Dedham, Mass., 1921

Araújo, L. Vanzetti

Sacred blood. Gippius, Z.

Sacred hearts. Curran, C.

Sacrifice

Ehn, E. 16670 (Maximilian Mary Kolbe)

Wilder, T. The Alcestiad

Sad hotel. Foley, D.

Sade, Marquis de, 1740-1814

about

Weiss, P. Marat/Sade

Sadism

Green, P. Hymn to the rising sun: a drama of man's waste

Neilson, A. Normal

The **safari** party. Firth, T.

Safdie, Oren

Private jokes, public places. Playwrights Canada 2001 58p

ISBN 0-88754-628-5

Safdie, Oren—*Continued*

Satire on academia, intellectual pretension, and postmodernism. Female architectural student presents her thesis to jury. 3m 1w 1 interior

The **saga** of the golden horseshoe. Cook, P.

Sagal, Peter

Game theory.

Two men try to learn corporate strategies while on retreat. 2m

> *In* 30 ten-minute plays for 2 actors from Actors Theatre of Louisville's National Ten-minute Play Contest

Happenstance.

Two ex-lovers bump into each other at O'Hare Airport. 1m 1w 1 interior

> *In* HB Playwrights short play festival 1999

Milton Bradley.

Rabbi tries to find nice things to say about deceased woman. 2m 1 interior

> *In* HB Playwrights short play festival 2000

The Taliban.

Congressman visits museum's controversial exhibit. 2m 1w

> *In* HB Playwrights short play festival 1998

Saigon: year of the cat. Hare, D.
Sailing to America. Bush, D.
Saint Francis of Esplanade. Skarstedt, S. A.
Saint George and the dragon at Christmas tide. Sigley, M.
Saint Lucy's eyes. Wimberly, B.
Saint Oscar. Eagleton, T.

Saint Petersburg (Russia)

Hare, D. The bay at Nice

Saints

Ehn, E. 16670 (Maximilian Mary Kolbe)
Ehn, E. Cedar (John of the Cross)
Ehn, E. Contemplacion (Mary and Martha)
Ehn, E. Dashboard (Christopher)
Ehn, E. The freak (George)
Ehn, E. The imp of simplicity (Thomas à Kempis)
Ehn, E. Locus (John the Baptist)

Ehn, E. Pain (Eulalia)
Ehn, E. Radio elephant (Barbara)
Ehn, E. Thistle
Ehn, E. Tree of hope, keep firm (Mary, the Annunciation)
Ehn, E. Una carroña (Rose of Lima)
Ehn, E. Wholly Joan's (Joan of Arc)
The four apparitions of Guadalupe (Las cuatro apariciones de Guadalupe)
Nigro, D. Joan of Arc in the autumn
Wilder, T. Brother Fire

Sales personnel and selling

Felder, L. Flight of fancy
Kareken, J. Hot Rod
Miller, A. Death of a salesman
Stickland, E. Sitting on paradise
Wilhelm, L. A pink Cadillac nightmare

Salieri, Antonio, 1750-1825

about

Pushkin, A. Mozart and Salieri

Salinas, Pablo

Picture perfect; tr. by Raul Moncada.

Drama set in Mexico City. Lonely single woman becomes involved with gigolo. 2 acts 11 scenes 1m 1w 1 interior

> *In* Five plays in translation from Mexican contemporary theater; ed. by S. Rodríguez del Pino

Sally Ann Thunder and Davey Crockett. Barchers, S. I.
Salmonberry: a West Coast fairy tale. Hoogland, C.
Salome. Wilde, O.
Salt. Murray, P.
Salt of the earth. Godber, J.
Salvage. Stoppard, T.
Salvoisy; or, The queen's lover. Gore, C.

Samson (Biblical figure)

c McCullough, L. E. Samson and Delilah
c Vogel, L. Samson
Samson. Vogel, L.
Samson and Delilah. McCullough, L. E.

Samuel (Biblical figure)

c Vogel, L. From cool to fool

Samurai

Huie, K. Yasuko and the young s-s-samurai
Hwang, D. H. The sound of a voice

San Francisco (Calif.)

Bell, N. McTeague: a tale of San Francisco

Culture Clash (Group). Mission magic mystery tour

MacLeod, W. Sin

San Francisco of course. Obermeir, G.

Sanatoriums

O'Neill, E. The straw

Sánchez, Edwin

Barefoot boy with shoes on. Broadway Play Pub. 2000 64p
ISBN 0-88145-178-9

Portrait of urban ghetto life. 5m 1w extra 1 setting

Clean.

Drama set in Bronx (N.Y.) and Puerto Rico about 30-year-old Catholic priest in love with 10-year-old boy. 2 acts 2 scenes 2b 2m 1w settings
    In Sánchez, E. Plays

Floorshow: Doña Sol and her trained dog.

Son, just released from mental institution, and former prostitute mother battle for truth regarding death of daughter who may never have existed. 1 act 1b 1g 2m 1w extras settings
    In Sánchez, E. Plays

Icarus. Broadway Play Pub. 1999 72p
ISBN 0-88145-155-X

Beauty, ugliness, reality, dreams, and symbolism motifs in drama about group of dysfunctional individuals seeking redemption. 3m 2w 1 exterior

Trafficking in broken hearts.

Look at New York street life focuses on hustler, lawyer, and young runaway. 1 act 3m 1 setting
    In Sánchez, E. Plays

Sanctuary. Williamson, D.

Sand castles. Larbey, B.

The **sandalwood** box. Wellman, M.

Sandberg, R. N.

Convivencia.

Muslim boy, Jewish girl, and Christian boy are caught up in civil turmoil of 15th century Spain. Music. Dancing. 2 acts 19 scenes 7m 2w 4 exteriors
    In International plays for young people

Sanders family Christmas. Ray, C.

Sanderson, Bill. See Thwaite, E. jt. auth.

Sandler, Susan

The burial society.

Set in funeral chapel. Actress converses with widower of colleague she despised. 1m 1w 1 interior
    In HB Playwrights short play festival 2000

Sanford, Karen

Ophelia.

Drama about religious girl who meets stranger with dubious intentions. Music. 1 act 1m 1w 1 setting
    In Off-Off Broadway festival plays, 24th ser.

Sangshuping chronicles. Chen Zidu, and others

Santa Claus

c McBride-Smith, B. Santaberry and the Snard

c Medoff, M. Kringle's window

Snyder, P. D. B. Miracle on 34th Street

Santaberry and the Snard. McBride-Smith, B.

The **Santaland** diaries. Mantello, J.

Santander, Felipe

The agronomist (El extensionista); translated by Lynne Alvarez.

Tragic love story highlights personal and political corruption in rural Mexico. 22m 6w extras 1 setting
    In Santander, F. Three plays

Mexico, USA; translated by Lynne Alvarez.

Murder mystery connects drug interdependence between Mexico and United States with Iran-Contra affair and corrupting force of violence. 2 acts Large mixed cast 2 interiors
    In Santander, F. Three plays

The unwritten law; translated by Lynne Alvarez.

Black comedy. Mexican official caught up in machinations of drug trade and political corruption. 2 acts 23 scenes Large mixed cast 12 interiors 4 exteriors
    In Santander, F. Three plays

Santanelli, Manlio

Emergency exit; translated from the Italian by Anthony Molino with Jane House. Xenos Bks. 1999 119p

ISBN 1-87937-840-X   LC 99-52460

Comedy. Two men living in condemned apartment in Naples wage psychological warfare on one another. 2 acts 4 scenes 2m extra

Sapergia, Barbara

Roundup.

On a drought-stricken ranch on the Canadian prairie, a couple debate their daughter's prospects, and their own. 1 scene 1m 2w 1 setting

In Short spells: scenes & monologues; ed. by V. Shantz

Sarah and Abraham. Norman, M.

Sarah, plain and tall. Robinette, J.

Sasaki, Sadako, 1943-1955

about

c Miller, K. S. A thousand cranes

Saskatchewan

Cairns, G. Danceland

Glass, J. M. Yesteryear

Sapergia, B. Roundup

Sater, Steven

Phone sex and a dumb show.

Man in New York apartment is harrassed by phone caller. 2m 1 setting

In take ten; ed. by E. Lane and N. Shengold

Satire

Al-Hakim, T. Fate of a cockroach

Albee, E. The American dream

Arden, J. Serjeant Musgrave's dance

Ardito, C. St. James's blues

Aristophanes. Acharnians

Aristophanes. Clouds

Aristophanes. Frogs

Aristophanes. Peace

Aristophanes. The sexual congress

Aristophanes. The suits

Aristophanes. Wasps

Aristophanes. Women in power

Armstrong, D. A Christmas Twist

Armstrong, D. Of grapes and nuts

Ayckbourn, A. Comic potential

Baraka, A. The election machine warehouse

y Barchers, S. I. A retrieved reformation

Barnes, P. The ruling class

Beaumont, F. The knight of the burning pestle

Bosakowski, P. Nixon apologizes to the nation

Breslin, J. Contract with Jackie

Bulgakov, M. Flight

Busch, C. Shanghai moon

Busch, C. The tale of the allergist's wife

Cajal, O.-M. Exchange at Cafe Mimosa

Carter, L. Gulliver

Carter, L. Gulliver redux

Chappell, E. Cut and dried

Chappell, E. We don't want to lose you

Chekhov, A. P. The dangers of tobacco

Chekhov, A. P. Ivanov

Chekhov, A. P. The wedding reception

Cheng, K. E. The China crisis

Corbett, B. The big slam

Crommelynck, F. A small-hearted woman

Culture Clash (Group). A bowl of beings

Culture Clash (Group). Radio mambo

De Angelis, A. The positive hour

Donaghy, T. The beginning of August

Dunbar, P. L. Jes lak white fo'ks

Durang, C. Baby with the bathwater

Durang, C. Beyond therapy

Durang, C. Laughing wild

Durang, C. The marriage of Bette and Boo

Durang, C. The Vietnamization of New Jersey

Edwards, G. Four walls

Elton, B. Gasping

Elton, B. Popcorn

Elton, B. Silly cow

Erdman, N. The suicide

Field, B. Pantagleize

Fo, D. Archangels don't play pinball

Fusco, C. Stuff

Godber, J. Bouncers

Gore, C. Quid pro quo; or, The day of the dupes

Gray, S. The late middle classes

Grazia, E. de. The vacuum cleaner

Guare, J. New York actor

Hall, C. The best little whorehouse goes public

Satire—*Continued*

Van Itallie, J.-C. Eat cake

Vidal, G. The best man

Wasserstein, W. Boy meets girl

Wilde, O. The importance of being Earnest

Williams, J. L. Why marry?

Williamson, D. Dead white males

Wong, E. Let the big dog eat

Wood, C. Dingo

Yacine, K. Intelligence powder

Yourgrau, T. TH FT

Saturday night. Shinn, C.

Saul (Biblical figure)

c Vogel, L. From cool to fool

c Vogel, L. What's up, rock?

Savage wilds. Reed, I.

Saved by the Serendipity Circus. Rust, J.

Scapin. Irwin, B., and O'Donnell, M.

The **scarlet** letter. Abbott, G. W.

Scene with celery. Hedges, P.

Scent of the roses. Ross, L. L.

Schalchlin, Steve

The last session; book by Jim Brochu;
music and lyrics by Steve Schalchlin.
French 1998 67p

ISBN 0-573-62295-7

Singer-composer, dying of AIDS, rents recording
studio to cut final record. 2 acts 3m 2w 1 interior

Scheffer, Will

Alien boy.

Monologue. Man remembers himself at thirteen,
suspecting that he was gay but afraid to tell his
mother. He finally resolves the question of who
betrayed his secret. 1 act 1m 1 setting

In Ensemble Studio Theatre marathon
2000: the one-act plays

Bel canto.

Two sisters and their gargoyle mother hide in
the basement while a hurricane passes overhead;
storms in the cellar as well. Music. 1 act 1 scene
3w 1 interior

In EST marathon '96: the one-act
plays; ed. by M. Smith

Easter. Dramatists 1999 45p

ISBN 0-8222-1667-1

Drama set in Kansas about criminal couple's
quest for catharsis and redemption. 2 acts 3m 1w
1 setting

Tennessee and me.

The spirit of Tennessee Williams moves into the
body of a New York hustler. Monologue, with
several voices. 1 act 1m 1 interior

In EST marathon '97: the one-act
plays; ed. by M. Smith

Scheherazade. Pargman, S.

Scheherazade. Roderer, E.

Schenkar, Joan

Burning desires.

Black comic reinvention of Joan of Arc story set
in 1950s Seattle. 2 acts entre-acte 4m 9w 1 setting

In Schenkar, J. Signs of life

Cabin fever.

Black comedy about degenerate lifestyles in isolated Southern mountain community. 2 acts 2m 1w
1 exterior

In Schenkar, J. Signs of life

Fulfilling Koch's postulate.

Black comedy. Typhoid Mary is live-in chef of
scientist who indentifies the bacillus she spreads.
2 acts 2m 2w 1 setting

In Schenkar, J. Signs of life

The last of Hitler.

Black comedy. Post-war Hitler and Eva Braun
trapped in Jewish retirement community in Florida.
2 acts entre-acte 3m 3w extras 1 setting

In Schenkar, J. Signs of life

Signs of life.

Symbolic surrealist drama. Scenes juxtaposing
Henry James's relationship with his sister Alice
and his fictional Dr. Sloper's relationship with a
freak Elephant Woman illustrate man's inhumanity
to woman. 1 act 3m 5w extras 1 setting

In Schenkar, J. Signs of life

The universal wolf.

Experimental play. Feminist version of Little
Red Riding Hood. 1m 2w extra 1 setting

In Schenkar, J. Signs of life

Schick, Alice

Santaberry and the Snard (dramatization)
See McBride-Smith, B. Santaberry and
the Snard

Schick, Joel, 1945-

Santaberry and the Snard (dramatization)
See McBride-Smith, B. Santaberry and
the Snard

Schiller, Friedrich

Mary Stuart; translated and with an introduction and notes by F. J. Lamport. Penguin Bks. 1998 150p

ISBN 0-14-044711-3

Tragedy. Last three days in the life of Mary Stuart, Queen of Scotland. Verse play. 5 acts 52 scenes 14m 6w extras 4 interiors 1 exterior

Schisgal, Murray

Fifty years ago.

Couple's first wedding anniversary coincides with 50th anniversany of V J Day when they first met. 1m 1w 1 interior

In The Best American short plays, 1996-1997

First love.

Successful literary agent's ex-husband returns looking for her help in getting his book published. 1m 1w 1 interior

In The Best American short plays 1999-2000

The man who couldn't stop crying.

Husband and wife attempt to cope with husband's compulsive crying. Music. 1m 1w 1 interior

In The Best American Short plays, 1997-1998

Playtime. Dramatists 1997 69p

ISBN 0-8222-1586-1

Comedy about stockbroker who reveals insider information to a successful Wall Street trader. 2 acts 10 scenes 2m 3w 2 settings

Schmiedl, Adaora Nzelibe

Ezigbo, the spirit child (dramatization) See Bush, M. Ezigbo, the spirit child

Schmitt, Eric-Emmanuel

Between worlds.

Set in a hotel that is literally between two worlds—this and the next; the souls of coma patients wait here until their fate is decided. 1 act 4m 3w 1 interior

In Schmitt, E.-E. Plays: 1

Don Juan on trial.

Five women stage a trial of Don Juan, who has seduced and abandoned them all. The Don parries their charges, but he is already a changed man, thanks to the brother of one of his victims. 3 acts 10 scenes 3m 7w 3 interiors 1 exterior

In Schmitt, E.-E. Plays: 1

Enigma variations. Dramatists 2003

ISBN 0-8222-1810-0

A reclusive writer learns that the "journalist" interviewing him is the husband of a woman with whom the writer once had an affair, a woman whose devoted letters have inspired him for years. 2m 1 interior setting

—Same

In Schmitt, E.-E. Plays: 1

The visitor.

Set in Vienna just after the Nazi takeover. A mysterious stranger visits Freud, who passionately denies that God could exist, given the evil in the world. 1 act 17 scenes 3m 1w 1 interior

In Schmitt, E.-E. Plays: 1

Schnitzler, Arthur, 1862-1931

La ronde (adaptation) See Hare, D. The blue room; Nelson, R. Jitterbugging: scenes of sex in a new society

Anatol; tr. by Carl R. Mueller.

Sequence of seven episodes about love affairs of Viennese playboy observed in dialogue with his philosophical friend and advisor. 7 scenes 4m 7w 6 interiors 1 exterior

In Schnitzler, A. Four major plays

Flirtation; tr. by Carl R. Mueller.

Variant titles: The game of love (Liebelei); Light-o'-love. Tragedy. Innocent Viennese girl is driven to suicide when she learns man she loves has been killed in duel provoked by his love for married woman. 3 acts 1g 4m 3w 2 interiors

In Schnitzler, A. Four major plays

The green cockatoo; tr. by Carl R. Mueller.

Tragic play-within-a-play set in France on eve of Revolution. Jealousy motivates murder in seedy tavern. 1 act 17m 5w extras

In Schnitzler, A. Four major plays

La Ronde; tr. by Carl R. Mueller.

Variant titles: Hands around; Merry-go-round; Round dance. Interlocking episodes of lovemaking and seduction in various strata of nineteenth century Viennese society. 10 scenes 5m 5w 8 interiors 2 exteriors

In Schnitzler, A. Four major plays

Scholtz, Pieter

c Tokoloshe. Anchorage Press 1998 65p

ISBN 0-87602-364-2

Play based on Zulu folktale about mischievous fun-loving imp. 2 acts 6m 2w extras 1 setting

The **school** for coquettes. Gore, C.

The **school** for wives. Molière
The **school** for wives criticized. Molière
Schools

Angus, Eric. The demon headmaster
Calarco, J. Shakespeare's R & J
c Deverell, R. Belonging
c Deverell, R. Weird kid
Keeffe, B. Gimme shelter: Gotcha
y Labey, R. New boy
McConnell, J. Short changed
c McCullough, L. E. Reach for the stars
c Vreeke, J. A little princess
Schoolyard games. Lazarus, J.
Schubert, Franz, 1797-1828
about

Gilbert, S. Schubert lied
Schubert lied. Gilbert, S.

Schulberg, Budd, and Silverman, Stan

On the waterfront. Dee, I. R. 2001 113p
ISBN 1-566-63367-2; 1-566-63368-0 (pa)
LC 00-47409

Melodrama about racketeering in 1950s New
York waterfront unions. 2 acts 25 scenes 22m extras 1 setting

Schulner, David

An infinite ache; music by Fabian Obis-
po. Dramatists 2003
ISBN 0-8222-1885-2

A love story between two lonely twenty-
somethings. Music. 1m 1w 1 interior setting
Schumann, Clara, 1819-1896
about

Jelinek, E. Clara S.

Schutzman, Steven

c Round the world tales. Pioneer Drama
Service 2001 30p

Cycle of three folktales from Japan, Sweden and
Nicaragua about how greed throws people out of
balance with their land and traditions. Variable
cast 1 setting
Schwartz, Delmore, 1913-1966

In dreams begin responsibilities (dramatization) See Margulies, D. Luna Park

Science fiction

Barnett, G. T for 2
Briggs, S. Terry Pratchett's Maskerade

Carlton, B. Return to the forbidden planet
Five Lesbian Brothers (Theater company). Brides of the moon
Frankel, R. Strange happenings
c Fredericks, A. D. Across the new frontier
c Fredericks, A. D. Alien teacher
c Fredericks, A. D. All the knowledge in
the universe
c Fredericks, A. D. Artifact
c Fredericks, A. D. Bubble trouble
c Fredericks, A. D. Do it yourself!
c Fredericks, A. D. Forever is a long time
c Fredericks, A. D. Heads/tails
c Fredericks, A. D. I am Slime
c Fredericks, A. D. I scream, you scream,
we all scream for ice cream
c Fredericks, A. D. Into, beyond, and back
again
c Fredericks, A. D. It's in the bag
c Fredericks, A. D. The Jovian pact
c Fredericks, A. D. Just a thought
c Fredericks, A. D. The last decision
c Fredericks, A. D. A long, long time
c Fredericks, A. D. The masters of all
c Fredericks, A. D. A matter of survival
c Fredericks, A. D. Me, myself, and I
c Fredericks, A. D. Once upon a time
y Jackson, K. High school dropouts from
outer space
c Jenkin, L. The invisible man
Madden, D. Drop
Pratchett, T. Carpe jugulum
Spencer, S. Resident alien
Wellman, M. Albanian softshoe
Scientists

Clark, R. Pierre and Marie
Field, B. Playing with fire
Hall, L. Genie
Hawdon, R. God and Stephen Hawking
Ludlam, C. Bluebeard
Parnell, P. QED
Reich, J. Proof
Schenkar, J. Fulfilling Koch's postulate
Stephenson, S. An experiment with an
air pump
Tasca, J. Deus-X
Vogel, L. A super scientific world
Walker, B. The moons of Alnyron
Scissors. Yew, C.

Scollard, Rose

c Firebird.

When Koshchei the Deathless abducts Firebird on Princess Irenka's command, the land of Zahr is laid to waste and Irenka is turned into wolf. 2 acts 3m 3w

   In TYA5: theatre for young audience

Scooping. Nelson, R.

Score. Bogart, A., and Clarke, J.

Scorn of women. London, J.

Scotland

y Gollobin, L. B. Selkie

  Greenhorn, S. Passing places

  McLean, D. Blackden

  McLean, D. Julie Allardyce

  McLean, L. Riddance

y Nielsen, K. Macbeth

  Schiller, F. Mary Stuart

Scott, Garet

  A town called Shame; music by Clark Gesner. French 1999 64p

    ISBN 0-573-62704-5

Western parody set in Kansas. Stranger helps widow save farm from evil judge. Music, singing. 2 acts 27 scenes 9m 2w 1 setting

Scott, Robert Falcon, 1868-1912

      about

  Brown, S. Toshie

Scottsboro, limited. Hughes, L.

Scottsboro Trial, Scottsboro, Ala., 1931

  Hughes, L. Scottsboro, limited

Scrape off the black. Ikoli, T.

Scrapple. Mattern, J.

Scribe, Augustin Eugène

  Salvoisy (adaptation) See Gore, C. The queen's champion; Gore, C. Salvoisy; or, The queen's lover

Scrooge. Bricusse, L.

Scruples. Jory, J.

The **sculptor** of masks. Crommelynck, F.

Sculptors

  Ibsen, H. When we dead awaken

Sea

  Ibsen, H. The lady from the sea

  O'Neill, E. Anna Christie

c Roberts, B. Angelica! . . . and the monstrous monster of the deep

The **seagull**. Chekhov, A. P.

Seamen

y Barchers, S. I. Captains courageous

  Baron, C. The blue room

  Fugard, A. The captain's tiger

  Gurney, A. R. Far East

  Levi, S. The gulf of crimson

c Mason, T. Treasure Island

c McCullough, L. E. Heave away, haul away! (tugboat captain)

  O'Neill, E. Anna Christie

  O'Neill, E. Bound east for Cardiff

  O'Neill, E. In the zone

  O'Neill, E. The moon of the Caribbees

Seance. Nigro, D.

Sears, Djanet

  The adventures of a black girl in search of God.

Drama set in Holland Township, Ontario. Black woman doctor blames herself for daughter's death and is about to divorce her minister husband. Prologue 2 acts 22 scenes epilogue 3m 4w extras

   In Testifyin' v2; ed. by D. Sears

  Harlem duet.

Uses Shakespeare's Othello as guide to black experience from 1860 to 1990. Music, singing. Prologue 2 acts 20 scenes 2m 3w 1 setting

   In Testifyin' v1; ed. by D. Sears

Season's greetings. Mantello, J.

Second class. Slaight, B.

The **second** shepherd's play. Harris, A.

The **second** shepherd's play (Los pastores); tr. by Larry Torres.

Shepherds encamped on a hillside engage in routine tasks and comic biplay before learning of Jesus's birth. Devil attempts to lead them astray but is vanquished by angel. Rhymed folk drama; bilingual edition. Music, singing. 1 scene 2b 9m 1w extras 1 exterior

   In Six nuevomexicano folk dramas for Advent season

Second time around. Benfield, D.

Secret agents in disguise. Hamlett, C.

Secret bridesmaids' business. Coleman, E.

The **secret** fall of Constance Wilde. Kilroy, T.

The **secret** garden. Duffield, N.

The **secret** garden. Sterling, P.

The **secret** rapture. Hare, D.

Secret service. Gillette, W.

The **secret** wife. York, Y.

The **secretaries**. Five Lesbian Brothers (Theater company)
Secrets. Lazarus, J.

Sedaris, Amy. See Sedaris, D. jt. auth.

Sedaris, David, and Sedaris, Amy
The book of Liz. Dramatists 2002
  ISBN 0-8222-1827-5
  Sister Elizabeth Donderstock is Squeamish. However, she feels unappreciated by her Squeamish brethren. She decides to try her luck in the outside world. 1m 2w settings

Seduction
  Ives, D. Foreplay; or, The art of the fugue
  Parker, S. Pratt's fall
  Pedrero, P. A night divided
  Schmitt, E.-E. Don Juan on trial
The **seduction** of Anne Boleyn. Luckham, C.
The **see-saw** tree. Wood, D.
See you in court! (Legal Aid lawyer). McCullough, L. E.
Seeing stars in Dixie. Osborne, R.
Seeing the light. McKay, R.

Self-service laundries
  Dunn, M. Gendermat

Selig, Paul
Slide show.
  Creepy/genteel monologue by a woman conducting a slide show of artifacts collected by her late husband, an archaeologist. Slide projections. 1 act 1w 1 interior
    In EST marathon '96: the one-act plays; ed. by M. Smith
Selim I, Sultan of the Turks
               about
  Greene, R. Selimus, emperor of the Turks
Selimus, emperor of the Turks. Greene, R.
Selkie. Gollobin, L. B.
Selkirk Avenue. McManus, B.
Semblance of madness! Newmeir, J. H.
Sensation(s). Beber, N.
Sense and sensibility. Parsley, R., and Graham, A.
The **sensuous** senator. Parker, M.
Sentences and words. Cooper, C. L.

September 11 terrorist attacks, 2001
  Kane, H. Snapshot: monument
  Mueller, L. Voices from September 11th
September in the rain. Godber, J.
Serbia
  Zellnik, D. Killing hand

Seremba, George
Come good rain.
  Autobiographical drama set in Uganda during murderous regimes of Idi Amin and Milton Obute. Account of author's politicalization, abduction and torture. 2 acts Large mixed cast
    In Testifyin' v1; ed. by D. Sears
Serenading Louie. Wilson, L.
Serjeant Musgrave's dance. Arden, J.
A **sermon**. Mamet, D.
The **serpent**: a ceremony. Van Itallie, J.-C.
Serra, Junípero, 1713-1784
               about
  c Fredericks, A. D. Mission San Juan Capistrano
The **servant** of two masters. Congdon, C.
The **servant** of two masters. Louise, D.

Servants
  Conquest, N. For they shall see God
  Ehn, E. Contemplacion (Mary and Martha)
  Louise, D. The servant of two masters
  Nielson, K. A true fool's folly
  Nigro, D. The malefactor's bloody register
  Nigro, D. Quint and Miss Jessel at Bly
Seurat, Georges
               about
  Sondheim, S. Sunday in the park with George
Seven against Thebes. Aeschylus
Seven days in the life of Simon Labrosse. Fréchette, C.
The **seventeenth** of June. Baker, E. A.

Sewell, Stephen
The sick room. Currency Press 1999 74p
  ISBN 0-86819-585-5   LC 99-487928
  Three generations of family gather under one roof to care for terminally ill teenage girl. 2 acts 38 scenes 4m 3w 1 setting

Sex

Ackerman, P. Things you shouldn't say past midnight
Adams, L. D. Greeks and centaurs
Brecht, B. Baal
De Angelis, A. The positive hour
Ensler, E. The Vagina monologues
Farrell, C. The once attractive woman
Godber, J. On a night like this
Godber, J. Unleashed
Griffiths, L. A game of inches
Gurney, A. R. Darlene
Hare, D. The blue room
Hedges, P. Scene with celery
Horovitz, I. Alfred the Great
Hwang, D. H. Bondage
Johnson, T. Dead funny
Lucas, C. Unmemorable
Marber, P. Closer
Margulies, D. New Year's Eve and Kibbutz
Miller, T. Naked breath
Neilson, A. The censor
Nelson, R. Jitterbugging: scenes of sex in a new society
Nigro, D. Quint and Miss Jessel at Bly
O'Neill, E. Anna Christie
Orton, J. What the butler saw
Parks, S.-L. In the blood
Ravenhill, M. Mother Clap's Molly house
Ravenhill, M. Shopping and fucking
Rebeck, T. Does this woman have a name?
Rebeck, T. Spike heels
Sater, S. Phone sex and a dumb show
Schnitzler, A. La Ronde
Silver, N. Claire
Silver, N. The Eros trilogy
Sleeping around
Upton, J. Stealing souls
Wedekind, F. Earth spirit
Wedekind, F. Lulu
Wedekind, F. Pandora's box
Wedekind, F. Spring's awakening

Sex crimes

Tropf, R. Shadow hour
Sex with the censor. Rebeck, T.
The **sexual** congress. Aristophanes
Shades of autumn. Paterson, D. L.

Shadow hour. Tropf, R.
The **shadow** of a gunman. O'Casey, S.

Shadowbox Cabaret (Theater group)

Shadowboxing. French 2002 104p
ISBN 0-573-62992-7
Comedy sketches. A variety of topics are satirized, including television and family values. 4 parts 6m 6w

Shadowboxing. Shadowbox Cabaret (Theater group)

Shafaat, Shahid

y Balcony.
Symbolic feminist drama set in Pakistan. 2w 1 interior
In International plays for young people
A **shaft** of sunlight. Joshi, A.
Shake, ripple & roll. Perkins, D.
Shakers. Godber, J.

Shakespeare, William, 1564-1616

Hamlet (adaptation) See Nielsen, K. Hamlet
Macbeth (adaptation) See Nielsen, K. Macbeth
Richard III (adaptation) See Cibber, C. The tragical history of King Richard III
The taming of the shrew (adaptation) See Christiansen, A. Best beware my sting
The tempest (adaptation) See Césaire, A. A tempest

about

Battlo, J. The little theater's production of Hamlet
Calarco, J. Shakespeare's R & J
Frankonis, W. The killings tale
c Hamlett, C. Where there's a Will, there's a play
Redgrave, L. Shakespeare for my father
Williamson, D. Dead white males

Parodies, imitations, etc.

Chaurette, N. The queens
Gurney, A. R. Overtime
y Karcz, L. R. The taming of LaRue
y LaVohn, R. W. A midsummer night's midterm
Levy, D. Pushing the prince into Denmark

Shakespeare, William, 1564-1616— about—Parodies, imitations, etc.—*Continued*

Ludlam, C. Stage blood

MacDonald, A.-M. Goodnight Desdemona (good morning Juliet)

c McBride-Smith, B. Twelfth night

y Miller, K. S. Shakespeare to go!

Robinson, K. The popular mechanicals

Sears, D. Harlem duet

Women's Theatre Group. Lear's daughters

Shakespeare for my father. Redgrave, L.

Shakespeare to go! Miller, K. S.

Shakespeare's R & J. Calarco, J.

The **Shamrock** road. Simmonds, R. N.

Shange, Ntozake

Hydraulics phat like mean.

Streetwise, hip-hop response to Shakespeare's Sonnet 128. Music. 1 act 1m 1w 1 setting

In Love's fire

I live in music.

Experimental theater piece incorporating music, dance and poetry. Music, dancing. 7 scenes variable cast

In Action; ed. by M. Algarin and L. Griffith

Shanghai (China)

Busch, C. Shanghai moon

Shanghai moon. Busch, C.

Shanley, John Patrick

Cellini; tr. by J. Addington Symonds. Dramatists 2002

ISBN 0-8222-1808-9

Adapted from his Autobiography, this play chronicles the life of Cellini, the sixteenth-century Italian sculptor and man-about-town. 7m 2w 1 interior setting

Psychopathia sexualis. Dramatists 1998 54p

ISBN 0-8222-1615-9   LC 98-158142

Comedy about Manhattan artist with sock fetish engaged to wealthy socialite from Texas. 2 acts 2m 2w

Welcome to the moon.

Old aquaintances meet in Bronx bar and reminisce about the past. 4m 1w 1 setting

In take ten; ed. by E. Lane and N. Shengold

Where's my money? Dramatists 2003

ISBN 0-8222-1865-8

A comedy about marriage and its discontents. It examines the emotional and physical scars of modern relationships. 3m 3w 1 setting

The **shape** of things. LaBute, N.

Shapiro, Norman R.

Take her, she's yours! or, Til divorce do us part; adaptation by Norman R. Shapiro. Applause 2000 102p

ISBN 1-557-83454-7

Comedy about disillusioned philandering husband's attempts to extricate himself from marriage of inconvenience, and his wife's fitting revenge at the expense of her twit of a would-be-lover. 3 acts Variable cast 2 interiors

The **Shapiros'** new adventure. Fredericks, A. D.

Sharkey, Jack, and Sharkey, Tom

Just say yes!. French 2002 79p

ISBN 0-573-60193-3

Comedy. Author of self-help books chooses the biggest of losers to help him prove his theories on success. 2 acts 6 scenes 2m 3w 1 interior

Sharkey, Tom. See Sharkey, J. jt. auth.

Sharland, Elizabeth

Love from Shakespeare to Coward. Applause 1999 63p

ISBN 1-55783-369-9

Combination of plays, poems, letters and diary extracts offer introduction into lives and careers of great Bristish dramatists and actors. Variable cast

Sharma, Tripurari

The wooden cart.

Drama about leprosy—the disease itself and the fear and ignorance that surround it. Presented in the style of street theater. Music, singing. 1 act 9 scenes 22m 8w extras settings

In DramaContemporary: India; ed. by E. B. Mee

Sharon and Billy. Bowne, A.

Shasta Rue. Martin, J.

Shattering word. Bass, A.

Shavout

c McCullough, L. E. The bird of happiness

Shaw, Bernard

The admirable Bashville (adaptation) See Valenti, M. Bashville in love

Caesar and Cleopatra.

Historical comedy. Aging Caesar teaches young Cleopatra to be queen while battling opponents in Egypt during Roman Civil War. Prologue 5 acts 8 scenes 11m 4w extras 3 interiors 6 exteriors

In Shaw, B. Three plays for Puritans

Captain Brassbound's conversion.

Comedy. Captain's plan for revenge on uncle, an English judge, by turning him over to Moroccan tribesmen, is changed by charming woman. 3 acts 12m 1w extras 3 interiors

In Shaw, B. Three plays for Puritans

The devil's disciple.

Comedy. "Devil's disciple" taking place of minister scheduled for hanging by Burgoyne's troops during American Revolution is rescued by minister-turned-soldier. 3 acts 10m 3w 4 interiors 1 exterior

In Shaw, B. Three plays for Puritans

Heartbreak House. Penguin Bks. 160p
ISBN 0-14-043787-8

Old sea captain takes a dim view of early 20th century English society. Music. 3 acts 6m 4w 1 setting

Man and superman. Penguin Bks. 264p
ISBN 0-14-043788-6

Philosophical romantic comedy. Modernized version of the Don Juan legend portraying man as quarry, woman as hunter. 4 acts 6 scenes 11m 5w extras 1 interior 3 exteriors

Mrs. Warren's profession.

Satirical comedy exposing hypocritical British society which condemns women it drives into prostitution. Well raised daughter learns mother heads brothel syndicate. 4 acts 4m 2w 2 interiors 2 exteriors

In Shaw, B. Plays unpleasant

The philanderer.

Satirical romantic comedy about "advanced" woman and English pseudo-Ibsenism. Philanderer in love with one woman, pursued by another, loses both. 3 acts 4m 3w extras 3 interiors

In Shaw, B. Plays unpleasant

Widowers' houses.

Young doctor discovers fiancee's father is slum landlord. 3 acts 4m 1w extras 2 interiors 1 exterior

In Shaw, B. Plays unpleasant

Shaw, Peggy

You're just like my father.

Humorous self-portrait about developing a butch identity while growing up in the conservative 1950s. 1w

In O solo homo; ed. by H. Hughes and D. Román

Shawn, Wallace

The designated mourner. Dramatists 2002
ISBN 0-8222-1848-8

Drama about self, art, and political oppression. Three interwoven monologues by renowned intellectual, his daughter, and her husband, a former English literature student. 2m 1w 1 setting

The designated mourner (condensation).

In The Best Plays of 1999-2000; ed. by Otis L. Guernsey, Jr.

She talks to Beethoven. Kennedy, A.

Shear, Claudia

Blown sideways through life. French 2002 28p
ISBN 0-573-62800-9

Comedic monologue. Woman recounts many jobs she has held. 1w 1 setting

Dirty blonde. French 2002 77p
ISBN 0-573-6283-8

Play based on life of Mae West. 2m 1w 1 setting

Shearer, Jill

Georgia. Currency Press 2000 75p
ISBN 0-86819-606-1

Drama about the American artist, Georgia O'Keeffe, and her relationship with a potter named Juan. 2 acts 11 scenes 2m 3w

Sheehy, John

Gave her the eye.

Paranoid sexual fantasy set in bar. 1m 2w 1 interior

In 30 ten-minutes plays for 3 actors from Actors Theatre of Louisville's National Ten-minute Play Contest

—Same

In Actors Theatre of Louisville. Ten-minute plays: v4

Sheila's day. Ndlovu, D.

Shelley, Mary Wollstonecraft, 1797-1851

Frankenstein (dramatization) See Field, B. Playing with fire

Frankstein (dramatization) See Barchers, S. I., and Kroll, J. L. Frankenstein

Shem, Samuel, and Surrey, Janet L.

Bill W. and Dr. Bob. French 2000 96p

ISBN 0-573-69174-6   LC 2002-279010

Drama about two men who pioneered Alcoholics Anonymous and their wives, who founded Al-Anon. Prologue 2 acts 24 scenes epilogue 2m 2w 1 setting

Shenandoah. Howard, B.

Shepard, Matthew, d. 1998

about

Kaufman, M. The Laramie Project

Shepard, Sam

Eyes for Consuela. Dramatists 1999 49p

ISBN 0-8222-1678-7   LC 00-703037

Down and out American in remote Mexican locale is haunted by strange story of love and sacrifice. Based on the The blue bouquet by Octavio Paz. 2 acts 2 scenes 4m 1w 1 setting

Shephard-Massat, S. M.

Waiting to be invited.

Drama about race relations set in 1964 Atlanta. Four black women convince themselves to visit previously whites-only restaurant. 2 acts 1m 5w 1 interior 1 exterior

In Women playwrights: the best plays of 2000

The **shepherd** and the troll. Barchers, S. I.

Shepherds

c Harris, A. The second shepherd's play

Sidney, Sir P. The Lady of May

y Swortzell, L. The shepherds of Saint Francis

The **shepherds** of Saint Francis. Swortzell, L.

Sheppard, Julian

Whatever. Dramatists 1998 68p

ISBN 0-8222-1610-8   LC 98-222982

Drama. Three friends discover that man they have all had unsafe sex with is HIV-positive. 2 acts 27 scenes 5m 3w 1 setting

Sher, Emil

Denial is a river.

Radio play. Canadian woman with AIDs takes on medical establishment after family doctor caused death of husband due to tainted blood. 5m 8w extras

In Sher, E. Making waves

Derailed.

Comic exploration of collapsing relationship. Fleeing financial disaster, businessman takes train trip with devoted wife and mistress/colleague. 2m 2w 1 setting

In Seven short plays from Theatre Ontario

Mourning dove.

Canadian farmer's decision to kill disabled daughter who has known nothing but pain. 8m 6w

In Sher, E. Making waves

Past imperfect.

Radio play about boundaries of forgiveness. Examines Jean-Louis Roux affair, when the former lieutenant governor of Quebec resigned his post upon revelations that, in his youth, he had worn a Nazi swastika at a rally. 4m 3w extras

In Sher, E. Making waves

Sherborne, Craig

Look at everything twice, for me. Currency Press 1999 46p

ISBN 0-86819-600-2

Woman seeks identity of organ donor, after receiving heart transplant. 2m 1w 1 setting

Sheridan, Richard Brinsley, 1751-1816

about

Grimm, D. Sheridan; or, Schooled in scandal

Sheridan; or, Schooled in scandal. Grimm, D.

Sherlock's secret life. Lange, E.

Sherman, James

Romance in D. Dramatists 2000 66p

ISBN 0-8222-1743-0

Romance about a musicologist and divorced poet who live in adjoining apartments in Chicago. Music. 2 acts 10 scenes 2m 2w 1 setting

Sherman, Jason

It's all true. Playwrights Canada 2000 122p

ISBN 0-88754594-7

Sherman, Jason—*Continued*

Drama about politics and theater set in 1937 New York. When government padlocks doors to theater where Marc Blitzstein's The Cradle Will Rock is set to open, the director, Orson Welles, marches cast and audience down Seventh Avenue to find new venue. 3 acts 19 scenes 4m 4w extras 5 interiors 2 exteriors

—Same

In Sherman, J. Six plays

The League of Nathans.

Three Canadian Jewish boys form club and grapple with their faith and identity. When one moves to Israel they are dispersed until years later when telegram summons members to synagogue in Spain. 2 acts 8 scenes 4m 4 interiors 2 exteriors

In Sherman, J. Six plays

Patience. Playwrights Canada 2000 113p
ISBN 0-88754-557-2   LC 00-456849

Man who thinks he has everything loses it all, and searches for an explanation. Music, singing. 2 acts 8 scenes 7m 4w extras 1 setting

—Same

In Sherman, J. Six plays

Reading Hebron.

Drama about 1994 massacre at Tomb of the Patriarchs in Hebron. Israel's government opens inquiry to determine whether Baruch Goldstein acted alone or with accomplices. 3m 2w

In Sherman, J. Six plays

The retreat.

Comedy set 1993 in Toronto and at artist's retreat in Canadian Rockies. Film producer drawn to young Jewish woman's screenplay about false Messiah. 2 acts 18 scenes 3m 1w 2 interiors

In Sherman, J. Six plays

Three in the back, two in the head.

Drama set in the Pentagon about ultimate cost of state and personal secrets. 14 scenes 4m 1w 1 exterior

In Sherman, J. Six plays

Sherman, Martin

Bent. Applause 1998 80p
ISBN 1-55783-336-2

Homosexuals imprisoned in German concentration camp during the Holocaust. 2 acts 11 scenes 9m 2 interiors 4 exteriors

A madhouse in Goa. French (London) 1998 108p
ISBN 0-573-62291-4   LC 98-234624

Deception unfolds among the visitors and expatriates staying on the Greek islands of Corfu and Santorini. 2 parts 4m 2w

Rose. French 2002 40p
ISBN 0-573-62922-6

One woman show. Life of feisty eighty-year-old Jewish woman from tiny Russian village, via the Warsaw ghetto to present day Miami Beach. 1w 1 setting

The **shield**. Menander

Shields, Carol

Larry's party (dramatization) See Norman, M. Larry's party

Shields, Carol, and Williamson, Dave

Anniversary; by Carol Shields and Dave Williamson. Blizzard Pub. 1998 60p
ISBN 0-921368-81-X   LC 98-216020

Ironic look at marriages of two upwardly mobile suburban Canadian couples. 2 acts 3m 2w 1 interior

Shimko, Rob

Specks. French 1999 40p il
ISBN 0-573-62663-4   LC 99-218310

Drama about a New Year's Eve party with a waitress, her mother, a regular patron, and a stranger. 1 act 2m 2w 1 interior

Shine!: the Horatio Alger musical. Anderson, Roger

Shinn, Christopher

Four. Dramatists 2002
ISBN 0-8222-1850-X

On the fourth of July in Hartford, a sixteen-year-old white boy meets a closeted, married black man. At the same time, a sixteen-year-old girl meets a twenty-year-old drug dealer. These two couples get to know each other. 3m 1w 1 setting

Other people. Dramatists 2002
ISBN 0-8222-1851-8

In the crucible of a tiny East village apartment, Stephen, Mark, and Petra struggle with questions of art, sex and each other as the impending New Year forces them to define how they want to live and love. 5m 1w 1 interior setting

Saturday night.

Couple argue about what to do on Saturday night. 1m 1w 1 interior

In 30 ten-minute plays for 2 actors from Actors Theatre of Louisville's National Ten-minute Play Contest

Shipman, Nell, 1893-1970
about
Pollock, S. Moving pictures
Shipwreck. Esson, L.
Shipwreck. Stoppard, T.

Shipwrecks
Kluger, S. Pilots of the purple twilight
Wilder, T. The angel on the ship
Wilder, T. Leviathan
A **shoe** is not a question. Stuart, K.
The **shoemaker's** holiday. Dekker, T.
Shop. Leivick, H.
Shopping and fucking. Ravenhill, M.

Shores, Del
Sordid lives. French 1998 120p
  ISBN 0-573-63043-7   LC 99-213834
Comedy about a woman who dies from banging
her head as a result of tripping over her lover's
wooden legs in a Texas motel room. 4 parts 6m
6w
Short changed. McConnell, J.

Shorty, Sharon
Trickster visits the old folks home.
Aging Tlingit woman makes transition from tra-
ditional bush life to non -native senior citizens
home in Whitehorse. 3 scenes 2w extras 1 interior
1 exterior
  In Staging the North; ed. by S. Grace,
      E. D'Aeth and L. Chalykoff
The **show-off**. Kelly, G.
Showdown on Rio Road. Medoff, M., and
  Marks, R.

Siamese twins
Gregg, S. A private moment
Krieger, H. Side show
Sib. Flacks, D., and Greenblatt, R.
The **sick** room. Sewell, S.
A **sick** world. Lopez, R.
Side man. Leight, W.
Side show. Krieger, H.
Siding 37. Lewis, G.

Sidney, Sir Philip
The Lady of May.
Country-house revel. Forester and shepherd en-
gage in singing match to win the Lady of May.
Elizabeth I is asked to determine winner. Singing.

5m 2w 1 setting
  In Renaissance drama; ed. by A. F.
      Kinney

Sierens, Arne
Drummers; tr. by Nadine Malfait.
Son's drum teacher helps poor single mother re-
call earlier, more carefree times. 1m 1w 1 interior
  In Dutch and Flemish plays, ed. by D.
      Couling

Sigley, Marjorie
c Saint George and the dragon at Christ-
  mas tide.
Modern adaptation of medieval mummers' play.
Music, singing, dancing. Prologue Variable cast
  In The twelve plays of Christmas; ed.
      by L. Swortzell

Sign language
y Zeder, S. The taste of sunrise
Signature. Henley, B.
A **significant** betrayal. Wilhelm, L.
Signs of life. Schenkar, J.

Silberman, Brian
Walkin' backward.
Story of three teenage boys running away from
home in small back-country Virginia town in
1965. Singing. 3m 1 exterior
  In The Best American short plays,
      2000-2001
Silhouette. Brett, S.

Sills, Paul
The blue light and other stories.
12 stories from repertoire. Introductory piece is
followed by dramatizations of folk tales, fables,
Arthurian legend, and Scottish balladry. Music. 2
acts 12 scenes variable cast settings
  In Sills, P. Paul Sills' story theater:
      four shows
A Christmas carol. Applause 2001 72p
  ISBN 1-557783-451-2
Dramatization of Dickens's classic holiday ghost
story. 2 acts 5 parts Large mixed cast 1 setting
—Same
  In Sills, P. Paul Sills' story theater:
      four shows

Sills, Paul—*Continued*

Rumi; tr. by Coleman Barks.

Dramatic adaptations of 19 stories by Jalal al-Din Rumi, a medieval Sufi poet and mystic. Stories draw on folklore, serve as parables. Music, singing. 19 scenes Variable cast settings

In Sills, P. Paul Sills' story theater: four shows

Stories of God; tr. by M. D. Herter Norton.

Dramatization of 8 tales composed by the poet Rilke in 1899. Some are drawn from Russian folklore, all reflect wonder and naive religious feeling. Music, singing. 2 acts 8 scenes Variable cast settings

In Sills, P. Paul Sills' story theater: four shows

Silly cow. Elton, B.

Silver, Nicky

The altruists. Dramatists 2001 63p

ISBN 0-8222-1806-2 LC 2002-275113

Satire. Explores passions and pretensions of Manhattan leftist do-gooders. 3m 2w 1 interior

Claire.

Monologue. Woman explores relationship with her mother and importance of sex. 1w 1 interior

In The Best American short plays 1999-2000

The Eros trilogy. Dramatists 1999 47p

ISBN 0-8222-1710-4 LC 00-502408

Trilogy. Four characters in three thematically connected pieces struggle to find refuge in the world through emotional intimacy or pure physical escape of sexual contact. 2m 2w

The maiden's prayer. Dramatists 1999 77p

ISBN 0-8222-1684-1

Comedy about arbitrariness of love. Collection of nervous wrecks ruin lives over unattainable love object. 2 acts 13 scenes 3m 2w

The **silver** tassie. O'Casey, S.

Silverman, Stan. See Schulberg, B. jt. auth.

Silverstein, Shel

Abandon all hope.

Two men debate meaning of sign. 2m 1 exterior setting

In Silverstein, S. Shel's shorts

All cotton.

Woman is furious because the guaranteed not-to-shrink blouse did and the store clerk will not give her a refund. 2w 1 interior 1 setting

In Silverstein, S. Shel's shorts

The best daddy.

Comedy about little girl, her sister, and their father. 1m 1w 1 setting

In Silverstein, S. An adult evening of Shel Silverstein

Blind Willie and the talking dog.

Blind Willie sings the blues to make money, but refuses to use his talking dog to make real money. Singing. 2m 1 exterior setting

In Silverstein, S. An adult evening of Shel Silverstein

Bus stop.

Man stands on corner with sign "bust stop." Passing woman listens to slang about busts, but turns tables on the man. 1m 1w 1 exterior setting

In Silverstein, S. An adult evening of Shel Silverstein

Buy one, get one free.

Hookers offer the deal of the century in rhyming song. Singing. 1m 2w 1 exterior

In Silverstein, S. An adult evening of Shel Silverstein

Click.

Woman takes a bath while husband sits on the toilet seat playing Russian roulette. 1m 1w 1 interior setting

In Silverstein, S. Shel's shorts

Do not feed the animal.

Woman sits next to man holding mysterious animal. 1m 1w 1 exterior setting

In Silverstein, S. Shel's shorts

Dreamers.

Plumbers who have symbolic dreams. 2m 1 setting

In Silverstein, S. Shel's shorts

Duck.

Man enters low doorway and finds ducks on other side. 2m 1w 1 setting

In Silverstein, S. Shel's shorts

Garbage bags.

Monologue. Woman sits between monstrous garbage bags, grocery bags, and cardboard boxes. As she recites her poem of refusing to take out the garbage, the bags move closer, until she disappears. 1w 1 setting

In Silverstein, S. Shel's shorts

Silverstein, Shel—*Continued*

Going once.

In a comic monologue, an auctioneer shows off a woman who is putting herself up for auction to the highest bidder. 1m 1w 1 interior setting

In Silverstein, S. An adult evening of Shel Silverstein

Gone to take a . . .

Woman is enraged when her employee leaves an explicit sign informing patrons that he has gone to take a . . . . 1m 1w 1 interior setting

In Silverstein, S. Shel's shorts

Hangnail.

Monologue. Woman tries to remove a hangnail. 1w 1 interior setting

In Silverstein, S. Shel's shorts

Hard hat area.

As one worker eats his lunch another tries to convince him to wear a hard hat so he will not be killed accidentally. 2m 1 exterior setting

In Silverstein, S. Shel's shorts

Have a nice day.

Three men try to combine the symbols for "peace" and "have a nice day." 2m 1 setting

In Silverstein, S. Shel's shorts

The lifeboat is sinking.

Comedy. Wife forces husband to make difficult decision. 1m 1w 1 interior setting

In Silverstein, S. An adult evening of Shel Silverstein

No dogs allowed.

Beach club manager claims that woman's husband is a dog. 2m 1w 1 setting

In Silverstein, S. Shel's shorts

No skronking.

A conversation between a customer and a waitress on the meaning of the posted sign that prohibits skronking. 1m 1w 1 interior setting

In Silverstein, S. Shel's shorts

No soliciting.

Brief sketch about sign salesman. 1m 1w 1 setting

In Silverstein, S. Shel's shorts

One tennis shoe.

A husband claims that his wife is becoming a bag lady. 1m 1w 1 setting

In Silverstein, S. An adult evening of Shel Silverstein

Smile.

Comedy. Two men have found the man responsible for the smiley face and the phrase, "have a nice day" and they are going to make him pay. 4m

1 exterior

In Silverstein, S. An adult evening of Shel Silverstein

Thinking up a new name for the act.

Farcical sketch about vaudeville act and murder. 1m 1w 1 interior 1 setting

In Silverstein, S. An adult evening of Shel Silverstein

The trio.

Maestro and cellist meet in restaurant to discuss their relationship, both personal and professional. 1m 1w extras 1 interior

In The Best American Short plays, 1997-1998

—Same

In EST marathon '98: the one-act plays; ed. by M. Smith

Wash and dry.

Comedy. Woman stops by the laundramat, but is horrified to discover that her laundry has not been cleaned. 2m 1w 1 interior

In Silverstein, S. An adult evening of Shel Silverstein

What are you doing in there?

Comedy. Mother and father harass son for being in bathroom too long. 2m 1w 1 interior

In The Best American short plays 1999-2000

Simmonds, Rae N.

c The Shamrock road. Anchorage Press 1998 46p

ISBN 0-87602-362-6

Musical set in rural Ireland in late 1800s. Young boy determined to get family's horse back from man who stole it after his father's death. Music, singing. 2 acts 9 scenes 1b 2g 4m 2w extras 1 setting

Simon, Ellen

Moonlight and Valentino. French 2003 74p

ISBN 0-573-62770-3

Comedy. Woman muddles through first year of widowhood 2 acts 6 scenes 1m 3w 1 setting

Simon, Mayo

At sea.

Comedy about a couple who swim in their kitchen with bucket of water. 1m 1w 1 interior

In Actors Theatre of Louisville. Ten-minute plays: v4

Simon, Neil

The dinner party. French 2002 64p

Comedy. Five people, who are complete strangers, are invited to a French dinner party at a first-rate restaurant. 3m 3w 1 interior

Neil Simon's 45 seconds from Broadway. French 2003 84p

ISBN 0-573-62850-5

A year in the lives of the people who frequent an unpretentious hotel coffee shop in New York's theater district, including a compulsively funny Jewish comedian, a loco WASP couple, and an aspiring African playwright. 2 acts 4 scenes 6m 6w 1 interior

Neil Simon's proposals. French 1998 109p

ISBN 0-573-65099-3   LC 00-703036

Family gathers at their retreat in the Poconos, Pennsylvania in the summer of 1953. Includes a workaholic father, his love-sick daughter and other interesting characters. 2 acts 7 scenes 5m 4w extras 1 setting

Simpson, Bland. See Herrick, J. jt. auth.

Simpson, Bland, and Wann, Jim

King Mackerel & the blues are running; by Bland Simpson & Jim Wann with Don Dixon and J.L. Mills. French 1998 61p

ISBN 0-573-69660-8

Musical about fishing buddies who stage a benefit concert to save a local inn. 2 acts 3m

Simpson, Ed

A point of order. French 1998 105p

ISBN 0-573-62621-9   LC 98-164559

Comedy about a small town committee in Pennsylvania which attempts to organize a media event to bolster the town's image. 2 acts 4m 2w 1 interior

Sin. MacLeod, W.

The sin-eater. Nigro, D.

Singapore

Ping, C. W. Details cannot body wants
Wood, C. Jingo

Race relations

Netto, L. Maria

Singapore. Palmer, J.

Singers

Cairns, G. Danceland

Chambers, R. Marg Szkaluba (Pissy's wife)

Clark, R. The incomparable LouLou

Laurence, C. The Ring sisters

c McCullough, L. E. Opening night at the opera, er, opry (piano tuner)

Parker, S. Catchpenny twist

Pugliese, F. The summer winds

Ray, C. Sanders family Christmas

Stolz, T. Mahalia

Wedekind, F. The tenor

Single women

Adams, G. Something blue

Auburn, D. Proof

Bowen, J. Singles

Brett, S. Putting the kettle on

Carmichael, F. Decisions, decisions

García Lorca, F. The house of Bernarda Alba

Kramer, S. The wall of water

Mann, S. The house of Bernarda Alba

Powell, D. Walking down Broadway

Powell, D. Women at four o'clock

Rebeck, T. Loose knit

Robson, J. Mr Wonderful

Salinas, P. Picture perfect

Townsend, J. Angels and saints

Williams, T. Lord Byron's love letter

Williams, T. A lovely Sunday for Creve Coeur

Singles. Bowen, J.

Singleton, the medal winner. Babe, T.

Siobhan. Augustine, J.

The **siren** song of Stephen Jay Gould. Bettenbender, B.

Sirera, Rodolf

The audition.

A marquis commands an actor to perform the death of Socrates and then, to ensure verisimilitude, initiates a sinister game of poisoning. 2m 1 interior

In Modern Catalan plays; ed. by J. London and D. George

Sistahs. Bailey, M., and Lewis, S. M.

Sisters

Ackermann, J. The batting cage

Auburn, D. Proof

Baker, E. A. The seventeenth of June

Sisters—*Continued*

Baker, E. A. Up, down, strange, charmed, beauty, and truth

Chekhov, A. P. Three sisters

Chen, K. Rowing to America

De Angelis, A. Hush

De Wet, R. Crossing

Dewberry, E. Happy mug

Greenberg, R. Everett Beekin

Hanes, M. The crimson thread

y Harden, V. Jessica and Jolene

Hare, D. The secret rapture

Hartman, K. Gum

Healy, A. M. Lonely

Henley, B. Crimes of the heart

Hollinger, M. Tiny island

Hughes, D. New morning

Ibsen, H. John Gabriel Borkman

Junyent, S. Packing up the past

Kossman, N. Miracles

Kramer, A. A treasure in a teacup

Lambert, A. Very heaven

MacIvor, D. Marion Bridge

McConnell, J. The guilt card

c Medoff, M. Kringle's window

Napier, E. The English teachers

Napier, E. Gone missing

Nigro, D. The great Gromboolian plain

Oates, J. C. Bad girls

Parsley, R. Sense and sensibility

Plautus, T. M. The wild, wild women (Bacchides)

Rayson, H. Hotel Sorrento

Redwood, J. H. The old settler

Rosenthal, A. Sitting pretty

Scheffer, W. Bel canto

y Shafaat, S. Balcony

Taylor, D. H. Only drunks and children tell the truth

Upton, J. Sunspots

Vogelstein, C. Sisters

Sisters. Vogelstein, C.

Sisters of the winter madrigal. Henley, B.

Sistren Theatre Collective

QPH.

Drama about 167 women who died in fire at Kingston Alms house in 1980. Speaking chorus. Prologue 2 acts 6 scenes 4w extras

In Postcolonial plays; ed. by H. Gilbert

Sisyphus. Barchers, S. I.

Sitting on paradise. Stickland, E.

Sitting pretty. Rosenthal, A.

Situation vacant. Vinaver, M.

Six characters in search of an author. Brustein, R.

Six characters in search of an author (Sei personaggi in cerca d'autore). Pirandello, L.

Six inch adjustable. Warmflash, S.

The **six** swans. McCullough, L. E.

The **Sixth** Floor museum. Long, Q.

Sixty below. Linklater, L., and Flather, P.

Sizwe Bansi is dead. Fugard, A., and others

Skarstedt, Sonja A.

Saint Francis of Esplanade. Empyreal Press 2000 113p

ISBN 0-921852-30-4

The denizens of a seedy boarding house include a religious fanatic and his unreconstructed opposite number, as well as a homophobe and a ghost. 2 acts 6m 4w 2 interiors 2 settings

Skin. Iizuka, N.

Skin. Kane, S.

Skin & ornaments. Hickman, C.

Skin and bones. Duffield, N.

Skitaletz (The wanderer). Lipkin, D.

A **skull** in Connemara. McDonagh, M.

Sky. Gault, C.

Skyscraper. Auburn, D.

Slabolepszy, Paul

Mooi Street moves.

Comedy set in rundown Johannesburg building. Streetwise black "Middle Man" and clueless white country bumpkin share room. 1 act 2m 1 interior

In Drama for a new South Africa; ed. by D. Graver

Slaight, Brad

Dancing by myself.

Series of short sketches dealing with a frustuated playwright, youth and a reunion in a coffee shop. 6 parts Large mixed cast settings

In New Plays; ed. by C. Slaight

y Second class.

Twenty-eight snippets of high school life. 28 scenes Variable cast

In New Plays from A.C.T.'s young conservatory v3

Slaughter City. Wallace, N.

Slavery

Bandele, 'Biyi. Aphra Behn's Oroonoko

Mayer, O. Ragged time

Plautus, T. M. Casina

Sondheim, S. A funny thing happened on the way to the forum

Canada

Clarke, G. E. Beatrice Chancy

Gale, L. Angélique

United States

Aiken, G. L. Uncle Tom's cabin

Beard, J. The Ornamental hermit

Boucicault, D. The octoroon; or, Life in Louisiana

Brown, W. W. The escape

Dove, R. The darker face of the earth

Gage, C. Harriet Tubman visits a therapist

Harper, L. An' push da wind down

c Hines, K. Home on the mornin' train

Luckham, C. The dramatic attitudes of Miss Fanny Kemble

Trowbridge, J. T. Neighbor Jackwood

Walcott, D. Walker

Slavs!. Kushner, T.

The **sleep** of reason. Buero-Vallejo, A.

Sleeping around; [by] Hilary Fannin [et al.] Methuen 1998 72p
ISBN 0-413-73270-3

Twelve scenes of sex and intimacy in face of potentially dehumanizing consumer culture in 1990s British Isles. 12 scenes 6m 6w settings

Sleeping beauty. Brett, S., and Travis, S.

The **sleeping** mountains. Winther, B.

Sleepy Hollow. Francoeur, B.

Slice of life. Brown, S. R.

Slide show. Selig, P.

A **slight** hangover. Ogilvy, I.

Slop-culture. Badlam, R.

Slotboom, Carl

The train. French (London) 1999 21p
ISBN 0-573-12332-2

An interruption in a train journey triggers an elderly couple's memories of an earlier trip, via cattle car, to a concentration camp. 1 act 2m 2w extras 1 interior

Slover, Tim

Joyful noise. French 2001 86p
ISBN 0-573-62759-2

Drama about George Frederick Handel's difficulties presenting his work Messiah to the court of King George II of England. 2 acts 20 scenes 5m 3w extras

The **slow** eviction of Ruby Rosenholtz. Rodin, T.

Small craft warnings. Williams, T.

A **small** delegation. Neipris, J.

A **small-hearted** woman. Crommelynck, F.

Smallpox

c McCullough, L. E. Edward Jenner and the gossip of milkmaids

The **smartest** woman in the kingdom. LaVohn, R. W.

Smashed eggs. Porter, P.

The **smell** of the kill. Lowe, M.

Smile. Silverstein, S.

A **smile** on the end of the line. Vinaver, M.

Smilow, David

Brights.

Two couples driving in car have conversation that reveals some secrets. 2m 2w 1 setting
In take ten; ed. by E. Lane and N. Shengold

Smith, Ali

Trace of Arc.

Joan appears as a comic to two modern young supermarket assistants. 4w extras 1 interior
In Mythic women/Real women

Smith, Charles

y City of gold.

Ghost figure interrupts Columbus Day celebration. Music, singing. 5m 1 setting
In International plays for young people

Knock me a kiss. Dramatic Publishing 2003 94p

Drama set during the Harlem Renaissance. Yolande Du Bois, daughter of W. E. B. Du Bois, marries homosexual poet Countee Cullen. Music, singing. 2 acts 12 scenes 3m 3w 5 interiors

—Same
In New playwrights: the best plays of 2000

Smith, Charles—*Continued*
The Sutherland. French 1999 62p
ISBN 0-573-62691-X

Drama about jazz musician who returns to his birthplace, Chicago, after living in Europe. 2 acts 6m 2w 1 interior

Takunda.

Drama incorporating Shona folk tales and songs. Singing. Variable cast 1 setting
In Multicultural theatre II; ed. by R. Ellis

Les trois Dumas. Dramatic Publishing 2003 112p

Drama about three generations of the internationally notorious Dumas family—General Thomas Dumas, Alexandre Dumas père (author of the Three Musketeers), and Alexandre Dumas fils. 3 acts 6m 3w 1 setting

Smith, Colin
Four-play. French (London) 2000 22p
ISBN 0-573-12248-2   LC 2002-279014

Comedy about two couples having an ordinary dinner in suburbia, until adulterous affair rises explosively to the surface. 2 scenes 2m 2w 1 setting

Smith, Evan
The uneasy chair. Dramatists 1999 71p
ISBN 0-8222-1699-X   LC 00-503534

Comedy of Victorian manners focusing on relationship of spinster and retired military man. 3 acts 3m 2w 1 interior

—Same
In New Playwrights: the best plays of 1998

Smith, Jack
Rehearsal for the destruction of Atlantis.

Experimental performance piece incorporating outlandish costumes, dance, film, and tape. 7m 3w 1 setting
In Theatre of the ridiculous; ed. by B. Marranca and G. Dasgupta

about
Vawter, R. Roy Cohn/Jack Smith

Smith, Jon McCauley
This is my story.

Worship program. A Holy Week Tenebrae Service. 1b 3m 2w extras
In The drama of Easter; ed. by R. Wray

Smith, Judy Gattis
c What the animals made known.

Little bird finds a voice upon joining other animals at the manger. Music, singing. 1 act Variable cast 1 setting
In 5 Christmas plays for children

Smith, Othniel
Giant steps.

Man dying in Cardiff AIDS hospice conducts final conversation with former drug dealer. 1 act 4 scenes 2m 1w 4 interiors
In New Welsh Drama II; ed. by J. Teare

Smith, Robert Holbrook, 1879-1950
about
Shem, S. Bill W. and Dr. Bob

Smith, Stephen
Background artiste. French (London) 2000 28p
ISBN 0-573-12044-7   LC 2002-279009

Comedy about agency for walk-on actors. 2m 3w 1 interior

On location. French (London) 2002 31p
ISBN 0-573-02353-0

A novice movie extra discovers the strange new world of low-budget filmmaking. 1 act 2m 3w extras 1 interior

Smith, Val
Breaking the chain.

Young woman refuses to send chain letter as her friends beg her to reconsider. 1m 2w
In 30 ten-minute plays for 3 actors from Actors Theatre of Louisville's National Ten-minute Play Contest

Marguerite Bonet.

Play about duality of fantasy and self-deception. Rebellious daughter of a psychic becomes the obsession of two physicists. Music. 2 acts 14 scenes 3m 1w settings
In Women playwrights: the best plays of 1998

Meow.

Two friends who work together meet after work on Fridays to discuss life. 3w 1 interior
In Actors Theatre of Louisville. Ten-minute plays; v5

—Same
In Humana Festival '98

Smith, Val, and Dixon, Michael Bigelow

The league of semi-super heroes.

Comedy about group of Super heroes looking for work. Variable cast 6 characters 1 interior

In 30 ten-minute plays for 4, 5 & 6 actors from Actors Theatre of Louisville's National Ten-Minute Play Contest

—Same

In Actors Theatre of Louisville. Ten-minute plays: v4

Smuggling

Darke, N. The King of Prussia

Smulewitz, Solomon

about

c McCullough, L. E. Di goldineh medineh (The golden land)

Smyth, Donna E.

Sole survivors.

Drama based on life and work of poet Elizabeth Bishop. 2 acts 26 scenes 2m 3w 1 setting

In Maiden voyages; ed. by S. Burke

Snake in fridge. Fraser, B.

The **snake** in the grass. Kelly, T.

Snakebit. Grant, D. M.

Snapshot: a quick tour of the monument. Wright, C.

Snapshot: American klepto. Moore, A.

Snapshot: becoming American. Nottage, L.

Snapshot: bomb squad. Wright, C.

Snapshot: defacing patriotic property. Barfield, T.

Snapshot: her first screen test. O'Brien, D.

Snapshot: here and now. Yew, C.

Snapshot: history lesson. Lindsay-Abaire, D.

Snapshot: little Pezidents. Dixon, M. B., and Smith, V.

Snapshot: monument. Kane, H.

Snapshot: night out. Kuruvilla, S.

Snapshot: on Lincoln's head. Jensen, J.

Snapshot: rock scissors paper. Margolin, D.

Snapshot: scene at Mount Rushmore. Long, Q.

Snapshot: the great father. Lodato, V.

Snapshot: thrift of the Magi. Weisman, A.

Snapshot: Tyler poked Taylor. Blessing, L.

Sneaky. Yellow Robe, W. S.

Snelgrove, Michael

Marking time. French (London) 1998 62p
ISBN 0-573-01828-6

Comedy about two competing teams of teachers grading papers at a residential teachers' center. 2 acts 3m 2w 1 setting

The **snow** ball. Gurney, A. R.

The **snow** palace. Gems, P.

The **snowflake** avalanche. York, Y.

Snyder, Geraldine Ann

c Johnny Appleseed. Dramatic Publishing 2003 41p

Musical. Based on life of John Chapman (Johnny Appleseed). Chronicle Johnny's adventure in early 1800s as he travels through Pennsylvania, Ohio and Indiana planting apple trees to feed the pioneers settling America's wilderness. Variable cast 1 setting

c Red Riding Hood. Dramatic Publishing 2003 56p

Musical version of classic tale set in city in th 1920s. Red is entrusted for the very first time to deliver a basket of goodies to her ailing grandmother. Variable cast 1 setting

Snyder, Patricia Di Benedetto

Miracle on 34th Street. French 2002 78p
ISBN 0-573-62892-0

A benevolent old man, employed by Macy's to act as Santa Claus, insists that he is Santa Claus and gradually convinces a skeptical world. A dramatization of the 1947 novel by Valentine Davies. Music, singing. 2 acts 33 scenes Large mixed cast 13 interiors 4 exteriors

So please be kind. Gilroy, F. D.

So tell me about this guy. Whiskeyman, D.

So what's new? Dike, F.

Soap opera. Ives, D.

Soccer

Farquhar, R. God's official

Oliver, C. Kicking out

y Oliver, C. Ooh ah Showab Khan

Social workers

De Angelis, A. The positive hour

Gardner, H. A thousand clowns

Socialism

Egloff, E. The devils

Socrates

about

Aristophanes. Clouds

Sodaro, Craig

c Chickenheart. Pioneer Drama Service 2001 44p

Medieval melodrama. Faced with marriage to despicable tax-collector Lady Emma and her maid flee in disguise. 2 acts 4 scenes 3m 10w 1 interior 1 exterior

y Hound of the Clackervilles. Pioneer Drama Service 1997 60p

Spoof of Sherlock Holmes mystery about family curse. 2 acts 7 scenes 10m 19w 1 interior

Murder by the book. Pioneer Drama Service 2000 66p

Murder takes place at meeting of mystery writers. 2 acts 6 scenes 4m 6w 1 interior

y Phantom of the campfire. Pioneer Drama Service 1999 60p

Comic mystery set at unusual Summer camp. 2 acts 7 scenes 10m 13w 1 exterior

Who poisoned his meatball? Pioneer Drama Service 2003 46p

Crime comedy. Town's wealthiest man murdered in Italian restaurant. 2 acts Variable cast 17 characters extras 1 interior

Sody Salleratus. McBride-Smith, B.

Soft click of a switch. Lewis, C. W.

Sokotra. Bullock, M.

The **solar** spectrum. Wedekind, F.

Soldiers

Gore, C. The maid of Croissey; or, Theresa's vow

Manzoni, A. The Count of Carmagnola: a tragedy

Oakes, M. Faith

Rachilde. The painted woman (La Femme peinte)

American

Babe, T. Singleton, the medal winner

c Fredericks, A. D. Two soldiers: talking, dying

Gilroy, F. D. Contact with the enemy

Gilroy, F. D. Getting in

Gilroy, F. D. The viewing

Paterson, D. L. Chutes

Wallace, N. In the heart of America

Wilkins, J. R. War letters

Australian

Hewett, D. The man from Mukinupin

British

Arden, J. Serjeant Musgrave's dance

Wood, C. Dingo

German

Büchner, G. Woyzeck

Israeli

Sunde, K. How his bride came to Abraham

Roman

Plautus, T. M. Major Blowhard (Miles gloriosus)

Soldiers will be soldiers. Rodriguez, E. S.

Sole survivors. Smyth, D. E.

Solis, Octavio

El otro.

Through peyote-induced experience young girl discovers her true father is drug-dealer, wife-beater and murderer on Tex-Mex border. 2 acts 6m 4w 1 exterior

In Latino plays from South Coast Repertory

Solomon, King of Israel

about

c McCullough, L. E. The wisdom of Solomon

c Vogel, L. Solomon—wise for a while

Solomon—wise for a while. Vogel, L.

Some golden states. Miller, T.

Some mother's son. O'Callaghan, J.

Some people. Hoch, D.

Somebody call 911. Nelson, J. L.

Somebody somebody's returning. Ward, F.

Someone save my Baby Ruth! St. John, B.

Someplace warm. Macklin, P.

Something blue. Adams, G.

Something in the air. Dresser, R.

Something special. Tait, L.

Something's burning. Chappell, E.

Somewhere over the balcony. Charabanc Theatre Company

Son, Diana

R. A. W. ('cause I'm a woman).

Experimental theater piece in which Asian American women react to sexual stereotypes. Background music. 4w

In take ten; ed. by E. Lane and N. Shengold

Stop kiss. Dramatists 2000 64p

ISBN 0-8222-1731-7   LC 99-37837

Romantic comedy about two women who meet, become friends, which leads to an unexpected attraction. 23 scenes 3m 3w 1 setting

—Same. Overlook Press 1999 141p

ISBN 0-87951-737-9   LC 99-37837

Sondheim, Stephen

Follies; book by James Goldman; music and lyrics by Stephen Sondheim. Theatre Communications Group 2001 87p

ISBN 1-55936-196-4

Former theater people meet in middle-age and end up kissing, but by night's end return to their respective spouses. 2 acts Large mixed cast 1 setting

A funny thing happened on the way to the forum; book by Burt Shevelove and Larry Gelbart; music and lyrics by Stephen Sondheim.

Musical comedy set in ancient Rome based on Plautus' Pseudolus. Man agrees to free slave upon delivery of courtesan. Mistaken identity and contrived funeral ceremony enter into vaudevillian scenario. 2 acts 7m 2w extras 1 setting

In Sondheim, S. Four by Sondheim

A little night music; book by Hugh Wheeler; music and lyrics by Stephen Sondheim.

Musical comedy based on Ingmar Bergman film Smiles of a summer night. Portrays romantic relationship in turn of the century Sweden. Prologue 2 acts 17 scenes 7m 10w 8 interiors 3 exteriors

In Sondheim, S. Four by Sondheim

Sunday in the park with George; book by George Lapine; music and lyrics by Stephen Sondheim.

Musical inspired by Georges Seurat's painting. Large mixed cast settings

In Sondheim, S. Four by Sondheim

Sweeney Todd; book by Hugh Wheeler; music and lyrics by Stephen Sondheim.

Musical adaptation of Christopher Bond's version of Sweeny Todd. Legendary barber murders clients and uses bodies to make pies. Prologue 2 acts epilogue 7m 3w extras settings

In Sondheim, S. Four by Sondheim

Song for the end. Ehn, E.

The **song** of one; or, The journey of Ti Marie. Hippolyte, K.

Sophiatown. Junction Avenue Theatre Company

Sophists (Greek philosophy)

Aristophanes. Clouds

Sophocles

Antigone (adaptation) See Anouilh, J. Antigone

Aias; tr. by Carl R. Mueller and Anna Krajewska-Wieczorek.

Greek tragedy in verse. Ajax, unable to reconcile himself to fact that Odysseus had been chosen leader of Greek forces in Trojan War, commits suicide.

In Sophocles. The complete plays

Ajax; tr. by Frederic Raphael and Kenneth McLeish.

Greek classical tragedy in verse. Ajax, unable to reconcile himself to the fact that Odysseus has been chosen leader of Greek forces in the Trojan War, commits suicide.

In Sophocles. Sophocles v1

Antigone; in a new translation by Nicholas Rudall. Dee, I. R. 1998 54p

ISBN 1-566-63210-2; 1-566-63211-0

LC 98-29136

Greek tragedy in verse. Disaster follows refusal of Creon, King of Thebes to permit burial of his enemy Antigone's brother. Speaking chorus.

—Same; tr. by Carl R. Mueller and Anna Krajewska-Wieczorek

In Sophocles. The complete plays

—Same; tr. by Kelly Cherry

In Sophocles. Sophocles v2

Electra; tr. by Frank McGuinness. French 1997 60p

ISBN 0-573-62695-2

The son and daughter of Agamemnon unite to kill their adulterous mother and thus avenge their father's murder.

Sophocles—*Continued*

—Same; tr. Henry Taylor

In Sophocles. Sophocles v1

Elektra; tr. by Carl R. Mueller and Anna Krajewska-Wieczorek.

Greek classical tragedy in verse. Based on the legend telling how Orestes and Electra, children of Agamemnon, avenged their father's murder.

In Sophocles. The complete plays

King Oedipus; tr. by Jascha Kessler.

Variant titles: Oedipus; Oedipus the King; Oedipus Rex; Oedipus Tyranos. Greek classical tragedy in verse. Oedipus, King of Thebes, is powerless to escape curse of earlier crime.

In Sophocles. Sophocles v2

Oedipus at Colonus; in a new translation by Nicholas Rudall. Dee, I. R. 2001 77p

ISBN 1-566-63407-5; 1-566-63406-7 (pa)
LC 2001-52564

Greek classical tragedy in verse. Conclusion to Oedipus saga. Oedipus pursued by Creon, milaculously passes from this world to become guardian spirit of Athens.

—Same; tr. by George Garrett

In Sophocles. Sophocles v2

Oedipus at Kolonos; tr. by Carl R. Mueller and Anna Krajewska-Wieczorek.

Greek classical tragedy in verse. Conclusion to Oedipus saga. Oedipus pursued by Creon, miraculously passes from this world to become guardian spirit of Athens.

In Sophocles. The complete plays

Oedipus the King; in a new translation by Nicholas Rudall. Dee, I. R. 2000 62p

ISBN 1-566-63307-9; 1-566-63308-7 (pa)
LC 00-25059

Variant titles: King Oedipus; Oedipus; Oedipus Rex; Oedipus Tyranos. Greek classical tragedy in verse. Oedipus, King of Thebes, is powerless to escape curse of earlier crime.

Oedipus Tyrannos; tr. by Carl R. Mueller and Anna Krajewska-Wieczorek.

Variant titles: King Oedipus; Oedipus; Oedipus Rex; Oedipus Tyranos. Greek classical tragedy in verse. Oedipus, King of Thebes, is powerless to escape curse of earlier crime. Speaking chorus

In Sophocles. The complete plays

Philoctetes; tr. by Armand Schwerner.

Greek classical tragedy in verse. Greeks send Neoptolemus and Odysseus to bring the banished Philoctetes to their aid in the siege of Troy.

In Sophocles. Sophocles v1

Philoktetes; tr. by Carl R. Mueller and Anna Krajewska-Wieczorek.

Greek classical tragedy in verse. Greeks send Neoptolemus and Odysseus to bring the banished Philoctetes to their aid in the siege of Troy.

In Sophocles. The complete plays

Women of Trachis; tr. by Brendan Galvin.

Greek classical tragedy in verse. Philandering Herakles returns from journey with captive women, one of whom he loves. His jealous wife, in attempt to win him back, mistakenly gives him a robe smeared with magic ointment which causes his death.

In Sophocles. Sophocles v1

—Same; tr. by Carl R. Mueller and Anna Krajewska-Wieczorek

In Sophocles. The complete plays

The **sorcerer's** apprentice. Lippa, L.

The **sorcerer's** apprentices. Kleberg, L.

Sordid lives. Shores, D.

Sorge, Reinhard

The beggar; tr. by Walter H. Sokel and Jacqueline Sokel.

Expressionist drama of a poet's spiritual pilgrimage. 3 acts 10m 4w extras 1 interior 1 exterior

In Theater of the avant-garde, 1890-1950; ed. by B. Cardullo and R. Knopf

Sorrows and rejoicings. Fugard, A.

Soul

Wilder, T. Leviathan

The **soul** of the white ant. Wilson, S.

The **sound** of a voice. Hwang, D. H.

The **sound** of stillness. Thomas, T. C.

Sounds of silents (The Essanay years). Peditto, P.

Sour grapes. Harding, M. P.

South Africa

Bailey, B. Ipi zombi?

Baitz, J. R. Film society

Conning, L. A Coloured place

De Wet, R. Crossing

Dike, F. So what's new?

Ellenbogen, N. Horn of sorrow

South Africa—*Continued*

Fugard, A. Sorrows and rejoicings
Fugard, A. Sizwe Bansi is dead
Mahomed, I. Cheaper than roses
Mahomed, I. Purdah
Maponya, M. The hungry earth
Maponya, M. Umongikazi (The nurse)
Mda, Z. And the girls in their Sunday dresses
Mhlophe, G. Have you seen Zandile?
Ndlovu, D. Sheila's day
Ross, L. L. Scent of the roses

Race relations

Gien, P. The syringa tree
Junction Avenue Theatre Company. Sophiatown
Lan, D. Painting a wall
Lan, D. Red earth
Slabolepszy, P. Mooi Street moves
Taylor, J. Ubu and the Truth Commission
Thompson, J. Pink
Wilson, S. The soul of the white ant

Southampton Insurrection, 1831

O'Hara, R. Insurrection

Southern States

Bailey, L. Baby doll
Brown, W. W. The escape
Gilman, R. The glory of living
Green, P. Hymn to the rising sun: a drama of man's waste
Green, P. In Abraham's bosom: the tragedy of a southern Negro
Henley, B. Crimes of the heart
Henley, B. The debutante ball
Herrick, J. Kudzu
Thorne, J. V. The exact center of the universe
Williams, T. Battle of angels
Williams, T. Period of adjustment
Williams, T. The rose tattoo
Williams, T. Suddenly last summer
Williams, T. Sweet bird of youth

Race relations

Childress, A. Wedding band: a love/hate story in black and white
Hughes, L. Mulatto: a tragedy of the Deep South

The **Southwark** Mysteries. Constable, J.

Southworth, Matthew

Damages to Tony.

Parents talk about son with broken leg and about life, while sitting in hospital cafeteria. 1m 1w 1 setting

In Actors Theatre of Louisville. Ten-minute plays; v5

Sovereign love. Murray, T. C.

Soyinka, Wole

Death and the king's horseman.

Tragedy based on events of 1946 in Oyo, Nigeria. English colonial officer intervenes to prevent ritual suicide of Yoruba chief. 5 acts 9m 3w extras 1 setting

In Modern African drama; ed. by B. Jeyifo

The strong breed.

Drama about Nigerian annual New Year purification rite where a stranger is scapegoat for the villagers' sins. 1g 7m 2w extras 1 setting

In Postcolonial plays; ed. by H. Gilbert

Space. Margulies, D.

Space junk. Ellison, L.

Spain

Junyent, S. Packing up the past
Mérimée, P. Inès Mendo; or, The defeat of prejudice (Inès Mendo; ou, Le préjugé vaincu)
Mérimée, P. Inès Mendo; or, The triumph of prejudice (Inès Mendo; ou, Le triomphe du préjugé)
Sandberg, R. N. Convivencia

Colonies

Hochwälder, F. The holy experiment

Social life and customs

Beaumarchais, P. A. D. The barber of Seville
García Lorca, F. The house of Bernarda Alba
Mann, S. The house of Bernarda Alba
The **Spanish** tragedy. Kyd, T.
Sparkleshark. Ridley, P.
Sparring partner. Bogdan, K.
Sparrow. Mooney, V.
Speak. Nelson, G.
Speaking in tongues. Bovell, A.

Spears, Elizabeth George

The witch of Blackbird Pond (dramatization) See York, Y. The witch of Blackbird Pond

Specks. Shimko, R.

Speeches, addresses, etc.

Elisha, R. The Goldberg variations
Wilson, A. The janitor

Speed-the-play. Ives, D.

Spencer, Stuart

In the western garden.

Two representatives of the present-day art world visit a reclusive old painter at his home in East Hampton and try to persuade him to reenter public life, under their auspices. 1 act 3m 1w 1 exterior

In Ensemble Studio Theatre marathon '99: the one-act plays

—Same

In Spencer, S. Plays

Resident alien.

Sci-fi comedy about space alien in small Wisconsin town. 2 acts 15 scenes 1b 4m 1w 4 interiors 1 exterior

In Humana Festival '98

—Same

In Spencer, S. Plays

The Rothko room.

A man encounters a woman from whom he has long been separated at an exhibition of Rothko's mystical late paintings. 1 act 1m 1w 1 interior

In Ensemble Studio Theatre marathon 2000: the one-act plays

Sudden devotion.

Portrays homosexual love affair. 2 acts 3m 1 setting

In Spencer, S. Plays

Sphinx and strawman. Kokoschka, O.

Spider flies to the feast. Barchers, S. I.

Spiderwoman Theater

Power pipes.

Episodic look at childhood of Native American woman. Music, singing, dancing. 22 scenes 6w

In Seventh generation; ed. by M. G. D'Aponte

Spies

Gillette, W. Secret service
Stoppard, T. Hapgood
York, Y. The secret wife

Spike heels. Rebeck, T.

Spinning into butter. Gilman, R.

Spirit. Nelson, G.

The **spirit** is willing. Quinn, N. B.

Spiritualism

Bush, M. Ezigbo, the spirit child
Coward, N. Blithe spirit
Glancy, D. American gypsy
Nigro, D. Seance

Spiro, Peter

Howya doin' Franky Banana?

Black comedy set in Brooklyn bar. Portrays hangers-on in fiefdom of local crime boss. 2 acts 3 scenes 4m 1w 1 interior

In Action; ed. by M. Algarin and L. Griffith

The **Spitfire** Grill. Valcq, J.

Spitz, Alison

Christus.

Worship program. Events of Christ's Passion, beginning with the betrayal and ending with his crucifixion at Golgotha. 8m extras 1 setting

In The drama of Easter; ed. by R. Wray

Splash hatch on the E going down. Corthron, K.

Splendora. Hoffman, S.

Split second: a play in two acts. McIntyre, D.

Spokesong; or, The common wheel. Parker, S.

Spoonface Steinberg. Hall, L.

Sportiello, Antony

Tickets, please!.

A successful woman executive has an unsettling encounter with one of Death's underlings, who may have mistaken her identity. Set on a commuter train. 1 act 1m 1w 1 interior

In Off-Off Broadway Festival plays, 26th ser.

Sports

y Francis, S. Body and soul
y Valentine, A. Swimming the globe
Williams, R. The No Boys Cricket Club

Spot's birthday party. Wood, D.

Spring storm. Williams, T.

Spring's awakening. Wedekind, F.

Spurboard. Enright, N.
The **spurt** of blood. Artaud, A.
Squaring the circle. Kataev, V.
Squeak and maiow! McCullough, L. E.
The **squire's** bride. McBride-Smith, B.
St. James's blues. Ardito, C.

St. John, Billy

The abduction. French 1999 68p
ISBN 0-573-62680-4
Thriller. Novelist's stepdaughter is kidnapped. 2 acts 5 scenes 5m 2w 1 interior

y Cindy Ella's going to the ball, baby!. French 1999 63p
ISBN 0-573-61715
Parody of Cinderella set in contemporary high school 7 scenes 3m 7w extras 3 interiors 1 exterior

Evil doings at Queen Toots' tomb. Pioneer Drama Service 2000 77p
Comic thriller set in 1920s. Expedition unseals tomb of Egyptian queen and unleashes ancient curses. Prologue 2 acts 9 scenes 6m 10w 1 setting

y Holder Posey, the felonious photographer. Pioneer Drama Service 1999 72p
Melodrama set in old west. Villainous traveling photographer attempts to rob vault of saloon. Prologue 2 acts 10 scenes Variable cast 21 characters extras 1 setting

Males order brides; or, Big Harry Deal's scandalous scheme! Pioneer Drama Service 1998 68p
Melodrama. Unscrupulous lawyer hires actresses to impersonate fiancées of quartet of love-starved citizens in 1870s Colorado Territory. 15 scenes 5m 4w extras

Murder can be habit-forming. Pioneer Drama Service 1999 72p
Comic mystery set in upstate New York convent. 2 acts 4 scenes 7m 9w 1 interior

The plot, like gravy, thickens. French 1999 84p
ISBN 0-573-60256-5
Comic murder mystery. A playwright's alter-ego demonstrates in the imagination how to commit murder, by using an unusual cast of characters. 2 acts 5m 9w 1 interior

The reunion. French 2000 84p il
ISBN 0-573-62747-9   LC 2001-270916
Thriller about high school reunion where one guest, the class weirdo, decides to practice his hobbies, hacking away into computers and people. 2 acts 3m 4w 1 setting

y Someone save my Baby Ruth!. Pioneer Drama Service 1999 40p
Melodrama. Villain kidnaps young widow's infant daughter in scheme to obtain valuable real estate. 5 scenes 5m 8m extras 1 interior

y Taming the wild, wild West in a dress. Pioneer Drama Service 2001 84p
Comedy set in 1895. Actor heads west thinking he inherited profitable saloon, when in fact he was bequeathed beauty salon. 2 acts 12 scenes 11m 10w 1 interior

The werewolf's curse; or, Hair today, gone tomorrow. French 2002 19p
ISBN 0-573-62968-4
Comedic spoof of horror films. American student in Rumania is bitten by werewolf cub. 2 acts 16 scenes 7m 8w 1 setting

y Wynn Fairly, champeen rassler! or, Get a grip on yourself!. Pioneer Drama Service 2001 56p
Local favorite set to wrestle for state championship faces opponent with unscrupulous, greedy manager. 2 acts 10 scenes 6m 10w extras 1 setting

You could die laughing!. French 2003 87p
ISBN 0-573-62972-2
Comedy murder mystery which takes place in a millionaire's lodge off the Canadian coast. 2 acts 5 scenes 7m 8w 1 interior
St. Kilda tales. Cortese, R.
St. Nicholas. McPherson, C.
Stage blood. Ludlam, C.
Stage door. Kaufman, G. S., and Ferber, E.
Stage fright. Marowitz, C.

Stair, Ernest R.

Parade without a permit.
Worship program focusing on familiar story of the entry of Jesus into Jerusalem from viewpoint of frustrated city official who is responsible for issuing parade permits. 1 act Variable cast 10 characters 1 setting
In The drama of Easter; ed. by R. Wray

Stairs to the roof. Williams, T.

Stamos, Dale Griffiths

The unintended video.

Set in a park in Seattle. Burn victim is befriended by lady tourist. 1m 1w
  In Actors Theatre of Louisville. Ten-minute plays: v4

Stanley, Jeffrey

Tesla's letters. French 1999 72p
  ISBN 0-573-62292-2

Political drama set in 1997 Belgrade. American woman graduate student arrives at Tesla Museum to do research and encounters museum's director, a Serb with family in Croatia. 2 acts 5 scenes 2m 2w 2 interiors 1 exterior

The **star** quilter. Yellow Robe, W. S.

Star sisters. Bruchac, J.

Stark naked. Marowitz, C.

Stars. Linney, R.

Starstruck. Williams, R.

Starvation

Jeffery, L. Who look in stove

Stealing souls. Upton, J.

Steel kiss. Fulford, R. W.

Steel pier. Kander, J., and Ebb, F.

Steele, Donald

The way to Miami.

Wife reluctant to move because house is her last connection to dead son. 1m 1w 1 interior
  In The Best American short plays 1999-2000
—Same
  In Off-Off Broadway Festival plays, 23rd ser.

Stein, Gertrude

Accents in Alsace: a reasonable tragedy.

Experimental anti-war play.
  In War plays by women; ed. by C. M. Tylee, E. Turner, and A. Cardinal

Doctor Faustus lights the lights.

Experimental drama about triumph of technology and role of God in modern life. Singing. 3 acts 5 scenes 2m 1w extras
  In Theater of the avant-garde, 1890-1950; ed. by B. Cardullo and R. Knopf

Please do not suffer.

Voice play. Self-absorbed chatter of civilians far from the front; underlying unease. 1 act 6m 7w 1 setting
  In War plays by women; ed. by C. M. Tylee, E. Turner, and A. Cardinal

The **Stendhal** syndrome. Strijards, F.

Stephenson, Shelagh

An experiment with an air pump. Dramatists 2000 77p
  ISBN 0-8222-1745-7

Drama about medical ethics focusing on two groups of people living in same Northern English house in 1799 and 1999. Prologue 2 acts 8 scenes 3m 4w 1 setting

Stepping Out. King, D.

Sterling, Pamela

The secret garden.

Dramatization of Frances Hodgson Burnett's children's classic. Orphan girl and invalid cousin are restored to health and happiness as they tend secret garden. Background music. Puppets. 3 acts 12 scenes 1b 1g 4m 2w 1 setting
  In Theatre for young audiences; ed. by C. A. Jennings

Stern, Nikki

Murder at Cafe Noir; [book by] David Landau ; music & lyrics by Nikki Stern. French 1999 60p
  ISBN 0-573-62664-2   LC 99-218316

Musical with audience participation. Comic tribute to Bogart movies of the 1940s. 5 scenes 4m 3w 1 interior

Stetson, Kent

The harps of God. Playwrights Canada 2001 135p
  ISBN 0-88754-606-4

Tragedy about Great Newfoundland Sealing Disaster of 1914. 3 acts 14m extras 1 setting

Stevenson, Robert Louis

The strange case of Dr. Jekyll and Mr. Hyde (dramatization) See Barchers, S. I., and Kroll, J. L. Dr. Jekyll and Mr. Hyde

Treasure Island (dramatization) See Mason, T. Treasure Island

The **steward** of Christendom. Barry, S.

Stewart-Brown, Christi

The gene pool.

Comedy. Lesbian couple's seemingly ideal family life begins to fall apaat. 2 acts 8 scenes 2m 3w 1 interior

In Plays from Woolly Mammoth; ed. by R. alexander and M. Kyrioglou

Stickland, Eugene

A guide to mourning.

Black comedy. Widow and three grown children plan funeral of their husband and father. 2 acts 8 scenes 5m 2w 3 interiors 1 exterior

In Stickland, E. Two plays

Sitting on paradise.

Selling off a beloved old couch, a woman reveals the emptiness of her life. 1 scene 1w extras 1 setting

In Short spells: scenes & monologues; ed. by V. Shantz

—Same

In Stickland, E. Two plays

Still, James

c Hush: an interview with America.

Metaphorical drama about life in United States amid news reports of social problems. 13 scenes Variable cast 1 setting

In Theatre for young audiences; ed. by C. A. Jennings

Still life with Iris. Dietz, S.

Stine, MacArthur

Theological zenith.

Comedy about two men who flip through TV channels and meet God. 4m 1 setting

In Blast from the future; ed. by D. Yeaton

Stinson, John

Median.

Three friends on median of busy highway. 2m 1w 1 exterior

In 30 ten-minute plays for 3 actors from Actors Theatre of Louisville's National Ten-minute Play Contest

—Same

In Actors Theatre of Louisville. Ten-minute plays: v4

Stockton, Frank R.

The lady, or the tiger? (dramatization) See Barchers, S. I., and Kroll, J. L. The lady, or the tiger?

Stockwell, Richard

Killing time. French (London) 1999 73p
ISBN 0-573-01818-9

Thriller about a man and woman who meet and then conspire to kill the woman's husband. 2 act 1m 1w 1 setting

Stohl, Hank

A play on letters. French 1999 48p
ISBN 0-573-62634-0

Comedy about seven characters corresponding with one another, resulting in near divorce for one couple. 5m 2w 1 setting

Stoker, Bram, 1847-1912
Parodies, imitations, etc.
Power, D. Tales of the undead

Stolen. Harrison, J.

Stolz, Tom

Mahalia; a gospel musical. French 1998 95p
ISBN 0-573-62626-X   LC 98-231833

Play with music. Story about the life of gospel singer Mahalia Jackson. Music, singing. 2 acts 1m 2w

The **stone** angel. Nichol, J. W.

The **stone** guest. Pushkin, A.

Stone the crows. Paterson, D. L.

Stones and bones. McClinton, M. I.

Stones in his pockets. Jones, M.

Stonewall Jackson's house. Reynolds, J.

Stoney Bowes. Ardito, C.

Stop kiss. Son, D.

Stop sending in the clowns. Cook, P.

Stop the presses! Kelly, T.

Stoppard, Tom

Arcadia.

Dramatic comedy set in English country house concurrently in present day and 1809. Landscape gardening, poetry, chaos theory, sex, and the end of the world are among topics discussed in exploration of clash between classical order and romantic ardor. 2 acts 7 scenes 8m 3w 1 setting

In Stoppard, T. Plays: five

Stoppard, Tom—*Continued*
Hapgood.
Women who runs British counter-espionage agency searches for source of information leak. 2 acts 12 scenes 8m 1w 5 interiors 2 exteriors
In Stoppard, T. Plays: five
Indian ink.
Drama based on author's radio play In the native state about cultural and political legacies of colonialism. Follows lives of British poet, Indian artist, and their descendants from 1930s India to 1980s London. 2 acts 11m 4w extras 2 interiors
In Stoppard, T. Plays: five
The invention of love. Grove Press 1998 102p
ISBN 0-8021-3581-1
Scenes from life of homosexual poet and classical scholar A. E Housman. 2 acts 19m 1w extras 1 setting
Night and day.
Fictional African country is faced with Soviet-backed revolution which brings in newsmen from around world, including Australian veteran reporter and idealistic young English journalist. At issue is extent of freedom of the press, which is ironically ultimately thwarted by labor strike of London printers. 2 acts 1b 6m 1w extra 1 interior
In Stoppard, T. Plays: five
The real thing.
Relationship between playwright's life and work is reflected in his rocky marriage to an actress. Background music. 2 acts 13 scenes 4m 3w 1 setting
In Stoppard, T. Plays: five
Salvage. Grove Press 2003 120p (The coast of Utopia, pt. 3)
ISBN 0-8021-4006-8 pb.; 0-8021-1762-7
Conclusion of trilogy. Action takes place between 1853 and 1865 in London and Geneva. Follows Alexander Herzen and group of Russian émigrés to London buzzing with plots and intrigues. 2 acts Large mixed cast settings
Shipwreck. Grove Press 2003 107p (The coast of Utopia, pt. 2)
ISBN 0-8021-1761-9; 0-8021-4005-X pb.
Second title in trilogy continues story of Mikhail Bakunin, critic Vissarion Belinsky, Ivan Turgenev, and their circle. Set in 1846-1852 in Russia, Salzbrunn, Paris, Dresden, and Nice. 2 acts 2b 1g 17m 7w extras settings
Voyage. Grove Press 2003 114p (The coast of Utopia, pt. 1)
ISBN 0-8021-1760-0; 0-8021-4004-1 pb.

First part of author's trilogy about 19th century European intellectual life. Set in 1833, follows career of future anarchist Mikhail Bakunin until his departure from Russia for Germany at age of twenty-six. 2 acts 17m 9w extras 1 setting
Stories of God. Sills, P.
The **stories** of Scheherazade. Francoeur, B.
Storks. Filloux, C.
The **story** of Hansel and Gretel. Francoeur, B.
The **story** of Peter Grimes. Beattie, A.
The **story** of Susanna. Kneubuhl, V. N.
Storytelling
c Espinosa, R. Ay, Carmelo! (Ay, Carmelo!)
Glancy, D. The women who loved house trailers
Hwang, D. H. Fob
c Kacmar, K. The oldest story ever told
c Mason, T. African tales: Kalulu and his monkey farm and Rumpelstiltskin
c Pargman, S. Scheherazade
y Ridley, P. Sparkleshark
Roderer, E. Scheherazade
Stowe, Harriet Beecher, 1811-1896
Uncle Tom's cabin (dramatization) See Aiken, G. L. Uncle Tom's cabin
Stowe-Gullen, Augusta, 1857-1943
about
Redhill, M. Building Jerusalem

Strachan, Keith
Large as life; book by Richard Harris; lyrics by Richard Harris and Keith Strachan; music by Keith Strachan. French (London) 2001 97p
ISBN 0-573-08114-X
First produced under the title: Baby love. Musical about one single woman and five couples where all the women are pregnant. Music, singing. 2 acts 5m 6w
Straight as a line. Alfaro, L.

Strand, John
Tom Walker. Dramatic Publishing 2003 72p
Comic drama set in colonial America. Chronically unemployed fiddler, is given the chance of a lifetime to turn his woeful fate around when he meets the Devil in a dimsal swamp outside Boston. 2 acts 3m 3w settings

Strand, Richard

The bug. Applause 2001 77p
ISBN 1-55783-461-X
Dark comedy about insecure employee who discovers a computer bug which will make his bosses very nervous. 2 acts 3m 2w 1 interior

The guest of honor.
Woman tries to smooth over conversation gone awry. 2m 2w
In 30 ten-minute plays for 4, 5 & 6 actors from Actors Theatre of Louisville's National Ten-minute Play Contest
—Same
In Actors Theatre of Louisville. Ten-minute plays: v4

Strange as it may seem. Milligan, J.

Strange happenings. Frankel, R.

Stranger. Lucas, C.

Strangers. Lhota, B.

Strangers on a train. Warner, C.

Strasberg, Lee, 1901-1982
about
Brustein, R. Nobody dies on Friday

Stratton, Allan

The Phoenix lottery. Playwrights Canada 2001 91p
ISBN 0-88754-600-5
Satire on art, commerce and family relationships. Businessman scrambles to avert bankruptcy. 2 acts 6 scenes 4m 2w extras 1 interior

Straughan, Peter

Bones. Methuen 2002 78p
ISBN 0-413-77204-7
Black comedy set in porn theater in 1960s Gateshead. Jewish brothers, their business on verge of collapse and in debt to local gangster, plot kidnapping. Prologue 2 acts 10 scenes 5m 1 interior

The straw. O'Neill, E.

Strawberry fields. Brofsky, K.

Stray cats. Leight, W.

Streeruwitz, Marlene

New York, New York.
Collage of choreographed and surreal scenes depict world of woman bathroom attendant. 20 scenes 5m 3w extras 1 interior
In Women's words, women's work; ed. by U. H. G. Borgert

A **streetcar** named Desire. Williams, T.

Strelich, Tom

BAFO (Best And Final Offer). French 2001 63p
ISBN 0-573-62771-1
Black comedy. Traces downward spiral of group of middle class white men and black woman in declining defense industry. 5m 1w 1 interior

Stretch marks. Miller, T.

Strijards, Frans

The Stendhal syndrome; tr. by Della Couling.
Funeral party for rich irresponsible financier who has committed suicide. 2 acts 3m 3w 1 interior
In Dutch and Flemish plays, ed. by D. Couling

Strikes and lockouts

Hughes, L. Harvest
Hwang, D. H. The dance and the railroad

Strindberg, August, 1849-1912

Miss Julie (adaptation) See McGuinness, F. Miss Julie; Tait, L. Miss Julie
The stronger (adaptation) See McGuinness, F. The stronger
A dream play; tr. by Carl R. Mueller.
Expressionistic play which symbolizes humanity's struggle against evil. Prologue 3 acts Large mixed cast
In Strindberg, A. Five major plays
The father; tr. by Carl R. Mueller.
Tragedy. Husband is driven to insanity by struggle with wife for control of daughter's destiny. 3 acts 5m 3w 1 interior
In Strindberg, A. Five major plays
—Same; tr. by Eivor Martinus
In Strindberg, A. The father, Lady Julie and Playing with fire
The ghost sonata; tr. by Carl R. Mueller.
Fantasy in symbolic form about the hidden guilt and failure of lives that lack the grace of God or man. 3 scenes 8m 7w extras 2 interiors 1 exterior
In Strindberg, A. Five major plays
—Same; tr. by Harry G. Carlson
In Theater of the avant-garde, 1890-1950; ed. by B. Cardullo and R. Knoph

Strindberg, August, 1849-1912—*Continued*

Lady Julie; tr. by Eivor Martinus.

Tragedy. Social problems of class distinction in 19th century Sweden exemplified in the relations between wealthy young woman and her manservant. Singing, dancing. 1 act 1m 2w extras 1 interior

In Strindberg, A. The father, Lady Julie and Playing with fire

Miss Julie; tr. by Carl R. Mueller.

Tragedy. Social problems of class distinction in 19th century Sweden exemplified in the relations between wealthy young woman and her manservant. Singing, dancing. 1 act 1m 2w extras 1 interior

In Strindberg, A. Five major plays

Playing with fire; tr. by Eivor Martinus.

Social comedy. Husband willing to let wife marry friend, who rejects offer. 1 act 21 scenes 3m 3w 1 interior

In Strindberg, A. The father, Lady Julie and Playing with fire

The stronger; tr. by Carl R. Mueller.

Social comedy. Wife versus "the other woman." 3w 1 interior

In Strindberg, A. Five major plays

about

Jenkins, M. Strindberg knew my father
Strindberg. Linney, R.
Strindberg knew my father. Jenkins, M.
The **strong** breed. Soyinka, W.
The **stronger**. McGuinness, F.
The **stronger**. Strindberg, A.

Stroppel, Frederick

Actor!. French 2003 65p
ISBN 0-573-62842-4

Comic odyssey about actor making his way through show biz jungle in search of fame and fortune. 3m 2w 1 interior

Judgment call.

Three baseball umpires prepare for coming seasons. 3m 1 setting

In Take ten; ed. by E. Lane and N. Shengold

Stuart, Kelly

A shoe is not a question.

Satire on Orpheus myth and fashion industry. Innocent yoga instructor pitted against aging, incestuous group of friends. 2 acts 3m 2w 1 interior

In New dramatists: best plays by the graduating class of 2000

Stuck. Goldberg, J.

Students

Beber, N. Misreadings
Halliwell, D. Little Malcolm and his struggle against the eunuchs
Margulies, D. Collected stories
Roth, A. Prelude to a crisis
Vaughan, R. L. Praying for rain
Studio portrait. Hutton, A.
Stuff. Fusco, C., and Bustamante, M. T.

Sturgill, Beverly

The enchantress of Ipswich. Anchorage Press 1998 95p
ISBN 0-87602-359-6

Story set in New England in 1692. Grandfather and granddaughter use magical powers to save the town of Ipswich from the horrors of nearby Salem. 3 acts 4 scenes 9m 9w 2 settings

Sturner, Lynda

Look what you made me do.

Monologue. Woman talks about her verbally abusive husband. 1w 1 interior

In Women's Project & productions; ed. by J. Miles

The **subject** was roses. Gilroy, F. D.
Subliminable. Allen, G.

Suburban life

Aerenson, B. The possum play
Cortese, R. St. Kilda tales
Farquhar, S. I do solemnly declare
O'Neill, T. A few roos loose in the top paddock
Wilson, L. Serenading Louie

Subways

Lauro, S. Railing it uptown
Pedrero, P. A night in the subway
Williams, B. C. Token to the moon
Success. Bishop, C., and Fuller, E.
Such foolish affected ladies. Molière
Sucking Dublin. Walsh, E.
Suddenly last summer. Williams, T.

Suffering fools. Goodden, H.

Suicide

Chekhov, A. P. Tatyana Repina

Crommelynck, F. Carine; or, The young woman who was crazy about her soul

Erdman, N. The suicide

Gilroy, F. D. Match point

Goodden, H. Suffering fools

Gough, L. Crossing the bar

Horovitz, I. Alfred dies

Hwang, D. H. The house of sleeping beauties

Kramer, S. David's redhaired death

Margulies, D. Anthony

Margulies, D. Misadventure

Miller, A. Death of a salesman

Nigro, D. Creatures lurking in the churchyard

Ogden, A. Johnny, don't jump

Rachilde. Madame La Mort

Suvorin, A. S. Tatyana Repina

Wedekind, F. Death and devil

The **suicide**. Erdman, N.

The **suitors**. Racine, J.

The **suits**. Aristophanes

Sullivan, Henry

about

Berger, G. I will go. . . I will go. . .

Summer and smoke. Williams, T.

Summer camps

y Sodaro, C. Phantom of the campfire

The **summer** sublet. Klavan, L.

The **summer** winds. Pugliese, F.

Summer's in the air. DeTurk, S.

Sun. Kennedy, A.

Sunday go to meetin'. Lauro, S.

Sunday in the park with George. Sondheim, S.

Sunday on the rocks. Rebeck, T.

Sunde, Karen

How his bride came to Abraham.

Drama set in South Lebanon. Israeli soldier in love with female Palestinian terrorist. 2m 2w 1 exterior

In Sunde, K. Plays

In a kingdom by the Sea.

Drama about abduction and subsequent death of Marine Lieutenant Colonel William R. Higgins who worked for UN peacekeeper. 2 acts 8m 1 setting

In Sunde, K. Plays

Truth takes a holiday.

President, First Lady, and his-and-hers aides engage in game of truth or dare. 2 acts 2m 2w settings

In Sunde, K. Plays

Sundown Alley. Kelly, T.

Sundstrom, Barbara

y The hundred penny box.

The African American experience, as reflected in the collection of pennies an old woman shares with her great-great-nephew. Adapted from the Newbery Honor book by Sharon Bell Mathis. Singing. 1 act 3 scenes 1b 1m 2w 1 setting

In EST marathon '98: the one-act plays; ed. by M. Smith

Sunset trail. Francoeur, B.

Sunshine, Gary

Al takes a bride.

Lesbian love affair in 19th century Memphis. 1 act 1m 2w 1 exterior

In The Best American short plays, 2000-2001

Sunspots. Upton, J.

A **super** scientific world. Vogel, L.

Superhighway. Pomerance, B.

Supernatural

De Wet, R. Crossing

Frankel, R. Strange happenings

McPherson, C. The weir

O'Casey, S. Cock-a-doodle dandy

Selig, P. Slide show

St. John, B. The werewolf's curse

Suppliant women. Euripides

The **suppliants**. Aeschylus

The **sure-success** twelve-step program to self-affirmation and esteem. Davis, K.

Surface, Mary Hall

y Blessings.

Originally performed under title Mixed blessings. Learning disabled teenaged girl gains confidence at mountain cabin with family and friends. Background music, singing. 8 scenes 3m 4w 1 setting

Surface, Mary Hall—*Continued*

In Surface, M. H. Most valuable player and four other all-star plays for middle and high school audiences

y Broken rainbows.

Budding friendship between African American and Jewish neighbors is shattered by teens' rivalry for internship. Singing, music. 12 scenes 2m 2w 1 setting

In Surface, M. H. Most valuable player and four other all-star plays for middle and high school audiences

y Dancing solo.

Teen dancer feels trapped in pattern of lies, deceit, and secrets in relationships with best friends, boyfriend, and alcoholic mother. 2m 3w 1 interior

In Surface, M. H. Most valuable player and four other all-star plays for middle and high school audiences

y Most valuable player.

Jackie Robinson overcomes race discrimination to become first African American major league baseball player. Variable cast 17 characters 1 setting

In Surface, M.H. Most valuable player and four other all-star plays for middle and high school students

c Prodigy.

Originally performed under title Young Mozart. Childhood of musical genius focuses on his relationship with his father. Music. Puppets. 1b 1g 4m 2w 1 setting

In Surface, M. H. Most valuable player and four other all-star plays for middle and high school audiences

Surfers

c Fry, G. Lockie Leonard, scumbuster

Surfin' Galilay. Vogel, L.

The **surgeon** of honour. Calderón de la Barca, P.

Surgeons

Norman, M. Traveler in the dark

Surrealism

Artaud, A. The spurt of blood

Bachmann, I. The good god of Manhattan

Bond, E. Early morning

Bosakowski, P. Chopin in space

Bullock, M. Sokotra

Churchill, C. This is a chair

Crommelynck, F. Golden guts

Darke, N. The body

Fennessy, A. Chilling and killing my Annabel Lee

García Lorca, F. As five years pass

García Lorca, F. Buster Keaton takes a walk

Orloff, R. Prague summer

Rivera, J. References to Salvador Dali make me hot

Schenkar, J. Signs of life

Tait, L. Jesus and the monkfish

Tremblay, L. A trick of fate

Vitrac, R. The mysteries of love

Weiss, P. The new trial

Wilner, S. Hunger

Wilson, S. The soul of the white ant

Witkiewicz, S. I. The cuttlefish; or, The Hyrcanian worldview

Survival (after airplane accidents, shipwrecks, etc.)

Kim, S. Dreamtime for Alice

Stetson, K. The harps of God

The **survivor**. Nanus, S.

Sutcliffe, William, 1971-

New boy (dramatization) See Labey, R. New boy

The **Sutherland**. Smith, C.

Sutton, Joe

Art for art's sake.

Author visits museum with his agent. 1m 1w extras

In HB Playwrights short play festival 1998

Layover.

Man watches two people making love in the airport lounge. 2m 3w 1 interior

In HB Playwrights short play festival 1999

Sutton, Michael, and Fingleton, Anthony

Over my dead body; suggested by the novel The murder league by Robert L. Fish. Dramatists 1998 70p

ISBN 0-8222-1601-9   LC 98-177800

Drama about murder mystery club in London, England fallen on hard times. 2 acts 2 scenes 7m 1w 1 setting

Suvorin, Alexei S.

Tatyana Repina.

Deserted by her lover, who must marry for money, a passionate actress takes poison and dies backstage, after a stunning performance. Music. 4 acts 33 scenes 12m 7w extras 3 interiors 1 exterior

In Tatyana Repina; ed. by J. Racin

Svevo, Italo, 1861-1928

Confessions of Zeno (dramatization) See Ardito, C. Confessions of Zeno

Svich, Caridad

Alchemy of desire/dead-man's blues.

A newly widowed woman's love for her late husband brings him back as a ghost. Bayou country setting. Music, singing. 1 act 19 scenes 1m 5w 1 setting

In Out of the fringe; ed. by C Svich and M. T. Marrero

But there are fires.

Married couple tries to reignite passion in their relationship. 10 scenes 2m 1w 1 interior 1 exterior

In Women's Project & productions; ed. by J. Miles

Prodigal kiss.

Drama with songs about immigrant experience in America. Singing. 2 parts 11 scenes 2m 2w extras settings

In New playwrights: the best plays of 1999

Swan song. Brooks, V.

Swan song. Chekhov, A. P.

Swayze, J. C.

Ossawattomie Brown.

Dramatization of John Brown's raid at Harper Ferry. 3 acts 18 scenes 1b 8m 6w extras 6 interiors 4 exteriors

In Fateful lightning; ed. by W. J. Meserve and M.A. Meserve

Sweatshop. LaRusso, L.

Sweeney Todd. Sondheim, S.

Sweet, Jeffrey

Cover.

Man asks friend to lie to is wife for him. 2m 1w 1 interior

In 30 ten-minute plays for 3 actors from Actors Theatre of Louisville's National Ten-minute Play Contest

Sweet bird of youth. Williams, T.

Sweet road. Oswald, D.

Sweet Sue. Gurney, A. R.

Swimming

Jordan, J. Nightswim

LeFevre, A. Waterbabies

Simon, M. At sea

The **swimming** pools of Paris. Tait, L.

Swimming the globe. Valentine, A.

Swindlers and swindling

Baitz, J. R. Mizlansky/Zilinsky

Magee, R. The green heart

y Ott, G. Minor leagues

Vickery, F. Pullin' the wool

Swingtime Canteen; book by Linda Thorsen Bond, William Repicci, and Charles Busch. French 1998 64p

ISBN 0-573-62333-3   LC 98-213917

Musical about Hollywood starlet and her all lady band performing in London in 1944. Music, singing. 2 acts 5w extras

Switching principals. Cook, P.

Swollen tongues. Oliver, K.

The **sword** in the stone. Miller, K. S.

Swortzell, Lowell

c The mischief makers.

Comedy based on folklore. Features tricksters Anansi the spider, Raven, and Reynard the fox. 1 act Unidentified cast 3 characters extras 1 exterior

In Theatre for young audiences; ed. by C. A. Jennings

c A partridge in a pear tree.

Musical one-act play based on the old Christmas carol. Music, singing. 1 act 4m 2w extras 1 setting

In The twelve plays of Christmas; ed. by L. Swortzell

y The shepherds of Saint Francis.

First christmas pageant staged in 1223 by Saint Francis in Greccio, Italy. 5 scenes Variable cast

In The twelve plays of Christmas; ed. by L. Swortzell

c A visit from St. Nicholas; or, The night before Christmas.

Story of the creation of Clement Moore's 1822 Christmas classic. 1b 2g 1m 2w

In The twelve plays of Christmas; ed. by L. Swortzell

The **sycamore** cross. Forsten, M. L.

Sydney (Australia)

y Valentine, A. Swimming the globe

Sylvia. Gurney, A. R.

Symbolism

Artaud, A. The spurt of blood

Blais, M.-C. Wintersleep

Briusov, V. The wayfarer

Darke, N. The body

Gao Xingjian. Bus stop

Gippius, Z. Sacred blood

Glaspell, S. The outside

Ibsen, H. The lady from the sea

Ibsen, H. When we dead awaken

Kennedy, A. Funnyhouse of a Negro

Levy, D. Pax

MacLeod, J. The hope slide

O'Casey, S. Purple dust

O'Casey, S. Red roses for me

O'Casey, S. Within the gates

Rachilde. Madame La Mort

Sánchez, E. Icarus

Schenkar, J. Signs of life

y Shafaat, S. Balcony

Strindberg, A. A dream play

Van Itallie, J.-C. War

Wellman, M. Allegory of whiteness

Wilson, L. Angels fall

Sympathetic magic. Wilson, L.

The **syringa** tree. Gien, P.

T

T for 2. Barnett, G.

Tabletop. Ackerman, R.

The **tail.** Gough, L.

A **tainted** dawn. Bhuchar, S., and Landon-Smith, K.

Tainted justice. Nigro, D.

Tait, Lance

The babysitter.

Experimental play about bizarre modern marriage. Music. 1m 3w 1 interior

In Tait, L. Miss Julie, David Mamet Fan Club, and other plays

Behave, my sorrow.

Comedy. Man and sock puppet discuss spiritual and romantic concerns. 1 act 1m 1 setting

In Tait, L. Miss Julie, David Mamet Fan Club, and other plays

Betsy Philadelphia.

Political drama set during 2000 election in Philadelphia. 1 act 3 scenes Variable cast 3 characters settings

In Tait, L. Mad cow disease in America; Something special and other plays

David Mamet fan club.

Dialogue between boyfriend and girlfriend on merits of David Mamet. 1 act 1m 1w 1 interior

In Tait, L. Miss Julie, David Mamet Fan Club, and other plays

Dmitri.

Suicidal waiter visited by hitman. 1 act 2m 1 setting

In Tait, L. Mad cow disease in America; Something special and other plays

East play.

Play about business and political prisoners. Action takes place simultaneously in Eastside Manhattan apartment and Chinese prison. 1 act 3m 2w 1 setting

In Tait, L. Miss Julie, David Mamet Fan Club, and other plays

Edwin Booth. Enfield Pub. 2001 189p

ISBN 1-893598-02-0

Explores private life and career of actor Edwin Booth, brother of John Wilkes Booth, from 1864 to 1884. 2 acts 19 scenes Large mixed cast settings

A family portrait.

Black comedy about eccentric family and their bad seed son. 1 act 2m 2w 1 setting

In Tait, L. Mad cow disease in America; Something special and other plays

Germany.

Afterpiece to The babysitter set in 1995 Leipzig. Woman exacts revenge on ex-brother-in-law for sister's death. 1m 3w 1 interior

In Tait, L. Miss Julie, David Mamet Fan Club, and other plays

The glass ceiling.

Satire on women's equality in the workplace and new age thinking. Set in San Francisco psychologist's office. 1 act 3w 1 interior

In Tait, L. Mad cow disease in America; Something special and other plays

Tasca, Jules—*Continued*

Judah's daughter. French 1999 63p

Two daughters in 15th century Venice, Italy, one legitimate and raised as an Orthodox Jew, the other illegitimate and raised Roman Catholic, both fall in love with the same man. 5m 4w 1 setting

Tasso, Torquato

Aminta; edited and translated by Charles Jernigan and Irene Marchegiani Jones. Italica Press 2000 180p

ISBN 0-934977-65-8   LC 00-63221

16th century pastoral play about shepherd's love for nymph. Speaking chorus Prologue 5 acts 10 scenes 4 interludes 6m 3w

The **taste** of sunrise. Zeder, S.

Tate, Judy

Mistaken for genius.

Comedy. Interview with playwright. Variable cast 1 interior

In Women's Project & productions; ed. by J. Miles

Tatjana in color. Jordan, J.

Tattersall, Clare

The last dance.

Comedy about woman who places classified ad for a dance partner. 1m 1w 1 interior

In Off-Off Broadway Festival plays, 22nd ser.

Tattoo. Martin, J.

Tattooing

Martin, J. Tattoo

Tatyana Repina. Chekhov, A. P.

Tatyana Repina. Suvorin, A. S.

Tatyana's golden doe. Paxton, K.

Tavel, Ronald

The life of Lady Godiva.

Experimental theater. Story of Lady Godiva, set in convent doubling as brothel. Background music, singing. 4m 2w extras 1 interior

In Theatre of the ridiculous; ed. by B. Marranca and G. Dasgupta

Taxes

Kushner, T. East coast ode to Howard Jarvis: a little teleplay in tiny monologues

Taxi cabs

Kern, W. Hellcab

Taylor, Drew Hayden

alterNatives. Talonbooks 2000 144p

ISBN 0-88922-428-5

A couple's dinner party clears the air but may end the relationship. She is a Jewish professor, he is an Ojibway sci-fi writer, and their guests, white liberals and Native radicals, disagree about practically everything, drawing the couple into the fray. 2 acts 3m 3w 1 interior

The baby blues. Talonbooks 1999 93p

ISBN 0-88922-406-4   LC 98-203658

Satiric look at fancy-dancers on the Pow wow trail. 2 acts 8 scenes 3m 3w 1 exterior

The boy in the treehouse.

Son of Ojibwa mother and British father embarks on vision-quest to reclaim late mother's culture. 9 scenes Variable cast 8 characters 1 setting

> *In* Taylor, D. H. The boy in the treehouse; Girl who loved her horses

Girl who loved her horses.

Native girl's only friend is her imagination. 11 scenes 2m 2w extras 1 setting

> *In* Taylor, D. H. The boy in the treehouse; Girl who loved her horses

Only drunks and children tell the truth. Talonbooks 1998 112p

ISBN 0-88922-384-X

A woman who was taken from her Native American family as a child and given to a white couple to raise makes a second attempt to come to terms with her divided heritage after her birth-mother dies. A sequel to the author's Someday (1993). 2 acts 6 scenes 2m 2w 2 interiors 1 exterior

—Same

> *In* Seventh generation; ed. by M. G. D'Aponte

Taylor, Edward

A rise in the market. French 1999 79p

ISBN 0-573-62674-X   LC 99-219506

Satire about the misadventures of an European Union politician seeking the support of a conservative elder statesman. 2 acts 5m 2w 1 interior

Television plays

Foote, H. Tomorrow

Gilroy, F. D. Far Rockaway

Griffiths, T. Food for ravens

Hare, D. Saigon: year of the cat

Hochwälder, F. Orders

Kane, S. Skin

Kushner, T. East coast ode to Howard Jarvis: a little teleplay in tiny monologues

Poliakoff, S. Caught on a train

Poliakoff, S. Perfect strangers

The **television** programme. Vinaver, M.

Television programs

Gardner, H. A thousand clowns

c Hamlett, C. Author! Author!

c McCullough, L. E. Lights, camera, traction! (television director)

Temporary. Wiltse, D.

The **temptations**. Vogel, L.

Tender offer. Wasserstein, W.

Tennessee and me. Scheffer, W.

Tennis

Woolley, J. You can't be serious

The **tenor**. Wedekind, F.

Terence

The brothers (Adelphoe); tr. by Deeena Berg.

Latin comedy, Adaptation of Monander's play of the same title. Two brothers raised separately; one by strict father, the other by permissive uncle. Prologue 5 acts

In Plautus and Terence, five Comedies

The mother-in-law (Hecyra); tr. by Deeena Berg.

Latin comedy. Adaptation of Apollodorus' The claimants. Scoundrel engineers double plot to win wives form two cousins. Prologue 5 acts

In Plautus and Terence, five Comedies

Phormio; translated by Timonthy J. Moore.

Variant title: The tricks of Phormio. Latin comedy. Adaptation of Apollodorus' the claimants. Scoundrel engineers double plot to win wives for two cousins. Prologue 5 acts

In Greek and Roman Comedy; ed. by S. O'Bryhim

Terkel, Studs, 1912-

Race: how Blacks and White think and feel about the American obsession (dramatization) See Pachino, J. Race

Terminal connection. Roth, A.

Terminal illness

Orton, J. The visitors

Terminating. Kushner, T.

Terms of abuse. Townsend, J.

Terra Australis. Esson, L.

The **terrible** false deception. Macpherson, R.

Terror and Erebus. MacEwen, G.

Terrorism

Brevoort, D. B. The women of Lockerbie

Gurr, M. Crazy brave

Parker, S. Catchpenny twist

Terry, Megan

Approaching Simone.

Dramatic portrayal of life of Simone Weil. 2 acts 5m 4w extras settings

In Terry, M. Plays

Babes in the bighouse.

Drama with music portraying life in a women's prison. Music, singing. 2 acts 2 scenes 4m 11w 1 setting

In Terry, M. Plays

Breakfast serial.

Exploration of gender roles. Violent youth preys on young boys. 1m 3w 1 exterior

In take ten; ed. by E. Lane and N. Shengold

Viet rock.

Anti-war satire with music about America's involvement in Vietnam. Music, singing. 2 acts 2 scenes 6m 7w 1 setting

In Terry, M. Plays

Terry Pratchett's Maskerade. Briggs, S.

Tesla's letters. Stanley, J.

The **test**. Caplan, P. J.

A **test** for Esther. Vogel, L.

Texas

Dunn, M. Cabin fever

Dunn, M. The deer and the antelope play

Foote, H. A coffin in Egypt

Foote, H. Getting Frankie married—and afterwards

Foote, H. Laura Dennis

Thérèse Raquin. Bell, N.

These flowers are for my mother. McGuire, M.

These two couples went to Italy. Rusconi, P.

Theseus (Greek mythology)

Euripides. Hippolytus

They can't take that away from me. Andersen, D. R.

Thiessen, Vern

Apple. Playwrights Canada 2002 85p
ISBN 0-88754-638-2

Unemployed man torn between seriously ill estranged wife and mysterious young woman he looks to for salvation. 2 acts 1m 2w 1 exterior

Blowfish. Playwrights Canada 1998 45p
ISBN 0-88754-547-5

Black comedy. Elegant caterer expounds on food, Canadian politics, and death. 2 acts 1m extras 1 setting

Thieves

y DeTurk, S. Summer's in the air

Lewis, C. W. The one-eyed man is king

Robinson, P. Red hot in Amsterdam

Thieves. Gardner, H.

Thin air: tales from a revolution. Alvarez, L.

Things that break. Kramer, S.

Things that go bump in the night. Nigro, D.

Things we do for love. Ayckbourn, A.

Things you shouldn't say past midnight. Ackerman, P.

Thinking up a new name for the act. Silverstein, S.

Thiong'o, Ngugi Wa, and Mirii, Ngugi Wa

I will marry when I want.

Poor man and his wife lose what little they have to greedy hypocrites. Music, singing, dancing. 3 acts 6 scenes 8m 5w extras 2 interiors

In Modern African drama; ed. by B. Jeyifo

Third and Oak. Norman, M.

This is a chair. Churchill, C.

This is how it is. Moses, B. P.

This is my story. Smith, J. M.

This lime tree bower. McPherson, C.

This old house. Murray, S.

This property is condemned. Williams, T.

Thistle, Louise

c The creation and birth of the Olympian gods.

Origin of Greek pantheon of gods. Prologue 6 scenes Variable cast

In Thistle, L. Dramatizing Greek mythology

c The labors of Hercules.

Depicts heroic feats of Hercules including destroying six-headed Hydra, capturing golden-horned deer, and getting jewelled belt of Amazon queen. Prologue 9 scenes Variable cast

In Thistle, L. Dramatizing Greek mythology

c The myth of Demeter and Persephone; or, The origin of the seasons.

Greek myth explaining origin of seasons. Prologues 6 scenes Variable cast

In Thistle, L. Dramatizing Greek mythology

c The myth of Orpheus and Eurydice; or, Descent into the underworld.

Depicts Orpheus' journey into underworld to convince King Hades to let his true love Eurydice return to land of the living. Prologue 8 scenes Variable cast

In Thistle, L. Dramatizing Greek mythology

c The Odyssey.

Dramatization of Homer's classic adventure epic. Prologue 3 scenes epilogue Variable cast

In Thistle, L. Dramatizing Greek mythology

Thistle. Ehn, E.

Thomas, Augustus

As a man thinks.

Husband's infidelity leads to wife's attempt to even the score. 4 acts 1b 6m 3w extras 3 interiors

In American plays of the new woman; ed. by K. Newlin

Thomas, Buddy

The crumple zone. French 2001 70p
ISBN 0-573-62767-3

Comedy. Three gay roommates during one frantic Christmas weekend. Music. 2 acts 4 scenes 5m 1 interior

Thomas, Dylan, 1914-1953

A child's Christmas in Wales (adaptation) See Brooks, J., and Mitchell, A. A child's Christmas in Wales

Return journey.

Narrator returns to his hometown of Swansea, Wales, and revisits his youth. 1 act Variable cast 1 setting

In Act one Wales; ed. by P. Clark

Thomas, Edward

Hiraeth.

Drama about two people seeking meaning and purpose in their lives. 1 act 1m 1w 1 interior

In Act one Wales; ed. by P. Clark

Thomas, Gwyer

Gazooka.

Set during summer 1926 in Rhonda Valley, Wales. Friends try to find costumes for local gazooka band. 1 act 12m 3w extras

In Act one Wales; ed. by P. Clark

Thomas, Robert

Trap for a lonely man. Weinberger, J. 1964 77p

ISBN 0-85676-029-3

Psychological thriller. Man contacts police to report missing wife. When woman claiming to be his wife surfaces he must convince police she is lying. 3 acts 4 scenes 3m 3w 1 interior

Thomas, Trevor C.

The sound of stillness.

Based on true events which occured during army manoeuvre in Wales in 1941. 1 act 6m

In Act one Wales; ed. by P. Clark

Thomas à Kempis, Saint

about

Ehn, E. The imp of simplicity (Thomas à Kempis)

Thompson, Judith

Habitat. Playwrights Canada 2001 80p

ISBN 0-88754-615-3

Group home for troubled adolescents struggles to survive in hostile neighborhood. 2 acts 30 scenes 2m 3w 1 setting

Lion in the street.

Psychological drama featuring ghost of murdered young girl. Women cope with cancer, poverty, childcare and weight problems. 2 acts 2m 4w 1 setting

In 7 cannons

Perfect pie. Playwrights Canada 2000 91p

ISBN 0-88754-590-4   LC 00-421184

Long buried memory resurfaces when two long estranged women are reunited. Singing. 2 acts 51 scenes 2g 2w 7 interiors 5 exteriors

Pink.

Monologue about apartheid. Ten-year-old white South African girl speaks to her dead black nurse. 1g 1 setting

In Postcolonial plays; ed. by H. Gilbert

Thompson-Scretching, Anne L.

You shouldn't have told. French 1998 94p

Domestic drama about middle-class black Brooklyn family. Mother refuses to believe her boyfriend is molesting her daughters until tragedy strikes. 2 acts 6 scenes 4m 5w 1 setting

Thomson, Katherine

Navigating. Currency Press 1998 84p

ISBN 0-86819-574-X   LC 99-460526

Drama about political corruption in Australian seaside town. Embattled female "whistleblower" finds herself in possession of damaging documentary evidence of local scandal. Music, singing. 2 acts 3m 4w

Thomson, R. H. (Ronald Hunter)

The lost boys. Playwrights Canada 2001 77p

ISBN 0-88754-634-X

One man play based on letters written by five Canadian brothers who served in Europe during World War I. 1m

Thomson, Tom, 1877-1917

about

Betts, J. Colour in the storm

Thoreau, Henry David, 1817-1862

about

Lee, R. E. The night Thoreau spent in jail

Oates, J. C. The passion of Henry David Thoreau

Thorne, Joan Vail

The exact center of the universe. Dramatists 2000 60p

ISBN 0-8222-1744-9   LC 00-703184

Comedy about Southern doyenne who is forced to cope with beloved son's elopement. 2 acts 5 scenes 1m 4w 1 setting

—Same

In Women playwrights: the best plays of 1999

A **thoroughly** modern Rapunzel. McBride-Smith, B.

Those damned ghosts. Filippo, E. de

Those learned ladies. Molière

A **thousand** clowns. Gardner, H.

A **thousand** cranes. Miller, K. S.

Three Americanisms. Wellman, M.

Three billy goats gruff: poetry-style. McBride-Smith, B.

Three days of rain. Greenberg, R.

Three fables. Lehan, R.

Three front. Owens, R.

Three gifts from gentle Jesus. Zapel, A. L.

Three Holocaust tales. McCullough, L. E.

Three in the back, two in the head. Sherman, J.

Three judgements in one. Calderón de la Barca, P.

The **Three** Kings (Los tres Reyes Magos); tr. by Larry Torres.

Rhymed folk drama about the Three Kings, Herod, and the infant Christ. Bilingual edition. Chorus. Music, singing. 8m 7w settings

In Six nuevomexicano folk dramas for Advent season

The **three** little pigs out west. Ellis, D.

Three monologues. Auburn, D.

The **three** musketeers—le panteau! Lloyd, R.

Three postcards. Lucas, C.

Three questions. Martin, M.

Three sisters. Chekhov, A. P.

Three sisters. Friel, B.

Three tables. Remmes, D.

The **three** wishes. Barchers, S. I.

The **throne** of Osiris. McCullough, L. E.

Throwaway. Bingham, S.

Throwing your voice. Lucas, C.

Thum, Nancy

The carpenter and the cross.

Worship program. Roman soldiers order carpenter to construct cross upon which Jesus will be crucified. 1 act 1b 1g 3m 3w extras

In The drama of Easter; ed. by R. Wray

Thunderation! (Alle Wetter!). Mühsam, E.

Thursday. Hochwälder, F.

Thwaite, Emily, and Sanderson, Bill

c Future perfect. French (London) 2000 35p

ISBN 0-573-15230-6

Drama set in future. Children try to save neighboring town from machines and pollution. Music, singing, dancing. Puppets. Prologue 15 scenes Variable cast

Ti-Jean. Cumming, P.

Ti Jean blues. Akalaitis, J.

Tibbetts, Mike

LittleBro morning and BigSis afternoon. French 1999 41p

ISBN 0-573-12154-0   LC 00-503528

Drama about twelve-year-old girl, who takes care of seven-year-old brother after their father abandons them. 1b 1g 3m 2w settings

The **Tibetan** book of the dead; or, How not to do it again. Van Itallie, J.-C.

Tichenor, Austin. See Long, A. jt. auth.

Tickets, please! Sportiello, A.

Tideline (Littoral). Mouawad, W.

Tidings of comfort and joy. Anderson, S. J.

Tidler, Charles

Red mango. Anvil Press 2001 61p

ISBN 1-895636-38-8

Monologue. Mid-40's divorced blues fanatic addicted to Victoria, British Columbia's dance clubs. Music. 15 scenes

A **tiger** in Central Park. Rivera, J.

Tightrope time: ain't nuthin' more than some itty bitty madness between twilight & dawn. Borden, W. M.

Tightwad. Angeles, T.

Till we meet again. Crowther, C., and Crowther, M.

Time flies. Ives, D.

The **time** machine. Miller, K. S.

Time, murderer, please. Dyer, C. R.

Time on fire. Mason, T.

Time to burn. Mee, C. L.

Time travel

Ayckbourn, A. Communicating doors

c Dodge, A. Joshua's egg

Levi, S. Hearts 'n kisses 'n Miss Vickers

c Miller, K. S. The time machine

Nigro, D. The great Gromboolian plain

O'Hara, R. Insurrection

Ting Tang mine. Darke, N.

Tiny island. Hollinger, M.

Tiny Thumbelina. Francoeur, B.

Tiny Tim is dead. Lebow, B.

Tiptoe through the tombstones. Robbins, N.

'Tis pity she's a whore. Ford, J.

Titanic (Steamship)

Kluger, S. Pilots of the purple twilight

Titus at the gates of Syon. Allison, B.

Tlingit Indians

Bruchac, J. The cannibal monster

Shorty, S. Trickster visits the old folks home

To meet Oscar Wilde. Holland, N.

To Rahtid. River, S. B.

To serve one another. Owens, J.

To the sun, moon, and wind. Barchers, S. I.

To wit and to whom. Wiltse, D.

The **toad** (another name for the moon) should have a bite. Glancy, D.

Toast. Bean, R.

Tobago

Philip, M. N. Coups and calypsos

Walcott, D. Pantomime

Today, I am a fountain pen. Horovitz, I.

Toddie, Jean Lenox

And send forth a raven. French 2002 87p

ISBN 0-573-62950-1

Mystery-drama. Five townspeople remain in run-down hostelry threatened by flood. 2 act 3m 2w 1 interior

By the name of Kensington. French 1998 35p

ISBN 0-573-62608-1   LC 00-502852

Comic drama. Well-bred cricket from London's Bond Street is dismayed to find himself playing doppelganger to an Appalachian woman. 1 act 2m 2w 1 setting

The juice of wild strawberries. French 2002 24p

ISBN 0-573-62881-5

Dialogue between a widow and her husband's ghost, as she walks away from the old family farm. 1 act 1m 1w 1 exterior

Token to the moon. Williams, B. C.

Tokoloshe. Scholtz, P.

Toksvig, Jenifer, and Perkins, David

c The curious quest for the sandman's sand. French (London) 1998 36p

ISBN 0-573-08109-3

Three wakeful children enter a magical world to recover the sandman's stolen sand. Music, singing, dancing. 1 act 6b 3g 1m 1w extras 1 setting

Tolan, Kathleen

The wax.

Middle-aged friends and lovers grapple with loneliness, inertia and regret about path not taken. 2m 4w 1 interior

In HB Playwrights short play festival 1997

Tolins, Johnathan

If memory serves. French 2000 79p

ISBN 0-573-62735-5

Satirical comedy about over-the-hill TV star and her son. 2 acts 20 scenes 4m 4w settings

Toller, Ernst, 1893-1939

Hinkemann (adaptation) See Hall, L. Bollocks

Bollocks (dramatization) See Hall, L. Bollocks

Tom Kitten and his friends. McNeff, S.

Tom Walker. Strand, J.

Tomorrow. Foote, H.

Tomorrowland. Jones, J. M.

Tom's midnight garden. Wood, D.

Tongue of a bird. McLaughlin, E.

Tongue twisted. Davies, C., and Fendrich, S.

Too wrapped up for Christmas. Brandl, D.

Tooth and consequences; or, Hortense said: "No skin off my ass!". Feydeau, G.

Top girls. Churchill, C.

Topor, Tom

Boundary County, Idaho.

Monologue by extremist involved in Christian identity movement. Singing. 1m

> *In* The Best American short plays 1998-1999

The **torch-bearers**. Kelly, G.

Toronto (Ont.)

Clarke, A. When he was free and young and he used to wear silks

Miles, K. I hate you on Mondays

Moodie, A. Riot

Walker, G. F. Beautiful city

Torres, Joan

Better half dead. French 1998 94p

ISBN 0-573-62654-5

Comedy thriller. Murder and blackmail result when unhappy wife attempts to return to first husband. 2 acts 6 scenes 3m 2w 1 interior

Torture

Nigro, D. The malefactor's bloody register

Toshie. Brown, S.

Totalitarianism

Blais, M.-C. Exile

Field, B. Monsieur de Molière

Kossman, N. Miracles

Raznovich, D. Disconcerted (El disconcierto)

Seremba, G. Come good rain

Yew, C. Red

Touched by an angle. Jackson, R. E.

Touching tomorrow. Plowman, G.

Tough!. Walker, G. F.

Tough guys. Palmieri, M.

Toussaint Louverture, 1743?-1803

about

Walcott, D. Drums and colours

Walcott, D. The Haitian earth

A **town** called Shame. Scott, G.

Townsend, Jessica

Angels and saints.

Middle-aged spinster burdened with invalid grandmother meets man who changes her life. 7 scenes 2m 2w 1 interior

> *In* Townsend, J. Angels and saints: two plays

Terms of abuse.

Drama based on Gloucester England's West murder trials. Explores ethics of selling stories of child abuse to gutter journalists. 3 acts 7 scenes 4m 2w 1 interior

> *In* Townsend, J. Angels and saints: two saints

Trace of Arc. Smith, A.

A **traditional** pageant. Anderson, S. J.

Traffic accidents

Oates, J. C. Black water

Roth, A. Jeffrey Slugworth: ex-embalmer

Trafficking in broken hearts. Sánchez, E.

Trafford Tanzi. Luckham, C.

Tragedy

Alvarez, L. The guitarrón

Anouilh, J. Antigone

Arden of Faversham. Arden of Faversham

Baitz, J. R. Hedda Gabler

Bandele, 'Biyi. Aphra Behn's Oroonoko

Bell, N. Thérèse Raquin

Boker, G. H. Francesca da Rimini

Boyd, G. E. Consecrated ground

Brustein, R. Enrico IV

Calderón de la Barca, P. The surgeon of honour

Calderón de la Barca, P. Three judgements in one

Champagne, L. Coaticook

Chekhov, A. P. Ivanov

Chikamatsu, M. The love suicides at Amijima

Chikamatsu, M. The love suicides at Sonezaki

Childress, A. Wedding band: a love/hate story in black and white

Dattani, M. Tara

Esson, L. Dead timber

Feliciano, G. Between blessings

Field, B. Camille

Field, B. Monsieur de Molière

Foote, H. Tomorrow

Ford, J. 'Tis pity she's a whore

García Lorca, F. The house of Bernarda Alba

Gilroy, F. D. That summer—that fall

Gonzalez, S. S. Boxcar

Green, P. Hymn to the rising sun: a drama of man's waste

Travis, Sarah

c The tale of Little Red Riding Hood; an untraditional pantomime; book and lyrics by Simon Brett; music by Sarah Travis. French (London) 1998 81p
ISBN 0-573-08106-9
Pantomime with music about aristocratic family in pre-revolutionary Russia. When evil fox condemns Siberia to eternal cold only brave woodcutter can help them. Music. 2 acts 21 scenes 3m 3w extras 1 setting
See also Brett, S. jt. auth.

Treason

Chikamatsu, M. The battles of Coxinga
The **treasure**. Pinski, D.
A **treasure** in a teacup. Kramer, A.
Treasure Island. Mason, T.
The **treatment**. Crimp, M.
Tree of hope, keep firm (Mary, the Annunciation). Ehn, E.
The **tree** that bled fish. Barchers, S. I.

Tremblay, Larry

Anatomy lesson; tr. by Sheila Fischman.
Monologue. Professor dissects and re-examines her long relationship with her abusive, slick, lawyer-politician husband. 1w
In Tremblay, L. Talking bodies

The dragonfly of Chicoutimi.
Forty years after trauma-induced aphasia, man loses his original maternal French and awakes from dream reinventing his life in English words using French syntax. Singing. 1m
In Tremblay, L. Talking bodies

Ogre; tr. by Sheila Fischman.
Media satire. Odious character's actions become ever more disgusting as he begins to believe hidden camera is recording his every move. 1m
In Tremblay, L. Talking bodies

A trick of fate; tr. by Sheila Fischman.
Surreal performance piece. Man's body increasingly abandons its "ordinary" place in the world. Music. 1m
In Tremblay, L. Talking bodies

Tremblay, Michel

For the pleasure of seeing her again.
Talonbooks 1998 78p
ISBN 0-88922-389-0
Drama about the relationship between a playwright and his mother. 1m 1w 1 setting

Tremulous. Wilhelm, L.

Treon, Phil. See Medoff, M. H. jt. auth.
Los **tres** ratoncitos: a chiste. Barchers, S. I.
Treseder's seeds. Woolf, C.
The **trestle** at Pope Lick Creek. Wallace, N.
The **trial** of the Arkansas bear. Glennon, W.

Trials

Ardov, V. The case of the entry room
Chepiga, M. J. Getting and spending
Goens, L. M. Resurrection on trial
y Harden, V. Big boys don't cry
Janes, H. The perfect murder
Kaufman, M. Gross indecency: the three trials of Oscar Wilde
Linney, R. A lesson before dying
Plata, M. C. Justice for whom?
Schmitt, E.-E. Don Juan on trial
Tropf, R. Shadow hour
Yeaton, D. Midwives

Trials (Murder)

Davis, T. Everybody's Ruby
Logan, J. Hauptmann
Logan, J. Never the sinner
Mann, E. Execution of justice
Neilson, A. Normal
Norton-Taylor, R. The colour of justice
Romero, E. If Susan Smith could talk
Vinaver, M. Portrait of a woman
Triangles for two. Wiltse, D.
A **trick** of fate. Tremblay, L.

Tricker, George

Life support. French 1999 79p
ISBN 0-573-62693-6
Tragicomedy about two people who meet and become friends in a hospital lounge, while awaiting the news of their ill spouses. 2 acts 9 scenes 1m 1w 1 interior
Trickster visits the old folks home. Shorty, S.

Trieschmann, Catherine

The bridegroom of Blowing Rock. French (London) 2003 76p
ISBN 0-573-62840-8

Trieschmann, Catherine—*Continued*

Set in Blowing Rock, North Carolina, immediately after the Civil War. Woman awaits return of Yankee fiancee, and must choose between him and Confederate family. 10 scenes 4m 4w 1 setting

Trifles. Glaspell, S.

Trinidad

Constable, J. Black mass

Hall, T. Jean and Dinah who have been locked away in a world famous calypso since 1956 speak their minds publicly

The **trio**. Silverstein, S.

Trip of a lifetime. Cashmore, B., and Powrie, A.

Tripp, Miles, 1923-. See McConnell, J. jt. auth.

Trips. Woods, S.

Tristan. Nigro, D.

The **triumph** of love. Marivaux, P. C. de C. de

Les **trois** Dumas. Smith, C.

Trojan War

c Barchers, S. I. Helen

Euripides. Iphigenia at Aulis

Euripides. The Trojan women

The **Trojan** women. Euripides

The **Trojan** women: a love story. Mee, C. L.

Tropf, Ralph

Shadow hour. French 1998 82p

ISBN 0-573-62714-2

Courtroom drama about young woman who accuses senator of sexual assault, and how each juror interprets the case. 2 acts 4m 8w 1 setting

Tropicana, Carmelita

Milk of amnesia (Leche de amnesia).

Monologue. Lesbian returns to Cuba in 1993 trying to restore her memory by revisiting sites of her childhoods; instead she is overwhelmed by economic devstation and human suffering she witnesses. 1w

    In O solo homo; ed. by H. Hughes and D. Román

Tropicana, Carmelita, and Parnes, Uzi

Memorias de la revolución.

A spoof of heroic socialist dramas, set in Cuba in 1955. Revolutionaries (most of them in the performing arts) try to assassinate a brutal police chief and do succeed in liberating themselves. Music, singing, dancing. Slide projections. Prologue 3 acts 6 scenes 4m 6w settings

    In Puro teatro; ed. by A. Sandoval-Sánchez and N. S. Sternbach

The **troth**. Mayne, R.

The **trouble** with Trent. Carmichael, F.

The **troublesome** reign and lamentable death of Edward the Second. Marlowe, C.

Trowbridge, John Townsend

Neighbor Jackwood.

Anti-slavery drama based on author's novel set in 1850s Vermont. 5 acts 30 scenes 13m 9w extras 9 interiors 9 extriors

    In Fateful lightning; ed. by W. J. Meserve and M.A. Meserve

Trudeau, Margaret

about

Griffiths, L. Maggie & Pierre

Trudeau, Pierre Elliot

about

Griffiths, L. Maggie & Pierre

Trudy Blue. Norman, M.

The **true** adventures of Pinocchio. Lippa, L.

True confessions of a go-go girl. Morley, J.

True crimes. Linney, R.

A **true** fool's folly. Nielson, K.

Trust. Mitchell, G.

Truth takes a holiday. Sunde, K.

Truthfulness and falsehood

Chappell, E. Double vision

Germann, G. The observatory

Gore, C. The king's seal

Horovitz, I. Alfred the Great

Laurence, C. The Ring sisters

MacLiammóir, M. The liar

Nelson, R. Jungle coup

Overmyer, E. Alki

Pirandello, L. Right you are (if you think you are) (Cosi è, se ui pare)

Truthfulness and falsehood—*Continued*

Poulton, M. Fortune's fool

Rintoul, H. Brave hearts

Schmitt, E.-E. Don Juan on trial

Sirera, R. The audition

Sweet, J. Cover

Wilder, T. Now the servant's name was Malchus

Wilson, L. Book of days

Trying to find Chinatown. Hwang, D. H.

Tryst. Crowther, C.

Tshai the brickmaker. McCullough, L. E.

Tuan, Alice

The technology project: F.E.T.C.H.

Carnivalesque theater piece involving three characters, "screnes," a flagpole, and a lively computer mouse. Prologue epilogue 1 act Unidentified cast 4 characters 1 setting

In Humana Festival 2002

Tuberculosis

O'Neill, E. The straw

Tubman, Harriet, 1815?-1913

about

Gage, C. Harriet Tubman visits a therapist

Tuesday. Bond, E.

Tunnel of love. Reingold, J.

Tunooniq Theatre

Changes.

Communal experiences of Inuit before and after arrival of traders and missionaries. Music, dance. 10 scenes 6m 3w 1 setting

In Staging the North; ed. by S. Grace, E. D'Aeth and L. Chalykoff

In search of a friend.

Troubled young Inuit man seeking refuge in drink and drugs is rescued by friend. 4 scenes 2m 4w extras 1 setting

In Staging the North; ed. by S. Grace, E. D'Aeth and L. Chalykoff

Turgenev, Ivan

Nakhlebnik (adaptation) See Poulton, M. Fortune's fool

about

Stoppard, T. Shipwreck

Turlish, Susan

Lafferty's wake. French 2000 62p

ISBN 0-573-627576

Comedy with audience participation. Deceased's widow, daughter, son-in-law, the parish priest, and innkeeper attend wake in local pub. Background music. 4m 3w 1 interior

The **turn** of the road. Mayne, R.

Turning points. Rye, M. S.

Turtle, Richard

Lunacy. French 1999 55p

ISBN 0-573-62640-5

Triptych set in apartment bathroom relates three scenes of angst, abuse and romance. 3 acts 2m 2w 1 interior

Twain, Mark, 1835-1910

The adventures of Huckleberry Finn (dramatization) See Francis, M. The adventures of Huckleberry Finn; Grauer, R., and Urquhart, J. Mark Twain's Huckleberry Finn

The adventures of Tom Sawyer (dramatization) See Mason, T. The adventures of Tom Sawyer

The diaries of Adam & Eve (dramatization) See Birney, D. The diaries of Adam & Eve

The prince and the pauper (dramatization) See Barchers, S. I., and Kroll, J. L. The prince and the pauper

about

c Miller, K. S. The Mark Twain show

'Twas brillig. Gilroy, F. D.

Twelfth night. McBride-Smith, B.

The **twelve** labors of Hercules. McBride-Smith, B.

The **twelve** months. McCullough, L. E.

Twelve strands of wool. Vanhecke, I.

Twenty-four years. Ayvazian, L.

Twins

Carr, M. Portia Coughlan

Dattani, M. Tara

Goldoni, C. The Venetian twins

y Harden, V. Jessica and Jolene

Ives, D. Enigma variations

Plautus, T. M. Double bind (Menaechmi)

Russell, W. Blood brothers

Vanhecke, I. Twelve strands of wool

Vogel, P. The Mineola twins

A **twist** of the tongue. Murray, S.

The **Twits**. Wood, D.

Two. Elisha, R.

Two and an orange. Hedges, P.

Two and two together. Benfield, D.

Two eclairs. Pintauro, J.

Two fat men. Gillian, P.

Two goats, two sisters, and a beggar king. McCullough, L. E.

Two-headed. Jensen, J.

Two horsemen. Bandele, B.

Two Jewish men in their seventies. Gersten-Vassilaros, A.

Two Marias. Lavery, B.

Two ships passing. Carley, D.

Two soldiers: talking, dying. Fredericks, A. D.

Two's company. Hall, L.

Typhoid Mary, d. 1938

about

Schenkar, J. Fulfilling Koch's postulate

Tzara, Tristan

The gas heart; tr. by Michael Benedikt.

Group of characters, named after parts of the head, carry on a conversation, generally at cross-purposes. 3 acts Unidentified cast 6 characters

In Theater of the avant-garde, 1890-1950; ed. by B. Cardullo and R. Knopf

U

Ubu and the Truth Commission. Taylor, J., and Kentridge, W.

Uganda

Seremba, G. Come good rain

Ukrainian tales. Mason, T.

Umongikazi (The nurse). Maponya, M.

Una **and** the goblin king. McCullough, L. E.

Una **carroña** (Rose of Lima). Ehn, E.

Unbroken. River, S. B.

Unchanging love. Linney, R.

Uncle Clete's toad. Nigro, D.

Uncle Eph's Christmas. Dunbar, P. L.

Uncle Tom's cabin. Aiken, G. L.

Uncle Vanya. Chekhov, A. P.

Uncles

Feffer, S. Little airplanes of the heart

Margulies, D. Death in the family

Wilhelm, L. A significant betrayal

Under Lubianka Square. Congdon, C.

Under plain cover. Osborne, J.

Underground railroad

Aiken, G. L. Uncle Tom's cabin

The **undertaking**. Osment, P.

Underworld

Havel, V. The beggar's opera

O'Rowe, M. Howie the rookie

The **uneasy** chair. Smith, E.

Unemployed

Keeffe, B. Barbarians: killing time

The **unerring** instinct. Wilder, T.

The **unexpected** man. Reza, Y.

Unfinished plays

Chekhov, A. P. The night before the trial

Unfinished women cry in no man's land while a bird dies in a gilded cage. Rahman, A.

The **unintended** video. Stamos, D. G.

United States

History—Civil War

Conquest, N. The widow's might

United States

Army—Military life

Wolf, M. Another American: asking and telling

Constitution

c Fredericks, A. D. The delegates speak out

c Fredericks, A. D. Equal Rights Amendment

History—Civil War

Babe, T. Singleton, the medal winner

Belasco, D. The heart of Maryland

Boucicault, D. Belle Lamar

Gillette, W. Secret service

Harrigan, E. The blue and the grey

Howard, B. Shenandoah

McCabe, J. D. J. The guerrillas

Pomerance, B. Quantrill in Lawrence

Trieschmann, C. The bridegroom of Blowing Rock

Woolf, B. E. Off to the war

History—Revolution

Mason, T. Time on fire

United States—History—Revolution—
Continued
Shaw, B. The devil's disciple
Race relations
Brown, W. Life during wartime
Cleage, P. Bourbon at the border
Graham, N. The basement at the bottom at the end of the world
Hughes, L. Angelo Herndon Jones
Hughes, L. Scottsboro, limited
Kennedy, A. Ohio State murders
Medley, C. Dearborn Heights
Ndlovu, D. Sheila's day
y Pachino, J. Race
Rahman, A. The Mojo and the Sayso
Reynolds, J. Stonewall Jackson's house
Shephard-Massat, S. M. Waiting to be invited
Walcott, D. The ghost dance
Walcott, D. Walker
Wilhelm, L. Meridian, Mississippi redux
Yew, C. A beautiful country
Social life and customs
Babe, T. Great day in the morning
Gearing, N. Dickens in America
c Still, J. Hush: an interview with America
United States. Central Intelligence Agency
Sherman, J. Three in the back, two in the head
The **universal** wolf. Schenkar, J.
The **unknown** woman. Blok, A.
Unleashed. Godber, J.
Unmarried couples
Griffiths, L. The Darling family
Unmemorable. Lucas, C.
Untouchables (India)
Bhagat, D. Routes and escape routes
Unwed mothers
Rahman, A. Unfinished women cry in no man's land while a bird dies in a gilded cage
Unwrap your candy. Wright, D.
The **unwritten** law. Santander, F.
The **unwritten** song. Linney, R.
Up and coming. Chappell, E.
Up, down, strange, charmed, beauty, and truth. Baker, E. A.
Up 'n' under. Godber, J.

Up on the roof. Martini, C.
The **uprooted** pine. Chikamatsu, M.

Upton, Judy
Ashes and sand.
Drama about violent girl gang in English seaside resort. 3 acts 6 scenes 3m 4w 1 setting
In Upton, J. Plays: 1
Confidence. Methuen 1998 96p
ISBN 0-413-77290-X
Drama about schemers and dreamers spending summer on English seafront. 10 scenes 3m 2w 1 setting
Everlasting rose.
Surreal look at modern vanity and self-perception set in England. Man's fourth wife challenges repetition and routine of male ego. 3 acts 2m 1w 1 interior
In Best of the Fest; ed. by Phil Setren
Know your rights.
Exploration of litigation culture. 2w 1 interior
In Upton, J. Plays: 1
People on the river.
Drama about victim T.V. and media exploitation. 3 acts 12 scenes 3m 3w extras settings
In Upton, J. Plays: 1
Stealing souls.
Set in Rio de Janeiro hotel. Magic realist s & m love story. 1m 1w 1 interior
In Upton, J. Plays: 1
Sunspots.
Drama set at English seaside. Explores relationship between sisters. 2 acts 7 scenes 2m 2w 1 setting
In Upton, J. Plays: 1
Urinetown the musical. Hollmann, M.

Urquhart, John
y Liza and the riddling cave. Anchorage Press 1999 54p
ISBN 0-87602-367-7
Adventure set in 1930s Appalachia about girl who can't speak, but has the ability to solve riddles. 6m 5w 1 setting
See also Grauer, R. jt. auth.

Urtusastegui, Tomas
Limited capacity; tr. by Raul Moncada.
Drama set in stalled elevator in Mexico City apartment building. What begins as funny incident escalates to tragic ending as people react to claus-

Urtusastegui, Tomas—*Continued*

trophobia and helplessness. 1b 2m 5w 1 interior

In Five plays in translation from Mexican contemporary theater; ed. by S. Rodríguez del Pino

Utopias

Aristophanes. Birds

Uyehara, Denise

Hello (sex) kitty: mad Asian bitch on wheels.

Comic monologue. Examines love, violence and respect among men and women, discusses HIV/AIDS, and women loving women. 1w

In O Solo homo; ed. by H. hughes and D. Román

V

Vacations

Aerenson, B. Paradise Island
Chappell, E. Heatstroke
Godber, J. Perfect pitch
Johnson, M. Jabiru
Larbey, B. Sand castles
McConnell, J. Cruise missile

Vaccination

c McCullough, L. E. Edward Jenner and the gossip of milkmaids

The **vacuum** cleaner. Grazia, E. de

Vagabond camp. Esson, L.

The **Vagina** monologues. Ensler, E.

Valcq, James

The Spitfire Grill; lyrics and book by Fred Alley, music and book by James Valcq. French 2002 79p

ISBN 0-573-62930-7

Musical based on film by Lee David Zlotoff about female parolee who ends up working as waitress at restaurant in small Wisconsin town. Music, singing. 2 acts 17 scenes 3m 4w 1 setting

Zombies from the beyond; music by James Valcq. Dramatists 1998 88p

ISBN 0-222-1611-6

Musical comedy set during Eisenhower era about flying saucer landing in Milwaukee. Music. singing, dancing. 2 acts 9 scenes 4m 3w 1 setting

Valenti, Michael

Bashville in love; adaptation and lyrics by Charles Marowitz; music by Michael Valenti. French 1998 80p

ISBN 0-573-62666-9

High-born lady falls in love with a bombastic prizefighter, to the dismay of her adoring butler. Adapted from The Admirable Bashville, a burlesque romamce by George Bernard Shaw. Music, singing, dancing. 2 acts 3 scenes 8m 2w 4 interiors 1 exterior

Quack; book and lyrics by Charles Marowitz; music by Michael Valenti. Dramatists 2002

ISBN 0-8222-1833-X

A vaudevillized musical version of Molière's The doctor in spite of himself. 6m 3w 1 setting

Valentine, Alana

y Swimming the globe. Currency Press 1999 78p

ISBN 0-86819-595-2

Journalist contrives to bring two swimming phenoms together for the 2000 Olympic games in Sydney, Australia. 21 scenes 2g 1m extras 2 settings

Valentine, Pam

Day of reckoning. French (London) 1999 64p

ISBN 0-573-01806-5

Comedy about British summer fete and hidden agendas of the villagers involved. 2 acts 4 scenes 1m 7w 1 setting

A dog's life. French (London) 2000 19p

ISBN 0-573-12175-3　　LC 2002-279013

Drama depicts moment when woman comes to animal shelter to chose between four dogs. Variable cast 6 characters 1 interior

Valparaiso. DeLillo, D.

Vampire. Wilson, S.

Vampire dreams. Charnas, S. M.

Vampire lesbians of Sodom. Busch, C.

Vampires

Busch, C. Vampire lesbians of Sodom
Charnas, S. M. Vampire dreams
Norman, M. Dracula
Warburton, N. Garlic and lavender
Welch, S. M. Earl the vampire

Van Druten, John

Make way for Lucia. French (London) 1999 80p
ISBN 0-573-01820-0

Based on the comic novels by E. F. Benson. War for supremacy between Lucia and Miss Mapp in small English coastal town. 3 acts 7 scenes 5m 6w 1 setting

Van Itallie, Jean-Claude

America hurrah (interview, TV, motel).

Satirical triptych of related scenes. Interview visits employment agency where all applicants are named Smith. TV dramatizes menace of mass media. Motel: a masque for three dolls explores mail-order-catologue surface of violent America. 3 parts 8m 7w settings

In Van Itallie, J. C. America hurrah and other plays

Bag lady.

Voices and memories assail lonely vagrant roaming New York streets with shopping bags. 1 act 1w 1 exterior

In Van Itallie, J. C. America hurrah and other plays

Eat cake.

Satire. Housewife confronted by eccentric rapist. 1m 1w 1 interior

In Van Itallie, J. C. America hurrah and other plays

The serpent: a ceremony.

Contemporary violence in society linked to ancient source. Experimental play reinterprets book of Genesis. Music, dancing. 1 act 7m 7w 1 setting

In Van Itallie, J. C. America hurrah and other plays

The Tibetan book of the dead; or, How not to do it again.

Experimental theater piece exploring Buddhist concept of transmigration of solos. Background music. 5m 2w 1 setting

In Van Itallie, J. C. America hurrah and other plays

The traveler.

Artist suffers and recovers from stroke. 4m 4w extras

In Van Itallie, J. C. America hurrah and other plays

War.

Two male actors who metamorphose into father and son visited by shimmering vision of great Edwardism actress. 2m 1w 1 interior

In Van Itallie, J. C. America hurrah and other plays

Van Zandt, Billy, and Milmore, Jane

Confessions of a dirty blonde. French 2000 91p
ISBN 0-573-62744-4

Famous movie icon attends gala tribute honoring her at Carnegie Hall. While recreating a famous magazine cover a lion bites her and exposes some interesting secrets. 2 acts 5 scenes 6m 2w 1 interior

Vanhecke, Ivan

Twelve strands of wool.

Based on Acadian mythology and children's story Le tapis de Grand-Pré by Réjean Aucoin and Jean-Claude Tremblay. Magical mailman helps twin brother and sister solve mystery of what happened to twelve special strands of wool for grandmother's rug. 1 act Variable cast 14 characters 1 setting

In Angels and anger; ed. by G. Nichols

Vanity fair. Donnellan, D.

Vanzetti, Bartolomeo, 1888-1927
about
Araújo, L. Vanzetti

Vanzetti. Araújo, L.

Vasilisa the fair. Lander, A.

Vaughan, R. M.

Camera, woman. Coach House Bks. 2000 71p
ISBN 1-552-45055-4   LC 2001-347136

Drama about woman Hollywood director Dorothy Arzner. Prologue 4 acts 1m 5w 1 setting

Vaughan, Robert Lewis

Praying for rain. Dramatists 2001 54p
ISBN 0-8222-1807-0   LC 2001-277819

After a crippling motorcycle accident, a high-school jock loses his identity, and starts a spiraling journey into self destruction 2 acts 4m 3w 1 setting

Vawter, Ron

Roy Cohn/Jack Smith.

One man piece about lawyer Roy Cohn and filmmaker Jack Smith. A double portrait of two complex minds, and two completely opposing approaches to gay sexuality. 1m
   In O Solo homo; ed. by H. Hughes and D. Román

Veber, Pierre. See Hennequin, M. jt. auth.
The **Venetian** twins. Goldoni, C.

Venice (Italy)

Jonson, B. Volpone
Tasca, J. Judah's daughter

Verdecchia, Guillermo

Fronteras Americanas (American borders).
One-man theater piece about Latin experience in North America. 2 acts 1m
   In Postcolonial plays; ed. by H. Gilbert

Verdi, Giuseppi

about

Chaurette, N. All the Verdis of Venice

Verga, Giovanni, 1840-1922

La lupa (dramatization) See Lan, D. La lupa

Vermont

Gilman, R. Spinning into butter
Trowbridge, J. T. Neighbor Jackwood
Yeaton, D. Mad River rising

Verne, Jules, 1828-1905

Around the world in eighty days (adaptation) See Willmott, Phil Around the world in eighty days

Vernon Early. Foote, H.

Very heaven. Lambert, A.

Vespucci, Amerigo, 1451-1512

about

c McCullough, L. E. Naming the unnamed: the strange saga of Amerigo Vespucci

Veterans

Gilroy, F. D. Getting in
Gilroy, F. D. The subject was roses

Veterans (Vietnamese Conflict, 1961-1975)

Durang, C. The Vietnamization of New Jersey
Epstein, D. Exact change

Kennedy, A. An evening with dead Essex
Wilson, L. Fifth of July

Veterans (World War, 1939-1945)

Holtzman, W. Hearts

Veterans; or, Hairs in the gates of Hellespont. Wood, C.
Via Dolorosa. Hare, D.

Vickery, Frank

The drag factor.
Couple visit son recuperating from from an accident, and discover he is a transvestite. 1 act 2m 1w 1 setting
   In Act one Wales; ed. by P. Clark

Pullin' the wool. French (London) 2002 96p
   ISBN 0-573-01959-2
Comedy. Three couples cope with stresses and strains of house buying and selling. 2 acts 3m 3w 2 settings

Vidal, Gore

The best man.
Political satire. Two candidates, one honorable and one ruthless, struggle for their party's presidential nomination. 12m 5w extras 2 interiors
   In Vidal, G. The essential Gore Vidal

Video wars. Deverell, R.

Vienna (Austria)

Horváth, Ö. von. Tales from the Vienna woods
Mee, C. L. Vienna: Lusthaus
Schmitt, E.-E. The visitor
Schnitzler, A. Anatol
Schnitzler, A. Flirtation
Schnitzler, A. La Ronde

Vienna: Lusthaus. Mee, C. L.
The **Vienna** notes. Nelson, R.
Viet rock. Terry, M.

Vietnamese Conflict, 1961-1975

c Fredericks, A. D. Two soldiers: talking, dying
Gilroy, F. D. Present tense
Hare, D. Saigon: year of the cat
Lequy, D. Meat party
Terry, M. Viet rock

The **Vietnamization** of New Jersey. Durang, C.
Vieux Carré. Williams, T.

A **view** from the roof. Carley, D.
View of the dome. Rebeck, T.
The **viewing**. Gilroy, F. D.
The **vile** veterinarian. Davidson, R.
Vilna's got a golem. Joselovitz, E.

Vinaver, Michel

Dissident, goes without saying; tr. by Peter Meyer.

Series of banal conversations reflect emotional distance between mother and son.
Together with Nina, that's something else, forms Chamber Theatre. 12 scenes 1m 1w 1 interior

In Vinaver, M. Plays: 1

High places; tr. by Gideon Y. Schein.

American business executives survive Andes plane crash by resorting to cannibalism. 7 scenes 7m 4w

In Vinaver, M. Plays: 2

The neighbours; tr. by Paul Antal.

Experimental drama utilizing elliptical dialogue to depict complexity of human relationships. 3 acts 3m 1m 1 setting

In Vinaver, M. Plays: 2

Nina, that's something else; tr. by Peter Meyer.

Girlfriend moving into apartment drastically changes balance between two brothers.
Together with Dissident, goes without saying, forms Chamber Theatre. 12 parts 2m 1w 1 interior

In Vinaver, M. Plays: 1

Overboard; tr. by Gideon Lester.

Play-within-a-play. World of big business seen through eyes of manager who is also author of play. Huge American company competes with small French family owned firm. 6 parts large mixed cast settings

In Vinaver, M. Plays: 1

Portrait of a woman; tr. by Donald Watson.

Drama based on 1950s Paris trial of female medical student accused of murdering lover. 8m 3w extras 1 setting

In Vinaver, M. Plays: 2

Situation vacant; tr. by John Burgess.

Experimental play about birth, initiation, transition, acceptance, rejection, self-affirmation, guilt, and loss of self-esteem. Parisian man loses his job. 2m 2w

In Vinaver, M. Plays: 1

A smile on the end of the line; tr. by Peter Meyer.

Play shows how repercussions of take-overs, strikes and fluctuating economy impact lives of French manufacturing firm's employees. 9 scenes 2m 3w

In Vinaver, M. Plays: 1

The television programme; tr. by David and Hannah Brady.

Two middle-aged couples at center of murder investigation. 20 scenes 5m 5w 6 interiors

In Vinaver, M. Plays: 2

Violence

Ayckbourn, A. Gizmo
Bernard, K. The magic show of Dr. Ma-Gico
Blomquist, E. Reality
Churchill, C. Far away
Clements, M. Now look what you made me do
Crimp, M. Play with repeats
Crow, A. G. A roomful of men
Finlayson, A. Winding the ball
y Frost, H. Why darkness seems so light
Fulford, R. W. Gulag
Keeffe, B. Barbarians: abide with me
Keeffe, B. Barbarians: in the city
Lewis, C. W. Soft click of a switch
London, J. The first poet
Margulies, D. Manny
Melski, M. Hockey mom, hockey dad
Mérimée, P. Carvajal's family (La famille de Carvajal)
Osborne, A. Redemption song
Pugliese, F. Aven'u boys
Ryan, T. Pig
Scheffer, W. Easter
Terry, M. Breakfast serial
Upton, J. Ashes and sand
Vaughan, R. L. Praying for rain
Williamson, D. Face to face
Wilson, S. Blowjob
Wilson, S. Pignight

Violinists

Río, M. del. On the way to the concert

Virtual reality

De Groen, A. The woman in the window
Virtual reality. Arkin, A.
Virtually yours. Bornstein, K.
The **visible** horse. Lathrop, M.

A **visit** from St. Nicholas; or, The night before Christmas. Swortzell, L.
Visiting Mr. Green. Baron, J.
The **visitor**. Schmitt, E.-E.
The **visitors**. Orton, J.

Viswananthan, Padma

House of sacred cows.

A graduate student from India is visited by the ghosts of his parents, who reproach him for eating meat. 1 scene 2m 1w 1 interior
In Short spells: scenes & monologues; ed. by V. Shantz

Vitrac, Roger

The mysteries of love; tr. by Ralph J. Gladstone.

Surrealistic drama. Plotless series of tableaux, with incessant lovers' quarrels, and attempts to involve audience in violent denouement. Prologue 3 acts 5 tableaux 18m 6w extras 1 exterior
In Theater of the avant-garde, 1890-1950; ed. by B. Cardullo and R. Knopf
Vladimir Mayakovsky. Mayakovsky, V.

Vogel, Larry

c An Ahab headache and a Jezebelly ache.

Worship program based on Bible story. Jezebel tells lies to gain neighbor's vineyard. Variable cast 1 setting
In Vogel, L. Fearless Pharaoh FooFoo and other dramas for children

The angels' locker room: A Christmas play.

Worship program. Like football coach, God directs angels to tell Mary of birth of Jesus. Variable cast 1 setting
In Vogel, L. Fearless Pharaoh FooFoo and other dramas for children

c The B-I-B-L-E is L-O-S-T.

Worship program based on Bible story. King Josiah rediscovers lost Bible. Variable cast 1 setting
In Vogel, L. Fearless Pharaoh FooFoo and other dramas for children

Be my guest.

Worship program. When guests refuse King's invitation to wedding, he invites the poor, crippled, blind, and lame. Singing. Variable cast 1 setting
In Vogel, L. Fearless Pharaoh FooFoo and other dramas for children

c Big little man.

Worship program based on Bible story of David and Goliath. Variable cast 1 setting
In Vogel, L. Fearless Pharaoh FooFoo and other dramas for children

Elijah's no good, horrible, very bad job.

Worship program based on Bible story. Discouraged Prophet Elijah is cheered by followers. Variable cast 1 setting
In Vogel, L. Fearless Pharaoh FooFoo and other dramas for children

c Everything's falling.

Worship program based on Bible stories. After many years of bad kings Jerusalem falls to Babylonians. Singing. Variable cast 1 setting
In Vogel, L. Fearless Pharaoh FooFoo and other dramas for children

Exiles.

Worship program based on Bible stories, children of exiles rebuild temple in Jerusalem. Singing. Variable cast 1 setting
In Vogel, L. Fearless Pharaoh FooFoo and other dramas for children

c The fall into sin.

Worship program based on Bible story of Adam and Eve's fall from grace. 1m 1w extras 1 exterior
In Vogel, L. Fearless Pharaoh FooFoo and other dramas for children

c Fearless Pharaoh FooFoo.

Worship program. Humorous version of Bible story of Seven Plagues of Egypt and escape of Moses and Israelites across Red Sea. Variable cast 1 setting
In Vogel, L. Fearless Pharaoh FooFoo and other dramas for children

c The flood.

Worship program based on Bible story of Tower of Babel. Variable cast 1 setting
In Vogel, L. Fearless Pharaoh FooFoo and other dramas for children

c From cool to fool.

Worship program based on Bible story of Samuel and foolish King Saul. Variable cast 1 setting
In Vogel, L. Fearless Pharaoh FooFoo and other dramas for children

Gracious goodness, great tongues of fire.

Worship program. God sends Holy Spirit to disciples. Variable cast 1 setting
In Vogel, L. Fearless Pharaoh FooFoo and other dramas for children

Vogel, Larry—*Continued*

He's so vain.

Worship program based on Bible. Jesus tells rich man what he must do to get into heaven. Singing. Variable cast 1 setting

In Vogel, L. Fearless Pharaoh FooFoo and other dramas for children

c Joseph.

Worship program based on biblical story of Joseph. Variable cast 1 setting

In Vogel, L. Fearless Pharaoh FooFoo and other dramas for children

c Judges—again.

Worship program based on Bible story. Judges help Israelites defeat enemies. 3m 2w extras 1 setting

In Vogel, L. Fearless Pharaoh FooFoo and other dramas for children

c Nay, nay, Naaman.

Worship program based on Bible story. Naaman attains faith in God when cured of leprosy by bathing in Jordan. Variable cast 1 setting

In Vogel, L. Fearless Pharaoh FooFoo and other dramas for children

Nick at night.

Worship program based on Bible story. Jesus explains to Nicodemus what it means to be born again. Singing. Variable cast 1 setting

In Vogel, L. Fearless Pharaoh FooFoo and other dramas for children

c The patriarchs.

Worship program based on Bible story of Abraham and Isaac. Singing. 4m 1w extras 1 setting

In Vogel, L. Fearless Pharaoh FooFoo and other dramas for children

c Rehoboam rubs 'em wrong.

Worship program based on Bible story. King Rehoboam's taxes lead to rebellion. 4m extras 1 setting

In Vogel, L. Fearless Pharaoh FooFoo and other dramas for children

c Ring around Jerusalem.

Worship program based on Bible story. God saves Jerusalem from Assyrians. Variable cast 1 setting

In Vogel, L. Fearless Pharaoh FooFoo and other dramas for children

Rockball, our natural pastime.

Worship program based on Bible story. Like a baseball umpire, Jesus throws sinners out of "game" of stoning woman. Variable cast 1 setting

In Vogel, L. Fearless Pharaoh FooFoo and other dramas for children

c Ruth.

Worship program based on Bible story of Ruth and Naomi. 4m 3w extras 1 setting

In Vogel, L. Fearless Pharaoh FooFoo and other dramas for children

c Samson.

Worship program based on Bible story of Samson and Delilah. 1m 1w extras 1 setting

In Vogel, L. Fearless Pharaoh FooFoo and other dramas for children

c Solomon—wise for a while.

Worship program based on Bible story about King Solomon. 3 parts Variable cast 1 setting

In Vogel, L. Fearless Pharaoh FooFoo and other dramas for children

A super scientific world.

Worship program. Three scientists attempt to create a world. 3m extras 1 setting

In Vogel, L. Fearless Pharaoh FooFoo and other dramas for children

c Surfin' Galilay.

Worship program based on Bible story. Jesus helps disciples cross water. Singing. 13m extras 1 exterior

In Vogel, L. Fearless Pharaoh FooFoo and other dramas for children

The temptations.

Worship program. Jesus, alone in desert, is tempted by Satan and demons. Singing. Variable cast 1 setting

In Vogel, L. Fearless Pharaoh FooFoo and other dramas for children

c A test for Esther.

Worship program. Queen Esther saves her people. 3m 1w extras 1 setting

In Vogel, L. Fearless Pharaoh FooFoo and other dramas for children

We're all shook up.

Worship program. People witness resurrection of Christ. Singing. Variable cast 1 setting

In Vogel, L. Fearless Pharaoh FooFoo and other dramas for children

Vogel, Larry—*Continued*

c What's up, rock?

Worship program based on Bible stories. David refrains from killing King Saul. Singing. Variable cast 1 setting

In Vogel, L. Fearless Pharaoh FooFoo and other dramas for children

c Wilderness wandering.

Worship program based on Bible story. God provides food and drink to Moses and Israelites wandering in desert. Singing. Variable cast 1 setting

In Vogel, L. Fearless Pharaoh FooFoo and other dramas for children

Yakety Yak: he won't talk back.

Worship program. Jesus in tried by priests and elders. Variable cast 1 setting

In Vogel, L. Fearless Pharaoh FooFoo and other dramas for children

Vogel, Paula

Hot'n' throbbing. Dramatists 2000 78p
ISBN 0-8222-1669-8

Drama about domestic violence. Feminist who writes erotica to support herself and her teenage children is murdered by husband after obtaining restraining order against him. 3m 3w 1 setting

How I learned to drive.

Middle-aged man's obssession with wife's teenaged niece. 1 act 1m 1w extras

In Vogel, P. The mammary plays

The Mineola twins. Dramatists 1999 55p
ISBN 0-8222-1622-1

Comedy about identical twins who argue about Vietnam and family values from the Eisenhower to Reagan/Bush era. 2 acts 6 scenes 3m 3w extras

—Same

In Vogel, P. The mammary plays

Vogelstein, Cherie

All about Al.

Two male friends discuss their hunger for intimacy. 2m 1w 1 interior

In The Best America short plays 1998-1999

—Same

In Ensemble Studio Theatre marathon '99: the one-act plays

—Same

In Four from E. S. T. Marathon '99

Cats and dogs.

Blind date from hell. 1 act 2m 3w extras 1 interior

In EST marathon '96: the one-act plays; ed. by M. Smith

Sisters.

Two sisters confide, quarrel, and make up while watching the U.S. Open. 1 act 1m 2w extras 1 exterior

In EST marathon '97: the one-act plays; ed. by M. Smith

Voice of blood (La voix du sang). Rachilde

Voices from September 11th. Mueller, L.

Voices in the dark. Pielmeier, J.

Volcanoes

c Winther, B. The sleeping mountains

Volpone. Jonson, B.

Vooght, Cherry

Bright interval. French (London) 2001 23p
ISBN 0-573-03386-2

Comedy about five vacationing women sitting on a terrace in the Austrian Alps exchanging stories, expressing feelings, and revealing worries. 6w 1 setting

The **voucher**. Pedrero, P.

Voyage. Stoppard, T.

Voyage to Lesbos. Five Lesbian Brothers (Theater company)

Voyages and travels

Woolf, C. Treseder's seeds

Vradenburg, Trish

The apple doesn't fall . . . Broadway Play Pub. 1998 84p
ISBN 0-88145-156-8

Relationship between woman diagnosed with Alzheimer's disease and her daughter. 2 acts 3m 4w 1 setting

Vreeke, John

The Canterville ghost. French 2002 94p
ISBN 0-573-62829-7

Vreeke, John—*Continued*

An American family in England flummox an Elizabethan ghost until, through a daughter's sympathy, he is finally laid to rest. Adapted from a story by Oscar Wilde. Music, dancing. Prologue 2 acts 28 scenes epilogue 2b 1g 5m 3w extras 7 interiors 6 exteriors

c A little princess. French 2002 87p

A rich man's thoughtful daughter at a fashionable London boarding school suffers considerable abuse after her father dies and she is left penniless. A dramatization of the children's classic by Frances Hodgson Burnett. Music, singing, dancing. Puppets. Prologue 2 acts 31 scenes 1b 7g 8m 5w extras 5 interiors 2 exteriors

Vvedensky, Aleksandr

Christmas at the Ivanovs'; tr. by Julia Listergarten and Karin Coonrod.

Absurdist comedy uses surreal and grotesque techniques to spoof conventions of Christmas celebrations and traditional drama. 4 acts 9 scenes 1b 1g 10m 7w extras

In Theater of the avant-garde, 1890-1950; ed. by B. Cardullo and R. Knopf

W

Wagner, Colleen

The monument.

Philosophical play about ambiguities of morality and justice. Young soldier convicted of war crimes "rescued" by woman from enemy side. 8 scenes 1m 1w 1 setting

In 7 cannons

Wain, Daniel

Look behind you. Weinberger, J. 2001 140p

ISBN 0-85676-241-5

Scenes from a traditional English pantomime alternate with backstage chaos at a provincial theater on the verge of collapse. Satirical portraits of theatrical types. Music, singing. 2 acts 14 scenes 5m 6w settings

Waiters

Tait, L. Dmitri

Waiting for Lefty. Odets, C.

Waiting for Philip Glass. Wasserstein, W.

Waiting for Ringo. Milligan, J.

Waiting for the barbarians. Ardito, C.

The **waiting** room. Loomer, L.

Waiting to be invited. Shephard-Massat, S. M.

Waitresses

Godber, J. Shakers

Shimko, R. Specks

Valcq, J. The Spitfire Grill

The **wake** of Jamey Foster. Henley, B.

Wake up and smell the coffee. Bogosian, E.

Walcott, Derek

Drums and colours.

Historical pageant forms second part of Haitian trilogy. Links lives of Columbus and Raleigh, Toussaint and George William Gordon. Prologue 17 scenes epilogue Large mixed cast

In Walcott, D. The Haitian trilogy

The ghost dance.

Historical drama set in North Dakota, 1890. Government agent is led to betray military secret to desperate Sioux. To redeem himself, he arranges assassination of Sitting Bull. Music, singing. 2 acts 18 scenes 10m 4w extras 7 interiors 4 exteriors

In Walcott, D. Walker and The ghost dance

The Haitian earth.

Conclusion of Haitian trilogy. Historical depiction of Toussaint Louverture's revolution. 2 acts 42 scenes 21m 6w settings

In Walcott, D. The Haitian trilogy

Henri Christophe.

First play in Haitian trilogy. Struggle between guerilla generals Henri Christophe and Jean Jacques Dessalines following imprisonment and death in exile of Toussaint L'Ouverture. 7 scenes 7m extras 2 interiors 3 exteriors

In Walcott, D. The Haitian trilogy

Pantomime.

In Tobago, British actor-hotel owner and servant plan show for hotel guests. Ensuing conflicts reflect problems of postcolonial life. Singing, dancing. 2 acts 2m 1 exterior

In Postcolonial plays; ed. by H. Gilbert

Walker.

Historical drama set in 1830 Boston. Black abolitionist David Walker is murdered when he persists in advocating slave revolt. Music, singing. 4 scenes 5m 2w extras 1 interior 1 exterior

In Walcott, D. Walker and The ghost dance

Wales

Blakeman, H. Caravan

c Brooks, J. A child's Christmas in Wales

Hunt, L. A night under canvas

Morgan, S. Magic threads

Osborne, A. Bull, rock, and nut

Rhys, T. The old petrol station

Thomas, D. Return journey

Thomas, G. Gazooka

Thomas, T. C. The sound of stillness

Way, C. Looking out to see

Walker, Brandy

The moons of Alnyron. French 2002 53p
  ISBN 0-573-62891-2

Drama about a young scientist obsessed with his research on a planet called Alnyron and its three moons. 2 acts 9 scenes 1m 1w 1 setting

Walker, David, 1785-1830

about

Walcott, D. Walker

Walker, George F.

Adult entertainment.

Police error results in boy's murder. 5 scenes 2m 2w 1 interior
  In Walker, G. F. Suburban motel

The art of war.

Concluding play in author's Power play trilogy. Reporter meets arch-enemy face to face representing battle between art and artlessness. Prologue 4m 2w 8 scenes 1 exterior
  In Walker, G. F. The power plays

Beautiful city.

Urban comedy set in Toronto. Lifestyles clash when trendy condo set meet more traditional neighbors. 11 scenes 5m 4w 1 setting
  In Walker, G. F. The East End plays, part 2

Better living.

Prequel to Criminals in love. Thought dead, man returns home forcing his wife and daughters to allow him to resume authority. 2 acts 3m 4w
  In Walker, G. F. The East End plays, part 1

Criminal genius.

Drama about arson for hire, fathers and sons, and revenge. 3 scenes 3m 2w 1 interior
  In Walker, G. F. Suburban motel

Criminals in love.

Two innocent teenagers in urban wasteland find themselves transformed into armed terrorists. 1 act 9 scenes 3m 3w settings
  In Walker, G. F. The East End plays, part 1

The end of civilization.

Policeman plants evidence in murder case to help old friend and her husband. 4 scenes 3m 2w 1 interior
  In Walker, G. F. Suburban motel

Escape from happiness.

Absurdist comedy about eccentric urban blue-collar family entangled with drug dealing, pornography and police corruption. 6 scenes 5m 5w 1 interior
  In Walker, G. F. The East End plays, part 1

Featuring Loretta.

Young unmarried pregnant woman weighs her options. 5 scenes 2m 2w 1 interior
  In Walker, G. F. Suburban motel

Filthy rich.

Second in the authors Power play trilogy. Comedy. Retired reporter is lured into investigating murder case involving corrupt businessmen and politicians. 8 scenes 4m 2w 1 interior
  In Walker, G. F. The power plays

Gossip.

First play in the author's Power play trilogy. Comic whodunit. Journalist solves mystery of murder of chic art patroness by unraveling web of rumors and innuendos. 9 scenes 6m 3w 6 interiors
  In Walker, G. F. The power plays

Love and anger.

Drama set in Canadian city. Once successful lawyer defends poor black woman against wealthy publisher of redneck tabloid. 7 scenes 3m 3w 1 interior
  In Walker, G. F. The East End plays, part 2

Problem child.

Young couple, charged with being unfit parents strive to regain custody of daughter. 7 scenes 2m 2w 1 interior
  In Walker, G. F. Suburban motel

Risk everything.

Mother's criminal activities endanger daughter and son-in-law. 4 scenes 2m 2w 1 interior
  In Walker, G. F. Suburban motel

Walker, George F.—*Continued*
Tough!.

Young, single pregnant woman and her girlfriend confront father of child. 1m 2w 1 exterior
  In Walker, G. F. The East End plays, part 2

Walker, Jeanne Murray

Inventing Montana. Dramatic Publishing 2003 79p

Play with a play. Discovery of lost manuscript leads Dickens scholar and young graduate student on an adventure across time and place. 2 acts 6m 10w 1 setting

Tales from the Daily Tabloid. Dramatic Publishing 2003 82p

Comedy. After losing his advertising job in New York, man is forced to take job writing for hometown newspaper. 2 acts 7m 8w 1 setting

Walker. Walcott, D.
Walkin' backward. Silberman, B.
Walking down Broadway. Powell, D.
Walking on the roof. Clarvoe, A.
The **wall** of water. Kramer, S.

Wallace, Naomi

In the fields of Aceldama.

Rural couple struggle to carry on following death of their 17-year-old daughter. 1 act 1m 2w 1 exterior
  In Best of the Fest; ed. by Phil Setren

In the heart of America.

Critique of American racism, militarism, and homophobia. Sister seeks truth about murder of gay soldier brother. 11 scenes 3m 2w settings
  In Wallace, N. In the heart of America, and other plays

One flea spare.

Set in plague-infested 1665 London. Wealthy elderly couple quarantined with 12-year-old girl and young sailor. 2 acts 21 scenes 1g 3m 1w 1 setting
  In Wallace, N. In the heart of America, and other plays

Slaughter City.

Drama about workers in American textile factory. Prelude 2 acts 28 scenes 5m 3w 1 setting
  In Wallace, N. In the heart of America, and other plays

The trestle at Pope Lick Creek. Broadway Play Pub. 2000 68p
  ISBN 0-88145-180-0

Tragic coming-of-age tale set in 1936 Kentucky. Teenage boy and his girlfriend hatch dangerous plan to race locomotive across bridge. Prologue 2 acts 20 scenes 1b 1g 2m 1w 1 setting
—Same
  In Humana Festival '98
—Same
  In Wallace, N. In the heart of America, and other plays

Walsh, Enda

Disco pigs.

Lifelong friends, an Irish boy and girl enjoy a night on the town, with dancing, sex, and violence. Music, dancing. 1 act 1m 1w settings
  In Walsh, E. Disco pigs & Sucking Dublin

Sucking Dublin.

The casual rape of a drunken girl at a party shatters illusions among a small group of disaffected Irish young people. Music. 1 act 2m 3w extras settings
  In Walsh, E. Disco pigs & Sucking Dublin

Walter, Marie-Thérèse, 1909-1977
  about
  McAvera, B. Marie-Therese

Walters, Larry
  about
  Cromelin, C. Man in the flying lawn chair

Wang Peigong

WM.

Group of educated Chinese youth from different social and family backgrounds adjust to societal changes from 1976 through 1984. Music. 4 acts 5m 4w 1 setting
  In Theater & society; ed. by Haiping Yan

Wann, Jim. See Simpson, B. jt. auth.

War

  Ardito, C. Waiting for the barbarians
  Bhuchar, S. A tainted dawn
  y Bond, E. Tuesday
  Box, M. Angels of war
  Bozzone, B. War
  Dempsey, S. Armagideon
  c Deverell, R. Video wars

War—*Continued*

Ensler, E. Necessary targets
Kane, S. Blasted
Kleist, H. von. The Prince of Homburg
Kraszewski, C. S. Iphigenia in Zagreb
Lask, B. Liberation (Die Befreiung)
Lenéru, M. Peace (La paix)
London, J. The acorn planter
Mayne, R. Phantoms
Oakes, M. Faith
Paterson, D. L. Chutes
Rachilde. The painted woman (La Femme peinte)
Rodriguez, E. S. Soldiers will be soldiers
Stein, G. Accents in Alsace: a reasonable tragedy
Wentworth, M. C. War brides
War. Bozzone, B.
War. Van Itallie, J.-C.
War brides. Wentworth, M. C.

War crime trials

Mann, A. Judgment at Nuremberg
Weiss, P. The investigation

War criminals

Wagner, C. The monument
Zellnik, D. Killing hand
War letters. Wilkins, J. R.
The **war** to end war. Mee, C. L.

Warburton, Nick

c Domby-Dom. French (London) 1999 21p
    ISBN 0-573-12221-0
Children put on a play about football match in space. Music. Variable cast

Garlic and lavender. French (London) 2001 34p
    ISBN 0-573-12306-3
Comedy about two English girls who visit Castle Drackenbert, owned by Count Drackenberg, who turns out to be a vampire. 7 scenes 8m 8w

Office song. French (London) 1998 26p
    ISBN 0-573-12174-5
Man waylaid in cloakroom at office Christmas party by co-worker who tries to get him to sing in talent contest. Music. Variable cast 1 interior
Warburton's Cook. Nigro, D.

Ward, Frederick

Somebody somebody's returning.
Tragicomedy about black Canadians. Depicts familial tension, disrupted relationships, fratricide and love betrayed. 13 scenes 1m 3w 2 interiors
    In Testifyin' v2; ed. by D. Sears
Warm love. Ryan, J.

Warmflash, Stuart

Six inch adjustable.
Older brother tries to prepare younger brother for the future, as they work on an old motorcycle after their father's death. 1 act 2m 1 setting
    In Off-Off Broadway Festival plays, 25th ser.

Warner, Craig

Strangers on a train. French (London) 2003 70p
    ISBN 0-573-01972-X
Thriller based on Patricia Highsmith's novel set in 1950s America. An architect and rich mother's boy meet in a dining-car and plan perfect murders. 2 acts 17 scenes 5m 2w 1 setting

Warner, Francis

Goethe's Weimar. Oxford Univ. Press 1997 116p
    ISBN 0-86140-406-8
Second play in author's Europe tetralogy. Verse play explores the secular saints of German Kulturreligion. 1b 19m 13w

Rembrandt's mirror. Smythe; Catholic Univ. of America Press 2000 138p (Oxford theater texts, 14)
    ISBN 0-8614-432-7
Title in author's Europe tetralogy. Historical verse play follows Rembrandt from his 1625 arrival in Amsterdam. Depicts art and life in Dutch Republic during period of political turmoil and religious intolerance. Slide projections. 2 acts 37 scenes 15m 8w

Warren, Robert Penn

All the king's men.
Based on author's Pulitzer Prize novel. Erstwhile grass roots politician uses unethical methods of political machine to get complete control of state, only to be killed by one of many betrayed. 14m 4w extras 1 interior
    In Warren, R. P. Robert Penn Warren's All the king's men

Warren, Robert Penn—*Continued*

Proud flesh.

Earliest version of author's tale of southern populist politics. 5 acts 10 scenes Large mixed cast

In Warren, R. P. Robert Penn Warren's All the king's men

Willie Stark.

Stage version of author's novel, All the king's men follows career of southern populist politician. Prologue 3 acts 12 scenes epilogue 11m 3w extras 1 setting

In Warren, R. P. Robert Penn Warren's All the king's men

Warsaw (Poland)

Nanus, S. The survivor

Wash and dry. Silverstein, S.

Washburn, Anne

The intervention.

Group of friends rehearse for planned intervention. 5 scenes Variable cast 6 characters 1 interior

In 30 ten-minute plays for 4, 5 & 6 actors from Actors Theatre of Louisville's National Ten-minute Play Contest

—Same

In Actors Theatre of Louisville. Ten-minute plays; v5

Wasp. Martin, S.

Wasps. Aristophanes

Wasserman, Dale

The bequest. French 2002 24p

ISBN 0-573-62816-5

Comic drama. Town playboy bequeaths fortune to wife of local newspaper reporter. 1 act 3m 3w 1 interior

Wasserstein, Wendy

An American daughter. Dramatists 1999 76p

ISBN 0-8222-1633-7

Political comedy. Woman nominated for U.S. surgeon general. 2 acts 8 scenes 8m 6w 1 interior

—Same. Harcourt Brace & Co. 1998 105p

ISBN 0-15-600645-6

Bette and me.

Comedy. Playwright's encounter with Bette Midler. 1 act 2w

In Wasserstein, W. Seven one-act plays

Boy meets girl.

Satire on New York City yuppies. Prologue 6 scenes epilogue 3m 3w 1 setting

In Wasserstein, W. Seven one-act plays

The man in a case.

Dramatization of Chekhov's short story. Conservative Russian schoolteacher is unnerved by fiancee's progressive ideas. 1 act 1m 1w 1 exterior

In Wasserstein, W. Seven one-act plays

Medea.

Tragic heroine and her chorus tries to figure out if it is appropriate to kill her children to punish her husband. 1 act 2m 4w

In Wasserstein, W. Seven one-act plays

Old money. French 2002 74p

ISBN 0-573-62793-2   LC 2002-512152

Drawing-room comedy spanning the 19th and 20th centuries about wealthy families living in a mansion in Manhattan, New York. 2 acts 3m 4w 1 interior

Tender offer.

Father picks up young daughter from dance recital that he has missed and they try to communicate. 1 act 1g 1m 1 interior

In Wasserstein, W. Seven one-act plays

Waiting for Philip Glass.

Inspired by Shakespeare's sonnet 94. Easthampton crowd waits for composer to show up as guest of honor at party. 2m 2w extras 1 interior

In The Best American short plays 1999-2000

—Same

In Love's fire

—Same

In Wasserstein, W. Seven one-act plays

Workout.

Comedy. During single workout, woman exercise instructor accomplishes great things. 1 act 1w

In Wasserstein, W. Seven one-act plays

Watch it come down. Osborne, J.

The **water** children. MacLeod, W.

Water, water will be mine. Barchers, S. I.

Waterbabies. LeFevre, A.

Waterhouse, Keith

Good grief. French (London) 1999 69p
ISBN 0-573-01777-8

Dramatization of the author's novel Tragicomedy
about widow who comes to terms with her be-
reavement by keeping talking diary. 2 acts 19
scenes 2m 2w extra

Watkins, Christine

Queen of hearts.

Monologue. Elderly Welsh woman imagines a
visit from Princess Diana. 1w 1 setting
In One woman, one voice; ed. by H.
    W. Davies

Welcome to my world.

Monologue. Woman who recently lost her mother, thinks her long lost sister has returned home.
1w 1 setting
In One woman, one voice; ed. by H.
    W. Davies

Watsonville: some place not here. Moraga,
    C.

The **Waverly** Gallery. Lonergan, K.

The **wax.** Tolan, K.

Way, Charles

Looking out to see.

Drama based on two poems by two boys, one
about going to college, the other about day trip off
Welsh coast. 1 act 6b 3g extras 1 setting
In Act one Wales; ed. by P. Clark

The **way** of all fish. May, E., and Arkin,
    A.

The **way** of the cross. Rhymes, B. G.

Way out west in a dress. Francoeur, B.

The **way** to Miami. Steele, D.

A **way** with words. Gilroy, F. D.

The **way** you look tonight. Williams, N.

The **wayfarer.** Briusov, V.

We don't want to lose you. Chappell, E.

We had a very good time. Auburn, D.

We the people. Cook, P.

We won't pay! We won't pay. Fo, D.

Wealth

Chambers, R. Pretty blue
Chappell, E. Double vision
Gates, T. Ladies who lunch
c Vreeke, J. A little princess
Walker, G. F. Filthy rich
Wasserstein, W. Old money
Williamson, D. Money and friends

Wealth. Aristophanes

Weaver, Lois

Faith and dancing.

Monologue. Mother shows daughter how to hang
laundry. 1w
In Mythic women/Real women

Webster, John

The Duchess of Malfi.

Elizabethan verse tragedy set in 16th century Italy. Chronicles secret marriage of widowed Duchess with her steward. 5 acts 19 scenes 13m 4w
In Renaissance drama; ed. by A. F.
    Kinney

The **wedding.** Chekhov, A. P.

Wedding band: a love/hate story in black
    and white. Childress, A.

The **wedding** bell blues. Hamlett, C.

Wedding day at the Cro-Magnons'
    (Journee de noces chez les Cro-
    Magnons). Mouawad, W.

The **wedding** party. Herzberg, J.

The **wedding** reception. Chekhov, A. P.

Weddings

Chekhov, A. P. Tatyana Repina
Chekhov, A. P. The wedding
Chekhov, A. P. The wedding reception
Dobrish, J. The handless maiden
c Hamlett, C. The wedding bell blues
Hawdon, R. Perfect wedding
Henley, B. Impossible marriage
Herzberg, J. The wedding party
Kemnitz, R. D. The processional
Mouawad, W. Wedding day at the Cro-
    Magnons' (Journee de noces chez les
    Cro-Magnons)
Osborne, J. The blood of the Bambergs

Wedekind, Frank

Death and devil; tr. by Carl R. Mueller.

German expressionist drama. Brothel keeper
driven to suicide when he realizes torment endured
by his prostitutes. 3 scenes 2m 2w extras 1 interior
In Wedekind, F. Four plays

Earth spirit; tr. by Carl R. Mueller.

German expressionist tragedy about Lulu, beautiful overtly sexual paradox of a heroine; who,
while exuding innocence causes disaster wherever
she goes as she rises in social status. Prologue 4
acts 9m 3w extras 4 interiors
In Wedekind, F. Four plays

Wedekind, Frank—*Continued*

Lulu; translated by Carl R. Mueller.

Translation of Wedekind's original which was later reworked as Earth spirit and Pandora's box. Set in 1890s Berlin, Paris and London. Life of Lulu, amoral woman of sexually voracious appetite. 5 acts 14m 3w settings

In Wedekind, F. Four major plays

The Marquis of Keith; translated by Carl R. Mueller.

Character study of an egotistical adventurer who exploited his friends and mistresses in an attempt to finance a new concert hall in Munich. 5 acts 14m 8w extras 3 interiors

In Wedekind, F. Four major plays

Pandora's box; tr. by Carl R. Mueller.

German expressionist tragedy. Continues exploits of Lulu begun in Earth-spirit. Lulu escapes from jail and flees to London where she is forced into poverty and prostitution and meets her end at murderer's hand. 3 acts 1g 13m 5w 3 interiors

In Wedekind, F. Four plays

The solar spectrum; tr. by Carl R. Mueller.

Expressionistic drama set in 1894 Berlin. Initiation of new girl into prostitution. Music, singing. 11m 8w 1 exterior

In Wedekind, F. Four plays

Spring's awakening; translated by Carl R. Mueller.

Tragedy results as three adolescents seek to balance their natural sexual desires with the dictates of repressive and hypocritical society. 3 acts 19 scenes Large mixed cast 7 interiors 6 exteriors

In Wedekind, F. Four major plays

The tenor; translated by Carl R. Mueller.

An egotistical Norwegian tenor places his career above everything including the only woman who really loved him. 1 act 5m 3w 1 interior

In Wedekind, F. Four major plays

Weekend breaks. Godber, J.
Weemen. Mtshali, T. S.

Wei Minglun

Pan Jinlian: the history of a fallen woman.

Realist redramatization of ancient Chinese story. Lascivious life of woman juxtaposed with various fictional and historical characters. Variable cast

In Theater & society; ed. by Haiping Yan

Weidman, John

Contact (condensation); by Susan Stroman and John Weidman; written by John Weidman; direction and choreography by Susan Stroman.

In The Best Plays of 1999-2000; ed. by Otis L. Guernsey, Jr.

Weil, Simone, 1909-1943

about

Terry, M. Approaching Simone

Weil, Virginia C.

Communication.

Drama about mother and daughter fighting while their Apollonian and Dionysian sides look on. 2g 2w 1 setting

In Blast from the future; ed. by D. Yeaton

Weimar (Germany)

Warner, F. Goethe's Weimar

Wein, Glenn, and Blumsack, Amy Lord

Grandma Sylvia's funeral; an interactive play in three acts; conceived by Glenn Wein and Amy Lord Blumsack; created by Glenn Wein and Amy Lord Blumsack and The Original Company and you. French 1998 149p

ISBN 0-573-62635-9   LC 99-195820

Interactive comedy. Grandmother's funeral brings fighting relatives and friends together. 3 acts 12m 10w 1 interior

Weiner, Wendy

Give me shelter.

Chronicles young woman's desperate, hilarious search for a livable New York apartment. Music. 1 w

In Women playwrights: the best plays of 1998

The **weir**. McPherson, C.
Weird kid. Deverell, R.

Weisman, Annie

Be aggressive. Dramatists 2002

ISBN 0-8222-1894-1

Vista Del Sol is a paradise, but everything changes for a 17-year-old cheerleader when her mother is killed and she becomes a caregiver for her younger sister and her brittle father. 1m 4w 1 setting

Weisman, Annie—*Continued*

Snapshot: thrift of the Magi.

A hip couple, pursuing retro gear, reenact O. Henry's classic story. 1 act 1m 1w 1 interior

In Humana Festival 2002

Weiss, Edith

c Hyronomous A. Frog. Pioneer Drama Service 1998 33p

Lonely frog prince must be kissed by maiden to break enchantment. 5 scenes 3m 4w settings

Weiss, Peter

The investigation.

Condensation of court record of trial of eighteen Germans accused of crimes at Auschwitz. 28m 2w 1 interior

In Weiss, P. Marat/Sade; The investigation; The shadow of the body of the coachman

Marat/Sade.

Takes place at the madhouse of Charenton, where the Marquis de Sade wrote plays and staged them with his fellow-inmates before audiences from Paris. 2 acts 33 divisions 20m 7w 1 setting

In Weiss, P. Marat/Sade; The investigation; The shadow of the body of the coachman

The new trial; translated, with an introduction, by James Rolleston and Kai Evers. Duke Univ. Press 2001 119p

ISBN 0-8223-2681-7; 0-8223-2690-6 (pa)

Loosely based on Kafka's novel The trial. Surreal world of attorney for multinational firm with fascistic intentions. 3 acts 32 scenes Variable cast

Welch, Sean Michael

Earl the vampire. French 2000 64p

ISBN 0-573-62731-2   LC 2002-275254

Comedy. Vampire appears on television, contracts to write book, and heads up movement to establish his kind as recognized minority group. 2 acts 9m 7w 1 interior

Welcome to Bedside Manor. Castle, G. V.

Welcome to my world. Watkins, C.

Welcome to the moon. Shanley, J. P.

Weldon, Fay

Flood warning. French (London) 2003 25p

ISBN 0-573-02361-1

Couple enlist the help of their two daughters to save the stock of their antique store during a flood. 2m 3w 1 setting

The reading group. French (London) 1999 26p

ISBN 0-573-12227-X

Participants reveal their personalities in all female reading group hosted by widowed astrologer. 3m 4w 1 setting

Weller, Michael

Buying time. French 2002 79p

ISBN 0-573-6281-3

Drama based on true story. Large Southwest law firm must decide between a big business client and pro bono environmental group. 2 acts 11 scenes 9m 4w settings

c Dogbrain.

When 6-year-old blames imaginary character for hitting incident at school, "Dogbrain" materializes and creates mischief. 10 scenes 2b 2m 2w extras 1 setting

In Eight plays for children; ed. by C.A. Jennings

Ghost on fire. French 1998 88p

ISBN 0573-69625-x

Tragicomedy about a failed Hollywood film director, who is approached by a terminally ill cameraman, to direct a horror film. 2 acts 7m 5w

The heart of art. French 2000 76p

Comedy. A struggling playwright is hired by an egomaniacal Off-Broadway producer to write a play. 2 acts 5m 3w 1 setting

Mistresses.

Two, eventually three, men locked out by their wives hang around a dumpster and discuss their extramarital affairs and how women are controlling their lives. 1 act 1 scene 3m 1 exterior

In EST marathon '97: the one-act plays; ed. by M. Smith

Welles, Orson, 1915-1985

about

Sherman, J. It's all true

Wellman, Mac

Albanian softshoe.

Experimental science fiction piece about double-dealing and homelessness. 2 acts 6m 2w extras settings

In Wellman, M. Cellophane

Wellman, Mac—*Continued*

Allegory of whiteness.

Symbolist play about haunted family. Music. 5m 5w extras 1 setting

In Humana Festival 2001

Bad penny.

Site specific theater piece for Bow Bridge in Central Park. Speaking chorus 4m 2w extras

In Wellman, M. Cellophane

Cat's-paw.

Experimental theater piece on Don Juan theme. 4w

In Wellman, M. Cellophane

Cellophane.

Experimental theater piece about language. Variable cast

In Wellman, M. Cellophane

Cleveland.

Adolescent girl's dreams. Music. 7 scenes 5m 7w 1 setting

In Wellman, M. Cellophane

Fnu Lnu.

Experimental site-specific piece set in Ybor City Florida about origin of political thinking. 6m extras

In Wellman, M. Cellophane

Girl gone.

Experimental dance play about group of schoolgirls. Music, dancing. 2m 11w extras 1 setting

In Wellman, M. Cellophane

Hypatia; or, The divine algebra.

Language experiment about Alexandrian mathematician and philosopher. 1g 7m 2w extras

In Wellman, M. Cellophane

Infrared; a play. French 2000 45p

ISBN 0-573-62729-0   LC 00-711144

Puppet play where narrator character loses shadow and travels to mirror-world to find it. Speaking chorus. Puppets. Variable cast 9 characters extras 1 setting

Mister Original Bugg.

Experimental piece about act of naming. 3w 1 setting

In Wellman, M. Cellophane

The sandalwood box.

Experimental drama. Troubled woman reacts to human cruelty. 2w extras

In Wellman, M. Cellophane

Three Americanisms.

Experimental theater piece about language. 2m 1w

In Wellman, M. Cellophane

Wells, H. G. (Herbert George), 1866-1946

The invisible man (dramatization) See Jenkin, L. The invisible man

Wells, Michael Louis

The "I" word: interns.

Interns at the Clinton White House, during the Lewinsky scandal. Disillusionment kept at bay by the sheer fascination of the political game. Music. 1 act 1m 3w 1 interior

In Ensemble Studio Theatre marathon '99: the one-act plays

Real real gone.

Two friends meet in a cemetery for the annual observance of their much-missed fathers' deaths. One involuntarily channels voices of the dead. 1 act 2m 1 exterior

In EST marathon '97: the one-act plays; ed. by M. Smith

Welsh

Australia

Williams, R. Killing kangaroos

Wentworth, Marion Craig

War brides.

Feminist anti-war play. 1 act 3m 4w extras 1 interior

In War plays by women; ed. by C. M. Tylee, E. Turner, and A. Cardinal

We're all shook up. Vogel, L.

The **werewolf's** curse. St. John, B.

Werfel, Franz

about

Ronzoni, M. 610 Bedford Drive

Wertenbaker, Timberlake

After Darwin. Faber & Faber 1998 73p

ISBN 0-571-19584-9

Play within a play. Portrays Darwin's conflict with Beagle's devoutly religious commander Robert Fitzroy. 2 acts 19 scenes 3m 1w 1 setting

The Ash Girl. Dramatic Publishing 2003 74p

Variation on Cinderella tale combining fairy tale, allegoric, and anthropomorphic elements. On way to palace Ashgirl must battle seven deadly sins. 2 acts Variable cast 21 characters 1 setting

Wertenbaker, Timberlake—*Continued*

Credible witness. Dramatic Publishing 2003 55p

Macedonian mother and son in England represent inherent clash between intransigent nationalism and necessary assimilation of exile. 8m 3w 1 setting

The love of the nightingale.

Drama based on Greek myth of Procne and Philomela depicting victimization of women. Chorus. 21 scenes Large mixed cast

In Mythic women/Real women

Wesker, Arnold

Annie Wobbler.

Portraits of three women; an eccentric bag lady, a gawky graduate student preparing for a date, and a successful novelist assuming persona for interview. 3 parts 1w

In Wesker, A. Plays: 2

Chicken soup with barley.

First play of the Wesker trilogy. Disillusionment of East End family over twenty-year period. 3 acts 6 scenes 6m 4w 2 interiors

In Wesker, A. Plays: 1

Four portraits—of mothers.

Set of vignettes in which one actress portrays four mothers of various ages from different ethnic and social backgrounds. 1w

In Wesker, A. Plays: 2

I'm talking about Jerusalem.

Conclusion of Wesker trilogy. Departure from city does not alleviate young couple's problems. Music, singing. 3 acts 5 scenes 8m 4w 1 setting

In Wesker, A. Plays: 1

Letter to a daughter.

Monologue by guilt-ridden single mother singer/composer. Singing. 6 parts 1w 1 setting

In Wesker, A. Plays: 2

The mistress.

Monologue by fashion designer mistress of historian. 1w 1 setting

In Wesker, A. Plays: 2

Roots.

Second play in the Wesker trilogy. Set in rural Norfolk, focuses on plight of displaced English farm laborers. Music, singing. 3 acts 4 scenes 5m 4w 3 interiors

In The Methuen book of sixties drama

—Same

In Wesker, A. Plays: 1

Whatever happened to Betty Lemon?

Monologue by eccentric elderly widow of philandering British socialist MP. 1w 1 setting

In Wesker, A. Plays: 2

Yardsale.

Radio play. Monologue by woman abandoned by husband of twenty five years. 8 scenes 1w

In Wesker, A. Plays: 2

West, Mae, 1892-1980

about

Shear, C. Dirty blonde

West, Cheryl

Jar the floor. Dramatists 2002

ISBN 0-8222-1809-7

A quartet of black women spanning four generations come together, with a white woman friend, to celebrate the matriarch's ninetieth birthday. 5w settings

West Indies

O'Neill, E. The Emperor Jones

Philip, M. N. Coups and calypsos

Williams, R. The No Boys Cricket Club

Williams, R. Starstruck

West of stupid. Cram, C.

West Virginia

Battlo, J. The little theater's production of Hamlet

Napier, E. The English teachers

Westerfield, Nancy G.

The morning of the Marys.

Resurrection story from the unique point of view of the mothers and wives of the key men in the Resurrection event. 7w 1 interior

In The drama of Easter; ed. by R. Wray

What are you afraid of? Dresser, R.

What are you doing in there? Silverstein, S.

What Corbin knew. Hatcher, J.

What do you believe about the future? Auburn, D.

What drove me back to reconsidering my father. Noonan, J. F.

What happened in the garden this summer? (Que paso en el jardin este verano?). Espinosa, R.

Whitemore, Hugh—*Continued*

Drama about four English tourists in Tuscany who encounter a fugitive claiming to have long-hidden knowledge involving the Vatican's secret archives. 2 acts 3m 2w 1 interior

Whitman, Walt, 1819-1892

about

Metcalf, P. The players

Whittington, Paul

c Rosie and the bad, bad apples; book and lyrics by Valerie Hall, music by Paul Whittington. French (London) 2001 84p

ISBN 0-573-08113-1

Story about a ceremony reuniting a daughter apple with her apple parents, disrupted by the bad apples. Music, singing. 2 acts 16 scenes Unidentified cast 15 characters

Who am I? Zapel, A. L.

Who look in stove. Jeffery, L.

Who poisoned his meatball? Sodaro, C.

Who shot Jacques Lacan? O'Donnell, D.

Who wins. Matthews, S.

Whodidit?. Harrison, N.

WhoDunit. . .and to whom? Frankel, R.

WhoDunit. . .and who's the big idea anyway? Frankel, R.

Who'll save the plowboy? Gilroy, F. D.

Wholly Joan's (Joan of Arc). Ehn, E.

Who's dying to be a millionaire? Cook, P.

Whose wives are they anyway? Parker, M.

Why ants carry burdens. Barchers, S. I.

Why bears no longer talk. McCullough, L. E.

Why darkness seems so light. Frost, H., and Cocks, H.

Why is John Lennon wearing a skirt? Dowie, C.

Why marry? Williams, J. L.

Whylah Falls: the play. Clarke, G. E.

A **wicked** woman. London, J.

Widowers

Aldridge, R. You're only young twice

Baron, J. Visiting Mr. Green

Margulies, D. Father and son

Parker, S. Nightshade

Widowers' houses. Shaw, B.

The **widowing** of Mrs. Holroyd. Lawrence, D. H.

Widows

Babe, T. Great day in the morning

Benjamin, K. A. Mary Macgregor

Donaghy, T. From above

Laurence, C. About Alice

Lipner, N. Pearls

Moore, R. The pain of pink evenings

Simon, E. Moonlight and Valentino

Toddie, J. L. The juice of wild strawberries

Waterhouse, K. Good grief

Williams, T. The rose tattoo

The **widow's** might. Conquest, N.

Wife abuse

Canino, F. The Angelina project

Crimp, M. The treatment

Rivera, C. Betty's garage

Vogel, P. Hot'n' throbbing

A **wife** to be lett: a comedy. Haywood, E. F.

Wihio's duck dance. Bruchac, J.

Wild Turkey. Penhall, J.

The **wild,** wild women (Bacchides). Plautus, T. M.

Wildboy. Bush, M.

Wilde, Constance, 1858-1898

about

Kilroy, T. The secret fall of Constance Wilde

Wilde, Oscar, 1854-1900

The Canterville ghost (dramatization) See Miller, C. The Canterville ghost; Vreeke, J. The Canterville ghost

The happy prince (dramatization) See Miller, C. The Canterville ghost; Wong, E. The happy prince

Lady Windermere's fan (adaptation) See Coward, N. After the ball

The picture of Dorian Gray (dramatization) See Hamlett, C. Picture perfect

A Florentine tragedy.

Fragment of unfinished play. Love, intrigue, and violent death in medieval Floence. 2m 1w 1 interior

In Wilde, O. The importance of being earnest and other plays

An ideal husband.

Social comedy. 19th century British government official's marriage and career are threatened by woman eager to regain social position. 4 acts 9m

Wilde, Oscar, 1854-1900—*Continued*

6w 3 interiors

In Wilde, O. The importance of being earnest and other plays

The importance of being Earnest.

Drawing room comedy exposing quirks and foibles of Victorian society with plot revolving around amorous pursuits of two young men who face social obstacles when they woo young ladies of quality. 3 acts 6m 4w 2 interiors

In Wilde, O. The importance of being earnest and other plays

Lady Windermere's fan.

Comedy of manners about 19th century English society. Woman with a past returns, saving daughter from ruin. 4 acts 7m 9w 3 interiors

In Wilde, O. The importance of being earnest and other plays

Salome.

Tragedy. Salome dances for Herod Antipas and as her reward claims head of John the Baptist. 1 act 11m 2w extras 1 exterior

In Wilde, O. The importance of being earnest and other plays

A woman of no importance.

Social comedy. Young Englishman's courtship of rich American orphan is complicated by the reappearance of his father after a twenty-five year absence. 4 acts 8m 7w 3 interiors 1 exterior

In Wilde, O. The importance of being earnest and other plays

about

Day, B. Aspects of Oscar

Eagleton, T. Saint Oscar

Hare, D. The Judas kiss

Holland, N. To meet Oscar Wilde

Kaufman, M. Gross indecency: the three trials of Oscar Wilde

Kilroy, T. The secret fall of Constance Wilde

Linney, R. Goodbye, Oscar

Linney, R. Oscar over here

Olmos, C. The dandy of the Savoy

Parodies, imitations, etc.

y Matera, J. The mirror of Dori Gray

Wilder, Thornton

The Alcestiad.

Three-part drama based on the Greek legend of Alcestis, the queen who took her husband's place in death. Performed with The Drunken Sisters. 3

acts 1b 18m 3w extras 1 exterior

In Wilder, T. The collected short plays of Thornton Wilder, v 2

And the sea shall give up its dead.

The dead, resurrected on Judgment Day, cling to their earthly identities. 1 scene 2m 1w 1 exterior

In Wilder, T. The collected short plays of Thornton Wilder, v 2

The angel on the ship.

The last survivors aboard a disabled ship pray to the ship's figurehead for mercy. 1 scene 2m 1w 1 exterior

In Wilder, T. The collected short plays of Thornton Wilder, v 2

The angel that troubled the waters.

Angel refuses to heal a heart-broken doctor. 1 scene 3m 1 setting

In Wilder, T. The collected short plays of Thornton Wilder, v 2

Brother Fire.

A visit from Saint Francis disrupts a peasant household. 1 scene 1g 1w 1m 1 interior

In Wilder, T. The collected short plays of Thornton Wilder, v 2

Centaurs.

The dead Shelley appears at an performance of The Master Builder and claims authorship of the work, and Ibsen agrees. 1 scene 2m 1w 1 interior

In Wilder, T. The collected short plays of Thornton Wilder, v 2

Childe Roland to the dark tower came.

Mortally wounded knight seeks admission to mysterious tower. 1 scene 1m 2w 1 exterior

In Wilder, T. The collected short plays of Thornton Wilder, v 2

The drunken sisters.

Comic pendant to the author's Alcestiad. Apollo gets the three Fates drunk to save the life of King Admetus, with ironic success. 1 act 1m 3w 1 setting

In Wilder, T. The collected short plays of Thornton Wilder, v 2

The Emporium.

Two scenes from an uncompleted play. An orphan, adopted from a surreal orphanage by a brutish farmer, aspires to a place in the fabulous Emporium, a store like nothing on earth. 2 scenes 3m 1w extras 2 interiors

In Wilder, T. The collected short plays of Thornton Wilder, v 2

Wilder, Thornton—*Continued*

Fanny Otcott.

Great actress sweeps aside clergyman's remorse over youthful affair. 1 scene 1m 2w 1 exterior

In Wilder, T. The collected short plays of Thornton Wilder, v 2

The flight into Egypt.

Christ child's survival depends on a garrulous donkey. 1 scene 1m 1w extra 1 setting

In Wilder, T. The collected short plays of Thornton Wilder, v 2

Hast thou considered my servant Job?

Satan loses a contest when his servant Judas foresakes evil. 1 scene 3m 1 setting

In Wilder, T. The collected short plays of Thornton Wilder, v 2

Leviathan.

A mermaid tries to catch a drowning prince's soul. 1 scene 2m 1w 1 exterior

In Wilder, T. The collected short plays of Thornton Wilder, v 2

The long Christmas dinner.

Fantasy. Ninety years of family life recalled during Christmas dinner. 5m 6w extras

In The twelve plays of Christmas; ed. by L. Swortzell

The marriage we deplore.

Social comedy. Boston grande dame entertains son and daughter-in-law, with shudders of disapproval. 1 act 2m 3w 1 interior

In Wilder, T. The collected short plays of Thornton Wilder, v 2

The message and Jehanne.

In Renaissance Paris, inscribed rings are delivered to the wrong parties, with dire results. 1 scene 2m 1w 1 interior

Wilder, T. The collected short plays of Thornton Wilder, v 2

Mozart and the gray steward.

A mysterious stranger commissions a requiem from Mozart. 1 scene 2m 1w 1 interior

In Wilder, T. The collected short plays of Thornton Wilder, v 2

Nascuntur poetae . . .

A not-yet-born soul learns of his fate: to be a poet. 1 scene 1b 2w 1 setting

In Wilder, T. The collected short plays of Thornton Wilder, v 2

Now the servant's name was Malchus.

In Heaven a minor figure from the New Testament is distressed because he looks ridiculous in the Bible account; the Lord sympathizes, having a similar problem. 1 scene 3m 1 setting

In Wilder, T. The collected short plays of Thornton Wilder, v 2

The penny that beauty spent.

A dancer, the king's new favorite, tries to give a royal present to her dying husband. 1 scene 2m 1w 1 interior

In Wilder, T. The collected short plays of Thornton Wilder, v 2

Proserpina and the devil: a play for marionettes.

Marionettes make the wrong moves and puppeteers quarrel at a Venetian street-show, where the Devil has entered Greek mythology. Puppet roles can be played by actors. 1 scene 5m 2w 1 setting

In Wilder, T. The collected short plays of Thornton Wilder, v 2

The unerring instinct.

A woman plays a trick to expose the foolishness of a friend's prejudices. Written in 1947 for the National Conference of Christians and Jews. 1 act 1m 2w 1 interior

In Wilder, T. The collected short plays of Thornton Wilder, v 2

Wilderness wandering. Vogel, L.

Wildwood Park. Wright, D.

Wiley and the Hairy Man. Zeder, S.

Wilhelm, Le

Meridian, Mississippi redux.

A visitor to the site of bloody confrontations during the Civil Rights era discovers that she may be more bigoted than the polite Southern lady who befriends her. 1 act 1 scene 2m 2w 1 interior

In Off-Off Broadway Festival plays, 23rd ser.

The parrot.

Two Southern teenagers from very different backgrounds start a complicated courtship. 1m 1w exterior

In Off-Off Broadway Festival plays, 27th series

A pink Cadillac nightmare.

Over-extended Mary Kay representative gives a hapless friend a facial and a sales pitch. 1 act 2w 1 interior

In Off-Off Broadway Festival plays, 25th ser.

Wilhelm, Le—*Continued*

A significant betrayal.

Drama about woman who turns to uncle who might shed light on her own past. 1 act 1m 1w 1 setting

In Off-Off Broadway festival plays, 24th ser.

Tremulous.

Tragicomedy about two teenage girls who talk about life while planning their suicides. 2g exterior

In Off-Off Broadway Festival plays, 22nd ser.

Wilkins, J. Robert

War letters. Pioneer Drama Service 2000 9p

Soldier on peacekeeping mission overseas corresponds with three women family members he left behind. 1 act 3w 1 interior

Williams, Brian Christopher

Token to the moon.

Comedy. Man who reads thoughts meets a woman in the New York subway. 1m 1w 1 setting

In Actors Theatre of Louisville. Ten-minute plays: v4

Williams, Caroline

Just be frank.

Comedy. Young woman tries to get promotion. 1m 4w 1 interior

In 30 ten-minute plays for 4, 5 & 6 actors from Actors Theatre of Louisville's National Ten-minute Play Contest

—Same

In Actors Theatre of Louisville. Ten-minute plays; v5

Williams, Jesse Lynch

Why marry?

Social comedy satiring the institution of marriage. 3 acts 7m 3w extras 1 interior

In American plays of the new woman; ed. by K. Newlin

Williams, Magi Noninzi

Kwa-landlady.

Young women tenants of a boarding house suffer abuse from the landlord and his bullying wife until a rape unites them in protest. 2 acts 9 scenes

1m 4w settings

In Black South African women; ed. by K. A. Perkins

Williams, Niall

The way you look tonight. New Island Bks. 2000 91p

ISBN 1-902602-31-5   LC 2001-326149

Domestic drama set in rural West Clare, Ireland about retired postmaster, his invalid wife, and three grown children. 2 acts 2m 3w 1 setting

Williams, Roger

Killing kangaroos.

Set in Sydney, Australia in 1999. Stereotypes collapse when Welsh trio arrives for backpacking holiday. 2 acts 8 scenes 5m 3w extras 1 interior

In New Welsh Drama II; ed. by J. Teare

Williams, Roy

Lift off.

When old time school chums begin to outgrow their lifelong friendship, prejudice brought to fore. 2 parts 4m 2w settings

In Williams, R. Plays: 1

The No Boys Cricket Club.

Beaten-down Jamaican born mother in London regains sense of self-worth when old friend helps her revisit her island girlhood. 2 acts 10 scenes 5g 2m 4w settings

In Williams, R. Plays: 1

—Same

In Williams, R. Starstruck and The No Boys Cricket Club

Starstruck.

Whole town goes crazy when Hollywood heart-throb Stewart Granger lands in Kingston, Jamaica to shoot lastest movie. 2 acts 8 scenes 1g 4m 2w 2 exteriors

In Williams, R. Plays: 1

—Same

In Williams, R. Starstruck and The No Boys Cricket Club

Williams, Simon

Kiss of death. French (London) 2003 65p

ISBN 0-573-01984-3

Thriller about actress who attends improvisation workshop and finds herself auditioning to be bait for real-life serial killer. 2 acts 6 scenes 3m 3w 1 setting

Williams, Simon—*Continued*

Laying the ghost. French (London) 2001 63p

ISBN 0-573-01854-5

Comedy about retired actress's ex-husband who dies during a performance, only to have his ghost return in act two. 2 acts 2m 5w 1 setting

Nobody's perfect. French (London) 2000 70p

ISBN 0-573-01819-7

Comedy about unsuccessful novelist who uses a female pseudonym to get his book published. 2 acts 3m 2w 1 setting

Williams, Tennessee, 1911-1983

Baby Doll (adaptation) See Bailey, L. Baby doll

27 wagons full of cotton.

Southern degenerate gets work for his cotton gin by setting fire to rival's plantation. 1 act 3 scenes 2m 1w extras 1 setting

In Williams, T. Plays, 1937-1955

And tell sad stories of the death of queens.

Drama about drag queen in New Orleans in early 1940s. 3 scenes 4m 1 setting

In Political stages; ed. by E. Mann and D. Roessel

Auto-da-fe.

In revolt against the degeneracy of his section of New Orleans, fanatical man sets fire to his mother's home. 1 act 1m 1w 1 exterior

In Williams, T. Plays, 1937-1955

Battle of angels.

Symbolic drama set in Southern town about storekeeper, unhappily married to invalid, who takes in handsome young hobo writer. Prologue 3 acts 5 scenes 11m 11w 1 interior

In Williams, T. Plays, 1937-1955

Camino Real.

Expressionistic drama set in desert town. Great romantic figures from literature and history languish under brutal control of unseen tyrant. Music, singing, dancing. Prologue 16 scenes Large mixed cast 1 exterior

In Williams, T. Plays, 1937-1955

The eccentricities of a nightingale.

Drama about promiscuous daughter of clergyman in small Mississippi town shortly before World War I. Music, singing. 3 acts 9 scenes epilogue 5m 5w 4 interiors 1 exterior

In Williams, T. Plays, 1957-1980

Fugitive kind; edited, with an introduction, by Allean Hale. New Directions 2001 147p

ISBN 0-8112-1472-9　　　　LC 00-67321

Drama set 1937 in St. Louis slum. Relationship develops between daughter of flop-house operator and most-wanted mobster on the lam. 8 scenes 17m 4w extras 1 interior

The glass menagerie.

Family drama set in run-down St. Louis tenement. Frustrated former Southern belle persuades rebellious son to provide "gentleman caller" for her grippled daughter. Background music. 2 parts 7 scenes 2m 2w 1 setting

In Williams, T. Plays, 1937-1955

I rise in flame, cried the phoenix.

D. H. Lawrence moments before death 1 act 1m 2w 1 interior

In Williams, T. Plays, 1937-1955

Kingdom of earth.

Domestic drama set on flood-threatened Mississippi farm. Woman caught between conflicting desires of transvestite husband and his virile brother. Singing. 2 acts 7 scenes 2m 1w 1 interior

In Williams, T. Plays, 1957-1980

The lady of Larkspur Lotion.

Wretchedly furnished room in New Orleans lodging house scene of confrontation between landlady, a faded Southern belle reduced to prostitution, and struggling writer. 1 act 1m 2w 1 interior

In Williams, T. Plays, 1937-1955

The last of my solid gold watches.

Aged traveling salesman in Mississippi attempts to come to terms with changes wrought by the passage of years. 1 act 3m 1 interior

In Williams, T. Plays, 1937-1955

Lord Byron's love letter.

Two old women claim that they possess one of Byron's love letters which they show to visitors for a small fee. Background music. 1m 3w 1 interior

In Williams, T. Plays, 1937-1955

A lovely Sunday for Creve Coeur.

St. Louis high school teacher spruned by principal for another woman. 2 scenes 4w extras 1 interior

In Williams, T. Plays, 1957-1980

The milk train doesn't stop here anymore.

Mysterious young poet helps dying musical comedy star prepare for her death. Prologue 6 scenes 5m 4w extras 1 setting

In Williams, T. Plays, 1957-1980

Williams, Tennessee, 1911-1983—*Continued*

The mutilated.

Interaction between two lonely prostitutes in fleabag hotel in New Orleans. One is an alcoholic, the other has be "muliated" by a mastectomy. Singing. 7 scenes 9m 4w 2 interiors 2 exteriors
In Williams, T. Plays, 1957-1980

The night of the iguana.

Renegade clergyman, dying poet, and sex-hungry teenager among lost souls whose lives intersect in shabby hotel on Mexican coast in 1940. Background music. 3 acts 8m 6w 1 exterior
In Williams, T. Plays, 1957-1980

Not about nightingales.

Drama about convicts on hunger strike locked in steam-heated cell and roasted to death. 3 acts 22 episodes 1b 13m 3w extras 1 setting
In Political stages; ed. by E. Mann and D. Roessel

—Same
In Williams, T. Plays, 1937-1955

—Same; Tennessee Williams; edited, with an introduction, by Allean Hale; foreword by Vanessa Redgrave. New Directions 1998 163p
ISBN 0-8112-1380-3   LC 97-47779

Not about nightingales (condensation).
In The Best Plays of 1998-1999; ed. by Otis L. Guernsey, Jr.

The notebook of Trigorin; the notebook of Trigorin based on a translation from the Russian by Ann Dunnigan. Dramatists 1997 67p
ISBN 0-8222-1597-7
Free adaptation of Chekhov's The Seagull. Story of young writer who seeks love and acceptance in his artistic endeavours. 4 acts 7m 6w

Out cry.

Variant title: The two-character play. Fantasy. Two actors abandoned by their troupe perform two-character play. 2 parts 1m 1w 1 setting
In Williams, T. Plays, 1957-1980

Period of adjustment.

Comedy of marital problems: a man and new bride drop in on army buddy whose wife has just left him. 3 acts 4m 5w 1 interior
In Williams, T. Plays, 1957-1980

Portrait of a Madonna.

Middle-aged, genteel spinster's delusions concerning youthful romantic disappointment finally culminates in insanity. 1 act 1m 2w extras 1 interior
In Williams, T. Plays, 1937-1955

The rose tattoo.

Drama set in Gulf Coast town about sexual salvation of Sicilian American widow. Music, singing. 3 acts 10 scenes 2b 2g 7m 12w 1 setting
In Williams, T. Plays, 1937-1955

Small craft warnings.

Tragedy. Cast-offs of society congregate in Monk's Place, a shabby bar off Pacific Coast of California. 2 acts 7m 2w 1 interior
In Williams, T. Plays, 1957-1980

Spring storm.

Tragedy set in small Mississippi town in 1937 about four young people whose love lives intertwine. 3 acts 7 scenes 7m 15w 2 interiors 2 exteriors
In Williams, T. Plays, 1937-1955

—Same; edited by Dan Isaac. New Directions 1999 166p
ISBN 0-8112-1422-2

Stairs to the roof; a prayer for the wild of heart that are kept in cages; edited, with an introduction, by Allean Hale. New Directions 2000 101p
ISBN 0-8112-1435-4
Expressionist comedy set in 1941 America. Wage-slave rebels against regimentation of office life, forsakes his pregnant wife and goes on urban, night prowl with secretary smitten by love for her boss. 19 scenes 17m 8w extras 5 interiors 4 exteriors

A streetcar named Desire.

Young widow warped by tragic marriage comes to live with sister and brother-in-law in New Orleans where further violence causes mental breakdown. Music. 11 scenes 6m 6w 2 interiors 1 exterior
In Williams, T. Plays, 1937-1955

Suddenly last summer.

Lurid tale of new Orleans matriarch who attempts to conceal truth about murder of decadent homosexual son. 4 scenes 2m 5w 1 interior
In Williams, T. Plays, 1957-1980

Williams, Tennessee, 1911-1983—*Continued*

Summer and smoke.

Puritanical minister's daughter in stagnant Mississippi town thwarted in her love for young doctor becomes promiscuous. Music. Prologue 2 parts 12 scenes 7m 6w 1b 1g extras 1 setting

In Williams, T. Plays, 1937-1955

Sweet bird of youth.

Tale of aging Hollywood diva and her gigolo, set against social background of Southern racist politics. Music, singing. 3 acts 5 scenes 12m 7w extras 3 interiors

In Williams, T. Plays, 1957-1980

This property is condemned.

Imaginative adolescent girl identifies with dead prostitute sister she adored. Singing. 1 act 1b 1g 1 exterior

In Williams, T. Plays, 1937-1955

Vieux Carré.

Writer recalls his stay at rooming house in New Orleans French Quarter in 1938, where he learns about life from the resident artists, homosexuals, drifters and other desperate characters. Music. 2 acts 12 scenes 5m 5w extras 1 interior

In Williams, T. Plays, 1957-1980

about

Foley, D. Sad hotel

Scheffer, W. Tennessee and me

Parodies, imitations, etc.

Morley, M. The glass mendacity

Williamson, Dave. See Shields, C. jt. auth.

Williamson, David

Corporate vibes.

An idealistic Human Resources Officer, hired to eliminate the "dead wood" at a failing firm, defies the ogrish boss and gives the demoralized staff a second chance. 2 acts 3m 4w 4 interiors 1 exterior

In Williamson, D. Two plays

Dead white males.

Academic satire aimed at political correctness, poststructuralism, radical feminism and multiculturalism. Australian coed and trendy critic cope with Shakespeare's legacy. 2 acts 5m 6w 1 setting

In Contemporary Australian plays; ed. by R. Vandenbroucke

Face to face.

A conference assembled to decide the fate of a young man likely to be charged with assault becomes a wrenching inquiry into workplace dynamics, teasing, and macho attitudes. 1 act 1 scene 6m 4w 1 interior

In Williamson, D. Two plays

The great man.

Family, friends and party faithful gather for funeral of grand old man of Australian Labor Party. 4m 3w 1 interior

In Williamson, D. The great man and Sancutary

Money and friends. Dramatists 1997 74p

ISBN 0-8222-1580-2   LC 98-115331

Drama about two Australian academics at a weekend getaway with wealthy friends. When one of the academics reveals his true feelings, emotions and friendship are tested. 2 acts 18 scenes 5m 4w 1 setting

Sanctuary.

Drama set in Queensland, Australia. Retired internatonally renowned investigative journalist beset by intrepid young biographer. 2 acts 2m 1 interior

In Williamson, D. The great man and Sancutary

Willie Stark. Warren, R. P.

Willmorth, Tom. See Armstrong, D. jt. auth.

Willmott, Phil

Around the world in eighty days; book, music and lyrics by Phil Willmott; additional music and arrangement by Annemarie Lewis Thomas. French (London) 2003 83p

ISBN 0-573-08120-4

Freely adapted from Jules Verne's novel. Story of adventures of Phileas Fogg and Passepartout. Music, singing. 2 acts 28 scenes Large mixed cast

Wills

Miller, E. Last will and testament

Wilner, Sheri

Bake off.

Baking contest brings out the worst in the contestants. 1 act 2m 1w 1 interior

In Humana Festival 2002

Hunger.

Surreal drama set on Nantucket about woman who has just accepted marriage proposal. 1 act 4 scenes 2m 1w 2 interiors 2 exteriors

In New playwrights: the best plays of 1999

Wilner, Sheri—*Continued*

Joan of Arkansas.

Two college students strike up conversation in reading room of large university. 1 act 1 interior 1m 1w
> *In* 30 ten-minute plays for 2 actors from Actors Theatre of Louisville's National Ten-minute Play Contest

Labor Day.

Friends attend annual Labor Day party. Variable cast 6 characters 1 setting
> *In* 30 ten-minute plays for 4, 5 & 6 actors from Actors Theatre of Louisville's National Ten-minute Play Contest

—Same
> *In* Actors Theatre of Louisville: Ten-minute plays; v5

Relative strangers.

Comedy. Young airline passenger decides woman seated next to her might be mother she never had. 3w 1 interior
> *In* The Best American short plays, 2000-2001

—Same
> *In* Women's Project & productions; ed. by J. Miles

Wilson, August

The janitor.

Middle-age janitor gives heart felt speech on youth in front of empty ballroom. 2m 1 setting
> *In* take ten; ed. by E. Lane and N. Shengold

Jitney. French 2002 80p
> ISBN 0-573-62795-9

Drama set in 1977 about gypsy cab drivers at a gypsy cab station in Pittsburgh, Pennsylvania. 2 acts 8 scenes 8m 1w 1 interior

Jitney (condensation).
> *In* The Best Plays of 1999-2000; ed. by Otis L. Guernsey, Jr.

Wilson, Cressida

Hurricane.

In series of scenes criss-crossing the country and culminating in Africa, women of today—of all ages and in all stages of life—struggle to make sense of their fragmented lives and find strength.

Prologue 5 scenes 2m 7w extras settings
> *In* Women playwrights: the best plays of 1998

Wilson, David Henry

How to make your theater pay. French (London) 2002 16p
> ISBN 0-573-02352-2

Comedy about a council official who wants to convert a theater into a storage space for files, in order to save the council money. 2m 1w

Wilson, Jonathan

Kilt. Playwrights Canada 1998 96p
> ISBN 0-88754-583-1

Family comedy. Dancer in gay strip club returns to Glasgow for funeral of his World War II vet grandfather and uncovers many family secrets. 2 acts 3m 2w 1 setting

Wilson, Lanford

Angels fall.

Road closing because of nuclear power plant accident strands group of people in remote New Mexico mission. 2 acts 4m 2w 1 interior
> *In* Wilson, L. Collected works v2, 1970-1983

Book of days. Dramatist Play Service 2001 82p
> ISBN 0-8222-1767-8

Drama about murder in Missouri town. Local woman searches for truth amid small town jealousies, religion, greed and lies. 2 acts 6m 5w Speaking chorus 1 setting

—Same. Grove Press 2000 105p
> ISBN 0-8021-3741-5

Fifth of July.

Set on Talley farmhouse in Missouri, Independence Day, 1977. Ken Talley, crippled in Vietnam war, plays host to group of former student activists. 2 acts 4m 4w 1 setting
> *In* Wilson, L. Collected works v3: the Talley trilogy

The Hot L Baltimore.

Residents of a hotel about to be demolished recall their lives and dreams. 3 acts 5m 7w extras 1 interior
> *In* Wilson, L. Collected works v2, 1970-1983

The mound builders.

Two archeologists, their families and assistants dig in Southern Illinois for cultural history of Indian mound builders. Interplay of characters and

Wilson, Lanford—*Continued*

contrast of Indian versus present culture is accentuated. 2 acts 1g 3m 3w 1 setting

> *In* Wilson, L. Collected works v2, 1970-1983

Serenading Louie.

Crisis point in lives of two young suburban couples. 2 acts 6 scenes 2m 2w 1 interior

> *In* Wilson, L. Collected works v2, 1970-1983

Sympathetic magic. Dramatists 1998 74p

> ISBN 0-8222-1630-2   LC 98-231835

Philosophical drama explores mysteries of the universe and of human and artistic creation. Young astrophysicist's life turned upside down when his lover has abortion against his wishes. 2 acts 5m 3w

Talley & son.

Earlier version produced under title: A tale told. Third play in Talley family cycle. Business decisions pit Eldon Talley against both his father and his older son. 2 acts 6m 6w 1 interior

> *In* Wilson, L. Collected works v3: the Talley trilogy

Talley's folly.

Part of cycle about Talley family of Lebanon, Missouri. Victorian boathouse known as Talley's Folly is setting for Jewish accountant's courtship of Sally Talley. 1 act 1m 1w 1 interior

> *In* Wilson, L. Collected works v3: the Talley trilogy

Your everyday ghost story.

As thirty-something man's gay friends suffer and evanesce physically, he becomes increasingly insubstantial spiritually. 2m 1 setting

> *In* The Best American short plays, 1996-1997

Wilson, Lauren

Chateau La Roach. Pioneer Drama Service 2002 72p

Farce. French proprietors of chateau on shores of American lake face infestation of cockroaches. 2 acts 5 scenes 8m 11w 1 setting

Wilson, Snoo

Blowjob.

Drama about violence and cost of role-playing. Two English skinheads bungle robbery in factory. 4m 1w

> *In* Wilson, S. Plays: 1

Darwin's flood.

Comic exploration of time and human personality featuring Charles Darwin, Friedrich Nietzsche, Jesus and Mary Magdalene. 3 acts 5m 4w 1 interior 1 exterior

> *In* Wilson, S. Plays: 1

The glad hand.

Fascist millionaire and group of unusual characters travel on oil tanker to Bermuda Triangle in hopes of travelling back in history to find and shoot Antichrist. Background music. 2 acts 8 scenes 9m 4w 1 interior

> *In* Wilson, S. Plays: 2

The grass widow.

Comedy. Following man's death, friends gather at his California estate to stake their claim to their inheritance: fifty acres of marijuana. 2 acts 2m 2w 1 exterior

> *In* Wilson, S. Plays: 2

More light.

Experimental drama about hypocrisy and paronoia. Portrays life of heretic Giordano Bruno, executed in 1600 for positing sun as center of universe. Set in heaven with cast of characters that includes Shakespeare, the Pope and Elizabeth I. 2 acts 4m 3w 1 setting

> *In* Wilson, S. Plays: 1

Pignight.

Sinister comedy about savagery and violence. Lincolnshire farm taken over by gangster and turned into machine for butchering and processing of swine. 5m extra 1 setting

> *In* Wilson, S. Plays: 1

Sabina.

Surreal look at founders of modern psychology. Freud and Jung portrayed as disturbed megalomaniacs. 2 acts 5m 3w settings

> *In* Wilson, S. Plays: 2

The soul of the white ant.

Surreal comedy about racial murder in South Africa and its subsequent cover-up. 1 act 6 scenes 3m 3w 1 setting

> *In* Wilson, S. Plays: 1

Vampire.

Experimental play spanning one hundred years, about how women have dealt with issues of sex, politics, war, death, religion, and social unrest. 3 acts 4 scenes Variable cast 26 characters 1 setting

> *In* Wilson, S. Plays: 2

Wilson, William Griffth

                         about

Shem, S. Bill W. and Dr. Bob

Wiltse, David

Otis proposes.

Aphasic old publisher struggles to propose to editor, who has decided she prefers women. 1 act 1m 1w 1 interior

In Wiltse, D. Triangles for two: failures in communication

Temporary. French 2000 79p

ISBN 0-573-62724-X   LC 2001-278087

Play noir about Nebraska farm couple who murder their hired hand. 2 acts 7 scenes 3m 1w 1 setting

To wit and to whom.

Black comedy. A conversation between husband and wife, with a decidedly sinsiter subtext. 1 act 1m 1w 1 interior

In Wiltse, D. Triangles for two: failures in communication

Triangles for two.

Husband and wife seem prepared to bicker over everything, including the differences between men and women and the nature of communication. 1 act 1m 1w 1 interior

In Wiltse, D. Triangles for two: failures in communication

Wimberly, Bridgette

Saint Lucy's eyes. French (London) 2003 57p

ISBN 0-573-62931-5

Drama set in Memphis, Tennessee in 1968, about issue of illegal abortions. 3 acts 2 scenes 1m 3w 1 interior

—Same

In Women playwrights: the best plays of 2001

Winding the ball. Finlayson, A.

Windshook. Gallagher, M.

Windsor, Wallis Warfield, Duchess of, 1896-1986

about

Griffiths, L. The Duchess, a.k.a. Wallis Simpson

Wing, Paula

c The King of Ireland's son.

Based on Irish folklore. King of Ireland's son finds girl held captive by giant. Singing. 2 acts 5m 3w 1 exterior

In Seattle Children's Theatre v2

The **winged** man. Rivera, J.

Wings. Kopit, A. L.

Winner takes all. Feydeau, G.

Wintersleep. Blais, M.-C.

Winther, Barbara

c Brother Rabbit sells corn.

Based on Hispanic folktale. Sly rabbit tries to trick friends into buying same barrel of corn again and again. 1 act 2 scenes Unidentified cast 5 characters 2 exteriors

In Winther, B. Plays from Hispanic tales

c El caballito of seven colors.

Based on Hispanic folktale. Boy granted three wishes by magic horse. 1 act 3 scenes 5m 2w extra 1 setting

In Winther, B. Plays from Hispanic tales

c The deer dance.

Drama with dancing about deer hurt based on Hispanic folklore. Music, dancing. 1 act 2b 1m 1w extras 1 exterior

In Winther, B. Plays from Hispanic tales

c The ghost of El Castillo.

Based on Hispanic folktale. Tinker uses common sense to rid castle of ghost. 1 act 4m 4m 1 interior 2 exteriors

In Winther, B. Plays from Hispanic tales

c A gift for Pachacuti Inca.

Based on Hispanic folktale. When new Pachacuti Inca king is crowned, every family must present him with a gift. 1 act 4 scenes Variable cast 10 characters 4 exteriors

In Winther, B. Plays from Hispanic tales

c The great hurricane.

Based on Hispanic folktale. Battle of wits between animals. 1 act Unidentified cast 5 characters 1 exterior

In Winther, B. Plays from Hispanic tales

c Latino trio: Hormiga's lawsuit.

Based on Hispanic folktale. Ant blames God for his misfortune. 1 act 1 scene 1m 1 interior

In Winther, B. Plays from Hispanic tales

Winther, Barbara—*Continued*

c Latino trio: Pedro's holey sombrero.

Based on Hispanic folktale. Poor man tricks wealthy man into buying old sombrero by telling him it's magic. 1 act 4m 1 exterior

In Winther, B. Plays from Hispanic tales

c Latino trio: Senorita Cucaracha finds a husband.

Pantomime based on Hispanic folktales. Cockroach is trying to find husband, but each potential suitor must sing for her. 1 act 4m 1w extra 1 setting

In Winther, B. Plays from Hispanic tales

c Macona, the honest warrior.

Based on Hispanic folktale. Warrior hides in the bushes to catch the thief who has been stealing his fish. 1 act 2 scenes 5m 2w extras 2 exteriors

In Winther, B. Plays from Hispanic tales

c Pedro de Urdemalas.

Trickster outwits wealthy landowner. Based on Hispanic folklore. 3m 3w extras 3 exteriors

In Winther, B. Plays from Hispanic tales

c The sleeping mountains.

Based on Hispanic folktale. Story of two volcanoes in Mexico and how they came to be. 1 act 3 scenes 7m 4w extras 3 exteriors

In Winther, B. Plays from Hispanic tales

—Same

In Winther, B. Plays from Hispanic tales

c The talking burro.

Based on Hispanic folktale. Burro granted human voice and takes off to see the world. Singing. 1 act 4 scenes Variable cast 12 characters 4 exteriors

In Winther, B. Plays from Hispanic tales

Winton, Tim

Cloudstreet (dramatization) See Enright, N., and Monjo, J. Cloudstreet

Lockie Leonard, scumbuster (dramatization) See Fry, G. Lockie Leonard, scumbuster

The **wisdom** of Solomon. McCullough, L. E.

The **wise** men and women of Chelm. McCullough, L. E.

The **wise** men of Chelm. Asher, S. F.

Wishes

c Winther, B. El caballito of seven colors

Wit. Edson, M.

Wit (condensation). Edson, M.

The **witch** of Blackbird Pond. York, Y.

Witchcraft

Bailey, B. Ipi zombi?

c Hamlett, C. Eat, drink, and be scary

c Korty, C. Baba Yaga and the black sunflower

Sturgill, B. The enchantress of Ipswich

c York, Y. The witch of Blackbird Pond

With the McMillans on the Oregon Trail. Fredericks, A. D.

Within the gates. O'Casey, S.

Without skin or breathlessness. Barfield, T.

Witkiewicz, Stanisław Ignacy

The cuttlefish; or, The Hyrcanian worldview; tr. by Daniel C. and Eleanor S. Gerould.

Surrealistic comedy. Artist/philosopher bored by life's mediocrity encounters ghost of Renaissance Pope who espouses absoluteness of art versus relativity of existence and king who seeks to impose absolutes on existence by creating realm for supermen. 1 act 6m 4w 1 interior

In Theater of the avant-garde, 1890-1950; ed. by B. Cardullo and R. Knopf

Wittgenstein, Ludwig, 1889-1951

about

Hall, L. Wittgenstein on Tyne

Wittgenstein on Tyne. Hall, L.

WM. Wang Peigong

Woldin, Judd

Murder in Baker Street. French 2003 63p

ISBN 0-573-62904-8

Comedy mystery. Murdered tycoon found in Sherlock Holmes' house. Dr. Watson is the prime suspect. 2 acts 23 scenes 1b 15m 4w 1 setting

Wolf, Marc

Another American: asking and telling.

Drama about gays and lesbians in the U.S. military. Prologue 2 acts Large mixed cast

In Political stages; ed. by E. Mann and D. Roessel

The **wolf** and its shadows. Asher, S. F.

The **wolf** and the seven kids. McBride-Smith, B.

Wolf child. Mast, E.

Wolff, Ruth

The abdication. Dramatic Publishing 2003 116p

In 1655, Christina of Sweden abdicates the throne, gives up Protestantism to become a Catholic and arrives in Rome expecting to be welcomed by the Pope. Instead, she is forced to face an intensive examination of her life and motives by Cadinal Assolino—with whom, shockingly and unexpectedly, she falls in love. 2 acts 6m 4w 1 setting

Wolfman, Judy

c The golden goose. Pioneer Drama Service 2001 26p

Dramatization of German folktale about simple woodsman who wins princess' hand by making her laugh. 3 scenes 8m 7w 1 interior 2 exteriors

Wolfsbane. Nigro, D.

A **woman** alone. Rame, F., and Fo, D.

Woman far walking. Ihimaera, W.

The **woman** from Samos. Menander

The **woman** in the window. De Groen, A.

A **woman** killed with kindness. Heywood, T.

A **woman** of no importance. Wilde, O.

The **woman** who was a red deer dressed for the deer dance. Glancy, D.

A **woman** without a name. Linney, R.

Woman's wit; or, The lady in fashion. Cibber, C.

Women

Anthony, T. 'Da kink in my hair

Bailey, M. Sistahs

Bogdan, K. Annette and Annette

Box, M. Angels of war

Bradley, J. Digging for ladies

Bush, D. Sailing to America

Carr, M. The Mai

Carter, R. A yearning

Clements, M. Now look what you made me do

Devlin, A. Ourselves alone

Ensler, E. The Vagina monologues

Five Lesbian Brothers (Theater company). The secretaries

Fréchette, C. The four lives of Marie

Griffiths, A. Bittergirl

Griffiths, L. Jessica

Hall, T. Jean and Dinah who have been locked away in a world famous calypso since 1956 speak their minds publicly

Hamilton, W. A. Bellies, knees and ankles

Hardin, H. Esker Mike & his wife, Agiluk

Hutton, A. The price you pay

Ibsen, H. The lady from the sea

Ihimaera, W. Woman far walking

Kreidl, M. Grateful women

Lask, B. Liberation (Die Befreiung)

Lauro, S. Railing it uptown

Lavery, B. Origin of the species

Laxdal, V. Cyber:/womb

Levy, D. The B file

Levy, D. Pax

Luckham, C. Trafford Tanzi

MacDonald, A.-M. Goodnight Desdemona (good morning Juliet)

Marnich, M. Quake

Martin, N. Women on the verge of HRT

McGuinness, F. The stronger

Orlandersmith, D. Beauty's daughter

Palmer, T. Body talk

Quilter, P. Respecting your piers

Rebeck, T. Sunday on the rocks

Redgrave, L. Shakespeare for my father

Shear, C. Blown sideways through life

Smith, A. Trace of Arc

Son, D. R. A. W. ('cause I'm a woman)

Stephenson, S. An experiment with an air pump

Strindberg, A. The stronger

Tait, L. Jesus and the monkfish

Van Druten, J. Make way for Lucia

Vooght, C. Bright interval

Walker, G. F. Better living

Wertenbaker, T. The love of the nightingale

Wesker, A. Annie Wobbler

Women artists

Cram, C. Landlocked

Glancy, D. The women who loved house trailers

LaBute, N. The shape of things

Women at four o'clock. Powell, D.

Women authors

Crothers, R. A man's world

Gow, D. Bea's niece

Griffiths, L. Alien creature

Norman, M. Trudy Blue

Pedrero, P. First star (Una estrella)

Rebeck, T. Does this woman have a name?

Sherman, J. The retreat

Taylor, R. Escape from paradise

Women in motion. Margulies, D.

Women in power. Aristophanes

The **women** of Lockerbie. Brevoort, D. B.

Women of the dust. Carter, R.

The **women** of Trachis. Sophocles

Women on the verge of HRT. Martin, N.

Women physicians

Romero, E. ¡Curanderas! serpents of the clouds

Women scientists

c McCullough, L. E. Mothers and daughters of invention: 4,000 years of women in science

The **women** who loved house trailers. Glancy, D.

Women's Theatre Group

Lear's daughters.

Prequel to Shakespeare's drama. Story of childhood in Lear's court and examination of effects of child abuse. 16 scenes 5w

In Mythic women/Real women

The **wonderful** tower of Humbert Lavoignet. Alvarez, L.

Wonderful world. Dresser, R.

Wonderland!. Francoeur, B.

Wonderland. Yew, C.

Wonders of the invisible world revealed. Nigro, D.

Wong, Elizabeth

c Boid & Oskar. Dramatic Publishing 2003 33p

Inspired by Oscar Wilder's The Happy Prince. With help of wisecracking sparrow, prince makes it his mission to help townspeople. Variable cast 1 setting

c The happy prince. Dramatic Publishing 2003 47p

Dramatization of Oscar Wilde's classic fairy tale. Tells the story of a migrating swallow who befriends a prince made of stone. Variable cast 10 characters 1 setting

Let the big dog eat.

Four wealthy friends discuss business and life during round of golf. 4m 1 exterior

In 30 ten-minute plays for 4, 5 & 6 actors from Actors Theatre of Louisville's National Ten-minute Play Contest

—Same

In Actors Theatre of Louisville. Ten-minute plays; v5

—Same

In Humana Festival '98

Letters to a student revolutionary.

Chinese woman and Chinese American woman chafe against societies that confine them. 1 act epilogue 3m 3w 1 setting

In Multicultural theatre II; ed. by R. Ellis

Wood, Charles

Across from the garden of Allah.

English screenwriter and bitter actress wife ridicule denizens of Hollywood hotel. 2 acts Variable cast 1 interior

In Wood, C. Plays: one

Dingo.

Satire about stupidity of war from perspective of British soldiers in desert during World War II. Music. 2 acts 6 scenes 10m extras 4 settings

In Wood, C. Plays: two

H; or, Monologues at front of burning cities.

Verse play about the British Army's involvement in Sepoy Rebellion in India. 2 Prologues 3 acts 24 scenes epilogue 16m 1w 1 setting

In Wood, C. Plays: two

Wood, Charles—*Continued*

Jingo.

Plight of British during fall of Singapore in 1942. Prologue 8 scenes epilogue 7m 2w 1 setting

In Wood, C. Plays: two

Veterans; or, Hairs in the gates of Hellespont.

Satire look at British film industry focuses on life on location in Turkey. 2 acts 7 scenes 7m 2w settings

In Wood, C. Plays: one

Wood, David

c The gingerbread man.

Musical play with audience participation. Salt cellar and paper-mill help cuckoo clock regain voice. 2 acts 4m 2w

In Wood, D. Plays: 1

c The ideal gnome expedition.

Musical play about two garden gnomes rescue stray ducks from dustbin. Unidentified cast 6 characters 2 acts 6 scenes 1 setting

In Wood, D. Plays: 1

c More adventures of Noddy; adapted by David Wood. French (London) 1998 67p

ISBN 0-573-05117-8

Musical fantasy based on Enid Blyton's children's books about a toy man and his Toyland friends. Puppets. 2 acts 14 scenes Variable cast 17 characters

c Mother Goose's golden Christmas.

Musical featuring nursery rhyme characters. Action centered on capture and rescue of Goose with the Golden eggs. 2 acts 11 scenes Variable cast

In Wood, D. Plays: 1

c The see-saw tree.

Musical about the ecological effects of cutting down a three-hundred-year old oak tree. 2 acts 4m 4w 1 interior 2 exteriors

In Wood, D. Plays: 1

c Spot's birthday party; based on the books by Eric Hill; music and lyrics by David Wood. French (London) 2002 58p

ISBN 0-573-05129-1

Play based on Eric Hill's series about Spot the puppy. Spot and his animal friends celebrate his birthday. Audience participation. Music, singing. 2 acts 5m 2w 1 interior

c Tom's midnight garden. French (London) 2001 74p

ISBN 0-573-05127-5

Time travel. Two lonely children who share a house become friends, although the boy is living in the twentieth century and the girl in the nineteenth. Adaptation of a children's book by Philippa Pearce. Music. 2 acts 23 scenes 5m 3w extras settings

c The Twits. Dramatic Publishing 2003 62p

Dramatization of Roald Dahl's tale. Set in circus ring. Narrator acts as ringmaster, bringing to life the story of grotesque satisfyingly unpleasant couple, who enjoy playing nasty tricks on each other. 2 acts Variable cast 9 characters 1 setting

—Same. French (London) 2000 45p

ISBN 0-573-05125-9

Wood, Silviana

And where was Pancho Villa when you really needed him?

Spanish-speaking children learn that their pretty sixth-grade teacher considers them hopeless cases, with consequences in later life. Singing. 1 act 2m 2w extra 1 setting

In Puro teatro; ed. by A. Sandoval-Sánchez and N. S. Sternbach

Wood, Tom

Claptrap. Buffalo, Simon & Pierre 1998 113p

ISBN 0-88924-279-8   LC 98-205977

Comedy about Canadian theater festival which turns its host town into an Ibsenesque period piece. 2 acts 9 scenes 8m 5w 1 setting

The **wood** demon. Chekhov, A. P.

The **wood** of the whispering. Molloy, M. J.

The **wooden** cart. Sharma, T.

Woodford, Karen

Cactus Pass. Pioneer Drama Service 2001 36p

Comedy set in Arizona. When their Rolls Royce motor home breaks down snooty family plays role in ending 80-year-old feud. 2 act 7 scenes 10m 15w 1 setting

c If the shoe fits. Pioneer Drama Service 2000 32p

Tradition dictates that prince attend ball and choose bride. 2 acts 10 scenes 12m 15w 1 interior

Woods, Jill

Inheritance. French (London) 2000 23p

ISBN 0-573-13255-0

Three sisters eagerly await mother's death following a fall which may not have been accidental. 4w 1 interior

Woods, Sarah

Trips. Oberon Bks. 1999 128p

ISBN 1-84002-110-1

Comedy about six Birmingham housemates on a night out searching for excitement. Music. 4 acts 14 scenes 3m 3w 1 setting

Wooed and viewed. Feydeau, G.

Woolf, Benjamin Edward

Off to the war.

Farce set during Civil War mixing romance with politics. 1 act 6m 3w 1 interior

In Fateful lightning; ed. by W. J. Meserve and M. A. Meserve

Woolf, Christine

Treseder's seeds. Playwrights Publishing Co. 17p

ISBN 1-873139-21-X

Drama about four women bound for New Zealand on a sailing ship in 1843. 1 act 6w 1 setting

Woolf, Wendy

y King Artie and the Knights of the Rad Table; book and lyrics by Pat Lydersen; music by Wendy Woolf. Pioneer Drama Service 1997 50p

Musical. Merlin wakes from 1,500 year nap and sweeps two teenagers away to days of chivalry. 7 scenes Variable cast 1 setting

Woolfson, Malcolm

c Bushveld bibble babble. Anchorage Press 2001 87p

ISBN 0-87602-375-8

Dramatization of eight traditional African animal tales. Music, singing, dancing. 2 acts 4b 4g extras 1 setting

Woolley, Joan

You can't be serious. Playwrights Canada 1998 86p

ISBN 1-873130-16-3

Members of a provincial British tennis club trade insults and innuendos in the course of a committee meeting and an important match. Background music. 2 acts 5 scenes 6m 5w 2 interiors 1 exterior

Woozey woo! Macadaeg, R.

A **word** from our sponsor. Pattison, J.

Working

Clark, R. Pierre and Marie

Cleveland, R. Jerry and Tom

Elwell, J. S. Evening education

Glass, J. M. Play memory

Lindsay-Abaire, D. Snapshot: history lesson

Wilhelm, L. A pink Cadillac nightmare

Williamson, D. Corporate vibes

Williamson, D. Face to face

Workout. Wasserstein, W.

World War, 1914-1918

Box, M. Angels of war

c Fredericks, A. D. March 1917: in a coffee shop

Handy, P. East of the sun and west of the moon

Lask, B. Liberation (Die Befreiung)

Massicotte, S. Mary's wedding

O'Casey, S. The silver tassie

Thomson, R. H. The lost boys

Naval operations

O'Neill, E. In the zone

World War, 1939-1945

Gilroy, F. D. Contact with the enemy

Gilroy, F. D. Getting in

Gilroy, F. D. The subject was roses

Gilroy, F. D. The viewing

Wood, C. Dingo

Wood, C. Jingo

Atrocities

Weiss, P. The investigation

Canada

Horovitz, I. A Rosen by any other name

Horovitz, I. Today, I am a fountain pen

Denmark

Mills, S. The Danish Play

France

y Jones, E. Y. Not on this night

Great Britain

Holman, R. Being friends

World War, 1939-1945—*Continued*
Ireland
McGuinness, F. Dolly West's kitchen
United States
Gurney, A. R. Ancestral voices: a family story

World without memory. Kramer, S.

Worship programs
Anderson, S. J. The big one
Anderson, S. J. Echoes of Christmas
Anderson, S. J. Epiphany mosaic
Anderson, S. J. Hanging on the tree
c Anderson, S. J. "Jingle bells" revisited
Anderson, S. J. Live from Bethlehem
Anderson, S. J. The night before pageant
Anderson, S. J. Now a shepherd, no longer a sheep
Anderson, S. J. Oh, come on, Emmanuel
Anderson, S. J. Tidings of comfort and joy
Anderson, S. J. A traditional pageant
Anderson, S. J. Traveling with reservations
Anderson, S. J. While you were out
Bass, A. The redeemer of minutes
Bass, A. Shattering word
Bass, T. Inventory
Bass, T. Letting Mikey go
Cheasebro, M. The empty tomb
Crumley, G. W. Death day/life day
Dixon, M. E. Into the light
y Evans, S. Jesus loved them
c Forsten, M. L. The sycamore cross
Gillies, J. Give us a sign
Goens, L. M. Resurrection on trial
Hill, R. Faces of the cross
Koopman, L. It is finished
Lewis, T. No vacancy
c McCullough, L. E. Chanukah: come light the menorah!
c McCullough, L. E. Dare to be a Daniel!
c McCullough, L. E. Hail, Queen Esther!
c McCullough, L. E. Jonah and the whale
c McCullough, L. E. King David's harp
c McCullough, L. E. Noah's ark: falsehood and wickedness hitch a ride
c McCullough, L. E. The prophet and the rabbi
c McCullough, L. E. Ruth and Naomi: the healing power of friendship

c McCullough, L. E. Samson and Delilah
c McCullough, L. E. Tales of angels
c McCullough, L. E. What is a brother?
c McCullough, L. E. The wisdom of Solomon
Owens, J. To serve one another
Rhymes, B. G. The way of the cross
Rogerson, P. B. While shepherds watched
Smith, J. M. This is my story
Spitz, A. Christus
Stair, E. R. Parade without a permit
Thum, N. The carpenter and the cross
c Vogel, L. An Ahab headache and a Jezebelly ache
Vogel, L. The angels' locker room: A Christmas play
c Vogel, L. The B-I-B-L-E is L-O-S-T
Vogel, L. Be my guest
c Vogel, L. Big little man
Vogel, L. Elijah's no good, horrible, very bad job
c Vogel, L. Everything's falling
Vogel, L. Exiles
c Vogel, L. The fall into sin
c Vogel, L. Fearless Pharaoh FooFoo
c Vogel, L. The flood
c Vogel, L. From cool to fool
Vogel, L. Gracious goodness, great tongues of fire
Vogel, L. He's so vain
c Vogel, L. Joseph
c Vogel, L. Judges—again
c Vogel, L. Nay, nay, Naaman
Vogel, L. Nick at night
c Vogel, L. The patriarchs
c Vogel, L. Rehoboam rubs 'em wrong
c Vogel, L. Ring around Jerusalem
Vogel, L. Rockball, our natural pastime
c Vogel, L. Ruth
c Vogel, L. Samson
c Vogel, L. Solomon—wise for a while
Vogel, L. A super scientific world
c Vogel, L. Surfin' Galilay
Vogel, L. The temptations
Vogel, L. We're all shook up
c Vogel, L. What's up, rock?
c Vogel, L. Wilderness wandering
Vogel, L. Yakety Yak: he won't talk back

Worship programs—*Continued*

Westerfield, N. G. The morning of the Marys

Younger, M. Making the rain stop

c Zapel, A. L. All things are bright and beautiful

c Zapel, A. L. Three gifts from gentle Jesus

c Zapel, A. L. Who am I?

Worsley, Victoria

Lift and separate.

Based on several pages in mail order catalog. Interior monologues of lingerie models. 6w

In Mythic women/Real women

Woudstra, Karst

Burying the dog; tr. by Della Couling.

Drama explores tortured relationship between two brothers and their partners. 2m 1w 1 interior

In Dutch and Flemish plays, ed. by D. Couling

The **would-be** gentleman. Molière

Woyzeck. Büchner, G.

Wrestling

Luckham, C. Trafford Tanzi

y St. John, B. Wynn Fairly, champeen rassler! or, Get a grip on yourself!

Wright, Craig

The pavilion. Dramatists 2003

ISBN 0-8222-1898-4

Man returns to his twenty-year high school reunion with dreams of winning back the girl he left behind after an unexpected pregnancy ruined their relationship. 2m 1w 1 setting

Snapshot: a quick tour of the monument.

Monologue by a guide at the Mount Rushmore national memorial, automatic but slightly perplexed. 1 act 1 scene 1 m 1 setting

In Humana Festival 2002

Snapshot: bomb squad.

Anarchic one-man demonstration at Mount Rushmore. Music, singing, dancing. 1 act 1m 1w 1 setting

In Humana Festival 2002

Wright, Doug

Baby talk.

A woman is unwound when her precocious baby begins to speak while still inside her womb. 1 act 3m 1w 1 setting

In Wright, D. Unwrap your candy

Lot 13: the bone violin.

A young violin prodigy skyrockets to international prominence, only to meet a shocking and supernatural fate. 1 act 3m 2w 1 setting

In Wright, D. Unwrap your candy

Unwrap your candy.

Five actors portray actual members of the theatre audience. 1 act 3m 2w 1 setting

In Wright, D. Unwrap your candy

Wildwood Park.

Real estate agent shows prospective buyer house that is notorious scene of recent crime. 1m 1w

In The Best American short plays, 1996-1997

—Same

In Wright, D. Unwrap your candy

Wright, Glenn, and Sebazco, Raul Santiago

The crime.

Mugger's victim turns out to be acquaintance from old neighborhood. 1 act 2m 1 exterior

In Action; ed. by M. Algarin and L. Griffith

Wright, Orville, 1871-1948

about

Giron, A. Flight

Wright, Wilbur

about

Giron, A. Flight

Wrong mountain. Hirson, D.

Wyld, Hazel. See Chinn, J. jt. auth.

Wymark, Olwen

Mothering Sunday. French (London) 2002 27p

ISBN 0-573-02354-9

Comedy. Swinging divorcee and estranged daughter reunite. Background music. 2m 2w 1 interior

Wynn Fairly, champeen rassler! or, Get a grip on yourself! St. John, B.

X

X-stacy. Forde, M.

Xerxes I, King of Persia, 519-465 or 4 B.C.

about

Aeschylus. The Persians
Cibber, C. Xerxes

Xerxes. Cibber, C.

Y

Yacine, Kateb

Intelligence powder.

Picaresque adventure of roguish philosopher and his many attempts to outwit sultan of North African Kingdom. 14m 1w extras 1 exterior

In Modern African drama; ed. by B. Jeyifo

Yagayah: two.black.womyn. griots. Young, D., and Belvett, N.

Yakety Yak: he won't talk back. Vogel, L.

Yalta (Russia)

Friel, B. The Yalta game

The **Yalta** game. Friel, B.

Yankee dawg you die. Gotanda, P. K.

Yankee Doodle had a brick (brick mason). McCullough, L. E.

Yard gal. Prichard, R.

A **yard** of sun. Fry, C.

Yardsale. Wesker, A.

Yasuko and the young s-s-samurai. Huie, K.

Yazbek, David

The full Monty; book by Terrence McNally; music & lyrics by David Yazbek. Applause 2002 148p

ISBN 1-55783-556-X

Musical set in Buffalo, N.Y. Laid-off mill workers decide to raise money with a striptease act. Adapted from a British film. Music, singing, dancing. 2 acts 1b 10m 8w extras settings

Year of the family. Neilson, A.

The **year** of the hiker. Keane, J. B.

Yearbook. Fendrich, S.

Yearbook reflections. DeTurk, S.

A **yearning**. Carter, R.

Yeaton, Dana

Helen at risk.

Short scene set in prison. Mask-making class turns deadly. 2m 1w 1 interior

In Take ten; ed. by E. Lane and N. Shengold

Mad River rising. PenStroke Press 1999 90p

ISBN 0-9669177-2-3

Tragedy about three generations of Vermont farm family devastated by the Great Flood of 1927. 2 acts 2b 4m 2w 1 setting

Midwives. PenStroke Press 2000 90p

ISBN 0-9669177-3-1

Dramatization of Chris Bohjalian's novel. Ferocious March ice storm forces respected midwife to make decision that leads to her facing criminal prosecution. 2 acts 4m 5w 2 interiors

The **yellow** boat. Saar, D.

Yellow Robe, William S.

The body guards.

Two Native Americans sit with corpse until sheriff arrives. 1 act 2m 1 interior

In Yellow Robe, W. S. Where the pavement ends

The council.

Native Americans' co-existence with animals. Music. Prologue 1 act 8 scenes epilogue Unidentified cast 7 characters 1 setting

In Yellow Robe, W. S. Where the pavement ends

The independence of Eddie Rose.

Native American teenager seeks to escape his dysfunctional family while at same time protecting his younger sister from abuse. Prologue 2 acts 10 scenes 1g 4m 2w 3 interiors 3 exteriors

In Seventh generation; ed. by M. G. D'Aponte

Rez politics.

Two ten-year-old mixed-blood boys argue about what makes one Native American. 1 act 2b 1 exterior

In Yellow Robe, W. S. Where the pavement ends

Sneaky.

American Indians in Montana steal their mother's body from funeral home so they can observe traditional Indian rituals. Prologue 4 scenes 1b 4m 1w 1 interior 2 exteriors

In Yellow Robe, W. S. Where the pavement ends

Yellow Robe, William S.—*Continued*

The star quilter.

Native American woman on Montana reservation creates traditional star quilts. 1 act 4 scenes 2w 1 interior

In Yellow Robe, W. S. Where the pavement ends

The **yellow** sound. Kandinsky, W.

Yes, sir, that's my baby. Andersen, D. R.

Yesterday's window. Miyagawa, C.

Yesteryear. Glass, J. M.

Yew, Chay

A beautiful country.

Dramatizes the history of anti-Asian prejudice in the United States. Slide projections. Music, singing. 23 scenes epilogue 7m 6w settings

In Yew, C. The hyphenated American

Red.

A popular Asian-American novelist revisits Shanghai, where she helped persecute her father, a star of the Chinese opera, during the Cultural Revolution. Music, singing, dancing. Prologue 27 scenes epilogue 1m 2w 2 1 setting

In Yew, C. The hyphenated American

Scissors.

Retired broker meets elderly immigrant barber in the park for a weekly haircut, a ritual that sustains both men. Set in New York during the Great Depression. 1 act 2m 1 exterior

In Yew, C. The hyphenated American

Snapshot: here and now.

Monologue about marriage and faded dreams. 1 act 1m extra 1 setting

In Humana Festival 2002

Wonderland.

Family tragedy about failure of American dream. Idealistic Chinese American father and romantic immigrant mother see their hopes destroyed nad their homosexual son alienated. Music. 1 act 3m 1w settings

In Yew, C. The hyphenated American

Yodellers. Healey, M., and Lynch, K.

The **Yoko** Ono project. Yoon, J.

Yoon, Jean

The Yoko Ono project; with instruction poems, music, and other texts by Yoko Ono. Broken Jaw Press 2002 80p (Velvet Touch, 4)

ISBN 1-55391-001-X

A multimedia meditation on the art of Yoko Ono, as it affects three Asian Canadian women. Music. 1 act 38 scenes 2m 4w settings

Yordy, Martha

c Little Red Riding Hood and The magic dragon; book by David and Julie Payne; lyrics by Julie Payne; music by Martha Yordy. Dramatic Publishing 2003 34p

Little Red Riding Hood dreads knowing that every time someone opens up her book she will be forced to relive the same old familiar tale. With the help magic dragon, she sets off for new adventure. Music, singing. 4m 4w extras 1 setting

York, Y.

Gerald's good idea.

Middle-aged guests at party let their hair down and their true feelings be known. Music. 2 acts 4 scenes 5m 5w 1 interior

In York, Y. Plays

Mask of the unicorn warrior. Dramatic Publishing 2003 48p

Mystic tale inspired by unicorn tapestries in Cluny Museum in Paris. Prince fears he is lacking courage necessary to properly rule kingdom and sets out on journey to prove his worthiness by killing unicorn. 2 acts 3m 2w

The secret wife.

Spy and his new bride move to West Germany in 1972. 2 acts 19 scenes 3m 4w 5 interiors 1 exterior

In York, Y. Plays

The snowflake avalanche.

Modern fable concerning ecological disaster, race relations, and the human condition. A native American fisherman's extreme response to an atrocious oil spill brings his family together with that of the African-American lawyer who defends him. 2 acts 40 scenes 1b 1g 2m 2w 3 interiors 1 exterior

In York, Y. Plays

c The witch of Blackbird Pond.

Dramatization of Elizabeth George Speare novel. Seventeen-year-old earns ire and suspicions of her Puritan village when she befriends banished healer believed to be witch. 2 acts 11 scenes 6m 8w settings

In Eight plays for children; ed. by C. A. Jennings

You can't be serious. Woolley, J.

You could die laughing! St. John, B.

You oughta be in pictures. Andersen, D. R.

You shouldn't have told. Thompson-Scretching, A. L.

Young, David

Clout. Coach House Bks. 2001 113p
ISBN 1-552-45077-5   LC 2001-347270
Drama about newspaper baron and his former employee, a burnt-out liberal journalist, both kidnapped by a terrorist and chained back to back in a dungeon cell. 2 acts 2m 1w 1 interior

Glenn. Coach House Bks. 1999 110p
ISBN 1-55245-058-9
Explores life and work of iconoclastic pianist Glenn Gould. Music. 2 acts 30 scenes 4m 1 setting

Young, Debbie, and Belvett, Naila

Yagayah: two.black.womyn. griots.
Traces friendship of two Jamaican women from 1984 to 1998. 16 scenes 2w
In Testifyin' v2; ed. by D. Sears

Young Cherokee. Miller, K. S.

The **young** chief who played the flute. Barchers, S. I.

The **young** girl and the monsoon. Ryan, J.

Young Olli and the trolls. McCullough, L. E.

Younger, Marshal

Making the rain stop.
Easter worship program about relevance of Christ's resurrection. 1b 3g 3m 1w 1 interior
In Jubilation: dramas for Easter

Your everyday ghost story. Wilson, L.

You're just like my father. Shaw, P.

You're only young twice. Aldridge, R.

Yourgrau, Tug

Cries from the cockpit.
Family must take over when owner of funeral home dies. 3m 1w 1 interior
In HB Playwrights short play festival 2000

Mid-life.
Older man and young woman have romantic tryst in motel room. 1m 1w 1 interior
In HB Playwrights short play festival 1997

Peanuts.
Man told he is dead at airport departure gate. 2m 3w 1 interior
In HB Playwrights short play festival 1999

TH FT.
Two potential art thieves find themselves participants in performance art piece. 7m 2w 1 interior
In HB Playwrights short play festival 1998

Youth

Ackermann, J. Off the map
Blessing, L. Reproduction
Chiasson, H. Cape Enrage
Corthron, K. Splash hatch on the E going down
Dean, P. 48 shades of brown
Dean, P. After January
Enright, N. Spurboard
y Foon, D. Chasing the money
y Francis, M. David Copperfield
y Francis, S. Body and soul
y Frost, H. Why darkness seems so light
Godber, J. Bouncers
Greenhorn, S. Passing places
Hairston, J. Forty-minute finish
Jordan, J. Mpls., St. Paul
Keeffe, B. Barbarians: abide with me
Keeffe, B. Barbarians: in the city
Keeffe, B. Barbarians: killing time
y Labey, R. New boy
Levi, S. Cherry and Little Banjo
Levi, S. Hearts 'n kisses 'n Miss Vickers
y Lopez, R. A sick world
Margulies, D. Collected stories
Margulies, D. New Year's Eve and Kibbutz
Martini, C. Illegal entry
y Mast, E. Wolf child
McClelland, C. E. Certain arrangements
Medoff, M. H. Crunch time
Miles, K. I hate you on Mondays
Miller, T. Some golden states
Nanus, S. The survivor
Oliver, C. Kicking out
Porter, C. Nymph errant
Rachilde. Pleasure (Volupté)
y Ridley, P. Sparkleshark
Rivera, J. The crooked cross
Rivera, J. The winged man

Youth—*Continued*

Sanford, K. Ophelia

Slaight, B. Dancing by myself

y Urquhart, J. Liza and the riddling cave

y Valentine, A. Swimming the globe

Walker, G. F. Tough!

Wallace, N. The trestle at Pope Lick Creek

Walsh, E. Disco pigs

Way, C. Looking out to see

Wellman, M. Cleveland

Wilhelm, L. The parrot

Wilhelm, L. Tremulous

Williams, T. Spring storm

Z

Zapel, Arthur L. (Arthur Lewis)

c All things are bright and beautiful.

Worship program. Symbolism of three Easter flowers is related through scripture readings. Singing. Variable cast

In The drama of Easter; ed. by R. Wray

c Three gifts from gentle Jesus.

Worship program. A children's Easter presentation. Music, singing. Variable cast 6 characters extras

In The drama of Easter; ed. by R. Wray

c Who am I?

Chancel play for Lent or Easter about Pontius Pilate. Variable cast

In The drama of Easter; ed. by R. Wray

Zeder, Suzan

c The taste of sunrise. Anchorage Press 1995 81p

ISBN 0-87602-401-0

Drama utilizing American Sign language about travails of young deaf man in Illinois, 1917-1928. 2 acts Variable cast 1 setting

—Same

In Seattle Children's Theatre v2

c Wiley and the Hairy Man.

Based on Southern folktale. With courage and resourcefulness boy outsmarts sinister Hairy Man. Speaking chorus. 1 act 2m 1w extra 1 setting

In Theatre for young audiences; ed. by C. A. Jennings

Zellnik, David

Killing hand.

At a social gathering, a visitor from Serbia is asked about his role in "ethnic cleansing." 1 act 4m 1w 1 interior

In EST marathon '98: the one-act plays; ed. by M. Smith

Zen Buddhism

Tait, L. Live free or die

Zeus and Hera. Barchers, S. I.

The **zig-zag** woman. Martin, S.

Zimbabwe

Lan, D. Desire

Lan, D. Flight

Zimmer. Margulies, D.

Zindel, Paul

Every seventeen minutes the crowd goes crazy!. Dramatists 2000 42p

ISBN 0-8222-1735-X

Sardonic comedy about modern family abandoned by their parents. Music. 8m 6w 1 setting

Zinn, Howard

Marx in Soho; a play on history. South End Press 1999 xxii, 55p

ISBN 0-89608-594-5; 0-89608-593-7 (pa)

LC 98-55072

Monologue. Karl Marx experiences "second coming" in contemporary New York. 1m 1 interior

Zionism

c McCullough, L. E. Next year in Jerusalem

Zola, Émile, 1840-1902

Thérèse Raquin (dramatization) See Bell, N. Thérèse Raquin; Bell, N. Thérèse Raquin

Zombies from the beyond. Valcq, J.

Zorin, Leonid

The guests.

Family drama set in small 1950s Soviet town. Intergenerational conflict contributes to decay of revolutionary spirit. 3 acts 5m 5w 1 setting

In Eight twentieth-century Russian plays; ed. by T. Langen and J. Weir

Zorro!; or, The curse of Capistrano. Barchers, S. I., and Kroll, J. L.

Part II

Cast Analysis

FEMALE CAST

1 character (1g)

Hall, L. Spoonface Steinberg

Thompson, J. Pink

1 character (1w)

Arizmendi, Y. Nostalgia maldita: 1-900-MEXICO, a Stairmaster piece

Aron, G. My brilliant divorce

Astor del Valle, J. Transplantations: straight and other jackets para mi

Auburn, D. Three monologues

Augustine, J. Siobhan

Ayvazian, L. Deaf day

Ayvazian, L. High dive

Ayvazian, L. Plan day

Barfield, T. Without skin or breathlessness

Bass, A. The redeemer of minutes

Blomquist, E. Reality

Bonel, W. Good grief, Lolita

Bornstein, K. Virtually yours

Brett, S. Putting the kettle on

Carlin, A. J. Jodie's body

Claff, R. Call waiting

Cleage, P. Chain

Cleage, P. Chain

Crow, A. G. A roomful of men

Curino, L. Passion

Dafydd, G. No regrets

Dempsey, S., and Millan, L. Mary Medusa

Dempsey, S., and Millan, L. Plastic bride

Diggs, E. How to plant a rose

Dowie, C. Adult child/dead child

Dowie, C. Drag act

Dowie, C. Leaking from every orifice

Dowie, C. Why is John Lennon wearing a skirt?

Durang, C. Mrs. Sorken

Durang, C. Mrs. Sorken

Enoch, W., and Mailman, D. The 7 stages of grieving

Gasteazoro, E. Amor de mis amores

Gien, P. The syringa tree

Glancy, D. The toad (another name for the moon) should have a bite

Gough, L. The tail

Grace-Smith, B. Nag pou wahine

Griffith, L. E. White sirens

Griffiths, L. Alien creature

Griffiths, L. A game of inches

Griffiths, L. Maggie & Pierre

Hughes, H. Clit notes

Kennedy, A. The film club (a monologue by Suzanne Alexander)

Kincaid, J. Girl

Korder, H. Geliebteh

Kron, L. 2.5 minute ride

Kron, L. 101 humiliating stories

Lill, W. The occupation of Heather Rose

Lindsay-Abaire, D. Snapshot: history lesson

Lipkin, J. The girl who lost her voice

Lucas, C. Credo

MacLeod, J. The hope slide

Magona, S. House-hunting unlike Soweto

Mahomed, I. Cheaper than roses

Mahomed, I. Purdah

Mantello, J. Season's greetings

Margolin, D. Snapshot: rock scissors paper

Margulies, D. I don't know what I'm doing

FEMALE CAST—*Continued*

Cleage, P. Late bus to Mecca
Cooper, C. L. Sentences and words
De Angelis, A. Ironmistress
De Matteo, D. The heart transplant
Dewberry, E. Happy mug
Dewberry, E. Head on
Feydeau, G. Ladies' man
Gage, C. Harriet Tubman visits a therapist
Glancy, D. The woman who was a red deer dressed for the deer dance
Glancy, D. The woman who was a red deer dressed for the deer dance
Hall, T. Jean and Dinah who have been locked away in a world famous calypso since 1956 speak their minds publicly
Hare, D. The breath of life
Healy, A. M. Kat and Eliza
Hewett, R. Goodbye Mrs. Blore
Hunt, L. A night under canvas
Ihimaera, W. Woman far walking
Ives, D. Lives of the saints
Jensen, J. Snapshot: on Lincoln's head
Jensen, J. Two-headed
Jensen, J. Two-headed
Jordan, J. Nightswim
Jordan, J. Nightswim
Junyent, S. Packing up the past
Kemnitz, R. D., and McMaster, J. Off the rack
Kemnitz, R. D., and McMaster, J. Off the rack
Kim, S. Dreamtime for Alice
Kim, S. Dreamtime for Alice
Kramer, A. A treasure in a teacup
Lauro, S. Railing it uptown
Lavery, B. Her aching heart
Lavery, B. Origin of the species
LeFevre, A. Waterbabies
LeFevre, A. Waterbabies
Levy, D. Pushing the prince into Denmark
Lipner, N. Pearls
Mack, C. K. After
Margulies, D. Collected stories
Margulies, D. Collected stories
Margulies, D. Women in motion
Martin, J. Beauty
Martin, J. Beauty

May, E., and Arkin, A. The way of all fish
McConnell, J. Cruise missile
McConnell, J. Cupboard love
McConnell, J. Day trippers
McConnell, J. The guilt card
McConnell, J. Last post
McConnell, J. Short changed
McConnell, J. Theatrical digs
McGee, J. A backward glance
Mckee, J. The daffodils
McKee, J. Invitation to a funeral
Mda, Z. And the girls in their Sunday dresses
Medley, C. Dearborn Heights
Mhlophe, G. Have you seen Zandile?
Morizono, L.-J. Freakish times
Morley, J. True confessions of a go-go girl
Murray-Smith, J. Love child
Nigro, D. The dead wife
Pedrero, P. The color of August
Prichard, R. Yard gal
Prichard, R. Yard gal
Quinn, N. B. The spirit is willing
Radano, L.-M. Bright angel
Rapp, A. Train story
Raznovich, D. MaTRIX, inc. (Casa matriz)
Reitz, D. Divulgence at Damarak 18
Reynolds, J. Physical therapy
y Shafaat, S. Balcony
Silverstein, S. All cotton
Son, D. Stop kiss
Upton, J. Know your rights
Wasserstein, W. Bette and me
Whiskeyman, D. So tell me about this guy
Wilhelm, L. A pink Cadillac nightmare
Yellow Robe, W. S. The star quilter
Young, D., and Belvett, N. Yagayah: two.black.womyn. griots

2 characters and extra (2w extra)

Foote, H. A coffin in Egypt

2 characters and extras (2w extras)

Cheasebro, M. The empty tomb
Kramer, S. David's redhaired death
Mack, C. K. After

FEMALE CAST—*Continued*

Shorty, S. Trickster visits the old folks home

Wellman, M. The sandalwood box

3 characters (1g 2w)

Hunt, M. Bread

Radano, L.-M. The divine child

3 characters (3g)

y Lazarus, J. Schoolyard games

3 characters (3w)

Brofsky, K. Strawberry fields

Charabanc Theatre Company Somewhere over the balcony

Dixcy, M. Eating out

Foote, H. The carpetbagger's children

Fricker, G. Buttonholes in silk

Glancy, D. The women who loved house trailers

Griffin, H. The ark

Hoffower, K. The office

Howes, L. Cathy's kitchen

Hutton, A. The price you pay

Jory, J. Heads

King, M. Bathory

Kreidl, M. Grateful women

Lauro, S. Sunday go to meetin'

Leonard, H. Love in the title

Mamet, D. Boston marriage

McGuinness, F. The stronger

McLeod, K. R. Broken hearts

Newmeir, J. H. Semblance of madness!

Nigro, D. Ballerinas

Nigro, D. The lost girl

Palmer, T. Body talk

Ruskin, A. L. The art of remembering

Scheffer, W. Bel canto

Smith, V. Meow

Smith, V. Meow

Strindberg, A. The stronger

Tait, L. The glass ceiling

Wellman, M. Mister Original Bugg

Wilkins, J. R. War letters

Wilner, S. Relative strangers

Wilner, S. Relative strangers

3 characters and extras (3w extras)

Gough, L. Our lady of shadows

4 characters (1g 3w)

Ehn, E. Una carroña (Rose of Lima)

Jensen, J. Old wives tale

4 characters (2g 2w)

Thompson, J. Perfect pie

Weil, V. C. Communication

4 characters (4w)

Danz, C., and others Fame takes a holiday

Dike, F. So what's new?

Dunn, M. The deer and the antelope play

George, M. The most massive woman wins

Gerstenberg, A. Overtones

Godber, J. Shakers

Hamilton, W. A. Bellies, knees and ankles

Lavery, B. Two Marias

Levy, D. Pax

Megna, K. An evening crossword

Rachilde The prowler (Le Rôdeur)

Rebeck, T. Sunday on the rocks

Son, D. R. A. W. ('cause I'm a woman)

Wellman, M. Cat's-paw

Woods, J. Inheritance

4 characters and extras (4w extras)

Sistren Theatre Collective QPH

Smith, A. Trace of Arc

Williams, T. A lovely Sunday for Creve Coeur

5 characters (5w)

Bailey, M., and Lewis, S. M. Sistahs

Bailey, M., and Lewis, S. M. Sistahs

De Angelis, A. Playhouse creatures

Five Lesbian Brothers (Theater company) Brave smiles . . . another lesbian tragedy

Five Lesbian Brothers (Theater company) Brides of the moon

Five Lesbian Brothers (Theater company) The secretaries

Five Lesbian Brothers (Theater company) Voyage to Lesbos

Hutton, A. A closer look

Kneubuhl, V. N. The conversion of Ka'ahumanu

Levy, D. The B file

FEMALE CAST—*Continued*

McLaughlin, E. Tongue of a bird
Mena, A. Las nuevas tamaleras
Quilter, P. Respecting your piers
Rogers, A. The life before/reconstruction/ reconstructing whiteness
West, Cheryl Jar the floor
Women's Theatre Group Lear's daughters

5 characters and extras (5w extras)

Swingtime Canteen

6 characters (6w)

Chaurette, N. The queens
Hanes, M. The crimson thread
Martin, J. Anton in show business
Murfitt, M., and Howie, B. Cowgirls
Spiderwoman Theater Power pipes
Vooght, C. Bright interval
Woolf, C. Treseder's seeds
Worsley, V. Lift and separate

7 characters (7w)

Ensler, E. Necessary targets
Highway, T. The Rez sisters
Martin, J. Anton in show business
Westerfield, N. G. The morning of the Marys

8 characters (7g 1w)

Kennedy, A. A lesson in a dead language

9 characters (9w)

Anthony, T. 'Da kink in my hair
Hutton, A. As it is in heaven

10 characters (10w)

Box, M. Angels of war
García Lorca, F. The house of Bernarda Alba

10 characters and extras (10w extras)

Mann, S. The house of Bernarda Alba

12 characters (12w)

Ndlovu, D. Sheila's day

16 characters (16w)

Churchill, C. Top girls

16 characters and extras (16w extras)

Ehn, E. The imp of simplicity (Thomas à Kempis)

MALE CAST

1 character (1b)

Hall, L. Child of our time: child of the snow
Margulies, D. Anthony
Wood, C. Jingo

1 character (1m)

Alfaro, L. Downtown
Barfield, T. Snapshot: defacing patriotic property
Bass, A. Shattering word
Bass, T. Letting Mikey go
Belke, D. The Maltese bodkin
Blessing, L. Chesapeake
Blessing, L. Snapshot: Tyler poked Taylor
Bogart, A., and Clarke, J. Score
Bogosian, E. Wake up and smell the coffee
Borden, W. M. Tightrope time: ain't nuthin' more than some itty bitty madness between twilight & dawn
Butler, D. The only thing worse you could have told me—
Chekhov, A. P. The dangers of tobacco
Chekhov, A. P. On the harmful effects of tobacco
Christenson, J., and Tremblay, J. Elephant wake
Clark, B. In pursuit of Eve
Couturier, G. My husband's an angel
Coxon, L. I am Angela Brazil
Drader, B. The fruit machine
Gearing, N. Dickens in America
Grassmann, B. Children of neon lights
Hall, L. Two's company
Hare, D. Via Dolorosa
Hare, D. Via Dolorosa
Hickman, C. Skin & ornaments
Hoch, D. Jails, hospitals and hip-hop
Hoch, D. Some people
Hunt, S. The white guy
Hunter, M. Atlantis
Kearns, M. Attachments
Kennedy, A. Sun

MALE CAST—*Continued*
Lucas, C. Boyfriend riff
Mamet, D. A sermon
Mantello, J. The Santaland diaries
Manzi, W. The award
Manzi, W. One for the money
Mapa, A. I remember Mapa
Margulies, D. Joey
Margulies, D. Louie
Margulies, D. Manny
Margulies, D. Zimmer
McLean, D. One sure thing
McPherson, C. The good thief
McPherson, C. The good thief
McPherson, C. Rum and vodka
McPherson, C. Rum and vodka
McPherson, C. St. Nicholas
McPherson, C. St Nicholas
Miller, T. Fruit cocktail
Miller, T. Glory box
Miller, T. My queer body
Miller, T. Naked breath
Miller, T. Naked breath
Miller, T. Some golden states
Miller, T. Stretch marks
Mode, B. Fully committed
Monge-Rafuls, P. R. Trash
Myatt, J. M. What he sent
Nelson, R. Scooping
Nigro, D. Broadway macabre
Nigro, D. Capone
Nigro, D. Childe Rowland to the dark
tower came
Nigro, D. Creatures lurking in the
churchyard
Nigro, D. Uncle Clete's toad
Nigro, D. Wolfsbane
Nottage, L. Snapshot: becoming
American
Oates, J. C. No next of kin
O'Donnell, D. Radio Rooster says that's
bad
Owens, R. Chucky's hunch
Panych, M. Earshot
River, S. B. To Rahtid
Rivera, J. Gas
Roth, A. Jeffrey Slugworth: ex-embalmer
Russell-King, C. Lucky four
Rutherford, S. The Chinese art of place-
ment
Scheffer, W. Alien boy

Scheffer, W. Tennessee and me
Tait, L. Behave, my sorrow
Thomson, R. H. The lost boys
Topor, T. Boundary County, Idaho
Tremblay, L. The dragonfly of Chicou-
timi
Tremblay, L. Ogre
Tremblay, L. A trick of fate
Vawter, R. Roy Cohn/Jack Smith
Verdecchia, G. Fronteras Americanas
(American borders)
Williams, T. I rise in flame, cried the
phoenix
c Winther, B. Latino trio: Hormiga's law-
suit
Wright, C. Snapshot: a quick tour of the
monument
Zinn, H. Marx in Soho

1 character and extra (1m extra)
Manzi, W. The audition
Tidler, C. Red mango
Yew, C. Snapshot: here and now

1 character and extras (1m extras)
Chan, M. Maggie's last dance
Garland, P. Brief lives
Luce, W. Barrymore
Maloney, P. Accident
Mueller, L. The confession of many
strangers
Palmieri, M. Prologue
Río, M. del On the way to the concert
Thiessen, V. Blowfish

2 characters (1b 1m)
Reitz, D. Mathematics

2 characters (2b)
Yellow Robe, W. S. Rez politics

2 characters (2m)
Adams, P. Free's point
Andersen, D. R. Everywhere
Anderson, S. J. Hanging on the tree
Anderson, S. J. Traveling with reserva-
tions
Arkin, A. Virtual reality
Arrabal, F. The body-builder's book of
love
Badlam, R. Guys

MALE CAST—*Continued*

Bandele, B. Two horsemen
Barlow, P. Love upon the throne
Baron, J. Visiting Mr. Green
Bogdan, K. Sparring partner
Brown, S. R. Slice of life
Caleb, J. R. The rehearsal
Caplan, P. J. The test
Chekhov, A. P. Swan song
Chekhov, A. P. Swan song
Cleveland, R. Jerry and Tom
Cunninghan, L. Flop cop
DiPietro, J. Executive dance
Donaghy, T. The dadshuttle
Elwell, J. S. Evening education
Feuer, J., and Boyd, G. The big bang
Gersten-Vassilaros, A. Two Jewish men in their seventies
Giancoli, E. The devil's parole
Gillies, J. Give us a sign
Goda, B. No crime
Gore, C. A good night's rest; or, Two in the morning
Gotanda, P. K. Yankee dawg you die
Hairston, J. Forty-minute finish
Hairston, J. Forty-minute finish
Hedges, P. Chicken potential
Hochwälder, F. 1003; or, Don Giovanni's back in town
Holman, R. Being friends
Hwang, D. H. The dance and the railroad
Hwang, D. H. Trying to find Chinatown
Hwang, D. H. Trying to find Chinatown
Jacker, C. A new life
Jones, M. Stones in his pockets
Jones, M. Stones in his pockets
Kavanagh, G. Ditch
Kleberg, L. The Aquarians
Kleberg, L. Ash Wednesday
Koltès, B.-M. In the solitude of cotton fields
Kushner, T. Notes on Akiba
Lane, E. A bowl of soup
Linney, R. Goodbye, Oscar
Linney, R. Goodbye, Oscar
Linney, R. Madmen
Loewenstern, M. A doctor's visit
Long, Q. Snapshot: scene at Mount Rushmore
y Lopez, R. A sick world

Lucas, C. Bad dream
Lucas, C. The boom box
Lucas, C. If Columbus does not figure in your travel plans
Macadaeg, R. Woozey woo!
Mamet, D. The disappearance of the Jews
Mamet, D. The disappearance of the Jews
Mamet, D. The jade mountain
Mamet, D. The jade mountain
Margulies, D. Death in the family
Margulies, D. Father and son
Margulies, D. Space
McLean, D. Rug comes to Shuv
Milligan, J. The genuine article
Milligan, J. Getting even
Mori, B. Adult fiction
Nelson, G. Speak
Odato, A. The profoundness of events
O'Donnell, D. White mice
Orlandersmith, D. The gimmick
Orloff, R. I didn't know you could cook
O'Rowe, M. Howie the rookie
O'Rowe, M. Howie the rookie
Palmieri, M. Makin' sense of nothin'
Palmieri, M. Tough guys
Paterson, D. L. Chutes
Paterson, D. L. Shades of autumn
Pelfrey, M. Drive angry
Pelfrey, M. Drive angry
Piatigorsky, A. The kabbalistic psychoanalysis of Adam R. Tzaddik
Pritchard, E. Chicken wings
Pushkin, A. Mozart and Salieri
Rebeck, T. The contract
Rebeck, T. The funeral play
Rebeck, T. What we're up against
Reich, J. Proof
Reitz, D. And that's how people burn to death in motel rooms
Rintoul, H. Brave hearts
Rowlands, I. The ogpu men
Sagal, P. Game theory
Sagal, P. Milton Bradley
Sater, S. Phone sex and a dumb show
Schmitt, E.-E. Enigma variations
Schmitt, E.-E. Enigma variations
Silverstein, S. Abandon all hope
Silverstein, S. Blind Willie and the talking dog

MALE CAST—*Continued*

Silverstein, S. Dreamers
Silverstein, S. Hard hat area
Silverstein, S. Have a nice day
Sirera, R. The audition
Slabolepszy, P. Mooi Street moves
Tait, L. Dmitri
Walcott, D. Pantomime
Warmflash, S. Six inch adjustable
Wells, M. L. Real real gone
Williamson, D. Sanctuary
Wilson, A. The janitor
Wilson, L. Your everyday ghost story
Wright, G., and Sebazco, R. S. The crime
Yellow Robe, W. S. The body guards
Yew, C. Scissors

2 characters and extra (2m extra)

Lucas, C. The dying gaul
Santanelli, M. Emergency exit

2 characters and extras (2m extras)

Curtis, D. Mesa
Finn, W. Painting you
Fuller, H. B. At Saint Judas's
Gardner, H. I'm with ya, Duke
Gorden, C. Guarding the bridge
Kalcheim, L. Defiled; or, The convenience of a shorthaired dog
Lewis, C. W. Soft click of a switch
Reingold, J. Joe and Stew's Theatre of Brotherly Love and Financial Success

3 characters (3m)

Aerenson, B. Lighting up the two-year-old
Anderson, S. J. The big one
Babe, T. Singleton, the medal winner
Babe, T. Singleton, the medal winner
Baker, E. A. Mafia on Prozac
Baker, J. Male bondage
Benet i Jornet, J. M. Legacy
Bouchard, M. M. Down Dangerous Passes Road
Brandt, A. 2 1/2 Jews
Carley, S. The edge
Culture Clash (Group) The mission
Culture Clash (Group) Radio mambo
Epstein, D. Exact change
Farquhar, R. God's official

Fugard, A., and others Sizwe Bansi is dead
Healey, M. The drawer boy
Ives, D. Mere mortals
Jeffery, L. Who look in stove
Keeffe, B. Barbarians: abide with me
Keeffe, B. Barbarians: in the city
Keeffe, B. Barbarians: killing time
Long, A., and others The Bible: the complete word of God (abridged)
Martini, C. Illegal entry
McKay, R. Seeing the light
McKay, R. Seeing the light
McPherson, C. Port Authority
McPherson, C. This lime tree bower
McPherson, C. This lime tree bower
Milligan, J. Men in suits
Milligan, J. Waiting for Ringo
Neilson, A. Penetrator
Nelson, R. Jungle coup
Owen, Gary Crazy Gary's mobile disco
Piatigorsky, A. The offering
Pushkin, A. The miserly knight
Rambo, D. God's man in Texas
Reza, Y. Art
Sánchez, E. Trafficking in broken hearts
Silberman, B. Walkin' backward
Simpson, B., and Wann, J. King Mackerel & the blues are running
Spencer, S. Sudden devotion
Stroppel, F. Judgment call
Thatcher, K. Among friends
Weller, M. Mistresses
Wilder, T. The angel that troubled the waters
Wilder, T. Hast thou considered my servant Job?
Wilder, T. Now the servant's name was Malchus
Williams, T. The last of my solid gold watches

3 characters and extras (3m extras)

Hatcher, J. Tango Delta
Machado, E. When the sea drowns in sand
Müller, H. Heracles 5
Ravenhill, M. Faust (Faust is dead)
Vogel, L. A super scientific world

MALE CAST—*Continued*
4 characters (4m)

Baron, J. Hershey: a space odyssey
Calarco, J. Shakespeare's R & J
Eagleton, T. The white, the gold and the gangrene
Feliciano, G. Between blessings
Fenton, E. From dream to ash
Foster, N. The foursome
Fulford, R. W. Steel kiss
Godber, J. Bouncers
Hoffman, J. Francis Brick needs no introduction
Lan, D. Painting a wall
MacEwen, G. Terror and Erebus
Moodie, A. A common man's guide to loving women
Osborne, A. The redemption song
Osborne, A. Redemption song
Palmieri, M. Rocks
Penhall, J. Wild Turkey
Ronzoni, M. 610 Bedford Drive
Sherman, J. The League of Nathans
Silverstein, S. Smile
Stine, M. Theological zenith
Williams, T. And tell sad stories of the death of queens
c Winther, B. Latino trio: Pedro's holey sombrero
Wong, E. Let the big dog eat
Wong, E. Let the big dog eat
Wong, E. Let the big dog eat
Young, D. Glenn

4 characters and extra (4m extra)

Metcalf, P. The players

4 characters and extras (4m extras)

c Vogel, L. Rehoboam rubs 'em wrong

5 characters (5m)

Churchill, C. A number
Gallagher, D. Howard Crabtree's when pigs fly
Kushner, T. G. David Schine in Hell
Martin, J. Good boys
Osment, P. The undertaking
Posner, A. The chosen
y Smith, C. City of gold
Straughan, P. Bones
Thomas, B. The crumple zone

5 characters and extra (5m extra)

Wilson, S. Pignight

5 characters and extras (5m extras)

River, S. B. Moor masterpieces

6 characters (6m)

c Barchers, S. I. Gawain and the Green Knight
Blessing, L. Thief river
Butterworth, J. Mojo
Ellenbogen, N. Horn of sorrow
Marber, P. Dealer's choice
Osborne, A. Bull, rock, and nut
Thomas, T. C. The sound of stillness

6 characters and extras (6m extras)

Wellman, M. Fnu Lnu

7 characters (1b 6m)

Esson, L. The drovers

7 characters (7m)

Bean, R. Toast
Bowne, A. Forty-deuce
The Christians and the Moors (Los moros y los cristianos)
Evans, A., and others Pageant
Logan, J. Never the sinner

7 characters and extras (7m extras)

Walcott, D. Henri Christophe

8 characters (8m)

Harding, M. P. Sour grapes
Noone, R. The lepers of Baile Baiste
O'Neill, E. In the zone
Sunde, K. In a kingdom by the Sea

8 characters and extras (8m extras)

c McCullough, L. E. Next year in Jerusalem
Spitz, A. Christus

9 characters (9m)

Kaufman, M. Gross indecency: the three trials of Oscar Wilde
Kaufman, M. Gross indecency: the three trials of Oscar Wilde
Leight, W. Stray cats
Sherman, M. Bent

MALE CAST—*Continued*

10 characters (10m)
Wood, C. Dingo

11 characters (11m)
Greenberg, R. Take me out
Kleberg, L. The sorcerer's apprentices
O'Neill, E. Bound east for Cardiff

12 characters and extras (1b 11m extras)
c Beattie, A. The looking-glass alchemist

12 characters and extras (12m extras)
Grimm, D. Kit Marlow

13 characters (13m)
Kramer, L. The normal heart
McNally, T. Corpus Christi
McNally, T. Corpus Christi

13 characters and extra (13m extra)
c Vogel, L. Surfin' Galilay

13 characters and extras (13m extras)
Green, P. Hymn to the rising sun: a drama of man's waste

14 characters and extras (14m extras)
Stetson, K. The harps of God

17 characters (17m)
Hochwälder, F. The holy experiment

22 characters and extras (22m extras)
Schulberg, B., and Silverman, S. On the waterfront

25 characters (25m)
Gilroy, F. D. The viewing

MIXED CAST

2 characters (1b 1g)
Williams, T. This property is condemned

2 characters (1b 1w)
Lathrop, M. The visible horse

2 characters (1g 1m)
Wasserstein, W. Tender offer

2 characters (1m 1w)
Alfaro, L. Straight as a line
Alvarez, L. On Sundays
Andersen, D. R. I'll take Manhattan
Andersen, D. R. Yes, sir, that's my baby
Anderson, S. J. Live from Bethlehem
Andrews, T. The admissions officers
Aronson, B. Dream
Auburn, D. Damage control
Auburn, D. The fifth planet
Auburn, D. Miss you
Auburn, D. We had a very good time
Baron, C. The blue room
Baron, C. The blue room
Basch, P. English (it's where the words are)
Beber, N. Adaptive ruse
Belluso, J. The technology project: voice properties
Benfield, D. Second time around
Benjamin, K. A. Mary MacGregor
Benjamin, K. A. Mary Macgregor
Bettenbender, B. The siren song of Stephen Jay Gould
Birney, D. The diaries of Adam & Eve
Bitterman, S. The price
Blais, M.-C. A couple
Blais, M.-C. Fever
Blais, M.-C. Ghost of a voice
Bogdan, K. Gunter's wife
Bogdan, K. My name is such and such
Breslin, J. Contract with Jackie
Briusov, V. The wayfarer
Brown, V. N. Roadtrip
Cameron, S. Flights
Cartwright, J. I liked a slag's deodorant
Chambers, R. Marg Szkaluba (Pissy's wife)
Christy, J. Creep
Courtney, E. Owls
Cram, C. West of stupid
Cristofer, M. Breaking up
De Matteo, D. The obit
Dietz, S. After you
Dietz, S. The Nina variations
Dixon, M. B., and Smith, V. Snapshot: little Pezidents
Dowie, C. Death and dancing
Dresser, R. What are you afraid of?
Elisha, R. Two
Farquhar, R. Kissing Sid James

MIXED CAST—*Continued*

Fechter, S. The last cigarette
Felder, L. Flight of fancy
Felder, L. The magic kingdom
Feydeau, G. Wooed and viewed
Feydeau, G. Wooed and viewed
Filloux, C. Photographs from S-21
Flacks, D., and Greenblatt, R. Sib
Foote, D. Farley and Betsy
Forbes, C. Courting Prometheus
Fraser, B. Poor Superman
Fréchette, C. Elisa's skin
Friel, B. The Yalta game
Gallagher, M. Brother
Germann, G. The observatory
Germann, G. The observatory
Gersten-Vassilaros, A. The airport play
Gersten-Vassilaros, A. Motel story
Gersten-Vassilaros, A. Rescue at the moment of death
Gilroy, F. D. Come next Tuesday
Gilroy, F. D. Present tense
Gilroy, F. D. Real to reel
Glancy, D. The lesser wars
Godber, J. April in Paris
Godber, J. Happy Jack
Godber, J. September in the rain
Goldstein, D. L. Burn
Gorisch, A. K. The individuality of streetlamps
Gough, L. The red room
Goyette, A. Marc and Marie
Graham, N. The basement at the bottom at the end of the world
Graziano, D. Acorn
Griffiths, L. The Darling family
Griffiths, L. The Darling family
Gurney, A. R. Darlene
Gurney, A. R. Darlene
Gurney, A. R. Love letters
Handy, P. East of the sun and west of the moon
Hare, D. The blue room
Hare, D. The blue room
Healey, M., and Lynch, K. Kreskinned
Healey, M., and Lynch, K. Yodellers
Hedges, P. Cake
Hedges, P. Noodles and peas
Hedges, P. Scene with celery
Holman, R. Lost
Howe, T. The divine fallacy

Huie, K. Yasuko and the young s-s-samurai
Hutton, A. I dream before I take the stand
Hutton, A. Last train to Nibroc
Hutton, A. Last train to Nibroc
Hutton, A. Studio portrait
Hwang, D. H. Bondage
Hwang, D. H. The house of sleeping beauties
Hwang, D. H. The sound of a voice
Ives, D. Bolero
Ives, D. Dr. Fritz; or, The forces of light
Ives, D. The green hill
Jordan, J. Mpls., St. Paul
Katims, J. The man who couldn't dance
Kennedy, A. She talks to Beethoven
Kuruvilla, S. Snapshot: night out
Lauro, S. Open admissions
Levi, S. Cherry and Little Banjo
Levi, S. The gulf of crimson
Levi, S. Red roses for my lady
Levy, D. Clam
Lhota, B. Romance
Lhota, B. Strangers
Li, A. Compatible
Linney, R. Stars
Lloyd, M. Dead certain
Lloyd, M. Dead certain
Lodato, V. Snapshot: the great father
Loewenstern, M. Carnality
London, J. The birthmark
Mamet, D. Deeny
Mamet, D. Deeny
Manzi, W. Moroccan travel guide
Manzi, W. The queen of the parting shot
Marcus, M. F. The gardens of Frau Hess
Margulies, D. L.A.
Margulies, D. Misadventure
Martin, J. Making the call
Martin, M. Three questions
Massicotte, S. Mary's wedding
Mastrosimone, W. Precipice
Mastrosimone, W. Precipice
Mattern, J. Scrapple
McKee, J. Jill on a recliner, reading
Melski, M. Hockey mom, hockey dad
Miller, A. Elegy for a lady
Miller, E. Last will and testament
Miller, M. Ferris wheel

MIXED CAST—*Continued*

Van Itallie, J.-C. Eat cake
Vinaver, M. Dissident, goes without saying
Wagner, C. The monument
Walker, B. The moons of Alnyron
Walsh, E. Disco pigs
Wasserstein, W. The man in a case
Weisman, A. Snapshot: thrift of the Magi
Wilhelm, L. The parrot
Wilhelm, L. A significant betrayal
Williams, B. C. Token to the moon
Williams, T. Auto-da-fe
Williams, T. Out cry
Wilner, S. Joan of Arkansas
Wilson, L. Talley's folly
Wiltse, D. Otis proposes
Wiltse, D. To wit and to whom
Wiltse, D. Triangles for two
Wright, C. Snapshot: bomb squad
Wright, D. Wildwood Park
Wright, D. Wildwood Park
Yourgrau, T. Mid-life

2 characters and extra (1g 1m extra)

Ehn, E. The freak (George)

2 characters and extra (1m 1w extra)

Reid, C. My name, shall I tell you my name
Wilder, T. The flight into Egypt

2 characters and extras (1m 1w extras)

García Lorca, F. Buster Keaton takes a walk
Guare, J. The talking dog
Hindman, J. Pete 'n' Keely
Kokoschka, O. The burning bush
Martin, J. Jack and Jill: a romance
Reingold, J. Creative development
Silverstein, S. The trio
Sutton, J. Art for art's sake
c Vogel, L. The fall into sin
c Vogel, L. Samson
Vogel, P. How I learned to drive

3 character (1m 2w)

Thiessen, V. Apple

3 characters (1b 1m 1w)

Holman, R. Making noise quietly

c Miller, K. S. The emperor's new clothes

3 characters (1b 2w)

c McDonnell, K. Loon boy
Wilder, T. Nascuntur poetae . . .

3 characters (1g 1b 1m)

c Jensen, L., and Wing, P. Coming around

3 characters (1g 1m 1w)

Filloux, C. The lessons of my father
Martini, C. House of glass
Wilder, T. Brother Fire

3 characters (1m 2w)

c Abela, D. Circus caravan
Baker, E. A. Up, down, strange, charmed, beauty, and truth
Berman, B. Dancing with a devil
Berman, B. Dancing with a devil
Brooks, V. Swan song
Burke, K. J. Charming & Rose: true love
Churchill, C. Far away
Congdon, C. Lips
Congdon, C. Under Lubianka Square
Congdon, C. Under Lubianka Square
Cruz, M. Fur
Cullen, M. Anna Weiss
Dempsey, S. Armagideon
c Duffield, N. Skin and bones
Edwards, G. Four walls
Elliot, T. Feed
Fill, S. Night visits
Filloux, C. Storks
Fosbrook, M. Remembering things
Frayn, M. Here
Galton, F. Nothing in the world like it
Gilroy, F. D. Match point
Glass, J. M. Play memory
Gurney, A. R. The golden age
Halvorson, K. One hundred women
Healy, A. M. Lonely
Healy, A. M. Lonely
Hedges, P. Good as new
Hughes, D. New morning
Ives, D. Arabian nights
Kareken, J. Hot Rod
Kramer, S. Hold for three
Laxdal, V. Karla and Grif
c Laxdal, V. Ruby and the rock
Levin, K. Just one night

MIXED CAST—*Continued*

Lowinger, R. The Encanto file
Marcato, R. Lunchtime
Marcato, R. Lunchtime
Martin, N. Women on the verge of HRT
Martin, S. Patter for the floating lady
McGuinness, F. Miss Julie
Meuller, L. The only woman general
c Miller, K. S. A thousand cranes
Milligan, J. Strange as it may seem
Mitchell, D. The hour of lamps
Miyagawa, C. Yesterday's window
Murray, P. Salt
Murray-Smith, J. Nightfall
Nigro, D. Seance
Nigro, D. The sin-eater
Nigro, D. The sin-eater
Nigro, D. The sin-eater
Nigro, D. Warburton's Cook
Orlandersmith, D. My red hand, my black hand
Owens, R. Three front
Philip, M. N. Coups and calypsos
Pintauro, J. Two eclairs
Rebeck, T. Does this woman have a name?
Rebeck, T. Great to see you
Ross, B. Little by little
Sapergia, B. Roundup
Sheehy, J. Gave her the eye
Sheehy, J. Gave her the eye
Silverstein, S. Buy one, get one free
Smith, V. Breaking the chain
Stinson, J. Median
Stolz, T. Mahalia
Sunshine, G. Al takes a bride
Taylor, R. Love poem #98
Walker, G. F. Tough!
Wallace, N. In the fields of Aceldama
Wilder, T. Childe Roland to the dark tower came
Wilder, T. Fanny Otcott
Wilder, T. The unerring instinct
Williams, T. The lady of Larkspur Lotion
Yew, C. Red

3 characters (1w 2m)
Boccioni, U. Genius and culture

3 characters (2b 1g)
y Lazarus, J. Night light
y Lazarus, J. Not so dumb

3 characters (2m 1w)
Adams, L. D. Greeks and centaurs
Andersen, D. R. In other words
Anderson, J. Lynette has beautiful skin
Apstein, T. The likeness
Araújo, L. Vanzetti
Asher, S. F. The wolf and its shadows
Auburn, D. Are you ready?
Bailey, F. Keeper
Bailey, F. Keeper
Beber, N. Sensation(s)
Belber, S. Tape
Bernard, L. The bear
Blais, M.-C. Exile
Bogosian, E. Bitter sauce
y Bond, E. Eleven vests
y Bond, E. Eleven vests & Tuesday
Bowne, A. Beirut
Bozzone, B. War
Brennan, K. Magpie
Cabal, F. Passage
Carley, D. Two ships passing
Cashin, C. C. Mail-order Annie
Cashmore, B., and Powrie, A. Trip of a lifetime
Chambers, R. Pretty blue
Chappell, E. Double vision
Chekhov, A. P. The bear
Chekhov, A. P. The bear
Chekhov, A. P. The proposal
Chekhov, A. P. The proposal
Chiasson, H. Cape Enrage
Clark, R. A bench in the sun
Crowther, C. Tryst
Cruz, N. A bicycle country
Daniels, J. Boom town
Darke, N. The dead monkey
Davis, K. The sure-success twelve-step program to self-affirmation and esteem
Davis, T. Lawyers, guns, & money
Davis, T. Lawyers, guns, & money
Farquhar, R. Dust to dust
Feydeau, G. Romance in a flat
y Foon, D. Chasing the money
Frayn, M. Copenhagen
Frayn, M. Copenhagen

MIXED CAST—*Continued*

Fréchette, C. Seven days in the life of Simon Labrosse
Frockt, D. L. Hard-boiled
Fugard, A. The captain's tiger
Fugard, A. The captain's tiger
Gadea, W. Brothers
Gilbert, S. The birth of Casper G. Schmidt
Gilbert, S. Schubert lied
Gilroy, F. D. Give the bishop my faint regards
Gilroy, F. D. The golf ball
Gilroy, F. D. The golf ball
Gilroy, F. D. Last licks
Gilroy, F. D. The next contestant
Gilroy, F. D. The only game in town
Gilroy, F. D. So please be kind
Gilroy, F. D. The subject was roses
Gilroy, F. D. A way with words
Godber, J. Weekend breaks
Gough, L. Crossing the bar
Graybill, C. Eye to eye
Greenberg, R. The author's voice
Greenberg, R. The dazzle
Greenberg, R. Three days of rain
Greenberg, R. Three days of rain
Grimsley, J. The lizard of Tarsus
Gromelski, B. Position available
Hannah, D. Fathers and sons
Hare, D. My zinc bed
Hatcher, J. Downtown
Hedges, P. Andy and Claire
Hedges, P. Oregon
Hedges, P. Two and an orange
Henkel, M. Corporate handbook line 11
Horovitz, I. Lebensraum
Howard, D. Electric roses
Hwang, D. H. Fob
Ives, D. The Philadelphia
Ives, D. Time flies
Jennings, C. S. Classyass
Johnson, M. Jabiru
y Jones, E. Y. Not on this night
Kane, S. Blasted
Kane, S. Blasted
Kops, B. Playing Sinatra
LaDue, T. Prom night
Lewis, T. No vacancy
Long, Q. The flight of the last Calhoon
Lucas, C. Grief

MacDonald, R. D. The ice house
MacLachlan, A. Dead eye boy
Madden, D. Drop
Mamet, D. Jolly
Mamet, D. Jolly
Marowitz, C. Stage fright
Martin, S. Guillotine
Martini, C. Up on the roof
McLean, L. Riddance
McPherson, C. Dublin carol
McPherson, C. Dublin carol
Mee, C. L. Limonade tous les jours
Miles, K. I hate you on Mondays
c Miller, K. S. The Mark Twain show
c Miller, K. S. The time machine
Milligan, J. Any friend of Percy D'Angelino is a friend of mine
Milligan, J. Exodus from McDonaldland
Milligan, J. Less said, the better
Milligan, J. Rivals
Murray, T. C. The briery gap
Neilson, A. Normal
Nelson, G. Speak
Nielson, K. A true fool's folly
Nigro, D. Gogol
Nigro, D. Lucy and the mystery of the vine-encrusted mansion
Nigro, D. Quint and Miss Jessel at Bly
Orloff, R. Prague summer
Palmieri, M. The departure of Brian O'Callahan
Palmieri, M. Poor fellas
Paterson, D. L. Stone the crows
Pedrero, P. A night divided
Penhall, J. Love and Understanding
Reitz, D. Where I come from
Rivera, J. Cloud tectonics
Rodriguez, E. Estorias del barrio: un ghost
y Roets, J. Cyrano
Sagal, P. The Taliban
Schenkar, J. Cabin fever
Shawn, W. The designated mourner
Shear, C. Dirty blonde
Sherborne, C. Look at everything twice, for me
Silverstein, S. Duck
Silverstein, S. No dogs allowed
Silverstein, S. Wash and dry
Silverstein, S. What are you doing in there?

MIXED CAST—*Continued*

Smith, O. Giant steps
Stinson, J. Median
Svich, C. But there are fires
Sweet, J. Cover
Tait, L. Jesus and the monkfish
Upton, J. Everlasting rose
Van Itallie, J.-C. War
Vickery, F. The drag factor
Vinaver, M. Nina, that's something else
Viswananthan, P. House of sacred cows
Vogelstein, C. All about Al
Vogelstein, C. All about Al
Vogelstein, C. All about Al
Wellman, M. Three Americanisms
Wilde, O. A Florentine tragedy
Wilder, T. And the sea shall give up its
  dead
Wilder, T. The angel on the ship
Wilder, T. Centaurs
Wilder, T. Leviathan
Wilder, T. The message and Jehanne
Wilder, T. Mozart and the gray steward
Wilder, T. The penny that beauty spent
Williams, T. Kingdom of earth
Wilner, S. Bake off
Wilner, S. Hunger
Wilson, D. H. How to make your theater
  pay
Woudstra, K. Burying the dog
Wright, C. The pavilion
Yeaton, D. Helen at risk
Young, D. Clout

3 characters and extra (1m 2w extra)

Rudolph, K. "Flickering images"
Schenkar, J. The universal wolf

3 characters and extra (2m 1w extra)

Bishop, C., and Fuller, E. Success
c Martini, C. The field

3 characters and extras (1m 2w extras)

Anderson, S. J. Tidings of comfort and
  joy
Fusco, C., and Bustamante, M. T. Stuff
Kennedy, A. A rat's mass
Nigro, D. The great Gromboolian plain
Rivera, J. A tiger in Central Park
Silverstein, S. The trio
Strindberg, A. Lady Julie

Strindberg, A. Miss Julie
Vogelstein, C. Sisters
Williams, T. Portrait of a Madonna

3 characters and extras (2b 1g extras)

c Rowland, B. T. The birthday gifts

3 characters and extras (2g 1m extras)

y Valentine, A. Swimming the globe

3 characters and extras (2m 1w extras)

Bruchac, J. Gluskabe and Old Man Win-
  ter
Carter, L. Gulliver
Constable, J. Iceman
Gems, P. Marlene
Harrigan, E. The blue and the grey
Howe, T. Rembrandt's gift
Ives, D. Time flies
Jonson, B. The masque of blackness
Jonson, B. The queen's masques: the
  first, of blackness
Kilroy, T. The secret fall of Constance
  Wilde
Klavan, L. The summer sublet
c Lippa, L. The sorcerer's apprentice
No room at the inn (Las posadas)
Stein, G. Doctor Faustus lights the lights
Williams, T. 27 wagons full of cotton
c Zeder, S. Wiley and the Hairy Man

4 characters (1b 1g 1m 1w)

Anderson, S. J. While you were out
Farquhar, S. I do solemnly declare
c Porter, P. Smashed eggs

4 characters (1b 1m 2w)

y Sundstrom, B. The hundred penny box

4 characters (1b 2m 1w)

c Miller, K. S. The sword in the stone
Norman, M. Traveler in the dark

4 characters (1b 3g)

c Rowland, B. T. Christmas hide and seek

4 characters (1g 2m 1w)

Ehn, E. Dashboard (Christopher)
García Lorca, F. Chimera
García Lorca, F. The maiden, the sailor,
  and the student

MIXED CAST—*Continued*

Goldberg, J. Refuge

4 characters (1m 3w)

Ackermann, J. The batting cage
Baker, E. A. The seventeenth of June
Compton, J. The big picture
Crowther, C. Footprints in the sand
De Wet, R. Crossing
Fugard, A. Sorrows and rejoicings
Gault, C. Sky
Gow, D. Bea's niece
Griffiths, A., and others Bittergirl
Hartman, K. The mother of modern censorship
Hollinger, M. Tiny island
Hollinger, M. Tiny Island
LeRoy, G. Not waving--
Levin, K. Just one night
Lill, W. The fighting days
Loomer, L. Accelerando
Medley, C. Maiden Lane
Merzer, G. Going nowhere apace
Nigro, D. The malefactor's bloody register
Overmyer, E. On the verge; or, The geography of yearning
Paterson, D. L. The king's horses
Rahman, A. Only in America
Real, C. The battle of Bull Run always makes me cry
Redwood, J. H. The old settler
Rivera, J. The winged man
Romero, E. If Susan Smith could talk
Romero, E. If Susan Smith could talk
Simon, E. Moonlight and Valentino
Tait, L. The babysitter
Tait, L. Germany
Terry, M. Breakfast serial
Ward, F. Somebody somebody's returning
Wells, M. L. The "I" word: interns
Wilder, T. The drunken sisters
Williams, T. Lord Byron's love letter
Wimberly, B. Saint Lucy's eyes
Wimberly, B. Saint Lucy's eyes

4 characters (2b 1m 1w)

McClelland, C. E. Certain arrangements

4 characters (2m 2w)

Frayn, M. Alarms & excursions

4 characters (2m 2w)

Albee, E. The play about the baby
Alexander, R. The last orbit of Billy Mars
Alfaro, L. Bitter homes and gardens
Alvarez, L. Hidden parts
Andersen, D. R. They can't take that away from me
Anderson, S. J. Now a shepherd, no longer a sheep
Aronson, B. Light years
Aronson, B. Light years
Auburn, D. Proof
Ayvazian, L. Twenty-four years
Badlam, R. Slop-culture
Badlam, R. Slop-culture
Barnett, G. T for 2
Barry, S. The steward of Christendom
Belbel, S. Fourplay
Benet i Jornet, J. M. Desire
Bishop, C., and Fuller, E. A friend from high school
Blessing, L. Reproduction
Bobrick, S. Remember me?
Bovell, A. Speaking in tongues
Bowne, A. Sharon and Billy
Brel, J. Jacques Brel is alive and well & living in Paris
Bullock, M. Sokotra
Bunin, K. Credeaux canvas
Busch, C. Queen Amarantha
Byerrum, E. Deja rendezvous
Byerrum, E. Remedial surveillance
Cairns, G. Danceland
Caputo, L. Birth marks
Chan, M. Mom, Dad, I'm living with a white girl
Charnas, S. M. Vampire dreams
Cheng, K. E. The China crisis
Chopin, K. M. Double take
Clarvoe, A. Walking on the roof
Cleage, P. Bourbon at the border
Cohen, D. J. No way to treat a lady
Conquest, N. A modern romance
Corbett, B. The big slam
Davidson, C. E. Mosquito dirigible aerosol deodorant
DeLillo, D. Valparaiso

MIXED CAST—*Continued*

c Deverell, R. Belonging
c Deverell, R. Video wars
c Deverell, R. Weird kid
Donaghy, T. Minutes from the blue route
Dunbar, P. L. Dream lovers
Dunn, M. Gendermat
Ekstrom, P., and DeBoy, D. Doctor! Doctor! a medical musical comedy revue
Evans, S. Little sister
Feibleman, P. S. Cakewalk
Feydeau, G. The boor hug
Fosbrook, M. Figuring things
Frayn, M. Alarms & excursions
Frisby, T. Funny about love
Gault, C. Otherwise Bob
Gilbert, S. Independence
Gilroy, F. D. Dreams of glory
Gilroy, F. D. 'Twas brillig
Glancy, D. Jump kiss
Glore, J. The Morpheus quartet
Godber, J. Perfect pitch
Godber, J. Perfect pitch
Goldberg, J. Refuge
Gomolvilas, P. Donut holes in orbit
Gregg, S. A private moment
Griffiths, L. Brother Andre's heart
Grimsley, J. The borderland
Gurney, A. R. Another Antigone
Gurney, A. R. The cocktail hour
Gurney, A. R. The fourth wall
Gurney, A. R. The fourth wall
Gurney, A. R. The guest lecturer
Gurney, A. R. The guest lecturer
Gurney, A. R. Later life
Gurney, A. R. Sweet Sue
Gurney, A. R. Sylvia
Guyer, M. Loyalties
Hall, L. Wittgenstein on Tyne
c Hamlett, C. Author! Author!
Hare, D. The bay at Nice
Harris, R. In two minds
Hawdon, R. God and Stephen Hawking
Henley, B. Control freaks
Henley, B. Control freaks
Herbert, K. Hit and run
Horovitz, I. Alfred dies
Horovitz, I. Alfred the Great
Horovitz, I. Our father's failing
Hunter, D. Un tango en la noche

Ikoli, T. Scrape off the black
Ives, D. Captive audience
Ives, D. Degas, c'est moi
c Kacmar, K. The oldest story ever told
Kane, S. Crave
Kushner, T. Terminating
Kushner, T. Terminating
LaBute, N. The shape of things
Laurence, C. About Alice
y Lazarus, J. Secrets
Lemoine, S. Evelyn Strange
Lewis, C. W. The one-eyed man is king
Lewis, D. Misconceptions
Lipkin, D. Pithecus
Long, Q. The Sixth Floor museum
Lucas, C. Stranger
Lucas, C. Throwing your voice
Lucas, C. What I meant was
Lucas, C. What I meant was
Lucas, C. What I meant was
Lucas, C. What I meant was
Macpherson, R. The terrible false deception
Marber, P. Closer
Margulies, D. Dinner with friends
Margulies, D. Dinner with friends
Margulies, D. Dinner with friends
Margulies, D. Luna Park
Martin, M. Once upon a time in Wigan
May, E. In and out of the light
McClinton, M. I. Stones and bones
McDonagh, M. The beauty queen of Leenane
McDonagh, M. The beauty queen of Leenane
McLean, D. I'd rather go blind
c Miller, K. S. Aladdin and the magic lamp
c Miller, K. S. Jack and the beanstalk
y Miller, K. S. Shakespeare to go!
Miller, Jesse Onionheads
Mueller, L. The mothers
Muschell, D. Amelia, once more
Neipris, J. Almost in Vegas
Nelson, R. Jitterbugging: scenes of sex in a new society
Nelson, R. Madame Melville
Nelson, R. The Vienna notes
Nigro, D. Doctor Faustus
Norman, M. Third and Oak
Oates, J. C. Good to know you

MIXED CAST—*Continued*

O'Donnell, M. Marred bliss
Oliver, K. Swollen tongues
y Pachino, J. Race
c Paxton, K. Tatyana's golden doe
Pedrero, P. The railing (El pasamanos)
Pielmeier, J. Pillow talk
Pollock, S. Angel's trumpet
Porter, R. M. Man, woman, dinosaur
Rebeck, T. Spike heels
Redwood, J. H. No niggers, no Jews, no dogs
Robins, J. D. Recipe for murder
Rodin, T. The slow eviction of Ruby Rosenholtz
Rosenfeld, S. Z. The flatted fifth
Schenkar, J. Fulfilling Koch's postulate
Sedaris, D., and Sedaris, A. The book of Liz
Shanley, J. P. Psychopathia sexualis
Shem, S., and Surrey, J. L. Bill W. and Dr. Bob
Sher, E. Derailed
Sherman, J. Romance in D
Shimko, R. Specks
Silver, N. The Eros trilogy
Smilow, D. Brights
Smith, C. Four-play
Stanley, J. Tesla's letters
Strand, R. The guest of honor
Strand, R. The guest of honor
Sunde, K. How his bride came to Abraham
Sunde, K. Truth takes a holiday
y Surface, M. H. Broken rainbows
Tait, L. A family portrait
Tait, L. The swimming pools of Paris
Taylor, D. H. Only drunks and children tell the truth
Taylor, D. H. Only drunks and children tell the truth
Toddie, J. L. By the name of Kensington
Townsend, J. Angels and saints
Turtle, R. Lunacy
Upton, J. Sunspots
Vinaver, M. Situation vacant
Walker, G. F. Adult entertainment
Walker, G. F. Featuring Loretta
Walker, G. F. Problem child
Walker, G. F. Risk everything
Wilhelm, L. Meridian, Mississippi redux

Williams, T. The glass menagerie
Wilson, L. Serenading Louie
Wilson, S. The grass widow
Wymark, O. Mothering Sunday

4 characters (3b 1w)

c Houston, V. H. Hula heart

4 characters (3m 1w)

Carmichael, F. Decisions, decisions
Chekhov, A. P. The night before the trial
Constable, J. Dead man's handle
Derrett, Bridget A light lunch
Donaghy, T. Northeast local
Dresser, R. The road to ruin
Ernst, P. The most perfect day
Esson, L. Mates
Gilroy, F. D. Fore
Goluboff, B. In-betweens
Gough, L. Head
Graham, B. Coyote on a fence
Grant, D. M. Snakebit
Grant, D. M. Snakebit
Healey, M. Plan B
Holloway, J. The dark
Johnson, T. Hysteria; or, Fragments of an analysis of an obsessional neurosis
Keeffe, B. Gimme shelter: Gem
Keeffe, B. Gimme shelter: Getaway
Keeffe, B. Gimme shelter: Gotcha
y Kornhauser, B. Lincoln's log; or Better angels
Krakower, B. 4 AM (open all night)
Leight, W. Glimmer, glimmer and shine
Lonergan, K. Lobby hero
Lucas, C. The dying Gaul
MacDonald, A. Eat me
Marcus, F. Matchstick dreams
Margulies, D. New Year's Eve and Kibbutz
Martin, S. The zig-zag woman
Mayne, R. The troth
McConnell, J., and Tripp, M. Death is catching
McDonagh, M. A skull in Connemara
McLean, D. Blackden
Merrill, J. The bait (1953)
Merrill, J. The bait (1988)
Moses, B. P. This is how it is
Neilson, A. The night before Christmas
Norman, M. The holdup

MIXED CAST—*Continued*

Obolensky, K. Lobster Alice
Pedrero, P. First star (Una estrella)
Piatigorsky, A. Easy Lenny Lazmon and the great western ascension
Pietri, E. R. P. El cabron
Rahman, A. The Mojo and the Sayso
Rhys, T. The old petrol station
Safdie, O. Private jokes, public places
Scheffer, W. Easter
Schmitt, E.-E. The visitor
Sherman, J. The retreat
Shinn, C. Four
Smith, V. Marguerite Bonet
Spencer, S. In the western garden
Vinaver, M. The neighbours
Wertenbaker, T. After Darwin
Wiltse, D. Temporary
Wright, D. Baby talk
Yew, C. Wonderland
Yourgrau, T. Cries from the cockpit

4 characters and extra (2m 2w extra)

Reza, Y. Life X 3
Taylor, D. H. Girl who loved her horses
Waterhouse, K. Good grief
Wood, S. And where was Pancho Villa when you really needed him?

4 characters and extra (3m 1w extra)

c Grauer, R., and Urquhart, J. Mark Twain's Huckleberry Finn
Kramer, S. World without memory

4 characters and extras (1b 1m 2w extras)

c McCullough, L. E. The bird of happiness

4 characters and extras (1b 2m 1w extras)

Margulies, D. Nocturne

4 characters and extras (1g 2m 1w extras)

Champagne, L. Coaticook

4 characters and extras (1m 3w extras)

Anderson, S. J. Oh, come on, Emmanuel
García Lorca, F. The love of Don Perlimplin for Belisa in the garden
Romero, E. ¡Curanderas! serpents of the clouds

4 characters and extras (2b 1m 1w extras)

c Winther, B. The deer dance

4 characters and extras (2m 2w extras)

Brustein, R. Nobody dies on Friday
Chekhov, A. P. The festivities
y Chislett, A. Then and now
Kopit, A. L. Oh Dad, poor dad, mamma's hung you in the closet and I'm feelin' so sad
Levy, D. Macbeth—false memories
MacLennan, M. L. Beat the sunset
Margulies, D. Pitching to the star
c McCullough, L. E. Rachel the clever
Slotboom, C. The train
Svich, C. Prodigal kiss
Wasserstein, W. Waiting for Philip Glass
Wasserstein, W. Waiting for Philip Glass
Wedekind, F. Death and devil

4 characters and extras (3m 1w extras)

Bachmann, I. A deal in dreams
Baraka, A. Dutchman
c Carlisle, B. The crane wife
Carpenter, B. Fall
Coen, L., and Crane, D. Epic proportions
Dozer, D. The milling crowd dies
Jonson, B. Mercury vindicated from the alchemists at court
Long, Q. Funeral home
Mastrosimone, W. Like totally weird
Orloff, R. Oedi
Osborne, J. Under plain cover
c Vogel, L. A test for Esther
Wilder, T. The Emporium

5 characters (1b 1g 1m 2w)

Bradbeer, S. Full bloom
Hannah, D. Rubber Dolly

5 characters (1b 1g 2m 1w)

Wallace, N. The trestle at Pope Lick Creek

5 characters (1b 1m 3w)

Ehn, E. Contemplacion (Mary and Martha)

5 characters (1b 2m 1w)

McGuire, M. These flowers are for my mother

5 characters (1b 2m 2w)

Gurney, A. R. Ancestral voices: a family story

MIXED CAST—*Continued*

Gurney, A. R. Ancestral voices: a family story

Hairston, J. a.m. Sunday

Milligan, J. Juris prudence

5 characters (1b 3m 1w)

Esson, L. Andeganora

5 characters (1g 2m 2w)

Ehn, E. Cedar (John of the Cross)

Heather Brothers Love bites

Rapp, A. Nocturne

Ryan, J. The young girl and the monsoon

5 characters (1g 3m 1w)

O'Neill, E. The rope

Wallace, N. One flea spare

5 characters (1m 4w)

Chapman, J., and Davidson, I. Late flowering

y Chislett, A. Flippin' in

DeChristopher, D. Fifteen minutes

Dundas, H. Cannibals

c Hamlett, C. Mother Goose gumshoe

Jory, J. Scruples

Lambert, A. Very heaven

MacIvor, D. Marion Bridge

Napier, E. Gone missing

Oates, J. C. Bad girls

Osborne, R. Seeing stars in Dixie

Thorne, J. V. The exact center of the universe

Weisman, A. Be aggressive

Williams, C. Just be frank

Williams, M. N. Kwa-landlady

5 characters (2b 2m 1w)

Sánchez, E. Clean

5 characters (2g 2m 1w)

Jordan, J. Tatjana in color

5 characters (2m 3w)

Adams, L. D. Poodle with guitar and dark glasses

Albee, E. The American dream

Ayckbourn, A. Things we do for love

Bowen, J. Singles

Busch, C. The tale of the allergist's wife

Carley, D. A view from the roof

Carr, M. Low in the dark

Chappell, E. Something's burning

Coward, N. Private lives

Cruz, N. Night train to Bolina

Curran, C. Maple Lodge

Dietz, S. Rocket man

Dresser, R. Bed & breakfast

Dresser, R. Wonderful world

Dresser, R. Wonderful world

Duarte, I. Bingo babes

Durang, C. Baby with the bathwater

Durang, C. Baby with the bathwater

Farrell, C. The once attractive woman

Gilman, R. Blue surge

Gilroy, F. D. That summer—that fall

Goldberg, J. Good thing

Goldberg, J. Stuck

Gurney, A. R. The perfect party

Hartman, K. Gum

Hawdon, R. The mating game

Hunter, M. Transit of Venus

Jackson, N. A hotel on Marvin Gardens

Jackson, N. A hotel on Marvin Gardens

Jeffries, B. Pastimes

Jenkins, M. Strindberg knew my father

Kane, A. Marriage can be hazardous to your health

Kerr, R. The Potato Creek chair of death

Lucas, C. Three postcards

Magee, R. The green heart

Maponya, M. Umongikazi (The nurse)

Martin, J. Tattoo

Martin, J. Tattoo

Martin, J. Tattoo

McManus, B. Selkirk Avenue

Mtshali, T. S. Weemen

Newmeir, J. H. Babysitting Calvin

O'Callaghan, J. Some mother's son

Pape, R. Hearts beating faster

Plowman, G. Touching tomorrow

Pollock, S. End dream

Pollock, S. Moving pictures

Redhill, M. Building Jerusalem

Reynolds, J. Stonewall Jackson's house

Rosen, S. Duet for bear and dog

Schisgal, M. Playtime

Sears, D. Harlem duet

Sharkey, J., and Sharkey, T. Just say yes!

MIXED CAST—*Continued*

Shearer, J. Georgia
Smith, S. Background artiste
Smyth, D. E. Sole survivors
Stewart-Brown, C. The gene pool
y Surface, M. H. Dancing solo
Sutton, J. Layover
Thompson, J. Habitat
Vinaver, M. A smile on the end of the line
Weldon, F. Flood warning
Wilder, T. The marriage we deplore
Williams, C. Just be frank
Williams, N. The way you look tonight
Yourgrau, T. Peanuts

5 characters (3m 2w)

Akalaitis, J. Ti Jean blues
Argall, T. G. A year in the death of Eddie Jester
Belke, D. Blackpool and Parrish
Bellusci, M. Born to be blue
Bourke, K. The hunt for Red Willie
Chambers, R. Dirt
Clark, R. Pierre and Marie
Cleage, P. Blues for an Alabama sky
Cleage, P. Blues for an Alabama sky
Constable, J. The false hairpiece
Crimp, M. Getting attention
Crimp, M. Play with repeats
Crip, N. J. That good night
Dixon, M. B., and Smith, V. The problem solver
Dixon, M. E. Into the light
Donaghy, T. The beginning of August
Donaghy, T. The beginning of August
Dresser, R. Something in the air
Elisha, R. The Goldberg variations
Elton, B. Silly cow
Elton, B. Silly cow
Esson, L. Dead timber
Fo, D. We won't pay! We won't pay
y Foote, D. When they speak of Rita
Foxton, D. Breakfast for one
y Frockt, D. L. The book of Ruth
c Fry, G. Lockie Leonard, scumbuster
Gibson, F. Belle
Glaspell, S. The outside
Glaspell, S. Trifles
Godber, J. Unleashed
Greenberg, R. The American plan

Gurney, A. R. Labor Day
Gurney, A. R. Labor Day
Harris, R. Ghosts
Harris, Z. Further than the furthest thing
Harvey, J. Beautiful thing
Hatcher, J. What Corbin knew
Henley, B. Abundance
Hoben, G. Telephone
Ives, D. Babel's in arms
Ives, D. Enigma variations
Ives, D. Lives of the saints
Ives, D. The mystery at Twicknam Vicarage
Ives, D. Soap opera
Johnson, T. Dead funny
Jones, J. M. The crazy plays
Kemnitz, R. D., and McMaster, J. The processional
Kemnitz, R. D., and McMaster, J. The processional
Keyes, S. Moonlight cocktail
Krakower, B. Mixed emotions
Kyle, C. Plunge
Letts, T. Killer Joe
Letts, T. Killer Joe
Levy, D. Honey, baby
Lill, W. The Glace Bay Miners' Museum
Linney, R. Oscar over here
Lonergan, K. The Waverly Gallery
Lonergan, K. The Waverly Gallery
Lucas, C. Unmemorable
Macklin, P. Someplace warm
Manno, K. The miracles of May
Marowitz, C. La Parisienne
Martin, M. The life and times of young Bob Scallion
y Mast, E. Wolf child
Neilson, A. Year of the family
Nigro, D. Beast with two backs
O'Neill, T. A few roos loose in the top paddock
Perez, F. Estorias del barrio: special people of international character
Plater, A. Peggy for you
Post, D. Drowning sorrows
Rachilde Voice of blood (La voix du sang)
Ravenhill, M. Shopping and fucking
Robinson, M. Colonial tongues
Robinson, M. The heart as it lived

MIXED CAST—*Continued*

Rusconi, P. These two couples went to Italy

Sánchez, E. Icarus

Schalchlin, S. The last session

Sherman, J. Reading Hebron

Shields, C., and Williamson, D. Anniversary

Silver, N. The maiden's prayer

Smith, E. The uneasy chair

Smith, E. The uneasy chair

Snelgrove, M. Marking time

Stickland, E. Sitting on paradise

Strand, R. The bug

Stroppel, F. Actor!

Stuart, K. A shoe is not a question

Tait, L. East play

Toddie, J. L. And send forth a raven

Torres, J. Better half dead

Upton, J. Confidence

Walker, G. F. Criminal genius

Walker, G. F. The end of civilization

Wallace, N. In the heart of America

Wallace, N. The trestle at Pope Lick Creek

Wallace, N. The trestle at Pope Lick Creek

White, E. N. Millennium 7

Whitemore, H. God only knows

Williams, S. Nobody's perfect

Wilson, J. Kilt

Wright, D. Lot 13: the bone violin

Wright, D. Unwrap your candy

York, Y. Mask of the unicorn warrior

5 characters (3w 2m)

Blakeman, H. Caravan

5 characters (4m 1w)

c Adamson-Klein, T. The frog in all of us

Alvarez, L. The wonderful tower of Humbert Lavoignet

Beane, D. C. Music from a sparkling planet

Beber, N. Afterthought

Bennett, S. Drummers

Bitterman, S. The job

Bitterman, S. The job

Chaurette, N. All the Verdis of Venice

Constable, J. Black mass

Culture Clash (Group) A bowl of beings

Cumming, P. Ti-Jean

Daniels, J. Apartment 3A

Fulford, R. W. Gulag

Giron, A. Flight

Guirgis, S. A. Jesus hopped the 'A' train

Halliwell, D. Little Malcolm and his struggle against the eunuchs

Holloway, J. The monkey's paw

Holtzman, W. Hearts

Kennedy, A. Motherhood 2000

Kopit, A. L. BecauseHeCan

Lan, D. Red earth

Linney, R. Lark

Linney, R. Love like fire

MacDonald, A. Chairmaker: the musical

Marowitz, C. Stark naked

Martini, C. Conversations with my neighbour's pit bull

Mayne, R. Red turf

McPherson, C. The weir

McPherson, C. The weir

Merrill, J. The birthday

Mitchell, G. In a little world of our own

Moffat, P. Iona rain

Murray, T. C. Birthright

Nassif, R. L. Honky-tonk highway

O'Brien, D. The Last Supper restoration

y Oliver, C. Ooh ah Showab Khan

Shanley, J. P. Welcome to the moon

Shepard, S. Eyes for Consuela

Sherman, J. Three in the back, two in the head

Silver, N. The altruists

Spiro, P. Howya doin' Franky Banana?

Wilson, S. Blowjob

Zellnik, D. Killing hand

5 characters and extra (3m 2w extra)

Gurney, A. R. Far East

5 characters and extra (4m 1w extra)

c Winther, B. Latino trio: Senorita Cucaracha finds a husband

5 characters and extras (1b 1g 1m 2w extras)

Grazia, E. de The vacuum cleaner

5 characters and extras (1b 1g 2m 1w)

Sánchez, E. Floorshow: Doña Sol and her trained dog

MIXED CAST—*Continued*

5 characters and extras (1b 2g 1m 1w extras)
Cruz, N. Night train to Bolina

5 characters and extras (1b 2m 2w extras)
Joshi, A. A shaft of sunlight

5 characters and extras (1g 1m 3w extras)
Rivera, C. Betty's garage

5 characters and extras (1g 3m 1w extras)
Gonzalez, S. S. The migrant farmworker's son

5 characters and extras (1g 4m extras)
Abse, D. The eccentric

5 characters and extras (1m 4w extras)
Adams, G. Something blue

5 characters and extras (2b 2g 1m extras)
c McCullough, L. E. Roll 'em up, roll 'em up! (pastry chef)

5 characters and extras (2b 3g extras)
c McCullough, L. E. How Quentzalcoatl found the sun

5 characters and extras (2g 2m 1w extras)
Ehn, E. Pain (Eulalia)

5 characters and extras (2m 3w extras)
c McCullough, L. E. Israel reborn
Mills, S. The Danish Play
Powell, D. Women at four o'clock
Smith, S. On location
Vogelstein, C. Cats and dogs
Walsh, E. Sucking Dublin

5 characters and extras (3b 2g extras)
c McCullough, L. E. The Monkey King

5 characters and extras (3m 2w extras)
Alonso de Santos, J. L. Hostages in the barrio
Cameron, M. Tear from a glass eye
Chekhov, A. P. The jubilee
Ehn, E. Radio elephant (Barbara)
Gilroy, F. D. Contact with the enemy
Gurney, A. R. Far east
Gurney, A. R. Human events

Kennedy, A. Dramatic circle
c McCullough, L. E. Counting, from quipu to googol
Morgan, E. Christopher Marlowe's Doctor Faustus
Murray, T. C. The pipe in the fields
c Vogel, L. Judges—again

5 characters and extras (4m 1w extras)
Chikamatsu, M. The love suicides at Sonezaki
Ehn, E. 16670 (Maximilian Mary Kolbe)
Esson, L. Australia felix
Guirgis, S. A. Jesus hopped the "A" train
Hansell, S. My Medea
Hirschberg, H. "Mistakes"
O'Neill, E. The Emperor Jones
O'Neill, E. The Emperor Jones
Rabe, D. A question of mercy
Romeril, J. Miss Tanaka
Shaw, B. Widowers' houses
c Vogel, L. The patriarchs

6 characters (1b 1g 2m 2w)
Pugliese, F. Hope is the thing with feathers
York, Y. The snowflake avalanche

6 characters (1b 2g 1m 2w)
Corthron, K. Splash hatch on the E going down
c Swortzell, L. A visit from St. Nicholas; or, The night before Christmas

6 characters (1b 2m 3w)
Gray, S. The late middle classes
Ibsen, H. Little Eyolf

6 characters (1b 3m 2w)
c Lebow, B. Tiny Tim is dead

6 characters (1b 4m 1w)
Foster, N. Ethan Claymore
Spencer, S. Resident alien
Yellow Robe, W. S. Sneaky

6 characters (1g 1m 4w)
O'Malley, G. Concertina's rainbow

6 characters (1g 2m 3w)
Bunyan, H. J. Prodigals in a promised land

MIXED CAST—*Continued*

6 characters (1g 3m 2w)

Ackermann, J. Off the map

Ayckbourn, A. It could be any one of us

6 characters (1g 4m 1w)

Lewis, G. Siding 37

6 characters (1m 5w)

Green, A. For tiger lilies out of season

Napier, E. The English teachers

Nelson, R. Conjuring an event

Shephard-Massat, S. M. Waiting to be invited

Svich, C. Alchemy of desire/dead-man's blues

Thorne, J. V. The exact center of the universe

Vaughan, R. M. Camera, woman

6 characters (2b 1g 1m 2w)

c Gollobin, L. B. The match girl's gift: A Christmas story

6 characters (2b 2g 1m 1w)

c McCullough, L. E. Reach for the stars

6 characters (2b 3m 1w)

The four apparitions of Guadalupe (Las cuatro apariciones de Guadalupe)

6 characters (2m 4w)

Ardito, C. Brief candle

Buttram, J. The Parker family circus

Chappell, E. Haywire

Cleage, P. Flyin' west

Ehn, E. Wholly Joan's (Joan of Arc)

Godber, J. It started with a kiss

Greenberg, R. Everett Beekin

c Hamlett, C. The wedding bell blues

Hardy, C. J. Let it be me

Hare, D. The secret rapture

Hawdon, R. Perfect wedding

Henley, B. Crimes of the heart

Henley, B. The Miss Firecracker contest

Hodges, A. Life goes on

Klein, J. Dimly perceived threats to the system

Margulies, D. July 7, 1994

Murphy, C. Beating heart cadaver

Murphy, L. Catch a falling star

O'Connell, S. Cartesian dreams

O'Rowe, M. From both hips

Raffle, D. Blue suede blues

Rayson, H. Life after George

Reingold, J. Tunnel of love

Romero, E. The fat-free Chicana and the Snow Cap queen

Taylor, R., and Bologna, J. Bermuda Avenue triangle

Thompson, J. Lion in the street

Tolan, K. The wax

Wasserstein, W. Medea

Yoon, J. The Yoko Ono project

6 characters (3b 2g 1m)

Oliver, C. Kicking out

6 characters (3m 3w)

Ackermann, J. Marcus is walking

Ardal, M. Midnight sun

Aronson, B. The art room

Auburn, D. Skyscraper

Ayckbourn, A. Communicating doors

Beane, D. C. As bees in honey drown

Benfield, D. In at the deep end

Crowther, C., and Crowther, M. Till we meet again

Curran, C. Sacred hearts

De Angelis, A. Hush

De Boer, L. The Buddha of Ceylon

Dixcy, M. Pyramid effect

Donaghy, T. From above

Edson, M. Wit

Edson, M. Wit

Ehn, E. Incide (Judas Iscariot)

Eldridge, D. Under the blue sky

Feffer, S. Little airplanes of the heart

Feydeau, G., and Desvallières, M. Mixed doubles

Firth, T. The safari party

Fox, Amy Summer cyclone

Gems, P. The snow palace

Green, G. M. Goodbye, Iphigenia

Griffiths, L. Jessica

Gurney, A. R. A Cheever evening

Gurney, A. R. The old boy

Hall, L. Cooking with Elvis

Hall, L. Cooking with Elvis

Hare, D. Amy's view

Hare, D. Amy's view

MIXED CAST—*Continued*

Feydeau, G. Caught with his trance down

Fo, D. Elizabeth: almost by chance a woman

Fry, C. A ringing of bells

Gilbert, S. The emotionalists

Glancy, D. American gypsy

Greig, D. The cosmonaut's last message to the woman he once loved in the former Soviet Union

Gurr, M. Crazy brave

Hall, L. Bollocks

c Hamlett, C. The ghost of Hemstead House

c Hamlett, C. The prince's dilemma

Hollinger, M. An empty plate in the Café du Grand Boeuf

Horovitz, I. A Rosen by any other name

Ives, D. The red address

Jannuzzi, L. Night of the foolish moon

Johnson, T. Imagine drowning

Kushner, T. Reverse transcription

Kushner, T. Reverse transcription

Linklater, L., and Flather, P. Sixty below

Mayne, R. Phantoms

McLean, D. Julie Allardyce

Melski, M. Miles from home

Meyer, M. The mystery of attraction

Molloy, M. J. The Paddy pedlar

Moodie, A. Riot

Ogilvy, I. A slight hangover

Orton, J. What the butler saw

Parker, S. Spokesong; or, The common wheel

Pinter, H. The room

Pollock, A. The death of cool

Pownall, D. Getting the picture

Rachilde Madame La Mort

Robinson, K. The popular mechanicals

Roche, B. The Cavalcaders

Ross, I. fareWel

Shaw, B. Mrs. Warren's profession

Sherman, M. A madhouse in Goa

Simpson, E. A point of order

Smith, V., and Dixon, M. B. The league of semi-super heroes

Teevan, C. Iph. . .

Townsend, J. Terms of abuse

Walker, G. F. The art of war

Walker, G. F. Filthy rich

Williams, R. Lift off

Wilson, L. Angels fall

c Wood, D. The gingerbread man

6 characters (5m 1w)

Ackerman, R. Tabletop

Daniels, J. Escanaba in da moonlight

del Valle, J. A. Fuchsia

Dulack, T. Diminished capacity

Elyot, K. The day I stood still

Field, B. Playing with fire

Gardner, H. The goodbye people

Gardner, H. A thousand clowns

Gould, H. M. Diva

Hill, R. Faces of the cross

Kennedy, A. An evening with dead Essex

McIntyre, D. Split second: a play in two acts

Mérimée, P. The gilded coach (Le carrosse du Saint-Sacrement)

Oakes, M. Faith

O'Rowe, M. The aspidistra code

Orton, J. Loot

Rapp, A. Finer noble gases

Shinn, C. Other people

Spencer, S. Resident alien

Strelich, T. BAFO (Best And Final Offer)

6 characters and extra (3m 3w extra)

Adamov, A. The invasion

6 characters and extra (4m 2w extra)

Kushner, T. Reverse transcription

Long, Q. The joy of going somewhere definite

6 characters and extras (1b 1g 2m 2w extras)

Ehn, E. Tree of hope, keep firm (Mary, the Annunciation)

Feffer, S. Little airplanes of the heart

6 characters and extras (1b 2g 3w extras)

Bush, M. Ezigbo, the spirit child

6 characters and extras (1b 3m 2w extras)

Kokoschka, O. Job

Smith, J. M. This is my story

6 characters and extras (1b 4m 1w extras)

O'Neill, E. Ile

MIXED CAST—*Continued*

6 characters and extras (1g 3m 2w extras)

Ehn, E. Thistle

6 characters and extras (1m 5w extras)

Coleman, E. Secret bridesmaids' business

6 characters and extras (2b 2g 1m 1w extras)

c McCullough, L. E. Call of the wild (park ranger)

6 characters and extras (2b 2m 2w extras)

c Weller, M. Dogbrain

6 characters and extras (2b 3m 1w)

Hall, L. I love you, Jimmy Spud

6 characters and extras (2b 4g extras)

c McCullough, L. E. King David's harp

6 characters and extras (2g 2m 2w extras)

Cromelin, C. Man in the flying lawn chair

6 characters and extras (2m 4w extras)

Green, M. Oedipus, King of Thebes
Hughes, L. Angelo Herndon Jones
Hwang, D. H. Golden child
Hwang, D. H. Golden child
Tunooniq Theatre In search of a friend

6 characters and extras (3b 3g extras)

c McCullough, L. E. Tshai the brickmaker

6 characters and extras (3m 3w extras)

c Congdon, C. Beauty and the beast
Coward, N. After the ball
Cram, C. Landlocked
Cruz, M., and Blecher, H. Frida: the story of Frida Kahlo
Durang, C. Betty's summer vacation
Elton, B. Gasping
Ibsen, H. When we dead awaken
Lowe, M. The smell of the kill
c McCullough, L. E. Aruman, hero of Java
Obermeir, G. San Francisco of course
Raznovich, D. Rear entry (De atrás para adelante)
Schenkar, J. The last of Hitler

Tait, L. Live free or die
c Travis, S. The tale of Little Red Riding Hood
Upton, J. People on the river
Vogel, P. The Mineola twins
c Winther, B. Pedro de Urdemalas

6 characters and extras (4b 2g extras)

c McCullough, L. E. The prophet and the rabbi

6 characters and extras (4m 2w extras)

Kharms, D. Elizaveta Bam
Kleist, H. von Amphitryon
Mann, K. Ania and Esther
McKay, G. In order of appearance
Murray, T. C. Maurice Harte
Pushkin, A. The stone guest
Stratton, A. The Phoenix lottery
c Swortzell, L. A partridge in a pear tree
Tasca, J. Deus-X
Tavel, R. The life of Lady Godiva
Wellman, M. Bad penny

6 characters and extras (5m 1w extras)

London, J. The first poet
Mérimée, P. Inès Mendo; or, The defeat of prejudice (Inès Mendo; ou, Le préjugé vaincu)
Quilter, P. Boyband
Sánchez, E. Barefoot boy with shoes on

7 characters (1b 1g 2m 3w)

c Dodge, A. Joshua's egg

7 characters (1b 1g 3m 2w)

Tibbetts, M. LittleBro morning and BigSis afternoon

7 characters (1b 3m 3w)

Alvarez, L. Eddie Mundo Edmundo
Feydeau, G. Going to pot (On purge Bébé)
Hannah, D. Running far back
Harelik, M. The legacy
Lucas, C. Missing persons

7 characters (1b 4m 2w)

Gilroy, F. D. Who'll save the plowboy?

7 characters (1g 3m 3w)

Martin, J. Mr. Bundy

MIXED CAST—*Continued*
Martin, J. Mr. Bundy
Martin, J. Mr. Bundy
Wilson, L. The mound builders

7 characters (1g 4m 2w)
Williams, R. Starstruck
Williams, R. Starstruck
Yellow Robe, W. S. The independence of Eddie Rose

7 characters (1m 6w)
Bush, M. Ezigbo, the spirit child
Norfolk, W. Caramba's revenge

7 characters (2b 3m 2w)
Hedges, P. Baby anger

7 characters (2g 4m 1w)
c McCullough, L. E. Una and the goblin king

7 characters (2m 5w)
Barry, S. Our lady of Sligo
Brevoort, D. B. The women of Lockerbie
Coward, N. Blithe spirit
Curran, C. Cake-walk
De Angelis, A. The positive hour
Hanes, M. Doin' time at the Alamo
Henley, B. The debutante ball
Henley, B. The debutante ball
Rebeck, T. Loose knit
Williams, S. Laying the ghost
Williams, T. Suddenly last summer

7 characters (3g 2m 2w)
y French, D. That summer

7 characters (3m 4w)
Aldridge, R. You're only young twice
Anderson, J. Defying gravity
Anderson, J. Defying gravity
Angeles, T. Tightwad
Baitz, J. R. Hedda Gabler
Baitz, J. R. Hedda Gabler
Beane, D. C. The country club
Bingham, S. Throwaway
Chernoff, M. Chaim's love song
Chiasson, H. Alienor
Finn, W. A new brain

Forde, M. X-stacy
Freed, A. The psychic life of savages
y Gollobin, L. B. Selkie
Gomolvilas, P. The theory of everything
Goupil, L. Dark owl; or, The renegade angel
c Hamlett, C. Secret agents in disguise
c Hamlett, C. Where there's a Will, there's a play
Henley, B. Am I blue
Henley, B. The wake of Jamey Foster
Ibsen, H. Hedda Gabler
y Newsome, M. The perfect night
Nigro, D. The circus animals desertion
O'Byrne, Joe En suite
Oswald, D. Sweet road
Parker, M. The Lone Star love potion
Parker, S. Catchpenny twist
Parker, Matt Celaine
Parsley, R., and Graham, A. Sense and sensibility
St. John, B. The reunion
Stephenson, S. An experiment with an air pump
y Surface, M. H. Blessings
Tait, L. Miss Julie
Thomson, K. Navigating
Upton, J. Ashes and sand
Valcq, J. The Spitfire Grill
Vradenburg, T. The apple doesn't fall . . .
Walker, G. F. Better living
Wasserstein, W. Old money
c Weiss, E. Hyronomous A. Frog
Weldon, F. The reading group
Williamson, D. Corporate vibes
York, Y. The secret wife

7 characters (4m 3w)
Benfield, D. Two and two together
Blake, W. D., and Blake, C. H. Jesus our brother is alive!
Boyd, G. E. Consecrated ground
Boyd, G. E. Consecrated ground
Carr, M. On Raftery's hill
Chepiga, M. J. Getting and spending
Clark, R. The incomparable LouLou
Cooney, R. Caught in the net
Corthron, K. Seeking the genesis
Dattani, M. Tara
Davis, B. C. Avow

MIXED CAST—*Continued*

Dean, P. After January

c Espinosa, R. Ay, Carmelo! (Ay, Carmelo!)

Gale, L. Angélique

Gale, L. Angelique

Gardner, H. Conversations with my father

Gardner, H. I'm not Rappaport

Gilman, R. Boy gets girl

Greig, D. The architect

Grimsley, J. Mr. Universe

Henley, B. Impossible marriage

Henley, B. Impossible marriage

Henley, B. The Lucky Spot

Henley, B. Revelers

Horovitz, I. Barking sharks

Jenkin, L. Pilgrims of the night

Kane, S. Cleansed

Keane, J. B. The year of the hiker

Laurence, C. The Ring sisters

Liebman, S. The Tale of Jemina Puddle-Duck

Lindsay-Abaire, D. Fuddy meers

Lindsay-Abaire, D. Fuddy meers

Marivaux, P. C. de C. de Changes of heart

Marivaux, P. C. de C. de The triumph of love

Martin, J. Flaming guns of the purple sage

Martin, J. Flaming guns of the purple sage

Martin, J. Flaming guns of the purple sage

Martin, J. Middle-aged white guys

c McCullough, L. E. Isaac Newton's poetry of the rainbow

McGuire, M. Helen's play

Miller, A. The ride down Mt. Morgan

Miller, A. The ride down Mt. Morgan

c Mitchell, W. Jolly Roger

Molière The school for wives criticized

Nagy, P. Never land

Neipris, J. The agreement

Nigro, D. Deflores

Norman, M. Sarah and Abraham

Nottage, L. Mud, river, stone

Ouellette, J. The marriage counselor

Pirandello, L. Naked

Plowman, G. There's none so blind

Poliakoff, S. Coming in to land

Rebeck, T. The family of Mann

Remmes, D. Three tables

c Saar, D. The yellow boat

Schmitt, E.-E. Between worlds

Sewell, S. The sick room

Stern, N. Murder at Cafe Noir

Stoppard, T. The real thing

Turlish, S. Lafferty's wake

Valcq, J. Zombies from the beyond

Vaughan, R. L. Praying for rain

Williamson, D. The great man

Wilson, S. More light

7 characters (5m 2w)

Ardito, C. Stoney Bowes

Ardito, C. Waiting for the barbarians

Chappell, E. Cut and dried

Chappell, E. Up and coming

Congdon, C. Dog opera

Conquest, N. For they shall see God

Conquest, N. The widow's might

Dunn, M. Cabin fever

Esson, L. Shipwreck

Gilman, R. Spinning into butter

Gilroy, F. D. Getting in

Gilroy, F. D. Getting in

Gore, C. The maid of Croissey; or, Theresa's vow

Harrower, David Kill the old torture their young

Hatcher, J. To fool the eye

Henley, B. Revelers

Hughes, D. Digging for fire

Hughes, L. De organizer

Johnston, S. Running dog, paper tiger

Kennedy, A. Electra (Euripides)

Kennedy, A. The owl answers

Kramer, L. The destiny of me

Linney, R. A lesson before dying

Logan, J. Hauptmann

Ludlam, C. Stage blood

Ludlam, C. Stage blood

Marivaux, P. C. de C. de The game of love and chance

Marivaux, P. C. de C. de The game of love and chance

Mitchell, G. Tearing the loom

Mitchell, G. Trust

Nagy, P. The talented Mr. Ripley

Norman, M. Dracula

MIXED CAST—*Continued*

Palmer, J. Singapore
Palmieri, M. Carl the Second
Parker, S. Pratt's fall
Rebeck, T. View of the dome
Rebeck, T. View of the dome
Robson, J. Mr Wonderful
Sidney, Sir P. The Lady of May
St. John, B. The abduction
Stickland, E. A guide to mourning
Stohl, H. A play on letters
Taylor, E. A rise in the market
Van Itallie, J.-C. The Tibetan book of the dead; or, How not to do it again
Warner, C. Strangers on a train
Wilder, T. Proserpina and the devil: a play for marionettes
c Wood, D. Spot's birthday party

7 characters (6m 1w)

Alvarez, L. The guitarrón
Godber, J. Up 'n' under
Goold, R., and Butler, C. The end of the affair
Hall, R. A return to the brink
Hare, D. The Judas kiss
McGuire, M. Hold me
O'Donnell, D. Who shot Jacques Lacan?
O'Neill, E. Where the cross is made
Rabe, D. A question of mercy

7 characters and extra (4m 3w extra)

Rebeck, T. The bar plays

7 characters and extra (5m 2w extra)

Grimsley, J. Math and aftermath
c Winther, B. El caballito of seven colors

7 characters and extra (6m 1w extra)

Rabe, D. The dog problem

7 characters and extras (1b 4m 2w extras)

Dymov, O. Bronx express

7 characters and extras (1g 4m 2w extras)

Iizuka, N. Skin

7 characters and extras (2b 2g 1m 2w extras)

c McCullough, L. E. The case of the purple pen (crime lab technician)
c McCullough, L. E. Lights, camera, traction! (television director)

7 characters and extras (2b 2g 2m 1w extras)

c McCullough, L. E. Heave away, haul away! (tugboat captain)

7 characters and extras (2b 2m 3w extras)

Miller, C. The Canterville ghost

7 characters and extras (3b 3g 1w extras)

c Espinosa, R. El bully (El valenton)

7 characters and extras (3m 4w extras)

Churchill, C. Heart's desire
Kennedy, A. June and Jean in concert (the concert of their lives)
Kramer, S. Things that break
Kuruvilla, S. Rice boy
Moraga, C. Watsonville: some place not here
Sears, D. The adventures of a black girl in search of God
Wentworth, M. C. War brides

7 characters and extras (4b 3g extras)

c McCullough, L. E. Why bears no longer talk

7 characters and extras (4m 3w extras)

Antonelli, L. A man confronts himself
Crommelynck, F. The merchant of regrets
Howe, T. Pride's Crossing
Kataev, V. Squaring the circle
Marivaux, P. C. de C. de Changes of heart
Murphy, G. The countess
Shaw, B. The philanderer
Sher, E. Past imperfect
Taylor, R. It ain't nothin' but the blues
c Vogel, L. Ruth

7 characters and extras (5b 2g extras)

c McCullough, L. E. Fionn in search of his youth
c McCullough, L. E. When a river cries: the myth of Oba and Oshun

7 characters and extras (5m 2w extras)

Calderón de la Barca, P. Life is a dream
Kessler, L. Robbers
c King, C. Really Rosie
Linney, R. A lesson before dying

MIXED CAST—*Continued*

Poliakoff, S. Caught on a train
Walcott, D. Walker
c Winther, B. Macona, the honest warrior

7 characters and extras (6m 1w extras)

Beaumarchais, P. A. D. The barber of
Seville
Bower, H. Natural life
Eagleton, T. Saint Oscar
Kuzmin, M. The dangerous precaution

8 characters (1b 1g 4m 2w)

Sterling, P. The secret garden
c Surface, M. H. Prodigy

8 characters (1b 2m 5w)

Urtusastegui, T. Limited capacity

8 characters (1b 3g 3m 1w)

Younger, M. Making the rain stop

8 characters (1b 4m 3w)

Crothers, R. A man's world
Esson, L. Mother and son
Horovitz, I. Today, I am a fountain pen

8 characters (1b 7w)

Moraga, C. The hungry woman: a Mexican Medea

8 characters (1g 4m 3w)

Bishop, C., and Fuller, E. Get happy
Schnitzler, A. Flirtation

8 characters (1g 5m 2w)

Lan, D. The end of the earth

8 characters (1m 7w)

Carr, M. The Mai
Carr, M. The Mai
Lavery, B. Nothing compares to you
Porter, C. Nymph errant
Valentine, P. Day of reckoning

8 characters (2b 2g 2m 2w)

c McCullough, L. E. Robots are everywhere (robotics engineer)

8 characters (2b 4m 2w)

Yeaton, D. Mad River rising

8 characters (2m 6w)

Battlo, J. The little theater's production of Hamlet
Carmichael, F. The trouble with Trent
Churchill, C. Blue kettle
Hoffman, S. Splendora
Kennedy, A. Funnyhouse of a Negro
Ledoux, P. Anne

8 characters (3m 5w)

Carmichael, F. Murder-go-round
Cristofer, M. Amazing grace
Gillian, P. Two fat men
Godber, J. On a night like this
c Hamlett, C. It's an okie-dokie life
Harper, L. An' push da wind down
Ibsen, H. John Gabriel Borkman
Kennedy, A. Funnyhouse of a Negro
Laxdal, V. Cyber:/womb
Lucas, C. God's heart
MacDonald, A.-M. Goodnight Desdemona (good morning Juliet)
Manktelow, B. Curtain call
Manktelow, B. Curtain up on murder
Parker, M. Whose wives are they anyway?
Racine, J. Phedre

8 characters (4m 4w)

Babe, T. Great day in the morning
Barry, P. J. Jump the train at Riverpoint
Basham, R. Lot's daughters
Beard, J. The Ornamental hermit
Bowen, J. Little boxes: Trevor
Carmichael, F. What if...?
Carter, L. Gulliver redux
Carter, L. Lemuel
Carter, R. A yearning
Chapman, J., and Lloyd, J. Business affairs
Crommelynck, F. Hot and cold; or, Mr. Dom's idea
Dunbar-Nelson, A. Mine eyes have seen
Edgar, D. Our own people
Flewitt, L. Is there anybody there?
Frayn, M. Now you know
Griffiths, L. O.D. on paradise
Guare, J. Lake Hollywood
Hedges, P. The age of pie
Hughes, D. Love and a bottle

MIXED CAST—*Continued*

Junction Avenue Theatre Company Sophiatown

Kane, R. Miss Roach's war

Kennedy, A. Ohio State murders

Khan-Din, A. Last dance at dum dum

Kokoschka, O. Murderer, hope of women

Kokoschka, O. Murderer, hope of women

Kops, B. Dreams of Anne Frank

Kramer, S. The wall of water

Lucie, D. Grace

Luckham, C. The seduction of Anne Boleyn

MacLeod, W. The water children

MacLeod, W. The water children

MacLiammóir, M. Ill met by moonlight

Mayer, O. Ragged time

Murray, T. C. Autumn fire

Nigro, D. Horrid massacre in Boston

Osborne, J. Watch it come down

Plata, M. C. Justice for whom?

Rayson, H. Hotel Sorrento

Rosen, L. Nighthawks

Sherman, J. It's all true

Tolins, J. If memory serves

Trieschmann, C. The bridegroom of Blowing Rock

Wilson, L. Fifth of July

c Winther, B. The ghost of El Castillo

c Wood, D. The see-saw tree

8 characters (5m 3w)

Alexander, R. A preface to the alien garden

Alvarez, L. The reincarnation of Jaime Brown

Ayckbourn, A. Body language

Bell, N. Thérèse Raquin

Bell, N. Thérèse Raquin

Bobrick, S. Death in England

Brett, S. Silhouette

Chekhov, A. P. Uncle Vanya

Crimp, M. Dealing with Clair

Dobrish, J. The handless maiden

Feydeau, G. Fit to be tried; or, Stepbrothers in crime

Gao Xingjian Bus stop

Gore, C. Salvoisy; or, The queen's lover

Greenberg, R. Hurrah at last

Guare, J. New York actor

Guare, J. New York actor

Hackenbrook, W. J. Conditions

Hollinger, M. Incorruptible

Horovitz, I. The Chopin playoffs

Kane, S. Skin

Keane, J. B. The highest house on the mountain

Kennedy, A. Orestes (Euripides)

Lange, E. Sherlock's secret life

Lawler, R. The Piccadilly bushman

Leight, W. Side man

Leight, W. Side man

Lequy, D. Meat party

Liebman, S. The tale of the Mandarin ducks

Mee, C. L. The investigation of the murder in El Salvador

Miller, A. Mr. Peters' connections

Molloy, M. J. The bachelor's daughter

Morley, M., and Willmorth, T. The glass mendacity

Murray, T. C. Appendix two: illumination

Neipris, J. A small delegation

Nigro, D. Tainted justice

Norman, M. Circus Valentine

Ogden, A. Johnny, don't jump

Poliakoff, S. Remember this

Strindberg, A. The father

Strindberg, A. The father

Wallace, N. Slaughter City

Wedekind, F. The tenor

Weller, M. The heart of art

Whelan, P. The herbal bed

Whitemore, H. Disposing of the body

Wilson, L. Sympathetic magic

Wilson, S. Sabina

c Wing, P. The King of Ireland's son

8 characters (6m 2w)

Ardito, C. St. James's blues

Busch, C. Vampire lesbians of Sodom

Corthron, K. Force continuum

Durang, C. The Vietnamization of New Jersey

Eagleton, T. Disappearances

Eagleton, T. God's locusts

Greig, D. Europe

Joselovitz, E. Vilna's got a golem

Kaplan, B. J. Landscape of desire

MIXED CAST—*Continued*

Lane, S. F., and Morehouse, W. If it was easy. . .
Lipkin, D. Skitaletz (The wanderer)
Lucie, D. Progress
MacLeod, W. Sin
MacLiammóir, M. Prelude in Kazbek Street
Nelson, G. Spirit
Racine, J. The suitors
Smith, C. The Sutherland
Van Zandt, B., and Milmore, J. Confessions of a dirty blonde

8 characters (7m 1w)

Baitz, J. R. Mizlansky/Zilinsky
Baitz, J. R. Mizlansky/Zilinsky
Nelson, T. B. The grey zone
Spencer, S. In the western garden
Sutton, M., and Fingleton, A. Over my dead body

8 characters and extra (1b 6m 1w extra)

Stoppard, T. Night and day

8 characters and extra (4m 4w extra)

Fennessy, A. Chilling and killing my Annabel Lee
Lenéru, M. Peace (La paix)

8 characters and extra (6m 2w extra)

c Espinosa, R. Where did they go? Where did I put them? (A donde se fueron? Donde las puse yo?)

8 characters and extras (1b 1g 3m 3w extras)

Thum, N. The carpenter and the cross

8 characters and extras (1b 1g 4m 2w extras)

c Jenkin, L. The invisible man

8 characters and extras (1b 2g 5m extras)

c Lavender, W. The invisible people

8 characters and extras (1g 3m 4w extras)

Jelinek, E. Clara S.

8 characters and extras (2b 2g 2m 2w extras)

c McCullough, L. E. Yankee Doodle had a brick (brick mason)

8 characters and extras (2m 6w extras)

Canino, F. The Angelina project

8 characters and extras (3m 5w extras)

Linney, R. Strindberg
McLeish, K. Orpheus
Powell, D. Walking down Broadway
Schenkar, J. Signs of life
Teale, P. Jane Eyre

8 characters and extras (4b 4g extras)

c Crowther, C., and Crowther, M. Noah's ark
c McCullough, L. E. Freya's golden necklace
c Woolfson, M. Bushveld bibble babble

8 characters and extras (4m 4w extras)

c Brett, S., and Travis, S. Sleeping beauty
Clarke, G. E. Whylah Falls: the play
Clarke, G. E. Whylah Falls: the play
y Grimsley, J. A bird of prey
Johnston, A. Melon farmer
Kokoschka, O. Orpheus and Eurydice
LaVohn, R. W. Murder at the banquet
Linney, R. True crimes
Neipris, J. A small delegation
Sherman, J. It's all true
Van Itallie, J.-C. The traveler
Wasserstein, W. An American daughter
c Yordy, M. Little Red Riding Hood and The magic dragon

8 characters and extras (5m 3w extras)

Busch, C. Red scare on Sunset
Crimp, M. The treatment
Gore, C. The queen's champion
Ibsen, H. The lady from the sea
Kleist, H. von The broken jug
c Leonard, J. Crow & Weasel
Russell, W. Blood brothers
Slover, T. Joyful noise
Streeruwitz, M. New York, New York
Williams, R. Killing kangaroos
c Wood, D. Tom's midnight garden

8 characters and extras (6m 2w extras)

Futcher, M., and Howard, H. A beautiful life
c McCullough, L. E. Di goldineh medineh (The golden land)
Mérimée, P. Carvajal's family (La famille de Carvajal)
Mouawad, W. Tideline (Littoral)

MIXED CAST—*Continued*

c Overmyer, E. Duke Kahanamoku vs. the surfnappers
Parker, S. Nightshade
c Scholtz, P. Tokoloshe
Wellman, M. Albanian softshoe

8 characters and extras (7m 1w extras)

Cibber, C. Xerxes

8 characters (5m 3w)

Sheppard, J. Whatever

9 characters (1b 3g 2m 3w)

Lauro, S. The contest

9 characters (1b 4m 4w)

Hirschbein, P. Green fields

9 characters (1b 5m 3w)

Marber, P. Howard Katz

9 characters (1g 3m 5w)

y Godber, J. Happy families

9 characters (2b 2g 2m 3w)

c McCullough, L. E. Opening night at the opera, er, opry (piano tuner)

9 characters (2m 7w)

Foote, H. The day Emily married
Orton, J. The visitors
Rahman, A. Unfinished women cry in no man's land while a bird dies in a gilded cage

9 characters (3g 3m 3w)

Congdon, C. The automata pieta

9 characters (3m 6w)

Brown, W. Life during wartime
Green, M. Cinderella
Nigro, D. November
Prida, D. Botánica
Rushforth, T. The Kerry dance

9 characters (4m 5w)

Bowen, J. Little boxes: the coffee lace
Coward, N. Hay fever
Crommelynck, F. A small-hearted woman

Elton, B. Popcorn
Elton, B. Popcorn
Friel, B. Give me your answer, do
Green, M. Trapped
c Hamlett, C. Picture perfect
y Harden, V. HIV positive
Horsler, P. Cut and run
Hwang, D. H. Family devotions
Linney, R. Gint
Nigro, D. Chronicles
Norman, M. Larry's party
Parker, M. Hotbed Hotel
Parker, M. The sensuous senator
Pattison, J. A word from our sponsor
Ryan, T. Pig
y Rye, M. S. Turning points
Thompson-Scretching, A. L. You shouldn't have told
Williams, T. Period of adjustment
Yeaton, D. Midwives

9 characters (5m 4w)

Anderson, J. Looking for normal
Bell, N. McTeague: a tale of San Francisco
Brossa, J. The quarrelsome party.
Chinn, J., and Wyld, H. The garden party
Dietz, S. Force of nature
y Dietz, S. Still life with Iris
Downing, M. Frankenstein's guests
Eng, A. The Goong Hay Kid
Feydeau, G. Tooth and consequences; or, Hortense said: "No skin off my ass!"
Finlayson, A. Winding the ball
Fraser, B. Snake in fridge
Gallagher, M. Windshook
Goodden, H. Suffering fools
Guare, J. The general of hot desire
Guare, J. The general of hot desire
Harvey, J. Guiding star
Harvey, J. Guiding star
Henley, B. Signature
Henley, B. Signature
Henley, B. Sisters of the winter madrigal
Kane, S. Phaedra's love
Kluger, S. Pilots of the purple twilight
Linney, R. A woman without a name
MacLiammóir, M. Where stars walk
McDonagh, M. The cripple of Inishmaan
McGuinness, F. Dolly West's kitchen

MIXED CAST—*Continued*

Moritz, D. Just the boys
Nelson, R. The return of Pinocchio
Nichol, J. W. The stone angel
Norman, M. 140
O'Hara, R. Insurrection
Pinter, H. Celebration
Pinter, H. Celebration
Robinson, R. No love lost
Tasca, J. Judah's daughter
Terry, M. Approaching Simone
Walker, G. F. Beautiful city
Wang Peigong WM
Wesker, A. Roots
Wesker, A. Roots
White, M. Far from the madding crowd
Williamson, D. Money and friends
Wilson, S. Darwin's flood

9 characters (6b 3g)

y Ridley, P. Sparkleshark

9 characters (6m 3w)

Chappell, E. Heatstroke
Clarke, A. When he was free and young and he used to wear silks
Gilroy, F. D. Any given day
Grimm, D. Sheridan; or, Schooled in scandal
Gurney, A. R. Overtime
Kelly, G. The show-off
Lucie, D. Fashion
MacLiammóir, M. The mountains look different
Mayne, R. The drone
Milligan, J. Family values
Murray, T. C. Sovereign love
Overmyer, E. Dark rapture
Rebeck, T. Abstract expression
Roth, A. Life in refusal
Smith, C. Les trois Dumas
Tasso, T. Aminta
Tunooniq Theatre Changes
Valenti, M. Quack
Walker, G. F. Gossip
Woolf, B. E. Off to the war

9 characters (7m 2w)

Euripides The Alcestis of Euripides
Guyer, M. World of mirth
Hare, D. Fanshen

Molière The school for wives
Nelson, R. An American comedy
Norman, M. Loving Daniel Boone
Osborne, A. In sunshine and in shadow
Pielmeier, J. Voices in the dark
Sandberg, R. N. Convivencia
Shanley, J. P. Cellini
Williams, T. Small craft warnings
Wood, C. Veterans; or, Hairs in the gates of Hellespont
Yourgrau, T. TH FT

9 characters (8m 1w)

Stoppard, T. Hapgood
Wilson, A. Jitney

9 characters and extra (1g 4m 4w extra)

Farias, J. Claudia meets Fulano Colorado

9 characters and extra (4m 5w extra)

Bean, R. Pride at Southanger Park

9 characters and extra (6m 3w extra)

c McCullough, L. E. Edward Jenner and the gossip of milkmaids

9 characters and extras (1b 2g 4m 2w extras)

c Simmonds, R. N. The Shamrock road

9 characters and extras (1b 5m 3w extras)

c Mason, T. The nightingale

9 characters and extras (1b 6m 2w extras)

Bhuchar, S., and Landon-Smith, K. A tainted dawn

9 characters and extras (1b 7m 1w extras)

c Mason, T. Kidnapped in London

9 characters and extras (2b 2g 2m 3w extras)

c McCullough, L. E. Monster in the basement (animal rescue agent)
c McCullough, L. E. See you in court! (Legal Aid lawyer)

9 characters and extras (2b 3m 4w extras)

McGuinness, F. A doll's house

9 characters and extras (2g 5m 2w extras)

Kraus, J. H. The ice wolf

9 characters and extras (2m 7w extras)

Wilson, C. Hurricane

MIXED CAST—*Continued*

9 characters and extras (3b 6g extras)

c McCullough, L. E. King Midas and the golden touch

9 characters and extras (3m 6w extras)

Powell, D. Jig saw

9 characters and extras (5b 4g extras)

c McCullough, L. E. Nitwits and numskulls: outwitting the oppressor

9 characters and extras (5m 4w extras)

c Heard, D. B. The love for three oranges
Molloy, M. J. Petticoat loose
Orton, J. Fred and Madge
Padmanabhan, M. Harvest
Simon, N. Neil Simon's proposals
St. John, B. Males order brides
Williams, T. The milk train doesn't stop here anymore

9 characters and extras (6b 3g extras)

Way, C. Looking out to see

9 characters and extras (6m 3w extras)

Dunbar, P. L. Uncle Eph's Christmas
Marowitz, C. Quack
c Mason, T. Pinocchio
Mérimée, P. Inès Mendo; or, The triumph of prejudice (Inès Mendo; ou, Le triomphe du préjugé)
Molière The affected damsels
Molière Such foolish affected ladies
Powell, D. Big night

9 characters and extras (7m 2w extras)

Boker, G. H. Francesca da Rimini
c Glennon, W. The trial of the Arkansas bear
Huxley, A. Now more than ever
Norman, M. Loving Daniel Boone
Sondheim, S. A funny thing happened on the way to the forum

10 characters (1b 1g 4m 4w)

Ayvazian, L. Nine Armenians

10 characters (1b 1g 5m 3w)

c Lippa, L. The true adventures of Pinocchio

10 characters (1b 1g 6m 2w)

c McCullough, L. E. The Golem of Belmont Boulevard

10 characters (1b 5m 4w)

Miller, A. All my sons

10 characters (1b 8m 1w)

c McCullough, L. E. Everyday science in Ben Franklin's America

10 characters (1m 9w)

Corthron, K. Breath, boom
King, D. Stepping Out

10 characters (2b 2g 2m 4w)

c McCullough, L. E. The big scoop (newspaper reporter)
c McCullough, L. E. It's an emergency! (emergency medical technician)

10 characters (2b 4g 2m 2w)

Dean, P. 48 shades of brown

10 characters (3b 3g 1m 3w)

y Labey, R. New boy

10 characters (3m 7w)

y Harden, V. The boardinghouse
y Harden, V. Jessica and Jolene
Schmitt, E.-E. Don Juan on trial

10 characters (4m 6w)

Bowen, J. Cold salmon
De Groen, A. The woman in the window
Lan, D. Desire
Lan, D. La lupa
MacLiammóir, M. The liar
Mee, C. L. The Trojan women: a love story
Robbins, N. Tiptoe through the tombstones
Rosenthal, A. Sitting pretty
Ross, L. L. Scent of the roses
Sodaro, C. Murder by the book
Tropicana, C., and Parnes, U. Memorias de la revolución

10 characters (5m 5w)

Ayckbourn, A. Comic potential
Cortese, R. St. Kilda tales

MIXED CAST—*Continued*

Durang, C. The marriage of Bette and Boo

Foote, H. The actor

Gilman, R. The glory of living

Gilman, R. The glory of living

c Keens-Douglas, R. The Nutmeg Princess

Kennedy, A. A movie star has to star in black and white

Kopit, A. L. Wings

Lan, D. Flight

Ludlam, C. Bluebeard

Oates, J. C. Black water

Pospisil, Craig Months on end

Schnitzler, A. La Ronde

Vinaver, M. The television programme

Walker, G. F. Escape from happiness

Williams, T. The eccentricities of a nightingale

York, Y. Gerald's good idea

Zorin, L. The guests

10 characters (6m 4w)

Chekhov, A. P. Uncle Vanya

Farley, Keythe, and Flemming, Brian Bat boy

y Field, B. Great expectations

Goldberg, J. The hologram theory

Griffiths, L. The Duchess, a.k.a. Wallis Simpson

Jones, J. M. The endless adventure of MCKAY; or, How they got from A to B

Linney, R. Unchanging love

c Lippa, L. Dreaming of Aloysius

c Mason, T. Beauty and the beast

Matthews, S. Who wins

May, E. Taller than a dwarf

O'Neill, E. Beyond the horizon

O'Neill, E. Beyond the horizon

Rodriguez, E. S. Soldiers will be soldiers

Shaw, B. Heartbreak House

Skarstedt, S. A. Saint Francis of Esplanade

Solis, O. El otro

Wesker, A. Chicken soup with barley

Wilde, O. The importance of being Earnest

Williamson, D. Face to face

Witkiewicz, S. I. The cuttlefish; or, The Hyrcanian worldview

Wolff, R. The abdication

10 characters (7m 3w)

Aerenson, B. The possum play

Al-Hakim, T. Fate of a cockroach

Clarvoe, A. The brothers Karamazov

Devlin, A. Ourselves alone

Dobrish, J. Notions in motion

Fo, D. Archangels don't play pinball

Gilroy, F. D. Far Rockaway

Glass, J. M. Yesteryear

Hughes, D. Halloween night

Mayne, R. The turn of the road

Molloy, M. J. The wood of the whispering

Nassar, M. The mayor's limo

Smith, J. Rehearsal for the destruction of Atlantis

10 characters (8m 2w)

Dunai, F. The parasol

Fo, D. About face

Hochwälder, F. Thursday

y McClelland, J. Blood lines

Pomerance, B. Melons

Valenti, M. Bashville in love

10 characters (9m 1w)

Dobrish, J. Blink of an eye

10 characters and extra (4m 6w extra)

Norman, M. Trudy Blue

10 characters and extra (7m 3w extra)

Anouilh, J. Antigone

Artaud, A. The spurt of blood

10 characters and extras (1b 1g 4m 4w extras)

Filippo, E. de Those damned ghosts

10 characters and extras (1b 4m 5w extras)

c McCullough, L. E. Two goats, two sisters, and a beggar king

10 characters and extras (1b 6m 3w extras)

Thomas, A. As a man thinks

10 characters and extras (1g 6m 3w extras)

Mee, C. L. Bobrauschenbergamerica

10 characters and extras (1g 7m 2w extras)

Soyinka, W. The strong breed

MIXED CAST—*Continued*

Wellman, M. Hypatia; or, The divine algebra

10 characters and extras (2m 8w extras)

y Matera, J. The mirror of Dori Gray

10 characters and extras (3m 7w extras)

y St. John, B. Cindy Ella's going to the ball, baby!

10 characters and extras (4m 6w extras)

c Cornett, E. Cinderella
Crommelynck, F. The childish lovers

10 characters and extras (5m 5w extras)

Dyer, C. R. Time, murderer, please
Gurney, A. R. The snow ball
c McCullough, L. E. Young Olli and the trolls
Wellman, M. Allegory of whiteness
Williams, T. Vieux Carré

10 characters and extras (6m 4w extras)

Brevoort, D. B. Into the fire
Calderón de la Barca, P. Three judgements in one
Hare, D. A map of the world
y Janaczewska, N. Madagascar lily
O'Casey, S. Juno and the paycock
O'Casey, S. Juno and the paycock
y Rabin, A. The man-child
c Reakes, P. Little Red Riding Hood

10 characters and extras (7b 3g extras)

c McCullough, L. E. Chanukah: come light the menorah!
c McCullough, L. E. Gilgamesh and the rose of eternal youth

10 characters and extras (7m 3w extras)

Chekhov, A. P. The wedding
Chekhov, A. P. The wedding reception
Crommelynck, F. The sculptor of masks
Filippo, E. de Christmas in Naples
Kops, B. The hamlet of Stepney Green
Rodgers, R. Flower drum song
Sondheim, S. Sweeney Todd
Williams, J. L. Why marry?

10 characters and extras (8m 2w extras)

Bosakowski, P. Bierce takes on the railroad!

Ibsen, H. An enemy of the people
Molière The bungler

11 characters (1g 2m 8w)

Bernhard, M., and others Bellyfruit

11 characters (1g 6m 4w)

Nowra, L. The language of the gods

11 characters (1g 8m 2w)

Congdon, C. The servant of two masters

11 characters (2b 1g 4m 4w)

Ibsen, H. A doll's house

11 characters (2g 3m 6w)

Childress, A. Wedding band: a love/hate story in black and white

11 characters (4m 7w)

y Davidson, R. The Pony Express
Edgar, D. That summer
Geiogamah, H. Body Indian
Lemoine, S. Cocktails at Pam's
Schnitzler, A. Anatol

11 characters (5g 2m 4w)

Williams, R. The No Boys Cricket Club
Williams, R. The No Boys Cricket Club

11 characters (5m 6w)

Alvarez, L. Deux marriages: Romola and Nijinsky
Busch, C. Psycho beach party
Carr, M. Portia Coughlan
Hennessy, M. A. Hazing the monkey
Kelly, G. Craig's wife
Louise, D. The servant of two masters
Paolucci, A. In the green room
Strachan, Keith Large as life
Van Druten, J. Make way for Lucia
Wain, D. Look behind you
Williamson, D. Dead white males

11 characters (6m 5w)

Carr, M. By the Bog of Cats. . .
Carr, M. By the bog of cats
Carr, M. By the Bog of Cats . . .
Carr, M. Portia Coughlan
Johnston, Bob, and Hochhauser, Jeff Theda Bara and the Frontier Rabbi

MIXED CAST—*Continued*

c McCullough, L. E. The wise men and women of Chelm

y Urquhart, J. Liza and the riddling cave

Wilson, L. Book of days

Woolley, J. You can't be serious

11 characters (7m 4w)

Carlton, B. Return to the forbidden planet

Field, B. Great expectations

Loomer, L. The waiting room

McCormack, Thomas Endpapers

Molloy, M. J. Daughter from over the water

Molloy, M. J. The king of Friday's men

Vinaver, M. High places

11 characters (8m 3w)

y Bond, E. Tuesday

Bosakowski, P. Chopin in space

Fishelson, D., and Leichter, A. The castle

Glass, J. M. Play memory

Keane, J. B. The change in Mame Fadden

Kushner, T. Homebody/Kabul

Molière The doctor despite himself

Molière The misanthrope

Molière The miser

O'Casey, S. Hall of healing

O'Casey, S. The shadow of a gunman

O'Casey, S. The shadow of a gunman

O'Neill, E. The long voyage home

Roche, B. Amphibians

Stoppard, T. Arcadia

Wertenbaker, T. Credible witness

11 characters (9m 2w)

Ardito, C. Da Ponte's last stand

Bhagat, D. Routes and escape routes

Brustein, R. Enrico IV

Scott, G. A town called Shame

11 characters and extras (1b 1g 8m 1w extras)

Bruchac, J. Pushing up the sky

11 characters and extras (1b 5g 3m 2w extras)

c Medoff, M. Kringle's window

11 characters and extras (1b 7m 3w extras)

Feydeau, G., and Desvallières, M. On the marry-go-wrong (Le mariage de Barillon)

c McCullough, L. E. Tale of the Baal Shem Tov

11 characters and extras (1b 8m 2w extras)

Beattie, A. The story of Peter Grimes

11 characters and extras (1g 7m 3w extras)

Gordin, J. God, man, and devil (got, mentsh, un tayvl)

11 characters and extras (2b 1g 5m 3w extras)

Vreeke, J. The Canterville ghost

11 characters and extras (2m 9w extras)

c McCullough, L. E. East of the sun, west of the moon

Naidoo, M. Flight from the Mahabarath

11 characters and extras (4m 7w extras)

y Barchers, S. I., and Kroll, J. L. Little women

Crommelynck, F. Carine; or, The young woman who was crazy about her soul

11 characters and extras (5m 6w extras)

London, J. Scorn of women

Wilder, T. The long Christmas dinner

11 characters and extras (6b 3g 1m 1w extras)

c Toksvig, J., and Perkins, D. The curious quest for the sandman's sand

11 characters and extras (6b 5g extras)

c McCullough, L. E. Hail, Queen Esther!

11 characters and extras (6m 5w extras)

Cibber, C. Woman's wit; or, The lady in fashion

Kraszewski, C. S. The archives at Kanonicza 5

11 characters and extras (7m 4w extras)

Ardov, V. The case of the entry room

Chikamatsu, M. The love suicides at Amijima

Crommelynck, F. The magnanimous cuckold

MIXED CAST—*Continued*

Lee, C. Carry the tiger to the mountain
Mee, C. L. Time to burn
Nicholson, W. Katherine Howard
Sherman, J. Patience
Sherman, J. Patience
c Winther, B. The sleeping mountains
c Winther, B. The sleeping mountains

11 characters and extras (8m 3w extras)

Chekhov, A. P. On the high road
Gore, C. Modern honor; or, The sharper in high life
Gore, C. The tale of a tub
Greenhorn, S. Passing places
Oates, J. C. The passion of Henry David Thoreau

11 characters and extras (8w 3w extras)

Vinaver, M. Portrait of a woman

11 characters and extras (9m 2w extras)

Bachmann, I. The cicadas
Clarke, G. E. Beatrice Chancy
Jonson, B. Pleasure reconciled to Virtue
Moraga, C. Heart of the earth: a Popol Vuh story

11 characters and extras (10m 1w extras)

Gonzalez, S. S. Boxcar
Metcalf, P. The confidence man

12 characters (1b 1g 3m 7w)

Aidoo, A. A. The dilemma of a ghost

12 characters (1b 1g 5m 7w)

Foote, H. Vernon Early

12 characters (1b 1g 6m 4w)

c McCullough, L. E. Geegaws and doo-hickeys: indispensible inventions and their forgotten inventors

12 characters (1b 1g 7m 3w)

Jefferson, J., and Boucicault, D. Rip Van Winkle

12 characters (1b 7m 4w)

Griffiths, T. Food for ravens

12 characters (1b 8m 3w)

Green, P. In Abraham's bosom: the tragedy of a southern Negro

12 characters (1g 5m 6w)

Kushner, T. Slavs!

12 characters (1g 9m 2w)

Molière The hypochondriac

12 characters (2b 5m 5w)

Herne, J. A. Margaret Fleming

12 characters (2m 10w)

LaRusso, L. Sweatshop

12 characters (4m 8w)

Tropf, R. Shadow hour

12 characters (5m 7w)

c Banks, J. Hercules—The panto!!
Blais, M.-C. Wintersleep
Mueller, L. Voices from September 11th
c Robinette, J. Sarah, plain and tall
Wellman, M. Cleveland

12 characters (6m 6w)

Devlin, A. After Easter
y Harden, V. Nobody heard mercy
Harding, M. Comfort and joy
Kelly, G. The torch-bearers
Learner, T. Miracles
c McCullough, L. E. "Lady of the Lamp": Florence Nightingale, founder of modern nursing
Mercier, P. Down the line
Nigro, D. Armitage
Shadowbox Cabaret (Theater group) Shadowboxing
Shores, D. Sordid lives
Simon, N. Neil Simon's 45 seconds from Broadway
Sleeping around
Williams, T. A streetcar named Desire
Wilson, L. Talley & son

12 characters (7m 5w)

Chekhov, A. P. The seagull
Hirson, D. Wrong mountain
Ludlam, C. Camille
Mason, T. Time on fire
Molière Tartuffe
Norman, M. Getting out
Weller, M. Ghost on fire
Wilson, L. Book of days

MIXED CAST—*Continued*

12 characters (8m 4w)

Field, B. Marriage

Guare, J. Chaucer in Rome

Guirgis, S. A. In Arabia we'd all be kings

Lawrence, D. H. The widowing of Mrs. Holroyd

Lloyd, J., and Croft, D. Are you being served?

c Lloyd, R. Arabian knights—The panto!

Wesker, A. I'm talking about Jerusalem

12 characters (9m 3w)

Bolger, D. The passion of Jerome

Bowen, J. After the rain

Fry, C. A yard of sun

Leonard, H. Great expectations

Nanus, S. The survivor

12 characters (10m 2w)

Buero-Vallejo, A. The sleep of reason

12 characters (11m 1w)

Boucicault, D. Belle Lamar

12 characters and extra (8m 4w extra)

Ehn, E. Locus (John the Baptist)

12 characters and extras (1b 7m 4w extras)

Brustein, R. Six characters in search of an author

Pirandello, L. Six characters in search of an author (Sei personaggi in cerca d'autore)

12 characters and extras (1g 5m 6w extras)

c Frankonis, W. A. A tale of Cinderella

12 characters and extras (1g 7m 4w extras)

Alvarez, L. Thin air: tales from a revolution

12 characters and extras (2b 4g 4m 2w extras)

c Medoff, M. Kringle's window

12 characters and extras (2b 5m 5w extras)

Bell, N. Ragged Dick

12 characters and extras (2b 9m 1w extras)

The second shepherd's play (Los pastores)

12 characters and extras (4m 8w extras)

Christiansen, A. The masked canary

Juana Inés de la Cruz The divine Narcissus (El divino Narciso)

12 characters and extras (5m 7w extras)

y Kelly, T. Stop the presses!

Wilson, L. The Hot L Baltimore

12 characters and extras (7m 5w extras)

Hennequin, M., and Veber, P. Anything to declare?

c McCullough, L. E. Three Holocaust tales

12 characters and extras (8m 4w extras)

Brown, S. Toshie

Chikamatsu, M. The uprooted pine

Lucas, C. Prelude to a kiss

Molière The miser

12 characters and extras (9m 3w extras)

Crommelynck, F. Golden guts

Gore, C. King O'Neil; or, The Irish Brigade

Irwin, B., and O'Donnell, M. Scapin

Janes, H. The perfect murder

Massinger, P. The renegado

Soyinka, W. Death and the king's horseman

Wedekind, F. Earth spirit

12 characters and extras (10m 2w extras)

Anderson, S. J. A traditional pageant

Jonson, B. The alchemist

Mayne, R. Bridge head

Mee, C. L. Orestes

12 characters and extras (11m 1w extras)

Hare, D. Saigon: year of the cat

13 characters (1b 8m 4w)

Cajal, O.-M. Exchange at Cafe Mimosa

13 characters (1g 4m 8w)

Carter, R. Women of the dust

13 characters (2b 2g 6m 3w)

Duffield, N. The secret garden

13 characters (3m 10w)

c Sodaro, C. Chickenheart

MIXED CAST—*Continued*

13 characters (4m 9w)

Schenkar, J. Burning desires

13 characters (5m 8w)

Davey, S. James Joyce's The dead
Foote, H. Laura Dennis
Gates, T. Ladies who lunch
c Hamlett, C. Eat, drink, and be scary

13 characters (6m 7w)

Bowen, J. The disorderly women
Chapman, J. Nil by mouth
Dee, P. English is a foreign language
Stein, G. Please do not suffer
Terry, M. Viet rock

13 characters (7m 6w)

Ardito, C. Confessions of Zeno
Chekhov, A. P. The sea gull
Chiarelli, L. The mask and the face
Daniels, S. Purple side coasters
Hischak, T. Molière's Tartuffe
Williams, T. The notebook of Trigorin
Yew, C. A beautiful country

13 characters (8m 5w)

Ardito, C. A bed for the knight
Filippo, E. de Filumena—a marriage Italian style
Gay, N. Radio times
Miller, A. Death of a salesman
Molière Those learned ladies
Reed, I. Savage wilds
Wood, T. Claptrap

13 characters (9m 4w)

Armstrong, D., and others Of grapes and nuts
Chekhov, A. P. The wood demon
Guare, J. A few stout individuals
Weller, M. Buying time
Williams, T. The mutilated
Wilson, S. The glad hand

13 characters (10m 3w)

Feydeau, G. Winner takes all
Langella, F. Frank Langella's Cyrano
Poulton, M. Fortune's fool
Shaw, B. The devil's disciple

13 characters (11m 2w)

Fishelson, D. The golem
O'Neill, E. Anna Christie
O'Neill, E. Anna Christie
Pirandello, L. Henry IV (Enrico IV)
Wilde, O. Salome

13 characters and extras (1b 1g 8m 3w extras)

c Roberts, B. Angelica! . . . and the monstrous monster of the deep

13 characters and extras (1b 1g 9m 2w extras)

c Clark, A. The red balloon

13 characters and extras (1b 10m 2w extras)

Hughes, L. Mulatto: a tragedy of the Deep South

13 characters and extras (2m 11w extras)

Wellman, M. Girl gone

13 characters and extras (3b 1g 5m 4w extras)

Aidoo, A. A. Anowa

13 characters and extras (5m 8w extras)

Sher, E. Denial is a river
y St. John, B. Someone save my Baby Ruth!

13 characters and extras (6m 7w extras)

Gray, J., and Raffalovich, M.-A. The blackmailers
Harvey, J. Hushabye Mountain
Harvey, J. Hushabye mountain
y McPherson, E. Legend of Sammy's Swamp

13 characters and extras (7b 6g extras)

c McCullough, L. E. The throne of Osiris

13 characters and extras (7m 6w extras)

c Ahlin, L. Cinderella: the true story
Cibber, C. Love's last shift; or, The fool in fashion
Durang, C. The idiots Karamazov

13 characters and extras (8b 2g 1m 2w extras)

Hughes, L. Scottsboro, limited

13 characters and extras (8m 5w extras)

Ludlam, C. Galas

MIXED CAST—*Continued*

Mowatt, A. C. Fashion; or, Life in New York

Thiong'o, N. W., and Mirii, N. W. I will marry when I want

13 characters and extras (9m 4w extras)

Cibber, C. Love makes a man; or, The fop's fortune

Cibber, C. The rival queans

Hochwälder, F. Orders

Mayakovsky, V. Vladimir Mayakovsky

c Reakes, P. Robinson Crusoe and the pirates

c Reakes, P. Robinson Crusoe and the pirates

13 characters and extras (10m 3w extras)

Goldoni, C. The Venetian twins

Molière The miser (short edition)

O'Casey, S. Purple dust

13 characters and extras (11m 2w extras)

Arden, J. Serjeant Musgrave's dance

13 characters and extras (12m 1w extras)

Shaw, B. Captain Brassbound's conversion

14 characters (1b 1g 5m 7w)

Foote, H. Vernon Early

14 characters (1b 8m 5w)

c McCullough, L. E. Naming the unnamed: the strange saga of Amerigo Vespucci

14 characters (1b 10m 3w)

Büchner, G. Woyzeck

14 characters (2b 3g 6m 3w)

Kang, M. J. Noran bang: the yellow room

14 characters (5m 9w)

Kneubuhl, V. N. The story of Susanna

St. John, B. The plot, like gravy, thickens

14 characters (6m 8w)

Foote, H. Getting Frankie married—and afterwards

y Hollingsworth, M. B. Johnny Brooke

Kushner, T. Hydriotaphia; or, The death of Dr. Browne

14 characters (6w 8m)

c York, Y. The witch of Blackbird Pond

14 characters (7m 7w)

Herzberg, J. The wedding party

Hewett, D. The man from Mukinupin

Van Itallie, J.-C. The serpent: a ceremony

14 characters (8m 6w)

Pomerance, B. Superhighway

Sher, E. Mourning dove

Wasserstein, W. An American daughter

Williams, T. The night of the iguana

Zindel, P. Every seventeen minutes the crowd goes crazy!

14 characters (9m 5w)

Friel, B. Three sisters

Kopit, A. L. Chad Curtiss, lost again

Nelson, R. Bal

14 characters (10m 4w)

Davis, T. Everybody's Ruby

Owens, R. Kontraption

14 characters (11m 3w)

Césaire, A. A tempest

Cibber, C. The tragical history of King Richard III

Hall, C. The best little whorehouse goes public

Molière Don Juan

Moody, W. V. The Great Divide

14 characters (12m 2w)

Kraszewski, C. S. Iphigenia in Zagreb

14 characters and extras (5m 9w extras)

Norman, M. Emily

14 characters and extras (6m 8w extras)

Ayckbourn, A. Garden

Ayckbourn, A. House

Frankel, R. WhoDunit. . .and who's the big idea anyway?

c Hines, K. Home on the mornin' train

MIXED CAST—*Continued*

14 characters and extras (7m 7w extras)

Murray, S. Tales of terror from Nightmare High School

14 characters and extras (8m 6w extras)

y Morreale, V. J. House of the Seven Gables

14 characters and extras (9m 5w extras)

Calderón de la Barca, P. The surgeon of honour
Chekhov, A. P. Three sisters
Mayne, R. Peter
O'Neill, E. The hairy ape
y Reader, C. The Oedipus plays

14 characters and extras (10m 4w extras)

Sorge, R. The beggar
Walcott, D. The ghost dance

14 characters and extras (11b 3g extras)

c McCullough, L. E. The flight of Icarus

14 characters and extras (11m 3w extras)

Gore, C. The king's seal
Herrick, J., and others Kudzu
Middleton, T., and Rowley, W. The changeling
Odets, C. Waiting for Lefty
Warren, R. P. Willie Stark

14 characters and extras (12m 2w extras)

Karnad, G. The fire and the rain
Osborne, J. The blood of the Bambergs

15 characters (1b 6m 8w)

c Hamlett, C. Once upon a fairy tale

15 characters (1b 9m 5w)

Harrison, N. Whodidit?

15 characters (2m 13w)

c McCullough, L. E. Mothers and daughters of invention: 4,000 years of women in science

15 characters (4m 11w)

y Davidson, R. The vile veterinarian
Terry, M. Babes in the bighouse

15 characters (7m 8w)

Enright, N. Spurboard
Kander, J., and Ebb, F. Steel pier
St. John, B. The werewolf's curse
St. John, B. You could die laughing!
Walker, J. M. Tales from the Daily Tabloid

15 characters (8m 7w)

Churchill, C. This is a chair
y Fuson, D. All the king's horses
c LaVohn, R. W. The smartest woman in the kingdom
The Three Kings (Los tres Reyes Magos)
Van Itallie, J.-C. America hurrah (interview, TV, motel)
Wilde, O. A woman of no importance
c Wolfman, J. The golden goose

15 characters (9m 6w)

Durang, C. A history of the American film
Egloff, E. The devils
Hardin, H. Esker Mike & his wife, Agiluk
Poliakoff, S. Talk of the city
Wilde, O. An ideal husband

15 characters (10b 4g 1m)

y Medoff, M., and Marks, R. Showdown on Rio Road

15 characters (10m 5w)

Gore, C. Quid pro quo; or, The day of the dupes
Holloway, J. Les miserables
Nelson, R. The killing of Yablonski: scenes of involvement in a current event
O'Casey, S. The plough and the stars
O'Casey, S. The plough and the stars
Owens, R. Futz

15 characters (12m 3w)

Bond, E. Early morning
Darke, N. The body
Gardner, H. Thieves
Reed, I. Hubba city

15 characters and extras (1b 1g 7m 6w extras)

Williams, T. Summer and smoke

MIXED CAST—*Continued*

15 characters and extras (1b 8m 6w extras)
Swayze, J. C. Ossawattomie Brown

15 characters and extras (5m 10w extras)
Larbey, B. Sand castles
McPherson, E. Divine Stella Devine

15 characters and extras (6b 9g extras)
c McCullough, L. E. The wisdom of Solomon

15 characters and extras (7m 8w extras)
y Francoeur, B. Oh, horrors! It's murder!

15 characters and extras (8m 7w extras)
c Art, S. S. The cotton blend horse
Christiansen, A. Best beware my sting
Strindberg, A. The ghost sonata
Strindberg, A. The ghost sonata

15 characters and extras (9m 6w extras)
Dobrish, J. Orpheus and Eurydice
Parks, S.-L. Fucking A

15 characters and extras (10m 5w extras)
Barras, C. M. The black crook
Leivick, H. Shop

15 characters and extras (11m 4w extras)
Ford, J. 'Tis pity she's a whore
Lee, R. E., and Lawrence, J. The night Thoreau spent in jail
Shaw, B. Caesar and Cleopatra
Stoppard, T. Indian ink

15 characters and extras (12m 3w extras)
Gabre-Medhin, T. Collision of altars
Molière Don Juan
Molière Don Juan

15 characters and extras (13m 2w extras)
Kleist, H. von The Prince of Homburg

15 characters and extras (14m 1w extras)
Yacine, K. Intelligence powder

16 characters (1b 12m 3w)
Frankonis, W. The killings tale

16 characters (2b 5g 5m 4w)
y Kral, B. Paper lanterns, paper cranes

16 characters (4m 12w)
c Hayes, S. The pomegranate seeds

16 characters (6m 10w)
García Lorca, F. Blood wedding
St. John, B. Evil doings at Queen Toots' tomb
Walker, J. M. Inventing Montana

16 characters (7m 9w)
St. John, B. Murder can be habit-forming
Wilde, O. Lady Windermere's fan

16 characters (8m 8w)
Warburton, N. Garlic and lavender

16 characters (9m 7w)
Arnault, M., and Arnault, A. The legend of Sleepy Hollow
Welch, S. M. Earl the vampire

16 characters (13m 3w)
Edelstein, Barry Race
Ives, D. Speed-the-play

16 characters (14m 2w)
Los Matachines unmasked (Los Matachines desenmascarados)

16 characters and extras (2g 7m 7w extras)
c McCullough, L. E. Around the world with Nellie Bly

16 characters and extras (4b 1g 9m 2w extras)
c Mason, T. The adventures of Tom Sawyer

16 characters and extras (6m 10w extras)
y St. John, B. Wynn Fairly, champeen rassler! or, Get a grip on yourself!

16 characters and extras (7b 6g 1m 2w extras)
y Francis, S. Body and soul

16 characters and extras (8m 8w extras)
Havel, V. The beggar's opera

16 characters and extras (9m 7w extras)
Pirandello, L. Right you are (if you think you are) (Cosi è, se ui pare)

16 characters and extras (10m 6w extras)
Feydeau, G. Not by bed alone (Un fil à la patte)

MIXED CAST—*Continued*

y Gieschen, C. How the West was Dun
London, J. Theft

16 characters and extras (11m 5w extras)

Haywood, E. F. The opera of operas; or, Tom Thumb the Great
Jonson, B. Epicoene
Shaw, B. Man and superman

16 characters and extras (12m 4w extras)

Molière The bourgeois gentleman
Molière The would-be gentleman

16 characters and extras (13m 3w extras)

Bandele, 'Biyi Aphra Behn's Oroonoko
Thomas, G. Gazooka

16 characters and extras (14m 2w extras)

Gore, C. Don Juan of Austria

16 characters and extras (15m 1w extras)

Mee, C. L. The war to end war

17 characters (7b 3g 7m)

Piñero, M. Playland blues

17 characters (7m 10w)

Sondheim, S. A little night music

17 characters (9m 8w)

Margulies, D. God of vengeance

17 characters (11m 6w)

Gore, C. The school for coquettes
Kaufman, G. S., and Ferber, E. The royal family

17 characters (12m 5w)

Nelson, R. The general from America

17 characters (13m 4w)

Webster, J. The Duchess of Malfi

17 characters (14m 3w)

Wedekind, F. Lulu

17 characters (15m 2w)

Arden of Faversham Arden of Faversham

17 characters (16m 1w)

Allison, B. Titus at the gates of Syon

Wood, C. H; or, Monologues at front of burning cities

17 characters and extras (1b 13m 3w extras)

Williams, T. Not about nightingales

17 characters and extras (1b 14m 2w extras)

Bailey, L. Baby doll

17 characters and extras (4b 2g 7m 4w extras)

c Brooks, J., and Mitchell, A. A child's Christmas in Wales

17 characters and extras (10m 7w extras)

Dove, R. The darker face of the earth

17 characters and extras (11m 6w extras)

Gore, C. Lords and commons

17 characters and extras (12m 5w extras)

Esson, L. The quest
Ohm, A. Night of the living dead
Osofisan, F. Once upon four robbers
Pomerance, B. Quantrill in Lawrence
Vidal, G. The best man

17 characters and extras (13m 4w extras)

Bosakowski, P. Nixon apologizes to the nation
Gillette, W. Secret service

17 characters and extras (14m 3w extras)

Friedman, G. W. The last supper
c Mason, T. Aladdin and the wonderful lamp

18 characters (7m 11w)

Edgar, D., and Todd, S. Teendreams

18 characters (9m 9w)

Sturgill, B. The enchantress of Ipswich

18 characters (11m 7w)

Cavacchioli, E. The bird of paradise
c Lander, A. Vasilisa the fair

18 characters (12m 6w)

Brown, C. The Negro of Peter the Great

18 characters (13m 5w)

Horváth, Ö. von Faith, love, hope

MIXED CAST—*Continued*

18 characters (14m 4w)
McCabe, J. D. J. The guerrillas

18 characters and extras (1b 11m 6w extras)
Whelan, P., and Alexander, B. Nativity

18 characters and extras (6m 12w extras)
y Jackson, K. High school dropouts from outer space

18 characters and extras (7m 11w extras)
Francoeur, B. Sunset trail
y Kelly, T. Sundown Alley

18 characters and extras (8m 10w extras)
Chekhov, A. P. Ivanov
Chekhov, A. P. Ivanov
Chekhov, A. P. Ivanov
c Francoeur, B. Sleepy Hollow

18 characters and extras (13b 5g extras)
c McCullough, L. E. What is a brother?

18 characters and extras (14m 4w extras)
Chekhov, A. P. Tatyana Repina
Warren, R. P. All the king's men

18 characters and extras (15m 3w extras)
Foote, H. Tomorrow
Kyd, T. The Spanish tragedy

19 characters (1g 13m 5w)
Wedekind, F. Pandora's box

19 characters (2g 9m 8w)
Howe, T. Pride's Crossing

19 characters (4b 5g 7m 3w)
Medoff, M. H., and Treon, P. Crunch time

19 characters (8m 11w)
Wilson, L. Chateau La Roach

19 characters (9m 10w)
Bernard, K. The magic show of Dr. MaGico

19 characters (11m 8w)
Wedekind, F. The solar spectrum

19 characters (13m 6w)
Anderson, Roger Shine!: the Horatio Alger musical

19 characters and extras (1b 1g 9m 8w extras)
c Howe, T. East of the sun and west of the moon

19 characters and extras (1b 1g 10m 7w extras)
Vvedensky, A. Christmas at the Ivanovs'

19 characters and extras (1b 8m 10w extras)
c DeTurk, S. The musical adventures of Oliver Twist

19 characters and extras (1b 10m 8w extras)
Yazbek, D. The full Monty

19 characters and extras (5m 14w extras)
c Frankel, R. Jurassic Park and Wreck

19 characters and extras (9m 10w extras)
y Francoeur, B. Rock around the block

19 characters and extras (10m 9w extras)
Hollmann, M. Urinetown the musical

19 characters and extras (12m 7w extras)
Suvorin, A. S. Tatyana Repina
Williams, T. Sweet bird of youth

19 characters and extras (15m 4w extras)
Chekhov, A. P. Tatyana Repina
Field, B. Monsieur de Molière
Nowra, L. Inside the island

19 characters and extras (16m 3w extras)
Field, B. Pantagleize

19 characters and extras (17m 2w extras)
Manzoni, A. The Count of Carmagnola: a tragedy

20 characters (1b 2g 10m 7w)
O'Neill, E. The straw

20 characters (1b 15m 4w)
Woldin, J. Murder in Baker Street

20 characters (16m 4w)
O'Casey, S. Cock-a-doodle dandy

MIXED CAST—*Continued*

20 characters and extras (6b 6g 5m 3w extras)
Angus, Eric, and Shostak, Cathy The demon headmaster

20 characters and extras (7m 13w extras)
Cook, P. The ghost of Christmas presents

20 characters and extras (8m 12w extras)
c Moriarty, J. Archie of the Amazon
y Murray, S. Inspector Incognito and the Kansas City Kid
Murray, S. Rocky of the rainforest

20 characters and extras (10m 10w extras)
Horváth, Ö. von Tales from the Vienna woods

20 characters and extras (14m 6w extras)
Boucicault, D. The octoroon; or, Life in Louisiana
Bulgakov, M. Flight
O'Casey, S. Within the gates
Schiller, F. Mary Stuart

20 characters and extras (15m 5w extras)
Chekhov, A. P. Platonov

20 characters and extras (17m 3w extras)
Williams, T. Not about nightingales
Williams, T. Not about nightingales

20 characters and extras (19m 1w extras)
Stoppard, T. The invention of love

21 characters (1b 4g 10m 6w)
Gien, P. The syringa tree

21 characters (7m 14w)
y Cook, P. Switching principals

21 characters (8m 13w)
y Cook, P. Stop sending in the clowns

21 characters (11m 10w)
y St. John, B. Taming the wild, wild West in a dress

21 characters (14m 7w)
Howard, B. Shenandoah

21 characters (15m 6w)
Ravenhill, M. Mother Clap's Molly house
y Romer, M. Rumble fish

21 characters (16m 5w)
O'Casey, S. Red roses for me

21 characters (18m 3w)
Morgan, E. The early years

21 characters and extras (1b 7g 8m 5w extras)
c Vreeke, J. A little princess

21 characters and extras (9m 12w extras)
Cook, P. Ax of murder

21 characters and extras (11m 10w extras)
y Francoeur, B. Way out west in a dress

21 characters and extras (13m 8w extras)
y Abbott, G. W. The scarlet letter
Field, B. Camille

21 characters and extras (17m 4w extras)
O'Neill, E. The moon of the Caribbees
Williams, T. Fugitive kind

21 characters and extras (20m 1w extras)
c Mason, T. Treasure Island

22 characters (3b 14m 5w)
Beaumont, F. The knight of the burning pestle

22 characters (7m 15w)
y Jackson, R. E. Touched by an angle
Williams, T. Spring storm
Williams, T. Spring storm

22 characters (11m 11w)
Williams, T. Battle of angels

22 characters (12m 10w)
Wein, G., and Blumsack, A. L. Grandma Sylvia's funeral

22 characters (17m 5w)
Barnes, P. The ruling class

22 characters (21m 1w)
c Hall, L. The adventures of Pinocchio

MIXED CAST—*Continued*

22 characters and extras (1b 18m 3w extras)
Wilder, T. The Alcestiad

22 characters and extras (2b 2g 12m 6w extras)
Sills, P. A Christmas carol

22 characters and extras (2b 14m 6w extras)
Chikamatsu, M. The battles of Coxinga

22 characters and extras (10m 12w extras)
Cook, P. The saga of the golden horse-shoe
c Pargman, S. Pollyanna

22 characters and extras (12m 10w extras)
Brittney, L. Pickwick papers

22 characters and extras (13m 9w extras)
Krieger, H. Side show
Trowbridge, J. T. Neighbor Jackwood

22 characters and extras (14m 8w extras)
Wedekind, F. The Marquis of Keith

22 characters and extras (15m 7w extras)
Howard, B. Shenandoah

22 characters and extras (17m 5w extras)
Schnitzler, A. The green cockatoo

22 characters and extras (18m 4m extras)
Dekker, T. The shoemaker's holiday

22 characters and extras (18m 4w extras)
Dekker, T. The shoemaker's holiday

22 characters and extras (20m 2w)
Manzoni, A. Adelchi: a tragedy

22 characters and extras (20m 2w extras)
Jonson, B. Volpone

23 characters (1b 13m 9w)
Field, B. A Christmas carol

23 characters (2b 2g 7m 12w)
Williams, T. The rose tattoo

23 characters (10m 13w)
y Sodaro, C. Phantom of the campfire

23 characters (15m 8w)
Warner, F. Rembrandt's mirror

23 characters (16m 7w)
Kushner, T. East coast ode to Howard Jarvis: a little teleplay in tiny monologues

23 characters (18m 5w)
O'Casey, S. The silver tassie

23 characters and extras (6m 17w extras)
Francoeur, B. The stories of Scheherazade
c Pargman, S. Scheherazade

23 characters and extras (17m 6w extras)
Brown, W. W. The escape

23 characters and extras (18m 5w extras)
Harrison, T. The passion

23 characters and extras (20m 3w extras)
Kopit, A. L. Indians

24 characters (2b 13m 9w)
Erdman, N. The suicide

24 characters (13m 11w)
Kaufman, G. S., and Ferber, E. Dinner at eight

24 characters (19m 5w)
Mann, A. Judgment at Nuremberg
Mann, A. Judgment at Nuremberg

24 characters and extras (1g 17m 6w extras)
Finlayson, A. Misfits

24 characters and extras (13m 11w extras)
Lloyd, R. The three musketeers—le panteau!

24 characters and extras (18m 6w extras)
Heywood, T. A woman killed with kindness
Vitrac, R. The mysteries of love

24 characters and extras (21m 3w extras)
Greene, R. Selimus, emperor of the Turks

MIXED CAST—*Continued*

25 characters (5b 11m 9w)

c Mason, T. The adventures of Huckleberry Finn

25 characters (7m 18w)

c Francoeur, B. Enchanted Sleeping Beauty

25 characters (10m 15w)

Woodford, K. Cactus Pass

25 characters and extras (7m 18w extras)

Cook, P. Who's dying to be a millionaire?

25 characters and extras (15m 8w extras)

Poskitt, K. Fawkes—the quiet guy

25 characters and extras (17m 8w extras)

Williams, T. Stairs to the roof

25 characters and extras (22m 3w extras)

Daborne, R. A Christian turned Turk

26 characters (1b 1g 17m 7w)

Chen Zidu, and others Sangshuping chronicles

26 characters (9m 17w)

Cook, P. Hillbilly hankerin'

26 characters (12m 14w)

Davis, M. R. Mystery at Shady Acres

26 characters (18m 8w)

Darke, N. Ting Tang mine

26 characters and extras (1b 2g 19m 4w extras)

c Bennett, A. Kenneth Grahame's The wind in the willows

26 characters and extras (8m 18w extras)

y Cook, P. Last one to survive is a rotten egg

26 characters and extras (10m 16w extras)

y Kelly, T. The snake in the grass

26 characters and extras (17m 9w extras)

Stoppard, T. Voyage

26 characters and extras (20m 6w extras)

Kraszewski, C. S. Peter the rock

27 characters (9m 18w)

y Davies, C., and Fendrich, S. Tongue twisted

y Murray, S. A twist of the tongue

27 characters (12m 15w)

c Woodford, K. If the shoe fits

27 characters (20m 7w)

Weiss, P. Marat/Sade

27 characters (21m 6w)

Walcott, D. The Haitian earth

27 characters and extras (2b 1g 17m 7w extras)

Stoppard, T. Shipwreck

27 characters and extras (8m 19w extras)

y Francoeur, B. Going. . .going. . .gone with the breeze

27 characters and extras (11m 16w extras)

y Francoeur, B. Groovy!

28 characters (1b 20m 7w)

Aiken, G. L. Uncle Tom's cabin

28 characters (11m 17w)

y Cook, P. Campaign capers at Taft High

28 characters and extras (22m 6w extras)

Santander, F. The agronomist (El extensionista)

29 characters (10m 19w)

y Sodaro, C. Hound of the Clackervilles

29 characters and extras (10m 19w extras)

y Francoeur, B. Kokonut Island

29 characters and extras (22m 7w extras)

Mühsam, E. Thunderation! (Alle Wetter!)

29 characters and extras (24m 5w extras)

Morgan, E. The execution

29 characters and extras (27m 2w extras)

Marlowe, C. The troublesome reign and lamentable death of Edward the Second

MIXED CAST—*Continued*

30 characters (18m 12w)
Haywood, E. F. A wife to be lett: a comedy.

30 characters (22m 8w)
Francis, M. The adventures of Huckleberry Finn

30 characters (28m 2w)
Weiss, P. The investigation

30 characters and extras (10m 20w extras)
y Murray, S. This old house

30 characters and extras (18m 12w extras)
Brecht, B. Baal

30 characters and extras (22m 8w extras)
Sharma, T. The wooden cart

30 characters and extras (23m 7w extras)
Jonson, B. Bartholomew Fair

30 characters and extras (26m 4w extras)
Belasco, D. The heart of Maryland

31 characters and extras (11m 20w extras)
y Francoeur, B. Kokonut kapers
y Kelly, T. Kokonut High

31 characters and extras (24m 7w extras)
Norton-Taylor, R. The colour of justice

32 characters (1g 23m 8w)
Morgan, E. The ministry

32 characters (11m 21w)
Francoeur, B. Charleston!
Francoeur, B. Flapper!

32 characters (15m 17w)
Kaufman, G. S., and Ferber, E. Stage door

32 characters and extras (11m 21w extras)
y DeTurk, S. Summer's in the air

32 characters and extras (13m 19w extras)
y Francoeur, B. Friday night fever

32 characters and extras (15m 17w extras)
Parnell, P. The cider house rules: part 1

33 characters (1b 19m 13w)
Warner, F. Goethe's Weimar

33 characters and extras (31m 2w extras)
Marlowe, C. The tragical history of Dr. Faustus

34 characters and extras (18m 16w extras)
Enright, N., and Monjo, J. Cloudstreet

35 characters and extras (17m 18w extras)
Poskitt, K. Nell's belles

Large cast
Alvarez, L. Don Juan of Seville
Bricusse, L. Scrooge
Briggs, S. Terry Pratchett's Maskerade
Brown, W. W. The escape
Constable, J. The Southwark Mysteries
Daniels, S. Dust
Dekker, T. The magnificent entertainment
Donnellan, D. Vanity fair
Edgar, D. Maydays
Filippo, E. de Naples gets rich
y Francis, M. David Copperfield
y Francoeur, B. DiscoKnights
Ganguli, U. Rudali
Green, P. The lost colony
Harrison, T. Doomsday
c Horovitz, I. A Christmas carol: Scrooge and Marley
Howe, L., and Gordon, R. Indian radio days
Hughes, L. Harvest
Ibsen, H. Emperor and Galilean: a world historical drama
Jarry, A. King Ubu
Jenkin, L. Like I say
Jenkins, M. F. All powers necessary and convenient
Kaufman, M. The Laramie Project
Kirshon, V. Grain
Kokoschka, O. Comenius
Kushner, T. A dybbuk, or between two worlds
Lask, B. Liberation (Die Befreiung)
Mann, E. Execution of justice

MIXED CAST—*Continued*

Mann, E. Execution of justice

c Meakin, P. The tales of Hans Andersen

Mendez Rodriguez, J. M. Autumn flower

Middleton, T. A chaste maid in Cheapside

Nelson, R. Rip Van Winkle; or, "The works"

Overmyer, E. Alki

Parnell, P. The cider house rules: part 2

y Perkins, D. Shake, ripple & roll

Pinski, D. The treasure

Poliakoff, S. Perfect strangers

Pratchett, T. Carpe jugulum

Santander, F. Mexico, USA

Santander, F. The unwritten law

Seremba, G. Come good rain

Sills, P. A Christmas carol

Slaight, B. Dancing by myself

Snyder, P. D. B. Miracle on 34th Street

Sondheim, S. Follies

Sondheim, S. Sunday in the park with George

Stoppard, T. Salvage

Strindberg, A. A dream play

Tait, L. Edwin Booth

Vinaver, M. Overboard

Walcott, D. Drums and colours

Warren, R. P. Proud flesh

Wedekind, F. Spring's awakening

Wertenbaker, T. The love of the nightingale

Williams, T. Camino Real

Willmott, Phil Around the world in eighty days

Wolf, M. Another American: asking and telling

PUPPETS

10 characters and extras

Taylor, J., and Kentridge, W. Ubu and the Truth Commission

18 characters

Beissel, H. Inuk and the sun

UNIDENTIFIED CAST

1 character

Kauffman, J. According to Coyote

2 characters

Kane, H. Snapshot: monument

3 characters

Rivera, J. Tape

3 characters and extras

c Swortzell, L. The mischief makers

4 characters

Anderson, S. J. The night before pageant

Tuan, A. The technology project: F.E.T.C.H.

5 characters

Lipkin, D. I am Laika

c Winther, B. Brother Rabbit sells corn

c Winther, B. The great hurricane

6 characters

Tzara, T. The gas heart

c Wood, D. The ideal gnome expedition

7 characters

c Barchers, S. I. The farmer and the animals

c Barchers, S. I. Fortunée

c Barchers, S. I. Spider flies to the feast

c Barchers, S. I. Los tres ratoncitos: a chiste

c McCullough, L. E. Marking time: clocks and calendars through the centuries

Yellow Robe, W. S. The council

8 characters

Bruchac, J. Possum's tail

8 characters and extras

Bruchac, J. Wihio's duck dance

9 characters

c McCullough, L. E. Ruth and Naomi: the healing power of friendship

11 characters

c McCullough, L. E. "Constellations then arise": astronomy in the age of Copernicus

13 characters

c Barchers, S. I. Water, water will be mine

UNIDENTIFIED CAST—*Continued*

c McCullough, L. E. Noah's ark: falsehood and wickedness hitch a ride

14 characters and extras

c Robinette, J. Charlotte's web

15 characters

c Whittington, P. Rosie and the bad, bad apples

16 characters

c Ellison, L. Space junk

21 characters

c McCullough, L. E. Dare to be a Daniel!

25 characters

c McCullough, L. E. The alphabet

VARIABLE CAST

Alexander, R. and others Heaven and hell (on earth): a divine comedy
Alvarez, L. Analiese
y Alvarez, L. Analiese
c Anderson, S. J. "Jingle bells" revisited
Armory The gentleman of the chrysanthemums
c Averill, R. Pixies, kings, and magical things
Bachmann, I. The good god of Manhattan
Baraka, A. The election machine warehouse
Baraka, A. Primitive world: an antinuclear jazz musical
y Barchers, S. I., and Kroll, J. L. A Christmas carol
y Barchers, S. I., and Kroll, J. L. Episodes from Don Quixote
Birch, M. Pratt of the Argus
Bishop, C., and Fuller, E. Dividing lines
Bishop, C., and Fuller, E. Family snapshots
y Bland, J. K. A tale of two cities
Blok, A. The unknown woman
Body, J. J. The Indian draft spirit
c Boettcher-Tate, K. Rapunzel
Bradley, J. Digging for ladies
Bruchac, J. Star sisters
c Bush, M. Wildboy

Chekhov, A. P. In Moscow
Chi, J. Bran nue dae
c A Christmas pageant
Chye, K. T. Here and now
Cohen, F. Amy Crockett: M.V.P.
Conning, L. A Coloured place
Cook, P. We the people
Crumley, G. W. Death day/life day
Culture Clash (Group) Anthems
Culture Clash (Group) Bordertown
Culture Clash (Group) Mission magic mystery tour
Culture Clash (Group) Nuyorican stories
c DeTurk, S. Let your hair down, Rapunzel
c DeTurk, S. The mad adventures of Mr. Toad
y DeTurk, S. Yearbook reflections
c DeVita, J. Looking glass land
Dunbar, P. L. Herrick
Dunbar, P. L. Jes lak white fo'ks
Ehn, E. Song for the end
Ensler, E. The Vagina monologues
c Espinosa, R. Clothes do not make the man (El habito no hace al monje)
c Espinosa, R. Don Quijote in America (Don Quijote en America)
c Espinosa, R. What happened in the garden this summer? (Que paso en el jardin este verano?)
y Fendrich, S. Yearbook
Foley, D. Sad hotel
c Francoeur, B. Cinderella's glass slipper
c Francoeur, B. Wonderland!
y Frost, H., and Cocks, H. Why darkness seems so light
c Garner, J. A giant's giant pizza
Gippius, Z. Sacred blood
Hall, L. Child of our time: children of the rain
c Harris, A. The orphan train
c Harris, A. The second shepherd's play
y Hippolyte, K. The song of one; or, The journey of Ti Marie
c Hoffman, E. T. A. The nutcracker and the mouse-king
Horváth, Ö. von Casimir and Caroline
Horváth, Ö. von The Italian evening
c Howard, C. The frog princess
y Hughes, L. Black nativity
Hughes, T. Euripides' Alcestis

VARIABLE CAST—*Continued*

c Vogel, L. Ring around Jerusalem

Vogel, L. Rockball, our natural pastime

c Vogel, L. Solomon—wise for a while

Vogel, L. The temptations

Vogel, L. We're all shook up

c Vogel, L. What's up, rock?

c Vogel, L. Wilderness wandering

Vogel, L. Yakety Yak: he won't talk back

c Warburton, N. Domby-Dom

Warburton, N. Office song

Wei Minglun Pan Jinlian: the history of a fallen woman

Weiss, P. The new trial

c Wong, E. Boid & Oskar

Wood, C. Across from the garden of Allah

c Wood, D. Mother Goose's golden Christmas

y Woolf, W. King Artie and the Knights of the Rad Table

c Zapel, A. L. All things are bright and beautiful

c Zeder, S. The taste of sunrise

1 character

Allen, G. Subliminable

Bayiates, A. Hype-r-connectivity

Tait, L. Mad cow disease in America

2 characters

Chinn, J. A different way home

Guare, J. Greenwich mean

Leight, W. The final interrogation of Ceauşescu's dog

Rivera, J. Tape

3 characters

Esson, L. Terra Australis

Graham, B. Desperate affection

Ives, D. Arabian nights

Kane, S. 4.48 psychosis

Lynch, J. Take two

Nelson, J. L. Somebody call 911

Tait, L. Betsy Philadelphia

Tate, J. Mistaken for genius

Taylor, R. Love poem #98

4 characters

Anderson, S. J. Echoes of Christmas

c Barchers, S. I. The three wishes

c Barchers, S. I. The white-haired old woman

c Fredericks, A. D. Columbus pleads his case

c Fredericks, A. D. Heads/tails

c Fredericks, A. D. I am Slime

c Fredericks, A. D. It's in the bag

c Fredericks, A. D. Me, myself, and I

Holland, N. To meet Oscar Wilde

Linney, R. Patronage

Oates, J. C. Poor Bibi

c Zapel, A. L. Who am I?

4 characters and extra

c Fredericks, A. D. Once upon a time

5 characters

c Barchers, S. I. Arion and his harp

y Barchers, S. I., and Kroll, J. L. The necklace

Bass, T. Inventory

Dietz, S. Private eyes

c Fredericks, A. D. All the knowledge in the universe

c Fredericks, A. D. A conversation with Thomas Jefferson

c Fredericks, A. D. A day in Mesa Verde

c Fredericks, A. D. Eight days, three hours, and eighteen minutes

c Fredericks, A. D. Long hours, long days

c Fredericks, A. D. A right to vote

c Fredericks, A. D. The Shapiros' new adventure

c Fredericks, A. D. Two soldiers: talking, dying

Harrison, J. Stolen

Kokoschka, O. Sphinx and strawman

c McCullough, L. E. Anthropology, the science of us

c Miller, K. S. Island son

Oates, J. C. The adoption

Oates, J. C. The adoption

Rivera, J. References to Salvador Dali make me hot

5 characters and extras

c Harris, A. The Arkansaw bear

6 characters

c Barchers, S. I. Aeolus and the winds

VARIABLE CAST—*Continued*

c Barchers, S. I. The clever daughter
c Barchers, S. I. Deucalion and Pyrrha
c Barchers, S. I. It could always be worse
c Barchers, S. I. Princess Sivatra
c Barchers, S. I. Sally Ann Thunder and Davey Crockett
c Barchers, S. I. Why ants carry burdens
c Barchers, S. I. The young chief who played the flute
c Barchers, S. I. Zeus and Hera
c Fredericks, A. D. Air to breathe, water to drink
c Fredericks, A. D. Do it yourself!
c Fredericks, A. D. I scream, you scream, we all scream for ice cream
c Fredericks, A. D. Into, beyond, and back again
c Fredericks, A. D. Leif Eriksson discovers Vinland
c Fredericks, A. D. The masters of all
c Fredericks, A. D. Mission San Juan Capistrano
c McBride-Smith, B. Demeter and Persephone
c McBride-Smith, B. Santaberry and the Snard
c McBride-Smith, B. The squire's bride
c McBride-Smith, B. Three billy goats gruff: poetry-style
Smith, V., and Dixon, M. B. The league of semi-super heroes
Valentine, P. A dog's life
Washburn, A. The intervention
Wilner, S. Labor Day

6 characters and extras

c Zapel, A. L. Three gifts from gentle Jesus

7 characters

c Barchers, S. I. Atalanta
c Barchers, S. I. Baba Yaga
c Barchers, S. I. The bee, the harp, the mouse, and the bum-clock
c Barchers, S. I. Daedalus and Icarus
c Barchers, S. I. Eos, Selene, and Helios
c Barchers, S. I. The giant in the garden
c Barchers, S. I. Hermes
c Barchers, S. I. The shepherd and the troll
c Barchers, S. I. Sisyphus

c Fredericks, A. D. A bowl of soup, a piece of bread
c Fredericks, A. D. Bubble trouble
c Fredericks, A. D. The delegates speak out
c Fredericks, A. D. Driving the final spike
c Fredericks, A. D. A long, long time
c Fredericks, A. D. March 1917: in a coffee shop
c Fredericks, A. D. A matter of survival
c Fredericks, A. D. With the McMillans on the Oregon Trail
Kern, W. Hellcab
Ludlam, C. The mystery of Irma Vep
c McBride-Smith, B. Atalanta
c McBride-Smith, B. Bill Erophon and his horse Peggy Sue
c McBride-Smith, B. Cat-skins
c McBride-Smith, B. Little Red Cowboy Hat
c McBride-Smith, B. A thoroughly modern Rapunzel
McKay, G. Me

7 characters and extras

c Barchers, S. I. Polly Ann and John Henry
c Espinosa, R. The coming of winter (La llegada del invierno)

8 characters

c Barchers, S. I. Ariadne
c Barchers, S. I. Artemis and Niobe
c Barchers, S. I. Athena
c Barchers, S. I. The doomed prince
c Barchers, S. I. Gifts of love
c Barchers, S. I. Leto
c Barchers, S. I. The magic table
c Barchers, S. I. The peach boy
c Barchers, S. I. Prometheus and Pandora
c Barchers, S. I. To the sun, moon, and wind
c Barchers, S. I. The tree that bled fish
y Barchers, S. I., and Kroll, J. L. The luck of Roaring Camp
y Barchers, S. I., and Kroll, J. L. Rappaccini's daughter
Clements, M. Now look what you made me do
c Fredericks, A. D. Across the new frontier
c Fredericks, A. D. Alien teacher

VARIABLE CAST—*Continued*

c Fredericks, A. D. Artifact

c Fredericks, A. D. December 7, 1941: aboard the USS Arizona

c Fredericks, A. D. Forever is a long time

c Fredericks, A. D. Just a thought

c Fredericks, A. D. The Mayflower Compact

Hoppe, G. Jackie, an American life

c Martini, C. Mouse

c McBride-Smith, B. Aaron Kelly is dead!

c McBride-Smith, B. Bubba the cowboy prince

c McBride-Smith, B. Henny Penny

c McBride-Smith, B. King Midas

c McBride-Smith, B. Sody Salleratus

c Miller, K. S. Beauty and the beast

c Miller, K. S. Young Cherokee

Orlandersmith, D. Monster

Pugliese, F. The summer winds

Taylor, D. H. The boy in the treehouse

8 characters and extras

y Hoogland, C. Salmonberry: a West Coast fairy tale

Rhymes, B. G. The way of the cross

9 characters

c Barchers, S. I. Catherine and her destiny

c Barchers, S. I. Demeter and Persephone

c Barchers, S. I. Eros and Psyche

c Barchers, S. I. King Midas

c Barchers, S. I. The master-maid

c Barchers, S. I. Molly Whuppie

c Barchers, S. I. Orpheus and Eurydice

c Barchers, S. I. Pan

y Barchers, S. I., and Kroll, J. L. The lady, or the tiger?

Bovell, A. Speaking in tongues

Busch, C. Shanghai moon

Fréchette, C. The four lives of Marie

c Fredericks, A. D. The Jovian pact

c Hamlett, C. The magic mermaid

c McBride-Smith, B. Arachne and Athena

c McBride-Smith, B. Finn M'Coul

River, S. B. Unbroken

c Wood, D. The Twits

9 characters and extras

c Forsten, M. L. The sycamore cross

c Mason, T. Ukrainian tales

Wellman, M. Infrared

c Wood, D. The Twits

10 characters

Auburn, D. What do you believe about the future?

c Barchers, S. I. Dick Whittington and his cat

c Barchers, S. I. How Fisher went to the skyland

c Barchers, S. I. Melampus

y Barchers, S. I., and Kroll, J. L. The oblong box

Bruchac, J. The cannibal monster

c Espinosa, R. Cinderella in modern times (Cenicienta en tiempos modernos)

c Espinosa, R. The princess is sad (La princesa esta triste)

y Evans, S. Jesus loved them

c Fredericks, A. D. December 1, 1955: Montgomery, Alabama

c Fredericks, A. D. Equal Rights Amendment

c Fredericks, A. D. An imaginary discussion

c McBride-Smith, B. Hershel and the Hanukkah goblins

c McBride-Smith, B. The miller and his donkey

c McCullough, L. E. Squeak and maiow!

c Reiser, D. The real story of Little Red Riding Hood

c Robbins, N. Red Riding Hood

Rogerson, P. B. While shepherds watched

Stair, E. R. Parade without a permit

c Winther, B. A gift for Pachacuti Inca

c Wong, E. The happy prince

10 characters and extra

c Fredericks, A. D. The last decision

10 characters and extras

c Espinosa, R. The farmer finds his true friends (El granjero descubre a sus verdaderos amigos)

c Ingram, S. L. Everywhere, everywhere, Christmas tonight

Paterson, D. L., and Liebman, S. The great Gilly Hopkins

VARIABLE CAST—*Continued*

11 characters

c Barchers, S. I. Finding the foolish
c Barchers, S. I. Helen
Godber, J. Salt of the earth
Houston, S. Message sent
y Kotwica, D. The great Denver railroad scam; or, If aunt May leaves, who'll weed the 'tunias?
Peditto, P. Sounds of silents (The Essanay years)
c Rosenberg, N. The gifts of Obidiah Oak

11 characters and extras

Ayckbourn, A. Gizmo
c Ingram, S. L. Christmas? Bah humbug!

12 characters

Anderson, S. J. Epiphany mosaic
c Barchers, S. I. Dionysus
c Barchers, S. I. Heracles
y Barchers, S. I., and Kroll, J. L. Dr. Jekyll and Mr. Hyde
y Barchers, S. I., and Kroll, J. L. A retrieved reformation
c McBride-Smith, B. The wolf and the seven kids
c Winther, B. The talking burro

12 characters and extras

c Art, S. S. Cindie Ellis
Owens, J. To serve one another
Rust, J. Saved by the Serendipity Circus

13 characters

c Art, S. S. Beulah and the feast
c Barchers, S. I. Jason and the golden fleece
y Barchers, S. I., and Kroll, J. L. Frankenstein
Betts, J. Colour in the storm
Busch, C. The lady in question
c Mast, E. Jungalbook
c McBride-Smith, B. Twelfth night
c McCullough, L. E. The magic ring

13 characters and extras

Marnich, M. Quake
y Zeder, S. The taste of sunrise

14 characters

c Ayckbourn, A. The champion of Paribanou

c Barchers, S. I. Oedipus
c Barchers, S. I. Perseus
Berger, G. I will go. . . I will go. . .
Casey, Gene, and Casey, Jan Hubba hubba
Głowacki, J. The fourth sister
c McBride-Smith, B. The contest for Athens
Vanhecke, I. Twelve strands of wool

15 characters

c Art, S. S. The Hatfields and the McCoys
y Barchers, S. I., and Kroll, J. L. Captains courageous
c McBride-Smith, B. The twelve labors of Hercules
c McCullough, L. E. The six swans

15 characters and extras

Bailey, B. Ipi zombi?
c Gavin, J. Monkey in the stars
Goens, L. M. Resurrection on trial
c Roman, J. Papa's angels: a Christmas story

16 characters

y Karcz, L. R. The taming of LaRue
Luckham, C. The dramatic attitudes of Miss Fanny Kemble

17 characters

Armstrong, D., and others A Christmas Twist
Bachmann, I. The good god of Manhattan
y Barchers, S. I., and Kroll, J. L. The legend of Sleepy Hollow
c Bush, M. The boy who left home to find out about the shivers
Foster, N. Office hours
Hanan, S. M. Jolson & company
y Harden, V. Big boys don't cry
Levi, S. Hearts 'n kisses 'n Miss Vickers
c McCullough, L. E. The great flying ship of Ivan the Impossible
c McCullough, L. E. The twelve months
y Surface, M. H. Most valuable player
c Wood, D. More adventures of Noddy

17 characters and extras

c Ellis, D. The three little pigs out west

VARIABLE CAST—*Continued*
Sodaro, C. Who poisoned his meatball?

18 characters
c Art, S. S. Joe Knight and the seven serfs
c Corey, I. L. The magic garden
Jackson, G., and Purcell, E. Q. Duet

18 characters and extras
c Francoeur, B. The story of Hansel and Gretel
y Jackson, R. E. Bad hair day

19 characters
y Barchers, S. I., and Kroll, J. L. Zorro!; or, The curse of Capistrano
c Francoeur, B. Babes in Toyland
Frankel, R. WhoDunit. . .and to whom?

19 characters and extras
y Nielsen, K. Hamlet
Pascal, J. Theresa

20 characters
y Barchers, S. I., and Kroll, J. L. Hard times
c Fredericks, A. D. One day in Gettysburg
c McCullough, L. E. The lost spear

20 characters and extras
c Castle, G. V. The Jungle Book: the musical
Cook, P. Last stop till Christmas
c Francoeur, B. Tiny Thumbelina
Koopman, L. It is finished
y Nielsen, K. Macbeth

21 characters
Aspengren, K. Flyer
y Barchers, S. I., and Kroll, J. L. The prince and the pauper
c DeTurk, S. Pocahontas
y Godber, J. Teechers
c Mason, T. African tales: Kalulu and his monkey farm and Rumpelstiltskin

c McCullough, L. E. Samson and Delilah
c McCullough, L. E. Tales of angels
Wertenbaker, T. The Ash Girl

21 characters and extras
c Morris, V. King Midas and the touch of gold
y St. John, B. Holder Posey, the felonious photographer

22 characters
Ayckbourn, A. Comic potential

23 characters and extras
Beevers, G. George Eliot's Silas Marner

24 characters
c McCullough, L. E. A cosmic bouquet: sun, moon and stars
Pomerance, B. Hands of light

25 characters
Boomer, L. Bocón
y Brandl, D. Too wrapped up for Christmas

25 characters and extras
Castle, G. V. Welcome to Bedside Manor

26 characters
y LaVohn, R. W. A midsummer night's midterm
Wilson, S. Vampire

27 characters
c Francoeur, B. Bah, humbug!

28 characters
Frankel, R. Strange happenings

33 characters
Harrison, T. The Nativity

37 characters and extras
Netto, L. Maria

PART III

List of Collections Indexed

Aeschylus

Aeschylus, 1; the Oresteia; edited and translated by David R. Slavitt. University of Pa. Press 1998 159p (Penn Greek drama series) ISBN 0-8122-3416-2; 0-8122-1627-X (pa) LC 97-28894

Contents: Agamemnon; The libation bearers; The Eumenides

Aeschylus, 2; edited by David R. Slavittand Palmer Davie. University of Pa. Press 1998 210p (Penn Greek drama series) ISBN 0-8122-3465-0; 0-8122-1671-7 (pa) LC 97-28894

Contents: The Persians; Seven against Thebes; The suppliants; Prometheus bound

Aeschylus: the complete plays v1; Oresteia; translated by Carl R. Mueller; introduction by Hugh Denard. Smith & Kraus 2002 313p (Great translations for actors series) ISBN 1-575-25312-7 LC 2002-70807

Contents: Agamemnon; Libation bearers; Eumenides

Aeschylus: the complete plays v2; four plays; translated by Carl R. Mueller; introduction by Hugh Denard. Smith & Kraus 2002 381p (Great translations for actors series) ISBN 1-57525-313-5 LC 2002-70807

Contents: Persians; Seven against Thebes; Suppliants; Prometheus bound

The Oresteia; a new translation by Ted Hughes. Farrar Straus Giroux 1999 197p ISBN 0-374-22721-7 LC 98-73704

Contents: Agamemnon; Choephori; The Eumenides

Alexander, Robert

(ed) Plays from Woolly mammoth. *See.* Plays from Woolly mammoth

Algarín, Miguel, 1941-

(ed) Action. *See* Action

Alvarez, Lynne

Collected plays: v1. Smith & Kraus 1998 384p (Contemporary playwrights series) ISBN 1-575-25146-9 LC 98-24129

America Hurrah and other plays. Van Itallie, J.-C.

American gypsy: six Native American plays. Glancy, D.

American plays of the new woman; edited by Keith Newlin. Dee, I. R. 2000 294p ISBN 1-56663-286-2

Contents: The Great Divide, by W. V. Moody; A man's world, by R. Crothers; As a man thinks, by A. Thomas; Overtones, by A. Gerstenberg; The outside, by S. Glaspell; Why marry?, by J. L. Williams.

Ancient Israel: legends from the Bible and Jewish folklore for grades K-3. McCullough, L. E.

Andersen, D. R.

Crazy and a half; six insane one-act comedies. French 2001 104p ISBN 0-573-62791-6

Anderson, Sheryl J., 1958-

The twelve plays of Christmas; original Christian dramas. Judson Press 1999 75p ISBN 0-8170-1312-1 LC 98-53386

Angels and anger; five Acadian plays; selected, edited and translated by Glen Nichols. Playwrights Canada 2003 255p ISBN 0-88754-660-9

Angels and saints: two plays. Townsend, J.

The **archives** at Kanonicza 5. Kraszewski, C. S.

Ardito, Carlo

Brief candle; Stoney Bowes; Da Ponte's last stand; Confessions of Zeno. Amber Lane 1998 256p ISBN 1-872868-23-1

Three plays. Amber Lane Press 2000 205p ISBN 1-872868-28-2

Aristophanes

Aristophanes, 1; edited by David R. Slavitt and Palmer Bovie. University of Pa. Press 1998-1999 322p (Penn Greek drama series) LC 98-8446

Contents: The Archarnians; Peace; Celebrating ladies; Wealth

Aristophanes, 2. University of Pa. Press 1999 360p (Penn Greek drama series) ISBN 0-8122-3483-9; 0-8122-1648-9 (pa)

Contents: Wasps; Lysistrata; Frogs; The sexual congress

Aristophanes—*Continued*
    Aristophanes, 3. University of Pa. Press 1999 308p (Penn Greek drama series) ISBN 0-8122-3501-0; 0-8122-1698-9
        Contents: The suits; Clouds; Birds
Arkin, Alan, 1934-
    Power plays. See May, Elaine, and Arkin, Alan, 1934-
Art, Suzanne Strauss
    Quintet; five lively plays for kids. Pemblewick Press 1998 125p ISBN 0-9656557-1-7 LC 99-216315
Auburn, David
    The fifth planet and other plays. Dramatists 2002 ISBN 0-8222-1825-9
Avoidance tactics. Gilbert, S.
The **award** and other plays. Manzi, W.
Ayckbourn, Alan, 1939-
    House & Garden. Faber & Faber 2000 222p ISBN 0-571-20593-3

B

Bachmann, Ingeborg, 1926-1973
    Three radio plays; translated by Lilian Friedberg. Ariadne Press 1999 222p ISBN 1-57241-079-5
Bachmann, Ingeborg, 1926-1973, and Wolf, Christa
    Selected prose and drama; edited by Patricia A. Herminghouse. Continuum 1998 283p (The German Library, v. 94) ISBN 0-8264-0956-3; 0-8264-0957-1 (pa) LC 98-6740
        Analyzed for plays only
        Contents: The good god of Manhattan, by I. Bachmann
Barchers, Suzanne I.
    From Atalanta to Zeus. Teacher Ideas Press 2001 203p ISBN 1-56308-815-0
    Multicultural folktales; readers theatre for elementary students. Teacher Ideas Press 2000 188p ISBN 1-563-08760-X LC 99-52879
Barchers, Suzanne I., and Kroll, Jennifer L.
    Classic readers theatre for young adults. Teachers Ideas Press 2002 243p ISBN 1-56308-881-9
Beauty's daughter; Monster; The gimmick. Orlandersmith, D.
The **beginning** of August and other plays. Donaghy, T.
Bell, Neal
    Plays. Broadway Play Pub. 1998 262p ISBN 0-88145-143-6
The **Best** American short plays, 1996-1997. Applause 1998 255p (Best American short plays series) ISBN 1-55783-316-8
The **Best** American short plays, 1997-1998; edited by Glenn Young. Applause 2000 227p ISBN 1-55783-426-1
The **Best** American short plays, 1999-2000; edited by Glenn Young. Applause 2001 201p (Best American short plays series) ISBN 1-55783-452-0
The **Best** American short plays, 2000-2001; edited by Mark Glubke. Applause 2002 296p ISBN 1-55783-480-6; 1-55783-481-4 ISSN 0067-6284
Best of the Fest; edited by Phil Setren. Aurora Metro Press (London) 1998 303p ISBN 0-9515877-8-1
The **Best** plays of 1997-1998; edited by Otis L. Guernsey, Jr.; illustrated with photographs and with drawings by Hirschfeld. Limelight Editions 1999 510p ISBN 0-87910-271-3
        "The Otis Guernsey/Burns Mantle Theater yearbook"
        Analyzed for condensed versions of plays only
        Contents: Gross indecency: The three trials of Oscar Wilde, by M. Kaufman; Pride's Crossing, by T. Howe; The beauty queen of Leenane, by M. LcDonagh; Art, by Y. Reza

The **Best** plays of 1998-1999; edited by Otis L. Guernsey, Jr.; illustrated with photographs and with drawings by Hirschfeld. Limelight Editions 1999 556p ISBN 0-87910-290-X
"The Otis Guernsey/Burns mantle Theater yearbook"
Analyzed for condensed versions of plays only
Contents: Side Man, by W. Leight; Wit, by M. Edson; Parade, by J. R. Brown; Not About Nightingales, by T. Williams; Closer, by P. Marber

The **Best** plays of 1999-2000; edited by Otis L. Guernsey, Jr.; illustrated with photographs and with drawings by Hirschfeld. Limelight Editions 2000 510p ISBN 0-87910-955-6
"The Otis Guernsey/Burns Mantel Theater yearbook"
Analyzed for condensed versions of plays only; beginning with 2000-2001 volume, condensations replaced with essays.
Contents: Contact, by J. Weidman; James Joyce's The Dead, by S. Davey; Dinner with Friends, by D. Margulies; Copenhagen, by M. Frayn; Jitney, by A. Wilson; The Designated Mourner, by W. Shawn

Bishop, Conrad, and Fuller, Elizabeth, 1940-
Seismic stages; five plays for teens : an anthology of plays and sketches created by The Independent Eye. WordWorkers 2000 249p ISBN 0-9624511-7-7 LC 99-91942

Black South African women; an anthology of plays; edited by Kathy A. Perkins. Routledge 1998 177p ISBN 0-415-18244-1

Blais, Marie-Claire, 1939-
wintersleep. Ronsdale Press 1998 144p ISBN 0-921870-60-4

Blasts from the future; an anthology of ten-minute plays from the Vermont young playwrights project; edited by Dana Yeaton; foreword by Congressman Bernie Sanders. PenStroke Press 1999 168p ISBN 0-9669177-0-7

Blessing, Lee
Chesapeake. Broadway Play Pub. 2000 49p ISBN 0-88145-179-7
Contents: Chesapeake; Reproduction

Blue heart. Churchill, C.

Body blows. Miller, T.

Bond, Edward
Eleven vests & Tuesday. Methuen 1997 117p ISBN 0-413-72120-5

Borgert, U. H. G.
(ed) Women's words, women's works. *See* Women's words, women's works

Bosakowski, Phil, d. 1994
Plays. Broadway Play Pub. 1999 144p ISBN 0-88145-165-7
Contents: Bierce takes on the railroad!; Chopin in space; Nixon Apologizes to the nation

Bowen, John
Plays: one. Oberon Bks. 1998 356p ISBN 1-84002-035-0
Contents: After the rain; The disorderly women; Little boxes; The coffee lace; Trevor; Singles

Bowne, Alan
Plays. Broadway Play Pub. 1997 149p ISBN 0-88145-142-8

The **boy** in the treehouse; Girl who loved her horses. Taylor, D. H.

Bruchac, Joseph, 1942-
Pushing up the sky; seven native American plays for children. Dial Books for Young Readers 2000 94p il ISBN 0-8037-2168-4; 0-8037-2535-3

Busch, Charles
The tale of the allergist's wife and other plays. Grove Press 2001 344p ISBN 0-821-3785-7

Byerrum, Eliot
Gumshoe rendezvous. French 2001 84p ISBN 0-573-62787-8
Contents: Remedial surveillance, by E. Byerrum; Deja rendezvous, by E. Eliot

C

Calderón de la Barca, Pedro, 1600-1681
Plays: one; translated and introduced by Gwynne Edwards. Methuen 2000 304p ISBN 0-413-63460-4
Contents: The surgeon of honour; Life is a dream; Three judgements in one
Carden, William
(ed) HB Playwrights Short Play Festival 1997: The motel Plays. *See* HB Playwrights Short Play Festival 1997: The motel Plays
(ed) HB Playwrights Short Play Festival 1998: The museum Plays. *See* HB Playwrights Short Play Festival 1998: The museum Plays
(ed) HB Playwrights Short Play Festival 1999: The airport Plays. *See* HB Playwrights Short Play Festival 1999: The airport Plays
(ed) HB Playwrights Short Play Festival 2000: The funeral plays. *See* HB Playwrights Short Play Festival 2000: The funeral plays
Cardinal, Agnes
(ed) War plays by women. *See* War plays by women
Cardullo, Bert
(ed) Theater of the avant-garde, 1890-1950: a critical anthology. *See* Theater of the avant-garde, 1890-1950: a critical anthology
Carr, Marina
Plays: one. Faber & Faber 1999 341p ISBN 0-571-20011-7
Contents: Low in the dark; The Mai; Portia Coughlan; By the Bog of Cats. . .
Carter, Lonnie, 1942-
Plays: the Gulliver trilogy. Broadway Play Pub. 1997 166p ISBN 0-88145-134-7
∅ **Celebration** and The room. Pinter, H.
∅ **Cellophane**. Wellman, M.
Chambers, Ron
Three nasty plays. Red Deer College Press 1997 192p ISBN 0-88734-928-5 LC 97-22595
Chappell, Eric
Fiddlers three. French (London) 2003 81p ISBN 0-573-01980-0
Contents: We don't want to lose you; Cut and dried
Chekhov, Anton Pavlovich, 1860-1904
7 short farces; a new translation by Paul Schmidt. Dramatists 1999 101p ISBN 0-8222-1645-0
Chekhov: the early plays; translated by Carol Rocamora. Smith & Kraus 1999 240p (Great translations series) ISBN 1-575-25152-3 LC 99-38692
The vaudevilles; and other short works; translated by Carol Rocamora. Smith & Kraus 1998 212p ISBN 1-575-25127-2 LC 97-42181
∅ **Chekhov**: the early plays. Chekhov, A. P.
∅ **Cherry** soda water. Levi, S.
∅ **Chesapeake**. Blessing, L.
Chikamatsu, Monzaemon
Four major plays of Chikamatsu; translated by Donald Keene. Columbia Univ. Press 1998 220p (UNESCO collection of representative works, Japanese series) ISBN 0-231-11101-0 LC 98-148374
Chislett, Anne
Flippin' in & Then and now. Playwrights Canada 1999 139p ISBN 0-88754-574-2 LC 00-304931
Churchill, Caryl
Blue heart. Theatre Communications Group 1998 69p ISBN 1-55936-154-9
Cibber, Colley, 1671-1757
The plays of Colley Cibber; volume 1; edited by Timothy J. Viator and William J. Burling. Fairleigh Dickinson Univ. Press; Associated Univ. Presses 2001 586p ISBN 0-8386-3624-1 LC 99-54768
∅ **Classic** readers theatre for young adults. Barchers, S. I., and Kroll, J. L.

Cleage, Pearl
Flyin' west and other plays. 1st ed. Theatre Communications Group 1999 339p il ISBN 1-559-36168-9 LC 99-18987

Coarse acting strikes back; edited by Michael Green. French (London) 2000 91p ISBN 0-573-10009-8

Cocktails at Pam's & Evelyn strange. Lemoine, S.

Collected novels and plays. Merrill, J.

The **collected** plays. Gardner, H.

Collected plays, 1984-1991. Gurney, A. R.

Collected plays, 1989-1998. Rebeck, T.

Collected plays, 1991-1995. Gurney, A. R.

Collected plays, 1992-1999. Gurney, A. R.

The **collected** plays of Bernard Pomerance. Pomerance, B.

Collected plays, v 2, 1996-2001. Martin, J.

Collected plays: v1. Alvarez, L.

Collected plays, v1. Norman, M.

Collected plays v1, 1980-1989. Henley, B.

Collected plays volume 2, 1990-1999. Henley, B.

The **collected** short plays of Thornton Wilder. Wilder, T.

Collected works v2, 1970-1983. Wilson, L.

Collected works v3: the Talley trilogy. Wilson, L.

Collected works: volume three, 1987-1997. Metcalf, P.

Complete full-length plays, 1962-1999. Gilroy, F. D.

Complete full-Length plays 1975-1995. Durang, C.

Complete plays. Kane, S.

The **complete** plays. Sophocles

Conquest, Ned
The widow's might: three plays. Apollonian Press 1997 105p ISBN 0-9627485-3-6

Constable, John
Sha-manic plays. Oberon Bks. 1997 241p ISBN 1-870259-90-4
Contents: Black mas; Dead man's handle; Iceman; The false hairpiece

Contemporary Australian Plays; edited and introduced by Russell Vandenbroucke. Methuen 2001 365p ISBN 0-413-76760-4
Contents: Hotel Sorrento, by H. Rayson; Dead white males, by D. Williamson; Two, by R. Elisha; The 7 stages of grieving, by W. Enoch & D. Mailman; The popular mechanicals, by K. Robinson & T. Taylor

Couling, Della
(ed) Dutch and Flemish plays. *See* Dutch and Flemish plays

Coward, Noel
Three plays; Blithe spirit, Hay fever, Private lives; introduction by Philip Hoare. 1st Vintage International ed. Vintage 1999 254p ISBN 0-679-78179-X LC 98-47414

Crazy and a half. Andersen, D. R.

Crimp, Martin, 1956-
Plays: one. Faber & Faber 2000 389p ISBN 0-571-20345-0
Contents: Dealing with Clair; Getting attention; Play with repeats; The treatment

Crommelynck, Fernand, 1886-1970
The theater of Fernand Crommelynck; eight plays; edited by Bert Cardullo; translation supervised by Alain Piette. Susquehanna Univ. Press 1998 421p ISBN 1-57591-002-0

Crossing the bar; Head; Our lady of shadows. Gough, L.

Culture Clash (Group)
Culture Clash in America. Theatre Communications Group 2003 225p ISBN 1-55936-216-2
Contents: Brodertown; Nuyorican stories; Mission magic mystery tour; Anthems
Culture Clash: life, death and revolutionary comedy. Theatre Communications Group 1998 164p ISBN 1-55936-139-5
Contents: The mission; A bowl of beings; Radio mambo

Culture Clash (Group)—*Continued*
Culture Clash in America. Culture Clash (Group)
Culture Clash: life, death and revolutionary comedy. Culture Clash
  (Group)

D

D'Aponte, Mimi Gisolfi
  (ed) Seventh Generation. *See* Seventh Generation
Darke, Nick, 1948-
  Plays: 1. Methuen 1999 342p ISBN 0-413-73720-9
    Contents: The Dead Monkey; The King of Prussia; The Body;
    Ting Tang Mine
  Darlene and The guest lecturer. Gurney, A. R.
Dasgupta, Gautam
  (ed) Theatre of the ridiculous. *See* Theatre of the ridiculous
  The **dazzle** and Everett Beekin. Greenberg, R.
De Angelo, April
  Plays: one. Faber & Faber 1999 323p ISBN 0-571-19709-4
    Contents: Ironmistress; Hush; Playhouse creatures; The positive
    hour
De Filippo, Eduardo, 1900-1984
  Four plays; translated by Maria Tucci; introduction by Ronald
    Harwood. Smith & Kraus 2001 171p (Great translations for actors
    series) ISBN 1-575-25229-5 LC 2001-49579
  Death and taxes. Kushner, T.
  Deckchairs II. McConnell, J.
  Deckchairs III. McConnell, J.
  Defiant acts (Actos desafiantes). Raznovich, D.
  Deflores and other plays. Nigro, D.
Deverell, Rex
  Plays of belonging; three plays. Playwrights Canada 1997 149p ISBN
    0-88754-531-9
    Contents: Belonging; Weird kid; Video wars
  Disco pigs & Sucking Dublin. Walsh, E.
Dixon, Michael Bigelow
  (ed) 30 ten-minute plays for 2 actors from Actors Theatre of
    Louisville's National Ten-Minute Play Contest. *See* 30 ten-minute
    plays for 2 actors from Actors Theatre of Louisville's National
    Ten-Minute Play Contest
  (ed) 30 ten-minute plays for 3 actors from Actors Theatre of
    Louisville's National Ten-Minute Play Contest. *See* 30 ten-minute
    plays for 3 actors from Actors Theatre of Louisville's National
    Ten-Minute Play Contest
  (ed) 30 ten-minute plays for 4, 5, and 6 actors from Actors Theatre
    of Louisville's National Ten-Minute Play Contest. *See* 30
    ten-minute plays for 4, 5, and 6 actors from Actors Theatre of
    Louisville's National Ten-Minute Play Contest
  (ed)
  Ten-minute plays: v4. *See* Actors Theatre of Louisville. Ten-minute
    plays: v4
  (ed)
  Ten-minute plays: v5. *See* Actors Theatre of Louisville. Ten-minute
    plays: v5
Dobrish, Jeremy
  Plays. Broadway Play Pub. 1999 148p ISBN 0-88145-157-6
  The **dogs** play and A few roos loose in the top paddock. O'Neill, T.
  Don Quijote in America: plays in English an Spanish grades 1-6.
    Espinosa, R.
Donaghy, Tom
  The beginning of August and other plays. Grove Press 2000 247p
    ISBN 0-8021-3724-5 LC 00-32143

Dowie, Claire
Why is John Lennon wearing a skirt?; and other stand-up theatre
plays. Methuen 1996 156p ISBN 0-413-71090-4
Down the line; The hunt for Red Willie. Methuen 2000 236p (The
Abbey Theatre Playscript Series) ISBN 0-413-76110-X
Drama for a new South Africa; seven plays; edited by David Graver.
Indiana Univ. Press 1999 228p (Drama and performance studies)
ISBN 0-253-33570-1; 0-253-21326-6 (pa) LC 99-25444
Contents: Sophiatown, by Junction Avenue Theatre Company;
Horn of sorrow, by N. Ellenbogen; And the girls in their Sunday
dresses, by Z. Mda; Mooi Street moves, by P. Slabolepszy; Purdah,
by I. Mahomed; Crossing, by R. de Wet; Ipi zombi?, by B. Bailey
The **drama** of Easter; an anthology of royalty-free Easter plays for all
ages; edited by Rhonda Wray. Meriwether Pub. 1999 337p ISBN
1-566-08051-7 LC 99-36985
DramaContemporary: India; edited by Erin B. Mee. Johns Hopkins
Univ. Press 2001 361p ISBN 0-8018-6622-7
Dramatizing Greek mythology. Thistle, L.
Durang, Christopher, 1949-
Complete full-Length plays 1975-1995. Smith & Kraus 1997
(Contemporary Playwrights Series) ISBN 1-57525-295-3
Dutch and Flemish plays; selected by Della Couling. Hern Bks. 1997
295p (International collection) ISBN 1-85459-289-0 LC 97-160285
The Buddha of Ceylon, by Lodewijk de Boer; The wedding
party, by Judith Herzberg; Drummers, by Arne Sierens; Burying the
dog, by Karst Woudstra; The Stendhal syndrome, by Frans Strijards
A **Dybbuk;** and, The dybbuk melody and other themes and variations.
Kushner, T.

E

Eagleton, Terry, 1943-
Saint Oscar and other plays. Blackwell 1997 225p ISBN
0-631-20452-0; 0-631-20453-9 (pa) LC 96-26957
Early plays. O'Neill, E.
The **East** end plays, part 1. Walker, G. F.
The **East** End plays, part 2. Walker, G. F.
Edgar, David
Plays: 3. Methuen 1997 418p ISBN 0-413-64850-8
Contents: Our Own People; Teendreams; Maydays; That Summer
Ehn, Erik
The saint plays. Johns Hopkins Univ. Press 2000 195p (PAJ Books)
ISBN 0-8018-6287-6
Eight Plays for Children: the new generation play project; edited by
Coleman A. Jennings. University of Texas Press 1999 479p ISBN
0-292-74057-3; 0-292-74056-5 (pa)
Eight twentieth-century Russian plays; translated from the Russian and
with an introduction by Timothy Langen and Justin Weir.
Northwestern Univ. Press 2000 354p ISBN 0-8101-1374-0;
0-8101-1374-0 LC 00-8680
Electra and other plays. Euripides
Eleven vests & Tuesday. Bond, E.
Ellis, Roger
(ed) International plays for young audiences. *See* International plays
for young audiences
(ed) Multicultural theatre II. *See* Multicultural theatre II
Elton, Ben, 1959-
Plays: 1; by Ben Elton. Methuen 1998 255p ISBN 0-413-73670-9
Contents: Gasping; Silly Cow; Popcorn
Engelman, Liz
(ed)
Ten-minute plays: v4. *See* Actors Theatre of Louisville. Ten-minute
plays: v4

⌀**Ensemble** Studio Theatre marathon 2000: the one-act plays. Faber & Faber 2001 218p ISBN 0-571-19993-3

⌀ **Ensemble** Studio Theatre Marathon '99: the one-act plays. Faber & Faber 2000 249p ISBN 0-571-19981-X

Espinosa, Resurrección

Don Quijote in America: plays in English an Spanish grades 1-6; book by Resurreccion Espinosa; drawings by Dorothy Louise Hall; music by Charles Frink. Teacher Ideas Press 2002 221p ISBN 1-56308-027-0

⌀ The **essential** Gore Vidal. Vidal, G.

Esson, Louis, 1878-1943

Plays 1: Terra Australis. Five Island Pree 1999 268p ISBN 0-86418-540-5

⌀**EST** marathon '96: the one-act plays; edited by Marisa Smith. Smith & Kraus 1998 174p ISBN 1-57525-134-5

⌀ **EST** marathon '97: the one-act plays; edited by Marisa Smith. Smith & Kraus 1998 155p ISBN 1-57525-135-3

⌀ **EST** marathon '98: the one-act plays; edited by Marisa Smith. Smith & Kraus 1999 135p ISBN 1-57525-165-5

Euripides, ca. 485-ca. 406 B.C.

Electra and other plays; translated by John Davie; with an introduction and notes by Richard Rutherford. Penguin Bks. 1998 l, 264p (Penguin classics) ISBN 0-14-044668-0 LC 99-179429

Euripides, 1; edited by David R. Slavitt and Palmer Bovie. University of Pa. Press 1998 298p (Penn Greek drama series) ISBN 0-8122-3415-4

Contents: vl Medea; Hecuba; Andromache; The Bacchae

Euripides, 2; edited by David R. Slavitt and Palmer Bovie. University of Pa. Press 1998 360p (Penn Greek drama series) ISBN 0-8122-1629-6

Contents: v2 Hippolytus; Suppliant women; Helen; Electra; Cyclops

Euripides, 3; edited by David R. Slavitt and Palmer Bovie. University of Pa. Press 1998 378p (Penn Greek drama series) ISBN 1-8122-1650-4

Contents: v3 Alcestis; Daughters of Troy; The Phoenician women; Iphigenia at Aulis; Rhesus

Euripides, 4; edited by David R. Slavitt and Palmer Bovie. University of Pa. Press 1999 408p (Penn Greek drama series) ISBN 0-8122-1697-0

Contents: v4: Ion; Children of Heracles; The madness of Heracles; Iphigenia in Tauris; Orestes

Iphigenia among the Taurians; Bacchae; Iphigenia at Aulis; Rhesus; translated with explanatory notes by James Morwood; with introduction by Edith Hall. Oxford Univ. Press 1998 liii, 227p ISBN 0-19-815094-6 LC 98-37702

F

⌀ **Fateful** lightning; America's Civil War plays; edited and introduced by Walter J. Meserve and Mollie Ann Meserve. Feedback Theatrebooks and Prospero Press 2000 550p ISBN 0-937657-50-6

⌀ The **father;** Lady Julie; Playing with fire. Strindberg, A.

⌀ **Fearless** Pharaoh FooFoo and other dramas for children. Vogel, L.

Feydeau, Georges, 1862-1921

Feydeau, first to last; eight one-act comedies; translated by Norman R. Shapiro. Applause 2001 316p ISBN 1-55783-463-6

Four farces. Applause 1998 346p (Tour de farce, 5) ISBN 1-55783-305-2

⌀**Feydeau,** first to last. Feydeau, G.

⌀ **Fiddlers** three. Chappell, E.

Field, Barbara
New classics from the Guthrie Theater; classical adaptations for the American stage. Smith & Kraus 2003 345p (Contemporary Playwrights Series) ISBN 1-57525-369-0
∅ The field mouse collection. Martini, C.
Finlayson, Alex
Plays. Oberon Bks. 1998 158p ISBN 1-870259-69-6
Contents: Misfits; Winding the ball
∅ First star and The railing. Pedrero, P.
∅ Five comedies; Plautus & Terence ; translated, with introductions, by Deena Berg & Douglass Parker. Hackett Pub. Co 1999 411p ISBN 0-87220-363-8; 0-87220-362-X (pa) LC 98-50732
∅ **Five Lesbian Brothers (Theater company)**
The Five Lesbian Brothers: four plays. Theatre Communications Group 2000 286p ISBN 1-55936-166-2
∅ Five major plays. Strindberg, A.
∅ Five plays in translation from Mexican contemporary theater; a new golden age; edited by Salvador Rodríguez del Pino. Edwin Mellen Press 2001 279p (Hispanic literature, v. 42) ISBN 0-7734-8274-1 LC 98-40428
∅ Flippin' in & Then and now. Chislett, A.
∅ Flyin' west and other plays. Cleage, P.
Fo, Dario
We won't pay! We won't pay! and other plays; by Dario Fo. Theatre Communications Group 2001 329p ISBN 1-55936-183-2; 1-55936-182-4 (pa)
Foote, Horton
Getting Frankie married—and afterwards, and other plays. Smith & Kraus 1998 288p ISBN 1-57525-136-1
"Horton Foote Collected plays volume 3"
∅ Four by Sondheim. Sondheim, S.
∅ Four farces. Feydeau, G.
∅ Four major plays. Schnitzler, A.
PT 2647 E26 A26 2000 Four major plays. Wedekind, F.
∅ Four plays. McPherson, C.
∅ Four plays. Powell, D.
Frayn, Michael
Plays: 3; by Michael Frayn. Methuen 2000 341p ISBN 0-413-75230-5 analyzed for plays only
Contents: Here; Now You Know; La Belle Vivette (libretto)
Fréchette, Carole, 1949-
Three plays; translated by John Murrell. Playwrights Canada 2002 181p ISBN 0-88754-629-3
Fredericks, Anthony D.
Readers theatre for American history. Teacher Ideas Press 2001 173p ISBN 1-56308-860-6
Science Fiction Readers Theatre. Teacher Ideas Press 2002 148p ISBN 1-56308-929-7
∅ From Atalanta to Zeus. Barchers, S. I.
Fulford, R. W. (Robin Wakelin),, 1950-
Faggot!. Blizzard Pub. 1999 74p ISBN 0-921368-88-7 LC 00-302172
Contents: Steel kiss; Gulag

G

García Lorca, Federico, 1898-1936
Federico García Lorca; impossible theater : five plays and thirteen poems; in new translations by Caridad Svich. Smith & Kraus 2000 168p (Great translations for actors series) ISBN 1-575-25228-7 LC 00-44571
Analyzed for plays only

Gardner, Herb, 1934-2003
The collected plays; and the screenplay Who is Harry Kellerman and why is he saying those terrible things about me? Applause 2000 489p il ISBN 1-557-83466-0; 1-557-83460-1
The **general** of hot desire and other plays. Guare, J.
George, David
(ed) Modern Catalan plays. *See* Modern Catalan plays
Getting Frankie married—and afterwards, and other plays. Foote, H.
Getting in and Contact with the enemy. Gilroy, F. D.
Giants have us in their books. Rivera, J.
Gilbert, Sky
Avoidance tactics. Broken Jaw Press 2001 112p ISBN 1-896647-50-2
Gilroy, Frank Daniel, 1925-
15 one-act plays. Smith & Kraus 2000 225p (Contemporary Playwrights Series) ISBN 1-57525-267-8
15 one-act plays. See Gilroy, Frank Daniel, 1925-
Complete full-length plays, 1962-1999. Smith & Kraus 2000 373p (Contemporary Playwrights Series) ISBN 1-57525-266-X
Getting in and Contact with the enemy. French 2000 86p ISBN 0-573-62730-4 LC 2001-278089
Glancy, Diane
American gypsy: six Native American plays. Univ. of Oklahoma Press 2002 218p (American Indian literature and critical studies series) ISBN 0-8061-3456-9
Glubke, Mark
(ed) The Best American short plays, 2000-2001. *See* The Best American short plays, 2000-2001
God, man, and devil; Yiddish plays in translation; translated and edited by Nahma Sandrow. Syracuse Univ. Press 1999 321p (Judaic traditions in literature, music, and art) ISBN 0-8156-2786-6; 0-8156-2787-4 (pa) LC 98-29003
Godber, John, 1956-
Plays: 1. Methuen 2001 ISBN 0-413-75810-9
Contents: Bouncers; Happy families; Shakers
Plays: 2. Methuen 2001 280p ISBN 0-413-75820-6
Contents: Teechers; Happy Jack; September in the rain; Salt of the earth
Plays: 3. Methuen 2003 ISBN 0-413-77304-3
Contents: April in Paris; Up'n'under; Perfect pitch
Gore, Catherine
Gore on stage; edited by John Franceschina. Garland 1999 533p ISBN 0-8153-2735-8
Gore on stage. Gore, C.
Gough, Lucy
Crossing the bar; Head; Our lady of shadows. Seren 2000 115p ISBN 1-85411-266-X
Graver, David, 1955-
(ed) Drama for a new South Africa. *See* Drama for a new South Africa
The **great** Gromboolian plain and other plays. Nigro, D.
The **great** man [and] Sanctuary. Williamson, D.
Greek and Roman Comedy; edited by Shawn O'Bryhim. University of Texas Press 2001 320p ISBN 0-202-76055-8
Green, Michael
(ed) Coarse acting strikes back. *See* Coarse acting strikes back
Green, Paul, 1894-1981
A Paul Green reader; edited with an introduction by Laurence G. Avery. University of N.C. Press 1998 297p ISBN 0-8078-2386-4; 0-8078-4708-9 (pa) LC 97-40365
Analyzed for plays only
Greenberg, Richard
The dazzle and Everett Beekin. Faber & Faber 2003 197p ISBN 0-571-21123-2

H

Horovitz, Israel
Two trilogies. Smith & Kraus 1994 375p (Contemporary playwrights series) ISBN 1-88039-951-2 LC 93-46378
"Collected plays volume IV"
Contents: The growing up Jewish trilogy; The Alfred trilogy
Horváth, Ödön von, 1901-1938, and Mitchell, Michael, 1941-
Tales from the Vienna Woods and other plays; translated and with an afterword by Michael Mitchell. Ariadne Press 2002 243p (Studies in Austrian literature, culture, and thought, Translation series) ISBN 1-572-41108-2 LC 2002-71746
House & Garden. Ayckbourn, A.
Hughes, Declan, 1963-
Plays: 1. Methuen 1998 289p (Methuen Contemporary Dramatists) ISBN 0-413-72380-1
Hughes, Holly
(ed) O solo homo. *See* O solo homo
Hughes, Langston, 1902-1967
The political plays of Langston Hughes; with introductions and analyses by Susan Duffy. Southern Ill. Univ. Press 2000 221p ISBN 0-8093-2295-1; 0-8093-2296-X ((pa)) LC 99-31502
Hughes, Ted
(tr) The Oresteia. *See* Aeschylus. The Oresteia
Humana Festival 2001; the complete plays; edited by Tanya Palmer and Amy Wegener. Smith & Kraus 2001 454p (Contemporary playwrights series) ISBN 1-57525-299-6
Humana Festival 2002; the complete plays; edited by Tanya Palmer and Amy Wegener. Smith & Kraus 2002 397p (Contemporary playwrights series) ISBN 1-57525-317-8
Humana Festival '98; the complete plays; edited by Michael Bigelow Dixon and Amy Wegener. Smith & Kraus 1998 367p (Contemporary playwrights series) ISBN 1-57525-142-6
Hwang, David Henry
Trying to find Chinatown: the selected plays; David Henry Hwang. 1st ed. Theatre Communications Group 2000 294p ISBN 1-559-36172-7 LC 99-44197
The hyphenated American. Yew, C.

I

Ibsen, Henrik, 1828-1906
Ibsen: four plays v3; translated by Brian Johnston with Rick Davis. Smith & Kraus 1998 235p (Great translations for actors) ISBN 1-57525-145-0
Ibsen: four plays v3. Ibsen, H.
The importance of being earnest and other plays. Wilde, O.
In his own voice; edited by Herbert Woodward Martin and Ronald Primeau. Ohio Univ. Press 2002 311p ISBN 0-8214-1421-6
In the heart of America, and other plays. Wallace, N.
Inoculations. O'Donnell, D.
International plays for young audiences; contemporary works from leading playwrights; edited by Roger Ellis. Meriwether Pub. 2000 419p ISBN 1-56608-065-7
Contents: Salmonberry: a west coast fairy tale, by C. Hoogland; Skin and bones, by N. Duffield; Circus caravan, by D. Abela; Blood lines, by J. McClelland; Convivencia, by R. N. Sandberg; The song of one or the journey of Ti Marie, by K. Hippolyte; City of gold, by C. Smith; Madagascar Lily, by N. Janaczewska; Race, by J. Pachino; Hunger, by H. McIntyre; Minor leagues, by G. Ott; Balcony, by S. Shafaat
Italian grotesque theater; translated with an introduction by Michael Vena. Fairleigh Dickinson Univ. Press; Associated Univ. Presses 2001 194p ISBN 0-8386-3894-5 LC 2001-18952

Ives, David
  Lives of the saints. Dramatists 2000 96p ISBN 0-8222-1746-5
  Mere mortals. Dramatists 1998 110p ISBN 0-8222-1632-9
  Time flies and other short plays. Grove Press 2001 222p ISBN 0-8021-3758-X LC 00-42993

J

Jails, hospitals & hip-hop, and Some people. Hoch, D.
Jenkin, Len
  Plays. Broadway Play Pub. 1999 153p ISBN 0-88145-158-4
    Contents: A Country Doctor; Like I Say; Pilgrims of the Night
Jenkins, Ron
  (tr) We won't pay! We won't pay! and other plays. *See* Fo, Dario. We won't pay! We won't pay! and other plays
Jennings, Coleman A., 1933-
  (ed) Theatre for young audiences. *See* Theatre for young audiences
Jeyifo, Biodun, 1946-
  (ed) Modern African drama. *See.* Modern African drama
Johnson, Terry
  Plays: 2. Methuen 1998 298p ISBN 0-413-72360-7
    Contents: Imagine Drowning; Hysteria; Dead Funny
Jones, Jeffrey M.
  Plays. Broadway Play Pub. 2000 230p ISBN 0-88145-183-5
Jonson, Ben, 1573?-1637
  Ben Jonson's plays and masques; authoritative texts of Volpone, Epicoene, The alchemist, The masque of blackness, Mercury vindicated from the alchemists at court, Pleasure reconciled to virtue: contexts, backgrounds and sources, criticism. 2nd ed, edited by Richard Harp. W.W. Norton 2001 203p ISBN 0-393-97638-6 LC 00-60906
Jubilation: dramas for Easter. Concordia Publishing House 1999 77p (InterMission scripts) ISBN 0-570-05390-0

K

Kaca, Bogdan
  My name is such and such and other plays. Currency Press 1998 121p ISBN 0-86819-556-1
Kane, Sarah, 1971-1999
  Complete plays; introduced by David Craig. Methuen 2001 268p ISBN 0-413-74260-1
    Contents: Blasted; Phaedra's Love; Cleansed; Crave; 4.48 Psychosis; Skin
Kaufman, George S., 1889-1961, and Ferber, Edna, 1887-1968
  Three comedies. Applause 1999 371p ISBN 1-55783-334-6
Keane, John B., 1928-2002
  Three plays. Mercier Press 2001 269p ISBN 1-85635-365-6 LC 2001-431242
    The year of the hiker; The change in Mame Fadden; The highest house on the mountain
Keeffe, Barrie, 1945-
  Plays: 1; by Barrie Keeffe. Methuen 2001 232p ISBN 0-413-76450-8
    Contents: Gimme Shelter: Gem; Gotcha; Getaway; Barbarians: Killing Time; Abide With Me; In the City
Kelly, George, 1887-1974
  Three plays; biographical and critical essays by William J. Lynch ; foreword by Wendy Wasserstein. Limelight Editions 1999 400p il ISBN 0-87910-282-9; 0-87910-279-9 (pa) LC 99-19841
Kennedy, Adrienne
  The Adrienne Kennedy reader; introduction by Werner Sollors. Univ. of Minnesota Press 2001 308p ISBN 0-8166-3603-6

Kinney, Arthur F., 1933-
(ed) Renaissance drama. *See* Renaissance drama
Kleberg, Lars
Starfall; a triptych; translated from the Swedish by Anselm Hollo. Northwestern Univ. Press 1997 77p ISBN 0-8101-1454-2 LC 97-41968
"A Hydra book"
Kleist, Heinrich von, 1777-1811
Three major plays; translated by Carl R. Mueller. Smith & Kraus 2000 151p (Great translations for actors series) ISBN 1-57525-230-9
Knopf, Robert, 1961-
(ed) Theater of the avant-garde, 1890-1950: a critical anthology. *See* Theater of the avant-garde, 1890-1950: a critical anthology
Kokoschka, Oskar, 1886-1980
Plays and poems; translated by Michael Mitchell ; afterword by Karl Leydecker. Ariadne Press 2001 250p (Studies in Austrian literature, culture, and thought, Translation series) ISBN 1-572-41041-8 LC 99-36779
Kopit, Arthur L.
Three plays; [by] Arthur Kopit. Hill & Wang 1997 270p ISBN 0-8090-1595-1 LC 97-7532
Kops, Bernard, 1926-
Plays: one; with an introduction by Mike Leigh. Oberon Bks. 1999 197p ISBN 1-84002-071-7
Contents: Playing Sinatra; The Hamlet of Stepney Green; Ezra
Kramer, Larry
The normal heart and The destiny of me. Grove Press 2000 252p ISBN 0-8021-3692-3
Kramer, Sherry
Plays. Broadway Play Pub. 2000 179p ISBN 0-88145-184-3
Kraszewski, Charles S.
The archives at Kanonicza 5. Libella Veritatis 2000 151p ISBN 1-930205-03-1
Kroll, Jennifer L.
Classic readers theatre for young adults. See Barchers, Suzanne I., and Kroll, Jennifer L.
Kron, Lisa
2.5 minute ride and, 101 humiliating stories. Theatre Communications Group 2001 73p ISBN 1-559-36181-6 LC 00-37755
Kushner, Tony
Death and taxes; Hydriotaphia and other plays. Theatre Communications Group 1998 316p ISBN 1-55936-156-5
A Dybbuk; and, The dybbuk melody and other themes and variations; adapted by Tony Kushner; translated from S. Ansky by Joachim Neugroschel; afterword by Harold Bloom. Theatre Communications Group 1998 198p ISBN 1-55936-1146-8; 1-55936-137-9
Kyrioglou, Michael
(ed) Plays from Woolly mammoth. *See.* Plays from Woolly mammoth

L

Lan, David, 1952-
Plays: 1. Methuen 1999 282p ISBN 0-413-73680-6
Contents: Painting a Wall; Red Earth; Flight; Desire; The Ends of the Earth
Lane, Eric
(ed) Take ten. *See* Take ten
Langen, Timothy
(ed) Eight twentieth-century Russian plays. *See* Eight twentieth-century Russian plays
Latino plays from South Coast Repertory; Hispanic Playwrights Project anthology. Broadway Play Pub. 2000 422p ISBN 1-88145-189-4

Lynch, Kate
The road to hell. See Healey, Michael, and Lynch, Kate

M

MacLiammóir, Micheál
Selected plays of Micheal MacLiammoir; chosen and with an introduction by John Barrett. Smythe; Catholic Univ. of America Press 1998 319p ISBN 0-8132-0888-2; 0-8132-0889-0
Mad cow disease in America; Something special and other plays. Tait, L.
Madame La Mort and other plays. Rachilde
Madame Melville and The general from America. Nelson, R.
Maiden voyages; Ships company theatre premieres 2000-2002; Scott Burke, editor. Broken Jaw Press 2003 191p ISBN 1-55391-023-0
Contents: Chairmaker: the musical, by A. Macdonald; Miles from home, by M. Melski; Sole survivors, by D. E. Smith
Making noise quietly. Holman, R.
Making waves. Sher, E.
Mamet, David
The old neighborhood. French 1998 70p ISBN 0-573-62653-7
The old neighborhood. Vintage Bks. 1998 100p ISBN 0-679-74652-8 LC 97-32224
The **mammary** plays. Vogel, P.
Mann, Emily, 1952-
(ed) Political stages: plays that shaped a century. See Political stages: plays that shaped a century
Mantello, Joe
The Santaland diaries and Season's greetings. Dramatists 1998 54p ISBN 0-8222-1631-0
Manzi, Warren
The award and other plays. French 1999 77p ISBN 0-573-62686-3
Manzoni, Alessandro, 1785-1873
Two plays; translated by Michael J. Curley. Lang, P. 2002 233p ISBN 0-8204-6158-X
Margulies, Donald
Luna Park; short plays and monologues. Theatre Communications Group 2002 241p ISBN 1-55936-206-5
Marivaux, Pierre Carlet de Chamblain de, 1688-1763
Marivaux, three plays; translated and adapted by Stephen Wadsworth. Smith & Kraus 1999 198p (Great translations for actors series) ISBN 1-575-25148-5 LC 98-38708
Marivaux, three plays. Marivaux, P. C. de C. de
Marowitz, Charles
Boulevard comedies; free adaptations of Becque, Feydeau and Molière. Smith & Kraus 2000 121p ISBN 1-57525-210-4
Marranca, Bonnie
(ed) Theatre of the ridiculous. See Theatre of the ridiculous
Marrero, María Teresa
(ed) Out of the fringe. See Out of the fringe
Martin, Jane
Collected plays, v 2, 1996-2001; ed. by Michael Bigelow Dixon. Smith & Kraus 2001 274p (Contemporary Playwrights Series) ISBN 1-57525-272-4
Martin, Steve
Wasp and other plays. Samuel French 1998 71p ISBN 0-573-60311-1
Martini, Clem
The field mouse collection. Playwrights Canada 2002 92p ISBN 0-88754-648-X
Contents: The field; Mouse
A three martini lunch. Red Deer College Press 2000 142p ISBN 0-88995-225-6

Menander

Menander; edited by David Slavitt and Palmer Bovie. University of Pa. Press 1998 277p (Penn Greek drama series) ISBN 0-8122-3444-8

Contents: The grouch; Desperately seeking justice; Closely cropped locks; The girl from Samos; The shield

Ø **Mere** mortals. Ives, D.

Mérimée, Prosper, 1803-1870

Plays on Hispanic themes; translated, edited, and introduced by Oscar Mandel. Lang, P. 2003 204p ISBN 0-8204-6308-6 LC 2002-41131

Merrill, James

Collected novels and plays; edited by J. D. McClatchy and Stephen Yenser. Knopf 2002 676p ISBN 0-375-41137-2

Analyzed for plays only

Metcalf, Paul, 1917-1999

Collected works: volume three, 1987-1997. Coffee House Press 1997 524p

Analyzed for plays only

Ø The **Methuen** Book of Modern Drama; introduced by Graham Whybrow. Methuen 2001 425p ISBN 0-413-76490-7

Contents: Top Girls, by C. Churchill; Hysteria, by T. Johnson; Blasted, by S. Kane; Shopping and Fucking, by M. Ravenhill; The Beauty Queen of Leenane, by M. McDonagh

Ø The **Methuen** book of Sixties drama; introduced by Graham Whybrow. Methuen 2001 530p ISBN 0-413-76280-7

Contents: Roots, by A. Wesker; Serjeant Musgrave's dance, by J. Arden; Loot, by J. Orton; Early morning, by E. Bond; The ruling class, by P. Barnes

Miles, Julia

(ed) The Women's Project & productions. *See* The Women's Project & productions

Miller, Tim, 1958-

Body blows; six performances; with a foreward by Tony Kushner; photographs by Dona Ann McAdams. University of Wis. Press 2002 xxix, 241p (Living out) ISBN 0-299-17680-0; 0-299-17684-3 (pa) LC 2001-5418

Milligan, Jason

Here, there & everywhere. French 2002 128p ISBN 0-573-62886-8

Men in suits; three plays about the mafia. French 1998 152p ISBN 0-573-62628-6

The **misanthrope** and other plays. Molière

The **miser** and other plays. Molière

Ø **Miss** Julie and The stronger. McGuinness, F.

Ø **Miss** Julie, David Mamet Fan Club, and other plays. Tait, L.

Mitchell, Gary

Tearing the loom and In a little world of our own. Hern Bks. 1998 124p ISBN 1-85459-403-6

Ø **Modern** Catalan plays; edited by John London and David George. Methuen 2000 238p ISBN 0-413-74440-X

Contents: The quarrelsome party, by J. Brossa; The audition, by R. Sirera; Desire, by J. M. Benet i Jornet; Fourplay, by S. Belbel

Moffat, Peter

Nabokov's gloves and Iona rain. Methuen 1999 171p ISBN 0-413-77108-6

Molière, 1622-1673

The misanthrope and other plays; translated by John Wood and David Coward, with an introduction and notes by David Coward. Penguin Bks. 2000 317p ISBN 0-14-044730-X

Contents: Tartuffe; The misanthrope; The doctor despite himself; The would-be gentleman; Those learned ladies

Molière, 1622-1673—*Continued*
The miser and other plays; translated by John Wood and David Coward ; with an introduction and notes by David Coward. Penguin Bks. 2000 304p (Penguin Classics) ISBN 0-14-044728-8 LC 2001-278482

Molière, four plays; translated by Carl Milo Pergolizzi; prologue by Claire Nicholas White. International Pocket Library 1999 333p ISBN 0-8283-2038-1 LC 99-18379
The bourgeois gentleman; The doctor in spite of himself; The affected damsels; The miser (regular edition); The miser (short edition)

Molloy, M. J. (Michael Joseph), 1917-
Selected plays of M.J. Molloy; chosen and with an introduction by Robert O'Driscoll. C. Smythe, Catholic University of America Press 1998 394p (Irish drama selections, 12) ISBN 0-8132-0933-1; 0-8132-0934-X (pa) LC 98-40761

Morgan, Edwin, 1920-
A.D.: trilogy of plays on the life of Jesus Christ. Carcanet Press 2000 224p ISBN 1-85754-498-6

Most valuable player and four other all-star plays for middle and high school audiences. Surface, M. H.

Moulds, Stephen
(ed) 30 ten-minute plays for 3 actors from Actors Theatre of Louisville's National Ten-Minute Play Contest. *See* 30 ten-minute plays for 3 actors from Actors Theatre of Louisville's National Ten-Minute Play Contest

Mr. Universe and other plays. Grimsley, J.

Müller, Heiner, 1929-1995
A Heiner Müller Reader; plays, poetry, prose; edited and translated by Carl Weber. Johns Hopkins Univ. Press 2001 xxiv, 244p (PAJ books) ISBN 0-8018-6577-8; 0-8018-6578-6 LC 00-62732
Analyzed for plays only

Multicultural folktales. Barchers, S. I.

Multicultural theatre II; contemporary Hispanic, Asian, and African-American plays; edited and with a critical introduction by Roger Ellis. Meriwether Pub. 1998 379p ISBN 1-566-08042-8 LC 98-28515

Murray, T. C. (Thomas Cornelius),, 1873-1959
Selected plays of T.C. Murray; chosen and with an introduction by Richard Allen Cave. Colin Smythe; Catholic Univ. of America Press 1998 274p (Irish drama selections, 10) ISBN 0-8132-0935-8; 0-8132-0936-6 (pa) LC 98-40763

My name is such and such and other plays. Kaca, B.

The **mystery** of Irma Vep and other plays. Ludlam, C.

Mythic women/real women; plays and performance pieces by women; selected and introduced by Lizbeth Goodman. Faber & Faber 2000 xl, 388p ISBN 0-571-19140-1 LC 2003-447840

N

Nabokov's gloves and Iona rain. Moffat, P.

Neilson, Anthony
Plays: 1. Methuen 1998 285p (Methuen Contemporary Dramatists, Anthony Neilson) ISBN 0-413-72460-3

Neipris, Janet
Plays. Broadway Play Pub. 2000 152p ISBN 0-88145-165-5

Nelson, Richard
Madame Melville and The general from America. Grove Press 2000 183p ISBN 0-8021-3844-6 LC 2001-40868
Plays by Richard Nelson, early plays volume one. Broadway Play Pub. 1998 1 132p ISBN 0-88145-150-9
Plays by Richard Nelson, early plays volume three. Broadway Play Pub. 1998 244p ISBN 0-88145-152-5

Nelson, Richard—*Continued*

Plays by Richard Nelson, early plays volume two. Broadway Play Pub. 1998 2 120p ISBN 0-88145-151-7

New classics from the Guthrie Theater. Field, B.

New dramatists: best plays by the graduating class of 2001; edited by Todd London. Smith & Kraus 2002 309p (Contemporary playwrights series) ISBN 1-57525-298-8

New dramatists: best plays of the graduating class of 2000; edited by Todd London. Smith & Kraus 2001 285p (Contemporary playwrights series) ISBN 1-57525-269-4

New plays. Oates, J. C.

New Plays: from A.C.T. young conservatory.

New plays from the Abbey theatre: volume two, 1996-1998; [by] Michael Harding [et. al.]; edited and with an introduction by Judy Friel and Sanford Sternlicht. Syracuse Univ. Press 2001 245p (Irish studies) ISBN 0-8156-2928-1

New playwrights: the best plays of 1998. Smith & Kraus 2000 380p (Contemporary playwrights series) ISBN 1-575-25171-X LC 00-29707

New playwrights: the best plays of 1999. Smith & Kraus 2001 342p (Contemporary playwrights series) ISBN 1-57525-225-2 LC 00-29707

New playwrights: the best plays of 2000. Smith & Kraus 2002 308p (Contemporary playwrights series) ISBN 1-57525-249-X

New Welsh Drama II; edited by Jeff Teare. Parthian Bks. 2001 416p ISBN 1-902638-13-1

Contents: Little sister, by S. Evans; Giant steps, by O. Smith; Killing kangaroos, by R. Williams

Newlin, Keith

(ed) American plays of the new woman. *See* American plays of the new woman

Nichols, Glen

(ed) Angels and anger. *See* Angels and anger

Nigro, Don

Deflores and other plays. French 2002 132p ISBN 0-573-62994-3

The great Gromboolian plain and other plays. French 1998 147p ISBN 0-573-60167-4

Tales from the Red Rose Inn. French 2000 152p ISBN 0-573-62720-7

Nine adaptations for the American stage. Linney, R.

Nineteenth century American plays; seven plays including The black crook; edited by Myron Matlaw. Applause 2001 511p ISBN 1-55783-464-4

The normal heart and The destiny of me. Kramer, L.

Norman, Marsha

Collected plays, v1. 1st ed. Smith & Kraus 1998 412p (Contemporary playwrights series) ISBN 1-575-25029-2 LC 97-7665

Not so dumb. Lazarus, J.

O

Oates, Joyce Carol, 1938-

New plays. Ontario Review Press 1998 284p ISBN 0-86538-089-9; 0-86538-090-2 (pa) LC 97-46802

O'Bryhim, Shawn

(ed) Greek and Roman Comedy. *See* Greek and Roman Comedy

O'Casey, Sean, 1880-1964

Plays: one; Introduced by Seamus Heaney. Faber & Faber 1998 420p ISBN 0-571-19181-9

Contents: Juno and the paycock; Within the gates; Red roses for me; Cock-a-doodle dandy

O'Casey, Sean, 1880-1964—*Continued*
Plays: two; introduced by Arthur Miller. Faber & Faber 1998 433p ISBN 0-571-19182-7
Contents: The shadow of a gunman; The plough and the stars; The silver tassie; Purple dust; Hall of healing
Three Dublin Plays. Faber & Faber 1998 247p ISBN 0-571-19552-0
O'Donnell, Darren, 1965
Inoculations; four plays. Coach House Bks. 2001 243p ISBN 1-55245-07-6
Off-off Broadway festival plays.
Off-Off Broadway Festival Plays, 22nd ser. French 1998 117p ISBN 0-573-60249-2
Contents: Brothers, by William Gadea; This Is How It Is, by Bryan Patrick Moses; Because I Wanted to Say, by Sean O'Donnell; Tremulous, by Le Wilhelm; The Last Dance, by Clare Tattersall; For Tiger Lilies out of Season, by Andrea Green; The Most Preferect Day, by Pete Ernst
Off-Off Broadway Festival plays, 23rd ser. French 1999 86p ISBN 0-573-62661-8
Contents: The way to Miami, by D. Steele; Harriet Tubman visits a therapist, by C. Gage; Meridian, Mississippi redux, by L. Wilhelm; Studio portrait, by A. Hutton; It's okay, honey, by B. Brown; Francis Brick needs no introduction, by J. Hoffman
Off-Off-Broadway Festival plays, 25th ser. French 2001 90p ISBN 0-573-62766-5
Strawberry fields, by K. Brofsky; Six inch adjustable, by S. Warmflash; Evening education, by J. S. Elwell; Hot Rod, by J. Kareken; A pink Cadillac nightmare, by L. Wilhelm; East of the sun and west of the moon, by P. Handy
Off-Off Broadway Festival plays, 26th ser. French 2002 95p ISBN 0-573-62910-2
Contents: Tickets, please!, by A. Sportiello; Someplace warm, by P. Macklin; The test, by P. J. Caplan; A closer look, by A. Hutton; A peace replaced, by B. Maloney; Three tables, by D. Remmes
The **offering** & The kabbalistic psychoanalysis of Adam R. Tzaddik. Piatigorsky, A.
The **old** neighborhood. Mamet, D.
One woman, one voice: a short collection; by Sharon Morgan [et. al.]; edited by Hazel Walford Davies. Parthian Bks. 2000 213p ISBN 1-902638-08-5
O'Neill, Eugene, 1888-1953
Early plays. Penguin Bks. 2001 395p ISBN 0-14-118670-4
Plays by Eugene O'Neill: early full-length plays. Broadway Play Pub. 2000 183p ISBN 0-88145-181-9
O'Neill, Tee
The dogs play and A few roos loose in the top paddock. Currency Press 1999 76p ISBN 0-86819-587-1
Oregon and other short plays. Hedges, P.
Orlandersmith, Dael
Beauty's daughter; Monster; The gimmick; three plays. Vintage 2000 110p ISBN 0-375-70871-5 LC 00-34946
The gimmick and other plays. Dramatists 2003 ISBN 0-8222-1881-X
O'Rowe, Mark
From both hips; two plays. Hern Bks. 1999 184p ISBN 1-85459-445-1 LC 99-491015
Contents: From both hips; The aspidistra code
Orton, Joe
The Visitors and Fred and Madge; by Joe Orton. Grove Press 1999 165p ISBN 0-8021-3628-1
Osborne, Alan
The Merthyr trilogy; three plays; Alan Osborne. Parthian Bks. 1998 172p ISBN 0-9521558-6-9 LC 98-192125

Osborne, John, 1929-1994
Plays for England. Oberon Bks. 1999 179p ISBN 1-84002-037-7
Contents: The blood of the Bambergs; Under plain cover; Watch it come down
Out of the fringe; contemporary Latina/Latino theatre and performance; edited by Caridad Svich and María Teresa Marrero. Theatre Communications Group 2000 461p ISBN 1-55936-171-9
Overmyer, Eric
Plays. Broadway Play Pub. 2000 201p ISBN 0-88145-153-3
Owens, Rochelle, 1936-
Plays. Broadway Play Pub. 2000 118p ISBN 0-88145-172-X

P

Palmer, Tanya
(ed) 30 ten-minute plays for 4, 5, and 6 actors from Actors Theatre of Louisville's National Ten-Minute Play Contest. *See* 30 ten-minute plays for 4, 5, and 6 actors from Actors Theatre of Louisville's National Ten-Minute Play Contest
(ed) Humana Festival 2001. *See* Humana Festival 2001
(ed) Humana Festival 2002. *See* Humana Festival 2002
Palmieri, Marc
Poor fellas. Dramatists 2001 69p ISBN 0-8222-1795-3
Parker, Stewart, 1941-1988
Plays: 1; introduced by Lynne Parker. Methuen 2000 334p ISBN 0-413-74340-3
Contents: Spokesong; Catchpenny Twist; Nightshade; Pratt's Fall
Parks, Suzan-Lori
The red letter plays. Theatre Communications Group 2001 225p ISBN 1-55936-195-6
Parting gesters with a night in the subway. Pedrero, P.
Paterson, David L.
Shades of autumn and Chutes. French 1998 80p ISBN 0-573-64246-X LC 99-169800
Paul Sills' story theater: four shows. Sills, P.
Pedrero, Paloma, 1957-
First star and The railing; translated by Rick Hite. Estreno 2001 59p ISBN 1-888463-11-2
Parting gesters with a night in the subway. Estreno 1999 60p ISBN 1-888463-06-6
Perkins, Kathy A., 1954-
(ed) Black South African women. *See* Black South African women
Petruska, Karen C.
(ed) 30 ten-minute plays for 2 actors from Actors Theatre of Louisville's National Ten-Minute Play Contest. *See* 30 ten-minute plays for 2 actors from Actors Theatre of Louisville's National Ten-Minute Play Contest
Piatigorsky, Anton
The offering & The kabbalistic psychoanalysis of Adam R. Tzaddik; two plays. Playwrights Canada 2001 133p ISBN 0-88754-624-2
Picasso's women. McAvera, B.
Pinter, Harold, 1930-
Celebration and The room. Grove Press 1999 125p ISBN 0-8021-3708-3 LC 99-87478
Pirandello, Luigi, 1867-1936
Luigi Pirandello; translated by Carl R. Mueller. 1st ed. Smith & Kraus 2000 163p (Great translations for actors series) ISBN 1-575-25231-7 LC 00-49681
Plautus, Titus Maccius
Five comedies. *See* Five comedies
Plays. Bell, N.
Plays. Bosakowski, P.

Plays from Mythology: Grades 4-6. McCullough, L. E.

Plays from Woolly mammoth.

Plays of belonging. Deverell, R.

The **plays** of Colley Cibber. Cibber, C.

Plays of exploration and discovery for grades 4-6. McCullough, L. E.

The **plays** of Jack London. London, J.

Plays of people at work: grades K-3. McCullough, L. E.

Plays of provocation; edited by Farley P. Richmond. Kendall/Hunt Pub. 1999 327p ISBN 0-7872-6007-X LC 00-504250

Contents: The American dream, by E. Albee; Baby with the bathwater, by C. Durang; Execution of justice, by E. Mann; Split second, by D. McIntyre; Wedding band, by A. Childress; What the butler saw, by J. Orton; Yankee dawg you die, by P. K. Gotanda

Plays on Hispanic themes. Mérimée, P.

Plays: one. Bowen, J.

Plays: one. Calderón de la Barca, P.

Plays: one. Carr, M.

Plays: one. Crimp, M.

Plays: one. De Angelo, A.

Plays: one. Kops, B.

Plays: one. O'Casey, S.

Plays: one. Wood, C.

Plays: one: the mysteries. Harrison, T.

Plays: the Gulliver trilogy. Carter, L.

Plays: two. O'Casey, S.

Plays: two. Wood, C.

Plays unpleasant. Shaw, B.

Poliakoff, Stephen

Plays: 3. Methuen 1998 300p ISBN 0-413-72320-8

Contents: Caught on a Train; Coming in to Land; Close My Eyes [Screenplay]

The **political** plays of Langston Hughes. Hughes, L.

PS 627 P65 P65 2002 **Political** stages: plays that shaped a century; edited by Emily Mann and David Roessel. Applause Bks. 2002 624p ISBN 1-55783-490-3

Pollock, Sharon

Three plays. Playwrights Canada 2003 224p ISBN 0-88754-656-0

Pomerance, Bernard

The collected plays of Bernard Pomerance. 1st ed. Grove Press 2001 343p ISBN 0-8021-3845-4 LC 2001-33239

Contents: Superhighway; Quantrill in Lawrence; Melons; Hands of light

Poor fellas. Palmieri, M.

Postcolonial plays; an anthology; edited by Helen Gilbert. Routledge 2001 469p ISBN 0-415-16448-6; 0-415-16449-4 (pa) LC 2001-31226

Powell, Dawn

Four plays; edited with an introduction by Michael Sexton and Tim Page. 1st ed. Steerforth Press 1999 454p ISBN 1-88364-261-2 LC 99-43314

Power plays. May, E., and Arkin, A.

Prelude to a kiss and other plays. Lucas, C.

Prerogatives; contemporary plays by women. Blizzard 1998 223p ISBN 0-921-368-69-0

Pugliese, Frank

Plays. Broadway Play Pub. 2001 170p ISBN 0-88145-193-2

Contents: Aven'U Boys; Hope is the Thing with Feathers; The Summer Winds

Puro teatro; a Latina anthology; edited by Alberto Sandoval-Sánchez and Nancy Saporta Sternbach. Univ. of Arizona Press 2000 440p ISBN 0-8165-1826-2; 0-8165-1827-0 pb

Pushing up the sky. Bruchac, J.

Pushkin, Aleksander, 1799-1837
The little tragedies; translated, with critical essays, by Nancy K.
Anderson. Yale Univ. Press 2000 227p (Russian literature and
thought) ISBN 0-300-08025-5; 0-300-08027-1 (pa) LC 99-46416

R

Rachilde, 1860-1953
Madame La Mort and other plays; translated and edited by Kiki
Gounaridou and Frazer Lively. Johns Hopkins Univ. Press 1998
163p ISBN 0-8018-5761-9; 0-8018-5762-7 (pa)
Racin, John
(ed) Tatyana Repina: two translated texts. *See* Tatyana Repina: two
translated texts
Rahman, Aishah
Plays. Broadway Play Pub. 1997 116p ISBN 0-88145-123-1
Raznovich, Diana, 1945-
Defiant acts (Actos desafiantes); four plays/cuatro obras. Bucknell
Univ. Press 2001 342p ISBN 0-8387-5479-1
Readers theatre for American history. Fredericks, A. D.
Rebeck, Theresa
Collected plays, 1989-1998. Smith & Kraus 1999 391p (Contemporary
playwrights series) ISBN 1-57252-172-8
"Complete plays v 1"
The **red** letter plays. Parks, S.-L.
Renaissance drama; an anthology of plays and entertainments; edited by
Arthur F. Kinney. Blackwell Publishers 1999 744p (Blackwell
anthologies) ISBN 0-631-20802-X; 0-631-20803-8 (pa)
LC 99-25286
Richmond, Farley P., 1938-
(ed) Plays of provocation. *See* Plays of provocation
River, Sol B.
Plays. Oberon Bks. 1997 69p ISBN 1-870259-82-3
Contents: Moor masterpieces; To Rahtid; Unbroken
Rivera, Jose, 1955-
Giants have us in their books; six naive plays. Broadway Play Pub.
1997 72p ISBN 0-88145-141-X
The **road** to hell. Healey, M., and Lynch, K.
Robert Penn Warren's All the kings's men. Warren, R. P.
Rodríguez del Pino, Salvador
(ed) Five plays in translation from Mexican contemporary theater. *See*
Five plays in translation from Mexican contemporary theater
Roessel, David
(ed) Political stages: plays that shaped a century. *See* Political stages:
plays that shaped a century
Román, David
(ed) O solo homo. *See* O solo homo
Rudolph, Kenny
Under Hemingway's Michigan sky; selected poems, prose and short
plays. Woodburn Avenue Bks. 2000 145p ISBN 0-9678088-0-4
Analyzed for plays only

S

Saint Oscar and other plays. Eagleton, T.
The **saint** plays. Ehn, E.
Sánchez, Edwin
Plays. Broadway Play Pub. 1997 144p ISBN 0-88145-129-0
Sandoval-Sánchez, Alberto, 1954-
(ed) Puro teatro. *See* Puro teatro
The **Santaland** diaries and Season's greetings. Mantello, J.

Santander, Felipe

Three plays; translated by Lynne Alvarez. Smith & Kraus 2002 169p (Great translations series) ISBN 1-57525-264-3 LC 2002-276539

Schenkar, Joan

Signs of life; edited and with an introduction by Vivian Patraka. Wesleyan Univ. Press 1998 285p il ISBN 0-8195-6322-6; 0-8195-6323-4 (pa) LC 97-17910

Schmitt, Eric-Emmanuel

Plays: 1. Methuen 2002 277p (Methuen Contemporary Dramatists) ISBN 0-413-76020-0

Schnitzler, Arthur, 1862-1931

Four major plays; translated by Carl R. Mueller. Smith & Kraus 1999 207p (Great translations series) ISBN 1-57525-180-9

Science Fiction Readers Theatre. Fredericks, A. D.

Sears, Djanet

(ed) Testifyin'. *See* Testifyin'

Seattle Children's theatre; six plays for young audiences; edited by Deborah Lynn Frockt. Smith & Kraus 2000 II 295p ISBN 1-57525-158-2

The **secret** rapture and other plays. Hare, D.

Seismic stages. Bishop, C., and Fuller, E.

Selected fiction and drama of Eliza Haywood. Haywood, E. F.

Selected plays of M.J. Molloy. Molloy, M. J.

Selected plays of Micheal MacLiammoir. MacLiammóir, M.

Selected plays of Rutherford Mayne. Mayne, R.

Selected plays of T.C. Murray. Murray, T. C.

Setren, Phil

(ed) Best of the Fest. *See* Best of the Fest

Seven one-act plays. Wasserstein, W.

Seven short plays from Theatre Ontario.

Seventh Generation; an anthology of Native American plays; edited by Mimi Gisolfi D'aponte. Theatre Communications Group 1999 385p ISBN 1-55936-147-6

Sha-manic plays. Constable, J.

Shades of autumn and Chutes. Paterson, D. L.

Shantz, Valerie

(ed) Short spells. *See* Short spells

Shaw, Bernard, 1856-1950

Plays unpleasant; definitive text under the editorial supervision of Dan H. Laurence ; with an introduction by David Edgar. Penguin Bks. 2000 291p (Penguin classics) ISBN 0-14-043793-2 LC 2001-266519

Three plays for Puritans; definitive text under the editorial supervision of Dan H.Laurence; withan introduction by Michael Billington. Penguin Bks. 2000 354p (Penguin Classics) ISBN 0-14-043792-4 LC 2001-266474

Sheer nerve. Griffiths, L.

Shengold, Nina

(ed) Take ten. *See* Take ten

Sher, Emil

Making waves; three radio plays. Simon & Pierre 1998 139p ISBN 0-88924-283-6

Sherman, Jason

Six plays. Playwrights Canada 2001 518p ISBN 0-88754-602-1

Contents: The League of Nathans; Reading Hebron; The retreat; Three inthe black, two in the head; It's all true; Patience

Shoreline. Hannah, D.

Short spells; scenes & monologues; edited by Valerie Shantz. Playwrights Canada 1998 120p ISBN 0-88754-559-9

Signs of life. Schenkar, J.

Sills, Paul, 1927-

Paul Sills' story theater: four shows; adapted for the stage by Paul Sills. Applause 2000 272p ISBN 1-55783-398-2

Silverstein, Shel

An adult evening of Shel Silverstein. Dramatists 2003 ISBN 0-8222-1873-9

Shel's shorts. Dramatists 2003 ISBN 0-8222-1897-6

Six Greek comedies; introduced by J. Michael Walton. Methuen 2002 358p ISBN 0-413-77130-X

Contents: Aristophanes: Birds; Frogs; Women in power; Menander: The woman from Samos; Euripides: Cyclops; Alkestis

Six nuevomexicano folk dramas for Advent season; translated by Larry Torres. Univ. of New Mexico Press 1999 194p (Pasó por aquí/Series on the Nuevo Mexicano literary heritage) ISBN 0-8263-1964-5

Six plays. Sherman, J.

Smith, Marisa

(ed) EST marathon '96: the one-act plays. *See* EST marathon '96: the one-act plays

(ed) EST marathon '97: the one-act plays. *See* EST marathon '97: the one-act plays

(ed) EST marathon '98: the one-act plays. *See* EST marathon '98: the one-act plays

(ed) Women playwrights: the best plays of 1997. *See* Women playwrights: the best plays of 1997

(ed) Women playwrights: the best plays of 1998. *See* Women playwrights: the best plays of 1998

(ed) Women playwrights: the best plays of 1999. *See* Women playwrights: the best plays of 1999

O solo homo; the new queer performance; edited by Holly Hughes & David Román. Grove Press 1998 481p ISBN 0-8021-3570-6 LC 98-5203

Sondheim, Stephen

Four by Sondheim; Wheeler, LaPine, Shevelove and Gelbart. Applause 2000 747p (Applause musical lib) ISBN 1-55783-407-5 LC 00-100279

Contents: A funny thing happened on the way to the forum; A little night music; Sweeney Todd; Sunday in the park with George

Sophocles

The complete plays; translated by Carl R. Mueller and Anna Krajewska-Wieczorek. Smith & Kraus 2000 479p (Great translations series) ISBN 1-575-25265-1 LC 00-44570

Sophocles, 1; edited by David R. Slavitt and Palmer Bovie. University of Pa. Press 1998 284p (Penn Greek drama series) ISBN 0-8122-3445-6; 0-8122-1653-9 (pa) LC 98-9962

Contents: v 1 Ajax; Women of Trachis; Electra; Philoctetes

Sophocles, 2; edited by David R. Slavitt and Palmer Bovie. University of Pa. Press 1999 258p (Penn Greek drama series) ISBN 0-8122-3462-6; 0-8122-1666-0 (pa) LC 98-9962

Spencer, Stuart

Plays. Broadway Play Pub. 2000 179p ISBN 0-88145-169-X

Contents: Sudden Devotion; Resident Alien; In the Western Garden

Staging the North: twelve Canadian plays; edited by Sherrill Grace, Eve D'Aeth, and Lisa Chalykoff. Playwrights Canada 1999 502p il ISBN 0-88754-564-5 LC 00-304684

Starfall. Kleberg, L.

Starstruck and The No Boys Cricket Club. Williams, R.

Sternbach, Nancy Saporta

(ed) Puro teatro. *See* Puro teatro

Stickland, Eugene, 1956-

Two plays. Red Deer College Press 1999 166p ISBN 0-88995-196-9 LC 99-39881

Stoppard, Tom
Plays: five. Faber & Faber 1999 593p ISBN 0-57119-751-5
Contents: Arcadia; Hapgood;The real thing; Night and day; India ink
Strindberg, August, 1849-1912
The father; Lady Julie; Playing with fire. Amber Lane Press 1998 192p ISBN 1-872868-20-7
Five major plays; translated by Carl R. Mueller. 1st ed. Smith & Kraus 1999 171p (Great translations for actors series) ISBN 1-575-25261-9 LC 99-89191
Ø **Suburban** motel. Walker, G. F.
Sunde, Karen
Plays. Broadway Play Pub. 2001 166p ISBN 0-88145-192-4
Surface, Mary Hall, 1958-
Most valuable player and four other all-star plays for middle and high school audiences. Smith & Kraus 1999 176p (Young actor series) ISBN 1-575-25178-7 LC 99-30018
Svich, Caridad, 1963-
(ed) Out of the fringe. *See* Out of the fringe

T

Tait, Lance
Mad cow disease in America; Something special and other plays; with an introduction by Michelle Powell. Enfield Pub. 2001 327p ISBN 1-893598-03-9
Miss Julie, David Mamet Fan Club, and other plays; with introductions by Yvonne Shafer and Frank Hoff. Enfield Pub. 2000 292p ISBN 0-9656184-9-8 LC 00-269228
PS 267 053 T35 1997 **Take** ten; new 10-minute plays; edited by Eric Lane and Nina Shengold. Vintage 1997 360p ISBN 0-679-77282-0 LC 96-53571
The **tale** of the allergist's wife and other plays. Busch, C.
Tales from the Red Rose Inn. Nigro, D.
Tales from the Vienna Woods and other plays. Horváth, Ö. von, and Mitchell, M.
Ø **Talking** bodies. Tremblay, L.
Tatyana Repina: two translated texts; translated and edited by John Racin. McFarland & Co. 1999 272p ISBN 0-7864-0575-9
Contents: Tatyana Repina, by Alexei S. Suvorin; Tatyana Repina, by Anton Chekhov
Taylor, Drew Hayden, 1962-
The boy in the treehouse; Girl who loved her horses. Talonbooks 2000 159p ISBN 0-88922-441-2
Teare, Jeff
(ed) New Welsh Drama II. *See* New Welsh Drama II
Tearing the loom and In a little world of our own. Mitchell, G.
Tell it together. McBride-Smith, B.
Ten plays for children. Mason, T.
Terence
Five comedies. *See* Five comedies
Terry, Megan, 1932-
Plays. Broadway Play Pub. 2000 168p ISBN 0-88145-185-1
Testifyin'; contemporary African Canadian drama volume I; edited by Djanet Sears. Playwrights Canada 2000 632p ISBN 0-88754-597-1 LC 00-340637
Testifyin'; contemporary African Canadian drama volume II; edited by Djanet Sears. Playwrights Canada 2003 632p il ISBN 0-88754-664-1
Theater and society; an anthology of contemporary Chinese drama; Haiping Yan, editor. Sharpe, M.E. 1998 xlvi, 328p (Asia and the Pacific) ISBN 0-7656-0307-1; 0-7656-0308-X (pa) LC 97-51561
"An East Gate Book"

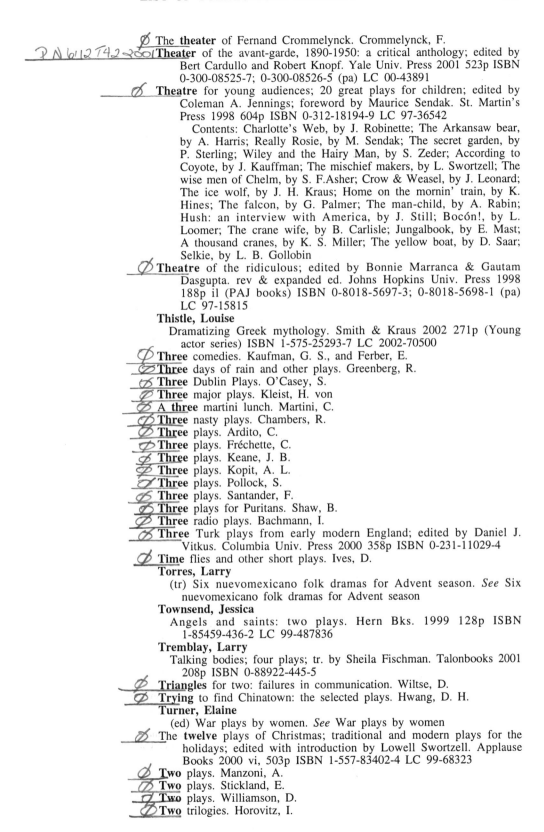

The **theater** of Fernand Crommelynck. Crommelynck, F.

Theater of the avant-garde, 1890-1950: a critical anthology; edited by Bert Cardullo and Robert Knopf. Yale Univ. Press 2001 523p ISBN 0-300-08525-7; 0-300-08526-5 (pa) LC 00-43891

Theatre for young audiences; 20 great plays for children; edited by Coleman A. Jennings; foreword by Maurice Sendak. St. Martin's Press 1998 604p ISBN 0-312-18194-9 LC 97-36542

Contents: Charlotte's Web, by J. Robinette; The Arkansaw bear, by A. Harris; Really Rosie, by M. Sendak; The secret garden, by P. Sterling; Wiley and the Hairy Man, by S. Zeder; According to Coyote, by J. Kauffman; The mischief makers, by L. Swortzell; The wise men of Chelm, by S. F.Asher; Crow & Weasel, by J. Leonard; The ice wolf, by J. H. Kraus; Home on the mornin' train, by K. Hines; The falcon, by G. Palmer; The man-child, by A. Rabin; Hush: an interview with America, by J. Still; Bocón!, by L. Loomer; The crane wife, by B. Carlisle; Jungalbook, by E. Mast; A thousand cranes, by K. S. Miller; The yellow boat, by D. Saar; Selkie, by L. B. Gollobin

Theatre of the ridiculous; edited by Bonnie Marranca & Gautam Dasgupta. rev & expanded ed. Johns Hopkins Univ. Press 1998 188p il (PAJ books) ISBN 0-8018-5697-3; 0-8018-5698-1 (pa) LC 97-15815

Thistle, Louise
Dramatizing Greek mythology. Smith & Kraus 2002 271p (Young actor series) ISBN 1-575-25293-7 LC 2002-70500

Three comedies. Kaufman, G. S., and Ferber, E.

Three days of rain and other plays. Greenberg, R.

Three Dublin Plays. O'Casey, S.

Three major plays. Kleist, H. von

A **three** martini lunch. Martini, C.

Three nasty plays. Chambers, R.

Three plays. Ardito, C.

Three plays. Fréchette, C.

Three plays. Keane, J. B.

Three plays. Kopit, A. L.

Three plays. Pollock, S.

Three plays. Santander, F.

Three plays for Puritans. Shaw, B.

Three radio plays. Bachmann, I.

Three Turk plays from early modern England; edited by Daniel J. Vitkus. Columbia Univ. Press 2000 358p ISBN 0-231-11029-4

Time flies and other short plays. Ives, D.

Torres, Larry
(tr) Six nuevomexicano folk dramas for Advent season. *See* Six nuevomexicano folk dramas for Advent season

Townsend, Jessica
Angels and saints: two plays. Hern Bks. 1999 128p ISBN 1-85459-436-2 LC 99-487836

Tremblay, Larry
Talking bodies; four plays; tr. by Sheila Fischman. Talonbooks 2001 208p ISBN 0-88922-445-5

Triangles for two: failures in communication. Wiltse, D.

Trying to find Chinatown: the selected plays. Hwang, D. H.

Turner, Elaine
(ed) War plays by women. *See* War plays by women

The **twelve** plays of Christmas; traditional and modern plays for the holidays; edited with introduction by Lowell Swortzell. Applause Books 2000 vi, 503p ISBN 1-557-83402-4 LC 99-68323

Two plays. Manzoni, A.

Two plays. Stickland, E.

Two plays. Williamson, D.

Two trilogies. Horovitz, I.

TYA5: theatre for young aduience; [edited by Mira Friedlander & Wayne Fairhead] Playwrights Canada 1998 268p ISBN 0-88754-577-7

Tylee, Claire M., 1946-
(ed) War plays by women. *See* War plays by women

U

Under Hemingway's Michigan sky. Rudolph, K.

Upton, Judy
Plays: 1. Methuen 2002 247p ISBN 0-413-77020-6
Contents: Ashes and Sand; Stealing Souls; Sunspots; People on the River; Know Your Rights

V

Van Itallie, Jean-Claude
America Hurrah and other plays; with an introduction by Bill Coco. Grove Press 2001 290p ISBN 0-8021-3761-X

Vandenbroucke, Russell
(ed) Contemporary Australian Plays. *See* Contemporary Australian Plays

The **vaudevilles**. Chekhov, A. P.

Via Dolorosa & When shall we live? Hare, D.

Vidal, Gore, 1925-
The essential Gore Vidal; edited by Fred Kaplan. Random House 1999 xxx, 988p ISBN 0-679-45746-1 LC 97-26590
Analyzed for play only

Vinaver, Michel, 1927-
Plays: 1; edited and introduced by David Bradby. Methuen 1997 359p ISBN 0-413-71780-1
Contents: Overboard; Situation Vacant; Dissident, Goes Without Saying; Nina, That's Something Else; A Smile on the End of the Line
Plays: 2; edited and introduced by David Bradby. Methuen 1997 319p ISBN 0-413-72070-5
Contents: Hugh Places; The Neighbors; Portrait of a Woman; The Television Programme

The **Visitors** and Fred and Madge. Orton, J.

Vitkus, Daniel J.
(ed) Three Turk plays from early modern England. *See* Three Turk plays from early modern England

Vogel, Larry, 1953-
Fearless Pharaoh FooFoo and other dramas for children. Concordia Pub. House 1998 159p ISBN 0-570-05332-3 LC 98-28472

Vogel, Paula
The mammary plays. Theatre Communications Group 1998 187p ISBN 1-559-36144-1 LC 97-40169
Contents: How I learned to drive; The Mineola twins

W

Walcott, Derek
The Haitian trilogy. Farrar Straus Giroux 2002 434p por ISBN 0-374-52813-6 LC 2001-23158
Contents: Henri Christophe; Drums and colours; The Haitian Walker and The ghost dance. Farrar, Strauss & Giroux 2002 246p ISBN 0-374-52814-4

Walker, George F.
The East end plays, part 1. Talonbooks 1999 255p ISBN 0-88922-413-7

PR9272.9 W3 W35 2002

Wesker, Arnold, 1932-—*Continued*
  Plays: 2; one-woman plays. Methuen 2001 189p ISBN 0-413-75840-0
      Contents: Annie Wobbler; Yardsale; Four portraits—of mothers;
      Whatever happened to Betty Lemon?; The mistress; Letter to a
      daughter
Ø **What** I meant was. Lucas, C.
Ø **Where** the pavement ends. Yellow Robe, W. S.
Ø The **widow's** might: three plays. Conquest, N.
Wilde, Oscar, 1854-1900
  The importance of being earnest and other plays. Penguin Bks. 2000
      431p ISBN 0-14-043606-5
Wilder, Thornton, 1897-1975
  The collected short plays of Thornton Wilder; edited by A. Tappan
      Wilder. Theatre Communications Group 1998 2 277p ISBN
      1-55936-148-4
Williams, Roy
  Plays: 1; introduced by Indhu Rubasingham. Methuen 2002 240p
      ISBN 0-413-77209-8
      Contents: The No Boys Cricket Club; Starstruck; Lift Off
  Starstruck and The No Boys Cricket Club; two plays; by Roy
      Williams. Methuen 1999 160p ISBN 0-413-73810-8
Williams, Tennessee, 1911-1983
  Plays, 1937-1955. Library of America 2000 1054p ISBN
      1-883011-86-8
  Plays, 1957-1980. Library of America 2000 999p ISBN 1-883011-87-6
Williamson, David
  The great man [and] Sanctuary. Currency Press 2000 128p ISBN
      0-86819-633-9
  Two plays. Currency Press 1999 125p ISBN 0-86819-596-0
Wilson, Lanford, 1937-
  Collected works v2, 1970-1983. Smith & Kraus 1998 249p
      (Contemporary playwrights series) ISBN 1-57525-119-1
  Collected works v3: the Talley trilogy. Smith & Kraus 1999 262p
      (Contemporary playwrights series) ISBN 1-57525-133-7
Wilson, Snoo, 1948-
  Plays: 1. Methuen 1999 260p ISBN 0-413-74180-X
      Contents: Pignight; Blowjob; The Soul of the White Ant; More
      Light; Darwin's Flood
  Plays: 2. Methuen 2000 312p ISBN 0-413-74400-0
      Contents: Vampire; The Glad Hand; The Grass Widow; Sabina
Wiltse, David
  Triangles for two: failures in communication. French 2002 51p ISBN
      0-573-62764-9
Ø **wintersleep.** Blais, M.-C.
Winther, Barbara
  Plays from Hispanic Tales. Plays, Inc. 1998 149p ISBN
      0-8238-0307-4
Wolf, Christa
  Selected prose and drama. See Bachmann, Ingeborg, 1926-1973, and
      Wolf, Christa
PS 628 W6 W674 1998 **Women** playwrights: the best plays of 1997; edited by Marisa Smith.
      Smith & Kraus 1998 190p ISBN 1-57525-131-0
Ø **Women** playwrights: the best plays of 1998; edited by Marisa Smith.
      Smith & Kraus 2000 318p ISBN 1-57525-181-7
Ø **Women** playwrights: the best plays of 1999; edited by Marisa Smith.
      Smith & Kraus 2001 335p ISBN 1-57525-274-0
Ø The **Women's** Project & productions; edited by Julia Miles. Smith &
      Kraus 2002 309p (Contemporary playwrights series) ISBN
      1-57525-271-6
Ø **Women's** words, women's works; an anthology of contemporary
      Austrian plays by women; edited by Udo Borgert. Ariadne Press
      2001 264p (Studies in Austrian literature, culture, and thought,
      Translation series) ISBN 1-572-41106-6 LC 2001-46230

Wood, Charles
Plays: one. Oberon Bks. 1997 276p ((Modern playwrights)) ISBN
1-870259-83-1
Contents: Veterans; Across from the Garden of Allah
Plays: two. Oberon Bks. 1999 375p ((Modern playwrights)) ISBN
1-870259-84-X
Contents: H; Jingo; Dingo
Wood, David
Plays: 1. Methuen 1999 324p ISBN 0-413-73700-4
Contents:The Gingerbread Man; The see-saw tree; The ideal
gnome expedition; Mother Goose's golden Christmas
Wray, Rhonda
(ed) The drama of Easter. *See* The drama of Easter
Wright, Doug
Unwrap your candy; an evening of one-act plays. Dramatists 2002
ISBN 0-8222-1871-2

Y

Yeaton, Dana
(ed) Blasts from the future. *See* Blasts from the future
Yellow Robe, William S., 1960-
Where the pavement ends; five Native American plays. Univ. of
Oklahoma Press 2000 169p (American Indian Literature and Critical
Studies Series, 37) ISBN 0-8061-3265-5 LC 00-23468
Yew, Chay
The hyphenated American. Grove Press 2002 454p ISBN
0-8021-3912-4
York, Y.
Plays. Broadway Play Pub. 2000 216p ISBN 0-88145-177-0
Young, Glenn
(ed) The Best American short plays, 1996-1997. *See* The Best
American short plays, 1996-1997
(ed) The Best American short plays, 1997-1998. *See* The Best
American short plays, 1997-1998
(ed) The Best American Short Plays, 1998-1999. *See.* The Best
American Short Plays, 1998-1999
(ed) The Best American short plays, 1999-2000. *See* The Best
American short plays, 1999-2000